FIFTH EDITION

EDWARD SIDLOW
Eastern Michigan University

BETH HENSCHEN
Eastern Michigan University

America at Odds

alternate
edition

THOMSON

WADSWORTH

Australia • Brazil • Canada • Mexico • Singapore • Spain • United Kingdom • United States

THOMSON

TM

WADSWORTH

America at Odds, Alternate **Fifth Edition**
Edward Sidlow and Beth Henschen

Publisher: Clark Baxter
Executive Editor: David Tatom
Senior Development Editor: Stacey Sims
Associate Development Editor: Rebecca Green
Editorial Assistant: Cheryl Lee
Technology Project Manager: Michelle Vardeman
Senior Marketing Manager: Janise Fry
Marketing Assistant : Teresa Jessen
Executive Advertising Project Manager: Nathaniel Bergson-Michelson
Permissions Editor: Joohee Lee
Print Buyer: Barbara Britton

Senior Project Manager: Ann Borman
Text Design: Bill Stryker
Illustrator: Bill Stryker
Cover Design: Laurie Anderson
Photo Researcher: Anne Sheroff
Copy Editor: Pat Lewis
Indexer: Bob Marsh
Compositor: Parkwood Composition Service
Text Printer: Courier Kendalville
Cover Printer: Phoenix Color
Cover Images: © Gary Hershorn/Reuters Newmedia Inc/Corbis

Printed in the United States of America
1 2 3 4 5 6 7 10 09 08 07 06

ExamView® and ExamView Pro® are registered trademarks of FSCreations, Inc. Windows is a registered trademark of the Microsoft Corporation used herein under license. Macintosh and Power Macintosh are registered trademarks of Apple Computer, Inc. Used herein under license.

WebTutor™ COPYRIGHT 2007 Thomson Learning, Inc. All Rights Reserved. Thomson Learning WebTutor™ is a trademark of Thomson Learning, Inc.

Library of Congress Control Number: 2005926361

Student Edition ISBN 0-534-60133-2

Instructor's Edition: ISBN 0-495-00182-1

Thomson Higher Education
10 Davis Drive
Belmont, CA 94002-3098
USA

For more information about our products, contact us at:
Thomson Learning Academic Resource Center
1-800-423-0563

For permission to use material from this text or product, submit a request online at **http://www.thomsonrights.com**.
Any additional questions about permissions can be submitted by e-mail to **thomsonrights@thomson.com**

To treasured aunts and uncles

contents in brief

contents

PART ONE
THE FOUNDATIONS OF OUR AMERICAN SYSTEM

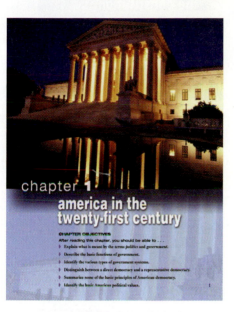

chapter 1
america in the
twenty-first century

CHAPTER OBJECTIVES
After reading this chapter, you should be able to . . .
▶ Explain what is meant by the terms *politics* and *government*.
▶ Describe the basic functions of government.
▶ Identify the various types of government systems.
▶ Distinguish between a direct democracy and a representative democracy.
▶ Summarize some of the basic principles of American democracy.
▶ Identify the basic American political values.

CHAPTER 1 FEATURES

THE POLITICS OF NATIONAL SECURITY
Terrorism Information Awareness 6

COMPARATIVE POLITICS
Theocracy in Iran 9

PERCEPTION VERSUS REALITY
Taking Property for Public Use 13

WHY DOES IT MATTER?
American Politics and Your Everyday Life 17

chapter 2
the constitution

CHAPTER OBJECTIVES
After reading this chapter, you should be able to . . .
> Describe some of the influences on the American political tradition in the colonial years.
> Indicate why and how Americans achieved independence from Great Britain.
> List some of the major compromises made by the delegates at the Constitutional Convention.
> Discuss the Federalist and Anti-Federalist positions with respect to ratifying the Constitution.
> Summarize the process by which the Constitution can be amended.

21

CHAPTER 2 FEATURES

PERCEPTION VERSUS REALITY
Why Didn't the Founders Ban Slavery? 35

THE POLITICS OF NATIONAL SECURITY
The Constitution and the War on Terrorism 39

COMPARATIVE POLITICS
Democracy in the Middle East 41

WHY DOES IT MATTER?
The Constitution and Your Everyday Life 45

CHAPTER 2
The Constitution 21

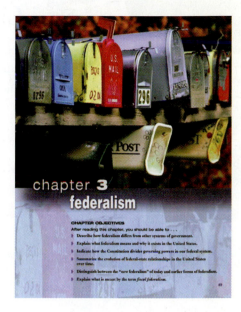

PART TWO
OUR LIBERTIES AND RIGHTS

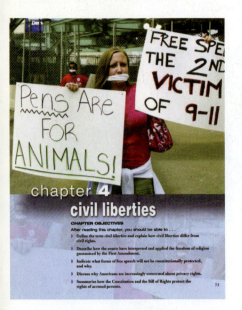

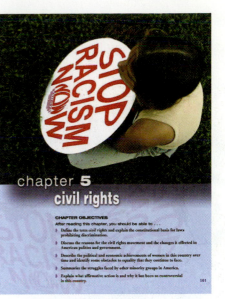

PART THREE
THE POLITICS OF DEMOCRACY

CHAPTER 6
Interest Groups 127

CHAPTER 6 FEATURES

THE POLITICS OF NATIONAL SECURITY
The Military-Industrial Complex 135

COMPARATIVE POLITICS
Gun Control in Britain and the United States— A Tale of Two Lobbies 140

PERCEPTION VERSUS REALITY
Dishing Out the Pork 144

WHY DOES IT MATTER?
Interest Groups and Your Everyday Life 146

CHAPTER 7
Political Parties 149

CHAPTER 7 FEATURES

THE POLITICS OF
NATIONAL SECURITY
War and Party Politics 158

PERCEPTION
VERSUS REALITY
Red versus Blue America 160

COMPARATIVE POLITICS
The German Greens 164

WHY DOES IT MATTER?
**Political Parties and
Your Everyday Life 168**

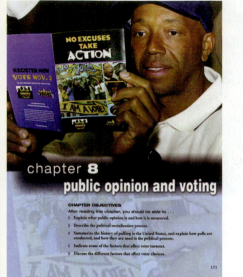

chapter **8**
public opinion and voting

CHAPTER OBJECTIVES

After reading this chapter, you should be able to . . .
‣ Explain what public opinion is and how it is measured.
‣ Describe the political socialization process.
‣ Summarize the history of polling in the United States, and explain how polls are conducted, and how they are used in the political process.
‣ Indicate some of the factors that affect voter turnout.
‣ Discuss the different factors that affect voter choices.

171

CHAPTER 8 FEATURES

THE POLITICS OF NATIONAL SECURITY
The "Perpetual War Campaign" 181

PERCEPTION VERSUS REALITY
Voting with One's Wallet 190

WHY DOES IT MATTER?
Voting and Your Everyday Life 192

CHAPTER 8
Public Opinion and Voting 171

CHAPTER 9
Campaigns and Elections 195

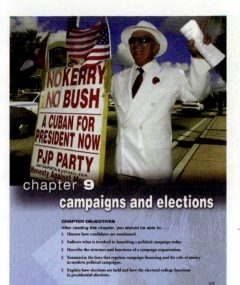

chapter **9**
campaigns and elections

CHAPTER OBJECTIVES
After reading this chapter, you should be able to . . .
▶ Discuss how candidates are nominated.
▶ Indicate what is involved in launching a political campaign today.
▶ Describe the structure and functions of a campaign organization.
▶ Summarize the laws that regulate campaign financing and the role of money in modern political campaigns.
▶ Explain how elections are held and how the electoral college functions in presidential elections.

195

CHAPTER 10 FEATURES

THE POLITICS OF NATIONAL SECURITY
What Is the Media's
Role in Wartime? **219**

COMPARATIVE POLITICS
When the State
Controls the Media **224**

PERCEPTION VERSUS REALITY
Does Online Information
Mean the Death of Traditional
News? **230**

WHY DOES IT MATTER?
Politics, the Media, and
Your Everyday Life **234**

CHAPTER 10
Politics and the Media 215

PART FOUR
INSTITUTIONS

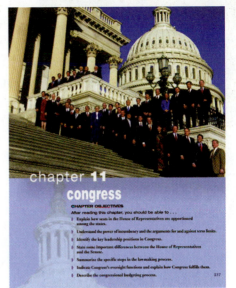

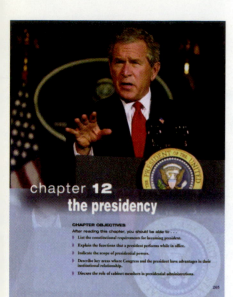

chapter 12
the presidency

CHAPTER OBJECTIVES
After reading this chapter, you should be able to . . .
- List the constitutional requirements for becoming president.
- Explain the functions that a president performs while in office.
- Indicate the scope of presidential powers.
- Describe key areas where Congress and the president have advantages in their institutional relationship.
- Discuss the role of cabinet members in presidential administrations.

265

CHAPTER 12 FEATURES

COMPARATIVE POLITICS
Having a Separate
Chief of State 272

**PERCEPTION
VERSUS REALITY**
Presidents and
the "Popular Vote" 279

**THE POLITICS OF
NATIONAL SECURITY**
Presidential Power
in a Time of Crisis 284

WHY DOES IT MATTER?
The Presidency and
Your Everyday Life 290

CHAPTER 12
The Presidency 265

CHAPTER 13
The Bureaucracy 293

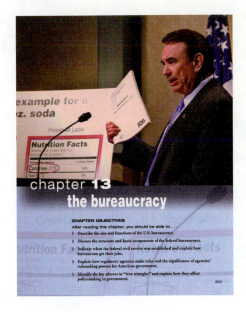

CHAPTER 13 FEATURES

COMPARATIVE POLITICS
The U.S. Bureaucracy
Really Is Special 298

**PERCEPTION
VERSUS REALITY**
Who Makes the Law? 307

**THE POLITICS OF
NATIONAL SECURITY**
Reforming U.S.
Intelligence Agencies 314

WHY DOES IT MATTER?
The Federal Bureaucracy
and Your Everyday Life 315

chapter **14**
the judiciary

CHAPTER OBJECTIVES
After reading this chapter, you should be able to . . .
▶ Summarize the origins of the American legal system and the basic sources of American law.
▶ Delineate the structure of the federal court system.
▶ Indicate how federal judges are appointed.
▶ Explain how the federal courts make policy.
▶ Describe the role of ideology and judicial philosophies in judicial decision making.

317

CHAPTER 14 FEATURES

COMPARATIVE POLITICS
Legal Systems
of the World 321

**PERCEPTION
VERSUS REALITY**
Judicial Appointments and
Presidential Legacies 329

**THE POLITICS OF
NATIONAL SECURITY**
Judicial Checks on
a Wartime President 332

WHY DOES IT MATTER?
The Judiciary and
Your Everyday Life 339

It does not take long for a student of American government to get the message: Americans are at odds over numerous political issues. The 2004 elections, for example, were bitterly partisan and contributed to an increasingly polarized political landscape in America. In 2005, Americans were deeply divided over Social Security reform. President George W. Bush's proposal to establish private investment accounts with a portion of Social Security withholdings met with significant opposition. The war on terrorism that began on September 11, 2001, also created new challenges for American democracy, as you will read throughout this text.

Political conflict and divergence of opinion have always characterized our political traditions and way of governing. Nonetheless, our democracy continues to endure. Indeed, the U.S. Constitution has been the model for most of the world's new democracies in the 1990s and early 2000s.

America at Odds: An Introduction to American Government, Fifth Edition, looks at government and politics in this country as a series of conflicts that have led to compromises. Along the way, your students will sometimes encounter a bit of irreverence—none of us should take ourselves so seriously all of the time!

This text was written with today's generation of students in mind. As such, it does the following:

- Forthrightly presents different perspectives on key issues being debated today, including how to ensure our nation's security against terrorism while protecting our civil liberties.
- Helps your students test their beliefs and assumptions.
- Assists your students in forming enlightened political values and opinions.
- Uses a thematic as well as an analytical approach, with emphasis on the various challenges that face our enduring democracy.
- Fully explains the major problems facing the American political system today.
- Integrates the global connections that exist between American politics and those of the rest of the world.
- Captures the excitement of cyberspace with respect to its effect on American politics and makes available numerous Web resources, ranging from a book-specific Web site to links to relevant Web sites that deal with questions raised in this text.

Politics in a Cyber Age

Cyberspace affects not only our home lives and the way we do business but also American politics. *America at Odds,* Fifth Edition, fully integrates the world of cyberspace into the study of American politics.

Throughout this text, your students are exposed to the numerous political issues that have arisen because of the rapid changes in communications technology. For example, Chapter 1 explores the question of how data-mining technology is being used in the war on terrorism. Chapter 4 examines the issues of privacy rights raised by new medical microchip technology.

Politics on the Web

The amount of information available to students of American government on the Web is almost without limits. Where do they start? And where do they go? We solve this thorny problem by providing, at the end of each chapter, an entire section entitled *Politics on the Web*. There your students can discover the best Web sites for each chapter's subject matter. Many of those Web sites offer additional hot links.

The *America at Odds,* Fifth Edition, Web Site

In addition to the *Politics on the Web* section, there is an *America at Odds* companion Web site at:

http://www.americaatodds.com

Here you and your students will find a wealth of information developed specifically for *America at Odds.* The Web site offers numerous helpful resources, including the following:

■ Chapter-by-chapter tutorial quizzes that allow students to test their knowledge.
■ Hyperlinks to relevant Web sites for each chapter—including URLs that update materials in the text.
■ Internet activities that relate to each chapter's material.
■ Glossaries, audio flash cards, and crossword puzzles.
■ Additional exercises related to the book's features, including *Comparative Politics* questions, *Perception versus Reality* "Critical Thinking" questions, and *Why Does It Matter?* activities.
■ A link to the Wadsworth American Government Resource Center at **http://politicalscience. wadsworth.com/amgov** for additional resources.

American Politics Now™ for Improved Study Techniques

This resource enhances the functionality of the book's companion Web site by providing a complete package of diagnostic quizzes and integrated media elements—including an *e-Book*—and an *Instructor Gradebook.* After students take a *Pre-Test* covering the chapter they have just read, American Politics Now™ calculates the results and generates a *Customized Study Plan.* The plan outlines those topics that require review and guides the student through the following media activities:

■ Simulations in which the student role-plays as state senator, adviser to the president, and others to encourage critical thinking and decision-making skills.
■ Video Case Studies that feature contemporary policy issues and conclude with provocative questions that encourage decision making.
■ MicroCase® Exercises that present issues in American government and direct students to pertinent data—helping them consider and interpret data.
■ Interactive Timelines, complete with photos and narrative.
■ *Post-Tests* that follow up on students' progress and help assess final mastery of the material.

Internet Activities

To make sure that your students not only master the Web but at the same time improve their understanding of American politics, we have a specially designed booklet that you can order for them. It is called *American Government Internet Activities,* Third Edition. Each exercise relates to topics that are covered in the text. The exercise takes your students on a navigation path and then asks them to complete various exercises related to the data that they discover.

The Modern Text—Features That Teach

Any American government text must present the basics of the American political process and its institutions. Any *modern* American government text, however, must go further: it must excite and draw the student into the subject materials. That is exactly what we do in *America at Odds,* Fifth Edition. Among other things, the Fifth Edition of *America at Odds* deals with current issues and events that are familiar to students. For example, in virtually every chapter there is a reference to, or discussion of, some aspect of the 2004 campaigns, elections, or election results.

Additionally, we present many of today's controversial political issues in special features. Each of these features is referred to within the text itself so that the student understands the connection between the feature and the topic being discussed. We describe below the various types of features that we have included in *America at Odds,* Fifth Edition.

- *America at Odds*—This chapter-opening feature examines a major controversy over which the public is divided and has strong views. Each of these features concludes with a section entitled *Where Do You Stand?* These sections, which consist of two questions, invite the student to form or express his or her own opinions on the arguments presented in the feature.

  Students can explore the issue further by accessing the Web site links provided in the *Explore This Issue Online* section. These links were chosen either to represent the opposing viewpoints posed in the feature or to provide a resource for further research. Some of the titles of these chapter-opening *America at Odds* features are as follows:

  - Is There Too Much Religion in American Politics? (Chapter 1).
  - Should Same-Sex Couples Be Allowed to Marry? (Chapter 5).
  - Do Colleges Shun Conservative Views? (Chapter 7).
  - Supreme Court Appointees: Does Partisan Ideology Matter? (Chapter 14).

- **In-Chapter *America at Odds*—**The theme of controversy continues in shorter features that are integrated within the text of every chapter. Each in-chapter *America at Odds* briefly introduces students in a concise yet thought-provoking manner to an issue that divides Americans. These features will keep your students thinking and questioning their own political attitudes and values. Some titles of these features include:

  - Has America Gone Too Far in "Exporting Liberty"? (Chapter 1).
  - Should States Be Allowed to Import Prescription Drugs? (Chapter 3).
  - Should Third-Party Candidates Debate? (Chapter 7).
  - A National Vote-by-Mail System (Chapter 8).
  - Redistricting for Competitive Elections (Chapter 11).

- *The Politics of National Security*—These features are designed to focus on the political implications of the effort to defend the nation against terrorist attacks. In the Fifth Edition, the scope of these features has broadened to include national security issues relating to foreign policy and American military engagements abroad. At the end of each of these features is a thought-provoking question that challenges students to consider whether we are safer as a result of a particular national security measure. Some of the titles of these features are as follows:

  - Can the States Afford to Defend the Homeland? (Chapter 3).
  - The Military-Industrial Complex (Chapter 6).
  - What Is the Media's Role in Wartime? (Chapter 10).
  - Judicial Checks on a Wartime President (Chapter 14).

- *Why Does It Matter?*—This feature gives a number of specific examples showing how the topic under study affects the student's everyday life. Each feature carries a subtitle including the chapter topic. For example, in Chapter 11 the feature's title is *Why Does It Matter? Congress and Your Everyday Life.* At the end of each feature is a section entitled *Taking Action.* These sections illustrate how ordinary Americans have made their voices heard on issues of importance to them.

- *Perception versus Reality*—Perhaps nowhere in our media-generated view of the world are there more misconceptions than in the area of American government and politics. This feature tries to help your students understand the difference between the public's general perception of a particular political event or issue and the reality of the situation.

The perception is often gleaned from responses to public opinion surveys. The reality usually is presented in the form of objective data that show that the world is not quite what the public often thinks it is. At the end of each of these features is a section entitled *What's Your Opinion?*, which encourages the student to think about why there is such a disparity between the perception and the reality. Some of the titles of these features are as follows:

- Churches, Politics, and the IRS (Chapter 4).
- Red versus Blue America (Chapter 7).
- Voting with One's Wallet (Chapter 8).
- Is Our Public Debt a Problem? (Chapter 11).

- *Comparative Politics*—One of the best ways to understand the American political system is by comparing it with other political systems. Students need to know that in much of the world, the political process is different. By understanding this, they can better understand and appreciate what goes on in this country, both in Washington, D.C., and in state capitals. Nearly every chapter has one of these features. At the end of each of these features, the student is asked to further examine some aspect of the topic under discussion in a question "For Critical Analysis." Some examples of the *Comparative Politics* features are as follows:

- Democracy in the Middle East (Chapter 2).
- France and Religious Dress in Schools (Chapter 4).
- The German Greens (Chapter 7).
- The "Orange Revolution" in Ukraine (Chapter 9).
- When the State Controls the Media (Chapter 10).

- *Chapter Objectives*—Every chapter-opening page includes a list of five learning objectives that let students know what concepts will be covered in the chapter.

Chapter-Ending Issues and Pedagogy

Every chapter ends with the following sections:

- **Key Terms.** This is a list of the terms that were boldfaced and defined within the chapter. Each term in the list is followed by the page number on which it first appeared and was defined.
- **Chapter Summary.** This point-by-point feature summarizes every important topic covered in the chapter.
- **Selected Readings.** Several books of recent scholarship, as well as some classic texts, are listed at the end of each chapter, along with annotations describing each book.
- **Politics on the Web.** As explained earlier, this section gives selected Web sites that students can access for more information.
- **Online Resources for This Chapter.** This section directs students to the text's Web site, where they can find links to additional related topics covered in the chapter.

The Supplements

Both instructors and students today expect, and indeed require, a variety of accompanying supplements to teach and learn about American government. *America at Odds,* Fifth Edition, takes the lead in providing the most comprehensive and user-friendly supplements package on the market today. These supplements include those listed below.

For Instructors

- Multimedia Manager with Instructor Resources CD-ROM, including, Instructor's Manual and Test Bank in Microsoft Word and ExamView computerized testing, written by Beth Henschen.

- An online Resource Center for political science at

  http://politicalscience.wadsworth.com/amgov

- A special, book-specific Web site for *America at Odds,* Fifth Edition, which can be accessed through the Resource Center or at

  http://www.americaatodds.com

- PowerPoint Lecture Outlines, with projectable digital images of charts, graphs, and tables.
- Video clips, the Resource Integration Guide, and Video Case Studies Instructor's Manual.
- WebTutor™, available on WebCT and Blackboard—A Web-based teaching and learning tool that allows you to provide virtual office hours, post your syllabi, set up threaded discussions, track student progress with the quizzing material, and more.
- *CNN Today: American Government videos and DVD.*
- A video library, including new selections.
- JoinIn™ on Turning Point Response Systems CD-ROM.
- TextChoice digital library for customized readers.
- InfoTrac® College Edition with InfoMarks.®
- Lecture Launchers—Video Case Studies in American Government—A set of twelve video case studies, produced by Baker/Losco Multimedia in 2002, that is available to qualified adopters in both video and DVD formats. A free *Instructor's Manual* provides brief summaries of each video, a set of key terms, three to five activities for each video, and suggestions on how best to use this exciting collection.

Printed Materials for Students

- *Study Guide,* written by Beth Henschen.
- *Readings in American Government,* Fourth Edition, edited by Mack C. Shelley, Erica Markley, and Steffen W. Schmidt, all of Iowa State University.
- *An Introduction to Critical Thinking and Writing in American Politics.*
- *American Government Internet Activities,* Third Edition.
- *Handbook of Selected Legislation and Other Documents,* Third Edition.
- *Handbook of Selected Court Cases,* Third Edition.
- *College Survival Guide.*
- *Thinking Globally, Acting Locally.*
- *Election 2004: An American Government Supplement,* by John Clark and Brian Schaffn.
- *The Quest for the 2004 Nomination and Beyond,* by Stephen Wayne.
- *Regime Change: Origins, Execution, and Aftermath,* by David Kinsella.
- *The California Governor Recall Election,* by David G. Lawrence.
- *9-11: The Giant Awakens,* by Jeremy Mayer.
- *American Government: Readings and Responses,* by Monica Bauer.
- *Critical Thinking and American Government,* Second Edition, by Kent M. Brudney, John H. Carver, and Mark E. Weber.

Multimedia Supplements for Students

- A special online Resource Center for American government at

  http://politicalscience.wadsworth.com/amgov

- A special, book-specific Web site for *America at Odds,* Fifth Edition, which can be accessed through the Resource Center or at

  http://www.americaatodds.com

- Opposing Viewpoints Resource Center.
- InfoTrac® College Edition, Student Guide for Political Science.
- Current Perspectives: Readings from InfoTrac® College Edition.
- American Government Internet Activities, Third Edition.

- HITS on the Web: Political Science 2004.
- *American Government:Using MicroCase® ExplorIt,* Ninth Edition—The Ninth Edition of this popular ancillary for American government courses includes computer-based assignments, a student version of MicroCase's ExplorIt software, and current real data sets. Each assignment is packed with dozens of issues that are guaranteed to grab student interest.
- WebTutor™ on WebCT and Blackboard, a Web-based teaching and learning tool.

What's New in the Fifth Edition?

We thought that those of you who have used the Fourth Edition of *America at Odds* would like to know what changes have been made for the Fifth Edition. Generally, all of the text, tables, figures, and features in this book have been rewritten or updated as necessary to reflect the most recent developments in American government and politics. The Fifth Edition incorporates the results of the most recent presidential and congressional elections throughout the text as they relate to chapter topics. This edition also presents an up-to-date discussion of the war on terrorism and the second Gulf War. Other key changes and additions for the Fifth Edition include those described below.

Significant Changes to the Chapters

As already indicated, each chapter in *America at Odds,* Fifth Edition, has been updated and revised in order to reflect the most current developments in American politics and government. When appropriate, new features have been added, and references to new laws and court decisions have been included. Throughout the text, we have incorporated references to the 2004 elections as appropriate. Here we list some other significant changes made to selected chapters.

- Chapter 1 (America in the Twenty-First Century)—The discussion of American political culture and ideology has been enhanced. A discussion of the British legacy, including the social contract theory of John Locke, has been moved to this chapter from Chapter 2.
- Chapter 2 (The Constitution)—This chapter has been revised to give greater clarity to the section discussing the events leading up to the Declaration of Independence. More attention has been given to the strengths and weaknesses of the Articles of Confederation.
- Chapter 4 (Civil Liberties)—New subsections on procedural and substantive due process have been added, along with an updated discussion of the right to privacy. A section about hate speech on campus has also been incorporated into the chapter.
- Chapter 5 (Civil Rights)—The section covering affirmative action has been largely rewritten and now includes a discussion of the 2003 Supreme Court decisions regarding admissions policies at the University of Michigan. The discussion of the political participation of Hispanics has been updated, and new data concerning wage discrimination is offered.
- Chapter 6 (Interest Groups)—This chapter now includes subsections on government interest groups and single-issue interest groups. A discussion of issue ads and partisan "527" groups has been added.
- Chapter 8 (Public Opinion and Voting)—The sections on polling were thoroughly revised, reflecting the failures of the exit polls during the 2004 presidential elections. There is an expanded discussion of educational attainment as a factor in voting behavior, along with an analysis of the narrower gender gap in the 2004 elections.
- Chapter 10 (Politics and the Media)—This chapter has been revised to place more emphasis on the rise of Internet media, such as blogs, and the increasing importance of Internet campaign fund-raising. A section on public-relations spending as political advertisement has been added.
- Chapter 11 (Congress)—A new section covering the representative function of Congress has been added, including different theories of the representative function. The redistricting controversy in Texas is discussed, as well as Tom DeLay's involvement in the controversy.
- Chapter 12 (The Presidency)—The discussion of executive privilege has been updated to reflect the recent developments with the 9/11 Commission. The section on presidential

pardons has been expanded, and a discussion of the role of the First Lady has been included.

- Chapter 13 (The Bureaucracy)—This chapter now includes the national intelligence reforms passed by Congress at the recommendation of the 9/11 Commission. A new section on issue networks was added.
- Chapter 14 (The Judiciary)—The section on federal judicial appointments has been thoroughly revised and now includes a discussion of the appointment tactics utilized by the Bush administration and 109th Congress. Recent criticism of the federal courts also receives significant attention.

Acknowledgments

A number of political scientists reviewed the previous editions of *America at Odds*. We remain indebted to the following scholars for their thoughtful suggestions on how to create a text that best suits the needs of today's students and faculty:

David Gray Adler
Idaho State University

Weston H. Agor
University of Texas, El Paso

Ross Baker
Highland Park, New Jersey

Glenn Beamer
University of Virginia

Lynn Brink
Northlake College, Texas

John Francis Burke
University of Houston

Rebecca Cartwright
Montgomery College

Brian Cherry
Northern Michigan University

Richard G. Chesteen
University of Tennessee at Martin

Richard Christofferson
University of Wisconsin, Stevens Point

Lane Crothers
Illinois State University

Larry Elowitz
Georgia College and State University

Craig Emmert
Texas Tech University

Terri Fine
University of Central Florida

Paul D. Foote
Abraham Baldwin Agricultural College, Georgia

Scott R. Furlong
University of Wisconsin, Green Bay

Gail E. Garbrandt
University of Akron, Ohio

J. Tobin Grant
Southern Illinois University

John Geer
Vanderbilt University

Christian Goergen
College of DuPage, Illinois

Paul Goren
Southern Illinois University

Jim Graves
Kentucky State University

Joanne Green
Texas Christian University

Richard Himelfarb
Hofstra University, New York

Marianne Ide
Monterey Peninsula College, California

William E. Kelly
Auburn University, Alabama

Matt Kerbel
Villanova University, Pennsylvania

Brian Kessel
Columbia College, Maryland

James D. King
University of Wyoming

Mel Laracey
University of Texas at San Antonio

Steven A. Light
University of North Dakota

James J. Lopach
University of Montana

Sam W. Mckinstry
East Tennessee State University

William McLauchlan
Purdue University, Indiana

Paz Pena
Austin Community College

Paul Savoie
Long Beach City College, California

Wendy E. Scattergood
University of Wisconsin, Green Bay

Linda J. Simmons
Northern Virginia Community College

Ruth Ann Strickland
Appalachian State University, North Carolina

Larry Taylor
Georgia Southern University

Gabriel Ume
Palo Alto College, Texas

Sharon G. Whitney
Tennessee Technological University

Bruce M. Wilson
University of Central Florida

J. David Woodard
Clemson University, South Carolina

Michele Zebich-Knos
Kennesaw State University, Georgia

In preparing the Fifth Edition of *America at Odds,* we benefited from the criticism and comments of a number of users and reviewers of the Fourth Edition. We thank the following reviewers for their conscientious work:

David Gray Adler
Idaho State University

Glen D. Hunt
Austin Community College, Texas

Carol Sears Botsch
University of South Carolina, Aiken

Melvin C. Laracey
University of Texas at San Antonio

Henry Bowers
Henry Ford Community College, Michigan

John D. Lees
Oakland University, Michigan

Luther F. Carter
Francis Marion University, South Carolina

Mark D. Maironis
Eastern Michigan University

M. Jeffrey Colbert
University of North Carolina, Greensboro

Anthony Perry
Henry Ford Community College, Michigan

Cecile D. Durish
Austin Community College, Texas

Our styles of teaching and mentoring students were shaped in important ways by our graduate faculty at Ohio State University. We thank Lawrence Baum, Herbert Asher, Elliot Slotnick, and Randall Ripley for lessons well taught. The students we have had the privilege of working with at many fine universities during our careers have also taught us a great deal. We trust that some of what appears on these pages reflects their insights, and we hope that what we have written will capture the interest of current and future students. Of course, we owe an immeasurable debt to our families, whose divergent views on political issues reflect an America at odds.

We thank Susan Badger, president of Wadsworth Publishing Company for all of her encouragement and support throughout our work on this project. We were also fortunate to have the editorial advice of Clark Baxter, publisher, and David Tatom, executive editor, and the assistance of Stacey Sims, senior developmental editor, who supervised all aspects of the supplements and the text. We thank Rebecca Green, assistant editor, for her handling of the supplements and related items. We also thank Paul Bartels and Lavina Leed Miller for their tremendous help in coordinating the project and for their research, copyediting, and proofreading assistance. We received additional copyediting and proofreading assistance from Pat Lewis, Mary Berry, and Suzie DeFazio. We are also grateful to Sue Jasin of K&M Consulting, Vickie Reierson, and Roxie Lee. We are especially indebted to the staff at Parkwood Composition. Their ability to generate the pages for this text quickly and accurately made it possible for us to meet our ambitious schedule. We appreciate the enthusiasm of Janise Fry, our hardworking marketing manager, and the cheerful support of Ann Borman, our project editor, at Wadsworth Publishing Company. We would also like to acknowledge Bill Stryker, our designer and production manager, for producing the most attractive and user-friendly American government text on the market today.

If you or your students have ideas or suggestions, you can write us directly or send us information through Wadsworth Publishing Company.

E.I.S.
B.M.H.

chapter 1

america in the twenty-first century

CHAPTER OBJECTIVES

After reading this chapter, you should be able to . . .

- Explain what is meant by the terms *politics* and *government*.

- Describe the basic functions of government.

- Identify the various types of government systems.

- Distinguish between a direct democracy and a representative democracy.

- Summarize some of the basic principles of American democracy.

- Identify the basic American political values.

Is There Too Much Religion in American Politics?

Moral values—along with jobs, education, and the war on terrorism—proved to be one of the greatest concerns among voters when they went to the polls in 2004. Issues such as abortion, gay marriage, and stem-cell research weighed on the minds of many Americans, and evangelical Christians continued to be a powerful bloc of voters. Certainly, the importance of religion and values in the 2004 elections helped the Republicans retain the White House and increase their majorities in both chambers of Congress.

In our increasingly multicultural and religiously diverse society, however, everyone does not share the same religious beliefs and values. Therefore, according to some Americans, political candidates and government policymakers should keep religion out of political campaigns and political decision making. Others disagree, contending that in a country in which a majority of the population claims to be Christian, we need a leader who upholds Christian values.

Keep Religion out of Politics, Say Some

Above all else, those in favor of keeping religion out of politics point to the U.S. Constitution. The Constitution mandates the separation of church and state. Indeed, the founders of this nation believed that protecting religious freedom for *all* Americans was so fundamental that they provided for this freedom in the very first clause of the Bill of Rights (the first ten amendments to the U.S. Constitution). In the founders' eyes, ensuring equal protection for the beliefs (or nonbeliefs) of all Americans should outweigh the desire of a religious majority to impose its values on the whole population.

Opponents of religion in politics believe that we need to follow the example of the decidedly more secular European nations. Most Europeans are surprised by President George W. Bush's public expressions of faith and are bewildered when he speaks of "praying about" decisions of national significance. In particular, they question the extent to which Bush's religious values have influenced proposed legislation to restrict stem-cell research and ban gay marriage. After all, the president represents *all* Americans, not just those who share his religious convictions. Declarations of faith should never be a condition for public office in our secular democracy. Separation of church and state must be guaranteed to protect Americans of every religious persuasion, as well as those who choose no affiliation at all.

Religion Is Ingrained in Our Political Tradition, Say Others

Other Americans argue that we are, after all, a nation based on Judeo-Christian culture and values and that there is nothing unusual about wanting our leaders to uphold those values. Furthermore, religion is deeply ingrained in our nation's past. Because most people in this country share a similar religious tradition, some argue that we should not discourage politicians from bringing religion into politics.

Indeed, religion routinely appears in our public life. Each time we look at a dollar bill, the phrase "In God We Trust" stares back at us. Public schoolchildren reciting the Pledge of Allegiance utter "one nation under God." Opening sessions of Congress often begin with a prayer, and numerous politicians speak of faith and religious values guiding their decisions.

Staunch supporters of mixing religion and politics argue that prayer should be allowed in public schools and that gay marriage should be banned. Everyone should be bound to values shared by most Americans, they claim. Indeed, a wide majority of Americans claim to be "fairly to very" religious, and many say that they would never vote for an atheist candidate. They argue that separating religion and politics would be very difficult, if not impossible. Religion has always been a part of our nation's story, from the moment the Puritans splashed ashore at Plymouth Rock to the present time.

Where Do You Stand?

1. Do you feel uncomfortable when politicians use religious language and speak of morals and values? Why or why not? When, if ever, is religion appropriate in the political arena?

2. Consider what it would be like to be a member of a religious minority. How would you feel if the dominant religious group enacted laws that were contrary to your beliefs?

Explore This Issue Online

- The Pew Forum on Religion and Politics, a project of the nonpartisan Pew Research Center, offers links to numerous perspectives on the topic of religion and politics. To access this site, go to **http://pewforum.org/religion-politics**.

- Another source to explore for a range of views on the role of religion in politics is the Librarians' Index to the Internet at **http://www.lii.org**. When you access the site, key the words "religion and politics" into the search box.

Introduction

Regardless of how Americans feel about government, one thing is certain: they can't live without it. James Madison (1751–1836) once said, "If men were angels, no government would be necessary." Today, his statement still holds true. People are not perfect. People need an organized form of government and a set of rules by which to live.

Note, though, that even if people were perfect, they would still need to establish rules to guide their behavior. They would somehow have to agree on how to divide up a society's resources, such as its land, among themselves and how to balance individual needs and wants against those of society generally. These perfect people would also have to decide *how* to make these decisions. They would need to create a process for making rules and a form of government to enforce those rules. It is thus not difficult to understand why government is one of humanity's oldest and most universal institutions. No society has existed without some form of government. The need for authority and organization will never disappear.

As you will read in this chapter, a number of different systems of government exist in the world today. In the United States, we have a democracy in which decisions about pressing issues ultimately are made by the people through their representatives in government. Because people rarely have identical thoughts and feelings about issues, it is not surprising that in any democracy citizens are often at odds with one another. Certainly, Americans are at odds over many political and social issues, including the issue discussed in the chapter-opening feature. Americans were also seriously at odds over the divisive character of the 2004 presidential campaigns. Many regarded the red-state/blue-state map of the nation as symbolic of a deep cultural divide between those who supported President George W. Bush and those who opposed him. Throughout this book, you will read about contemporary issues that have brought various groups of Americans into conflict with one another.

Realize, though, that the aim of this book is not to depict a nation that is falling apart at the seams. Rather, it is to place the conflicting views currently being expressed by Americans in a historical perspective. Having citizens at odds with one another is nothing new in this country. Indeed, throughout this nation's history, Americans have had strikingly different ideas about what decisions should be made, and by whom. Differences in opinion are part and parcel of a democratic government. Ultimately, these differences are resolved, one way or another, through the American political process and our government **institutions.**

institution An ongoing organization that performs certain functions for society.

U.S. President George W. Bush takes the oath of office at the 55th Presidential Inauguration in Washington, D.C., on January 20, 2005. Pictured next to him are First Lady Laura Bush and their two daughters, Barbara and Jenna. Then chief justice William Rehnquist administered the oath.

Dennis Brack/*Bloomberg News/Landov*

What Are Politics and Government?

Politics means many things to many people. To some, politics is an expensive and extravagant game played in Washington, D.C., in state capitols, and in city halls, particularly during election time. To others, politics involves all of the tactics and maneuvers carried out by the president and Congress. Most formal definitions of politics, however, begin with the assumption that **social conflict**—disagreements among people in a society over what the society's priorities should be—is inevitable. Conflicts will naturally arise over how the society should use its scarce resources and who should receive various benefits, such as wealth, status, health care, and higher education. Resolving such conflicts is the essence of **politics.** Political scientist Harold Lasswell perhaps said it best when he defined politics as the process of determining "who gets what, when, and how" in a society.[1]

There are also many different notions about the meaning of government. From the perspective of political science, though, **government** can best be defined as the individuals and institutions that make society's rules and that also possess the *power* and *authority* to enforce those rules. Although this definition of government sounds remote and abstract, what the government does is very real indeed. As one scholar put it, "Make no mistake. What Congress does directly and powerfully affects our daily lives."[2] The same can be said for decisions made by state legislators and local government officials, as well as for decisions rendered by the courts—the judicial branch of government. Of course, a key question remains: How do specific individuals obtain the power and authority to govern? As you will read shortly, the answer to this question varies from one type of political system to another.

To understand what government is, you need to understand what it actually does for people and society. Generally, in any country government serves at least three essential purposes: (1) it resolves conflicts; (2) it provides public services; and (3) it defends the nation and its culture against attacks by other nations.

Resolving Conflicts

Even though people have lived together in groups since the beginning of time, none of these groups has been free of social conflict. As mentioned, disputes over how to distribute a society's valued resources inevitably arise because valued resources, such as property, are limited, while people's wants are unlimited. To resolve such disputes, people need ways to determine who wins and who loses, and how to get the losers to accept those decisions. Who has the legitimate power and authority to make such decisions? This is where government steps in.

Governments decide how conflicts will be resolved so that public order can be maintained. Governments have **power**—the ability to influence the behavior of others. Power is getting someone to do something he or she would not do otherwise. Power may involve the use of force (often called coercion), persuasion, or rewards. Governments also have **authority,** which they can exercise only if their power is legitimate. As used here, the term *legitimate power* means power that is collectively recognized and accepted by society as legally and morally correct. Power and authority are central to a government's ability to resolve conflicts by making and enforcing laws, placing limits on what people can do, and developing court systems to make final decisions.

For example, the judicial branch of government—specifically, the United States Supreme Court—resolved the conflict over whether the votes in certain Florida counties could be recounted after the 2000 presidential elections. Because of the Court's stature and authority as a government body, there was little resistance to its decision not to allow the recounting—although the decision was strongly criticized by many.

Providing Public Services

Another important purpose of government is to provide **public services**—essential services that many individuals cannot provide for themselves. Governments undertake projects that individuals usually would not or could not do on their own, such as building and maintaining roads, providing welfare programs, operating public schools, and preserving national parks. Governments also provide such services as law enforcement, fire protection, and public health and safety programs. As Abraham Lincoln once stated:

---

social conflict Disagreements among people in a society over what the society's priorities should be with respect to the use of scarce resources.

politics The process of resolving conflicts over how society should use its scarce resources and who should receive various benefits, such as public health care and public higher education. According to Harold Lasswell, politics is the process of determining "who gets what, when, and how" in a society.

government The individuals and institutions that make society's rules and that also possess the power and authority to enforce those rules.

power The ability to influence the behavior of others, usually through the use of force, persuasion, or rewards.

authority The ability to exercise power, such as the power to make and enforce laws, legitimately.

public services Essential services that individuals cannot provide for themselves, such as building and maintaining roads, providing welfare programs, operating public schools, and preserving national parks.

The legitimate object of government is to do for a community of people whatever they need to have done but cannot do at all, or cannot so well do for themselves in their separate and individual capacities. But in all that people can individually do for themselves, government ought not to interfere.

Some public services are provided equally to all citizens of the United States. For example, government services such as national defense and domestic law enforcement allow all citizens, at least in theory, to feel that their lives and property are safe. Laws governing clean air and safe drinking water benefit all Americans. Other services are provided only to citizens who are in need at a particular time, even though they are paid for by all citizens through taxes. Examples of such services include health and welfare benefits, and public housing. Laws such as the Americans with Disabilities Act explicitly protect the rights of people with disabilities, although all Americans pay for such protections whether they are disabled or not.

Defending the Nation and Its Culture

Historically, matters of national security and defense have been given high priority by governments and have demanded considerable time, effort, and expense. The U.S. government provides for the common defense and national security with its Army, Navy, Air Force, Marines, and Coast Guard. The State Department, Defense Department, Homeland Security Department, Central Intelligence Agency, National Security Agency, and other agencies also contribute to this defense network. As part of an ongoing policy of national security, many departments and agencies in the federal government are constantly dealing with other nations. The Constitution gives our national government exclusive power over relations with foreign nations. No individual state can negotiate a treaty with a foreign nation.

Of course, in defending the nation against attacks by other nations, a government helps to preserve the nation's culture, as well as its integrity as an independent unit. Failure to defend successfully against foreign attacks may have significant consequences for a nation's culture. For example, consider what happened in Tibet in the 1950s. When the former government of that country was unable to defend itself against the People's Republic of China, the conquering (mainland) Chinese set out on a systematic program to destroy Tibet's culture.

Since the terrorist attacks on the World Trade Center and the Pentagon in 2001, defending the homeland against future terrorist attacks has become a priority of our government. One of the many issues over which Americans are at odds today has to do with antiterrorism policies and programs that threaten to curb our civil liberties. (See, for example, the program discussed in this chapter's *The Politics of National Security* feature on the next page.)

Different Systems of Government

Through the centuries, the functions of government just discussed have been performed by many different types of government structures. A government's structure is influenced by a number of factors, such as history, customs, values, geography, climate, resources, and human experiences and needs. No two nations have exactly the same form of government. Over time, however, political analysts have developed various ways of classifying different systems of government. One of the most meaningful ways of classifying governments is according to *who* governs. Who has the power to make the rules and laws that all must obey?

Rule by One: Autocracy

In an **autocracy,** the power and authority of the government are in the hands of a single person. At one time, autocracy was a common form of government, and it still exists in some parts of the world. Autocrats usually obtain their power either by inheriting it or by force.

Monarchy   One form of autocracy, known as a **monarchy,** is government by a king, queen, emperor, empress, tsar, or tsarina. In a monarchy, the monarch, who usually acquires power through inheritance, is the highest authority in the government.

autocracy A form of government in which the power and authority of the government are in the hands of a single person.

monarchy A form of autocracy in which a king, queen, emperor, empress, tsar, or tsarina is the highest authority in the government; monarchs usually obtain their power through inheritance.

The POLITICS of national SECURITY

You are here

Terrorism Information Awareness

In the aftermath of the terrorist attacks on September 11, 2001, government officials and citizens alike asked why government agencies designed to protect us had failed to stop the terrorists before they acted. As information about the terrorists' activities before September 11 was revealed, the government's answer was that it "failed to connect the dots." Since then, the government has been working on systems that could monitor the actions of potential terrorists and thwart a terrorist attack before it occurs.

To tie together the actions of hundreds, if not thousands, of potential terrorists would require a sophisticated computer database that could track everything from applications for passports, visas, and driver's licenses to credit-card transactions, car rentals, airline ticket purchases, gun purchases, arrest records, e-mail, and more. And to monitor the activity of every potential terrorist, the government would need to monitor the activity of, well, just about everyone. The government is creating such a "data-mining" system. It is called the Terrorism Information Awareness system, or TIA.

LIBERTY VERSUS NATIONAL SECURITY

As this chapter explains, a fundamental political value of all Americans is liberty—the freedom of individuals to believe, act, and express themselves freely. As you will read in Chapter 4, this liberty is protected by the First Amendment to the Constitution. If the government creates a system that could monitor the transactions, purchases, and records of all Americans, this fundamental tenet of our democracy could be violated. Yet part of the definition of liberty is

that one person's freedom should not infringe on the rights of others, such as the right to be secure in our persons. How can the government balance the need to protect our liberties with its duty to provide national security?

In countries with fewer constitutionally protected rights than we enjoy, the war against terrorism has been proceeding more quickly. Paradoxically, the U.S. government often finds it easier to monitor potential terrorists abroad than within the United States. On numerous occasions, the Central Intelligence Agency and the National Security Agency have captured suspected terrorists in foreign countries by using methods that would have been deemed illegal within America's borders.

TECHNOLOGY AND "BIG BROTHER"

TIA officials claim that they can develop data-mining technology that will be effective against potential terrorists and yet pose few risks to American civil liberties. John Poindexter, the former director of the Information Awareness Office, has argued that ordinary Americans have little to fear from systems designed to sift through seemingly infinite banks of electronic data. Champions of such technology say that ordinary Americans' identities can remain protected while analysts mine financial and other "public" records for suspicious activities.

Businesses, financial institutions, and medical organizations share records on a daily basis. TIA analysts desire access to these same channels of information, claiming they can use the data to protect citizens against potential terrorist acts. For example, the proposed TIA system could discover that a person had purchased nitrate fertilizer, diesel fuel, and a rental truck. By connecting the dots between these transactions, an analyst could alert the proper authorities to suspicious activity.

For many Americans, the thought of "Big Brother" peering into their daily lives makes them feel personally violated. Those who are skeptical of the TIA system argue that the government could potentially abuse the technology to snoop into Americans' private lives. An example cited by many is government access to bookstore records. Under TIA guidelines, an individual's purchase of books about chemical reactions might be considered sufficiently suspicious to spawn an investigation. The American Civil Liberties Union has taken an aggressive stance against the TIA system, saying that it is an illegal intrusion and could potentially be misused by "Big Brother."

New technology is making it possible for the government to monitor extensively the activities of private individuals. Here, agents in the Central Intelligence Agency's "Fusion Center" monitor and coordinate actions against terrorists. Many Americans worry that new data-mining technology will compromise their privacy rights to an unacceptable extent.

© Roger Ressmeyer/Corbis

Are We Safer?

How effective do you think data-mining technology can be in the war on terrorism? To what degree—if any—should Americans forfeit their privacy rights and other civil liberties in the interests of national security?

---

divine right theory A theory that the right to rule by a king or queen was derived directly from God rather than from the consent of the people.

Historically, many monarchies were *absolute monarchies,* in which the ruler held complete and unlimited power as a matter of divine right. Prior to the eighteenth century, the theory of divine right was widely accepted in Europe. The **divine right theory,** variations of which had existed since ancient times, held that God gave those of royal birth the unlimited right to govern other men and women. In other words, those of royal birth had a "divine right" to rule. According to this theory, only God could judge those of royal birth. Thus, all citizens were bound to obey their monarchs, no matter how unfair or unjust they seemed to be. Challenging this power was regarded not only as treason against the government but also as a sin against God.

Most modern monarchies, however, are *constitutional monarchies,* in which the monarch shares governmental power with elected lawmakers. The monarch's power is limited, or checked, by other government leaders and perhaps by a constitution or a bill of rights. These constitutional monarchs serve mainly as *ceremonial* leaders of their governments, as in Great Britain, Denmark, and Sweden.

Dictatorship Another form of autocracy is a **dictatorship,** in which a single leader rules, although not through inheritance. Dictators often gain supreme power by using force, either through a military victory or by overthrowing another dictator or leader. Dictators hold absolute power and are not accountable to anyone else.

A dictatorship can also be *totalitarian,* which means that the leader (or group of leaders) seeks to control almost all aspects of social and economic life. The needs of the nation come before the needs of individuals, and all citizens must work for the common goals established by the government. Examples of this form of government include Adolf Hitler's government in Nazi Germany from 1933 to 1945, Benito Mussolini's rule in Italy from 1923 to 1943, and Josef Stalin's rule in the Soviet Union from 1929 to 1953. More contemporary examples of totalitarian dictators include Fidel Castro in Cuba, Kim Jong Il in North Korea, and, until his government was dismantled in 2003, Saddam Hussein in Iraq.

Rule by Many: Democracy

The most familiar form of government to Americans is **democracy,** in which the supreme political authority rests with the people. The word *democracy* comes from the Greek *demos,* meaning "the people," and *kratia,* meaning "rule." The main idea of democracy is that government exists only by the consent of the people and reflects the will of the majority.

The Athenian Model of Direct Democracy Democracy as a form of government began long ago. **Direct democracy** exists when the people participate directly in government decision making. In its purest form, direct democracy was practiced in Athens and other ancient Greek city-states about 2,500 years ago. Every Athenian citizen participated in the governing assembly and voted on all major issues. Although some consider the Athenian form of direct democracy ideal because it demanded a high degree of citizen participation, others point out that most residents in the Athenian city-state (women, foreigners, and slaves) were not deemed to be citizens and thus were not allowed to participate in government.

Clearly, direct democracy is possible only in small communities in which citizens can meet in a chosen place and decide key issues and policies. Nowhere in the world does pure direct democracy exist today. Some New England town meetings, though, and a few of the smaller political subunits, or cantons, of Switzerland still use a modified form of direct democracy.

Representative Democracy Although the founders of the United States were aware of the Athenian model and agreed that government should be based on the consent of the governed, many feared that a pure, direct democracy would deteriorate into mob rule. They believed that large groups of people meeting together would ignore the rights and opinions of people in the minority and would make decisions without careful thought. They concluded that a representative democracy would be the better choice because it would enable public decisions to be made in a calmer and more deliberate manner.

In a **representative democracy,** the will of the majority is expressed through a smaller group of individuals elected by the people to act as their representatives. These representatives are responsible to the people for their conduct and can be voted out of office. Our founders preferred to use the term **republic,** which means essentially a representative democracy—with one difference. A republic, by definition, has no king or queen; rather, the people are sovereign. In contrast, a representative democracy may be headed by a monarch. For example, as Britain evolved into a representative democracy, it retained its monarch as the head of state.

dictatorship A form of government in which absolute power is exercised by a single person who has usually obtained his or her power by the use of force.

democracy A system of government in which the people have ultimate political authority. The word is derived from the Greek *demos* (people) and *kratia* (rule).

direct democracy A system of government in which political decisions are made by the people themselves rather than by elected representatives. This form of government was practiced in some areas of ancient Greece.

representative democracy A form of democracy in which the will of the majority is expressed through smaller groups of individuals elected by the people to act as their representatives.

republic Essentially, a term referring to a representative democracy—in which there is no king or queen and the people are sovereign. The people elect smaller groups of individuals to act as the people's representatives.

This New Hampshire town meeting is an example of direct democracy.

Farrell Grehan/Photo Researchers

In the modern world, there are two forms of representative democracy: presidential and parliamentary. In a *presidential democracy*, the lawmaking and law-enforcing branches of government are separate but equal. For example, in the United States, Congress is charged with the power to make laws, and the president is charged with the power to carry them out. In a *parliamentary democracy*, the lawmaking and law-enforcing branches of government overlap. In Great Britain, for example, the prime minister and the cabinet are members of the legislature, called Parliament. Parliament thus both enacts the laws and carries them out.

Other Forms of Government

Autocracy and democracy are but two of many forms of government. Traditionally, other types of government have included those that are ruled "by the few." For example, an aristocracy (from the Greek word *aristos*) is a government in which the "best," or a small privileged class, rule. A *plutocracy* is a government in which the wealthy (*ploutos* in Greek means "wealth") exercise ruling power. A *meritocracy* is a government in which the rulers have earned, or merited, the right to govern because of their special skills or talents.

A difficult form of government for Americans to understand is a *theocracy*—a term derived from the Greek words meaning "rule by the deity" or "rule by God." In a theocracy, there is no separation of church and state. Rather, the government rules according to religious precepts. For a closer look at one theocracy in today's world, see this chapter's *Comparative Politics* feature.

American Democracy

> This country, with all its institutions, belongs to the people who inhabit it. Whenever they shall grow weary of the existing government, they can exercise their constitutional right to amend it, or their revolutionary right to dismember or overthrow it.

With these words, Abraham Lincoln underscored the most fundamental concept of American government: that the people, not the government, are ultimately in control.

The British Legacy

In writing the U.S. Constitution, the framers incorporated two basic principles of government that had evolved in England: *limited government* and *representative government.* In a sense, then, the beginnings of our form of government are linked to events that occurred centuries earlier in England. They are also linked to the writings of European philosophers, particularly the English political philosopher John Locke. From these writings, the founders of our nation derived ideas to justify their rebellion against Britain and the establishment of a "government by the people."

Limited Government   At one time, the English monarch had virtually unrestricted powers. This changed in 1215, when King John was forced by his nobles to accept the Magna Carta, or Great Charter. This monumental document provided for a trial by a jury of one's peers (equals). It prohibited the taking of a person's life, liberty, or property except by the lawful judgment of that person's peers. The Magna Carta also forced the king to obtain the nobles' approval of any taxes he imposed on his subjects. Government thus became a contract between the king and his subjects.

The importance of the Magna Carta to England cannot be overemphasized, because it clearly established the principle of **limited government**—a government on which strict limits are placed, usually by a constitution. Hence, the Magna Carta signaled the end of the monarch's absolute power. Although the rights provided under the Magna Carta originally applied only to the nobility, the document formed the basis of the future constitutional government for all individuals in England and eventually in the United States.

The principle of limited government was expanded four hundred years later, in 1628, when King Charles I signed the Petition of Rights. Among other things, this petition prohibited the monarch from imprisoning political critics without a jury trial. Perhaps more important, the petition declared that even the king or queen had to obey the law of the land.

The National Archives

The Magna Carta

limited government A form of government based on the principle that the powers of government should be clearly limited either through a written document or through wide public understanding; characterized by institutional checks to ensure that government serves public rather than private interests.

comparative politics

Theocracy in Iran

As discussed elsewhere, many different governmental frameworks exist around the globe. Consider Iran, an Islamic nation in the Middle East. In most Muslim (Islamic) countries, government and religion are intertwined to a degree that is quite startling to both Europeans and Americans. Church and state are not separated in a theocracy, as they are in the United States and in many other nations.

GOVERNMENT BASED ON ISLAM

The Koran (or Qur'an), not the national constitution, serves as the basis for the law in Iran. The Koran consists of sacred writings that Muslims (those of the Islamic faith) believe were revealed to the prophet Muhammad by Allah through the angel Gabriel. In Iran, church and state are not separate. The Council of Guardians, an unelected group of clerics (religious leaders), ensures that laws and lawmakers conform to the teachings of Islam.

OBSTACLES TO REFORM MOVEMENTS

Iran's national constitution vests supreme power in the hands of a single religious leader, a position currently held by Ayatollah Ali Khamenei. The result is a clerical dictatorship. The country has elections, a legislature, and a president. Iran even calls itself an "Islamic democracy." Yet despite years of effort by Iranian President Mohammad Khatami and reformist elements in the parliament, the nation remains under the ultimate control of Khamenei and the Council of Guardians. Their power was evident in 2000, when reform-oriented candidates swept national elections only to have their victories overturned by the clerics. A total of 2,500 candidates, including eighty legislators, were barred from holding office. The 2000 election sparked a 67 percent voter turnout. The people had spoken, but the clerics ultimately refused to listen. As much as three-fourths of the Iranian population is thought to support an end to clerical rule, but Khamenei controls the military—a formidable obstacle to reformist efforts.

For Critical Analysis

Is it possible to have a theocratic form of government in a democracy? Why or why not?

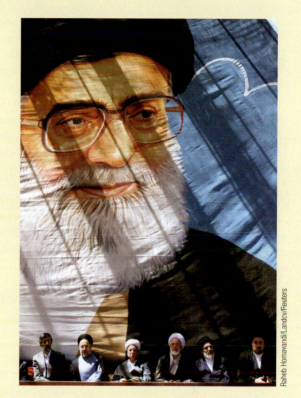

Raheb Homavandi/Landov/Reuters

Members of Iran's leadership sit beneath a portrait of Iran's religious leader, Ayatollah Ali Khamenei, during a ceremony to mark the fifteenth anniversary of the death of Ayatollah Ruhollah Khomeini, the founder of the Islamic Republic, in June 2004.

In 1689, the English Parliament (described shortly) passed the English Bill of Rights, which further extended the concept of limited government. This document included several important ideas:

■ The king or queen could not interfere with parliamentary elections.
■ The king or queen had to have Parliament's approval to levy (collect) taxes or to maintain an army.
■ The king or queen had to rule with the consent of the people's representatives in Parliament.
■ The people could not be subjected to cruel or unusual punishment or to excessive fines.

The English colonists in North America were also English citizens, and thus the English Bill of Rights of 1689 applied to them as well. As a result, virtually all of the major concepts in the English Bill of Rights became part of the American system of government.

Representative Government In a representative government, the people, by whatever means, elect individuals to make governmental decisions for all of the citizens. Usually, these representatives of the people are elected to their offices for specific periods of time.

parliament The name of the national legislative body in countries governed by a parliamentary system, as in Britain and Canada.

bicameral legislature A legislature made up of two chambers, or parts. The United States has a bicameral legislature, composed of the House of Representatives and the Senate.

social contract A voluntary agreement among individuals to create a government and to give that government adequate power to secure the mutual protection and welfare of all individuals.

natural rights Rights that are not bestowed by governments but are inherent within every man, woman, and child by virtue of the fact that he or she is a human being.

John Locke (1632–1704), an English philosopher. Locke argued that human beings were equal and endowed by nature with certain rights, such as the right to life, liberty, and property. The purpose of government, according to Locke, was to protect those rights. Locke's theory of natural rights and his contention that government stemmed from a social contract among society's members were an important part of the political heritage brought to this country by the English colonists.

The Granger Collection

This group of representatives is often referred to as a **parliament,** which is a **bicameral** (two-house) **legislature.** The English Parliament consists of the House of Lords (upper chamber) and the House of Commons (lower chamber). The English form of government provided a model for Americans to follow. Many of the American colonies had bicameral legislatures—as did, eventually, the U.S. Congress that was established by the Constitution.

Political Philosophy—Social Contracts and Natural Rights

Our democracy resulted from what can be viewed as a type of **social contract** among early Americans to create and abide by a set of governing rules. Social-contract theory was developed in the seventeenth and eighteenth centuries by philosophers, such as John Locke (1632–1704) and Thomas Hobbes (1588–1679) in England and Jean-Jacques Rousseau (1712–1778) in France. According to this theory, individuals voluntarily agree with one another, in a "social contract," to give up some of their freedoms to obtain the benefits of orderly government; the government is given adequate power to secure the mutual protection and welfare of all individuals. Generally, social-contract theory, in one form or another, provides the theoretical underpinnings of most modern democracies, including that of the United States.

Although Hobbes and Rousseau also posited social contracts as the bases of governments, neither theorist was as influential in America as John Locke was. John Locke argued that people are born with **natural rights** to life, liberty, and property. He theorized that the purpose of government was to protect those rights; if it did not, it would lose its legitimacy and need not be obeyed. Locke's assumption that people, by nature, are rational and are endowed with certain rights is an essential component of his theory that people can govern themselves. As you will read in Chapter 2, when the American colonists rebelled against British rule, such concepts as "natural rights" and a government based on a "social contract" became important theoretical tools in justifying the rebellion.

Principles of American Democracy

American democracy is based on five fundamental principles:

- *Equality in voting.* Citizens need equal opportunities to express their preferences about policies or leaders.
- *Individual freedom.* All individuals must have the greatest amount of freedom possible without interfering with the rights of others.
- *Equal protection of the law.* The law must entitle all persons to equal protection of the law.
- *Majority rule and minority rights.* The majority should rule, while guaranteeing the rights of minorities so that the latter may sometimes become majorities through fair and lawful means.
- *Voluntary consent to be governed.* The people who make up a democracy must agree voluntarily to be governed by the rules laid down by their representatives.

These principles frame many of the political issues that you will read about in this book. They also frequently lie at the heart of America's political conflicts. Does the principle of minority rights mean that minorities should receive preferential treatment in hiring and firing decisions? Does the principle of individual freedom mean that individuals can express whatever they want on the Internet, including hateful, racist comments? Such conflicts over individual rights and freedoms and over society's priorities are natural and inevitable. Resolving these conflicts is what politics is all about. What is important is that Americans are able to reach acceptable compromises—because of their common political heritage.

American Political Values

Historically, as the nations of the world emerged, the boundaries of each nation normally coincided with boundaries of a population that shared a common ethnic heritage, language, and culture. From its beginnings as a nation, however, America has been defined less by the culture shared by its diverse population than by a set of ideas, or its political culture. A **political culture** can be defined as a patterned set of ideas, values, and ways of thinking about government and politics.

political culture The set of ideas, values, and attitudes about government and the political process held by a community or a nation.

The ideals and standards that constitute American political culture are embodied in the Declaration of Independence, one of the founding documents of this nation, which is discussed further in Chapter 2 and presented in its entirety in Appendix B. The political values outlined in the Declaration of Independence include natural rights (to life, liberty, and the pursuit of happiness), equality under the law, government by the consent of the governed, and limited government powers. In some ways, the Declaration of Independence defines Americans' sense of right and wrong. It presents a challenge to anyone who might wish to overthrow our democratic processes or deny our citizens their natural rights.

Fundamental political values shared by most Americans include liberty, equality, and property. These values provide a basic framework for American political discourse and debate because they are shared by most Americans, yet individual Americans often interpret their meaning quite differently.

Liberty The term **liberty** refers to a state of being free from external controls or restrictions. In the United States, the Constitution sets forth our civil liberties (see Chapter 4), including the freedom to practice whatever religion we choose and to be free from any state-imposed religion. Our liberties also include the freedom to speak freely on any topics and issues. Because people cannot govern themselves unless they are free to voice their opinions, freedom of speech is a basic requirement in a true democracy.

liberty The freedom of individuals to believe, act, and express themselves freely so long as doing so does not infringe on the rights of other individuals in the society.

Clearly, though, if we are to live together with others, there have to be some restrictions on individual liberties. If people were allowed to do whatever they wished, without regard for the rights or liberties of others, pandemonium would result. Hence, a more accurate definition of liberty would be as follows: *liberty is the freedom of individuals to believe, act, and express themselves freely so long as doing so does not infringe on the rights of other individuals in the society.*

AMERICA at odds

Has America Gone Too Far in "Exporting Liberty"?

President Bush's decision to go to war against Iraq in March 2003 was a controversial move that divided Americans and caused a major rift within the world community. Many Americans, despite their concern about future terrorist attacks, believed that we should proceed cautiously in the war on terrorism. Although faulty intelligence indicated prior to the war that Iraq had weapons of mass destruction and links to the al Qaeda terrorist network, Iraq had not shown overt hostility toward the United States. Furthermore, many felt that the United States should not act alone but rather should address the problem jointly with its European allies and the United Nations. In the view of these Americans, Bush's plans to attack Iraq would only stir up resistance in the Middle East and encourage more terrorist activity. They feared that any American attempt to influence the social and political structure of Iraq would be viewed with extreme suspicion by the Iraqi people, who did not have a particularly favorable opinion of America to begin with.

Bush's overarching goal was to "export liberty" to the Middle East, creating free democratic societies in nations that had been ruled by stifling despots and religious fundamentalists. Bush reiterated this goal in his inaugural address in January 2005. By bringing liberty and democracy to these nations, Bush has argued that he will be making America safer from future terrorist attacks while improving the lives of people in the Middle East. Even when it became clear that Iraq had never posed an immediate threat to the United States (that it had possessed no weapons of mass destruction or identifiable links to al Qaeda), Bush and his supporters argued that the war was justified. The war liberated Iraq from its oppressive government and made it possible to establish a democratic government in that country.

A U.S. Marine hands out school supplies and gifts to Iraqi students as part of Operation Iraqi Freedom's security and stabilization efforts.

AP Photo/USMC, LCpl Andrew D. Young

No doubt, most Americans would like nations that are now suffering from oppressive political regimes to enjoy liberty and democracy. Yet how far should America go in "exporting liberty" through preemptive wars? If furthering the cause of liberty and democracy was a sufficient justification for the war against Iraq, as the Bush administration has claimed, this opens the door to preemptive wars against all other nations headed by cruel dictators.

equality A concept that holds, at a minimum, that all people are entitled to equal protection under the law.

Equality

The goal of **equality** has always been a central part of American political culture. Many of the first settlers came to this country to be free of unequal treatment and persecution. They sought the freedom to live and worship as they wanted. They believed that anyone who worked hard could succeed, and America became known as the "land of opportunity." The Declaration of Independence confirmed the importance of equality to early Americans by stating, "We hold these Truths to be self-evident, that all Men are created equal." Because of the goal of equality, the Constitution prohibited the government from granting titles of nobility. Article I, Section 9, of the Constitution states, "No Title of Nobility shall be granted by the United States." (The Constitution did not prohibit slavery, however—see Chapter 2.)

But what, exactly, does equality mean? Does it mean simply political equality—the right to vote and run for political office? Does it mean that individuals should have equal opportunities to develop their talents and skills? What about those who are poor, suffer from disabilities, or are otherwise at a competitive disadvantage? Should it be the government's responsibility to ensure that these groups also have equal opportunities? Although most Americans believe that all persons should have the opportunity to fulfill their potential, few contend that it is the government's responsibility to totally eliminate the economic and social differences that lead to unequal opportunities. Indeed, some contend that efforts to achieve equality, in the sense of equal justice for all, are misguided attempts to create an ideal society that can never exist.[3]

Property

As noted earlier, the English philosopher John Locke asserted that people are born with "natural" rights and that among these rights are life, liberty, and *property*. The Declaration of Independence makes a similar assertion: people are born with certain "unalienable" rights, including the right to life, liberty, and the *pursuit of happiness*. For Americans, property and the pursuit of happiness are closely related. Americans place a great value on land ownership, on material possessions, and on the monetary value of their jobs. Property gives its owners political power and the liberty to do whatever they want—within limits. (For one limitation on property ownership, see this chapter's *Perception versus Reality* feature.)

Political Values in a Multicultural Society

From the earliest British and European settlers to the numerous cultural groups who today call America their home, American society has always been a multicultural society. Until recently, most Americans viewed the United States as the world's melting pot. They accepted that American society included numerous ethnic and cultural groups, but they expected that the members of these groups would abandon their cultural distinctions and assimilate the language and customs of Americans. One of the outgrowths of the civil rights movement of the 1960s, however, was an emphasis on *multiculturalism,* the belief that the many cultures that make up American society should remain distinct and be protected—and even encouraged—by our laws.

The ethnic make-up of the United States has changed dramatically in the last two decades, however, and will continue to change (see Figure 1–1 on the following page). Already, whites are a minority in California. For the nation as a whole, non-Hispanic whites will be in the minority by the year 2060 or shortly thereafter. Some Americans fear that rising numbers of immigrants will threaten traditional American political values and culture.

perception versus REALITY

Taking Property for Public Use

An important limitation on the private ownership of land is set forth in the "takings clause" of the Fifth Amendment to the U.S. Constitution. That clause states that the government may take private property for *public use,* but on one condition: the government must pay the property owner "just compensation." This power of the government to take private property for public use is known as *eminent domain.*

THE PERCEPTION

Many Americans assume that the phrase *public use* means just what it says—that private property taken by the government will be used by the public. For example, governments often take private property to construct or expand a road or to build a dam. Private property has also been taken to alleviate urban congestion by creating a public park. If the community (public) benefits from the taking, it may even make sense for the government to take property in a slum area so that the land can be put to better use.

THE REALITY

In reality, governments can and do take private property for any number of reasons. State and local governments have often used their power of eminent domain to "take" private property in blighted neighborhoods and turn the land over to private developers for urban renewal projects. In the 1950s, Washington, D.C., became a pioneer in such efforts, and communities across America followed Washington's example. The courts upheld such projects as legitimate "public purposes" for takings. By the 1980s, various courts had expanded the "public use" definition even further to include private projects that would increase state tax revenues and job opportunities. Governments have "taken" oceanfront property from its owners and turned the land over to a private developer to build condominiums. Companies such as Costco, Target, and Wal-Mart have all benefited from this broadened interpretation of "public use" to obtain land for their superstores.

Is it constitutionally permissible for a city to condemn unoffending private property for private business development? In 2004, the

The homeowners in this working-class neighborhood in New London, Connecticut, asked the United States Supreme Court to decide whether the Fifth Amendment to the U.S. Constitution permitted the city government to "take" their land and turn it over to private land developers.

United States Supreme Court agreed to review a case raising just this question.[4] The case involved Susette Kelo and other homeowners in the city of New London, Connecticut. Kelo and her neighbors live along the Thames River in ordinary working-class homes, and they would like to stay there. The city of New London, however, wants to "take" the land and then give it to a private developer to build condominiums (thus giving the city more tax dollars for that land). The Court's decision on this controversial question will have a tremendous impact on Americans' property rights.

What's Your Opinion?

Should the government be able to take private property from one person just to turn it over to another private party, such as a company that wants to build a sports arena or a superstore? What's your position on this issue?

FIGURE 1-1

Distribution of the U.S. Population by Race and Hispanic Origin, 1980 to 2075

By about 2060, minorities will constitute a majority of the U.S. population.

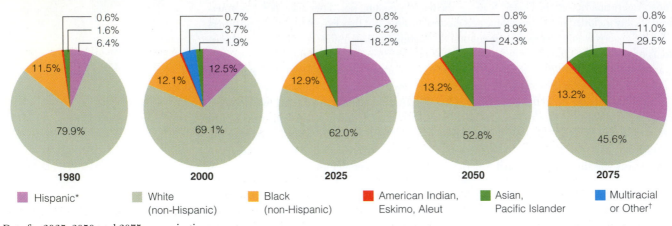

Data for 2025, 2050, and 2075 are projections.

*Persons of Hispanic origin can be of any race.

†The "multiracial or other" category in 2000 is not an official census category but represents all non-Hispanics who chose either "some other race" or two or more races in the 2000 census.

SOURCE: U.S. Bureau of the Census.

AMERICA at odds

A Nation Divided?

Supporters of multiculturalist policies believe that Americans must be tolerant of other cultures and ways of life. They argue that in the past, too much of what was taught in our educational institutions about history, art, and literature dealt with the achievements of "dead white men." Consequently, they have supported the elimination of standard Western civilization requirements at colleges and universities in favor of more emphasis on American minority groups and non-Western cultures. Multiculturalists have also been among the strongest supporters of bilingual education (see Chapter 5).

Opponents of multiculturalism argue that such policies promote moral relativism by implying that no one group's values are superior to those of another. As noted in this chapter's opening *America at Odds* feature, a sizable number of Americans claim to be Christians. Some within this group reject the notion of moral relativism and would like to see the government endorse Christian values in its policies. A multiculturalist, however, would raise the following questions: What about Muslims? What about Jews? What about those who hold no religious beliefs at all? Should these minority groups be subject to the will of a Christian majority?

Harvard University scholar Samuel P. Huntington has suggested that multiculturalism may lead to a bilingual, and thus divided, nation. Huntington bases this conclusion on the observation that the descendants of Mexican immigrants tend to hold on to their language far more than do the children and grandchildren of immigrants from other areas and cultures. Because language is intertwined with a nation's culture and identity, Huntington believes increased immigration from Mexico poses a grave threat to traditional American values and our national identity.[5]

Despite the fears that cultural diversity will destroy American values, there is no real evidence that these fears are being realized. In fact, some studies suggest that the ties that bind the nation may be stronger than is often thought.[6]

ideology A set of beliefs about human nature, social inequality, and government institutions that forms the basis of a political or economic system.

American Political Ideology

An **ideology** can be defined broadly as a comprehensive set of beliefs about human nature and government institutions. Generally, assumptions as to what the government's role should be with respect to basic values, such as liberty or equality, are important determinants of one's political ideology. Americans tend to fall into two broad camps with respect to political ideology: conservatives and liberals. The meanings of these terms have changed over the years and will continue to change as political attitudes and ideologies evolve. Traditionally, liberalism and conservatism have been regarded as falling within a political spectrum that ranges from the far left (extremely liberal) to the far right (extremely conservative). People who hold very strong political opinions are sometimes called **ideologues.** Most Americans, however, are not interested in all political issues and have a mixed set of opinions that do not fit neatly under the liberal or conservative label.

Figure 1–2 illustrates the spectrum of political attitudes and its relationship to the two major American political parties—Democrats and Republicans. As you can see, those with liberal views tend to identify with and vote for the Democratic Party, whereas those with conservative views tend to identify with and vote for the Republican Party.

Liberalism   Liberals usually believe in such ideals as constitutionally guaranteed civil liberties, political equality, free political competition, and separation of church and state. Modern **liberalism** generally supports the notion that the national government should take an active role in solving the nation's domestic problems. Further, today's liberals feel that the national government must look out for the interests of the individual against the majority. They generally support social-welfare programs that assist the poor and the disadvantaged.

There is a close relationship between those holding liberal views and those identifying themselves politically as Democrats. Keep in mind, though, that not all Democrats share all of the liberal views just discussed. Rather, those with liberal views simply tend to find that on the whole the Democratic Party's positions on issues are more acceptable than those of the Republican Party. Ideology, therefore, is not a perfect indicator of how someone will vote.

Conservatism   Conservatives, as the term implies, seek to conserve tradition and the ways of the past. **Conservatism,** as a political philosophy, thus defends traditional institutions and practices. It places a high value on the principles of community, continuity, law and order, and—in some countries—the preservation of rule by the privileged classes. In the United States, today's conservatives seek to preserve such traditions as states' rights, family values, individual initiative, and free enterprise. They want to minimize government interference in the business affairs of the nation. They believe that the federal government is already too big and should not be expanded further. Indeed, many conservatives believe that the share of annual national income going to government should fall from the current 40 percent to a much lower proportion.

In terms of party affiliation and voting, conservatives tend to identify with the Republican Party. Again, however, you need to be careful about associating the term *conservative* with the Republican Party. Republicans do not constitute a cohesive group that is consistently in favor of a fixed array of political, social, and economic policy prescriptions.

The Political Center   People whose views fall in the middle of the political spectrum are generally called **moderates.** Moderates rarely classify themselves as either liberal or conservative, and they may vote for either Republicans or Democrats. Many moderates do not belong to either major political party and often describe themselves as independents (see Chapter 7).

ideologue An individual who holds very strong political opinions.

liberalism A set of political beliefs that includes the advocacy of active government, including government intervention to improve the welfare of individuals and to protect civil rights.

conservatism A set of beliefs that includes a limited role for the national government in helping individuals, support for traditional values and lifestyles, and a cautious response to change.

moderate A person whose views fall in the middle of the political spectrum.

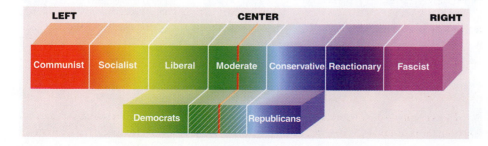

FIGURE 1–2
The Political Spectrum

radical left Persons on the extreme left side of the political spectrum who would like to significantly change the political order, usually to promote egalitarianism.

radical right Persons on the extreme right side of the political spectrum. The radical right includes reactionaries (who would like to return to the values and social systems of some previous era) and libertarians (who believe in no regulation of the economy and individual behavior, except for defense and law enforcement).

The Extreme Left and Right On both ends of the political spectrum are those who espouse radical views. The **radical left** consists of those who would like significant changes to the political order, usually to promote egalitarianism. Often, members of the radical left do not wish to work within the established political processes to reach their goals. They may even accept or advocate using violence or overthrowing the government in order to obtain those goals. Socialists believe in equality and, usually, active government involvement in the economy to bring about this goal. Communists believe in total equality and base their beliefs on the political philosophy of Karl Marx (1818–1883).

The **radical right** includes reactionaries, those who wish to turn the clock back to some previous era when there weren't, for example, so many civil rights for the nation's minorities and women. Reactionaries strongly oppose liberal and progressive politics and resist political and social change. Like those on the radical left, members of the radical right may even advocate the use of violence to achieve their goals. A less extreme right-wing ideology is libertarianism. Libertarians believe in virtually total political and economic liberty for individuals and no government regulation of the economy or individual behavior (except for defense and law enforcement).

American Democracy at Work

By now, you may have decided that Americans are at odds over every possible issue. But even the most divisive issues can be and are resolved through the political process. How does this process work? Who are the key players? These questions will be answered in the remaining chapters of this book. In the meantime, though, it is helpful to have some kind of a "road map" to guide you through these chapters so that you can see how each topic covered in the text relates to the big picture.

The Big Picture

The U.S. Constitution is the supreme law of the land. It sets forth basic governing rules by which Americans, when they ratified the Constitution, agreed to abide. It is appropriate, then, that we begin this text, following this introductory chapter, with a discussion of how and why the Constitution was created, the type of governing structure it established, and the rights and liberties it guarantees for all Americans. These topics, covered in Chapters 2 through 5, are necessarily the point of departure for any discussion of our system of government. As you will

Reciting the Pledge of Allegiance in school is one way that American children learn about their political heritage and values.

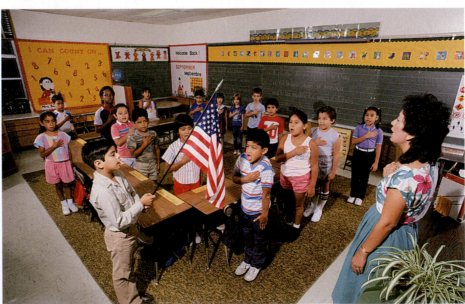

Bob Daemmrich/Stock Boston

see, some of the most significant political controversies today have to do with how various provisions in this founding document should be applied, over two hundred years later, to modern-day events and issues.

Who Governs?

Who acquires the power and authority to govern, and how do they obtain that power and authority? Generally, of course, the "winners" in our political system are the successful candidates in elections. But the electoral process is influenced by more than just the issue positions taken by the candidates. As you read Chapters 6 through 10, keep the following questions in mind: How do interest groups influence elections? How essential are political parties to the electoral process? To what extent do public opinion and voting behavior play a role in determining who the winners and losers will be? Why are political campaigns so expensive, and what are the implications of high campaign costs for our democracy? Finally, what role do the media, including the Internet, play in fashioning the outcomes of campaigns?

Once a winning candidate assumes a political office, that candidate becomes a part of one of the institutions of government. In Chapter 11 and the remaining chapters of this text, we examine these institutions and the process of government decision making. You will learn how those who govern the nation make laws and policies to decide "who gets what, when, and how" in our society. Of course, the topics treated in these chapters are not isolated from the materials covered earlier in the text. For example, when formulating and implementing federal policies, as well as state and local policies, the wishes of interest groups cannot be ignored, particularly those of wealthy groups that can help to fund policymakers' reelections. And public opinion and the media not only affect election outcomes but also influence which issues will be included on the policymaking agenda.

The political system established by the founders of this nation has endured for over two hundred years. The challenge facing Americans now is how to make sure that it will continue to endure.

why does it MATTER?

American Politics and Your Everyday Life

From the time you are born until you reach your final resting place, government affects your everyday life. This was not always the case. In the early years of this nation, government at both the state and federal levels was a relatively small undertaking. The extensive presence of government in the average American's everyday life truly began only in the twentieth century, when, as the nation grew and faced new problems, the government began to regulate economic and social life. Today, government affects virtually all of your activities.

The American government provides the essential framework for nearly everything you do, and in turn American political culture provides the essential framework for American government. Virtually all Americans believe in private property. Most believe in freedom of speech and religion. Few Americans today would advocate the violent overthrow of the government. Almost no Americans believe that taxes are theft. Universal education is accepted by all. The peaceful transition from one administration to the next is taken as a given. For the most part, decisions made by the Supreme Court are accepted, even if reluctantly, by those they concern.

Thus, in spite of Americans' diverse backgrounds, we share certain beliefs about the role of government and citizens in the United States. This common political culture creates an environment that maximizes the possibility that Americans will live peaceful and fulfilling lives.

Taking Action

Although the government of the United States is a *representative* democracy, our political culture encourages *direct* participation in government by citizens. Much is said in the media about low voter turnout in elections and other examples of Americans' lack of political participation. In fact, though, Americans have, and take advantage of, a vast array of methods for influencing their government. In the remaining chapters of this book, *Why Does It Matter?* features will discuss how government and politics affect your daily life. These features will also give examples of how citizens can take action to make a difference when they are at odds with their government on an issue.

Key Terms

authority 4	equality 12	moderate 15	radical left 16
autocracy 5	government 4	monarchy 5	radical right 16
bicameral legislature 10	ideologue 15	natural rights 10	representative democracy 7
conservatism 15	ideology 14	parliament 10	republic 7
democracy 7	institution 3	political culture 11	social conflict 4
dictatorship 7	liberalism 15	politics 4	social contract 10
direct democracy 7	liberty 11	power 4	
divine right theory 6	limited government 8	public services 4	

Chapter Summary

1 Politics can be formally defined as the process of resolving social conflict—disagreements over how the society should use its scarce resources and who should receive various benefits, such as wealth, status, health care, and higher education.

2 Government can be defined as the individuals and institutions that make society's rules and that also possess the power and authority to enforce those rules. Government serves at least three major purposes: (1) it resolves conflicts; (2) it provides public services; and (3) it defends the nation and its culture against attacks by other nations.

3 In an autocracy, the power and authority of the government are in the hands of a single person. Monarchies and dictatorships, including totalitarian dictatorships, are all forms of autocracy. In a constitutional monarchy, however, the monarch shares power with elected lawmakers. In an aristocracy, "the best," or a privileged class, rule. Other forms of government characterized by "rule by the few" include plutocracy (rule by the wealthy) and meritocracy (rule by a skilled and talented group). A theocracy is a form of government in which church and state are combined—the nation is ruled by religious principles.

4 Democracy is a form of government in which the government exists only by the consent of the people and reflects the will of the majority. In a direct democracy, the people participate directly in government decision making. In a representative democracy, or republic, people elect representatives to government office to make decisions for them. Forms of representative democracy include presidential democracy and parliamentary democracy.

5 The British legacy to American democracy consisted of the principle of limited government, the principle of representative government, and the political theory of John Locke and other European philosophers.

6 The five principles of American democracy are (1) equality in voting, (2) individual freedom, (3) equal protection of the law, (4) majority rule and minority rights, and (5) voluntary consent to be governed.

7 A political culture can be defined as a patterned set of ideas, values, and ways of thinking about government and politics. Three deeply rooted values in American political culture are liberty, equality, and property.

8 Americans seem to be in agreement as to what the basic political values of this country are. Although many Americans have expressed fears that multiculturalist policies and programs tend to erode American political values, there is no evidence that this has happened.

9 American political ideology is often viewed as including a spectrum of beliefs ranging from the far left (extremely liberal) to the far right (extremely conservative). Although liberals are often Democrats and conservatives are often Republicans, this association between ideology and political party affiliation does not always hold true.

RESOURCES FOR FURTHER STUDY

Selected Readings

Chua, Amy. *World on Fire: How Exporting Free Market Democracy Breeds Ethnic Hatred and Global Instability.* New York: Bantam Doubleday, 2004. The author warns that the dual exportation of capitalism and democracy can cause huge strains in the developing world, leading to intense disdain for outside influence and power.

Cullen, Jim. *The American Dream: A Short History of an Idea That Shaped a Nation.* New York: Oxford University Press, 2003. The author explores the history of "the American dream," how the dream has evolved, and how it remains an expression of Americans' shared ideals.

D'Souza, Dinesh. *What's So Great about America?* Washington, D.C.: Regnery Publishing, 2002. The author presents his arguments, from the perspective of an immigrant and now a citizen, for why America is "the greatest, freest, and most decent society in existence."

Roberts, Sam. *Who We Are Now: The Changing Face of America in the Twenty-First Century.* New York: Henry Holt & Co., 2004. The author uses the results of the 2000 census to identify and illuminate trends and social transformations that are changing the face of America.

Politics on the Web

Each chapter of *America at Odds*, Fifth Edition, concludes with a list of Internet resources and addresses. Once you are on the Internet, you can use the addresses, or uniform resource locators (URLs), listed in the *Politics on the Web* sections in this book to access the ever-growing number of resources available on the Internet relating to American politics and government.

Internet sites tend to come and go, and there is no guarantee that a site included in some of the *Politics on the Web* features will be there by the time this book is in print. We have tried, though, to include sites that have so far proved to be fairly stable. If you do have difficulty reaching a site, do not immediately assume that the site does not exist. First, recheck the URL shown in your browser. Remember, you have to type the URL exactly as written: upper case and lower case are important. If the URL appears to be keyed in correctly, then try the following technique: delete all of the information to the right of the forward slash mark that is farthest to the right in the address, and press enter. Sometimes, this will allow you to reach a home page from which you can link to the topic at issue.

A seemingly infinite number of sites on the Web offer information on American government and politics. A list of even the best sites would fill pages. For reasons of space, in this chapter and in those that follow, the *Politics on the Web* sections will include references to only a few selected sites. Following the links provided by these sites will take you to a host of others. The Web sites listed below all provide excellent points of departure for those who wish to learn more about American government and politics today.

- The U.S. government's "official" Web site offers extensive information on the national government and the services it

provides for citizens. To access this site, go to **http://www.firstgov.gov**

- National Issues Forum, a nonpartisan Web site, provides articles discussing the pros and cons of several controversial issues currently facing Americans. The URL for this site's home page is **http://www.nifi.com**

- Another nonpartisan site dealing with current political questions is This Nation. To access this site, go to **http://www.thisnation.com**

- To find news on the Web, you can go to the site of any major news organization or even your local newspaper. Links to online newspapers, both within the United States and in other countries, are available at **http://www.newspapers.com**

- Additionally, CNN's AllPolitics offers a wealth of news, news analysis, polling data, and news articles dating back to 1996. Go to **http://www.cnn.com/ALLPOLITICS**

- To learn how new computer and communications technologies are affecting the constitutional rights and liberties of Americans, go to the Web site of the Center for Democracy and Technology at **http://www.cdt.org**

- The Pew Research Center for the People and the Press offers survey data online on a number of topics relating to American politics and government. The URL for the center's site is **http://people-press.org**

- Yale University Library, one of the great research institutions, has an excellent collection of sources relating to American politics and government. Go to **http://www.library.yale.edu/socsci**

Online Resources for This Chapter

This text's Companion Web Site, at **http://www.americaatodds.com**, offers links to numerous resources that you can utilize to learn more about the topics covered in this chapter. For a list describing these resources, see the inside front cover of this book.

chapter 2

the constitution

CHAPTER OBJECTIVES

After reading this chapter, you should be able to . . .

▶ Describe some of the influences on the American political tradition in the colonial years.

▶ Indicate why and how Americans achieved independence from Great Britain.

▶ List some of the major compromises made by the delegates at the Constitutional Convention.

▶ Discuss the Federalist and Anti-Federalist positions with respect to ratifying the Constitution.

▶ Summarize the process by which the Constitution can be amended.

Should We Elect the President by Popular Vote?

When Americans go to the polls every four years to cast their ballots for president, many do not realize that they are not, in fact, voting directly for the candidates. Rather, they are voting for *electors*—individuals chosen in each state by political parties to cast the state's electoral votes for the candidate who wins that state's popular vote. The system by which electors pledge their votes for president is known as the *electoral college*.

Each state is assigned electoral votes based on its number of representatives in Congress. Although each state has the same number of representatives in the U.S. Senate (two), the number of representatives a state has in the U.S. House of Representatives is determined by the size of its population. That means that, in all, there are currently 538 electoral votes.[1]

To become president, a candidate must win 270 of these 538 electoral votes. Most states have a "winner-take-all" system in which the candidate who receives the most votes in a state receives *all* of that state's electoral votes, even if the margin of victory is very slight. The winner-take-all system means that a candidate who wins the popular vote nationally may yet lose in the electoral college—and vice versa. Many Americans believe that we should let the popular vote, not the electoral college, decide who becomes president. Others are not so sure.

Let the People Elect Our President

In 2000, Democratic candidate Al Gore won the popular vote yet narrowly lost to Republican George W. Bush in the electoral college. Many Americans questioned the legitimacy of Bush's election. They also decried the electoral college as an outdated invention of the late 1700s. To be sure, the system was originally designed to ensure that the interests of smaller states were not totally overshadowed by their more populous neighbors. Yet the electoral college gives the smaller states a disproportionate amount of clout. Consider, for example, that one electoral vote in California now corresponds to roughly 645,000 people, while an electoral vote in more sparsely settled Wyoming represents only 167,000 individuals. Clearly, the votes of Americans are not weighted equally, and this voting inequality is contrary to the "one person, one vote" principle of our democracy.

According to its critics, the electoral college also provides imaginary majorities. Under the system, it is possible for a candidate to win narrow majorities in numerous states (and thus all of the electoral votes in those states), lose significantly in other states, and yet still emerge with an overwhelming majority of electoral votes. For example, Bill Clinton garnered only 43 percent of the popular vote in 1992 but won by a landslide in the electoral college (370 votes, compared to 168 for George H. W. Bush).

The Electoral College Protects the Small States and Ensures Stability

Supporters of the electoral college argue that if the system were abolished, small states would suffer. Because each state has as many electors as its total number of representatives in Congress, the electoral college helps to protect the small states from being overwhelmed by the large states.

The electoral college also helps to maintain a relatively stable and coherent party system. If the president were elected by popular vote, we would have countless parties vying for the nation's highest office—as occurs in such nations as France, Italy, and Germany. Moreover, the system also provides another benefit: it helps to prevent single-issue or regional candidates—candidates who are not focused on the interests of the nation as a whole—from being elected to the presidency. To prevail in the electoral college, a candidate must build a national coalition, campaign in Santa Fe as well as New York City, and propose policies that unite, rather than divide, the nation.

Finally, the electoral college vote has diverged from the popular vote in only three elections during our nation's history—in 1876, 1888, and 2000. These exceptions do not justify abolishing the system.

Where Do You Stand?

1. Do you believe that a candidate elected by the popular vote would be more representative of the entire nation than a candidate elected by the electoral college? Why or why not?

2. Suppose that instead of using the "winner-take-all" system, all states awarded their electoral votes according to the proportion of the popular vote each candidate received. How would this affect the final outcome in the electoral college?

Explore This Issue Online

- For critical views of the electoral college, go to the Web site of the Center for Voting and Democracy at **http://www.fairvote.org/e-college**.

- For an article making a case for the electoral college, go to the Web site of Accuracy in Media (a media watchdog group) at **http://www.aim.org**. Select "Briefings" from the menu on the left and then click on "December 2004."

Protesters against the current system of voting hold signs outside the statehouse in Boston, where the Electoral College of Massachusetts was scheduled to meet on December 13, 2004.

AP Photo/Michael Dwyer

Introduction

Whether the electoral college should be abolished is just one of many debates concerning the government established by the U.S. Constitution. The Constitution, which was written over two hundred years ago, continues to be the supreme law of the land. Time and again, its provisions have been adapted to the changing needs and conditions of society. The challenge before today's citizens and political leaders is to find a way to apply those provisions to an information age that could not possibly have been anticipated by the founders. Will the Constitution survive this challenge? Most Americans assume that it will—and with good reason: no other written constitution in the world today is as old as the U.S. Constitution. To understand why, you have to go back to the beginnings of our nation's history.

The Beginnings of American Government

When the framers of the Constitution met in Philadelphia in 1787, they brought with them some valuable political assets. One asset was their English political heritage (see Chapter 1). Another was the hands-on political experience they had acquired during the colonial era. Their political knowledge and experience enabled them to establish a constitution that could meet not only the needs of their own time but also the needs of generations to come.

The American colonies were settled by individuals from many nations, including England, France, Spain, Holland, Sweden, and Norway. The majority of the colonists, though, came from England. The British colonies in North America were established by private individuals and private trading companies and were under the rule of the British Crown. The British colonies, which were located primarily along the Atlantic seaboard of today's United States, eventually numbered thirteen.

Although American politics owes much to the English political tradition, the colonists actually derived most of their understanding of social compacts, the rights of the people, limited government, and representative government from their own experiences. Years before Parliament adopted the English Bill of Rights or John Locke wrote his *Two Treatises on Government* (1690), the American colonists were putting the ideas expressed in those documents into practice.

The Granger Collection, New York

This 1859 engraving illustrates the pilgrims aboard the *Mayflower* signing the Mayflower Compact on November 11, 1620.

Mayflower Compact A document drawn up by Pilgrim leaders in 1620 on the ship *Mayflower*. The document stated that laws were to be made for the general good of the people.

Bill of Rights The first ten amendments to the U.S. Constitution. They list the freedoms—such as the freedoms of speech, press, and religion—that a citizen enjoys and that cannot be infringed on by the government.

FIGURE 2-1

The Thirteen Colonies
Georgia, the last of the thirteen colonies, was established in 1732. By this time, each of the thirteen colonies had developed its own political system, complete with necessary political documents and a constitution.

*Maine was part of Massachusetts until 1832.

The First British Settlements

In the 1580s, Sir Walter Raleigh convinced England's queen, Elizabeth I, to allow him to establish the first English outpost in North America on Roanoke Island, off the coast of what is now North Carolina. The attempted settlement was unsuccessful, however. The first permanent English settlement in North America was Jamestown, in what is now Virginia.[2] Jamestown was established in 1607 as a trading post of the Virginia Company of London.[3]

The first New England colony was founded by the Plymouth Company in 1620 at Plymouth, Massachusetts. The settlers at Plymouth, who called themselves Pilgrims, were a group of English Protestants who came to the New World on the ship *Mayflower*. Even before the Pilgrims went ashore, they drew up the **Mayflower Compact,** in which they set up a government and promised to obey its laws. The reason for the compact was that the group was outside the jurisdiction of the Virginia Company, which had arranged for them to settle in Virginia, not Massachusetts. Fearing that some of the passengers might decide that they were no longer subject to any rules of civil order, the leaders onboard the *Mayflower* agreed that some form of governmental authority was necessary. The Mayflower Compact, which was essentially a social contract, has historical significance because it was the first of a series of similar contracts among the colonists to establish fundamental rules of government.[4]

The Massachusetts Bay Company established another trading outpost in New England in 1630. In 1639, some of the Pilgrims at Plymouth, who felt that they were being persecuted by the Massachusetts Bay Colony, left Plymouth and settled in what is now Connecticut. They developed America's first written constitution, which was called the Fundamental Orders of Connecticut. This document called for the laws to be made by an assembly of elected representatives from each town. The document also provided for the popular election of a governor and judges. Other colonies, in turn, established fundamental governing rules. The Massachusetts Body of Liberties protected individual rights. The Pennsylvania Frame of Government, passed in 1682, and the Pennsylvania Charter of Privileges of 1701 established principles that were later expressed in the U.S. Constitution and **Bill of Rights** (the first ten amendments to the Constitution).

By 1732, all thirteen colonies had been established, each with its own political documents and a constitution (see Figure 2–1).

Colonial Legislatures

As mentioned, the British colonies in America were all under the rule of the British monarchy. Britain, however, was thousands of miles away (it took two months to sail across the Atlantic). Thus, to a significant extent, colonial legislatures carried on the "nuts and bolts" of colonial government. These legislatures, or *representative assemblies,* consisted of representatives elected by the colonists. The earliest colonial legislature was the Virginia House of Burgesses, established in 1619. By the time of the American Revolution, all of the colonies had representative assemblies, many of which had been in existence for more than a hundred years.

Through their participation in colonial governments, the colonists gained crucial political experience. Colonial leaders became familiar with the practical problems of governing. They learned how to build coalitions among groups with diverse interests and how to make compromises. Indeed, according to Yale University professor Jon Butler, by the time of the American Revolution in 1776 Americans had formed a complex, sophisticated political system. They had also created a wholly new type of society characterized, among other things, by ethnic and religious diversity.[5] Because of their political experiences, the colonists were quickly able to set up their own constitutions and state systems of government—and eventually a new national government—after they declared their independence from Great Britain in 1776.

The Rebellion of the Colonists

Scholars of the American Revolution point out that, by and large, the American colonists did not want to become independent of Great Britain. For the majority of the colonists, Britain was the homeland, and ties of loyalty to the British monarch were strong. Why, then, did the colonists revolt against Britain and declare their independence? What happened to sever the political, economic, and emotional bonds that tied the colonists to Britain? The answers to these questions lie in a series of events in the mid-1700s that culminated in a change in British policy with respect to the colonies. Table 2–1 shows the chronology of the major political events in early U.S. political history.

One of these events was the Seven Years' War (1756–1763) between Britain and France, which Americans often refer to as the French and Indian War. The Seven Years' War and its aftermath permanently changed the relationship between Britain and the American colonists. To pay its war debts and to finance the defense of its expanded empire, Britain needed revenues. The British government decided to obtain some of these revenues by imposing taxes on the American colonists and exercising more direct control over colonial trade. At the same time, Americans were beginning to distrust the British. Having fought alongside British forces, Americans thought they deserved some credit for the victory. The British, however, attributed the victory solely to the British war effort.

Additionally, Americans began to develop a sense of identity separate from the British. Americans were shocked at the behavior of some of the British soldiers and the cruel punishments meted out to enforce discipline among the British troops. The British, in turn, had little good to say about the colonists with whom they had fought, considering them brutish, uncivilized, and undisciplined. It was during this time that the colonists began to use the word *American* to describe themselves.

"Taxation without Representation"

In 1764, in an effort to obtain needed revenues, the British Parliament passed the Sugar Act, which imposed a tax on all sugar imported into the American colonies. Some colonists, particularly in Massachusetts, vigorously opposed this tax and proposed a boycott of certain British imports. This boycott launched a "nonimportation" movement that soon spread to other colonies.

The Stamp Act of 1765

The following year, Parliament passed the Stamp Act, which imposed the first direct tax on the colonists. Under the act, all legal documents, newspapers, and other items, including playing cards and dice, had to use specially embossed (stamped) paper that was purchased from the government.

The Stamp Act generated even stronger resentment among the colonists than the Sugar Act had aroused. James Otis, Jr., a Massachusetts attorney, declared that there could be "no taxation without representation." The American colonists could not vote in British elections and therefore were not represented in the British Parliament. They viewed Parliament's attempts to tax them as contrary to the principle of representative government. The British saw the matter differently. From the British perspective, it was only fair that the colonists pay taxes to help support the costs incurred by the British government in defending its American territories and maintaining the troops that were permanently stationed in the colonies following the Seven Years' War.

In October 1765, nine of the thirteen colonies sent delegates to the Stamp Act Congress in New York City. The delegates prepared a declaration of rights and grievances, which they sent to King George III. This action marked the first time that a majority of the colonies had joined together to oppose British rule. The British Parliament repealed the Stamp Act.

Further Taxes and the Coercive Acts

Soon, however, Parliament passed new laws designed to bind the colonies more tightly to the central government in London. Laws that imposed taxes on glass, paint, lead, and many other items were passed in 1767. The colonists protested by boycotting all British goods. In 1773, anger over taxation reached a powerful climax at the Boston Tea Party, in which colonists dressed as Mohawk Indians dumped almost 350 chests of British tea into Boston Harbor as a gesture of tax protest.

The British Parliament was quick to respond to the Tea Party. In 1774, Parliament passed the Coercive Acts (sometimes called the "Intolerable Acts"), which closed the harbor and placed the government of Massachusetts under direct British control.

TABLE 2–1

Significant Events in Early U.S. Political History

1585	British outpost set up in Roanoke.
1607	Jamestown established; Virginia Company lands settlers.
1620	Mayflower Compact signed.
1630	Massachusetts Bay Colony set up.
1639	Fundamental Orders of Connecticut adopted.
1641	Massachusetts Body of Liberties adopted.
1682	Pennsylvania Frame of Government passed.
1701	Pennsylvania Charter of Privileges written.
1732	Last of thirteen colonies established.
1756	French and Indian War declared.
1765	Stamp Act; Stamp Act Congress meets.
1770	Boston Massacre.
1773	Boston Tea Party.
1774	First Continental Congress.
1775	Second Continental Congress; Revolutionary War begins.
1776	Declaration of Independence signed.
1777	Articles of Confederation drafted.
1781	Last state signs Articles of Confederation.
1783	"Critical period" in U.S. history begins; weak national government until 1789.
1786	Shays' Rebellion.
1787	Constitutional Convention.
1788	Ratification of Constitution.
1791	Ratification of Bill of Rights.

Patrick Henry addressing the First
Continental Congress.

First Continental Congress The first
gathering of delegates from twelve of the
thirteen colonies, held in 1774.

Second Continental Congress The
congress of the colonies that met in
1775 to assume the powers of a central
government and establish an army.

The Continental Congresses

In response to the "Intolerable Acts," Rhode Island, Pennsylvania, and New York proposed a colonial congress. The Massachusetts House of Representatives requested that all colonies select delegates to send to Philadelphia for such a congress.

The First Continental Congress
The **First Continental Congress** met on September 5, 1774, at Carpenter's Hall in Philadelphia. Of the thirteen colonies, Georgia was the only one that did not participate. The First Continental Congress decided that the colonies should send a petition to King George III to explain their grievances, which they did. The congress also passed other resolutions continuing the boycott of British goods and requiring each colony to establish an army.

To enforce the boycott and other trading sanctions against Britain, the delegates to the First Continental Congress urged that "a committee be chosen in every county, city and town, by those who are qualified to vote for representatives in the legislature, whose business it shall be attentively to observe the conduct of all persons." Over the next several months, all colonial legislators supported this action. The committees of "safety" or "observation," as they were called, organized militias, held special courts, and suppressed the opinion of those who remained loyal to the British Crown. Committee members spied on neighbors' activities and reported to the press the names of those who violated the trading sanctions against Britain. The names were then printed in the local papers, and the transgressors were harassed and ridiculed in their communities.

The Second Continental Congress
Almost immediately after receiving the petition, the British government condemned the actions of the First Continental Congress as open acts of rebellion. Britain responded with even stricter and more repressive measures. On April 19, 1775, British soldiers (Redcoats) fought with colonial citizen soldiers (Minutemen) in the towns of Lexington and Concord in Massachusetts, the first battles of the American Revolution. The battle at Concord was memorialized by the poet Ralph Waldo Emerson as the "shot heard round the world." Less than a month later, delegates from all thirteen colonies gathered in Pennsylvania for the **Second Continental Congress,** which immediately assumed the powers of a central government. The Second Continental Congress declared that the militiamen who had gathered around Boston were now a full army. It also named George Washington, a delegate to the Second Continental Congress who had some military experience, as its commander in chief.

The delegates to the Second Continental Congress still intended to reach a peaceful settlement with the British Parliament. One declaration stated specifically that "we [the congress] have not raised armies with ambitious designs of separating from Great Britain, and establishing independent States." The continued attempts to effect a reconciliation with Britain, even after the outbreak of fighting, underscore the colonists' reluctance to sever their relationship with the home country. As one scholar put it, "Of all the world's colonial peoples, none became rebels more reluctantly than did Anglo-Americans in 1776."[6]

Breaking the Ties: Independence

Public debate about the problems with Great Britain continued to rage, but the stage had been set for declaring independence. One of the most rousing arguments in favor of independence was presented by Thomas Paine, a former English schoolmaster and corset maker,[7] who wrote a pamphlet called *Common Sense*. In that pamphlet, which was published in Philadelphia in January 1776, Paine addressed the crisis using "simple fact, plain argument, and common sense." He mocked King George III and attacked every argument that favored loyalty to the king. He called the king a "royal brute" and a "hardened, sullen-tempered Pharaoh [Egyptian king in ancient times]."[8]

Paine's writing went beyond a personal attack on the king. He contended that America could survive economically on its own and no longer needed its British connection. He wanted the developing colonies to become a model nation for democracy in a world in which other nations were oppressed by strong central governments.

None of Paine's arguments was new; in fact, most of them were commonly heard in tavern debates throughout the land. Instead, it was the pungency and eloquence of Paine's words that made *Common Sense* so effective:

> A government of our own is our natural right: and when a man seriously reflects on the precariousness of human affairs, he will become convinced, that it is infinitely wiser and safer, to form a constitution of our own in a cool and deliberate manner, while we have it in our power, than to trust such an interesting event to time and chance.[9]

Many historians regard Paine's *Common Sense* as the single most important publication of the American Revolution. The pamphlet became a best seller; more than 100,000 copies were sold within a few months after its publication.[10] It put independence squarely on the agenda. Above all, *Common Sense* severed the remaining ties of loyalty to the British monarch, thus removing the final psychological barrier to independence. Indeed, later John Adams would ask,

> What do we mean by the Revolution? The War? That was no part of the Revolution. It was only an effect and consequence of it. The Revolution was in the minds of the people, and this was effected, from 1760 to 1775, in the course of fifteen years before a drop of blood was drawn at Lexington.[11]

Independence from Britain—The First Step

By June 1776, the Second Continental Congress had voted for free trade at all American ports for all countries except Britain. The congress had also suggested that all colonies establish state governments separate from Britain. The colonists realized that a formal separation from Great Britain was necessary if the new nation was to obtain supplies for its armies and commitments of military aid from foreign governments. On June 7, 1776, the first formal step toward independence was taken when Richard Henry Lee of Virginia placed the following resolution before the congress:

> RESOLVED, That these United Colonies are, and of right ought to be, free and independent States, that they are absolved from allegiance to the British Crown, and that all political connection between them and the state of Great Britain is, and ought to be, totally dissolved.

The congress postponed consideration of Lee's resolution until a formal statement of independence could be drafted. On June 11, a "Committee of Five" was appointed to draft a declaration that would present to the world the colonies' case for independence.

The Declaration of Independence

Thomas Jefferson, a member of the Committee of Five, drafted the declaration in just under three weeks. After two other committee members, Benjamin Franklin and John Adams, had made some changes to the document, it was submitted to the congress for consideration on July 2. On that day, the congress adopted Lee's resolution of independence and immediately began considering the draft of the Declaration of Independence. Further alterations were made to the document, and it was formally adopted on the afternoon of July 4, 1776.

The Significance of the Declaration of Independence

The Declaration of Independence is one of the world's most famous documents. Like Paine, Thomas Jefferson, who wrote most of the document, elevated the dispute between Britain and the American colonies to a universal level. Jefferson opened the second paragraph of the declaration with the following words, which have since been memorized by countless American schoolchildren and admired the world over:

Thomas Paine (1737–1809). In addition to his successful pamphlet *Common Sense,* Paine also wrote a series of sixteen pamphlets, under the title *The Crisis,* during the American Revolution. He returned to England and, in 1791 and 1792, wrote *The Rights of Man,* in which he defended the French Revolution. Paine returned to the United States in 1802.

Library of Congress

The committee chosen to draft a declaration of independence is shown at work in this nineteenth-century engraving. They are, from the left, Benjamin Franklin, Thomas Jefferson, John Adams, Philip Livingston, and Roger Sherman.

AP Photo

We hold these Truths to be self-evident, that all Men are created equal, that they are endowed by their Creator with certain unalienable Rights, that among these are Life, Liberty, and the Pursuit of Happiness—That to secure these Rights, Governments are instituted among Men, deriving their just Powers from the Consent of the Governed, that whenever any Form of Government becomes destructive of these Ends, it is the Right of the People to alter or to abolish it, and to institute new Government. . . .

The concepts expressed in the Declaration of Independence clearly reflect Jefferson's familiarity with European political philosophy, particularly the works of John Locke.[12] Locke's philosophy, though it did not cause the American Revolution, provided the philosophical underpinnings by which it could be justified.

AMERICA at odds

What Happened to the Promise of Equality?

For some Americans, the political concepts that are set forth in the Declaration of Independence—particularly the concept of equality—have become standards by which American institutions should be measured. As you will see, however, the Constitution did not allow for equal treatment for many Americans, including African Americans (who were not considered citizens) and women. The disparity between the declaration's promise of equality and the Constitution's unequal treatment of Americans set the stage for future conflicts over the issue of equality.

Neither Thomas Jefferson nor the framers of the Constitution interpreted the word *equality* to mean equal income. Rather, they envisioned a nation in which all citizens had what we would now call equal opportunity. Equal opportunity promotes other American ideals, such as individualism and self-reliance. It also often leads to a meritocracy based on individual talent and effort. Those who have the advantage of more education, more money to invest in an enterprise, greater talent, and higher levels of energy will have a competitive edge and come out the winners.

In recent times, some people have been unwilling to accept the results of simple equality of opportunity if it creates a gross maldistribution of wealth. Some have argued that the founders, who lived in a largely agrarian economy, could not have envisioned the huge disparities in income in an industrial age and certainly would not have thought them consistent with democratic government.[13] Some reformers have thus backed the creation of a welfare safety net by which the government protects and promotes the economic security of its citizens. Other reformers have tried to level the playing field through programs known as "affirmative action." These programs give preferences to minorities and other groups to make up for past discrimination. Those who favor affirmative action view its opponents as heartless individualists, who would let other Americans remain in poverty because they lack the talent, luck, or education to rise above it. Opponents of affirmative action argue that such programs perpetuate unequal treatment and emphasize racial divisions in society. We discuss this debate further in Chapter 5.

From Colonies to States

Even before the Declaration of Independence, some of the colonies had transformed themselves into sovereign states with their own permanent governments. In May 1776, the Second Continental Congress had directed each of the colonies to form "such government as shall . . . best be conducive to the happiness and safety of their constituents [those represented by the government]." Before long, all thirteen colonies had created constitutions. Eleven of the colonies had completely new constitutions; the other two colonies, Rhode Island and Connecticut, made minor modifications to old royal charters. Seven of the new constitutions contained bills of rights that defined the personal liberties of all state citizens. All constitutions called for limited governments.

Many citizens were fearful of a strong central government because of their recent experiences under the British Crown. They opposed any form of government that resembled monarchy in any way. Consequently, wherever such antiroyalist sentiment was strong, the legislature—composed of elected representatives—itself became all-powerful. In Pennsylvania and Georgia, for example, **unicameral** (one-chamber) **legislatures** were unchecked by any executive authority. Indeed, antiroyalist sentiment was so strong that the executive branch was extremely weak in all thirteen states. This situation would continue until the ratification of the U.S. Constitution.

unicameral legislature A legislature with only one chamber.

The Confederation of States

Antiroyalist sentiments also influenced the thinking of the delegates to the Second Continental Congress, who formed a committee to draft a plan of confederation. A **confederation** is a voluntary association of *independent* states (see Chapter 3). The member states agree to let the central government undertake a limited number of activities, such as forming an army, but the states do not allow the central government to place many restrictions on the states' own actions. The member states typically can still govern most state affairs as they see fit.

confederation A league of independent states that are united only for the purpose of achieving common goals.

On November 15, 1777, the Second Continental Congress agreed on a draft of the plan, which was finally signed by all thirteen colonies on March 1, 1781. The **Articles of Confederation,** the result of this plan, served as this nation's first national constitution and represented an important step in the creation of our governmental system.[14]

The Articles of Confederation established the Congress of the Confederation as the central governing body. This congress was a unicameral assembly of representatives, or ambassadors, as they were called, from the various states. Although each state could send anywhere from two to seven representatives to the congress, each state, no matter what its size, had only one vote. The issue of sovereignty was an important part of the Articles of Confederation:

Articles of Confederation The nation's first national constitution, which established a national form of government following the American Revolution. The Articles provided for a confederal form of government in which the central government had few powers.

> Each State retains its sovereignty, freedom, and independence, and every power, jurisdiction, and right, which is not by this Confederation expressly delegated to the United States in Congress assembled.

The structure of government under the Articles of Confederation is shown in Figure 2–2.

Powers of the Government of the Confederation

Congress had several powers under the Articles of Confederation, and these enabled the new nation to achieve a number of accomplishments, as shown in Figure 2–3 on the next page. The Northwest Ordinance settled states' claims to western lands and established a basic pattern for

FIGURE 2-2

American Government under the Articles of Confederation

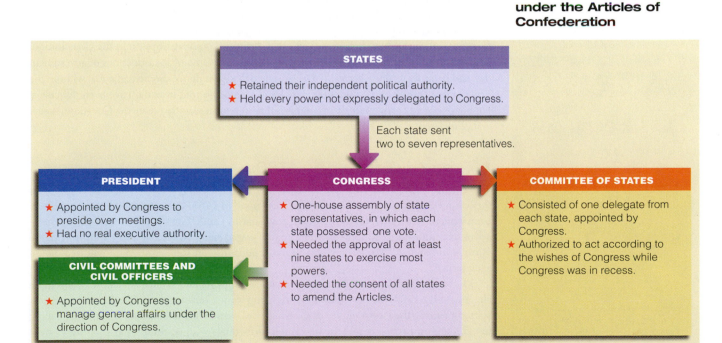

STATES
- ★ Retained their independent political authority.
- ★ Held every power not expressly delegated to Congress.

Each state sent two to seven representatives.

PRESIDENT
- ★ Appointed by Congress to preside over meetings.
- ★ Had no real executive authority.

CONGRESS
- ★ One-house assembly of state representatives, in which each state possessed one vote.
- ★ Needed the approval of at least nine states to exercise most powers.
- ★ Needed the consent of all states to amend the Articles.

COMMITTEE OF STATES
- ★ Consisted of one delegate from each state, appointed by Congress.
- ★ Authorized to act according to the wishes of Congress while Congress was in recess.

CIVIL COMMITTEES AND CIVIL OFFICERS
- ★ Appointed by Congress to manage general affairs under the direction of Congress.

Williamsburg: Printed by Alexander Purdie [1777], Library of Congress

FIGURE 2-3

Powers of the Central Government under the Articles of Confederation

Although the Articles of Confederation were later scrapped, they did allow the early government of the United States to achieve several important goals, including winning the Revolutionary War.

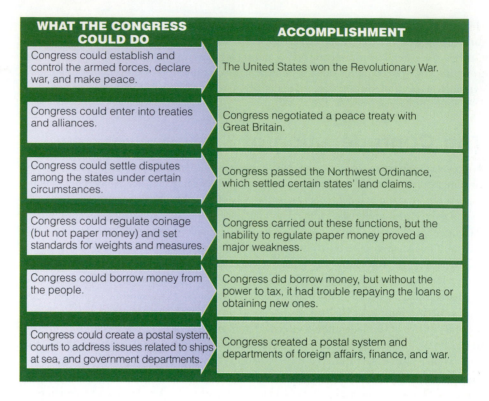

WHAT THE CONGRESS COULD DO	ACCOMPLISHMENT
Congress could establish and control the armed forces, declare war, and make peace.	The United States won the Revolutionary War.
Congress could enter into treaties and alliances.	Congress negotiated a peace treaty with Great Britain.
Congress could settle disputes among the states under certain circumstances.	Congress passed the Northwest Ordinance, which settled certain states' land claims.
Congress could regulate coinage (but not paper money) and set standards for weights and measures.	Congress carried out these functions, but the inability to regulate paper money proved a major weakness.
Congress could borrow money from the people.	Congress did borrow money, but without the power to tax, it had trouble repaying the loans or obtaining new ones.
Congress could create a postal system, courts to address issues related to ships at sea, and government departments.	Congress created a postal system and departments of foreign affairs, finance, and war.

The Articles of Confederation, signed by all thirteen colonies on March 1, 1781, was America's first national constitution.

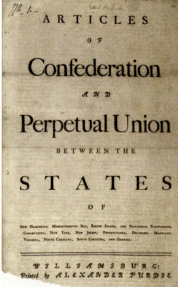

the government of new territories. Also, the 1783 peace treaty negotiated with Great Britain granted to the United States all of the territory from the Atlantic Ocean to the Mississippi River and from the Great Lakes and Canada to what is now northern Florida.

In spite of these accomplishments, the central government created by the Articles of Confederation was, in fact, quite weak. The Congress of the Confederation had no power to raise revenues for the militia or to force the states to meet military quotas. Essentially, this meant that the new government did not have the power to enforce its laws. Even passing laws was difficult because the Articles of Confederation provided that nine states had to approve any law before it was enacted.[15] Figure 2–4 lists these and other powers that the central government lacked under the Articles of Confederation.

Nonetheless, the Articles of Confederation proved to be a good "first draft" for the Constitution, and at least half of the text of the Articles would later appear in the Constitution. The Articles were an unplanned experiment that tested some of the principles of government that had been set forth earlier in the Declaration of Independence. Some argue that without the experience of government under the Articles of Confederation, it would have been difficult, if not impossible, to arrive at the compromises that were necessary to create the Constitution several years later.

A Time of Crisis—The 1780s

The Revolutionary War ended on October 18, 1781. The Treaty of Paris, which confirmed the colonies' independence from Britain, was signed in 1783. Peace with the British may have been won, but peace within the new nation was hard to find. The states bickered among themselves and refused to support the new central government in almost every way. As George Washington stated, "We are one nation today and thirteen tomorrow. Who will treat us on such terms?"

The states also increasingly taxed each other's imports and at times even prevented trade altogether. By 1784, the new nation was suffering from a serious economic depression. States started printing their own money at dizzying rates, which led to inflation. Banks were calling in old loans and refusing to issue new ones. Individuals who could not pay their debts were often thrown into prison.

WHAT THE CONGRESS COULD NOT DO	RESULT
Congress could not force the states to meet military quotas.	The central government could not draft soldiers to form a standing army.
Congress could not regulate commerce between the states or with other nations.	Each state was free to set up its own system of taxes on goods imported from other states. Economic quarrels among the states broke out. There was difficulty in trading with other nations.
Congress could enter into treaties, but could not enforce its power or control foreign relations.	The states were not forced to respect treaties. Many states entered into treaties independent of Congress.
Congress could not directly tax the people.	The central government had to rely on the states to collect and forward taxes, which the states were reluctant to do. The central government was always short of money.
Congress had no power to enforce its laws.	The central government depended on the states to enforce its laws, which they rarely did.
Nine states had to approve any law before it was enacted.	Most laws were difficult, if not impossible, to enact.
Any amendment to the Articles required all thirteen states to consent.	In practice, the powers of the central government could not be changed.
There was no national judicial system.	Most disputes among the states could not be settled by the central government.
There was no executive branch.	Coordinating the work of the central government was almost impossible.

FIGURE 2-4

Powers That the Central Government Lacked under the Articles of Confederation

The government's lack of certain powers under the Articles of Confederation taught the framers of the Constitution several important lessons, which helped them create a more effective government under that new document.

Shays' Rebellion   The tempers of angry farmers in western Massachusetts reached the boiling point in August 1786. Former Revolutionary War captain Daniel Shays, along with approximately two thousand armed farmers, seized county courthouses and disrupted the debtors' trials. Shays and his men then launched an attack on the national government arsenal in Springfield. **Shays' Rebellion** continued to grow in intensity and lasted into the winter, when it was finally stopped by the Massachusetts volunteer army, paid by private funds.[16]

Similar disruptions occurred throughout most of the New England states and in some other areas as well. The upheavals, and particularly Shays' Rebellion, were an important catalyst for change. The revolts scared American political and business leaders and caused more and more Americans to realize that a *true* national government had to be created.

The Annapolis Meeting   The Virginia legislature called for a meeting of representatives from all of the states at Annapolis, Maryland, on September 11, 1786, to address the problems facing the nation. Five of the thirteen states sent delegates, two of whom were Alexander Hamilton of New York and James Madison of Virginia. Both of these men favored a strong central government.[17] They persuaded the other delegates to issue a report calling on the states to hold a convention in Philadelphia in May of the following year.

The Congress of the Confederation at first was reluctant to give its approval to the Philadelphia convention. By mid-February 1787, however, seven of the states had named delegates to the Philadelphia meeting. Finally, on February 21, the congress called on the states

Shays' Rebellion A rebellion of angry farmers in western Massachusetts in 1786, led by former Revolutionary War captain Daniel Shays. This rebellion and other similar uprisings in the New England states emphasized the need for a true national government.

Constitutional Convention The convention (meeting) of delegates from the states that was held in Philadelphia in 1787 for the purpose of amending the Articles of Confederation. In fact, the delegates wrote a new constitution (the U.S. Constitution) that established a federal form of government to replace the governmental system that had been created by the Articles of Confederation.

to send delegates to Philadelphia "for the sole and express purpose of revising the Articles of Confederation." That Philadelphia meeting became the **Constitutional Convention.**

Drafting the Constitution

Although the convention was supposed to start on May 14, 1787, few of the delegates had actually arrived in Philadelphia on that date. The convention formally opened in the East Room of the Pennsylvania State House on May 25, after fifty-five of the seventy-four delegates had arrived.[18] Only Rhode Island, where feelings were strong against creating a more powerful central government, did not send any delegates.

Who Were the Delegates?

Among the delegates to the Constitutional Convention were some of the nation's best-known leaders. George Washington was present, as were Alexander Hamilton, James Madison, George Mason, Robert Morris, and Benjamin Franklin (then eighty-one years old), who had to be carried to the convention on a portable chair. Some notable leaders were absent, including Thomas Jefferson and John Adams, who were serving as ambassadors in Europe, and Patrick Henry, who did not attend because he "smelt a rat." (Henry favored local government and was wary that the convention might favor a stronger central government.)

For the most part, the delegates were from the best-educated and wealthiest classes. Thirty-three delegates were lawyers, nearly half of the delegates were college graduates, three were physicians, seven were former chief executives of their respective states, six owned large plantations, at least nineteen owned slaves, eight were important business owners, and twenty-one had fought in the Revolutionary War. In other words, the delegates to the convention constituted an elite assembly. No ordinary farmers, workers, women, African Americans, or Native Americans were present. Indeed, in his classic work on the Constitution, Charles Beard maintained that the Constitution was produced primarily by wealthy property owners who wanted a stronger government that could protect their property rights.[19]

The Virginia Plan

James Madison had spent months reviewing European political theory before he went to the Philadelphia convention. When his Virginia delegation arrived before anybody else, he immediately put its members to work. On the first day of the convention, Governor Edmund Randolph of Virginia was able to present fifteen resolutions outlining what was to become known as the *Virginia Plan.* This was a masterful political stroke on the part of the Virginia delegation. Its proposals immediately set the agenda for the remainder of the convention.

James Madison (1751–1836). Madison's contributions at the Constitutional Convention in 1787 earned him the title "Master Builder of the Constitution." As a member of Congress from Virginia, he advocated the Bill of Rights. He was secretary of state under Thomas Jefferson (1801–1809) and became our fourth president in 1809.

Library of Congress

The fifteen resolutions contained in the Virginia Plan proposed an entirely new national government under a constitution. The plan, which favored large states such as Virginia, called for the following:

- A bicameral legislature. The lower house was to be chosen by the people. The smaller upper house was to be chosen by the elected members of the lower house. The number of representatives would be in proportion to each state's population (the larger states would have more representatives). The legislature could void any state laws.
- A national executive branch, elected by the legislature.
- A national court system, created by the legislature.

The smaller states immediately complained because they would have fewer representatives in the legislature. After two weeks of debate, they offered their own plan—the *New Jersey Plan.*

The New Jersey Plan

William Paterson of New Jersey presented an alternative plan favorable to the smaller states. He argued that because each state had an equal vote under the Articles of Confederation, the convention had no power to change this arrangement. The New Jersey Plan proposed the following:

- Congress would be able to regulate trade and impose taxes.
- Each state would have only one vote.
- Acts of Congress would be the supreme law of the land.
- An executive office of more than one person would be elected by Congress.
- The executive office would appoint a national supreme court.

The Compromises

Most delegates were unwilling to consider the New Jersey Plan. When the Virginia Plan was brought up again, delegates from the smaller states threatened to leave, and the convention was in danger of dissolving. On July 16, Roger Sherman of Connecticut broke the deadlock by proposing a compromise plan. Compromises on other disputed issues followed.

The Connecticut Plan: The Great Compromise
Sherman's plan, which has become known as the **Great Compromise** (or the Connecticut Compromise), called for a legislature with two houses:

- A lower house (the House of Representatives), in which the number of representatives from each state would be determined by the number of people in that state.
- An upper house (the Senate), which would have two members from each state; the members would be elected by the state legislatures.

The Great Compromise gave something to both sides: the large states would have more representatives in the House of Representatives than the small states, yet each state would be granted equality in the Senate—because each state, regardless of size, would have two senators. The Great Compromise thus resolved the small-state/large-state controversy.

The Three-Fifths Compromise
A second compromise had to do with how many representatives each state would have in the House of Representatives. Although slavery was legal in parts of the North, most slaves and slave owners lived in the South. Indeed, in the southern states, slaves constituted about 40 percent of the population. Counting the slaves as part of the population would thus greatly increase the number of southern representatives in the House. The delegates from the southern states wanted the slaves to be counted as persons; the delegates from the northern states disagreed. Eventually, the **three-fifths compromise** settled this deadlock: each slave would count as three-fifths of a person in determining representation in Congress. (The three-fifths compromise was eventually overturned in 1868 by the Fourteenth Amendment, Section 2.)

Slave Importation
The three-fifths compromise did not satisfy everyone at the Constitutional Convention. Many delegates wanted slavery to be banned completely in the United States. The delegates compromised on this question by agreeing that Congress could not prohibit the importation of slaves into the country until the year 1808. The issue of slavery itself, however, was never really addressed by the delegates to the Constitutional Convention. As a result, the South won twenty years of unrestricted slave trade and a requirement that escaped slaves who had fled to the northern states be returned to their owners. Domestic slave trading was untouched.

Banning Export Taxes
The South's economic health depended in large part on its exports of agricultural products. The South feared that the northern majority in Congress might pass taxes on these exports. This fear led to yet another compromise: the

Great Compromise A plan for a bicameral legislature in which one chamber would be based on population and the other chamber would represent each state equally. The plan, also known as the Connecticut Compromise, resolved the small-state/large-state controversy.

three-fifths compromise A compromise reached during the Constitutional Convention by which it was agreed that three-fifths of all slaves were to be counted for purposes of representation in the House of Representatives.

This woodcut of slaves before the Civil War shows the slave overseer with a whip in his hand. During the fifteenth and sixteenth centuries, the British, French, Dutch, Spanish, and Portuguese engaged in a brutal slave trade along the African coast. Slaves were first brought to Virginia in 1619. Britain outlawed the slave trade in 1807 and abolished slavery in the entire British Empire in 1833.

The Granger Collection

interstate commerce Trade that involves more than one state.

South agreed to let Congress have the power to regulate **interstate commerce** as well as commerce with other nations; in exchange, the Constitution guaranteed that no export taxes would ever be imposed on products exported by the states. Today, the United States is one of the few countries that does not tax its exports.

The Final Draft Is Approved

The Great Compromise was reached by mid-July. Still to be determined was the make-up of the executive branch and the judiciary. A five-man Committee of Detail undertook the remainder of this work and on August 6 presented a rough draft to the convention. On September 8, a committee was named to "revise the stile [style] of, and arrange the Articles which had been agreed to" by the convention. The Committee of Stile was headed by Gouverneur Morris of Pennsylvania.[20] On September 17, 1787, the final draft of the Constitution was approved by thirty-nine of the remaining forty-two delegates.

Looking back on the drafting of the Constitution, an obvious question emerges: Why didn't the founders ban slavery outright? Certainly, as already mentioned, many of the delegates thought that slavery was morally wrong and that the Constitution should ban it entirely. This group, as well as many other Americans, regarded the framers' failure to deal with the slavery issue as a betrayal of the Declaration of Independence, which proclaimed that "all Men are created equal." Others pointed out how contradictory it was that the framers of the Constitution complained about being "enslaved" by the British yet ignored the problem of slavery in this country.

Perhaps the most compelling argument supporting the framers' action (or lack of it) with respect to slavery is that they had no alternative but to ignore the issue. If they had taken a stand on slavery, the Constitution certainly would not have been ratified. Indeed, if the antislavery delegates had insisted on banning slavery, the delegates from the southern states might have walked out of the convention—and there would have been no Constitution to ratify. Many delegates, including Benjamin Franklin, thought that any government would be a blessing for the people, so long as it was not despotic. Perhaps delegate Gunning Bedford said it best when he stated, "The condition of the United States requires that something should be immediately done. It will be better that a defective plan should be adopted, than that none should be recommended."[21] Note, though, that the framers would have had to resolve significant practical questions if they had banned slavery outright. For a discussion of some of these questions, see this chapter's *Perception versus Reality* feature.

The Debate over Ratification

The ratification of the Constitution set off a national debate of unprecedented proportions. The battle was fought chiefly by two opposing groups—the **Federalists** (those who favored a strong central government and the new Constitution) and the **Anti-Federalists** (those who opposed a strong central government and the new Constitution).

Federalists A political group, led by Alexander Hamilton and John Adams, that supported the adoption of the Constitution and the creation of a federal form of government.

Anti-Federalists A political group that opposed the adoption of the Constitution because of the document's centralist tendencies and because it did not include a bill of rights.

The Federalists Argue for Ratification

In the debate over ratification, the Federalists had several advantages. They assumed a positive name, leaving their opposition with a negative label. The Federalists also had attended the Constitutional Convention and thus were familiar with the arguments both in favor of and against various constitutional provisions. The Anti-Federalists, in contrast, had no actual knowledge of those discussions because they had not attended the convention. The Federalists also had time, money, and prestige on their side. Their impressive list of political thinkers and writers included Alexander Hamilton, John Jay, and James Madison. The Federalists could communicate with each other more readily because they were mostly bankers, lawyers, and merchants who lived in urban areas, where communication was easier. The Federalists organized a quick and effective ratification campaign to elect themselves as delegates to each state's ratifying convention.

perception versus REALITY

Why Didn't the Founders Ban Slavery?

Thomas Jefferson, a slave owner, pronounced that "all Men are created equal" as he wrote the Declaration of Independence. Jefferson considered slavery a "hideous blot" on America. George Washington, also a slave owner, regarded the institution of slavery as "repugnant." Why, then, didn't Jefferson and the other founders stay true to the declaration and free the slaves?

THE PERCEPTION

Most Americans assume that southern economic interests and racism alone led the founders to abandon the principles of equality expressed in the Declaration of Independence. African slaves were the backbone of American agriculture, particularly for tobacco, the most profitable export. Without their slaves, southern plantation owners would not have been able to turn such high profits. Presumably, southerners would not have ratified the Constitution unless it protected the institution of slavery.

THE REALITY

In reality, the debate over slavery during the Constitutional Convention (and later, during the First Congress) involved a host of other, more practical issues. These issues were particularly challenging because of the sheer number of slaves involved. When the first national census was taken in 1790, just a few years after the Constitutional Convention, South Carolina's population of 249,073 included 107,094 slaves, while Virginia's 292,627 slaves made up 39 percent of its residents. If the slaves were freed, where would they go? How would they fit into American society? Many slave owners felt responsible for their slaves, believing that they needed to care for the slaves as if they were dependent children. Because of such feelings of condescending paternalism, the founders worried about the social consequences of freeing the slaves. Furthermore, how would the slave owners be compensated for the loss of their slave labor? The issue of compensation posed special difficulties because the new government already faced mounting debts from the Revolutionary War and a currency crisis.

Because of the founders' inability to resolve the issue of slavery at the Constitutional Convention, slavery dominated the American political landscape until the Civil War a century later. To this day, we are dealing with the damage slavery caused to African Americans and to American society.

What's Your Opinion?

In what ways does the founders' failure to abolish slavery during the Constitutional Convention still haunt America today?

The *Federalist Papers*   Alexander Hamilton, a leading Federalist, started answering the Constitution's critics in New York by writing newspaper columns under the pseudonym "Caesar." The Caesar letters appeared to have little effect, so Hamilton switched his pseudonym to "Publius" and enlisted John Jay and James Madison to help him write the papers. In a period of less than a year, these three men wrote a series of eighty-five essays in defense of the Constitution. These essays, which were printed not only in New York newspapers but also in other papers throughout the states, are collectively known as the *Federalist Papers*.

Allaying the Fears of the Constitution's Critics   Generally, the papers attempted to allay the fears expressed by the Constitution's critics. One fear was that the rights of minority groups would not be protected. Another was that a minority might block the passage of measures that the majority felt were in the national interest. Many critics also feared that a republican form of government would not work in a nation the size of the United States. Various groups, or **factions,** would struggle for power, and chaos would result. Madison responded to the latter argument in *Federalist Paper* No. 10 (see Appendix F), which is considered a classic in political theory. Among other things, Madison argued that the nation's size was actually an advantage in controlling factions: in a large nation, there would be so many diverse interests and factions that no one faction would be able to gain control of the government.[22]

faction A group of persons forming a cohesive minority.

The Anti-Federalists' Response

Perhaps the greatest advantage of the Anti-Federalists was that they stood for the status quo. Usually, it is more difficult to institute changes than it is to stay with what is already known, experienced, and understood. Among the Anti-Federalists were such patriots as Patrick Henry and Samuel Adams. Patrick Henry said of the proposed Constitution: "I look upon that paper as the most fatal plan that could possibly be conceived to enslave a free people."

In response to the *Federalist Papers*, the Anti-Federalists published their own essays, using such pseudonyms as "Montezuma" and "Philadelphiensis." They also wrote brilliantly,

This satirical eighteenth-century engraving touches on some of the issues in Connecticut politics on the eve of the Constitution's ratification. The two factions shown are the "Federals," who represented the trading interests and were for tariffs on imports, and the "Antifederals," who favored agrarian interests and were more receptive to paper money. The artist clearly sides with the Federalist cause.

The National Archives

tyranny The arbitrary or unrestrained exercise of power by an oppressive individual or government.

attacking nearly every clause of the new document. Many Anti-Federalists contended that the Constitution had been written by aristocrats and would lead the nation to aristocratic **tyranny** (the exercise of absolute, unlimited power). Other Anti-Federalists feared that the Constitution would lead to an overly powerful central government that would limit personal freedom.[23]

The Anti-Federalists strongly argued that the Constitution needed a bill of rights. They warned that without a bill of rights, a strong national government might take away the political rights won during the American Revolution. They demanded that the new Constitution clearly guarantee personal freedoms. The Federalists generally did not think that a bill of rights was all that important. Nevertheless, to gain the necessary support, the Federalists finally promised to add a bill of rights to the Constitution as the first order of business under the new government. This promise turned the tide in favor of the Constitution.

Ratification

The contest for ratification was close in several states, but the Federalists finally won in all of the state conventions. After unanimous ratifications in Delaware, New Jersey, and Georgia, Pennsylvania voted in favor of the Constitution by a margin of two to one, and Connecticut by a margin of three to one. Even though the Anti-Federalists were perhaps the majority in Massachusetts, a successful political campaign by the Federalists led to ratification by that state on February 6, 1788.

New Hampshire became the ninth state to ratify the Constitution on June 21, 1788, by a fifty-seven to forty-six margin, thus formally putting the Constitution into effect. New York and Virginia had not yet ratified, however, and without them the Constitution would have no true power. Those worries were dispelled in the summer of 1788, when both Virginia and New York ratified the new Constitution. North Carolina waited until November 21 of the following year to ratify the Constitution, and Rhode Island did not ratify until May 29, 1790.

The Constitution's Major Principles of Government

The framers of the Constitution were fearful of the powerful British monarchy, against which they had so recently rebelled. At the same time, they wanted a central government strong enough to prevent the kinds of crises that had occurred under the weak central authority of the Articles of Confederation. The principles of government expressed in the Constitution reflect both of these concerns.

Limited Government and Popular Sovereignty

The Constitution incorporated the principle of limited government, which means that government can do only what the people allow it to do through exercise of a duly developed system of laws. This principle can be found in many parts of the Constitution. For example, while Articles I, II, and III indicate exactly what the national government *can* do, the first nine amendments to the Constitution list the ways in which the government *cannot* limit certain individual freedoms.

Implicitly, the principle of limited government rests on the concept of popular sovereignty. Remember the phrases that frame the Preamble to the Constitution: "We the People of the United States . . . do ordain and establish this Constitution for the United States of America." In other words, it is the people who form the government and decide on the powers that the government can exercise. If the government exercises powers beyond those granted to it by the Constitution, it is acting illegally. The idea that no one is above the law, including government officers, is often called the **rule of law.**

rule of law A basic principle of government that requires both those who govern and those who are governed to act in accordance with established law.

The Principle of Federalism

The Constitution also incorporated the principle of federalism. In a **federal system** of government, the central (national) government shares sovereign powers with the various state governments. Federalism was the solution to the debate over whether the national government or the states should have ultimate sovereignty.

The Constitution gave to the national government significant powers—powers that it had not had under the Articles of Confederation. For example, the Constitution expressly states that the president is the nation's chief executive as well as the commander in chief of the armed forces. The Constitution also declares that the Constitution and the laws created by the national government are supreme—that is, they take precedence over conflicting state laws. Other powers given to the national government include the power to coin money, to levy and collect taxes, and to regulate interstate commerce, granted by the **commerce clause.** (For a discussion of how the national government's powers under the commerce clause affect our daily lives, see the *Why Does It Matter?* feature at the end of this chapter.) Finally, the national government was authorized to undertake all laws that are "necessary and proper" to carrying out its expressly delegated powers.

Because the states feared too much centralized control, the Constitution also allowed for numerous states' rights. These rights include the power to regulate commerce within state borders and generally the authority to exercise any powers that are not delegated by the Constitution to the central government. (See Chapter 3 for a detailed discussion of federalism.)

federal system A form of government that provides for a division of powers between a central government and several regional governments. In the United States, the division of powers between the national government and the fifty states is established by the Constitution.

commerce clause The clause in Article I, Section 8, of the Constitution that gives Congress the power to regulate interstate commerce (commerce involving more than one state).

Separation of Powers

As James Madison (1751–1836) once said, after you have given the government the ability to control its citizens, you have to "oblige it to control itself." To force the government to "control itself" and to prevent the rise of tyranny, Madison devised a scheme, the **Madisonian Model,** in which the powers of the national government were separated into different branches: the legislative, executive, and judicial.[24] The legislative branch (Congress) passes laws; the executive branch (the president) administers and enforces the laws; and the judicial branch (the courts) interprets the laws. By separating the powers of government, no one branch would have enough power to dominate the others. This principle of **separation of powers** is laid out in Articles I, II, and III of the Constitution.

Madisonian Model The model of government devised by James Madison in which the powers of the government are separated into three branches: executive, legislative, and judicial.

separation of powers The principle of dividing governmental powers among the executive, the legislative, and the judicial branches of government.

Checks and Balances

A system of **checks and balances** was also devised to ensure that no one group or branch of government can exercise exclusive control. Even though each branch of government is

checks and balances A major principle of American government in which each of the three branches is given the means to check (to restrain or balance) the actions of the others.

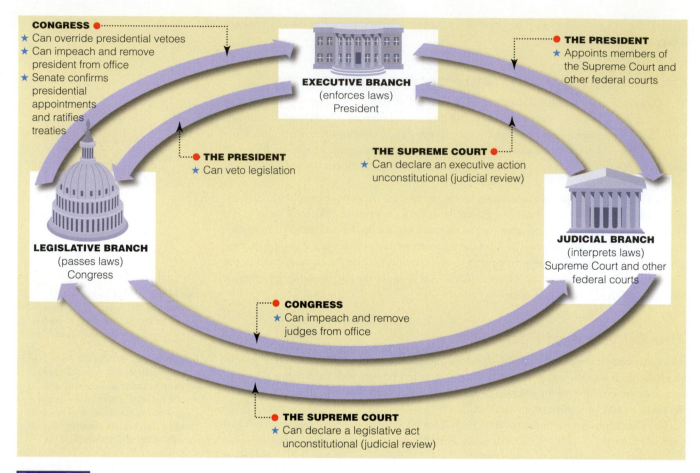

CONGRESS ●
- ★ Can override presidential vetoes
- ★ Can impeach and remove president from office
- ★ Senate confirms presidential appointments and ratifies treaties

EXECUTIVE BRANCH
(enforces laws)
President

THE PRESIDENT ●
- ★ Appoints members of the Supreme Court and other federal courts

THE PRESIDENT ●
- ★ Can veto legislation

THE SUPREME COURT ●
- ★ Can declare an executive action unconstitutional (judicial review)

LEGISLATIVE BRANCH
(passes laws)
Congress

JUDICIAL BRANCH
(interprets laws)
Supreme Court and other federal courts

CONGRESS ●
- ★ Can impeach and remove judges from office

THE SUPREME COURT ●
- ★ Can declare a legislative act unconstitutional (judicial review)

FIGURE 2–5

Checks and Balances among the Branches of Government

veto power A constitutional power that enables the chief executive (president or governor) to reject legislation and return it to the legislature with reasons for the rejection. This prevents or at least delays the bill from becoming law.

independent of the others, it can also check the actions of the others. (See this chapter's *The Politics of National Security* feature for a discussion of the system of checks and balances in the war on terrorism.) Look at Figure 2–5, and you can see how this is done. As the figure shows, the president checks Congress by holding a **veto power,** which is the ability to return bills to Congress for reconsideration. Congress, in turn, controls taxes and spending, and the Senate must approve presidential appointments. The judicial branch of government can also act as a check on the other branches of government through its power of *judicial review*—the power to rule congressional or presidential actions unconstitutional.[25] In turn, the president and the Senate exercise some control over the judiciary through the president's power to appoint federal judges and the Senate's role in confirming presidential appointments.

Among the other checks and balances built into the American system of government are staggered terms of office. Members of the House of Representatives serve for two years, members of the Senate for six, and the president for four. Federal court judges are appointed for life but may be impeached and removed from office by Congress for misconduct. Staggered terms and changing government personnel make it difficult for individuals within the government to form controlling factions. The American system of government also includes numerous other checks and balances, many of which you will read about in later chapters of this book. We look next at another obvious check on the powers of government: the Bill of Rights.

The Bill of Rights

To secure the ratification of the Constitution in several important states, the Federalists had to provide assurances that amendments would be passed to protect individual liberties against violations by the national government. At the state ratifying conventions, delegates set forth specific rights that should be protected. James Madison considered these recommendations as he labored to draft what became the Bill of Rights.

The Constitution and the War on Terrorism

In the wake of the terrorist attacks of September 11, 2001, our government has been forced to find a balance between strengthening national security and upholding the Constitution. The attacks revealed serious flaws in the government's ability to protect the American homeland. To combat terrorism, the government established the Department of Homeland Security and enacted legislation that has made it easier for government agents to access information. These steps have created some friction, however, because they encroached on time-honored provisions in the Constitution.

TAMPERING WITH THE SYSTEM OF CHECKS AND BALANCES

Early in 2002, President George W. Bush proposed a Department of Homeland Security that would incorporate some of the largest agencies in the government. The earliest protests from Congress concerned the size and power of this new executive branch department. The proposed department would consist of 170,000 employees from twenty-two federal agencies and command a budget of nearly $38 billion.

The creation of the Department of Homeland Security marked the largest reorganization of the executive branch since 1947. Supporters claimed that the new department would streamline the efforts of the different agencies that protect the homeland. Yet many argued that the department's size and scope could upset the system of checks and balances established by the Constitution. A compromise was struck: the new department could be created, but only if Congress retained significant oversight of its activities.

CIVIL LIBERTIES UNDER FIRE

Notable measures to improve national security included increased government access to individuals' personal information and the curtailment of the legal rights of suspected terrorists. For example, the USA Patriot Act, which was passed in 2001 shortly after the terrorist attacks, grants the government great latitude to investigate not only suspected terrorists but also persons who are only vaguely associated with terrorists. The act even allows government agents to conduct searches and seize evidence without probable cause or a warrant. This means that the government can find out what periodicals you read, where you travel, and how you spend your income. And, for the

Newhouse News Service /Landov

A protester demonstrating against the USA Patriot Act kneels outside the Fleet Center during the 2004 Democratic Convention in Boston.

first time in this nation's history, the government has the legal right to read your mail before you receive it.

Most Americans have nothing to hide and therefore have no reason to fear prosecution (or even snooping by the government). Moreover, the Constitution protects every U.S. resident's right to privacy and ensures that we will not be subject to unreasonable searches and seizures. Legislation such as the USA Patriot Act, however, allows the government to curb many basic civil liberties guaranteed by the Constitution. Therefore, a central issue before Americans is whether national security can be protected without sacrificing privacy rights.

Are We Safer?

Do you feel that the government has curtailed too many civil liberties in an attempt to protect America against future terrorist attacks? Have increased security measures made you feel safer? Why or why not?

After sorting through more than two hundred state recommendations, Madison came up with sixteen amendments. Congress tightened the language somewhat and eliminated four of the amendments. Of the remaining twelve, two—one dealing with the apportionment of representatives and the other with the compensation of the members of Congress—were not ratified by the states during the ratification process.[26] By 1791, all of the states had ratified the ten amendments that now constitute our Bill of Rights. Table 2–2 on the following page presents the text of the first ten amendments to the Constitution, along with explanatory comments. (Note that neither a constitution nor a bill of rights, in itself, is any guarantee that civil liberties will be enforced or that American-style democracy will flourish. See this chapter's *Comparative Politics* feature on page 41 for a discussion of this topic.)

TABLE 2-2
The Bill of Rights

Amendment I.
Religion, Speech, Press, Assembly, and Petition

Congress shall make no law respecting an establishment of religion, or prohibiting the free exercise thereof; or abridging the freedom of speech, or of the press; or the right of the people peaceably to assemble, and to petition the Government for a redress of grievances.

Congress may not create an official church or enact laws limiting the freedom of religion, speech, the press, assembly, and petition. These guarantees, like the others in the Bill of Rights (the first ten amendments), are not absolute—each may be exercised only with regard to the rights of other persons.

Amendment II.
Militia and the Right to Bear Arms

A well regulated Militia, being necessary to the security of a free State, the right of the people to keep and bear Arms, shall not be infringed.

To protect itself, each state has the right to maintain a volunteer armed force. States and the federal government regulate the possession and use of firearms by individuals.

Amendment III.
The Quartering of Soldiers

No Soldier shall, in time of peace be quartered in any house, without the consent of the Owner, nor in time of war, but in a manner to be prescribed by law.

Before the Revolutionary War, it had been common British practice to quarter soldiers in colonists' homes. Military troops do not have the power to take over private houses during peacetime.

Amendment IV.
Searches and Seizures

The right of the people to be secure in their persons, houses, papers, and effects, against unreasonable searches and seizures, shall not be violated, and no Warrants shall issue, but upon probable cause, supported by Oath or affirmation, and particularly describing the place to be searched, and the persons or things to be seized.

Here the word warrant *means "justification" and refers to a document issued by a magistrate or judge indicating the name, address, and possible offense committed. Anyone asking for the warrant, such as a police officer, must be able to convince the magistrate or judge that an offense probably has been committed.*

Amendment V.
Grand Juries, Self-Incrimination, Double Jeopardy, Due Process, and Eminent Domain

No person shall be held to answer for a capital, or otherwise infamous crime, unless on a presentment or indictment of a Grand Jury, except in cases arising in the land or naval forces, or in the Militia, when in actual service in time of War or public danger; nor shall any person be subject for the same offense to be twice put in jeopardy of life or limb; nor shall be compelled in any criminal case to be a witness against himself, nor be deprived of life, liberty, or property, without due process of law; nor shall private property be taken for public use, without just compensation.

There are two types of juries. A grand jury considers physical evidence and the testimony of witnesses and decides whether there is sufficient reason to bring a case to trial. A petit jury hears the case at trial and decides it. "For the same offense to be twice put in jeopardy of life or limb" means to be tried twice for the same crime. A person may not be tried for the same crime twice or forced to give evidence against herself or himself. No person's right to life, liberty, or property may be taken away except by lawful means, called the due process of law. Private property taken for public purposes must be paid for by the government.

Amendment VI.
Criminal Court Procedures

In all criminal prosecutions, the accused shall enjoy the right to a speedy and public trial, by an impartial jury of the State and district wherein the crime shall have been committed, which district shall have been previously ascertained by law, and to be informed of the nature and cause of the accusation; to be confronted with the witnesses against him; to have compulsory process for obtaining witnesses in his favor, and to have the Assistance of Counsel for his defence.

Any person accused of a crime has the right to a fair and public trial by a jury in the state in which the crime took place. The charges against that person must be so indicated. Any accused person has the right to a lawyer to defend him or her and to question those who testify against him or her, as well as the right to call people to speak in his or her favor at trial.

Amendment VII.
Trial by Jury in Civil Cases

In Suits at common law, where the value in controversy shall exceed twenty dollars, the right of trial by jury shall be preserved, and no fact tried by a jury, shall be otherwise reexamined in any Court of the United States, than according to the rules of the common law.

A jury trial may be requested by either party in a dispute in any case involving more than $20. If both parties agree to a trial by a judge without a jury, the right to a jury trial may be put aside.

Amendment VIII.
Bail, Cruel and Unusual Punishment

Excessive bail shall not be required, nor excessive fines imposed, nor cruel and unusual punishments inflicted.

Bail is that amount of money that a person accused of a crime may be required to deposit with the court as a guarantee that she or he will appear in court when requested. The amount of bail required or the fine imposed as punishment for a crime must be reasonable compared with the seriousness of the crime involved. Any punishment judged to be too harsh or too severe for a crime shall be prohibited.

Amendment IX.
The Rights Retained by the People

The enumeration in the Constitution, of certain rights, shall not be construed to deny or disparage others retained by the people.

Many civil rights that are not explicitly enumerated in the Constitution are still held by the people.

Amendment X.
Reserved Powers of the States

The powers not delegated to the United States by the Constitution, nor prohibited by it to the States, are reserved to the States respectively, or to the people.

Those powers not delegated by the Constitution to the federal government or expressly denied to the states belong to the states and to the people. This clause in essence allows the states to pass laws under their "police powers."

comparative politics

Democracy in the Middle East

The Taliban has been flushed out of Kabul and into hiding in southern Afghanistan. Saddam Hussein now stares at the walls of a jail cell after twenty-five years of ruthless rule in Iraq. American soldiers are on the march across the Middle East, but U.S. success on the battlefield begs a larger question: How do we rebuild war-torn nations such as Afghanistan and Iraq after years of tyrannical rule by despots?

AMERICA'S ROLE IN NATION BUILDING

President George W. Bush and his top foreign policy advisers believe that the answer to the troubles in these nations is a democratic form of government. Bush has outlined three "deficits" affecting the Middle East: freedom, women's rights, and knowledge. He insists that democracy will eventually erase these deficits by encouraging political participation, market economies, personal liberty, and the free exchange of ideas through an uncensored media.

American-led democratization worked superbly following World War II in Japan and Germany. Both nations emerged from the ashes of brutal dictatorships to become shining examples of free societies in the latter half of the twentieth century. The jury remains out in the Middle East, however. Afghans have gone to the polls for the first time and elected a president. In addition, one-fifth of the representatives drawing up the Afghan constitution are women. The people of Iraq cast ballots of their own. Indeed, even the Kurdish ethnic minority has a voice in Iraqi politics after years of persecution.

THE PATH TO DEMOCRACY WILL NOT BE EASY

Many obstacles to democracy in Afghanistan and Iraq remain, however. Dangerous warlords and large-scale drug wholesalers still control much of the desolate rural areas of Afghanistan despite the progress made in the cities. In Iraq, Muslim fundamentalists and rebel groups are engaging in a guerrilla war and attempting to resist "Americanization." Some scholars of the Middle East argue that the religion of Islam and Western ideas of democracy cannot coexist. Other detractors claim that anti-American sentiment is so strong in

An Iraqi university student passes by a poster urging the people of Iraq to participate in the January 30, 2005, national elections. In spite of threats by insurgents that voters risked death if they went to the polls, the elections were a stunning success, with voter turnout being much higher than expected.

the region that fledgling democratic governments will survive only as long as the United States maintains a strong military presence. Bush and his advisers remain confident, however, that democracy will slowly take root in Afghanistan and Iraq. Those nations, he argues, will then serve as examples to the peoples of other despotic nations and eventually lead to the spread of freedom and liberty across the entire Middle East.

For Critical Analysis

Should the United States attempt to spread democracy throughout the Middle East? Why or why not? Do you believe that attempts at nation building will lead to greater freedom and liberty in the Middle East, or will America's efforts backfire and encourage another generation of terrorists?

The Constitution Compared to the Articles of Confederation

As mentioned earlier, the experiences under the government of the Confederation, particularly the weakness of the central government, strongly influenced the writing of the U.S. Constitution. The Constitution shifted many powers from the states to the central government—the Constitution's division of powers between the states and the national government is discussed at length in Chapter 3.

One of the weaknesses of the Confederation had been the lack of an independent executive authority. The Constitution remedied this problem by creating an independent executive—the president—and by making the president commander in chief of the army and navy and of the state militias when called into national service. The president was also given extensive appointment powers, although Senate approval was required for certain appointments.

Another problem under the Confederation was the lack of a judiciary that was independent of the state courts. The Constitution established the United States Supreme Court and authorized Congress to establish other "inferior" federal courts.

To protect against possible wrongdoing, the Constitution also provided for a way to remove federal officials from office—through the impeachment process. The Constitution provides that a federal official who commits "Treason, Bribery, or other high Crimes and Misdemeanors" may be impeached (accused, or charged with wrongdoing) by the House of Representatives and tried by the Senate. If found guilty of the charges by a two-thirds vote in the Senate, the official can be removed from office and prevented from ever assuming another federal government post. The official may also face judicial proceedings for the alleged wrong-doing after removal from office.

The Constitution—A Document for the Ages

The Constitution that was drafted by the framers and ratified by the states has proved to be a lasting foundation for American government. At the time the Constitution was created, how-ever, there was a great deal of doubt about whether the arrangement would actually work. James Madison, among others, hoped that the framers had created a government "for the ages." Indeed, Madison's vision has been realized, in large part because of the checks and bal-ances that were incorporated into the Constitution and have safeguarded the nation from tyranny—one of the greatest fears of the founders.

Another reason for the Constitution's long life is the brevity of its wording. Rather than set forth the details of government, the founders established broad principles that could be—and have been—applied to changing conditions over time. Moreover, for all the stress on private property in the founding era, the framers did not require any property qualification for hold-ing political office. The Constitution also provides that compensation be given for elective posts, meaning that, at least in theory, anyone—no matter how poor—could hold a federal office.

The Constitution also provided for an easier amendment process than that provided under the Articles of Confederation. Under the Articles of Confederation, amendments to the Arti-cles required the unanimous consent of the states. As a result, it was virtually impossible to amend the Articles. The framers of the Constitution provided for an amendment process that requires the approval of only three-fourths of the states. Although the process is still extraor-dinarily cumbersome, it is easier to amend the Constitution than it was to change the Articles of Confederation.

AMERICA at odds

The Constitution—A Blueprint for Future Controversy

When the Constitution was ratified in 1788, many issues remained unresolved. During the rev-olutionary period, those who opposed British rule had little difficulty agreeing on the meaning of such terms as *liberty* and *equality*. Once the Revolutionary War was won, however, it became apparent that consensus on the meaning of these terms was far from solid. Consider the debate over slavery at the Constitutional Convention. Clearly, there was disagreement over whether the slaves should enjoy the liberty or equality for which the American revolutionaries had fought. The three-fifths compromise, mentioned elsewhere, left the issue of slavery to be debated by future generations.

A fundamental—and divisive—issue during the founding era had to do with the national government's role in the new republic. One group, the Federalists, desired a strong central gov-ernment that would act in the interests of Americans collectively. Another group, the Anti-Federalists, championed the rights of individuals and states over national interests. Since that time, the issue of individual or states' rights versus the national government has surfaced again and again. Indeed, during the 2004 presidential campaigns, Republican candidate George W. Bush presented himself as the champion of individual liberty. He often warned that Democratic candidate John Kerry's health plan and other policies would lead to "big government"—more government intrusion into affairs that should be handled by the private sector. Only once in our nation's history did this ongoing debate lead to bloodshed rather than discussion and compromise. In the 1860s, the issue of slavery proved too divisive and led to the Civil War.

How did the early American republic surmount the challenges and potential instability caused by such divisive attitudes? The answer to this question lies in the emergence of the political parties (see Chapter 7). Essentially, the party system provided a framework that allowed controversy and differences of opinion to become an integral part of our body politic. In many respects, then, the founding generation passed a political tug-of-war down through American history, and the Constitution served, in part, as a blueprint for future controversy.

Amending the Constitution

Since the Constitution was written, more than 11,000 amendments have been introduced in Congress. Sometimes, amendments have been proposed to counter perceived antimajoritarian provisions of the Constitution. Immediately after the 2000 elections, for example, an amendment was introduced in Congress to abolish the electoral college. As noted in the chapter-opening *America at Odds* feature, many Americans believe that the electoral college is an archaic institution that thwarts the popular will. After all, Democratic candidate Al Gore received a half-million more popular votes than George W. Bush; yet the electoral college vote, not the popular vote, determined the outcome of the race. Other suggested amendments have called for term limits for members of Congress, prayer in the public schools, English as the nation's official language, the prohibition of flag-burning, the banning of abortion, equal rights for women, and rights for crime victims during criminal proceedings.

It is often contended that members of Congress use the amendment process simply as a political ploy. By proposing an amendment, a member of Congress can show her or his position on an issue, knowing that the odds *against* the amendment's being adopted are high. After all, in the years since the ratification of the Bill of Rights, the first ten amendments to the Constitution, only seventeen proposed amendments have actually survived the amendment process and become a part of our Constitution.

One of the reasons there are so few amendments is that the framers, in Article V, made the formal amendment process extremely difficult—although it was much easier than it was under the Articles of Confederation, as just discussed. There are two ways to propose an amendment and two ways to ratify one. As a result, there are only four possible ways for an amendment to be added to the Constitution.

Methods of Proposing an Amendment

The two methods of proposing an amendment are as follows:

1. A two-thirds vote in the Senate and in the House of Representatives is required. All of the twenty-seven existing amendments have been proposed in this way.
2. If two-thirds of the state legislatures request that Congress call a national amendment convention, then Congress could call one. The convention could propose amendments to the states for ratification. There has yet to be a successful amendment proposal using this method.

The notion of a national amendment convention is exciting to many people. Many national political and judicial leaders, however, are uneasy about the prospect of convening a body that conceivably could do what the Constitutional Convention did—create a new form of government.

In two separate instances, the call for a national amendment convention almost became reality. Between 1963 and 1969, thirty-three state legislatures (out of the necessary thirty-four) attempted to call a convention to amend the Constitution to eliminate the Supreme Court's

The Process of Amending the Constitution

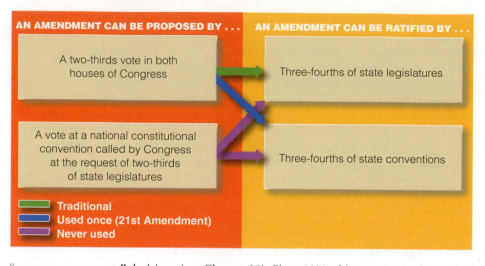

"one person, one vote" decisions (see Chapter 11). Since 1975, thirty-two states have asked for a national convention to propose an amendment requiring that the federal government balance its budget. Generally, the major national convention campaigns have reflected dissatisfaction, on the part of certain conservative and rural groups, with the national government's social and economic policies.

Methods of Ratifying an Amendment

There are two methods of ratifying a proposed amendment:

1. Three-fourths of the state legislatures can vote in favor of the proposed amendment. This method is considered the "traditional" ratification method and has been used twenty-six times.
2. The states can call special conventions to ratify the proposed amendment. If three-fourths of the states approve, the amendment is ratified. This method has been used only once—to ratify the Twenty-first Amendment.

You can see the four methods for proposing and ratifying amendments in Figure 2–6. As you can imagine, to meet the requirements for proposal *and* ratification, any amendment must have wide popular support in all regions of the country.

The Constitution and Your Everyday Life

The U.S. Constitution is the supreme law of the land. Perhaps this is not enough to convince you that the Constitution is important to you and does affect your everyday life. To show that the Constitution does matter and that it directly affects your daily life, we look here at just two constitutional provisions—it would take a book to discuss them all.

Congress Regulates Interstate Commerce

Article 1, Section 8, Clause 3, of the Constitution expressly delegates to the national government the power:

> [T]o regulate Commerce with foreign Nations, and among the several States, and with the Indian Tribes.

The framers included this clause, known as the commerce clause, to prevent states from establishing laws or regulations that would interfere with trade among the states, as had happened under the Articles of Confederation. But the commerce clause has had much broader implications. Today, it applies to nearly every aspect of your life.

- If you had breakfast this morning, chances are the food you ate was inspected by a federal government agency.
- As for the clothes you wear, the federal government regulates the way the fabric is manufactured and the way clothes are shipped to the store where you buy them.
- If you have a job, your workplace is governed by myriad federal laws and regulations, such as laws protecting employees against unsafe working conditions and against discriminatory treatment in the workplace.

A complete list could fill all the pages in this book. Suffice it to say that the power granted to the national government by the commerce clause and broadly interpreted by the Supreme Court affects every American throughout his or her life.

You Can Move from State to State and Not Lose Any of Your Rights

Consider Article IV, Section 1, Clause 1, which states as follows:

> Full Faith and Credit shall be given in each State to the Public Acts, Records, and judicial Proceedings of every other State.

Now consider the words of Article IV, Section 2, Clause 1:

> The Citizens of each State shall be entitled to all Privileges and Immunities of Citizens in the several States.

These clauses concern relationships among the states in our system of government. Among other things, the "full faith and credit" clause means that if you are married in one state, you are considered legally married in all other states. If you are divorced in one state, you are considered divorced in all states. If you have signed a contract in one state, such as to purchase a car, that contract is valid no matter where you move within the United States.

The "privileges and immunities" clause means that if you apply for a job in another state, that state cannot discriminate against you simply because it would prefer to hire only state citizens so as to reduce the state's unemployment rate. In short, states normally must consider actions legally undertaken in other states to be valid and cannot discriminate against out-of-state residents.

Taking Action

As you have read, the founders envisioned that the Constitution, to remain relevant, would need to be changed over time. It has been amended twenty-seven times, but many more amendments have been proposed. You can take action in a debate over the Constitution by supporting or opposing a proposed amendment, such as the Federal Marriage Amendment (FMA). The FMA would define marriage as between "one man and one woman" in the Constitution, thereby making marriage for same-sex couples impossible. You could also become involved in opposing such a controversial amendment. As you will read in Chapter 5, the issue of gay marriage has divided Americans. The battle over the issue has primarily taken place in state courts and legislatures and through votes on state ballot initiatives. If the FMA is adopted, however, it would become part of the federal Constitution and thus the supreme law of the land. You can take action by writing your representatives and senators in Congress or by forming protest groups to voice your concerns.

A gay group's version of an American flag blocks a supporter of the Federal Marriage Amendment (FMA). The FMA supporter is participating in a march in San Francisco in 2004 to affirm that marriage should be between a man and a woman.

Key Terms

Anti-Federalists 34	faction 35	Mayflower Compact 24	tyranny 36
Articles of Confederation 29	federal system 37	rule of law 37	unicameral legislature 29
Bill of Rights 24	Federalists 34	Second Continental Congress 26	veto power 38
checks and balances 37	First Continental Congress 26	separation of powers 37	
commerce clause 37	Great Compromise 33	Shays' Rebellion 31	
confederation 29	interstate commerce 34	three-fifths compromise 33	
Constitutional Convention 32	Madisonian Model 37		

Chapter Summary

1 The first successful English colonies were established at Jamestown (Virginia) in 1607 and at Plymouth (Massachusetts) in 1620. The Mayflower Compact created the first formal government in the colonies. By 1732, all thirteen colonies had been established.

2 For all their distance from Britain, the colonists had strong ties of loyalty to the home country and to the British monarch. A series of events during and following the Seven Years' War (1756–1763) served to loosen, and finally sever, these ties.

3 The colonies eventually transformed themselves into sovereign states, each having its own permanent government. The first national government was created by the Articles of Confederation.

4 General dissatisfaction with the Articles of Confederation prompted the states to send delegates to a meeting in Philadelphia in 1787, which is now referred to as the Constitutional Convention. The Constitution created by the convention delegates provided for limited government and popular sovereignty, a federal system of government, the separation of government powers among the three branches of government, and a system of checks and balances.

5 The Federalists, who favored a strong central government, and the Anti-Federalists, who opposed ratification, intensely debated the ratification issue. By 1790, however, all of the states had ratified the Constitution. The Anti-Federalists' fears of a strong central government prompted the addition of the Bill of Rights (the first ten amendments) to the Constitution.

6 The Constitution addressed several problems that the Articles of Confederation had not resolved and shifted many powers from the states to the central government, including the power to regulate interstate commerce.

7 The Constitution has proved to be an enduring document, in part because of the checks and balances that were incorporated into it and that have safeguarded the nation from tyranny. In addition, the Constitution's brevity and establishment of broad principles of government have allowed it to be adapted to the needs of a changing nation over the years. At the same time, the Constitution was, in a sense, a blueprint for future controversy. From the beginning of this nation, the broad language of the Constitution has contributed to differing interpretations of its provisions. Ultimately, the political parties provided a framework within which conflicting interpretations of constitutional provisions could be resolved.

8 A constitutional amendment may be proposed either by a two-thirds vote in each house of Congress or by a national convention called by Congress at the request of two-thirds of the state legislatures. Ratification of an amendment can occur either by a positive vote in three-fourths of the legislatures of the various states or by a positive vote in three-fourths of special conventions called in the states for the specific purpose of ratifying the proposed amendment.

RESOURCES FOR FURTHER STUDY

Selected Readings

Dahl, Robert A. *How Democratic Is the American Constitution?* New Haven, Conn.: Yale University Press, 2002. The author compares the American Constitution—the world's first great democratic experiment—to other democratic systems. He focuses on the more unusual, and potentially undemocratic, aspects of the American system, such as federalism and the electoral college.

Edwards, George C. *Why the Electoral College Is Bad for America.* New Haven, Conn.: Yale University Press, 2004. The author argues that the electoral college does not provide presidents with effective coalitions for governing and fails in its purpose—protecting the interests of small states and minorities.

Ellis, Joseph J. *Founding Brothers: The Revolutionary Generation.* New York: Knopf Publishing, 2002. The author explores the decade of the 1790s and the men who made decisions that would forever shape and influence our nation.

Hamilton, Alexander, James Madison, and John Jay. *The Federalist Papers.* Cambridge, Mass.: Harvard University Press, 1961. The book contains the complete set of columns from the *New York Packet* defending the new Constitution.

Storing, Herbert J. *The Complete Anti-Federalist.* 7 vols. Chicago: University of Chicago Press, 1981. An analysis of the views of those who argued against the adoption of the Constitution.

Politics on the Web

- The World Wide Web version of the Constitution provides hypertext links to amendments and other changes. Go to **http://www.law.cornell.edu/constitution/constitution. overview.html**

  - The National Constitution Center in Philadelphia has a Web page at **http://www.constitutioncenter.org** The site offers an online version of the *Federalist Papers,* a Constitution quiz, basic facts about the Constitution, and other information.

- James Madison's notes are one of our most important sources for the debates and exchanges that took place during the Constitutional Convention. These notes are now online at **http://www.thisnation.com/library/madison/index.html**

- An online version of the Anti-Federalist Papers is now available at the Web site of the West El Paso Information Network (WEPIN). Go to **http://wepin.com/articles/afp/index.htm**

- For information on the effect of new computer and communications technologies on the constitutional rights and liberties of Americans, go to the Center for Democracy and Technology at **http://www.cdt.org**

- The Cyberspace Law Institute (CLI) also focuses on law and communications technology. Go to **http://www.cli.org/papers.html**

- The constitutions of almost all of the states are now online. You can find them at **http://www.findlaw.com/11stategov**

- To find historical documents from the founding period, including the charter to Sir Walter Raleigh in 1584, the Royal Proclamation of 1763, and writings by Thomas Paine, go to **http://www.yale.edu/lawweb/avalon/alfalist.htm**

- You can find constitutions for other countries at **http://www.oefre.unibe.ch/law/icl/home.html**

Online Resources for This Chapter

This text's Companion Web Site, at **http://www.americaatodds.com**, offers links to numerous resources that you can utilize to learn more about the topics covered in this chapter. For a list describing these resources, see the inside front cover of this book.

chapter 3
federalism

CHAPTER OBJECTIVES

After reading this chapter, you should be able to . . .

▶ Describe how federalism differs from other systems of government.

▶ Explain what federalism means and why it exists in the United States.

▶ Indicate how the Constitution divides governing powers in our federal system.

▶ Summarize the evolution of federal-state relationships in the United States over time.

▶ Distinguish between the "new federalism" of today and earlier forms of federalism.

▶ Explain what is meant by the term *fiscal federalism*.

Should the States Decide the Medical-Marijuana Issue?

In recent years, voters in eleven states have approved laws permitting the use of marijuana for medical purposes. Such laws allow physicians to prescribe marijuana for patients suffering from AIDS and other terminal or chronic illnesses.

These states and the national government are at odds with one another over the medical-marijuana issue, however. As you will read in this chapter, the United States has a *federal system* of government. In our federal model, the power to create and implement policy is shared by the national government and the state governments. In 2004, the United States Supreme Court agreed to revisit the medical-marijuana question as a states' rights issue. Does the federal government have the authority to enforce a national drug policy, or should the states be allowed to regulate drugs within their own borders?

Let the National Government Regulate Drugs

Opponents of state laws authorizing the use of marijuana for medical purposes claim that such laws should not be allowed to stand because they are contrary to national drug policy. In all states, the possession of marijuana continues to be subject to a national law governing drugs: the Comprehensive Drug Abuse Prevention and Control Act of 1970, as amended. The national government's authority to control drugs is ultimately based on the commerce clause of the Constitution. That clause, as interpreted by the United States Supreme Court, gives the national government the exclusive power to regulate interstate commerce. Because the sale and distribution of drugs affect interstate commerce, the provisions of the 1970 federal act should take priority over state laws regulating the use of marijuana.

To be sure, growing marijuana for one's own use (not for sale or distribution) does not directly affect interstate commerce. Nonetheless, allowing medical-marijuana laws would be dangerous. It would be difficult to determine whether people were growing marijuana for its stated medical purpose or for wider recreational use. A general fear of those opposed to state medical-marijuana laws is that such laws would put drug control efforts on a slippery slope toward more relaxed drug policies. In any given year, more than forty million Americans violate some drug law at least once. To have varying state laws regulating drugs would create a lack of uniformity that would make it extremely difficult to control illegal drug use and trafficking.

Let the States Create Their Own Policies

Angel Raich has suffered from tumors in her brain and uterus, spasms, seizures, and nausea. Her physician prescribed numerous painkillers, but Raich did not experience any relief from her ailments until she tried marijuana. Raich, a resident of California, may lose access to the drug because the national government is attempting to overturn the 1996 state law that allows for the "compassionate use" of marijuana. She and many other Americans claim that because growing and using marijuana for medical purposes does not involve commerce, the national government cannot regulate it. Most of the state medical-marijuana laws allow patients and their "caregivers" to grow and possess small amounts of the drug. If a caregiver is involved, that individual cannot charge a fee for the marijuana. Thus, no commercial transaction takes place.[1]

Supporters of the medical-marijuana initiatives argue that states need to relax laws on possession and distribution of the drug so that patients may readily obtain it. Even some states without medical-marijuana laws have criticized the federal government's position. Alabama, Louisiana, and Mississippi issued a statement to the United States Supreme Court supporting other states' prerogatives within our federal system of government to serve as "laboratories for experimentation." Those in favor of permitting the medical use of marijuana are part of a larger group who think that drug policy should be formed by the states and cities in which we live, rather than by the national government.

Where Do You Stand?

1. What would result if the states were allowed to control drug policy?

2. If the states exercised ultimate control over drug policy, how could they arrange to handle the problem of interstate and international drug trafficking?

Explore This Issue Online

- Medical Marijuana ProCon, a nonpartisan, nonprofit organization, explores whether medical marijuana should be a legal option on its Web site. Go to **http://medicalmarijuanaprocon.org**.
- The American Medical Marijuana Association advocates the use of marijuana for medical purposes. For its views on this controversial subject, go to **http://americanmarijuana.org**.

Introduction

Whether drug policy should be controlled by the national government or by state governments is just one example of how different levels of government in our federal system can be at odds with one another. Let's face it—those who work for the national government based in Washington, D.C., probably would not like to see power taken away from Washington and given to the states. At the same time, those who work in state governments don't like to be told what to do by the national government. Finally, those who work in local governments would like to run their affairs with the least amount of interference from both their state governments and the national government.

Such conflicts arise because our government is based on the principle of **federalism,** which means that government powers are shared by the national government and the states. When the founders of this nation opted for federalism, they created a practical and flexible form of government capable of enduring for centuries. At the same time, however, they planted the seeds for future conflict between the states and the national government over how government powers should be shared. As you will read in this chapter—and throughout this book—many of today's most pressing issues have to do with which level of government should exercise certain powers, such as the power to control drug policy.

The relationship between the national government and the governments at the state and local levels has never been free of conflict. Indeed, even before the Constitution was adopted, the Federalists and Anti-Federalists engaged in a heated debate over the issue of national versus state powers. As you learned in Chapter 2, the Federalists won the day by convincing Americans to adopt the Constitution. The Anti-Federalists' concern for states' rights, however, has surfaced again and again in the course of American history. Today, for example, we see the concern for states' rights reflected in arguments supporting **devolution**—the transfer to the states of some of the responsibilities assumed by the national government since the 1930s.

federalism A system of shared sovereignty between two levels of government—one national and one subnational—occupying the same geographic region.

devolution The surrender or transfer of powers to local authorities by a central government.

Federalism and Its Alternatives

There are various ways of ordering relations between central governments and local units. Federalism is one of these ways. Learning about federalism and how it differs from other forms of government is important to understanding the American political system.

Angel Raich gestures beside jars of marijuana at her home in Oakland, California. Legal drugs have done little to help Raich, who is beset by numerous ailments, including cancer. In a case that reached the U.S. Supreme Court, Raich argued that growing marijuana on one's own property for one's own medical use did not involve interstate commerce and thus was not subject to federal regulation.

AP Photo/Ben Margot

TABLE 3-1
Countries That Have a Federal System Today

COUNTRY	POPULATION (IN MILLIONS)
Argentina	36.9
Australia	19.2
Austria	8.1
Brazil	172.9
Canada	31.3
Germany	82.8
India	1,014.0
Malaysia	21.8
Mexico	100.3
Switzerland	7.3
United States	295.4

SOURCE: Central Intelligence Agency, *The World Fact Book, 2001* (Washington, D.C.: U.S. Government Printing Office, 2000); plus authors' update.

What Is Federalism?

Nowhere in the Constitution does the word *federalism* appear. This is understandable, given that the concept of federalism was an invention of the founders. Since the Federalists and the Anti-Federalists argued more than two hundred years ago about what form of government we should have, hundreds of definitions of federalism have been offered. Basically, though, as mentioned in Chapter 2, in a *federal system*, government powers are divided between a central government and regional, or subdivisional, governments.

Although this definition seems straightforward, its application certainly is not. After all, virtually all nations—even the most repressive totalitarian regimes—have some kind of subnational governmental units. Thus, the existence of national and subnational governmental units by itself does not make a system federal. *For a system to be truly federal, the powers of both the national units and the subnational units must be specified in a constitution.* Under true federalism, individuals are governed by two separate governmental authorities (national and state authorities) whose expressly designated constitutional powers cannot be altered without rewriting or altering (by amendment, for example) the constitution. The Central Intelligence Agency estimates that only eleven countries, constituting 32 percent of the world's population, have a truly federal system (see Table 3-1).[2]

Federalism in theory is one thing; federalism in practice is another. As you will read shortly, the Constitution sets forth specific powers that can be exercised by the national government and provides that the national government has the implied power to undertake actions necessary to carry out its expressly designated powers. All other powers are "reserved" to the states. The broad language of the Constitution, though, has left much room for debate over the specific nature and scope of certain powers, such as the national government's implied powers and the powers reserved to the states. Thus, the actual workings of our federal form of government have depended, to a great extent, on the historical application of the broad principles outlined in the Constitution.

To further complicate matters, the term *federal government,* as it is currently used, refers to the national, or central, government. When individuals talk of the federal government, they mean the national government; they are not referring to the federal *system* of government, which is made up of both the national government and the state governments.

Alternatives to Federalism

Perhaps an easier way to define federalism is to discuss what it is *not.* Most of the nations in the world today have a **unitary system** of government. In such a system, the constitution vests all powers in the national government. If the national government so chooses, it can delegate certain activities to subnational units. The reverse is also true: the national government can take away, at will, powers delegated to subnational governmental units. In a unitary system, any subnational government is a "creature of the national government." The governments of Britain, France, Israel, Japan, and the Philippines are examples of unitary systems. In the United States, because the Constitution does not mention local governments (cities and counties), we say that city and county governmental units are "creatures of state government." That means that state governments can—and do—both give powers to and take powers from local governments. (For further discussion of how unitary systems differ from federal systems, see this chapter's *Comparative Politics* feature.)

The Articles of Confederation created a confederal system (see Chapter 2). In a **confederal system,** the national government exists and operates only at the direction of the subnational governments. During the Civil War, eleven southern states formed the Confederate States of America, or the Confederacy. Invoking the ideology of the Anti-Federalists, the members of the Confederacy desired an expansion of states' rights and greater autonomy. These states resented the authority of a strong national government, especially on the issue of slavery, so they decided to leave the Union. (For a further discussion of the Civil War era and secession, see page 60 in this chapter.) Few true confederal systems are in existence today.

unitary system A centralized governmental system in which local or subdivisional governments exercise only those powers given to them by the central government.

confederal system A league of independent sovereign states, joined together by a central government that has only limited powers over them.

comparative politics

Life in a Unitary System

Even in a country with a unitary system, the central government must delegate some power to regional or local administrative units. No matter how small the country, it usually doesn't make sense for the central government to decide such things as the speed limit on every city street. Note, though, that under a unitary system, once the decision about speed limits is made on the local level, the central government can override that decision if it chooses. Local governments in a unitary system have only as much or as little power as the central government decides they should have, and the central government can give or take away that power at its discretion.

AN EXAMPLE—JAPAN'S POSTWAR CONSTITUTION

Japan contains forty-seven prefectures—subdivisional units that manage local affairs—but the central government maintains a large amount of control over them. Japan's present constitution was written in 1946 when the country was under U.S. occupation following World War II. The United States, therefore, greatly influenced Japan's postwar constitution. Despite the U.S. preference for a federal system, however, the tradition of strong central power in Japan prevailed. The Japanese islands were unified 1,500 years ago and were ruled by an emperor, considered divine by the Japanese people. After World War II, the emperor renounced his divinity and today serves only as a political figurehead, but centuries of centralized government left their mark on Japan.

The 1946 constitution created a representative democracy in which the National Diet, elected by the people, wields legislative power. A prime minister and cabinet are chosen by the Diet from its own members. As is typical in a unitary system, the central government in Japan controls local taxation, collecting nearly two-thirds of the nation's taxes and sending half back to local governments. These transferred revenues are targeted for specific programs that reflect national policies, not local initiatives.

EVEN UNITARY SYSTEMS ARE DECENTRALIZING

In spite of Japan's unitary system, its prefectures collect one-third of the taxes for local use, and the constitution does prescribe certain autonomous functions for local government. Such decentralization is

Members of the lower chamber of Japan's parliament, the National Diet, are vociferously debating a 2004 proposed plan to reform the country's troubled pension system.

also occurring in other countries with unitary systems, such as France and Great Britain. France has recently decreased the degree of its government centralization, and Britain has allowed a degree of regional autonomy in Northern Ireland, Wales, and Scotland.

The key difference between a federal and a unitary system, then, is that the central government in a unitary system has the power to grant, and to take away, local autonomy.

For Critical Analysis

Why might the central government in a unitary system relinquish some of its power over regional governments? Conversely, why might the central government take power away from regional governments?

Federalism—An Optimal Choice for the United States?

The Articles of Confederation failed because they did not allow for a sufficiently strong central government. The framers of the Constitution, however, were fearful of tyranny and a too-powerful central government. The natural outcome had to be a compromise—a federal system.

The appeal of federalism was that it retained state powers and local traditions while establishing a strong national government capable of handling common problems, such as national defense. A federal form of government also furthered the goal of creating a division of powers (to be discussed shortly). There are other reasons why the founders opted for a federal system, and a federal structure of government continues to offer many advantages (as well as some disadvantages) for U.S. citizens.

Advantages of Federalism One of the reasons a federal form of government is well suited to the United States is its large size compared to many other countries. Even in the days when the United States consisted of only thirteen colonies, its geographic area was larger than that of France or England. In those days, travel was slow and communication was difficult, so people in outlying areas were isolated. The news of any particular political decision could take several weeks to reach everyone. Therefore, even if the framers of the Constitution had wanted a more centralized system (which most of them did not), such a system would have been unworkable.

Look at Figure 3–1. As you can see, to a great extent the practical business of governing this country takes place not in Washington, D.C., but in state and local governmental units. Federalism, by providing a multitude of arenas for decision making, keeps government closer to the people and helps make democracy possible.

The existence of numerous government subunits in the United States also makes it possible to experiment with innovative policies and programs at the state or local level. Many observers, including Supreme Court Justice Louis Brandeis, have emphasized that in a federal system, state governments can act as "laboratories" for public-policy experimentation. When a state adopts a program that fails, any negative effects are relatively limited. A program that succeeds can be copied by other states. For example, several states today are experimenting with new educational programs, including voucher systems. Depending on the outcome of a specific experiment, other states may (or may not) implement similar programs. State innovations can also serve as models for federal programs. For example, California was a pioneer in air-pollution control. Many of that state's regulations were later adapted by the federal government to federal regulatory programs.

We have always been a nation of different political subcultures. The Pilgrims who founded New England were different from the settlers who established the agricultural society of the South. Both of these groups were different from those who populated the Middle Atlantic states. The groups who founded New England were religiously oriented, while those who populated the Middle Atlantic states were more business oriented. Those who settled in the South were more individualistic than the other groups; that is, they were less inclined to act

---

FIGURE 3–1

Governmental Units in the United States Today

The most common type of governmental unit in the United States is the special district, which is generally concerned with issues such as solid waste disposal, mass transportation, fire protection, or similar matters. Often, the jurisdiction of special districts crosses the boundaries of other governmental units, such as cities or counties. They also tend to have fewer restrictions than other local governments as to how much debt they can incur and so are created to finance large building projects.

THE NUMBER OF GOVERNMENTS IN THE UNITED STATES TODAY

Government	Number
Federal government	1
State governments	50
Local governments	
Counties	3,034
Municipalities (mainly cities or towns)	19,431
Townships (less extensive powers)	16,506
Special districts (water, sewer, and so on)	35,356
School districts	13,522
Subtotal local governments	87,849
Total	**87,900**

PERCENTAGE OF ALL GOVERNMENTS IN THE UNITED STATES TODAY

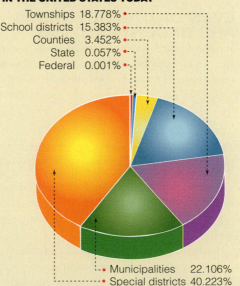

Townships 18.778%
School districts 15.383%
Counties 3.452%
State 0.057%
Federal 0.001%

Municipalities 22.106%
Special districts 40.223%

SOURCE: U.S. Census Bureau, *Preliminary Report, 2004 Census of Governments.*

as a unit and more inclined to act independently of each other. A federal system of government allows the political and cultural interests of regional groups to be reflected in the laws governing those groups.

Some Drawbacks to Federalism Federalism offers many advantages, but it also has some drawbacks. For example, although federalism in many ways promotes greater self-rule, or democracy, some scholars point out that local self-rule may not always be in society's best interests. These observers argue that the smaller the political unit, the higher the probability that it will be dominated by a single political group, which may or may not be concerned with the welfare of the majority of the local unit's citizens. For example, entrenched segregationist politicians in southern states denied African Americans their civil rights and voting rights for decades, as you will read further in Chapter 5.

Federalism also poses the danger that national powers will be expanded at the expense of the states. President Ronald Reagan (1981–1989) once said, "The Founding Fathers saw the federalist system as constructed something like a masonry wall. The States are the bricks, the national government is the mortar. . . . Unfortunately, over the years, many people have increasingly come to believe that Washington is the whole wall."[3]

At the same time, powerful state and local interests can block progress and impede national plans. State and local interests often diverge from those of the national government. For example, as you will read later in this chapter, the state of Oregon and the federal government are at odds over Oregon's physician-assisted suicide law. Finding acceptable solutions to such a conflict has not always been easy. Indeed, as will be discussed shortly, in the 1860s, war—not politics—decided the outcome of a struggle over states' rights.

Federalism has other drawbacks as well. One of them is the lack of uniformity of state laws, which can complicate business transactions that cross state borders. Another problem is the difficulty of coordinating government policies at the national, state, and local levels. Simultaneous regulation of business by all levels of government creates considerable red tape that imposes substantial costs on the business community.

The Constitutional Division of Powers

The founders created a federal form of government by dividing sovereign powers into powers that could be exercised by the national government and powers that were to be reserved to the states. Although there is no systematic explanation of this **division of powers** between the national and state governments, the original Constitution, along with its amendments, sets forth what the national and state governments can (and cannot) do.

division of powers A basic principle of federalism established by the U.S. Constitution. In a federal system, powers are divided between units of government (such as the federal and state governments).

The Powers of the National Government

The Constitution delegates certain powers to the national government. It also prohibits the national government from exercising certain powers.

Powers Delegated to the National Government The Constitution grants three types of powers to the national government: expressed powers, implied powers, and inherent powers. Article I, Section 8, of the Constitution expressly enumerates twenty-seven powers that Congress may exercise. Two of these **expressed powers** are the power to coin money and the power to regulate interstate commerce. Constitutional amendments have provided for other expressed powers. For example, the Sixteenth Amendment, added in 1913, gives Congress the power to impose a federal income tax. Article II, Section 2, of the Constitution expressly delegates certain powers to the president. These powers include making treaties and appointing certain federal officeholders.

The constitutional basis for the **implied powers** of the national government is found in Article I, Section 8, Clause 18, often called the **necessary and proper clause.** This clause states that Congress has the power to make "all Laws which shall be necessary and proper for carrying into Execution the foregoing [expressed] Powers, and all other Powers vested by this Constitution in the Government of the United States, or in any Department or Officer

expressed powers Constitutional or statutory powers that are expressly provided for by the Constitution or by congressional laws.

implied powers The powers of the federal government that are implied by the expressed powers in the Constitution, particularly in Article I, Section 8.

necessary and proper clause Article I, Section 8, Clause 18, of the Constitution, which gives Congress the power to make all laws "necessary and proper" for the federal government to carry out its responsibilities; also called the elastic clause.

One of the expressed powers of Congress is the power to coin money. On April 2, 1792, Congress established the Mint of the United States in Philadelphia. Congress subsequently established mints in Denver and San Francisco.

States have the power to protect the health, safety, morals, and welfare of their citizens.

inherent powers The powers of the national government that, although not always expressly granted by the Constitution, are necessary to ensure the nation's integrity and survival as a political unit. Inherent powers include the power to make treaties and the power to wage war or make peace.

thereof." The necessary and proper clause is often referred to as the *elastic clause*, because it gives elasticity to our constitutional system.

The national government also enjoys certain **inherent powers**—powers that governments have simply to ensure the nation's integrity and survival as a political unit. For example, any national government must have the inherent ability to make treaties, regulate immigration, acquire territory, wage war, and make peace. Although the national government's inherent powers are few, they are important.

Powers Prohibited to the National Government   The Constitution expressly prohibits the national government from undertaking certain actions, such as imposing taxes on exports, and from passing laws restraining certain liberties, such as the freedom of speech or religion. Most of these prohibited powers are listed in Article I, Section 9, and in the first eight amendments to the Constitution. Additionally, the national government is prohibited from exercising powers, such as the power to create a national public school system, that are not included among its expressed and implied powers.

The Powers of the States

The Tenth Amendment to the Constitution states that powers that are not delegated to the national government by the Constitution, nor prohibited to the states, "are reserved to the States respectively, or to the people."

police powers The powers of a government body that enable it to create laws for the protection of the health, morals, safety, and welfare of the people. In the United States, most police powers are reserved to the states.

Police Powers   The Tenth Amendment thus gives numerous powers to the states, including the power to regulate commerce within their borders and the power to maintain a state militia. In principle, each state has the ability to regulate its internal affairs and to enact whatever laws are necessary to protect the health, morals, safety, and welfare of its people. These powers of the states are called **police powers.** The establishment of public schools and the regulation of marriage and divorce are uniquely within the purview of state and local governments.

Because the Tenth Amendment does not specify what powers are reserved to the states, these powers have been defined differently at different times in our history. In periods of widespread support for increased regulation by the national government, the Tenth Amendment tends to recede into the background of political discourse. When the tide turns the other way, as it has in recent years (see the discussion of the new federalism later in this chapter), the Tenth Amendment is resurrected to justify arguments supporting increased states' rights. Because the Supreme Court is the ultimate arbiter of the Constitution, the outcome of disputes over the extent of state powers often rests with the Court.

AMERICA at odds

Should States Be Allowed to Import Prescription Drugs?

With prescription drug costs climbing rapidly, Canadian pharmacies have become an increasingly popular alternative for Americans seeking to reduce prescription costs. The Food and Drug Administration (FDA), which ensures the quality of pharmaceuticals before they are marketed, has warned the states that importing Canadian drugs is illegal by federal mandate. Yet many states are defying the national government, claiming that American prices are out of control and that their citizens need "affordable" drugs.

Those in favor of importing Canadian drugs point out that many Americans, especially senior citizens on fixed incomes, struggle to purchase the drugs that help keep them alive. A number of states lacking physical proximity to Canada, such as Alabama, have even set up Web sites that allow their citizens to purchase Canadian drugs online. Other states, such as Minnesota, have tapped into the Canadian market to drive down the cost of prescriptions for state employees. Proponents of importing Canadian drugs claim that the Canadian equivalent of the FDA, Health Canada, has safety and quality-control standards comparable to U.S. standards. This group argues that as long as consumers obtain drugs from brick-and-mortar Canadian pharmacies or approved Canadian Web sites, Americans can have confidence in the safety of the products being purchased. Indeed, many of the drugs obtained from Canada are the same brand-name pharmaceuticals that are available in the United States with different labels and packaging. The only real difference is in the price.

Opponents of importing drugs from Canada stress that the reason such imports have been banned is that they may be unsafe. During a random three-day inspection in 2003, FDA officials intercepted nearly two thousand packages en route to the United States from Canadian pharmacies. The FDA claims that the inspectors found over 1,700 unapproved drugs. Some of the drugs were produced in Thailand and India, while others came loosely wrapped in sandwich bags. Most of these examples were purchased over the Internet from unapproved Web sites. Opponents of importing Canadian drugs also argue that the pharmaceutical industry needs the large profits earned in the United States to fund its medical research. They claim that without the billions of dollars in profits reaped from the sale of prescription drugs in the United States at higher prices, research and development for future drugs and better versions of existing pharmaceuticals will be slowed. Thus, American citizens must decide whether they want less expensive drugs now or the continued availability of cutting-edge (and possibly, lifesaving) pharmaceuticals in the future.

Pfizer, Inc., a New York–based pharmaceutical corporation, comes under fire from a group of U.S. citizens who object to Pfizer's efforts to block Americans from buying prescription drugs at lower prices from Canadian pharmacies.

AP Photo/James A. Finley

Powers Prohibited to the States   Article I, Section 10, denies certain powers to state governments, such as the power to tax goods that are transported across state lines. States also are prohibited from entering into treaties with other countries. In addition, the Thirteenth, Fourteenth, Fifteenth, Nineteenth, Twenty-fourth, and Twenty-sixth Amendments also prohibit certain state actions. (The complete text of these amendments is included in Appendix A.)

Interstate Relations

The Constitution also contains provisions relating to interstate relations. The states have constant commercial and social interactions among themselves, and these interactions often do not directly involve the national government. The relationships among the states in our federal system of government are sometimes referred to as *horizontal federalism.*

The Constitution outlines a number of rules for interstate relations. For example, the Constitution's full faith and credit clause requires each state to honor every other state's public acts, records, and judicial proceedings. The issue of gay marriage, however, has made this constitutional mandate difficult to follow. If a gay couple legally married in Massachusetts decides to move to Georgia, they may experience difficulty. Georgia passed a state constitutional amendment banning gay marriage in 2004. Which state's law would take priority in this example? The United States Supreme Court may ultimately have to decide this issue.

Concurrent Powers

concurrent powers Powers held by both the federal and state governments in a federal system.

Concurrent powers can be exercised by both state governments and the federal government. Generally, a state's concurrent powers apply only within the geographic area of the state and do not include functions that the Constitution delegates exclusively to the national government, such as the coinage of money and the negotiation of treaties. An example of a concurrent power is the power to tax. Both the states and the national government have the power to impose income taxes—and a variety of other types of taxes. States, however, are prohibited from imposing tariffs (taxes on imported goods), and the federal government may not tax articles exported by any state. Figure 3–2, which summarizes the powers granted and denied by the Constitution, lists other concurrent powers.

The Supremacy Clause

supremacy clause Article VI, Clause 2, of the Constitution, which makes the Constitution and federal laws superior to all conflicting state and local laws.

The Constitution makes it clear that the federal government holds ultimate power. The **supremacy clause** in Article VI, Clause 2, states that the U.S. Constitution and the laws of the federal government "shall be the supreme Law of the Land." In other words, states cannot use their reserved or concurrent powers to counter national policies. Whenever state or local officers, such as judges or sheriffs, take office, they become bound by an oath to support the U.S. Constitution. National government power always takes precedence over any conflicting state action.[4]

The Struggle for Supremacy

Much of the political and legal history of the United States has involved conflicts between the supremacy of the national government and the desires of the states to remain independent. The most extreme example of this conflict was the Civil War in the 1860s. Through the years, because of the Civil War and several key Supreme Court decisions, the national government has increased its power.

Early U.S. Supreme Court Decisions

John Marshall, chief justice of the United States Supreme Court from 1801–1835, was instrumental in establishing the supremacy of the national government.

The Granger Collection/New York

Two Supreme Court cases, both of which were decided in the early 1800s, played a key role in establishing the constitutional foundations for the supremacy of the national government. Both decisions were issued while John Marshall was chief justice of the Supreme Court. In his thirty-four years as chief justice (1801–1835), Marshall did much to establish the prestige and the independence of the Court. In *Marbury v. Madison,*[5] he clearly enunciated the principle of judicial review, which has since become an important part of the checks and balances in the American system of government. Under his leadership, the Supreme Court also established, through the following cases, the superiority of federal authority under the Constitution.

McCulloch v. Maryland **(1819)**   The issue in *McCulloch v. Maryland,*[6] a case decided in 1819, involved both the necessary and proper clause and the supremacy clause. When the state of Maryland imposed a tax on the Baltimore branch of the Second Bank of the

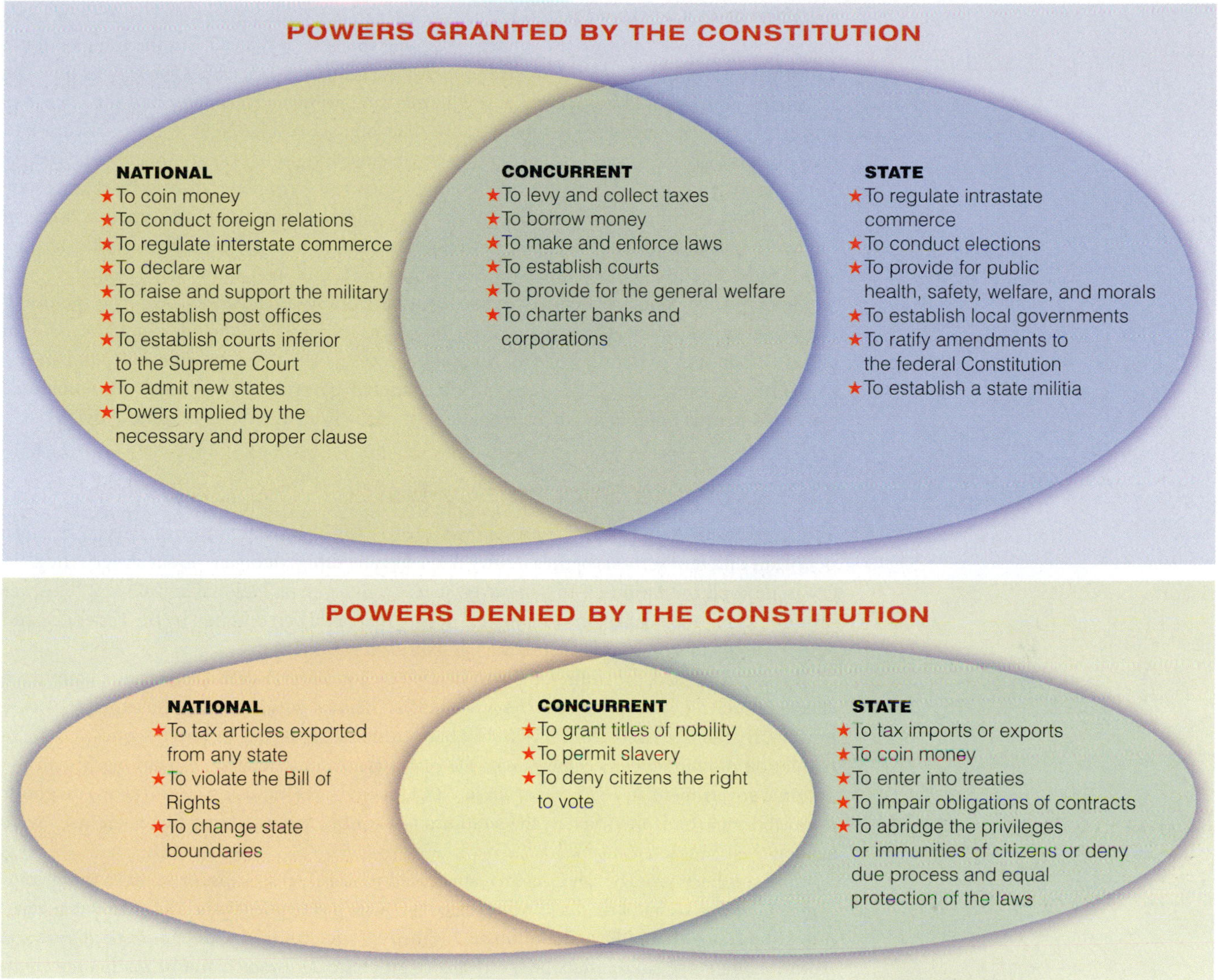

POWERS GRANTED BY THE CONSTITUTION

NATIONAL
★ To coin money
★ To conduct foreign relations
★ To regulate interstate commerce
★ To declare war
★ To raise and support the military
★ To establish post offices
★ To establish courts inferior to the Supreme Court
★ To admit new states
★ Powers implied by the necessary and proper clause

CONCURRENT
★ To levy and collect taxes
★ To borrow money
★ To make and enforce laws
★ To establish courts
★ To provide for the general welfare
★ To charter banks and corporations

STATE
★ To regulate intrastate commerce
★ To conduct elections
★ To provide for public health, safety, welfare, and morals
★ To establish local governments
★ To ratify amendments to the federal Constitution
★ To establish a state militia

POWERS DENIED BY THE CONSTITUTION

NATIONAL
★ To tax articles exported from any state
★ To violate the Bill of Rights
★ To change state boundaries

CONCURRENT
★ To grant titles of nobility
★ To permit slavery
★ To deny citizens the right to vote

STATE
★ To tax imports or exports
★ To coin money
★ To enter into treaties
★ To impair obligations of contracts
★ To abridge the privileges or immunities of citizens or deny due process and equal protection of the laws

FIGURE 3-2

The Constitutional Division of Powers
As illustrated here, the Constitution grants certain powers to the national government and to the state governments, while denying them other powers. Some powers, called *concurrent powers,* can be exercised at either the national or the state level, but generally the states can exercise these powers only within their own borders.

United States, the branch's chief cashier, James McCulloch, decided not to pay the tax. The state court ruled that McCulloch had to pay it, and the national government appealed to the United States Supreme Court. The case involved much more than a question of taxes. At issue was whether Congress had the authority under the Constitution's necessary and proper clause to charter and contribute capital to the Second Bank of the United States. A second constitutional issue was also involved: If the bank was constitutional, could a state tax it? In other words, was a state action that conflicted with a national government action invalid under the supremacy clause?

Chief Justice Marshall pointed out that no provision in the Constitution grants the national government the *expressed* power to form a national bank. Nevertheless, if establishing such a bank helps the national government exercise its expressed powers, then the authority to do so could be implied. Marshall also said that the necessary and proper clause included "all means that are appropriate" to carry out "the legitimate ends" of the Constitution.

Having established this doctrine of implied powers, Marshall then answered the other important constitutional question before the Court and established the doctrine of national supremacy. Marshall declared that no state could use its taxing power to tax an arm of the national government. If it could, the Constitution's declaration that the Constitution "shall be the supreme Law of the Land" would be empty rhetoric without meaning. From that day on, Marshall's decision became the basis for strengthening the national government's power.

Gibbons v. Ogden (1824)

As you learned in Chapter 2, Article I, Section 8, gives Congress the power to regulate commerce "among the several States." But the framers of the Constitution did not define the word *commerce.* At issue in *Gibbons v. Ogden*[7] was how the *commerce clause* should be defined and whether the national government had the exclusive power to regulate commerce involving more than one state. The New York legislature had given Robert Livingston and Robert Fulton the exclusive right to operate steamboats in New York waters, and they licensed Aaron Ogden to operate a ferry between New York and New Jersey. Thomas Gibbons, who had a license from the U.S. government to operate boats in interstate waters, decided to compete with Ogden, but he did so without New York's permission. Ogden sued Gibbons in the New York state courts and won. Gibbons appealed.

Chief Justice Marshall defined *commerce* as including all business dealings, including steamboat travel. Marshall also stated that the power to regulate interstate commerce was an *exclusive* national power and had no limitations other than those specifically found in the Constitution. Since this 1824 decision, the national government has used the commerce clause numerous times to justify its regulation of virtually all areas of economic activity.

The Ultimate Supremacy Battle—The Civil War

The great issue that provoked the Civil War (1861–1865) was the future of slavery. Because people in different sections of the country had radically different beliefs about slavery, the slavery issue took the form of a dispute over states' rights versus national supremacy. The war brought to a bloody climax the ideological debate that had been outlined by the Federalist and Anti-Federalist factions even before the Constitution was ratified.

As just discussed, the Supreme Court headed by John Marshall interpreted the commerce clause in such a way as to increase the power of the national government at the expense of state powers. By the late 1820s, however, a shift back to states' rights began, and the question of the regulation of commerce became one of the major issues in federal-state relations. When the national government, in 1823 and again in 1830, passed laws imposing tariffs (taxes) on goods imported into the United States, the southern states objected, believing that such taxes were against their best interests.

One southern state, South Carolina, attempted to *nullify* the tariffs, or to make them void. South Carolina claimed that in conflicts between state governments and the national government, the states should have the ultimate authority to determine the welfare of their citizens. Additionally, some southerners believed that democratic decisions could be made only when all the segments of society affected by those decisions were in agreement. Without such agree-

The Civil War is known in the South as the War between the States, but the official Union designation was the War of the Rebellion. The first shot of the Civil War was fired on April 12, 1861, at Fort Sumter, South Carolina.

Library of Congress

ment, a decision should not be binding on those whose interests it violates. This view was used to justify the **secession**—withdrawal—of the southern states from the Union.

When the South was defeated in the war, the idea that a state has a right to secede from the Union was defeated also. Although the Civil War occurred because of the South's desire for increased states' rights, the result was just the opposite—an increase in the political power of the national government.

secession The act of formally withdrawing from membership in an alliance; the withdrawal of a state from the federal Union.

From the Civil War to the 1930s—Dual Federalism

Scholars have devised various models to describe the relationship between the states and the national government at different times in our history. These models are useful in describing the evolution of federalism after the Civil War. The model of **dual federalism** assumes that the states and the national government are more or less equals, with each level of government having separate and distinct functions and responsibilities. The states exercise sovereign powers over certain matters, and the national government exercises sovereign powers over others.

dual federalism A system of government in which both the federal and state governments maintain diverse but sovereign powers.

For much of our nation's history, this model of federalism prevailed. Certainly, after the Civil War the courts tended to support the states' rights to exercise their police powers and concurrent powers to regulate intrastate activities. In 1918, for example, the Supreme Court ruled unconstitutional a 1916 federal law excluding from interstate commerce the products created through the use of child labor. The law was held unconstitutional because it attempted to regulate a local problem.[8] The era of dual federalism came to an end in the 1930s, when the United States was in the depths of the greatest economic depression it had ever experienced.

Cooperative Federalism and the Growth of the National Government

The model of **cooperative federalism,** as the term implies, involves cooperation by all branches of government. This model views the national and state governments as complementary parts of a single governmental mechanism, the purpose of which is to solve the problems facing the entire United States. For example, federal law enforcement agencies, such as the Federal Bureau of Investigation (FBI), lend technical expertise to solve local crimes, and local officials cooperate with federal agencies.

cooperative federalism The theory that the states and the federal government should cooperate in solving problems.

Cooperative federalism grew out of the need to solve the pressing national problems caused by the Great Depression, which began in 1929. In 1933, to help bring the United States out of the depression, President Franklin D. Roosevelt (1933–1945) launched his **New Deal,** which involved many government spending and public-assistance programs. Roosevelt's New Deal legislation not only ushered in an era of cooperative federalism, which has more or less continued until the present day, but also marked the real beginning of an era of national supremacy.

New Deal A program ushered in by the Roosevelt administration in 1933 to bring the United States out of the Great Depression. The New Deal included many government spending and public-assistance programs, in addition to thousands of regulations governing economic activity.

Was the Expansion of National Powers Inevitable?
Some scholars argue that even if the Great Depression had not occurred, we probably would still have witnessed a growth in the powers of the national government. As the country became increasingly populated, industrialized, and interdependent with other nations, problems and situations that once were treated locally began to have a profound impact on Americans hundreds or even thousands of miles away. Environmental pollution does not respect state borders, nor do poverty, crime, and violence. National defense, space exploration, and an increasingly global economy also call for national—not state—action. Thus, the ascendancy of national supremacy in the twentieth century had a logical set of causes.

Cooperative Federalism and the Welfare State
Certainly, the 1960s and 1970s saw an even greater expansion of the national government's role in domestic policy. The Great Society legislation of President Lyndon Johnson's administration (1963–1969) created Medicaid, Medicare, the Job Corps, Operation Head Start, and other programs. The Civil Rights Act of 1964 prohibited discrimination in public accommodations, employment,

In a 1938 radio broadcast, President Franklin D. Roosevelt called upon the nation's voters to elect New Deal candidates. The Roosevelt administration's New Deal programs played a key role in lifting the country out of the Great Depression of the 1930s and ushered in an era of national supremacy as well as cooperative federalism.

© Bettmann/Corbis

picket-fence federalism A model of federalism in which specific policies and programs are administered by all levels of government—national, state, and local.

President Johnson displays his signature on the War on Poverty bill after he signed it into law in a ceremony in the Rose Garden at the White House on August 20, 1964.

Getty News Images

and other areas on the basis of race, color, national origin, religion, or gender. In the 1970s, national laws protecting consumers, employees, and the environment imposed further regulations on the economy. Today, few activities are beyond the reach of the regulatory arm of the national government.

Nonetheless, the massive social programs undertaken in the 1960s and 1970s also precipitated greater involvement by state and local governments. The national government simply could not implement those programs alone. For example, Head Start, a program that provides preschool services to children of low-income families, is administered by local nonprofit organizations and school systems, although it is funded by federal grants. The model in which every level of government is involved in implementing a policy is sometimes referred to as **picket-fence federalism.** In this model, the policy area is the vertical picket on the fence, while the levels of government are the horizontal support boards. America's welfare system has relied on this model of federalism, although, as you will read, recent reforms have attempted to give more power to the state and local levels.

Supreme Court Decisions and Cooperative Federalism   The two Supreme Court decisions discussed earlier (*McCulloch v. Maryland* and *Gibbons v. Ogden*) became the constitutional cornerstone of the regulatory powers the national government enjoys today. From the 1930s to the mid-1990s, the Supreme Court consistently upheld Congress's power to regulate domestic policy under the commerce clause. Even activities that occur entirely within a state were rarely considered outside the regulatory power of the national government. For example, in 1942 the Supreme Court held that wheat production by an individual farmer intended wholly for consumption on his own farm was subject to federal regulation, because the home consumption of wheat reduced the demand for wheat and thus could have a substantial effect on interstate commerce.[9]

By 1980, the Supreme Court acknowledged that the commerce clause had "long been interpreted to extend beyond activities actually in interstate commerce to reach other activities, while wholly local in nature, which nevertheless substantially affect interstate commerce."[10] Today, Congress can regulate almost any kind of economic activity, no matter where it occurs. Increasingly, though, as you will read shortly, the Supreme Court is curbing Congress's regulatory powers under the commerce clause.

AMERICA at odds

Should Direct Wine Shipments Be Legalized?

Many vacationing wine connoisseurs have left a vineyard in a state of confusion. Why couldn't they have a case of that wonderful merlot shipped to their homes? American consumers are not accustomed to being told that they cannot legally purchase something. Yet this is what happens when a state law bans the direct shipment of wine to consumers' home states. Some Americans have become exasperated with the current web of state wine-shipment laws. This group argues that such laws violate the Constitution's commerce clause, which stipulates that states cannot enact laws that pose barriers to the free exchange of goods between the states.

Consumers and vineyards alike have tired of laws that they believe are largely designed to protect state wine wholesalers. They contend that such barriers need to be torn down so that free trade can flourish. Some proponents of abolishing existing state laws banning interstate wine shipments want to extend the rights of consumers to Internet and telephone orders as well. Twenty-six states currently allow direct shipment of wine. Thus, a wine lover in Idaho who wants to purchase a California chardonnay can simply point and click, and the bottle is immediately shipped to his or her doorstep.

Other Americans cringe at the thought of consumers being able to place an order for wine in the same way that they purchase a book or a DVD by phone or over the Internet. Who would ensure that the consumer was of legal drinking age, for example? Opponents of legalizing direct wine shipments argue that states are well within their rights to ban the shipment of alcohol across state borders. They point to the Twenty-first Amendment, which repealed Prohibition (the ban on sales of alcoholic beverages, which had been imposed by the Eighteenth Amendment) but gave the states the right to regulate the sale and distribution of alcohol. To these Americans, the Twenty-first Amendment should take priority over the commerce clause in this instance. Ultimately, this spirited debate will likely be resolved by the United States Supreme Court, which in 2004 agreed to review a case involving this issue.[11]

Linda and Patrick Elliott-Smith of Napa, California, pack a gift box featuring their Elan Vineyards wine. Their vineyard ships about one-third of the wine that it produces to out-of-state buyers. Many people believe that state laws barring people from buying wine directly from out-of-state suppliers should be struck down as unconstitutional.

AP Photo/Eric Risberg

John Marshall's validation of the supremacy clause of the Constitution has also had significant consequences for federalism. One important effect of the supremacy clause today is that the clause allows for federal **preemption** of certain areas in which the national government and the states have concurrent powers. When Congress chooses to act exclusively in an area in which the states and the national government have concurrent powers, Congress is said to have *preempted* the area. When Congress preempts an area, such as aviation, the courts have held that a valid federal law or regulation takes precedence over a conflicting state or local law or regulation covering the same general activity.

preemption A doctrine rooted in the supremacy clause of the Constitution that provides that national laws or regulations governing a certain area take precedence over conflicting state laws or regulations governing that same area.

Federalism Today

By the 1970s, some Americans began to question whether the national government had acquired too many powers. Had the national government gotten too big? Was it too deeply in debt as a result of annual budget deficits that created a national debt running into the trillions? Should steps be taken to reduce the regulatory power and scope of the national government? Today's model of federalism reflects these concerns.

The New Federalism—More Power to the States

new federalism A plan to limit the federal government's role in regulating state governments and to give the states increased power to decide how they should spend government revenues.

During the 1970s and 1980s, several administrations attempted to revitalize the doctrine of dual federalism, which they renamed the "new federalism." The **new federalism** involves a shift from *nation-centered* federalism to *state-centered* federalism. One of the major goals of the new federalism is to return to the states certain powers that have been exercised by the national government since the 1930s. The term *devolution*—the transfer of powers to political subunits—is often used to describe this process. Although a product of conservative thought and initiated by Republicans, the devolutionary goals of the new federalism were also espoused by the Clinton administration (1993–2001). (See this chapter's *Perception versus Reality* feature for a discussion of where the current Republican administration stands on the issue of the national government versus states' rights.)

An example of the new federalism is the welfare reform legislation passed by Congress in 1996, which gave the states more authority over welfare programs. In the late 1990s, Congress also managed to balance its budget for the first time in decades, but deficits returned in the 2000s. As you will read in Chapter 13, reducing the size of the national government has proved difficult, as have attempts to reduce government spending.

The Supreme Court and the New Federalism

During and since the 1990s, the Supreme Court has played a significant role in furthering the cause of states' rights. In a landmark 1995 decision, *United States v. Lopez*,[12] the Supreme Court held, for the first time in sixty years, that Congress had exceeded its constitutional authority under the commerce clause. The Court concluded that the Gun-Free School Zones

perception versus REALITY

The GOP and States' Rights

The issue of states' rights has been a constant source of debate since the early days of American history. The first defenders of states' rights in our system of government were the Anti-Federalists, who argued against ratification of the Constitution. The Anti-Federalists claimed that the Constitution gave too much authority to the national government. How do today's political parties line up on the issue of states' rights?

THE PERCEPTION

The Republican Party (sometimes called the Grand Old Party, or GOP) is often viewed as the champion of states' rights. Certainly, the Republican Party has claimed such a role. For example, when the Republicans took control of both chambers of Congress in 1995, they promised *devolution*—a shifting of power from the national level to the individual states. In contrast, Democrats have usually sought greater centralization of power in Washington, D.C.

Generally, from the civil rights movement of the 1960s to more recent attempts at welfare reform, the Republicans have amassed a track record of favoring states' rights. Smaller central government and a state-centered federalism are purported to be the twin pillars of Republican ideology.

THE REALITY

In reality, Republicans—following the lead of the Bush administration—have abandoned the states' rights camp on numerous occasions. For example, educational assessment has long been regarded as a prerogative of state governments. Nonetheless, in 2002 President George W. Bush signed the No Child Left Behind Act into law, forcing schools to meet national testing benchmarks to receive federal funding.

Consider also that marriage and family law has traditionally been under the purview of state government. Yet the Bush administration has backed the Federal Marriage Amendment (FMA) to the U.S. Constitution, which would define marriage as being between one man and one woman. The FMA would subvert state court decisions in favor of civil unions and marriage rights for same-sex couples. Administration officials have also attempted to assert their authority in environmental matters. Numerous states have more stringent environmental regulations than the federal government requires, but their authority is being questioned by pro-business Republicans in Washington, D.C. In addition, former Attorney General John Ashcroft made numerous attempts to block California's medical-marijuana initiative and Oregon's physician-assisted suicide law. After decades of championing states' rights, the Republicans seem to be redefining their party's approach to federalism.

What's Your Opinion?

Should states willingly allow the federal government to regulate areas, such as education and marriage, that have traditionally been regulated by the states? Why or why not?

Act of 1990, which banned the possession of guns within one thousand feet of any school, was unconstitutional because it attempted to regulate an area that had "nothing to do with commerce." In a significant 1997 decision, the Court struck down portions of the Brady Handgun Violence Prevention Act of 1993, which obligated state and local law enforcement officers to do background checks on prospective handgun buyers until a national instant check system could be implemented. The Court stated that Congress lacked the power to "dragoon" state employees into federal service through an unfunded **federal mandate** of this kind.[13]

In its 2000–2001 term, the Court continued to limit the national government's regulatory powers. In 2000, for example, the Court invalidated a key provision of the federal Violence Against Women Act of 1994, which allowed women to sue in federal court when they were victims of gender-motivated violence, such as rape. The Court upheld a federal appellate court's ruling that the commerce clause did not justify national regulation of noneconomic, criminal conduct.[14]

> **federal mandate** A requirement in federal legislation that forces states and municipalities to comply with certain rules. If the federal government does not provide funds to the states to cover the costs of compliance, the mandate is referred to as an *unfunded* mandate.

The Shifting Boundary between Federal and State Authority

Clearly, the boundary between federal and state authority is shifting. Notably, issues relating to the federal structure of our government, which in the past several decades have not been at the forefront of the political arena, are now the subject of heated debate among Americans and their leaders. The federal government and the states seem to be in a constant tug-of-war over federal regulation, federal programs, and federal demands on the states.

Federalism under the Bush Administration

For example, at the beginning of George W. Bush's administration, the new president announced the creation of a task force on federalism that would consult with governors on federal rulemaking and draft an executive order on federalism requiring federal departments and agencies to "respect the rights of our states and territories."[15] The executive order was never issued, however.

Since the September 11, 2001, terrorist attacks, the Bush administration has increased demands on state and local governments to participate in homeland security. (For more on how homeland security efforts have influenced the balance of power between the federal government and the states, see this chapter's *The Politics of National Security* feature on the next page.) Furthermore, in 2002, President Bush signed a sweeping new education bill, called the No Child Left Behind Act (NCLB), which significantly expands the federal government's role in education, an area long regarded as the purview of the states. The NCLB Act requires

U.S. soldiers brandish their M4 firearms with M203 grenade launchers in a show of increased security during President George W. Bush's inauguration ceremony in January 2005. In post–September 11, 2001, America, the Bush administration has focused on the need to combat terrorism and provide for homeland security at both the federal and state levels.

Jason Reed/Reuters/Landov

The POLITICS of
national SECURITY

You are here

Can the States Afford to Defend the Homeland?

The U.S. Constitution gives Congress the power and authority to provide for the common defense. But much of the burden of homeland defense falls on state and local governments. These governments are the "first responders" to crises, including terrorist attacks. Additionally, state and local governments are responsible for detecting, preparing for, preventing, and recovering from terrorist attacks.

THE COST OF HOMELAND DEFENSE

Homeland defense is necessarily a costly undertaking. Firefighting departments need more equipment and training. Emergency communications equipment must be purchased. Funds are necessary to secure ports, ensure water safety and airport security, obtain new bomb-detecting equipment, and increase security at nuclear plants and laboratories. Additional law enforcement resources must be obtained. But who should pay for this increased security—the states or the national government?

Clearly, in view of the financial crises that many state governments are facing, this is not the ideal time for those governments to incur additional costs. Yet the Bush administration has required state and local governments to play larger roles in homeland security. Each time the country has been placed on a heightened state of alert, city and state governments must ask police officers, firefighters, and emergency medical crews to work overtime. The U.S. Conference of Mayors estimates that each "Code Orange" (high) alert costs a total of $70 million per week nationwide. As yet, however, the fed-

eral government has been slow to provide the billions of dollars that it promised the states to help in their efforts.

WASHINGTON TURNS ITS BACK

Many governors had hoped that the federal government would come to their assistance. At the least, the states thought that the federal government should reimburse the states for homeland security costs already incurred and provide adequate funding for future efforts at the state and local levels. President Bush, however, has not offered much help. He told the governors that the federal government also has budget problems, so the states would simply have to work out their problems on their own.

The war in Iraq has also depleted the ranks of state and local police, firefighters, and other emergency personnel. Many individuals in these professions are also in the National Guard and have been called up to active duty. Additionally, western governors have expressed concern that their states might become more vulnerable to wildfires because they had relied on the National Guard to help extinguish fires in the past. Neither the Bush administration nor Congress has offered any ideas to help solve such problems.

Are We Safer?

Would it be in the best interests of national security for the states or the federal government to bear the greater financial and personnel burden for defending the homeland? Why?

---

schools to provide public school choice for students in failing schools, to issue annual report cards on schools, and to implement annual, standards-based assessment tests. It also sets strict time lines for the states to show improvement in poorly performing schools. The federal government has spent $26.5 billion to help the states implement the act.

Federalism and Public Opinion   Although many U.S. political leaders, as well as many average Americans, believe that the national government does too much and has too much power, the issues become more complex when it comes to specific government programs. According to one study, most Americans support government spending on such programs as job training, medical research, subsidies for teachers, aid for college students, clean-air standards, Head Start, job-safety regulations, Medicaid, and housing assistance. In all, fewer than 10 percent of those interviewed wanted the government to do or spend less on these programs, and about half of those interviewed thought the government should do more.[16]

The Fiscal Side of Federalism

As everybody knows, big government is costly. But how can government spending be reduced without sacrificing government programs that many feel are essential? This question, which to a significant extent frames the debate over federalism today, requires an understanding of the fiscal side of federalism.

Since the advent of cooperative federalism in the 1930s, the national government and the states have worked hand in hand to implement programs mandated by the national government. Whenever Congress passes a law that preempts a certain area, the states are, of course, obligated to comply with the requirements of that law. As already noted, a requirement that a state provide a service or undertake some activity to meet standards specified by a federal law is called a federal mandate. Many federal mandates concern civil rights or environmental protection. Recent federal mandates require the states to provide persons with disabilities with access to public buildings, sidewalks, and other areas; to establish minimum water-purity and air-purity standards for specific localities; and to extend Medicaid coverage to all poor children.

To help the states pay for some of the costs associated with implementing national policies, the national government gives back some of the tax dollars it collects to the states—in the form of grants. As you will see, the states have come to depend on grants as an important source of revenue.

Federal Grants

Even before the Constitution was adopted, the national government granted lands to the states to finance education. Using the proceeds from the sale of these lands, the states were able to establish elementary schools and later, *land-grant colleges.* Cash grants started in 1808, when Congress gave money to the states to pay for the state militias. Federal grants were also made available for other purposes, such as building roads and railroads.

Only in the twentieth century, though, did federal grants become an important source of funds to the states. The major growth began in the 1960s, when the dollar amount of grants quadrupled to help pay for the Great Society programs of the Johnson administration. Grants became available for education, pollution control, conservation, recreation, highway construction and maintenance, and other purposes.

There are two basic types of federal grants: categorical grants and block grants. A **categorical grant** is targeted for a specific purpose as defined by federal law—the federal government defines hundreds of categories of state and local spending. Categorical grants give the national government control over how states use the money by imposing certain conditions. For example, a categorical grant may require that the funds not be used for purposes that discriminate against any group or for construction projects that pay below the local union wage. Depending on the project, the government might require that an environmental impact statement be prepared.

categorical grant A federal grant targeted for a specific purpose as defined by federal law.

In contrast, a **block grant** is given for a broad area, such as criminal justice or mental-health programs. First started in 1966, block grants now constitute a growing percentage of all federal aid programs. The block grant is one of the tools of the new federalism because it gives the states more discretion over how the funds will be spent. Nonetheless, the federal government can exercise control over state decision making through these grants by using *cross-cutting requirements.* Title VI of the 1964 Civil Rights Act, for example, bars discrimination in the use of all federal funds, regardless of their sources.

block grant A federal grant given to a state for a broad area, such as criminal justice or mental-health programs.

Many public services and projects carried out by the states are actually funded, at least in part, by federal grants. Our interstate highway system is a case in point.

Bridging the Tenth Amendment—Fiscal Federalism

Grants of funds to the states from the national government are one way that the Tenth Amendment to the U.S. Constitution can be bridged. Remember that the Tenth Amendment reserves all powers not delegated to the national government to the states and to the people. You might well wonder, then, how the federal government has been able to exercise control over matters that traditionally have been under the control of state governments, such as the minimum drinking age. The answer involves the giving or withholding of federal grant dollars. The power of the national government to influence state policies through grants is often referred to as **fiscal federalism.**

fiscal federalism The power of the national government to influence state policies through grants.

For example, during President Ronald Reagan's administration (1981–1989), the national government wanted the states to raise the minimum drinking age to twenty-one years. States that refused to do so were threatened with the loss of federal highway construction funds. The threat worked—it was not long before all states had changed their minimum-drinking-age laws accordingly.[17] In the 1990s, Congress used this same threat to encourage the states to lower their blood-alcohol limits for drunk driving to .08 percent by 2004. Those states that failed to comply with the .08 percent limit would face reductions in federal highway funds.

The education reforms embodied in the NCLB Act rely on fiscal federalism for their implementation. The states receive block grants for educational purposes and, in return, must meet federally imposed standards relating to testing and accountability. A common complaint, however, is that the existing NCLB Act is an underfunded federal mandate. Critics argue that the national government does not provide sufficient funds to implement it. Furthermore, many state education officials express concern that the fiscal federalism used to put the act into practice is the beginning of a fundamental shift toward the national government's assumption of control over public schools.

The Cost of Federal Mandates

As mentioned, when the national government passes a law preempting an area in which the states and the national government have concurrent powers, the states must comply with that law in accordance with the supremacy clause of the Constitution. Thus, when such laws require the states to implement certain programs, the states must comply—but compliance with federal mandates can be costly.

For example, the estimated total cost of complying with federal mandates concerning water purity, over just a four-year period, is in the vicinity of $29 billion. In all, the estimated cost of federal mandates to the states in the early 2000s was over $70 billion annually. Although Congress passed legislation in 1995 to curb the use of "unfunded" federal mandates (that is, mandates that are not funded by the federal government), the legislation was more rhetoric than reality.

Competitive Federalism

The debate over federalism is sometimes reduced to a debate over taxes. Which level of government will raise taxes to pay for government programs, and which will cut services to avoid raising taxes?

competitive federalism A model of federalism devised by Thomas R. Dye in which state and local governments compete for businesses and citizens, who in effect "vote with their feet" by moving to jurisdictions that offer a competitive advantage.

How states answer that question gives citizens an option: they can move to a state with fewer services and lower taxes, or to a state with more services but higher taxes. Political scientist Thomas R. Dye calls this model of federalism **competitive federalism.** State and local governments compete for business and citizens. If the state of Ohio offers tax advantages for locating a factory there, for example, a business may be more likely to do so, providing more jobs for Ohio residents. If Ohio has very strict environmental regulations, however, that same business may choose not to build its factory there, no matter how beneficial the tax advantages, because complying with the regulations will be costly. Although Ohio citizens lose the opportunity for more jobs, they may enjoy better air and water quality than citizens of the state where the new factory is ultimately built.

Some observers consider the competitive nature of federalism an advantage: Americans have several variables to consider when they choose a state in which to live. Others consider it a disadvantage: a state that offers more social services or lower taxes may suddenly experience an increase in population as people "vote with their feet" to take advantage of that state's laws. This population increase can overwhelm the state's resources and force it to cut social services or raise taxes.

It appears likely, then, that the debate over how our federal system functions, as well as the battle for control between the states and the federal government, will continue. The Supreme Court, which has played umpire in this battle, will also likely continue to issue rulings that influence the balance of power.

why does it MATTER?

Federalism and Your Everyday Life

Most students of American government believe that the rather abstract concept of federalism has nothing to do with the realities they encounter in their everyday lives. Nothing could be further from the truth. On a broad scale, the fact that we have a federal form of government allows the fifty states to have significant influence over such matters as the level of taxation, the regulation of business, the creation and enforcement of criminal laws, and so on. What does that mean for you, as an individual? Most important, it means that you can pack up and move from one state to another in search of a business or working environment, a social and moral environment, or a legal environment that is more appealing to you than the one offered by your state.

Consider some examples of how state laws differ. In Nevada, you can purchase alcoholic beverages 24 hours a day, 365 days a year. In the neighboring state of Utah, the purchase of alcoholic

beverages is severely restricted. With respect to so-called soft drugs, such as marijuana, there are also differences in state laws. Many states now do not prosecute an individual who is found with a small amount of marijuana. (Federal law still has not decriminalized marijuana.) Certainly, your ability to carry a gun or to be protected from those who do carry guns is a function of the state where you live. This is because in our federal system, the states can currently regulate the sale and use of concealed firearms. In some states, concealed firearms are allowed; in others, they are strictly forbidden. You have the ability under our federal system to move to a jurisdiction that suits your tastes.

In nations that have a unitary form of government, such as France, this is not the case. Basically, you pay the same taxes no matter where you live in France. You go to exactly the same school system, and you face exactly the same criminal laws no matter where you live in that country.

Taking Action

As you have read, our federal system frequently creates tension between state or local concerns and national priorities. Often, individuals and groups take the initiative to assure that state or local governments respond to their particular wishes, regardless of how the nation as a whole might feel about it. The issue of physician-assisted suicide is a case in point. Oregonians have repeatedly voted for the right of terminally ill patients to seek help from a physician in ending their lives. In 2001, however, then U.S. Attorney General John Ashcroft issued a directive prohibiting physicians from prescribing lethal doses of federally controlled drugs. In response to this attempt, James Romney, shown in the photo on the left, took action. He brought a suit in federal court, claiming that the federal government did not have the authority to nullify Oregon's law. The court agreed with Romney and issued a restraining order against the federal government.

AP Photo/Don Ryan

Key Terms

block grant 67

categorical grant 67

competitive
  federalism 68

concurrent powers 58

confederal system 52

cooperative
  federalism 61

devolution 51

division of powers 55

dual federalism 61

expressed powers 55

federal mandate 65

federalism 51

fiscal federalism 68

implied powers 55

inherent powers 56

necessary and proper
  clause 55

New Deal 61

new federalism 64

picket-fence
  federalism 62

police powers 56

preemption 63

secession 61

supremacy clause 58

unitary system 52

Chapter Summary

1 The United States has a federal form of government, in which governmental powers are shared by the national government and the states. Alternatives to federalism include a unitary system and a confederal system. Federalism has been viewed as well suited to the United States for several reasons, but it also has some drawbacks.

2 The powers delegated by the Constitution to the national government include expressed powers, such as the power to coin money and to regulate interstate commerce; implied powers, or powers that are "necessary and proper" to the carrying out of the expressed powers; and inherent powers, which are necessary for any nation to survive and be a member of the community of nations.

3 All powers not delegated to the national government are "reserved" to the states, or to the people. State powers include police powers, which enable the states to enact whatever laws are necessary to protect the health, safety, morals, and welfare of their citizens. The Constitution prohibits both the national government and the states from exercising certain powers and provides for concurrent powers—powers that can be exercised by both state governments and the national government. The supremacy clause provides that national laws are supreme—they take priority over any conflicting state laws.

4 Two early Supreme Court cases that increased the powers of the national government are *McCulloch v. Maryland* (1819) and *Gibbons v. Ogden* (1824). The power struggle between the states and the national government ultimately resulted in the Civil War.

5 Federalism has evolved through several stages since the Civil War, including dual federalism, which prevailed until the 1930s,

and cooperative federalism, which involves cooperation by all branches of government and launched an era of national government growth. The new federalism, which involves returning to the states some of the powers assumed by the national government, dates to the 1970s and has continued, in varying degrees, to the present.

6 For much of the twentieth century, the Supreme Court by and large held that the national government had not overreached the powers given to it by the commerce clause and the supremacy clause of the Constitution. In the 1990s and early 2000s, however, a more conservative Supreme Court has shown a willingness to support the new federalism by holding certain national government actions unconstitutional and emphasizing state sovereignty.

7 To help the states pay for the costs associated with implementing policies mandated by the national government, the national government awards grants to the states. Through the awarding of grants, the federal government can also influence activities that constitutionally are regulated by the states under their reserved powers.

8 Today, the federal government and the states seem to be in a constant tug-of-war over power, with the Supreme Court sometimes acting as umpire. Although the Supreme Court has ruled in favor of state sovereignty in many cases, the federal government continues to wield enormous power. Controversial issues today concern federal preemption of state laws and the use of unfunded federal mandates. Homeland security concerns have also led the federal government to impose greater demands on the states.

RESOURCES FOR FURTHER STUDY

Selected Readings

Karmis, Dimitrios, and Wayne Norman, eds. *Theories of Federalism: A Reader.* New York: Palgrave MacMillan, 2005. This reader brings together the most significant writings on federalism from the late eighteenth century to the present.

Light, Paul Charles. *Government's Greatest Achievements: From Civil Rights to Homeland Defense.* Washington, D.C.: Brookings Institution Press, 2002. The author acknowledges that the federal government is rarely credited with policy successes, particularly in the debate over how much power it should share with the states. Nonetheless, the federal government has made achievements, and they are chronicled in this book.

Nagel, Robert F. *The Implosion of American Federalism.* New York: Oxford University Press, 2002. The author argues that even recent Supreme Court decisions returning some power to the states will not save the nation from the dangers of increasingly centralized power. Indeed, he argues, the Court cannot, and is not, leading a revival of federalism.

Simon, James F. *What Kind of Nation: Thomas Jefferson, John Marshall, and the Epic Struggle to Create a United States.* New York: Simon & Schuster, 2002. The author compares the states' rights views of Jefferson and the Federalist beliefs of Marshall in the early decades of the nation and describes how Marshall's views eventually prevailed.

Politics on the Web

- You can access the *Federalist Papers,* as well as state constitutions, information on the role of the courts in resolving issues relating to federalism, and information on international federations, at the following site: **http://www.constitution.org/cs_feder.htm**

- You can find information on state governments, state laws and pending legislation, and state issues and initiatives at **http://www.statescape.com**

- Supreme Court opinions, including those discussed in this chapter, can be found at the Court's official Web site. Go to **http://www.supremecourtus.gov**

- A good source for information on state governments and issues concerning federalism is the Web site of the Council of State Governments. Go to **http://www.statenews.org**

- The Electronic Policy Network offers "timely information and leading ideas about federal policy and politics." It also has links to dozens of sites providing materials on federalism and public policy. Go to **http://www.movingideas.org**

- The Brookings Institution, the nation's oldest think tank, is a good source for information on emerging policy challenges, including federal-state issues, and for practical recommendations for dealing with those challenges. To access the institution's home page, go to **http://www.brook.edu**

- If you are interested in a libertarian perspective on issues such as federalism, the Cato Institute has a Web page at **http://www.cato.org**

- You can find comparative statistics and public-policy information for all fifty states at the following Web site. Recent news and information are organized by state and by topic. Go to **http://www.stateline.org/stateline**

- *Governing* magazine, an excellent source for state and local news, can be found online at **http://www.governing.com**

Online Resources for This Chapter

This text's Companion Web Site, at **http://www.americaatodds.com**, offers links to numerous resources that you can utilize to learn more about the topics covered in this chapter. For a list describing these resources, see the inside front cover of this book.

chapter **4**

civil liberties

CHAPTER OBJECTIVES

After reading this chapter, you should be able to . . .

▶ Define the term *civil liberties* and explain how civil liberties differ from civil rights.

▶ Describe how the courts have interpreted and applied the freedom of religion guaranteed by the First Amendment.

▶ Indicate what forms of free speech will not be constitutionally protected, and why.

▶ Discuss why Americans are increasingly concerned about privacy rights.

▶ Summarize how the Constitution and the Bill of Rights protect the rights of accused persons.

73

Should the Death Penalty Be Abolished?

In 2003, hours before leaving office, Illinois governor George Ryan commuted death sentences to life imprisonment for all 167 inmates on the state's death row. Death penalty opponents hailed the actions as the first steps toward reforming or even repealing a process that they believe is seriously flawed. Supporters of capital punishment criticized Ryan for arbitrarily discontinuing a practice favored by a majority of citizens in Illinois.

As you will read in this chapter, the Eighth Amendment to the U.S. Constitution prohibits cruel and unusual punishment. The United States Supreme Court has held that the question of whether an execution is "cruel and unusual" is determined by the "changing norms and standards of society."[1] Today, roughly 70 percent of Americans support the death penalty. Many others, though, argue that the death penalty should be abolished.

Keep the Death Penalty— It Maintains Order and Fairness

Former U.S. assistant district attorney and novelist Scott Turow believes that the real reason most Americans support the death penalty is that it seems to restore "moral order." Some crimes are so horrible that executing the person responsible seems to be the only fitting response. The criminal justice system would not be "just" if it treated murder like any other crime. Indeed, in many states prisons are so overfilled that criminals are routinely returned to society before serving all of their sentences. Capital punishment helps to ensure that those who commit the most heinous crimes never endanger the lives of citizens again.

Death penalty supporters question the arguments and evidence offered by those opposed to capital punishment. For example, death row inmates whose sentences are overturned based on legal technicalities or the deaths of key witnesses during the prolonged appeals process are often incorrectly said to have been shown to be "innocent." Proponents of the death penalty point out that since 1976, not a single executed convict has been subsequently proved innocent.

Capital punishment is also central to the victims' rights movement. The strongest condemnation of Governor Ryan's decision to commute all death sentences came from the victims' loved ones. The victims' rights movement is premised on the idea that society owes something more than a seat at a trial to those who have experienced the trauma of a murdered family member or friend. Victims' families often speak of the sense of "closure" or "justice" that a murderer's execution brings.

Abolish the Death Penalty— It Is Inhumane and Discriminatory

A driving force behind Governor Ryan's decision to commute death sentences was the evidence of misconduct on the part of law enforcement officials while pursuing a conviction. The increased participation of victims' families and friends in the prosecutorial process has placed greater public pressure on police officers, prosecutors, and judges to bring about satisfactory resolutions to violent crimes—sometimes even at the expense of justice.

Opponents of the death penalty argue that poor defendants who cannot afford to hire an attorney are more likely to be found guilty because they must depend on the often inexperienced or overburdened legal counsel provided by the state. Race also appears to play a role in the likelihood that the death penalty will be imposed. Evidence shows that when white victims are involved, a defendant is more likely to be convicted of a crime punishable with the death penalty. Furthermore, although African Americans constitute only 12 percent of the general population, they make up 42 percent of those on death row.

Opponents of capital punishment also point out that the United States stands alone among Western nations in utilizing the death penalty. Western European nations in particular have criticized the United States on human rights grounds. In some instances, foreign countries have refused to extradite alleged criminals back to the United States, fearing that the death penalty might be imposed on the individual. Clearly, those convicted of capital crimes can be detained in prison for their natural lives to prevent them from harming society.

Where Do You Stand?

1. Do you think that the death penalty deters people from committing violent crimes? Why or why not?

2. How much consideration should the wishes of the victim's family and friends be given in determining how a convict is punished?

Explore This Issue Online

- For more arguments and evidence opposing the use of capital punishment, go to **http://www.deathpenaltyinfo.org**.

- To learn more about arguments in favor of the death penalty, visit **http://www.prodeathpenalty.org**.

Introduction

The debate over the death penalty, which we looked at in the chapter-opening *America at Odds* feature, is but one of many controversies concerning our civil liberties. Civil liberties are legal and constitutional rights that protect citizens from government actions. For example, the First Amendment to the U.S. Constitution prohibits Congress from making any law that abridges the right to free speech. The First Amendment also guarantees freedom of religion, freedom of the press, and freedom to assemble (to gather together for a common purpose, such as to launch a protest against a government policy or action). These and other freedoms and guarantees set forth in the Constitution and the Bill of Rights are essentially *limits* on government action.

Perhaps the best way to understand what civil liberties are and why they are important to Americans is to look at what might happen if we did not have them. If you were a student in China, for example, you would have to exercise some care in what you say and do. That country prohibits speech that is contrary to the socialist ideology or the cultural aims of the nation. If you criticized the government in e-mail messages to your friends or on your Web site, you could end up in court on charges that you had violated the law—and perhaps even go to prison.

Note that some Americans confuse *civil liberties* (discussed in this chapter) with *civil rights* (discussed in the next chapter) and use the terms interchangeably. Nonetheless, scholars make a distinction between the two. They point out that whereas civil liberties are limitations on government action, setting forth what the government *cannot do*, civil rights specify what the government *must* do—to ensure equal protection under the law for all Americans, for example.

The Constitutional Basis for Our Civil Liberties

The founders believed that the constitutions of the individual states contained ample provisions to protect citizens from government actions. Therefore, the founders did not include many references to individual civil liberties in the original version of the Constitution. These references were added by the Bill of Rights, ratified in 1791. Nonetheless, the original Constitution did include some safeguards to protect citizens against an overly powerful government.

Safeguards in the Original Constitution

Article I, Section 9, of the Constitution provides that the writ of *habeas corpus* (a Latin phrase that roughly means "produce the body") will be available to all citizens except in times of rebellion or national invasion. A writ of *habeas corpus* is an order requiring that an official bring a specified prisoner into court and show the judge why the prisoner is being kept in jail. If the court finds that the imprisonment is unlawful, it orders the prisoner to be released. If our country did not have such a constitutional provision, political leaders could jail their opponents without giving them the opportunity to plead their cases before a judge. Without this opportunity, many opponents might conveniently disappear or be left to rot away in prison.

The Constitution also prohibits Congress and the state legislatures from passing bills of attainder. A bill of attainder is a legislative act that directly punishes a specifically named individual (or a group or class of individuals) without a trial. For example, no legislature can pass a law that punishes a named Hollywood celebrity for unpatriotic statements.

The Constitution also prohibits Congress from passing *ex post facto* laws. The Latin term *ex post facto* roughly means "after the fact." An *ex post facto* law punishes individuals for committing an act that was legal when it was committed but that has since become a crime.

The Bill of Rights

As you read in Chapter 2, one of the contentious issues in the debate over ratification of the Constitution was the lack of protections for citizens from government actions. Although many state constitutions provided such protections, the Anti-Federalists wanted more. The promise of the addition of a bill of rights to the Constitution assured its ratification.

civil liberties Individual rights protected by the Constitution against the powers of the government.

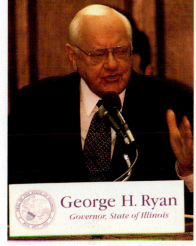

Frank Polich/Reuters/Landov

George H. Ryan
Governor, State of Illinois

Former Illinois governor George Ryan sparked further debate over the death penalty when he commuted the death sentences of 167 state inmates on death row to life imprisonment just before leaving office in 2003.

writ of *habeas corpus* An order that requires an official to bring a specified prisoner into court and explain to the judge why the person is being held in prison.

bill of attainder A legislative act that inflicts punishment on particular persons or groups without granting them the right to a trial.

***ex post facto* law** A criminal law that punishes individuals for committing an act that was legal when the act was committed but that has since become a crime.

The Bill of Rights was ratified by the states and became part of the Constitution on December 15, 1791. Look at the text of the Bill of Rights in Chapter 2 on page 40. As you can see, the first eight amendments grant the people specific rights and liberties. The remaining two amendments reserve certain rights and powers to the people and to the states.

Basically, in a democracy, government policy tends to reflect the view of the majority. A key function of the Bill of Rights, therefore, is to protect the rights of minority groups against the will of the majority. When there is disagreement over how to interpret the Bill of Rights, the courts step in—particularly the Supreme Court, which has become known as the guardian of individual liberties. Ultimately, though, the responsibility for protecting minority rights lies with the American people. Each generation has to learn anew how it can uphold its rights by voting, expressing opinions to elected representatives, and bringing cases to the attention of the courts when constitutional rights are threatened.

The Incorporation Issue

For many years, the protections against government actions in the Bill of Rights were applied only to actions of the federal government, not those of state or local governments. The founders believed that the states, being closer to the people, would be less likely to violate their own citizens' liberties. Moreover, state constitutions, most of which contain bills of rights, protect citizens against state government actions. The United States Supreme Court upheld this view when it decided, in *Barron v. Baltimore* (1833), that the Bill of Rights did not apply to state laws.[2]

due process clause The constitutional guarantee, set out in the Fifth and Fourteenth Amendments, that the government will not illegally or arbitrarily deprive a person of life, liberty, or property.

due process of law The requirement that the government use fair, reasonable, and standard procedures whenever it takes any legal action against an individual; required by the Fifth and Fourteenth Amendments.

The Right to Due Process
In 1868, three years after the end of the Civil War, the Fourteenth Amendment was added. The **due process clause** of this amendment ensures that state governments will protect their citizens' rights. The due process clause reads, in part, as follows:

No State shall . . . deprive any person of life, liberty, or property, without due process of law.

The right to **due process of law** is simply the right to be treated fairly under the legal system. That system and its officers must follow "rules of fair play" in making decisions, in determining guilt or innocence, and in punishing those who have been found guilty.

Procedural Due Process
Procedural due process requires that any governmental decision to take life, liberty, or property be made equitably. For example, the government must use fair procedures in determining whether a person will be subjected to punishment or have some burden imposed on him or her. Fair procedure has been interpreted as requiring that the person have at least an opportunity to object to a proposed action before an impartial, neutral decision maker (which need not be a judge).

Substantive Due Process
Substantive due process focuses on the content, or substance, of legislation. If a law or other governmental action limits a *fundamental right,* it will be held to violate substantive due process, unless it promotes a *compelling or overriding state interest.* All First Amendment rights, plus the rights to interstate travel, privacy, and voting are considered fundamental. Compelling state interests could include, for example, the public's safety.

Other Liberties Incorporated
The Fourteenth Amendment also states that no state "shall make or enforce any law which shall abridge the privileges or immunities of citizens of the United States." For some time, the Supreme Court considered the "privileges and immunities" referred to in the amendment to be those conferred by state laws or constitutions, not the federal Bill of Rights.

Starting in 1925, however, the Supreme Court gradually began using the due process clause to say that states could not abridge a civil liberty that the national government could not abridge. In other words, the Court *incorporated* the protections guaranteed by the national Bill of Rights into the liberties protected under the Fourteenth Amendment. As you can see in Table 4–1, the Supreme Court was particularly active during the 1960s in broadening its interpretation of the due process clause to assure that states and localities cannot infringe on civil

TABLE 4-1

Incorporating the Bill of Rights into the Fourteenth Amendment

Year	Issue	Amendment Involved	Court Case
1925	Freedom of speech	I	*Gitlow v. New York,* 268 U.S. 652.
1931	Freedom of the press	I	*Near v. Minnesota,* 283 U.S. 697.
1932	Right to a lawyer in capital punishment cases	VI	*Powell v. Alabama,* 287 U.S. 45.
1937	Freedom of assembly and right to petition	I	*De Jonge v. Oregon,* 299 U.S. 353.
1940	Freedom of religion	I	*Cantwell v. Connecticut,* 310 U.S. 296.
1947	Separation of church and state	I	*Everson v. Board of Education,* 330 U.S. 1.
1948	Right to a public trial	VI	*In re Oliver,* 333 U.S. 257.
1949	No unreasonable searches and seizures	IV	*Wolf v. Colorado,* 338 U.S. 25.
1961	Exclusionary rule	IV	*Mapp v. Ohio,* 367 U.S. 643.
1962	No cruel and unusual punishments	VIII	*Robinson v. California,* 370 U.S. 660.
1963	Right to a lawyer in all criminal felony cases	VI	*Gideon v. Wainwright,* 372 U.S. 335.
1964	No compulsory self-incrimination	V	*Malloy v. Hogan,* 378 U.S. 1.
1965	Right to privacy	Various	*Griswold v. Connecticut,* 381 U.S. 479.
1966	Right to an impartial jury	VI	*Parker v. Gladden,* 385 U.S. 363.
1967	Right to a speedy trial	VI	*Klopfer v. North Carolina,* 386 U.S. 213.
1969	No double jeopardy	V	*Benton v. Maryland,* 395 U.S. 784.

liberties protected by the Bill of Rights. Today, the liberties still not incorporated include the right to bear arms, the right to refuse to quarter soldiers, and the right to a grand jury hearing.

Freedom of Religion

The First Amendment prohibits Congress from passing laws "respecting an establishment of religion, or prohibiting the free exercise thereof." The first part of this amendment is known as the **establishment clause.** The second part is called the **free exercise clause.**

That the freedom of religion was the first freedom mentioned in the Bill of Rights is not surprising. After all, many colonists came to America to escape religious persecution. Nonetheless, these same colonists showed little tolerance for religious freedom within the communities they established. For example, in 1610 the Jamestown colony enacted a law requiring attendance at religious services on Sunday "both in the morning and the afternoon." Repeat offenders were subjected to particularly harsh punishments. For those who twice violated the law, for example, the punishment was a public whipping. For third-time offenders, the punishment was death. The Maryland Toleration Act of 1649 declared that anyone who cursed God or denied that Jesus Christ was the son of God was to be punished by death. In all, nine of the thirteen colonies had established official religions by the time of the American Revolution.

This context is helpful in understanding why, in 1802, President Thomas Jefferson, a great proponent of religious freedom and tolerance, wanted the establishment clause to be "a wall of separation between church and state." The context also helps to explain why even state leaders who supported state religions might have favored the establishment clause—to keep the national government from interfering in such state matters. After all, the First Amendment states only that *Congress* can make no law respecting an establishment of religion; it says nothing about whether the *states* could make such laws. And, as noted earlier, the protections in

establishment clause The section of the First Amendment that prohibits Congress from passing laws "respecting an establishment of religion." Issues concerning the establishment clause often center on prayer in public schools, the teaching of fundamentalist theories of creation, and government aid to parochial schools.

free exercise clause The provision of the First Amendment stating that the government cannot pass laws "prohibiting the free exercise" of religion. Free exercise issues often concern religious practices that conflict with established laws.

the Bill of Rights initially applied only to actions taken by the national government, not the state governments.

The Establishment Clause

The establishment clause forbids the government to establish an official religion. This makes the United States different from countries that are ruled by religious governments, such as the Islamic government of Iran. It also makes us different from nations that have in the past strongly discouraged the practice of any religion at all, such as the People's Republic of China.

What does this separation of church and state mean in practice? For one thing, religion and government, though constitutionally separated in the United States, have never been enemies or strangers. The establishment clause does not prohibit government from supporting religion in *general;* it remains a part of public life. (See this chapter's *Comparative Politics* feature for a discussion of how another country, France, approaches the question of religion in public life.) Most government officials take an oath of office in the name of God, and our coins and paper currency carry the motto "In God We Trust." Clergy of different religions serve with each branch of the armed forces. Public meetings and even sessions of Congress open with prayers. Indeed, the establishment clause often masks the fact that Americans are, by and large, religious and would like their political leaders to be people of faith.

The First Amendment to the Constitution mandates separation of church and state. Nonetheless, references to God are common in public life—and on our currency, as the phrase "In God We Trust" on this coin illustrates.

The "wall of separation" that Thomas Jefferson referred to, however, does exist and has been upheld by the Supreme Court on many occasions. An important ruling by the Supreme Court on the establishment clause came in 1947 in *Everson v. Board of Education.*[3] The case involved a New Jersey law that allowed the state to pay for bus transportation of students who attended parochial schools (schools run by churches or other religious groups). The Court stated as follows: "No tax in any amount, large or small, can be levied to support any religious activities or institutions." The Court upheld the New Jersey law, however, because it did not aid the church *directly* but provided for the safety and benefit of the students. The ruling both affirmed the importance of separating church and state and set the precedent that not *all* forms of state and federal aid to church-related schools are forbidden under the Constitution.

A full discussion of the various church-state issues that have arisen in American politics would fill volumes. Here we examine three of these issues: prayer in the schools, evolution versus creationism, and government aid to parochial schools.

Prayer in the Schools
On occasion, some schools have promoted a general sense of religion without proclaiming allegiance to any particular church or sect. Whether the states have a right to allow this was the main question presented in 1962 in *Engel v. Vitale,*[4] also known as the "Regents' Prayer case." The State Board of Regents in New York had composed a nondenominational prayer (a prayer not associated with any particular religion) and urged school districts to use it in classrooms at the start of each day. The prayer read as follows:

> Almighty God, we acknowledge our dependence upon Thee, and we beg Thy blessings upon us, our parents, our teachers, and our Country.

Some parents objected to the prayer, contending that it violated the establishment clause. The Supreme Court agreed and ruled that the Regents' Prayer was unconstitutional. Speaking for the majority, Justice Hugo Black wrote that the First Amendment must at least mean "that in this country it is no part of the business of government to compose official prayers for any group of the American people to recite as a part of a religious program carried on by government."

Prayer in the Schools—The Debate Continues
Since the *Engel v. Vitale* ruling, the Supreme Court has continued to shore up the wall of separation between church and state in a number of decisions. Generally, the Court has had to walk a fine line between the wishes of those who believe that religion should have a more prominent place in our public institutions and those who do not. For example, in a 1980 case, *Stone v. Graham,*[5]

comparative politics

France and Religious Dress in Schools

In September 2004, Muslim girls across France were banned from wearing their religiously mandated head scarves, or *hijabs,* to school. The French government, citing the need to uphold its national commitment to a secular (nonreligious) culture, had passed a law restricting religious symbols and dress in public schools earlier that year. The law covered a variety of attire, including Muslim head scarves, Jewish skull caps (*yarmulkes*), and large Christian crosses. Although numerous religious groups were affected, French Muslims believed that they had been specifically targeted by the law.

THE MUSLIM WORLD REACTS

France has Western Europe's largest Muslim population, estimated at five million. Many opponents of the ban believe that the French government instituted the law to combat the growing presence of Islamic fundamentalism. With international terrorism a viable threat throughout Europe and the United States, as well as in Western outposts around the globe, nations have struggled with how to handle their Muslim populations. France has also recently seen increases in violence toward Jews by Muslim fundamentalists.

Like Muslim girls in France, a high school girl in Muskogee, Oklahoma, was barred from wearing a *hijab* (traditional head scarf) to her public school. The school district later revised its dress code as part of a settlement in a lawsuit brought by the girl's parents and a civil rights group.

While Muslims outside France strongly protested the ban on head scarves, reactions among French Muslims were mixed. Polls suggested that French Muslim women were evenly divided in their opinion of the ban. Many women viewed the ban as liberating because, to them, head scarves represent the second-class status of women within their religion. Others felt that the ban discriminated against Muslims on the basis of their religious faith. Most demonstrations against the ban were peaceful, though, and French Muslim groups uniformly denounced the kidnappers of two French journalists in Iraq who demanded that the ban be rescinded in return for releasing the hostages.[6]

THE AMERICAN RESPONSE TO BANNING HEAD SCARVES

Traditionally, France has encouraged the assimilation of its immigrants into mainstream secular culture, a philosophy especially anti-

thetical to Muslim belief. The United States, despite its checkered past with regard to the treatment of immigrants, largely promotes diversity and multiculturalism in public life. When an Oklahoma school attempted to bar a young Muslim girl, Nashala Hearn, from wearing a head scarf to school in 2004, President George W. Bush intervened. The Bush administration stated that Hearn had the constitutionally protected right to wear religious garb to school.

For Critical Analysis

Why would the U.S. government protect the right to wear religious symbols in public schools when we have a constitutionally mandated separation of church and state? What other civil liberties ensured by the U.S. Constitution might protect the right to wear religious dress in public schools?

the Supreme Court ruled that a Kentucky law requiring that the Ten Commandments be posted in all public schools violated the establishment clause. Many groups around the country opposed this ruling. Currently, a number of states have passed or proposed laws permitting (but not *requiring,* as the Kentucky law did) the display of the Ten Commandments on public property, including public schools. Supporters of such displays contend that they will help

A teacher leads her students in a prayer. While many Americans contend that school prayer should be allowed in public schools, the United States Supreme Court has held that school-sponsored prayer is constitutionally impermissible.

Karim Shambi-Basha/Corbis Sygma

reinforce the fundamental religious values that are a part of the American heritage. Opponents claim that the displays blatantly violate the establishment clause.

Another controversial issue is whether "moments of silence" in the schools are constitutional. In 1985, the Supreme Court ruled that an Alabama law authorizing a daily one-minute period of silence for meditation and voluntary prayer was unconstitutional. Because the law specifically endorsed prayer, it appeared to support religion.[7] Since then, the lower courts have generally held that a school may require a moment of silence but only if it serves a clearly secular purpose (such as to meditate on the day's activities).[8] Yet another issue concerns prayers said before public school sporting events, such as football games. In 2000, the Supreme Court held that student-led pregame prayer using the school's public-address system was unconstitutional.[9]

In sum, the Supreme Court has ruled that the public schools, which are agencies of government, cannot sponsor religious activities. It has *not,* however, held that individuals cannot pray, when and as they choose, in schools or in any other place. Nor has it held that the Bible cannot be studied as a form of literature in the schools.

Evolution versus Creationism

Certain religious groups, particularly in the southern states, have long opposed the teaching of evolution in the schools. These groups contend that evolutionary theory, a scientific theory with overwhelming support, directly counters their religious belief that human beings did not evolve but were created fully formed, as described in the biblical story of the creation. The Supreme Court, however, has held unconstitutional state laws that forbid the teaching of evolution in the schools.

For example, in *Epperson v. Arkansas,*[10] a case decided in 1968, the Supreme Court held that an Arkansas law prohibiting the teaching of evolution violated the establishment clause because it imposed religious beliefs on students. In 1987, the Supreme Court also held unconstitutional a Louisiana law requiring that the biblical story of the creation be taught along with evolution. The Court deemed the law unconstitutional, in part because it had as its primary purpose the promotion of a particular religious belief.[11]

Some state and local groups, however, continue their efforts against the teaching of evolution. Recently, for example, Alabama approved a disclaimer to be inserted in biology textbooks, stating that evolution is "a controversial theory some scientists present as a scientific explanation for the origin of living things." A school district in Georgia adopted a policy that creationism could be taught along with evolution. No doubt, these laws and policies will eventually be challenged on constitutional grounds.

Aid to Parochial Schools

Americans have long been at odds over whether public tax dollars should be used to fund activities in parochial schools—private schools that have religious affiliations. Over the years, the courts have often had to decide whether specific types of aid do or do not violate the establishment clause. Aid to church-related schools in the form of transportation, equipment, or special educational services for disadvantaged students has been held permissible. Other forms of aid, such as funding teachers' salaries and paying for field trips, have been held unconstitutional.

Since 1971, the Supreme Court has held that, to be constitutional, a state's school aid must meet three requirements: (1) the purpose of the financial aid must be clearly secular (not religious); (2) its primary effect must neither advance nor inhibit religion; and (3) it must avoid an "excessive government entanglement with religion." The Court first used this three-part test in *Lemon v. Kurtzman*,[12] and hence it is often referred to as the **Lemon test.** In the *Lemon* case, the Court denied public aid to private and parochial schools for the salaries of teachers of secular courses and for textbooks and instructional materials in certain secular subjects. The Court held that the establishment clause is designed to prevent three main evils: "sponsorship, financial support, and active involvement of the sovereign [the government] in religious activity."

A Recent Application of the *Lemon* Test

In 2000, the Supreme Court applied the *Lemon* test to a federal law that gives public school districts federal funds for special services and instructional equipment. The law requires that the funds be shared with all private schools in the district. A central issue in the case was whether using the funds to supply computers to parochial schools had a clearly secular purpose. Some groups claimed that it did not, because students in parochial schools could use the computers to access religious materials online. Others, including the Clinton administration (1993–2001), argued that giving high-tech assistance to parochial schools did have a secular purpose and was a religiously neutral policy. The Supreme Court sided with the latter argument and held that the law did not violate the establishment clause.[13]

School Voucher Programs

Another contentious issue has to do with the use of **school vouchers**—educational certificates provided by state governments that students can use at any school, public or private. In an effort to improve their educational systems, several

Lemon **test** A three-part test enunciated by the Supreme Court in the 1971 case of *Lemon v. Kurtzman* to determine whether government aid to parochial schools is constitutional. To be constitutional, the aid must (1) be for a clearly secular purpose; (2) in its primary effect, neither advance nor inhibit religion; and (3) avoid an "excessive government entanglement with religion." The *Lemon* test has also been used in other types of cases involving the establishment clause.

school voucher An educational certificate, provided by the government, that allows a student to use public funds to pay for a private or a public school chosen by the student or his or her parents.

School voucher proponent Jackie Meeks of Cleveland takes part in a rally outside the United States Supreme Court in February 2002, when the Court heard arguments on Cleveland's six-year-old school voucher program. The Supreme Court subsequently ruled that the program was constitutional.

AP Photo/Rick Bowmer

school districts have been experimenting with voucher systems. President George W. Bush also proposed vouchers as part of his plan to reform education. The courts, however, have been divided on the issue of whether school vouchers violate the establishment clause when they enable public funds to be used to pay for education at parochial schools.

For example, in one case a federal appellate court held that a voucher program in Cleveland, Ohio, was unconstitutional. Under the program, the state provided up to $2,250 to low-income families, who could use the funds to send their children to either public or private schools. The court held that the program did not meet the three prongs of the *Lemon* test and thus violated the establishment clause.[14] The case was appealed to the United States Supreme Court, and in 2002 the Court ruled that the Ohio voucher program was constitutional. The Court concluded that the taxpayer-paid voucher program does not unconstitutionally entangle church and state because the funds go to parents, not to schools. The parents theoretically can use the vouchers to send their children to secular private academies or charter schools, even though 95 percent use the vouchers at religious schools.[15]

Despite the Supreme Court ruling, several constitutional questions surrounding school vouchers remain unresolved. For example, some state constitutions are more explicit in denying the use of public funds for religious education than is the federal Constitution. Even after the Supreme Court ruling in the Ohio case, a Florida court ruled in 2002 that a voucher program in that state violated Florida's constitution.[16]

AMERICA at odds

Is America One Nation "under God"?

Although by law no person can be required to say the Pledge of Allegiance, children routinely recite it in classrooms across the nation every day. When the pledge was first published in a youth magazine in 1892, it did not contain the words "under God." Those were added by congressional legislation in 1954, at the urging of President Dwight D. Eisenhower (1952–1961). In 2002, however, the Ninth Circuit Court of Appeals, using the *Lemon* test, ruled that the words "under God" in the pledge violated the establishment clause of the First Amendment.

Michael Newdow, the plaintiff in the case, argued that his daughter's constitutional rights were violated when she was forced to "watch and listen" as her teacher led her classmates "in a ritual proclaiming that there is a God."[17] The federal appellate court agreed, stating that

Michael Newdow sued the Elk Grove Unified School District in Sacramento, California, for violating the establishment clause of the Constitution by requiring his second-grade daughter to recite the phrase "under God" in the Pledge of Allegiance. Although a federal appellate court ruled in his favor, the United States Supreme Court later overturned the decision on technical grounds.

AP Photo/Rich Pedroncelli

"a profession [declaration] that we are a nation 'under God' is identical, for Establishment Clause purposes, to a profession that we are a nation 'under Jesus,' a nation 'under Vishnu,' a nation 'under Zeus,' or a nation 'under no god,' because none of these professions can be neutral with respect to religion." The court further argued that to recite the pledge "is to swear allegiance to the values for which the flag stands: unity, indivisibility, liberty, justice, and—since 1954—monotheism."

In contrast, proponents of the pledge as it now reads argue that the words "under God" merely acknowledge the religious heritage of the nation. Other proponents say the pledge is purely ceremonial—it recognizes a higher power that supports the nation but does not endorse any particular religious belief.[18] In a *Newsweek* poll following the appellate court's decision, 87 percent of respondents said they support including "under God" in the pledge, and 84 percent said they think references to God are acceptable in schools, government buildings, and other public settings, so long as no specific religion is mentioned.[19] Nonetheless, 29 million Americans identify themselves as nonreligious, atheist, or agnostic, and another one million are affiliated with religions generally not considered monotheistic, such as Buddhism or Hinduism. In 2004, the United States Supreme Court overturned the Ninth Circuit's decision. The Court stated that Newdow lacked standing to file suit in the first place, as he did not have custody of his daughter.[20] In its decision, however, the Court did not rule on whether the phrase "under God" was constitutional. The question thus remains whether such a public ritual proclaiming the existence of a God violates the rights of the 30 million Americans who disagree.

The Free Exercise Clause

As mentioned, the second part of the First Amendment's statement on religion consists of the free exercise clause, which forbids the passage of laws "prohibiting the free exercise of religion." This clause protects a person's right to worship or believe as he or she wishes without government interference. No law or act of government may violate this constitutional right. (For an example of how First Amendment rights surfaced in the 2004 election, see this chapter's *Perception versus Reality* feature on the following page.)

Belief and Practice Are Distinct
The free exercise clause does not necessarily mean that individuals can act in any way they want on the basis of their religious beliefs. There is an important distinction between belief and practice. The Supreme Court has ruled consistently that the right to hold any *belief* is absolute. The government has no authority to compel you to accept or reject any particular religious belief. The right to *practice* one's beliefs, however, may have some limitations. As the Court itself once asked, "Suppose one believed that human sacrifice were a necessary part of religious worship?"

The Supreme Court first dealt with the issue of belief versus practice in 1878 in *Reynolds v. United States*.[21] Reynolds was a Mormon who had two wives. Polygamy, or the practice of having more than one spouse at a time, was encouraged by the customs and teachings of his religion. Polygamy was also prohibited by federal law. Reynolds was convicted and appealed the case, arguing that the law violated his constitutional right to freely exercise his religious beliefs. The Court did not agree. It said that to allow Reynolds to practice polygamy would be to make the doctrines of religious beliefs superior to the law.

Religious Practices and the Workplace
The free exercise of religion in the workplace was bolstered by Title VII of the Civil Rights Act of 1964, which requires employers to accommodate their employees' religious practices unless such accommodation causes an employer to suffer an "undue hardship." Thus, if an employee claims that his or her religious beliefs prevent him or her from working on a particular day of the week, such as Saturday or Sunday, the employer must attempt to accommodate the employee's needs.

Several cases have come before lower federal courts concerning employer dress codes that contradict the religious customs of employees. For example, in 1999 the Third Circuit Court of Appeals ruled in favor of two Muslim police officers in Newark, New Jersey, who claimed that they were required by their faith to wear beards and would not shave them to comply with

Churches, Politics, and the IRS

Numerous political commentators claimed that the 2004 presidential elections were influenced greatly by Americans who voted according to their religious and moral beliefs. And many churchgoing voters were no doubt influenced strongly by the views of their religious leaders and others in their faith communities. Indeed, on a number of occasions prior to the elections, religious leaders made their views clear. Some of these leaders even endorsed specific candidates or encouraged their congregations to vote a certain way on specific ballot measures. Are such actions permissible, given that churches have tax-exempt status under federal law?

THE PERCEPTION

By and large, although some church-goers are uncomfortable hearing politically charged pronouncements from the pulpit, most of them do not perceive such actions to be unusual or illegal. After all, churchgoers commonly seek direction from their religious leaders, both in terms of spirituality and in how they live their daily lives. Members of many religious denominations see politics and voting as important ways of spreading the influence and message of their beliefs. "Moral" issues—such as abortion, capital punishment, and aiding the poor and disadvantaged—are frequent topics of sermons and conversations among churchgoers. To mobilize their members, churches have frequently staged voting drives, and some have even passed out voting pamphlets or literature.

THE REALITY

Legally, churches are barred from championing political causes or candidates. If churches are found to be overtly engaging in political activities, the Internal Revenue Service (IRS) can strip them of their tax-exempt status as nonprofit organizations. Most churches rely heavily on their tax-exempt privilege to fund their operating costs as well as the social services that they provide to their congregations and the community as a whole. All nonprofit organizations, regardless of whether they are religiously affiliated, are held to the same standard by the IRS.

Many churches may be in danger of losing their nonprofit classification after the 2004 elections. The campaign organizers for Presi-

AP Photo/April L. Brown

A volunteer places a voter-registration form into a bag inside the trailer of an iVote.Values.com truck parked outside a Baptist church in Springdale, Arkansas. The voter-registration rally prior to the 2004 presidential elections coincided with a nationwide telecast called "Battle for Marriage, We Vote Values" by Dr. James Dobson. Dobson is a leader of the religious right and a strong supporter of President Bush.

dent George W. Bush, for example, asked numerous conservative churches across the country to help register voters in their congregations and to endorse Bush's candidacy. Some religious groups turned over their mailing lists to the Bush campaign staff, and others passed out literature encouraging churchgoers to vote for candidates and measures that best mirrored their church's political and moral ideology.

To be sure, such practices are not without precedent. Democrats have long used African American churches to help campaign organizers increase voter participation and affiliation with the Democratic Party. Republicans, although they have complained about these practices in the past, seemed to have mimicked the tactics in mobilizing their own religious voting base prior to the 2004 elections.

What's Your Opinion?

Some attorneys have claimed that the IRS standards threaten church leaders' right to freedom of speech. Do you agree with this assessment? Should the government ensure that churches, as nonprofit organizations, refrain from political activity? Why or why not?

the police department's grooming policy. A similar case was brought in 2001 by Washington, D.C., firefighters who were suspended for violating their department's safety regulations regarding long hair and beards. Muslims, Rastafarians, and others refused to change the grooming habits required by their religions and were successful in court.[22]

Freedom of Expression

No one in this country seems to have a problem protecting the free speech of those with whom they agree. The real challenge is protecting unpopular ideas. The protection needed is, in Justice Oliver Wendell Holmes's words, "not free thought for those who agree with us but freedom for the thought that we hate." The First Amendment is designed to protect the freedom to express *all* ideas, including those that may be unpopular or different.

The First Amendment has been interpreted to protect more than merely spoken words; it also protects **symbolic speech**—speech involving actions and other nonverbal expressions. Some common examples include picketing in a labor dispute or wearing a black armband in protest of a government policy. Even burning the American flag as a gesture of protest has been held to be protected by the First Amendment.

symbolic speech The expression of beliefs, opinions, or ideas through forms other than speech or print; speech involving actions and other nonverbal expressions.

The Right to Free Speech Is Not Absolute

Although Americans have the right to free speech, not *all* speech is protected under the First Amendment. Our constitutional rights and liberties are not absolute. Rather, they are what the Supreme Court—the ultimate interpreter of the Constitution—says they are. Although the Court has zealously safeguarded the right to free speech, at times it has imposed limits on speech in the interests of protecting other rights of Americans. These rights include security against harm to one's person or reputation, the need for public order, and the need to preserve the government.

Generally, throughout our history, the Supreme Court has attempted to balance our rights to free speech against these other needs of society. As Justice Holmes once said, even "the most stringent protection of free speech would not protect a man in falsely shouting fire in a theatre and causing a panic."[23] We look next at some of the ways that the Court has limited the right to free speech.

Early Restrictions on Expression

At times in our nation's history, various individuals have not supported our form of democratic government. Our government, however, has drawn a fine line between legitimate criticism and the expression of ideas that may seriously harm society. Clearly, the government may pass laws against violence, espionage, sabotage, and treason. **Espionage** is the practice of spying for a foreign power. **Sabotage** involves actions normally intended to hinder or damage the nation's defense or war effort. **Treason** is specifically defined in the Constitution as levying war against the United States or adhering (remaining loyal) to its enemies (Article III, Section 3). But what about **seditious speech,** which urges resistance to lawful authority or advocates overthrowing the government?

As early as 1798, Congress took steps to curb seditious speech when it passed the Alien and Sedition Acts, which made it a crime to utter "any false, scandalous, and malicious" criticism against the government. The acts were considered unconstitutional by many but were never tested in the courts. Several dozen individuals were prosecuted under the acts, and some were actually convicted. In 1801, President Thomas Jefferson pardoned those sentenced under the acts, and Congress soon repealed them. During World War I, Congress passed the Espionage Act of 1917 and the Sedition Act of 1918. The 1917 act prohibited attempts to interfere with the operation of the military forces, the war effort, or the process of recruitment. The 1918 act made it a crime to "willfully utter, print, write, or publish any disloyal, profane, scurrilous [insulting], or abusive language" about the government. More than two thousand persons were tried and convicted under this act, which was repealed at the end of World War I.

espionage The practice of spying on behalf of a foreign power to obtain information about government plans and activities.

sabotage A destructive act intended to hinder a nation's defense efforts.

treason As enunciated in Article III, Section 3, of the Constitution, the act of levying war against the United States or adhering (remaining loyal) to its enemies.

seditious speech Speech that urges resistance to lawful authority or that advocates the overthrowing of a government.

In 1940, Congress passed the Smith Act, which forbade people from advocating the violent overthrow of the U.S. government. The Supreme Court first upheld the constitutionality of the Smith Act in *Dennis v. United States*,[24] which involved eleven top leaders of the Communist Party who had been convicted of violating the act. The Court found that their activities went beyond the permissible peaceful advocacy of change. According to the Smith Act, these activities threatened society's right to national security. Subsequently, however, the Court modified its position. Since the 1960s, the Court has defined seditious speech to mean only the advocacy of imminent and concrete acts of violence against the government.[25]

Limited Protection for Commercial Speech

commercial speech Advertising statements that describe products. Commercial speech receives less protection under the First Amendment than ordinary speech.

Advertising, or **commercial speech,** is also protected by the First Amendment, but not as fully as regular speech. Generally, the Supreme Court has considered a restriction on commercial speech to be valid as long as the restriction "(1) seeks to implement a substantial government interest, (2) directly advances that interest, and (3) goes no further than necessary to accomplish its objective." Problems arise, though, when restrictions on commercial advertising achieve one substantial government interest yet are contrary to the interest in protecting free speech and the right of consumers to be informed. In such cases, the courts have to decide which interest takes priority.

Liquor advertising is a good example of this kind of conflict. For example, in one case, Rhode Island argued that its law banning the advertising of liquor prices served the state's goal of discouraging liquor consumption (because the ban discouraged bargain hunting and thus kept liquor prices high). The Supreme Court, however, held that the ban was an unconstitutional restraint on commercial speech. The Court stated that the First Amendment "directs us to be especially skeptical of regulations that seek to keep people in the dark for what the government perceives to be their own good."[26] In contrast, restrictions on tobacco advertising are the result of a policy choice that free speech can be restrained in the interests of protecting the health of society, particularly the health of young Americans.

Unprotected Speech

Certain types of speech receive no protection under the First Amendment. These types of speech include libel and slander, "fighting words," and obscenity.

libel A published report of a falsehood that tends to injure a person's reputation or character.

slander The public utterance (speaking) of a statement that holds a person up for contempt, ridicule, or hatred.

Libel and Slander   No person has the right to libel or slander another. **Libel** is a published report of a falsehood that tends to injure a person's reputation or character. **Slander** is the public utterance (speaking) of a statement that holds a person up for contempt, ridicule, or hatred. To prove libel and slander, however, certain criteria must be met. The statements made must be untrue, must stem from an intent to do harm, and must result in actual harm.

The Supreme Court has ruled that public figures (public officials and others in the public limelight) cannot collect damages for remarks made against them unless they can prove the remarks were made with "reckless" disregard for accuracy. Generally, it is believed that because public figures have greater access to the media than ordinary persons do, they are in a better position to defend themselves against libelous or slanderous statements.

"fighting words" Words that, when uttered by a public speaker, are so inflammatory that they could provoke the average listener to violence.

"Fighting Words"   Another form of speech that is not protected by the First Amendment is what the Supreme Court has called **"fighting words."** This is speech that is so inflammatory that it will provoke the average listener to violence. The Court has ruled that "fighting words" must go beyond merely insulting or controversial language. The words must be a clear invitation to immediate violence or breach of the peace. Sometimes, however, determining when hateful speech becomes an actual threat against a person or an invitation to start a riot can be difficult. For example, an individual was arrested for allegedly praising the World Trade Center terrorist attacks to a crowd in Times Square just a few days after September 11, 2001. His arrest was upheld in court by a judge who noted that his words "were plainly intended to incite the crowd to violence, and not simply to express a point of view." Nonetheless, some legal experts argue that upholding this arrest on the "fighting words" doctrine is untenable because the defendant was expressing political speech.[27]

Obscenity

Obscene speech is another form of speech that is not protected under the First Amendment. Although the dictionary defines **obscenity** as that which is offensive and indecent, the courts have had difficulty defining the term with any precision. Supreme Court Justice Potter Stewart's famous statement, "I know it when I see it," certainly gave little guidance on the issue.

One problem in defining obscenity is that what is obscene to one person is not necessarily obscene to another; what one reader considers indecent, another reader might see as "colorful." Another problem is that society's views on obscenity change over time. Major literary works of such great writers as D. H. Lawrence (1885–1930), Mark Twain (1835–1910), and James Joyce (1882–1941), for example, were once considered obscene in most of the United States.

After many unsuccessful attempts to define obscenity, in 1973 the Supreme Court came up with a three-part test in *Miller v. California*.[28] The Court decided that a book, film, or other piece of material is legally obscene if it meets the following criteria:

1. The average person applying contemporary [present-day] standards finds that the work taken as a whole appeals to the prurient interest—that is, tends to excite unwholesome sexual desire.
2. The work depicts or describes, in a patently [obviously] offensive way, a form of sexual conduct specifically prohibited by an antiobscenity law.
3. The work taken as a whole lacks serious literary, artistic, political, or scientific value.

The very fact that the Supreme Court has had to set up such a complicated test shows how difficult defining obscenity is. The Court went on to state that, in effect, local communities should be allowed to set their own standards for what is obscene. What is obscene to many people in one area of the country might be perfectly acceptable to those in another area.

Obscenity in Cyberspace

One of the most controversial issues in regard to free speech in cyberspace concerns obscene and pornographic materials. Such materials can be easily accessed by anyone of any age anywhere in the world at numerous Web sites. Many people strongly believe that the government should step in to prevent obscenity on the Internet. Others believe, just as strongly, that speech on the Internet should not be regulated.

The issue came to a head in 1996, when Congress passed the Communications Decency Act (CDA). The law made it a crime to transmit "indecent" or "patently offensive" speech or images to minors (those under the age of eighteen) or to make such speech or images available online to minors. Violators of the act could be fined up to $250,000 or imprisoned for up to two years. In 1997, the Supreme Court held that the law's sections on indecent speech were unconstitutional. According to the Court, those sections of the CDA were too broad in their scope and significantly

obscenity Indecency or offensiveness in speech or expression, behavior, or appearance. Whether specific expressions or acts constitute obscenity normally is determined by community standards.

restrained the constitutionally protected free speech of adults.[29] Congress made a further attempt to regulate Internet speech in 1998 with the Child Online Protection Act. The act imposed criminal penalties on those who distribute material that is "harmful to minors" without using some kind of age-verification system to separate adult and minor Web users. The law has been under a court injunction barring its enforcement until the First Amendment issues are resolved in the courts.[30]

Having failed twice in its attempt to regulate online obscenity, Congress decided to try a different approach. In late 2000, it passed the Children's Internet Protection Act (CIPA). This act requires schools and libraries to use Internet **filtering software** to protect children from pornography or risk losing federal funds for technology upgrades. The CIPA was also challenged on constitutional grounds, but in 2003 the Supreme Court held that the act did not violate the First Amendment. The Court concluded that because libraries can disable the filters for any patrons who ask, the system was reasonably flexible and did not burden free speech to an unconstitutional extent.[31]

In 1996, with the Child Pornography Prevention Act, Congress also attempted to prevent the distribution and possession of "virtual" child pornography—computer-generated images of children engaged in lewd and lascivious behavior. These images, when digitally rendered, are amazingly real, even though they are created entirely on a computer, with no child actors involved. In 2002, the Supreme Court reviewed the 1996 act and found it unconstitutional. The Court ruled that the act did not establish the necessary link between "its prohibitions and the affront to community standards prohibited by the obscenity definition."[32]

filtering software Computer programs designed to block access to certain Web sites.

Hate Speech on Campus

A difficult question, faced by many universities today, is whether the right to free speech includes the right to make hateful remarks about others based on their race, gender, or sexual orientation. Some claim that allowing people with extremist views to voice their opinions can lead to violence. In response to this question, several universities have gone so far as to institute speech codes to minimize the disturbances that hate speech might cause. For example, the student assembly at Wesleyan University passed a resolution in 2002 stating that the "right to speech comes with implicit responsibilities to respect community standards."[33] Campus rules governing speech and expression, however, can foster the idea that "good" speech should be protected, but "bad" speech should not. Furthermore, who should decide what is considered "hate speech"?

Freedom of the Press

The framers of the Constitution believed that the press should be free to publish a wide range of opinions and information, and generally the free speech rights just discussed also apply to the press. The courts have placed certain restrictions on the freedom of the press, however. Over the years, the Supreme Court has developed various guidelines and doctrines to use in deciding whether freedom of speech and the press can be restrained.

Clear and Present Danger

One guideline the Court has used resulted from a case in 1919, *Schenck v. United States*.[34] Charles T. Schenck was convicted of printing and distributing leaflets urging men to resist the draft during World War I. The government claimed that his actions violated the Espionage Act of 1917, which made it a crime to encourage disloyalty to the government or resistance to the draft. The Supreme Court upheld both the law and the convictions. Justice Holmes, speaking for the Court, stated as follows:

> The question in every case is whether the words used are used in such circumstances and are of such a nature as to create a *clear and present danger* that they will bring about the substantive evils that Congress has a right to prevent. It is a question of proximity [closeness] and degree. [Emphasis added.]

Thus, according to the *clear and present danger test,* government should be allowed to restrain speech only when that speech clearly presents an immediate threat to public order.

AP Photo/Nick Ut

Students at Claremont McKenna College in California held a rally to protest a rash of hate incidents at colleges in the area in 2004.

It is often hard to say when speech crosses the line between being merely controversial and being a "clear and present danger," but the principle has been used in many cases since *Schenck*.

The clear and present danger principle seemed too permissive to some Supreme Court justices. Several years after the *Schenck* ruling, in the case of *Gitlow v. New York*,[35] the Court held that speech could be curtailed even if it had only a *tendency* to lead to illegal action. Since the 1920s, however, this guideline, known as the *bad-tendency test*, has generally not been supported by the Supreme Court.

The Preferred-Position Doctrine

Another guideline, called the *preferred-position doctrine*, states that certain freedoms are so essential to a democracy that they hold a preferred position. According to this doctrine, any law that limits these freedoms should be presumed unconstitutional unless the government can show that the law is absolutely necessary. Thus, freedom of speech and the press should rarely, if ever, be diminished, because spoken and printed words are the prime tools of the democratic process.

Prior Restraint

Stopping an activity before it actually happens is known as *prior restraint*. With respect to freedom of the press, prior restraint involves *censorship*, which occurs when an official removes objectionable materials from an item before it is published or broadcast. An example of censorship and prior restraint would be a court's ruling that two paragraphs in an upcoming article in the local newspaper had to be removed before the article could be published. The Supreme Court has generally ruled against prior restraint, arguing that the government cannot curb ideas *before* they are expressed.

On some occasions, however, the Court has allowed prior restraint. For example, in a 1988 case, *Hazelwood School District v. Kuhlmeier*,[36] a high school principal deleted two pages from the school newspaper just before it was printed. The pages contained stories on students' experiences with pregnancy and discussed the impact of divorce on students at the school. The Supreme Court, noting that students in school do not have exactly the same rights as adults in other settings, ruled that high school administrators *can* censor school publications. The Court said that school newspapers are part of the school curriculum, not a public forum. Therefore, administrators have the right to censor speech that promotes conduct inconsistent with the "shared values of a civilized social order."

Freedom of Assembly

The First Amendment also protects the right of the people "peaceably to assemble" and communicate their ideas on public issues to government officials, as well as to other individuals. Parades, marches, protests, and other demonstrations are daily events in this country and allow groups to express and publicize their ideas. The Supreme Court often has put this freedom of assembly, or association, on a par with freedom of speech and freedom of the press. In the interests of public order, however, the Court has allowed municipalities to require permits for parades, sound trucks, demonstrations, and the like.

Like unpopular speech, unpopular assemblies or protests often generate controversy. One controversial case arose in 1977, when the American Nazi Party decided to march through the largely Jewish suburb of Skokie, Illinois. The city of Skokie enacted three ordinances designed to prohibit the types of demonstrations that the Nazis planned to undertake. The American Civil Liberties Union (ACLU) sued the city on behalf of the Nazis, defending their right to march (in spite of the ACLU's opposition to the Nazi philosophy). A federal district court agreed with the ACLU and held that the city of Skokie had violated the Nazis' First Amendment guarantees by denying them a permit to march. The appellate court affirmed that decision. The Supreme Court refused to review the case, thus letting the lower court's decision stand.[37]

All groups—even the racially intolerant Ku Klux Klan—are guaranteed the freedom of assembly under the First Amendment.

AP Photo/Rogelio Solis

What about laws that prevent gang members from assembling on city streets? Do such laws violate the gang members' First Amendment rights or other constitutional guarantees? Courts have answered this question differently, depending in part on the nature of the laws in question.

In some cases, for example, "antiloitering" laws have been upheld by the courts. In others, they have not. In 1999, the Supreme Court held that Chicago's antiloitering ordinance violated the right to due process because, among other things, it left too much "lawmaking" power in the hands of the police, who had to decide what constitutes "loitering."[38] How a particular court balances gang members' right of assembly against the rights of society may also come into play. In 1997, for example, the California Supreme Court had to decide whether court injunctions barring gang members from appearing in public together in certain areas of San Jose, California, were constitutional. The court upheld the injunctions, declaring that society's rights to peace and quiet and to be free from harm outweighed the gang members' First Amendment rights to gather together in public.[39]

The Right to Privacy

Supreme Court Justice Louis Brandeis stated in 1928 that the right to privacy is "the most comprehensive of rights and the right most valued by civilized men."[40] The majority of the justices on the Supreme Court at that time did not agree. In 1965, however, in the landmark case of *Griswold v. Connecticut,*[41] the justices on the Supreme Court held that a right to privacy is implied by other constitutional rights guaranteed in the First, Third, Fourth, Fifth, and Ninth Amendments. For example, consider the words of the Ninth Amendment: "The enumeration in the Constitution, of certain rights, shall not be construed to deny or disparage others retained by the people." In other words, just because the Constitution, including its amendments, does not specifically mention the right to privacy does not mean that this right is denied to the people.

Since then, the government has also passed laws ensuring the privacy rights of individuals. For example, in 1966 Congress passed the Freedom of Information Act, which, among other things, allows any person to request copies of any information about her or him contained in government files. In 1974, Congress passed the Privacy Act, which restricts government disclosure of data to third parties. In 1994, Congress passed the Driver's Privacy Protection Act, which prevents states from disclosing or selling a driver's personal information without the driver's consent.[42] In late 2000, the federal Department of Health and Human Services issued a regulation ensuring the privacy of a person's medical information. Health-care providers and insurance companies are restricted from sharing confidential information about their patients.

Although Congress and the courts have acknowledged a constitutional right to privacy, the nature and scope of this right are not always clear. For example, Americans continue to debate whether the right to privacy includes the right to have an abortion or the right of terminally ill persons to commit physician-assisted suicide. Americans are also at odds over how to deal with what is perhaps one of the most difficult challenges of our time—how to protect privacy rights in cyberspace. Since the terrorist attacks of September 11, 2001, another pressing privacy issue has been how to monitor potential terrorists to prevent another attack without violating the privacy rights of all Americans.

The Abortion Controversy

One of the most divisive and emotionally charged issues being debated today is whether the right to privacy means that women can choose to have abortions.

Abortion and Privacy In 1973, in the landmark case of *Roe v. Wade*,[43] the Supreme Court, using the *Griswold* case as a precedent, held that it did. According to the Court, the "right of privacy . . . is broad enough to encompass a woman's decision whether or not to terminate her pregnancy." The right is not absolute throughout pregnancy, however. The Court also said that any state could impose certain regulations to safeguard the health of the mother after the first three months of pregnancy and, in the final stages of pregnancy, could act to protect potential life.

Since the *Roe v. Wade* decision, the Supreme Court has adopted a more conservative approach and has upheld restrictive state laws requiring counseling, waiting periods, notification of parents, and other actions prior to abortions.[44] Yet the Court has never overturned the *Roe* decision. In fact, in 1997 and again in 2000, the Supreme Court upheld laws requiring "buffer zones" around abortion clinics to protect those entering the clinics from unwanted counseling or harassment by antiabortion groups.[45] In 2000, the Supreme Court invalidated a Nebraska statute banning "partial-birth" abortions, a procedure used during the second trimester of pregnancy.[46] Undeterred by the fate of the Nebraska law, President George W. Bush signed the Partial Birth Abortion Ban Act in 2003. In 2004, however, a federal judge ruled the law unconstitutional because it failed to provide any exception if a woman's health was at stake and could be interpreted to ban more than a single procedure.[47]

Even with the *Roe* decision intact and the Court's rulings upholding "buffer zones," a woman's right to privacy in seeking an abortion remains an issue before the courts. Since 2001, protesters opposed to abortions have positioned themselves outside abortion clinics with cameras, photographed clinic patients, and then posted the photos, along with license-plate numbers and other identifying information, on Web sites. The question that the courts face is whether women entering a clinic lose their privacy protection because they are in a public place or, to the contrary, are afforded additional privacy protection because they are seeking medical attention.

Abortion and Politics American opinion on the abortion issue has become more nuanced than the labels "pro-life" and "pro-choice" would indicate. For example, 41 percent of respondents in a 2005 Gallup poll would like to see laws regulating abortion "remain the same," while 19 percent would prefer "less strict" laws and 38 percent would want "more strict" laws. These numbers seem to show that a majority favors the *Roe* decision. Yet a 2004 Gallup poll found that 61 percent of respondents believed that abortion should either be "illegal in all circumstances" or "legal only in a few circumstances." Many Americans who otherwise disagree with abortion believe that a woman should have access to one if her life is at stake or if the pregnancy resulted from rape or incest. Even more notably, a 2000 *Los Angeles Times* poll revealed that while 57 percent of respondents considered abortion "murder," roughly half of them still believed that women should possess the right to choose. Understandably, politicians find it difficult to respond to these conflicting perspectives.

Some scholars contend, though, that the reelection of George W. Bush and the Republican victories in the Senate in 2004 signaled a shift in the ideological bent of federal judges. Conservative judges, opposed to abortion rights, are more likely to be nominated to the Supreme Court and approved by the Senate. Some observers have even predicted that *Roe v. Wade* could be overturned.

Do We Have the "Right to Die"?

Whether it is called euthanasia (mercy killing), assisted suicide, or a dignified way to leave this world, it all comes down to one basic question: Do terminally ill persons have, as part of their civil liberties, a right to die and to be assisted in the process by physicians or others? Phrased another way, are state laws banning physician-assisted suicide in such circumstances unconstitutional?

In 1997, the issue came before the Supreme Court, which characterized the question as follows: Does the liberty protected by the Constitution include a right to commit suicide, which itself includes a right to assistance in doing so? The Court's clear and categorical answer to this question was no. To hold otherwise, said the Court, would be "to reverse centuries of legal doctrine and practice, and strike down the considered policy choice of almost every state."[48] (Suicide, including attempts to aid or promote suicide, is defined as a crime in most, if not all, states.) Although the Court upheld the states' rights to ban such a practice, the Court did not hold that state laws *permitting* assisted suicide were unconstitutional. In 1997, Oregon became the first state—and so far, the only one—to implement such a law.

The Supreme Court's enunciation of its opinion on this topic has not ended the debate, though, just as the debate over abortion did not stop after the 1973 *Roe v. Wade* decision legalizing abortion. And Americans continue to be at odds over this issue.

Privacy Rights in an Information Age

Perhaps one of the most pressing issues facing Americans and their political leaders today is how to protect privacy rights in cyberspace. Indeed, in today's online world, some people believe that privacy rights are quickly becoming a thing of the past. "Cookies" tell the hosts of a Web site what you did the last time you visited their site. Furthermore, any person who wants to purchase goods from online merchants or auctions inevitably must reveal some personal information, including (often) a credit-card number. One of the major concerns of consumers in recent years has been the increasing value of personal information for online marketers—who are willing to pay a high price to those who collect and sell them such information.

The problem for today's citizens is that they cannot even know what kind of information on their personal lives and preferences is being collected by Internet companies and other online users. Nor can they know how that information will be used. According to a report recently published by the University of California at Los Angeles (UCLA), Americans are quite aware of—and concerned about—their lack of privacy on the Internet. The study found that almost two-thirds (63.6 percent) of Internet users and more than three-quarters (76.1 percent) of nonusers either agreed or strongly agreed with the statement that "people who go online put their privacy at risk."[49]

The federal government has yet to take any decisive step toward regulating the acquisition and sale of personal information by online businesses. This is largely because most Web firms have implemented privacy policies on their Web sites that inform Internet users as to how their personal information will and will not be used and sometimes allow users to opt out of any disclosure of personal information. In view of these developments, the Federal Trade Commission has decided to allow the online industry to regulate itself, with only minimal oversight by the federal government.

AMERICA at odds

Medical Microchips and Privacy Rights

A tiny electronic capsule that can be injected into patients' arms recently won approval by the Food and Drug Administration (FDA). Physicians could scan you just as a supermarket cashier scans a box of cereal. Rather than seeing a price come up on a screen, health-care professionals can access your medical records from the embedded microchip. While many hail the medical microchip as a potential lifesaver, others denounce it as a possible tool for identity theft and invasion of privacy.

Proponents of medical microchips look to the potentially lifesaving benefits of the new technology. For an unconscious patient being rushed to the hospital, an embedded medical microchip would allow emergency room staff to immediately access such information as the patient's allergies, prior adverse reactions to medication, and health history. Indeed, the time saved by having records readily available could ultimately save countless lives. The microchips would also help create up-to-date, accurate, and portable medical records. Each time an individual visited a physician or ordered prescription drugs, that individual's records could be updated on a universal computer database. The medical microchip would serve as a "bar code" or a "personal identification number (PIN)" to access and update the patient's files.

To be sure, the technology could prove very helpful. Critics of medical microchips argue, however, that unintended consequences, such as identity theft, could result. Medical records are confidential and need to be closely safeguarded. In addition, many privacy advocates oppose medical microchips because they could be used to monitor a person's actions. Over one million American cats and dogs already have similar identification chips implanted under their skin, allowing pet owners to track down lost animals. In post–9/11 America, privacy advocates argue, the government could use medical microchip technology as a surveillance tool. "Big Brother" would be watching our every movement.

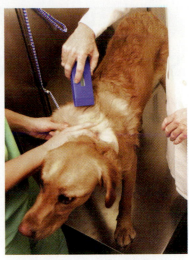

Implanted microchips are becoming a common, effective way to locate lost or stolen pets. Many medical professionals would like to see the same technology used in patients as a potentially life-saving tool, but others see the microchip as an invasion of privacy.

Personal Privacy and National Security

Since the terrorist attacks of September 11, 2001, one of the most common debates in the news media and on Capitol Hill has been how the United States can address the urgent need to strengthen national security while still protecting civil liberties, particularly the right to privacy. As you will read throughout this book, various programs have been proposed or attempted, and some have already been dismantled after public outcry. For example, the Homeland Security Act passed in late 2002 included language explicitly prohibiting a controversial program called Operation TIPS (Terrorism Information and Prevention System). Operation TIPS was proposed to create a national reporting program for "citizen volunteers" who regularly work in neighborhoods and communities, such as postal carriers and meter readers, to report suspicious activity to the government. The public backlash against the program was quick and resolute—neighbors would not spy on neighbors.

Other programs that infringe on Americans' privacy rights were enacted in the months following the September 11 attacks, however. The Federal Bureau of Investigation (FBI) sought and received legislation permitting "roving" wiretaps, which allow the government to monitor a person under suspicion no matter what form of electronic communication he or she uses. When, how, and where such roving wiretaps are used is left entirely up to the FBI. Such taps may lead to the invasion of the privacy of hundreds of third parties who believe their telephone conversations or e-mails are private. Another type of monitoring system that has been much debated since September 11 is the use of national identification cards. We explore this issue in this chapter's *The Politics of National Security* feature on the next page.

Concerns over privacy rights have been so pronounced that both the House and the Senate have proposed bills that would require all federal agencies putting forward new rules or regulations to produce a "privacy impact analysis" explaining how the new rules will affect Americans' privacy. Some civil libertarians are so concerned about the erosion of privacy rights that they wonder why the public outcry has not been even more vehement.

The Rights of the Accused

The United States has one of the highest murder rates in the industrialized world. It is therefore not surprising that many Americans have extremely strong opinions about the rights of persons accused of criminal offenses. Indeed, some Americans complain that criminal defendants have too many rights.

Why do criminal suspects have rights? The answer is that all persons are entitled to the protections afforded by the Bill of Rights. If criminal suspects were deprived of their basic constitutional liberties, all people would suffer the consequences. In fact, these liberties take

Should We Carry National Identification Cards?

Most of you probably carry a driver's license, a Social Security card, a student identification card, credit cards, and possibly even a passport. Today, the majority of these documents contain a magnetic strip that can be scanned to access your data from the relevant database and add new information about you. With so much information about all of us readily available, why do worries over a national identification card continue to surface?

ID CARDS WILL CATCH MORE TERRORISTS

Using appropriate technology, a national identification (ID) system would help the government monitor the activities of potential terrorists and catch them before they act. State driver's licenses are notoriously easy to forge, and at least seven of the September 11 airplane hijackers were able to obtain Virginia ID cards or driver's licenses. "Smart cards" that use some type of biometric identification system, such as face scans, retinal scans, or thumbprints, would reduce the prevalence of forged ID cards. In addition, sophisticated "back-end" technology would ensure that when you board a plane, buy a gun, or cross a border, your ID card is linked to a central database that will prove you are not a threat.

More than one hundred nations already use a national ID card system. Great Britain, the key ally of the United States in the "war on terrorism," recently adopted a national identity card. MORI, a polling agency, found that over the past decade, 75 to 85 percent of Britons supported such a card.

Some suggest that even a voluntary system of ID cards might give us a measure of security. Those who feel that they have nothing to hide could obtain the card, while those who do not want a card could go without it and face stricter scrutiny when boarding planes or entering or exiting the country. A uniform national ID card might also decrease such nationwide problems as identity theft and the use of social services by illegal immigrants.

ID CARDS, PRIVACY RIGHTS, AND DISCRIMINATION

One of the concerns about a national ID card system is that it would mark the beginning of a national surveillance system in America. Your ID card could be requested at any time or any place and

Protesters in London reveal their opposition to the British government's plans to introduce a national identity card for each citizen by burning a mock ID card for Tony Blair, the British prime minister.

scanned into a master database that logs your movements, your purchases, your bank deposits and withdrawals—almost everything about you. Even if safeguards were put in place to prevent such intrusive uses of the system, those safeguards could be ignored or abandoned months or years from now, especially if the terrorist threat becomes more severe. The original Social Security Act, which was enacted in 1935, prohibited using Social Security cards for unrelated purposes, but those strictures are routinely ignored today. Consider how often you use your Social Security number as your student ID or are asked for the last four digits of your number by your bank or credit-card company.

In addition, a national ID card system would likely increase the harassment of minorities and foreigners. If identity checks were left to the discretion of police, banks, and merchants, then the likely targets would be people who look or sound "foreign." According to the American Civil Liberties Union, one of the most vocal opponents of national ID cards, "the stigma and humiliation of constantly having to prove that they are Americans or legal immigrants would weigh heavily on such groups."[50]

Are We Safer?

How might a national ID card system help prevent a terrorist attack? Do you believe that such cards would also pose a significant threat to our privacy rights? Why or why not?

on added significance in the context of criminal law. After all, in a criminal case, a state official (such as the district attorney, or D.A.) prosecutes the defendant, and the state has immense resources that it can bring to bear against the accused person. By protecting the rights of accused persons, the Constitution helps to prevent the arbitrary use of power on the part of the government.

The Rights of Criminal Defendants

The basic rights, or constitutional safeguards, provided for criminal defendants are set forth in the Bill of Rights. These safeguards include the following:

- The Fourth Amendment protection from unreasonable searches and seizures.
- The Fourth Amendment requirement that no warrant for a search or an arrest be issued without **probable cause** (cause for believing that there is a substantial likelihood that a person has committed or is about to commit a crime).
- The Fifth Amendment requirement that no one be deprived of "life, liberty, or property, without due process of law." (As discussed earlier in this chapter, this requirement is also included in the Fourteenth Amendment, which protects persons against actions by state governments.)
- The Fifth Amendment prohibition against **double jeopardy** (being tried twice for the same criminal offense).
- The Fifth Amendment provision that no person can be required to be a witness against (incriminate) himself or herself. (This is often referred to as the constitutional protection against **self-incrimination.** It is the basis for a criminal suspect's "right to remain silent" in criminal proceedings.)
- The Sixth Amendment guarantees of a speedy trial, a trial by jury, a public trial, and the right to confront witnesses.
- The Sixth Amendment guarantee of the right to counsel at various stages in some criminal proceedings. (The right to counsel was established in 1963 in *Gideon v. Wainwright*.[51] The Supreme Court held that if a person is accused of a felony and cannot afford an attorney, an attorney must be made available to the accused person at the government's expense.)
- The Eighth Amendment prohibitions against excessive bail and fines and against cruel and unusual punishments.

probable cause Cause for believing that there is a substantial likelihood that a person has committed or is about to commit a crime.

double jeopardy To prosecute a person twice for the same criminal offense; prohibited by the Fifth Amendment in all but a few circumstances.

self-incrimination Providing damaging information or testimony against oneself in court.

The Exclusionary Rule

Any evidence obtained in violation of the constitutional rights spelled out in the Fourth Amendment normally is not admissible at trial. This rule, which has been applied in the federal courts since at least 1914, is known as the **exclusionary rule.** The rule was extended to state court proceedings in 1961.[52] The reasoning behind the exclusionary rule is that it forces law enforcement personnel to gather evidence properly. If they do not, they will be unable to introduce the evidence at trial to convince the jury that the defendant is guilty.

exclusionary rule A criminal procedural rule requiring that any illegally obtained evidence not be admissible in court.

The *Miranda* Warnings

In the 1950s and 1960s, one of the questions facing the courts was not whether suspects had constitutional rights—that was not in doubt—but how and when those rights could be exercised. For example, could the right to remain silent (under the Fifth Amendment's prohibition against self-incrimination) be exercised during pretrial interrogation proceedings or only during the trial? Were confessions obtained from suspects admissible in court if the suspects had not been advised of their right to remain silent and other constitutional rights? To clarify these issues, in 1966 the Supreme Court issued a landmark decision in *Miranda v. Arizona*.[53] In that case, the Court enunciated the *Miranda* **warnings** that are now familiar to virtually all Americans:

> Prior to any questioning, the person must be warned that he has a right to remain silent, that any statement he does make may be used against him, and that he has a right to the presence of an attorney, either retained or appointed.

***Miranda* warnings** A series of statements informing criminal suspects, on their arrest, of their constitutional rights, such as the right to remain silent and the right to counsel; required by the Supreme Court's 1966 decision in *Miranda v. Arizona*.

This police officer is reading the accused his *Miranda* warnings. Since the 1966 *Miranda* decision, the Supreme Court has relaxed its requirements in some situations, such as when a criminal suspect who is not under arrest enters a police station voluntarily.

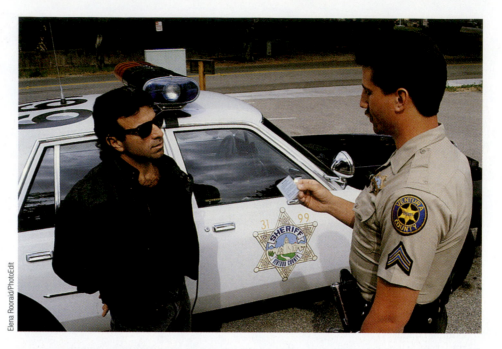

Elena Rooraid/PhotoEdit

The Erosion of *Miranda*

As part of a continuing attempt to balance the rights of accused persons against the rights of society, the Supreme Court has made a number of exceptions to the *Miranda* ruling. In 1986, for example, the Court held that a confession need not be excluded even though the police failed to inform a suspect in custody that his attorney had tried to reach him by telephone.[54] In an important 1991 decision, the Court stated that a suspect's conviction will not be automatically overturned if the suspect was coerced into making a confession. If the other evidence admitted at trial was strong enough to justify the conviction without the confession, then the fact that the confession was obtained illegally can be, in effect, ignored.[55] In yet another case, in 1994 the Supreme Court ruled that a suspect must unequivocally and assertively state his right to counsel in order to stop police questioning. Saying, "Maybe I should talk to a lawyer" during an interrogation after being taken into custody is not enough. The Court held that police officers are not required to decipher the suspect's intentions in such situations.[56]

In 1999, the U.S. Court of Appeals for the Fourth Circuit stunned the nation's legal establishment by enforcing a long-forgotten provision, Section 3501, of the Omnibus Crime Control Act of 1968. Congress passed the act two years after the Supreme Court's *Miranda* decision in an attempt to reinstate a rule that had been in effect for 180 years before *Miranda*—namely, that statements by defendants can be used against them as long as they are voluntarily made. The Justice Department immediately disavowed Section 3501 as unconstitutional. The Fourth Circuit, however, decided to enforce the provision. After all, Congress has the "unquestioned power to establish the rules of procedure and evidence in federal courts," and there is no explicit constitutional requirement that defendants be told of their rights to counsel and to remain silent. In 2000, however, when the Supreme Court reviewed the case, the high court held that the *Miranda* rights were based on the Constitution. Thus, these rights could not be overruled by legislative act.[57]

Civil Liberties and Your Everyday Life

The sad fact is that most Americans take their civil liberties so much for granted that they do not even consider how these liberties affect their everyday lives. But they do. The Bill of Rights—the first ten amendments to the Constitution—sets forth a number of basic liberties that are enjoyed by all Americans. Because our civil liberties are so important to our everyday lives, individuals and organizations are constantly fighting to make sure that federal, state, and local governments do not infringe on those liberties. Consider some obvious ones:

◆ Freedom of speech—We all take for granted that we can read just about any point of view that we want to in newspapers, magazines, and even brochures. What you read every day of your life is clearly a function of our freedom of speech. Throughout history, many nations have severely curtailed this important civil liberty. Today, citizens of the United States still enjoy perhaps the freest press in the world.

◆ Freedom of religion—We have enjoyed religious freedom for so long that we tend to take this liberty for granted. Although there are restrictions on how the state can or cannot be involved in religious activities, virtually any of you can practice just about any religion you wish. For many Americans, that is an important aspect of their everyday lives. In contrast, in some countries—for example, Iran and Saudi Arabia—an official state religion dominates all aspects of everyday life. In other countries—for example, Cuba and the People's Republic of China—religious activities are often curtailed by government.

AP Photo/Rod Mikinski/*The Manhattan Mercury*

Taking Action

Americans frequently get involved in protecting their civil liberties. Some have said it is part of the American character to fight the intrusion of government into our private lives. Groups such as the American Civil Liberties Union (ACLU), the Center for Democracy and Technology, and the Electronic Privacy Information Center monitor government regulation and pending legislation, organize letter-writing campaigns and protests, and bring lawsuits—all in defense of our civil liberties. But even individuals acting alone can make a difference. For example, consider Cliff Cookman, shown in the photo above. When he was a junior at Manhattan High School in Manhattan, Kansas, he proclaimed himself to be a priest of Satanism. He decided to wear his "priestly vestments" to school, believing that he had a right, under the First Amendment, to express his beliefs through his clothing. His high school principal disagreed, however, and told him that he would have to change his clothes. The ACLU later came to his assistance in asserting his right to wear his priestly symbols in school.

Key Terms

bill of attainder 75	establishment clause 77	libel 86	self-incrimination 95
civil liberties 75	*ex post facto* law 75	*Miranda* warnings 95	slander 86
commercial speech 86	exclusionary rule 95	obscenity 87	symbolic speech 85
double jeopardy 95	"fighting words" 86	probable cause 95	treason 85
due process clause 76	filtering software 88	sabotage 85	writ of *habeas*
due process of law 76	free exercise clause 77	school voucher 81	*corpus* 75
espionage 85	*Lemon* test 81	seditious speech 85	

Chapter Summary

1 The Bill of Rights (the first ten amendments to the Constitution) sets forth our civil liberties. Other civil liberties are specified in the Constitution itself. Although originally the Bill of Rights limited only the power of the national government, not that of the states, today most of the liberties guaranteed by the national Constitution apply to state government actions as well.

2 The First Amendment prohibits government from passing laws "respecting an establishment of religion, or prohibiting the free exercise thereof." The first part of this statement is referred to as the establishment clause; the second part is known as the free exercise clause. Issues involving the establishment clause often focus on prayer in the schools, the teaching of evolutionary theory, and aid to parochial schools.

3 Although citizens have an absolute right to hold any religious beliefs they choose to hold, their right to engage in religious practices may be limited if those practices violate the laws or threaten the health, safety, or morals of the community. Employers must accommodate the religious needs of employees unless to do so would cause the employer to suffer an "undue hardship."

4 The First Amendment also protects freedom of speech, including symbolic (nonverbal) speech, although the Supreme Court has at times imposed limits on speech in the interests of protecting other rights of society. Some forms of speech—including libel and slander, "fighting words," and obscenity—are not protected by the First Amendment.

5 The First Amendment freedom of the press generally protects the right to publish a wide range of opinions and information. Guidelines have been developed by the courts to decide in what situations freedom of expression can be restrained.

6 The Supreme Court has held that a right to privacy is implied by other constitutional rights set forth in the Bill of Rights. The nature and scope of this right are not always clear, however. Whether this right encompasses a right to have an abortion or to commit assisted suicide, and how privacy rights can be protected while increasing national security, are issues on which Americans have still not reached consensus.

7 The Fourth, Fifth, Sixth, and Eighth Amendments protect the rights of persons accused of crimes. Any evidence obtained in violation of the constitutional rights of criminal defendants normally is not admissible in court.

RESOURCES FOR FURTHER STUDY

Selected Readings

Bollinger, Lee C., and Geoffrey R. Stone, eds. *Eternally Vigilant: Free Speech in the Modern Era.* Chicago: University of Chicago Press, 2002. This book examines the philosophical underpinnings of free speech. It also contains a history of some of the most contentious free speech disputes, drawing on the work of several legal scholars.

Gottlieb, Roger S. *Joining Hands: Politics and Religion Together for Social Change.* Boulder, Colo.: Westview Press, 2002. In this book, the author examines such movements for social change as the civil rights movement, feminism, and environmentalism to reveal how religion and progressive politics share a common vision.

Johnson, John W. *Griswold v. Connecticut: Birth Control and the Constitutional Right to Privacy.* Lawrence, Kans.: University Press of Kansas, 2005. Part of the "Landmark Law Cases and American Society" series, the book delves into the case that serves as the precedent for our current privacy rights. The *Griswold* case is also very important for those seeking greater understanding of the *Roe v. Wade* decision.

Stone, Geoffrey R. *Perilous Times: Free Speech in Wartime from the Sedition Act of 1798 to the War on Terrorism.* New York: W. W. Norton, 2004. The author investigates the history of civil liberties in wartime.

Politics on the Web

■ Almost three dozen First Amendment groups have launched the Free Expression Network Clearinghouse, which is a Web site designed to feature legislation updates, legal briefings, and news on cases of censorship in local communities. Go to **http://www.FREEExpression.org**

■ The leading civil liberties organization, the American Civil Liberties Union (ACLU), can be found at **http://www.aclu.org**

■ A group named the Liberty Counsel calls itself "a nonprofit religious civil liberties education and legal defense organization established to preserve religious freedom." You can access this organization's home page at **http://www.lc.org**

- For information on the effect of new computer and communications technologies on the constitutional rights and liberties of Americans, go to the Center for Democracy and Technology at **http://www.cdt.org**

- For information on privacy issues relating to the Internet, go to the Electronic Privacy Information Center's Web site at **http://www.epic.org/privacy**

- To access Supreme Court decisions on civil liberties, go to the Supreme Court's official Web site at **http://supremecourtus.gov**

Online Resources for This Chapter

This text's Companion Web Site, at **http://www.americaatodds.com**, offers links to numerous resources that you can utilize to learn more about the topics covered in this chapter. For a list describing these resources, see the inside front cover of this book.

chapter 5
civil rights

CHAPTER OBJECTIVES

After reading this chapter, you should be able to . . .

▸ Define the term *civil rights* and explain the constitutional basis for laws prohibiting discrimination.

▸ Discuss the reasons for the civil rights movement and the changes it effected in American politics and government.

▸ Describe the political and economic achievements of women in this country over time and identify some obstacles to equality that they continue to face.

▸ Summarize the struggles faced by other minority groups in America.

▸ Explain what affirmative action is and why it has been so controversial in this country.

Should Same-Sex Couples Be Allowed to Marry?

Pressure for the extension of marriage rights to gay and lesbian couples has mounted considerably in recent years. The controversy began at least a decade ago, when the Hawaii Supreme Court ruled that Hawaii's law banning same-sex marriages violated the state constitution's equal protection clause. In 2000, Vermont began allowing same-sex couples to form *civil unions,* thereby granting to same-sex couples the same state-level bene-fits afforded to married couples.

In November 2003 and again in February 2004, a Massachusetts court ruled that only full marriage rights for gay couples, rather than civil unions, would conform to the state constitution's equal protection mandate. Yet thirty-nine other U.S. states have declared that marriage may be only between one man and one woman.

We Should Not Discriminate against Same-Sex Couples

Proponents of same-sex marriage argue that the right to marry, like other rights, is an issue of basic equality. Why should heterosexual couples be permitted to marry and same-sex couples not be allowed to do so? Civil unions and other "separate-but-equal" arrangements, they argue, do not suffice. Many maintain that one's choice in marriage is a private, individual decision; it should not be the subject of public scrutiny.

Others point to the skyrocketing divorce rates and the growing number of single-parent families among heterosexuals. They suggest that same-sex couples' determination to secure the rights and status of marriage may, in fact, strengthen the decaying institution. Marriage would give same-sex couples access to government benefits at both the federal and state levels. Married partners would also gain the right to inherit a deceased partner's property, the authority to make decisions in medical emergencies, and the right to share custody of children.

Many supporters of same-sex marriage believe that the United States Supreme Court offers the best venue for a fair hearing of this issue. They point to the Court's leading role, during the 1950s and 1960s, in ending segregation in the public schools and other discriminatory policies. Supporters of same-sex couples' right to marry believe that the Court should extend equal protection under the law to homosexuals. Belgium, the Netherlands, and Canada have all allowed same-sex couples to marry without disastrous consequences. In those nations, life carried on largely as usual after the controversy faded.

Marriage Should Be between One Man and One Woman

Some opponents of same-sex marriages argue against such marriages on religious grounds. Various conservative Christian groups, for instance, claim that the Bible regards homosexual conduct as sinful. Although these groups often receive the most public attention, religious sentiment does not account for all of the opposition to gay marriage. Polls show that a considerable majority of Americans, perhaps over 60 percent, oppose gay marriage. Sensing this popular disapproval, even numerous liberal politicians have declared their opposition to same-sex marriage.

Some politicians and political groups have undertaken action to ban gay marriage definitively. The 1996 Defense of Marriage Act denies federal recognition of same-sex marriages. In addition, in 2004 thirteen states amended their constitutions to ban same-sex marriage. Such amendments will be unnecessary, however, if President George W. Bush's proposed Federal Marriage Amendment (FMA) to the U.S. Constitution is adopted. That proposed amendment, which defines marriage as "a union between a man and a woman," would effectively ban same-sex marriages throughout the nation.

In a speech supporting the FMA, President Bush stated that a policy of "live and let live" would not do because "marriage cannot be severed from its cultural, religious and natural roots without weakening the good influence of society." Going even further, some have argued that civil rights such as freedom of speech, assembly, and worship could be jeopardized by legalizing same-sex marriage. If such marriages were legal, objecting religious groups could be stripped of the marriage-licensing function or prohibited, by means of hate speech legislation, from preaching against same-sex marriage.

Where Do You Stand?

1. Is same-sex marriage a valid public concern, or is it an exclusively private matter?

2. Do you believe that same-sex marriages should be allowed? Why or why not?

Explore This Issue Online

- There are a variety of state stances and laws regarding same-sex marriage, civil unions, and domestic partnerships. To compare state policies, go to **http://www.stateline.com** and enter a search for "gay marriage."

- For the most up-to-date articles and information on the same-sex marriage debate, visit **http://www.gaymarriagenews.com**.

Introduction

Whether gay and lesbian couples should be allowed to marry is one issue in an ongoing debate over the nature of our civil rights. As noted in Chapter 4, people sometimes confuse civil rights with civil liberties. Generally, though, the term **civil rights** refers to the rights of all Americans to equal treatment under the law, as provided for by the Fourteenth Amendment. One of the functions of our government is to ensure—through legislation or other actions—that this constitutional mandate is upheld.

Although the democratic ideal is for all people to have equal rights and equal treatment under the law, and although the Constitution guarantees those rights, this ideal has often remained just that—an ideal. It is people who put ideals into practice, and as James Madison (1751–1836) once pointed out (and as we all know), people are not angels. As you will read in this chapter, the struggle of various groups in American society to obtain equal treatment has been a long one, and it still continues today.

In a sense, the history of civil rights in the United States is a history of discrimination against various groups. Discrimination against women, African Americans, and Native Americans dates back to the early years of this nation, when the framers of the Constitution refused to grant these groups rights that were granted to others (that is, to white, property-owning males). During our subsequent history, as peoples from around the globe immigrated to this country at various times and for various reasons, each of these immigrant groups has faced discrimination in one form or another. More recently, other groups, including older Americans, persons suffering from disabilities, and gay men and lesbians, have struggled for equal treatment under the law.

Central to any discussion of civil rights is the interpretation of the equal protection clause of the Fourteenth Amendment to the Constitution. For that reason, we look first at that clause and how the courts, particularly the Supreme Court, have interpreted it and applied it to civil rights issues.

civil rights The rights of all Americans to equal treatment under the law, as provided for by the Fourteenth Amendment to the Constitution.

The Equal Protection Clause

Equal in importance to the due process clause of the Fourteenth Amendment is the **equal protection clause** in Section 1 of that amendment, which reads as follows: "No State shall . . .

equal protection clause Section 1 of the Fourteenth Amendment, which states that no state shall "deny to any person within its jurisdiction the equal protection of the laws."

Same-sex marriage advocates protest at a rally in Chicago. They are opposed to President George W. Bush's proposed amendment to the U.S. Constitution (the Federal Marriage Amendment), which, if adopted, would effectively ban same-sex marriage nationwide.

John Gress/Reuters/Landov

deny to any person within its jurisdiction the equal protection of the laws." Section 5 of the amendment provides a legal basis for federal civil rights legislation: "The Congress shall have power to enforce, by appropriate legislation, the provisions of this article."

The equal protection clause has been interpreted by the courts, and especially the Supreme Court, to mean that states must treat all persons in an equal manner and may not discriminate *unreasonably* against a particular group or class of individuals unless there is a sufficient reason to do so. The task of distinguishing between reasonable discrimination and unreasonable discrimination is difficult. Generally, in deciding this question, the Supreme Court balances the constitutional rights of individuals to equal protection against government interests in protecting the safety and welfare of citizens. Over time, the Court has developed various tests, or standards, for determining whether the equal protection clause has been violated.

Strict Scrutiny

fundamental right A basic right of all Americans, such as all First Amendment rights. Any law or action that prevents some group of persons from exercising a fundamental right will be subject to the "strict-scrutiny" standard, under which the law or action must be necessary to promote a compelling state interest and must be narrowly tailored to meet that interest.

If the law or action prevents some group of persons from exercising a **fundamental right** (such as all First Amendment rights), the law or action will be subject to the "strict-scrutiny" standard. Under this standard, the law or action must be necessary to promote a *compelling state interest* and must be narrowly tailored to meet that interest. A law based on a **suspect classification,** such as race, is also subject to strict scrutiny by the courts, meaning that the law must be justified by a compelling state interest.

suspect classification A classification, such as race, that provides the basis for a discriminatory law. Any law based on a suspect classification is subject to strict scrutiny by the courts—meaning that the law must be justified by a compelling state interest.

Intermediate Scrutiny

Because the Supreme Court had difficulty deciding how to judge cases in which men and women were treated differently, another test was developed—the "intermediate-scrutiny" standard. Under this standard, laws based on gender classifications are permissible if they are "substantially related to the achievement of an important governmental objective." For example, a law punishing males but not females for statutory rape is valid because of the important governmental interest in preventing teenage pregnancy in those circumstances and because virtually all of the harmful and identifiable consequences of teenage pregnancies fall on young females.[1] A law prohibiting the sale of beer to males under twenty-one years of age and to females under eighteen years would not be valid, however.[2]

Generally, since the 1970s, the Supreme Court has scrutinized gender classifications closely and has declared many gender-based laws unconstitutional. In 1979, the Court held that a state law allowing wives to obtain alimony judgments against husbands but preventing husbands from receiving alimony from wives violated the equal protection clause.[3] In 1982, the Court declared that Mississippi's policy of excluding males from the School of Nursing at Mississippi University for Women was unconstitutional.[4] In a controversial 1996 case, *United States v. Virginia,*[5] the Court held that Virginia Military Institute, a state-financed institution, violated the equal protection clause by refusing to accept female applicants. The Court said that the state of Virginia had failed to provide a sufficient justification for its gender-based classification. Nonetheless, the goal of equal treatment for women, which dates back to the Constitution, has yet to be fully achieved.

The Rational Basis Test (Ordinary Scrutiny)

rational basis test A test (also known as the "ordinary-scrutiny" standard) used by the Supreme Court to decide whether a discriminatory law violates the equal protection clause of the Constitution. Few laws evaluated under this test are found invalid.

A third test used to decide whether a discriminatory law violates the equal protection clause is the **rational basis test.** When applying this test to a law that classifies or treats people or groups differently, the justices ask whether the discrimination is rational. In other words, is it a reasonable way to achieve a legitimate government objective? Few laws tested under the rational basis test—or the "ordinary-scrutiny" standard, as it is also called—are found invalid, because few laws are truly unreasonable. A municipal ordinance that prohibits certain vendors from selling their wares in a particular area of the city, for example, will be upheld if the city can meet this rational basis test. The rational basis for the ordinance might be the city's legitimate government interest in reducing traffic congestion in that particular area.

African Americans

The equal protection clause was originally intended to protect the newly freed slaves after the Civil War (1861–1865). In the early years after the war, the U.S. government made an effort to protect the rights of blacks living in the former states of the Confederacy. The Thirteenth Amendment (which granted freedom to the slaves), the Fourteenth Amendment (which guaranteed equal protection under the law), and the Fifteenth Amendment (which stated that voting rights could not be abridged on account of race) were part of that effort. By the late 1880s, however, southern legislatures began to pass a series of segregation laws—laws that separated the white community from the black community. Such laws were commonly called "Jim Crow" laws (from a song that was popular in black minstrel shows). Some of the most common Jim Crow laws involved the use of public facilities such as schools, railroads, and, later, buses. They also affected housing, restaurants, hotels, and many other facilities.

Separate but Equal

In 1892, a group of Louisiana citizens decided to challenge a state law that required railroads to provide separate railway cars for African Americans. A man named Homer Plessy, who was seven-eighths Caucasian and one-eighth African, boarded a train in New Orleans and sat in the railway car reserved for whites. When Plessy refused to move at the request of the conductor, he was arrested for breaking the law.

Four years later, in 1896, the Supreme Court provided a constitutional basis for these segregation laws. In *Plessy v. Ferguson*,[6] the Court held that the law did not violate the equal protection clause because *separate* facilities for blacks were *equal* to those for whites. The lone dissenter, Justice John Marshall Harlan, disagreed: "Our Constitution is colorblind, and neither knows nor tolerates classes among citizens." The majority opinion, however, established the **separate-but-equal doctrine**, which was used to justify segregation in many areas of American life for nearly sixty years.

In the late 1930s and 1940s, the Supreme Court gradually moved away from this doctrine. The major breakthrough, however, did not come until 1954, in a case involving an African American girl who lived in Topeka, Kansas.

The *Brown* Decisions and School Integration

In the 1950s, Topeka's schools, like those in many cities, were segregated. Mr. and Mrs. Oliver Brown wanted their daughter, Linda Carol Brown, to attend a white school a few blocks from their home instead of an all-black school that was twenty-one blocks away. With the help of lawyers from the National Association for the Advancement of Colored People (NAACP), Linda's parents sued the board of education to allow their daughter to attend the nearby school.

In *Brown v. Board of Education of Topeka*,[7] the Supreme Court reversed *Plessy v. Ferguson*. The Court unanimously held that segregation by race in public education was unconstitutional. Chief Justice Earl Warren wrote as follows:

> Does segregation of children in public schools solely on the basis of race, even though the physical facilities and other "tangible" factors may be equal, deprive the children of the minority group of equal educational opportunities? We believe that it does. . . . [Segregation generates in children] a feeling of inferiority as to their status in the community that may affect their hearts and minds in a way unlikely ever to be undone. . . . We conclude that in the field of public education the doctrine of "separate but equal" has no place. Separate educational facilities are inherently unequal.

The following year, in *Brown v. Board of Education*[8] (sometimes called *Brown II*), the Supreme Court ordered desegregation to begin "with all deliberate speed," an ambiguous phrase that could be (and was) interpreted in a variety of ways.

Reactions to School Integration   The Supreme Court ruling did not go unchallenged. Bureaucratic loopholes were used to delay desegregation. Another reaction was "white flight." As white parents sent their children to newly established private schools, some formerly

Library of Congress/Photo by Danny Lyon/1963

Signs such as the ones shown here over drinking fountains were commonplace in the South from the 1870s to the 1960s. The "separate-but-equal" doctrine, enunciated by the Supreme Court in 1896, justified "Jim Crow" laws that permitted racial segregation.

separate-but-equal doctrine A Supreme Court doctrine holding that the equal protection clause of the Fourteenth Amendment did not forbid racial segregation as long as the facilities for blacks were equal to those provided for whites. The doctrine was overturned in the *Brown v. Board of Education of Topeka* decision of 1954.

President Bill Clinton, Arkansas governor Mike Huckabee, and Little Rock mayor Jim Daley (top row, going from right to left) stand on the steps of Central High School in Little Rock, Arkansas, behind the "Little Rock Nine." The occasion was the fortieth anniversary of the integration of the high school. All nine of the black students who entered the all-white high school under armed escort in 1957 attended the 1997 anniversary ceremony.

AP Photo/Danny Johnston

de jure segregation Racial segregation that is legally sanctioned—that is, segregation that occurs because of laws or decisions by government agencies.

de facto segregation Racial segregation that occurs not as a result of deliberate intentions but because of past social and economic conditions and residential patterns.

busing The transportation of public school students by bus to schools physically outside their neighborhoods to eliminate school segregation based on residential patterns.

white-only public schools became 100 percent black. Arkansas's Governor Orval Faubus used the state's National Guard to block the integration of Central High School in Little Rock in 1957, which led to increasing violence in the area. The federal court demanded that the troops be withdrawn. Only after President Dwight D. Eisenhower federalized the Arkansas National Guard and sent in troops to help quell the violence did Central High finally become integrated.

By 1970, school systems with **de jure segregation**—segregation that is legally sanctioned—had been abolished. That is not to say that **de facto segregation** (actual segregation, produced by circumstances even though no law requires it) was eliminated. It meant only that no public school could legally identify itself as being reserved for all whites or all blacks.

Busing   Attempts to eliminate *de facto* segregation have included redrawing school district lines and reassigning pupils. **Busing**—the transporting of students by bus to schools physically outside their neighborhoods—to achieve racially desegregated schools has also been tried. The Supreme Court first sanctioned busing in 1971 in a case involving the school system in Charlotte, North Carolina.[9] Following this decision, the Court upheld busing in several northern cities, as well as in Denver, Colorado.[10] Proponents believe that busing improves the educational and career opportunities of minority children and also enhances the ability of children from different ethnic groups to get along with each other.

Opposition to Busing   Nevertheless, busing was unpopular with many groups from its inception. Parents and children complained that they lost the convenience of neighborhood schools. Local governments and school boards resented having the courts tell them what to do. Some black parents argued that busing exposed their children to the hostility of white students in the schools to which they were bused. Some blacks also resented the implication that minority children can learn only if they sit next to white children. Opposition to busing was so pronounced in some areas that bused students had to be escorted by police to prevent potential violence.

By the mid-1970s, the courts had begun to retreat from their former support for busing. In 1974, the Supreme Court rejected the idea of busing children across school district lines.[11] In 1986, the Court refused to review a lower court decision to end a desegregation plan in Norfolk, Virginia.[12] By the 1990s, some large-scale busing programs were either being cut back or terminated. In *Missouri v. Jenkins*[13] in 1995, the Supreme Court ruled that the state of Missouri could stop spending money to attract a multiracial student body through major educational improvements, called magnet schools. Today, busing orders to end *de facto* segregation are not upheld in court. Indeed, *de facto* segregation in America's schools is still widespread.

The Civil Rights Movement

In 1955, one year after the first *Brown* decision, an African American woman named Rosa Parks, a longtime activist in the NAACP, boarded a public bus in Montgomery, Alabama. When it became crowded, she refused to move to the "colored section" at the rear of the bus. She was arrested and fined for violating local segregation laws. Her refusal and arrest spurred the local African American community to organize a year-long boycott of the entire Montgomery bus system. The protest was led by a twenty-seven-year-old Baptist minister, Dr. Martin Luther King, Jr. During the protest period, he was jailed and his house was bombed. Despite the hostility and the overwhelming odds, the protesters were triumphant.

In 1956, a federal court prohibited the segregation of buses in Montgomery, and the era of the **civil rights movement**—the movement by minorities and concerned whites to end racial segregation—had begun. The movement was led by a number of diverse groups and individuals, including Dr. Martin Luther King and his Southern Christian Leadership Conference (SCLC). Other groups, such as the Congress of Racial Equality (CORE), the NAACP, and the Student Nonviolent Coordinating Committee (SNCC), also sought to secure equal rights for African Americans.

civil rights movement The movement in the 1950s and 1960s, by minorities and concerned whites, to end racial segregation.

Nonviolence as a Tactic   Civil rights protesters in the 1960s began to apply the tactic of nonviolent **civil disobedience**—the deliberate and public refusal to obey laws considered unjust—in civil rights actions throughout the South. For example, in 1960, in Greensboro, North Carolina, four African American students sat at the "whites only" lunch counter at Woolworth's and ordered food. The waitress refused to serve them and the store closed early, but more students returned the next day to sit at the counter, with supporters picketing outside. **Sit-ins** spread to other lunch counters across the South. In some cases, students were heckled or even dragged from the store by angry whites. But the protesters never reacted with violence. They simply returned to their seats at the counter, day after day. Within months of the first sit-in, lunch counters began to reverse their policies of segregation.

civil disobedience The deliberate and public act of refusing to obey laws thought to be unjust.

Civil rights activists were trained in the tools of nonviolence—how to use nonthreatening body language, how to go limp when dragged or assaulted, and how to protect themselves from clubs or police dogs. As the civil rights movement gained momentum, the media images of nonviolent protesters being attacked by police, sprayed with fire hoses, and attacked by dogs shocked and angered Americans nationwide. This public backlash led to nationwide demands for reform. The March on Washington for Jobs and Freedom, led by Martin Luther King, Jr., in 1963, aimed in part to demonstrate the widespread public support for legislation to ban discrimination in all aspects of public life.

sit-in A tactic of nonviolent civil disobedience. Demonstrators enter a business, college building, or other public place and remain seated until they are forcibly removed or until their demands are met. The tactic was used successfully in the civil rights movement and other protest movements in the United States.

Civil Rights Legislation in the 1960s   As the civil rights movement demonstrated its strength, Congress began to pass civil rights laws. It became clear that while the Fourteenth Amendment prevented the *government* from discriminating against individuals or groups, the private sector—businesses, restaurants, and so on—could still freely refuse to employ and serve nonwhites.

On February 2, 1960, a group of black college students in Greensboro, North Carolina, staged a sit-in because they were refused service at a lunch counter reserved for whites.

The Civil Rights Act of 1964 was the first and most comprehensive civil rights law. It forbade discrimination on the basis of race, color, religion, gender, and national origin. The major provisions of the act were as follows:

- It outlawed discrimination in public places of accommodation, such as hotels, restaurants, snack bars, movie theaters, and public transportation.
- It provided that federal funds could be withheld from any federal or state government project or facility that practiced any form of discrimination.
- It banned discrimination in employment.
- It outlawed arbitrary discrimination in voter registration.
- It authorized the federal government to sue to desegregate public schools and facilities.

Library of Congress

Other significant laws passed by Congress during the 1960s included the Voting Rights Act of 1965, which made it illegal to interfere with anyone's right to vote in any election held in this country (see Chapter 8 for a discussion of the historical restrictions on voting that African Americans faced), and the Civil Rights Act of 1968, which prohibited discrimination in housing.

The Black Power Movement   Not all African Americans embraced nonviolence. Several outspoken leaders in the mid-1960s were outraged at the slow pace of change in the social and economic status of blacks. Malcolm X, a speaker and organizer for the Nation of Islam (also called the Black Muslims), rejected the goals of integration and racial equality espoused by the civil rights movement. He called instead for black separatism and black pride. Although he later moderated some of his views, his rhetorical style and powerful message influenced many African American young people. Among them was Stokely Carmichael. Carmichael had been a leader in the civil rights movement, a freedom rider, and later chairman of the SNCC, but by 1966 he had become frustrated with the tactic of nonviolence. He began to exhort civil rights activists to defend themselves, to demand political and economic power, and to demonstrate racial pride.

By the late 1960s, with the assassinations of Malcolm X in 1965 and Martin Luther King, Jr., in 1968, the era of mass acts of civil disobedience in the name of civil rights came to an end. Some civil rights leaders ceased to believe that further change was possible. Some left the United States altogether. Stokely Carmichael emigrated to Guinea in West Africa. Others entered politics and worked to advance the cause of civil rights from within the system.

Political Participation

As you will read in Chapter 8, African Americans were restricted from voting for many years after the Civil War, despite the Fifteenth Amendment (1870). These discriminatory practices persisted in the twentieth century. In the early 1960s, only 22 percent of African Americans of voting age in the South were registered to vote, compared with 63 percent of voting-age whites. In Mississippi, the most extreme example, only 6 percent of voting-age African Americans were registered to vote. Such disparities led to the enactment of the Voting Rights Act of 1965, which ended discriminatory voter-registration tests and gave federal voter registrars the power to prevent racial discrimination in voting.

Today, the percentages of voting-age blacks and whites registered to vote are nearly equal. As a result of this dramatic change, political participation by African Americans has increased,

Black Muslim leader Malcolm X speaks to an audience at a Harlem rally in 1963. His talk, in which he restated the Black Muslim theme of complete separation of whites and African Americans, outdrew a nearby rally sponsored by a civil rights group ten to one.

Bettmann/Corbis

Martin Luther King, Jr., shakes hands with President Lyndon B. Johnson just after Johnson had signed the Civil Rights Act of 1964. At the signing, Johnson asked all Americans to join in the effort "to bring justice and hope to all our people and to bring peace to our land."

as has the number of African American elected officials. Today, more than 8,500 African Americans serve in elective office in the United States. At least one congressional seat in each southern state is held by an African American, as are more than 15 percent of the state legislative seats in the South.

Nonetheless, only two African Americans have been elected to a state governorship, and only three African Americans have been elected to the U.S. Senate since 1900. Although several African Americans have aspired to the presidency, none has come close to winning the nomination of one of the major political parties. The increase in political participation by African Americans is thus somewhat more illusory than the numbers suggest. Some argue that a great deal more progress needs to be made.

Women

The failure of the framers of the Constitution to give women political rights was viewed by many early Americans as an act of betrayal. Not only did the Constitution betray the Declaration of Independence's promise of equality, but it also betrayed the women who had contributed to the making of that independence during the Revolutionary War. Nonetheless, not until the 1840s did women's rights groups begin to form.

The Struggle for Voting Rights

In 1848, Lucretia Mott and Elizabeth Cady Stanton organized the first "woman's rights" convention in Seneca Falls, New York. The three hundred people who attended approved a Declaration of Sentiments: "We hold these truths to be self-evident: that all men *and women* are created equal." In the following years, other women's groups held conventions in various cities in the Midwest and the East. With the outbreak of the Civil War, though, women's rights advocates devoted their energies to the war effort.

The movement for political rights again gained momentum in 1869, when Susan B. Anthony and Elizabeth Cady Stanton formed the National Woman Suffrage Association. **Suffrage**—the right to vote—became their goal. For members of the National Woman Suffrage Association, suffrage was only one step on the road toward greater social and political rights for

suffrage The right to vote; the franchise.

TABLE 5–1

Years, by Country, in Which Women Gained the Right to Vote

1893:	New Zealand
1902:	Australia
1913:	Norway
1918:	Britain
1918:	Canada
1919:	Germany
1920:	United States
1930:	South Africa
1932:	Brazil
1944:	France
1945:	Italy
1945:	Japan
1947:	Argentina
1950:	India
1952:	Greece
1953:	Mexico
1956:	Egypt
1963:	Kenya
1971:	Switzerland
1984:	Yemen

women. Lucy Stone and other women, who had founded the American Woman Suffrage Association, thought that the right to vote should be the only goal. By 1890, the two organizations had joined forces, and the resulting National American Woman Suffrage Association had indeed only one goal—the enfranchisement of women. When little progress was made, small, radical splinter groups took to the streets. Parades, hunger strikes, arrests, and jailings soon followed.

World War I (1914–1918) marked a turning point in the battle for women's rights. The war offered many opportunities for women. Thousands of women served as volunteers, and about a million women joined the workforce, holding jobs vacated by men who entered military service. After the war, President Woodrow Wilson wrote to Carrie Chapman Catt, one of the leaders of the women's movement, "It is high time that [that] part of our debt should be acknowledged." Two years later, in 1920, seventy-two years after the Seneca Falls convention, the Nineteenth Amendment to the Constitution was ratified: "The right of citizens of the United States to vote shall not be denied or abridged by the United States or by any State on account of sex." Although the United States may seem slow in having given women the vote, it was really not far behind the rest of the world (see Table 5–1).

Women in American Politics Today

More than ten thousand members have served in the U.S. House of Representatives. Only 1 percent of them have been women. Women continue to face a "men's club" atmosphere in Congress, although in 2002, for the first time in history, a woman, Nancy Pelosi (D., Calif.), was elected minority leader of the House of Representatives. In the 109th Congress, 16 percent of the 435 members of the House of Representatives and 14 percent of the 100 members of the Senate are women. Considering that eligible female voters outnumber eligible male voters, women are vastly underrepresented in the U.S. Congress.

Federal Offices   The same can be said for the number of women receiving presidential appointments to federal offices. Franklin Roosevelt (1933–1945) appointed the first woman to a cabinet post—Frances Perkins, who was secretary of labor from 1933 to 1945. In recent administrations, several women have held cabinet posts. In addition, Ronald Reagan (1981–1989) appointed the first woman ever to sit on the Supreme Court, Sandra Day O'Connor. Bill Clinton (1993– 2001) appointed Ruth Bader Ginsburg to the Supreme Court, and, in his second term, he appointed Madeleine Albright as secretary of state, the first woman

Women gathered to protest the incarceration of Alice Paul, a leader of the American Woman Suffrage Association, who was arrested in July 1917 for disturbing the peace in demonstrations calling for women's suffrage (voting rights).

to hold that position. President George W. Bush has appointed several women to cabinet positions and other significant federal offices.

State Politics   Women have made greater progress at the state level, and the percentage of women in state legislatures has been rising steadily. Women now constitute nearly one-fourth of state legislators. Notably, in recent elections gender seemed to be less of an issue than it had been in the past. In fact, in 1998, women won races for each of the top five offices in Arizona, the first such occurrence in U.S. history. Generally, women have been more successful politically in the western states than elsewhere. In Washington, over one-third of the state's legislative seats are now held by women. At the other end of the spectrum, though, are states such as Alabama. In that state, less than 10 percent of the lawmakers are women.

Today, various women's organizations are attempting to increase the number of women in government. These organizations include the National Coalition for Women's Appointments, the Women's Political Caucus, Black Women Organized for Action, and the Fund for a Feminist Majority. Additionally, women have formed political action committees (PACs—discussed in Chapter 6) to support female candidates for political office. One of the largest PACs is EMILY's List, which promotes and supports Democratic women candidates running for seats in Congress and state governorships. (EMILY stands for "Early Money Is Like Yeast—It Makes the Dough Rise.")

Women in the Workplace

An ongoing challenge for American women is to obtain equal pay and equal opportunity in the workplace. In spite of federal legislation and programs to promote equal treatment of women in the workplace, women continue to face various forms of discrimination.

Wage Discrimination   In 1963, Congress passed the Equal Pay Act. The act requires employers to pay an equal wage for substantially equal work—males cannot be paid more than females who perform essentially the same job. The following year, Congress passed the Civil Rights Act of 1964, Title VII of which prohibits employment discrimination on the basis of race, color, national origin, gender, and religion. Women, however, continue to face wage discrimination.

It is estimated that for every dollar earned by men, women earn about 76 cents. Although the wage gap has narrowed significantly since 1963, when the Equal Pay Act was enacted (at that time women earned 58 cents for every dollar earned by men), it still remains. This is particularly true for women in management positions and older women. Female managers now earn, on average, only 70 percent of what male managers earn. And women between the ages of forty-five and fifty-four make, on average, only 73 percent of what men in that age group earn. Also, when a large number of women are in a particular occupation, the wages that are paid in that occupation continue to be relatively low.

Additionally, even though an increasing number of women now hold business and professional jobs once held by men, relatively few of these women are able to rise to the top of the career ladder in their firms due to the lingering bias against women in the workplace. This bias has created the so-called **glass ceiling**—the often subtle obstacles to advancement that professional women encounter on the job. A recent study conducted by the U.S. Census Bureau shows that women hold only 7 percent of the top corporate management positions in this country.

Sexual Harassment   Title VII's prohibition of gender discrimination has also been extended to prohibit sexual harassment. **Sexual harassment** occurs when job opportunities, promotions, salary increases, or even the ability to retain one's job depends on whether an employee complies with demands for sexual favors. A special form of sexual harassment, called hostile-environment harassment, occurs when an employee is subjected to sexual conduct or comments in the workplace that interfere with the employee's job performance or that create an intimidating, hostile, or offensive environment.

The Supreme Court has upheld the right of persons to be free from sexual harassment on the job on a number of occasions. In 1986, the Court indicated that creating a hostile environment

House Minority Leader Nancy Pelosi addresses the Democratic National Committee in Washington, D.C., in 2003. Pelosi was the first woman ever to be elected to a leadership position in Congress.

glass ceiling   The often subtle obstacles to advancement faced by professional women in the workplace.

sexual harassment   Unwanted physical contact, verbal conduct, or abuse of a sexual nature that interferes with a recipient's job performance, creates a hostile environment, or carries with it an implicit or explicit threat of adverse employment consequences.

FIGURE 5–1

Hispanics Living in the United States by Place of Origin

As you can see in this chart, most Hispanics (just over two-thirds) are from Mexico.

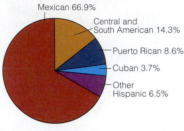

Mexican 66.9%
Central and South American 14.3%
Puerto Rican 8.6%
Cuban 3.7%
Other Hispanic 6.5%

SOURCE: U.S. Bureau of the Census.

by sexual harassment violates Title VII, even when job status is not affected, and in 1993 the Court held that to win damages in a suit for sexual harassment a victim did not need to prove that the harassment caused psychological harm.[14] In 1998, the Court made it clear that sexual harassment includes harassment by members of the same sex.[15] In the same year, the Court held that employers are liable for the harassment of employees by supervisors in their workplaces unless the employers can show that (1) they exercised reasonable care in preventing such problems (by implementing antiharassment policies and procedures, for example) and (2) the employees failed to take advantage of any corrective opportunities provided by the employers.[16] Additionally, the Civil Rights Act of 1991 greatly expanded the remedies available for victims of sexual harassment. Under the act, victims can seek damages as well as back pay, job reinstatement, and other compensation previously unavailable.

Hispanics

Like African Americans and women, other groups in American society continue to fight for equal treatment. Hispanics, or Latinos, as they are often called, constitute the largest ethnic minority in the United States. Whereas African Americans represent about 12.8 percent of the U.S. population, Hispanics now constitute about 13.6 percent of the population. Each year, the Hispanic population grows by nearly one million people, one-third of whom are newly arrived legal immigrants. By 2050, Hispanics are expected to constitute about one-fourth of the U.S. population.

Hispanics can be of any race, and to classify them as a single minority group is misleading. Spanish-speaking individuals tend to identify themselves by their country of origin, rather than as Hispanics. As you can see in Figure 5–1, the largest Hispanic group consists of Mexican Americans, who constitute over 66 percent of the Hispanic population living in the United States. Close to 9 percent of Hispanics are Puerto Ricans, and approximately 4 percent are Cuban Americans. A significant number of the remaining Hispanics are from Latin American countries.

Economically, Hispanic households seem to have become entrenched as this country's working poor. About 22 percent of Hispanic families now live below the poverty line, compared with 8 percent of white families. Researchers have found it difficult to pinpoint any reasons for such extensive poverty among Hispanics. Hispanic leaders, however, tend to attribute the low income levels to language problems, lack of job training, and continuing immigration. (Immigration disguises statistical progress because language problems and lack of job training

Columba Bush, wife of Florida governor Jeb Bush, is applauded as she addresses a Hispanic rally for President George W. Bush in Orlando, Florida, prior to the 2004 presidential elections. Governor Jeb Bush stands behind her, flanked by other Republican officials.

are usually more notable among new immigrants than among those who have lived in the United States for several years.)

Party Identification and Electoral Significance

In their party identification, Hispanics tend to follow some fairly well-established patterns. Generally, Mexican Americans and Puerto Ricans tend to identify with the Democratic Party, which traditionally has favored more government assistance and support programs for disadvantaged groups. Cubans, in contrast, tend to identify with the Republican Party. This is largely because of a different history. Cuban émigrés fled from that country during and after the Communist revolution led by Fidel Castro. The strong anti-Communist sentiments of the Cubans propelled them toward the more conservative party—the Republicans. Today, relations with Castro-led Cuba continue to be the dominant political issue for Cuban Americans.

Given their increasing numbers, the electoral importance of Hispanics cannot be denied. Significantly, Latinos tend to be located in some of the most populous states, including California, Florida, Illinois, New York, and Texas. In the 2004 elections, these states accounted for 168 electoral college votes. Understandably, in the 2004 presidential campaigns both candidates tried to woo Hispanic voters.

Political Participation

Generally, Hispanics in the United States have a comparatively low level of political participation. This is understandable, given that one-third of Hispanics are below voting age, and another one-fourth are not citizens and thus cannot vote. Voter turnout among Hispanics is only about 27 percent, compared with about 50 percent for the population at large. Yet the Hispanic voting rate is rising as more immigrants become citizens and as more Hispanics reach voting age. Notably, when comparing citizens of equal incomes and educational backgrounds, Hispanic citizens' participation rate is higher than average. Even poor Hispanics are more likely to vote than poor whites.

Increasingly, Hispanics are holding political offices, particularly in those states with large Hispanic populations. Today, more than 5 percent of the state legislators in Arizona, California, Colorado, Florida, New Mexico, and Texas are of Hispanic ancestry. Cuban Americans have been notably successful in gaining local political power, particularly in Dade County, Florida.

President George W. Bush has appointed a number of Hispanics to federal offices, including some cabinet positions. In his second administration, for example, he nominated Alberto Gonzales to head the Justice Department and Carlos Gutierrez as secretary of commerce. Hispanics are also increasing their presence in Congress, albeit slowly. Following the 2004 elections, there were twenty-three Hispanics in the House of Representatives and two Hispanics in the Senate. In all, though, Hispanics constitute only about 5 percent of the members of the 109th Congress. As with African Americans and women, Hispanic representation in Congress is notably disproportionate to the size of the Hispanic population in the United States.

Asian Americans

Asian Americans have also suffered, at times severely, from discriminatory treatment. The Chinese Exclusion Act of 1882 prevented persons from China and Japan from coming to the United States to prospect for gold or to work on the railroads or in factories in the West. After 1900, immigration continued to be restricted—only limited numbers of persons from China and Japan were allowed to enter the United States. Those who were allowed into the country faced racial prejudice by Americans who had little respect for their customs and culture. In 1906, after the San Francisco earthquake, Japanese American students were segregated into special schools so that white children could use their buildings.

The Japanese bombing of Pearl Harbor in 1941, which launched the entry of the United States into World War II (1939–1945), intensified Americans' fear of the Japanese. Actions taken under an executive order issued by President Franklin D. Roosevelt in 1942 subjected many Japanese Americans to curfews, excluded them from certain "military areas," and evacuated them to internment camps (also called "relocation centers").[17] In 1988, Congress provided

In what many consider to be one of America's low points, 120,000 Japanese Americans were moved to "internment camps" during World War II. Shown here is Manzanar Camp in California.

Library of Congress

funds to compensate former camp inhabitants—$1.25 billion for approximately 60,000 people.

Today, Japanese Americans and Chinese Americans lead other ethnic groups in median income and median education. Indeed, Asians who have immigrated to the United States since 1965 represent the most highly skilled immigrant group in American history. Nearly 40 percent of Asian Americans over the age of twenty-five have college degrees.

More recently, immigrants from Asia, particularly from Southeast Asia, have faced discrimination. More than a million Indochinese war refugees, most from Vietnam, have immigrated to the United States since the 1970s. Like their predecessors, the newer immigrants quickly increased their median income. Most came with relatives and were sponsored by American families or organizations. Thus, they had good support systems to help them get started.

Immigrants' Rights

Hispanic Americans and Asian Americans are joined every day by a steady stream of immigrants to the United States, some also from Latin America and Asia and others from the Middle East, Africa, and Europe. Approximately one million immigrants entered the United States in 2004. Thirty-three million people born outside the United States currently live here, the highest percentage of foreign-born residents since 1930. The percentage of immigrants who eventually become citizens has been on the rise in recent years. Today, naturalized citizens account for approximately 6 percent of eligible voters. This trend has focused more political attention on the rights of immigrants. Issues such as access to public services, health care, and education have dominated the debate. As you will read shortly, one issue over which Americans are at odds is whether bilingual education should be offered to the children of immigrants.

The terrorist attacks of September 11, 2001, centered particular attention on U.S. immigration policy and the rights of immigrants. Several of the hijackers were here legally on student visas. In the weeks following the attacks, the federal government detained nearly 1,500 immigrants of Middle Eastern descent. Although many civil rights advocates decry the treatment of Arab Americans and immigrants, the response of the nation as a whole has been muted because the fear of future terrorist attacks is so great.

racial profiling A form of discrimination in which law enforcement assumes that people of a certain race are more likely to commit crimes. Racial profiling has been linked to more frequent traffic stops of African Americans by police and increased security checks of Arab Americans in airports.

Racial profiling, a form of discrimination that occurs when, for example, a police officer pulls a driver over for no reason other than the driver's skin color, has received attention mainly in how it has been applied to African Americans. The practice has also been used in the prosecution of the war on terrorism. Civil rights groups claim that immigrants from the Middle East, North Africa, India, Pakistan, Indonesia, and the Philippines have been singled out by airport security workers, border guards, and immigration officials for searches and detention. Airlines have removed passengers from flights solely because they were of Middle Eastern or Asian appearance. We examine the issue of racial profiling and the war on terrorism further in this chapter's *The Politics of National Security* feature on page 116.

AMERICA at odds

Should Bilingual Education Be Abolished?

In the 1960s, many Americans became concerned over the language difficulties faced by immigrant children. In an effort to accommodate these children, bilingual schools were established. Because Hispanics form the largest non-English-speaking group in the United States, the majority of these schools were created to teach Spanish-speaking immigrant children. The long-term benefits of bilingual education have never been proved, however. Some argue that bilingual education has actually impeded children's progress in learning English—and thus made it difficult for them to compete in college and in the job market. Others disagree.

Proponents of bilingual education point out that the United States has a history of multilingual education. In the 1800s, children were taught in a variety of languages, including German,

Dutch, and Polish. During World War I, anti-German sentiment led most states to prohibit schools from teaching in a language other than English. But in 1968, Congress passed the Bilingual Education Act, which was intended to help Hispanic children learn English. In *Lau v. Nichols*,[18] the Supreme Court ordered a California school district to provide special programs for Chinese students with limited English proficiency. English will always be the language of the nation, say bilingual education supporters. Teaching students to be proficient in more than one language will not change that fact, but it may help students in the long run.

Opponents of bilingual education argue that schools should be concerned only with their students' achievement levels. As a result of a 1998 ballot initiative banning bilingual education in California, in that state children who did not speak English were placed in "English-immersion" programs. Two years later, test results showed dramatic improvement in English-language proficiency. Even the co-founder of the California Association of Bilingual Educators, Ken Noonan, admitted that if the new law had not passed, "We would not have learned how quickly and how well kids can learn English."

Native Americans

During the last few centuries, the populations of most groups in America—including African Americans—increased rapidly. In contrast, the Native American population in the United States was cut in half. That population dropped from about one million in 1600 to half a million in 1925, the demographic low point.

Today, more than two million people in the United States identify themselves as Native Americans. Most Native Americans live in Arizona, California, New Mexico, and Oklahoma, about half of them on reservations. Of all of the groups that have suffered discriminatory treatment in the United States, Native Americans stand out because of the unique nature of their treatment.

In 1789, Congress designated the Native American tribes as foreign nations so that the government could sign land and boundary treaties with them. As members of foreign nations, Native Americans had no civil rights under U.S. laws. This situation continued until 1924, when citizenship rights were extended to all persons born in the United States.

Early Policies toward Native Americans

The Northwest Ordinance, passed by the Congress of the Confederation in 1787, stated that "the utmost good faith shall always be observed towards the Indians; their lands and property shall never be taken from them without their consent; and in their property, rights, and liberty, they shall never be invaded or disturbed, unless in just and lawful wars authorized by Congress." Over the next hundred years, many agreements were made with the Indian tribes; many were also broken by Congress, as well as by individuals who wanted Indian lands for settlement or exploration.

In the early 1830s, the government followed a policy of separation. To prevent conflicts, boundaries were established between lands occupied by Native Americans and those occupied by white settlers. In 1830, Congress instructed the Bureau of Indian Affairs (BIA), which Congress had established in 1824 as part of the War Department, to remove all tribes to lands (reservations) west of the Mississippi River in order to free land east of the Mississippi for white settlement.

In the late 1880s, the U.S. government changed its policy. The goal became the "assimilation" of Native Americans into American society. Each family was given a parcel of land within the reservation to farm. The remaining acreage was sold to whites, thus reducing the number of acres in reservation status

Young men from a variety of tribes pose for a photograph in 1872 on their arrival at a Virginia boarding school for Native Americans. Later, they donned school uniforms, and another photo was taken (to be used for "before and after" comparisons). This was a typical practice at Native American boarding schools.

Duke University The Rare Book, Manuscript and Special Collections Library

Racial Profiling in the War on Terrorism

Racial profiling by police has been a controversial practice for some time. Former president Bill Clinton called racial profiling, as it has been applied to African Americans and Hispanics, a "morally indefensible, deeply corrosive practice." Since September 11, 2001, Arab Americans have also become victims of this practice, but with little public outcry. Private citizens and public officials alike have "profiled" people of Middle Eastern appearance as potential terrorists. Does this violate their constitutionally protected civil rights?

RACIAL PROFILING AT AIRPORTS

As expected, several instances of racial profiling of Arab Americans have taken place at airports. Not only have Arab Americans been targeted, but so have many individuals of Middle Eastern appearance. For example, on December 31, 2001, three men were removed from a Continental Airlines flight after a passenger told the captain that "those brown-skinned men are behaving suspiciously." In fact, none of the men was an Arab: one was Filipino, one was Sri Lankan, and one was Latino. Of the many passengers removed from airplanes since September 11, none has been charged with a crime or found to have terrorist connections.

During President George W. Bush's first presidential term, then U.S. attorney general John Ashcroft announced the National Security Entry-Exit Registration System. The system was created to expand America's scrutiny of foreign visitors who might pose a national security problem.

RACIAL PROFILING BY THE FEDERAL GOVERNMENT

In December 2002, the government began implementing the National Security Entry-Exit Registration System, which requires foreign visitors from specific countries,[19] most of them in the Middle East, to report to a U.S. Citizenship and Immigration Services office to register. Registrants are fingerprinted and photographed, and some are forced to answer questions under oath about their religious beliefs and political affiliations. In the system's first month of operation, the government detained hundreds of people, most of them on minor immigration violations. Many registrants reported mistreatment and have sought legal recourse.

A thornier legal issue has been how to treat U.S. citizens alleged to be "enemy combatants" or associated with the terrorist network al Qaeda. Two U.S. citizens fighting with the Taliban in Afghanistan in 2001 were captured and detained, but they were treated quite differently under the law. One, John Walker Lindh, is from a white, middle-class family from affluent Marin County, California. He converted to Islam as a teenager and later moved to Yemen. Lindh was charged with conspiring to kill Americans and received legal counsel. With the aid of legal representation, he pled guilty to a lesser charge of supplying services to the Taliban and is now serving twenty years in prison.

The other, Yaser Hamdi, was born in the United States to Saudi parents and moved to Saudi Arabia as a child. He was originally held as an "enemy combatant" without being charged with a crime and thus was denied access to an attorney. The United States Supreme Court, however, later ruled that U.S. citizens held as "enemy combatants" have the right to be told the reasons for their detention and to have an opportunity to rebut those claims before a judge.[20] In a settlement with the U.S. government, Hamdi was released in exchange for renouncing his U.S. citizenship and returning to Saudi Arabia.

Are We Safer?

In your opinion, is racial profiling an effective practice in preventing future acts of terrorism? Why or why not? How should we balance respect for individuals' civil rights and the interests of national security?

from 140 million to about 47 million acres. Tribes that would not cooperate with this plan lost their reservations altogether. To further the goal of cultural assimilation, agents from the BIA, which runs the Indian reservation system with the tribes, set up Native American boarding schools for the children to remove them from their parents' influence. In these schools, Native American children were taught to speak English, to practice Christianity, and to dress like white Americans.

Native Americans Today

Native Americans have always found it difficult to obtain political power. In part, this is because they have no official representation. Additionally, the tribes are small and scattered, making organized political movements difficult. Today, Native Americans remain a frag-

A dealer named Michaela works behind a blackjack table at Casino Hollywood on New Mexico's Pueblo San Felipe. Today, many Native American tribes run lucrative gambling operations. Some critics argue that the casinos are wrongfully transforming the traditional Native American way of life.

mented political group because large numbers of their population live off the reservations. Nonetheless, by the 1960s, some Native Americans succeeded in forming organizations to strike back at the U.S. government and to reclaim their heritage, including their lands.

The first militant organization was called the National Indian Youth Council. In the late 1960s, a small group of persons identifying themselves as Indians occupied Alcatraz Island, claiming that the island was part of their ancestral lands. Other militant actions followed. For example, in 1973, supporters of the American Indian Movement took over Wounded Knee, South Dakota, where about 150 Sioux Indians had been killed by the U.S. Army in 1890.[21] The occupation was undertaken to protest the government's policy toward Native Americans and to call attention to the injustices they had suffered.

Compensation for Past Injustices

As more Americans became aware of the concerns of Native Americans, Congress started to compensate them for past injustices. In 1990, Congress passed the Native American Languages Act, which declared that Native American languages are unique and serve an important role in maintaining Indian culture and continuity. Under the act, the government and the Indian community share responsibility for the survival of native languages and native cultures. Courts, too, have shown a greater willingness to recognize Native American treaty rights. For example, in 1985, the Supreme Court ruled that three tribes of Oneida Indians could claim damages for the use of tribal land that had been unlawfully transferred in 1795.[22]

The Indian Gaming Regulatory Act of 1988 allows Native Americans to have gambling operations on their reservations. Although the profits from casino gambling operations have helped to improve the economic and social status of many Native Americans, some Native Americans feel that the casino industry has irreparably hurt traditional culture. Poverty and unemployment remain widespread on the reservations.

AMERICA at odds

Native American Gaming

Evidence of Native American gambling can be found in tribal oral histories, literature, and archaeological studies. Although many native groups had a history of gaming in one form or another, it was not until the 1980s that the lucrative era of Native American casinos arrived. A multibillion-dollar industry has exploded on many previously economically depressed reservations. The establishment of casinos has created divisions in Native American communities, however, as well as causing friction with antigambling groups and state governments.

Proponents of Native American casinos argue that the gambling establishments are an economic necessity for tribal groups. In the 1980s, the Reagan administration significantly cut back on federal aid to Native Americans living on reservations. Casinos emerged as a logical solution to economic hardship. Native American groups could negotiate exclusive gambling compacts in many states because they were considered sovereign nations within the United States. Supporters also argue that Native Americans deserve the right to operate casinos, while enjoying special tax arrangements, because of past wrongs and damages inflicted on them by the U.S. government and people. Many Native Americans have heralded the casino as "the new buffalo," or the path to a brighter future. They argue that gambling establishments have helped them gain self-respect and self-sufficiency. Additionally, the profits can be used to improve their quality of life and to invest in nongambling business ventures as well.

Many Americans oppose Native American casinos, contending that gambling leads to increased crime, alcoholism, drug addiction, and corruption. Others argue that Native Americans should not be permitted to hold exclusive rights to operating casinos in states that otherwise restrict gambling. These critics question the status of tribes as sovereign nations within the United States. Many Native Americans also oppose gambling, believing that it harms their culture and degrades their traditional values. Intratribal violence even broke out among the Mohawk in 1990; during the series of conflicts that ensued, two men were killed, and a casino was burned down.

Securing Rights for Other Groups

In addition to those groups already discussed, other groups in American society have faced discriminatory treatment. Older Americans have been victims of discrimination. So have persons with disabilities and gay men and lesbians.

Protecting Older Americans

Today, about 38 million Americans (nearly 13 percent of the population) are aged sixty-five or over. By the year 2040, it is estimated that this figure will almost double. Clearly, as the American population grows older, the problems of aging and retirement will become increasingly important national issues. Because many older people rely on income from Social Security, the funding of Social Security benefits continues to be a major issue on the national political agenda.

Many older people who would like to work find it difficult because of age discrimination. Some companies have unwritten policies against hiring, retaining, or promoting people they feel are "too old," making it impossible for some older workers to find work or to continue with their careers. At times, older workers have fallen victim to cost-cutting efforts by employers. To reduce operational expenses, companies may replace older, higher-salaried employees with younger workers who are willing to work for less pay. As part of an effort to protect the rights of older Americans, Congress passed the Age Discrimination in Employment Act (ADEA) in 1967. This act prohibits employers, employment agencies, and labor organizations from discriminating against individuals over the age of forty on the basis of age.

In 2000, the Supreme Court limited the applicability of the ADEA somewhat when it held that lawsuits under this act could not be brought against a state government employer.[23] Essentially, this means that this act does not protect state employees against age-based discrimination by their state employers. (Note, though, that most states also have laws prohibiting age-based discrimination, and state employees can sue in state courts under those laws.)

Obtaining Rights for Persons with Disabilities

Like age discrimination, discrimination based on disability crosses the boundaries of race, ethnicity, gender, and religion. Persons with disabilities, especially physical deformities or

Americans with disabilities demonstrate in Washington, D.C., in support of the Americans with Disabilities Act (ADA), which was signed into law by President George H. W. Bush in 1990.

Terry Ashe/Getty News Images

severe mental impairments, have to face social bias against them because they are "different." Although attitudes toward persons with disabilities have changed considerably in the last several decades, persons with disabilities continue to suffer from discrimination in all its forms.

Persons with disabilities first became a political force in this country in the 1970s, and in 1973, Congress passed the first legislation protecting this group of persons—the Rehabilitation Act. This act prohibited discrimination against persons with disabilities in programs receiving federal aid. The Individuals with Disabilities Education Act (formerly called the Education for All Handicapped Children Act of 1975) requires public schools to provide children with disabilities with free, appropriate, and individualized education in the least restrictive environment appropriate to their needs. Further legislation in 1978 led to regulations for ramps, elevators, and the like in all federal buildings. The Americans with Disabilities Act (ADA) of 1990, however, is by far the most significant legislation protecting the rights of this group of Americans.

The ADA requires that all public buildings and public services be accessible to persons with disabilities. The act also mandates that employers "reasonably accommodate" the needs of workers or job applicants with disabilities who are otherwise qualified for particular jobs unless to do so would cause the employer to suffer an "undue hardship." The ADA defines persons with disabilities as persons who have physical or mental impairments that "substantially limit" their everyday activities. Health conditions that have been considered disabilities under federal law include blindness, alcoholism, heart disease, cancer, muscular dystrophy, cerebral palsy, paraplegia, diabetes, and acquired immune deficiency syndrome (AIDS). The ADA, however, does not require employers to hire or retain workers who, because of their disabilities, pose a "direct threat to the health or safety" of their co-workers.

In 2001, the Supreme Court reviewed a case raising the question of whether suits under the ADA could be brought against state employers. The Court concluded, as it did with respect to the ADEA, that states are immune from lawsuits brought to enforce rights under this federal law.[24]

Gay Men and Lesbians

Until the late 1960s and early 1970s, gay men and lesbians tended to keep quiet about their sexual preferences because to expose them usually meant facing harsh consequences. This attitude began to change after a 1969 incident in New York City, however. When the police raided the Stonewall Inn—a bar popular with gay men and lesbians—on June 27 of that year, the bar's patrons responded by throwing beer cans and bottles at the police. The riot continued for two days. The Stonewall Inn incident launched the gay power movement. By the end of the year, gay men and lesbians had formed fifty organizations, including the Gay Activist Alliance and the Gay Liberation Front.

A Changing Legal Landscape

The number of gay and lesbian organizations has grown from fifty in 1969 to several thousand today. These groups have exerted significant political pressure on legislatures, the media, schools, and churches. In the decades following the Stonewall incident, more than half of the forty-nine states that had sodomy laws—laws prohibiting homosexual conduct—repealed them. In seven other states, the courts invalidated such laws. Then, in 2003, the United States Supreme Court issued a ruling that effectively invalidated all remaining sodomy laws in the country. In *Lawrence v. Texas,*[25] the Court ruled that sodomy laws violated the Fourteenth Amendment's due process clause. According to the Court, "The liberty protected by the Constitution allows homosexual persons the right to choose to enter upon relationships in the confines of their homes and their own private lives and still retain their dignity as free persons."

Today, twelve states and more than 230 cities and counties in the United States have laws prohibiting discrimination against homosexuals in housing, education, banking, employment, and public accommodations. In a landmark case in 1996, *Romer v. Evans,*[26] the Supreme Court held that a Colorado amendment that would have invalidated all state and local laws protecting homosexuals from discrimination violated the equal protection clause of the Constitution. The Court stated that the amendment would have denied to homosexuals in Colorado—but to no other Colorado residents—"the right to seek specific protection from the law."

Changing Attitudes

Laws and court decisions protecting the rights of gay men and lesbians reflect social attitudes that are much changed from the days of the Stonewall incident. Liberal political leaders have been supporting gay rights for at least two decades. In 1984, presidential candidate Walter Mondale openly sought the gay vote, as did Jesse Jackson in his 1988 presidential campaign. Former president Bill Clinton strongly supported gay rights.

Even conservative politicians have softened their stance on the issue. For example, during his 2000 presidential campaign, George W. Bush met with representatives of gay groups to discuss issues important to them. Although Bush stated that he was opposed to the idea of gay marriage, he promised that he would not disqualify anyone from serving in his administration on the basis of sexual orientation.

By 2005, Gallup polls showed that a wide majority (89 percent) of Americans believed that gays and lesbians should have equal rights in terms of job opportunities. Nevertheless, strong opposition to gay and lesbian marriages persists. As noted in the chapter-opening *America at Odds* feature, a majority of Americans oppose same-sex marriages. Many states have banned such marriages, and the Bush administration is pushing for an amendment to the federal Constitution that would prohibit same-sex marriages throughout the nation.

Beyond Equal Protection— Affirmative Action

One provision of the Civil Rights Act of 1964 called for prohibiting discrimination in employment. Soon after the act was passed, the federal government began to legislate programs of **equal employment opportunity.** Such programs require that employers' hiring and promotion practices guarantee the same opportunities to all individuals. Experience soon showed that minorities often had fewer opportunities to obtain education and relevant work experience than did whites. Because of this, they were still excluded from many jobs. Even though discriminatory practices were made illegal, the change in the law did not make up for the results of years of discrimination. Consequently, under President Lyndon B. Johnson (1963–1969), a new strategy was developed.

Called **affirmative action,** this policy requires employers to take positive steps to remedy *past* discrimination. Affirmative action programs involve giving special consideration, in jobs and college admissions, to members of groups that have been discriminated against in the

equal employment opportunity A goal of the 1964 Civil Rights Act to end employment discrimination based on race, color, religion, gender, or national origin and to promote equal job opportunities for all individuals.

affirmative action A policy calling for the establishment of programs that give special consideration, in jobs and college admissions, to members of groups that have been discriminated against in the past.

"Larry is a white male, but he hasn't
been able to do much with it."

B. Smaller

past. Until recently, all public and private employers who received federal funds were required to adopt and implement these programs. Thus, the policy of affirmative action has been applied to all agencies of the federal, state, and local governments and to all private employers who sell goods to or perform services for any agency of the federal government. In short, it has covered nearly all of the nation's major employers and many of its smaller ones.

Affirmative Action Tested

The Supreme Court first addressed the issue of affirmative action in 1978 in *Regents of the University of California v. Bakke.*[27] Allan Bakke, a white male, had been denied admission to the University of California's medical school at Davis. The school had set aside sixteen of the one hundred seats in each year's entering class for applicants who wished to be considered as members of designated minority groups. Many of the students admitted through this special program had lower test scores than Bakke. Bakke sued the university, claiming that he was a victim of **reverse discrimination**—discrimination against whites. Bakke argued that the use of a **quota system,** in which a specific number of seats were reserved for minority applicants only, violated the equal protection clause.

The Supreme Court was strongly divided on the issue. Some justices believed that Bakke had been denied equal protection and should be admitted. A majority on the Court, however, concluded that both the Constitution and the Civil Rights Act of 1964 allow race to be used as a factor in making admissions decisions, although race could not be the *sole* factor. Because the university's quota system was based solely on race, it was unconstitutional.

reverse discrimination The assertion that affirmative action programs that require special consideration for minorities discriminate against those who have no minority status.

quota system A policy under which a specific number of jobs, promotions, or other types of placements, such as university admissions, must be given to members of selected groups.

Strict Scrutiny Applied

In 1995, the Supreme Court issued a landmark decision in *Adarand Constructors, Inc. v. Peña.*[28] The Court held that any federal, state, or local affirmative action program that uses racial classifications as the basis for making decisions is subject to "strict scrutiny" by the courts. As discussed earlier in this chapter, this means that, to be constitutional, a discriminatory law or action must be narrowly tailored to meet a *compelling* government interest. In effect, the *Adarand* decision narrowed the application of affirmative action programs. An affirmative action program can no longer make use of quotas or preferences and cannot be maintained simply to remedy past discrimination by society in general. It must be narrowly tailored to remedy actual discrimination that has occurred, and once the program has succeeded, it must be changed or dropped.

The Diversity Issue

Following the *Adarand* decision, several lower courts faced cases raising the question of whether affirmative action programs designed to achieve diversity on college campuses were constitutional. For example, in a 1996 case, *Hopwood v. State of Texas*,[29] two white law school applicants sued the University of Texas School of Law in Austin, claiming that they had been denied admission because of the school's affirmative action program. The program allowed admissions officials to take racial and other factors into consideration when determining which students would be admitted. A federal appellate court held that the program violated the equal protection clause because it discriminated in favor of minority applicants. In its decision, the court directly challenged the *Bakke* decision by stating that the use of race even as a means of achieving diversity on college campuses "undercuts the Fourteenth Amendment." In other words, race could never be a factor, even though it was not the sole factor, in such decisions.

In 2003, the United States Supreme Court reviewed two cases involving issues similar to that in the *Hopwood* case. Both cases involved admissions programs at the University of Michigan. In *Gratz v. Bollinger*,[30] two white applicants who were denied undergraduate admission to the university alleged reverse discrimination. The school's policy gave each applicant a score based on a number of factors, including grade point average, standardized test scores, and personal achievements. The system *automatically* awarded every "underrepresented" minority (African American, Hispanic, and Native American) applicant twenty points—one-fifth of the points needed to guarantee admission. The Court held that this policy violated the equal protection clause.

In contrast, in *Grutter v. Bollinger*,[31] the Court held that the University of Michigan Law School's admissions policy was constitutional. In that case, the Court concluded that "[u]niversities can, however, consider race or ethnicity more flexibly as a 'plus' factor in the context of individualized consideration of each and every applicant." The significant difference between the two admissions policies, in the Court's view, was that the law school's approach did not apply a mechanical formula giving "diversity bonuses" based on race or ethnicity. In short, the Court concluded that diversity on college campuses was a legitimate goal and that limited affirmative action programs could be used to attain this goal. (For a discussion of who has benefited from affirmative action programs with respect to college admissions and African Americans, see this chapter's *Perception versus Reality* feature.)

State Actions

Beginning in the mid-1990s, some states have taken actions to ban affirmative action programs or replace them with alternative policies. For example, in 1996, by a ballot initiative, California amended its state constitution to prohibit any "preferential treatment to any individual or group on the basis of race, sex, color, ethnicity, or national origin in the operation of public employment, public education, or public contracting." Two years later, voters in the state of Washington approved a ballot measure ending all state-sponsored affirmative action in that state.

Some states have attempted to increase diversity on college campuses through "race-neutral" alternatives to affirmative action. For example, in 1998 the state of Texas implemented what became known as the "10 percent solution." Under this program, students in the top 10 percent of the graduating class in all private and public schools within the state are guaranteed admission to Texas colleges and universities. Today, the "10 percenters" constitute more than 70 percent of freshman college admissions. After banning affirmative action, California adopted a similar plan.

As noted earlier, the 2003 Supreme Court decision in *Grutter v. Bollinger* in effect validated the use of race-conscious programs to achieve a diverse student body. In view of this decision, some states that had banned affirmative action in college admissions may revive those programs.

Who Benefits from Affirmative Action?

In the forty years since the inception of affirmative action, considerable progress has been made in increasing the number of African Americans at America's best universities. This increase is important to the goal of creating equality in America because college education often opens the door to future success. Yet which African Americans are truly benefiting from today's affirmative action programs?

THE PERCEPTION

The common perception is that the African Americans who are benefiting from affirmative action programs are black Americans whose ancestors were slaves. The initial goal of affirmative action was to make up for past discrimination against this group of Americans by giving them special consideration in college admissions as well as in the workplace. In the past, higher education was virtually segregated, with only a handful of blacks and other minorities studying at the country's best universities. This situation has changed, however, especially in the last two decades, and African Americans now constitute a prominent minority on American college campuses. The Harvard class of 2008, to take one of America's most elite universities as an example, is 9.2 percent African American. Although this figure still falls short of the approximately 12 percent of Americans who are African American, it nevertheless represents a significant change from the days when hardly any African Americans studied at Ivy League universities. Other universities besides Harvard have made similar changes, redressing some of the imbalance that has long marked American higher education.

THE REALITY

Currently, about two-thirds of the African American students at Harvard are the children of West Indian and recent African immigrants. These immigrants often arrive in the United States with professional experience and above-average levels of education. Only about one-third of the African Americans at Harvard come from families in which all four grandparents were born in this country as descendants of slaves. Many argue that it is the latter group of African Americans—those who have been disadvantaged by the legacy of Jim Crow laws, segregation, and decades of racism, poverty, and inferior schools—who were intended to be the principal beneficiaries of affirmative action in university admissions.

In reality, though, the majority of African Americans at schools such as Harvard do not come from poor, inner-city backgrounds. Indeed, this reflects a growing trend in American higher education: as *racial* diversity on university campuses has increased in the last two decades, *economic* diversity has plummeted. Of the freshmen entering the top 250 colleges in the country in 2000, 55 percent came from the highest-earning one-fourth of the population, up from 46 percent fifteen years earlier.

What's Your Opinion?

Is the purpose of affirmative action being served if individuals of African heritage with predominantly American roots benefit only minimally? Why or why not?

Civil Rights and Your Everyday Life

In the twenty-first century, we tend to take for granted the civil rights of virtually all Americans, including women, African Americans, Hispanics, and all other minorities. Yet these rights, relatively speaking, are of fairly recent vintage. We all know, of course, that compared to hundreds of years ago, when only white males had full civil rights, the rights that citizens enjoy today are extensive. But consider what America was like a little over fifty years ago, in 1950.

- In 1950, the prevailing view was that "a woman's place is in the home." Women in the workplace faced far more discrimination than they do today, and there was no such thing as a lawsuit for gender discrimination or sexual harassment.
- At that time, segregation in public schools and in colleges and universities was pervasive—and legal. Today, segregation in public schools cannot be required by law.
- There were no laws requiring that special accommodations be made for persons with disabilities. Today, several laws and policies protect this group of Americans.
- Older Americans who were fired from their jobs and replaced with younger workers had little recourse under the law. Today, both federal and state laws prohibit age discrimination in employment.
- Gay males and lesbians had no political voice; there were no special laws protecting their rights, and many laws outlawed homosexual behavior. Today, these groups have much more protection against discrimination.
- There were no equal employment opportunity guarantees for minorities and women. Today, equal employment opportunity for all is required by law.
- At that time, few civil and political rights were guaranteed for minority groups. Today, equal rights for minority groups are mandated by federal laws and by many state laws.

Your Educational Everyday Life

Because of changing laws and changing court interpretations of the laws, you most likely are going to school in a much different environment than students experienced fifty years ago. Indeed, it is probably hard for you to imagine a college classroom in which all students are of the same race or ethnic background. Yet if our laws and their application had not changed, it is likely you would be surrounded on a daily basis by only those of your race. You would not be exposed to the cultural backgrounds of members of other minority groups. Now, this is not to say that all of you are attending institutions whose student bodies are fully diversified. But certainly, the majority of American college and university students find themselves surrounded by more ethnic diversity than their counterparts did fifty years ago.

Taking Action

Despite the progress that has been made toward attaining equal treatment for all groups of Americans, much remains to be done. Discriminatory practices have not vanished from the nation, to be sure. Countless activist groups continue to pursue the goal of equality for all Americans. Individuals can also take action in various ways to make their voices heard. For example, the student shown in the photo below made his views on affirmative action known to all who came near the steps of the Student Union on the University of Michigan campus. The student was reacting to a federal appellate court's decision, which had upheld the university's affirmative action policies with respect to law school admissions. The United States Supreme Court later affirmed that decision, while declaring that the University of Michigan's undergraduate admissions policy was unconstitutional.

AP Photo/Danny Moloshok

Key Terms

Chapter Summary

1 Civil liberties limit the government by stating what the government cannot do. Civil rights, in contrast, are constitutional provisions and laws specifying what the government must do. Generally, civil rights refer to the right to equal treatment under the laws, as guaranteed by the Fourteenth Amendment to the Constitution.

2 The Fourteenth Amendment was added in 1868 to protect the newly freed slaves from discriminatory treatment. Soon, however, southern states began to pass laws that required racial segregation ("Jim Crow" laws). In 1896, the Supreme Court held that "separate-but-equal" treatment of the races did not violate the equal protection clause. The separate-but-equal doctrine justified segregation for the next sixty years.

3 In the landmark case of *Brown v. Board of Education of Topeka,* the Supreme Court held that segregation in the schools violated the equal protection clause. Forced integration of the schools was begun, and court-ordered busing of schoolchildren from white to black schools and vice versa was undertaken in an attempt to integrate the schools. By the 1980s and 1990s, the courts were allowing cities and states to discontinue busing efforts.

4 The civil rights movement was a movement by minorities and concerned whites to end racial segregation. In response, Congress passed a series of civil rights laws, including the Civil Rights Act of 1964, the Voting Rights Act of 1965, and the Civil Rights Act of 1968.

5 The struggle of women for equal treatment initially focused on gaining the franchise—voting rights. In 1920, the Nineteenth Amendment, which granted voting rights to women, was ratified. Today, women remain vastly underrepresented in Congress and political offices, even though eligible female voters outnumber male voters. In the workplace, women continue to face discrimination in the form of sexual harassment and wage discrimination.

6 Hispanics, or Latinos, constitute the largest minority group in the United States, and their numbers are climbing. The largest Hispanic groups are Mexican Americans, Puerto Ricans, and Cuban Americans. Relative to other groups, a disproportionate number of Hispanics live below the poverty line. Politically, Hispanics have been gaining power in some states, and their electoral significance is increasing.

7 Asian Americans have suffered from racial bias and discrimination since they first began to immigrate to this country in the late 1800s. The worst treatment of Japanese Americans occurred during World War II, when they were placed in internment camps. Economically, Asian Americans have the highest median income and median education of any ethnic group in the United States.

8 The United States absorbs more than one million new immigrants every year. New immigrants lack citizenship and voting rights, but they are still guaranteed equal protection under the laws. Since September 11, 2001, the civil rights of immigrants have been particularly threatened, as they face arbitrary and sometimes discriminatory changes in immigration laws and the fear and hostility of some Americans worried about future terrorist attacks.

9 U.S. policy toward Native Americans was first one of separation—removing them to lands separate from those occupied by whites—and then one of assimilation. By the late 1980s and 1990s, federal policy had changed, and legislation was passed that allowed gambling on reservation lands and encouraged the survival of Native American languages.

10 Other groups have also suffered discrimination and unequal treatment in America. The Age Discrimination in Employment Act of 1967 was passed in an attempt to protect Americans over the age of forty from age discrimination in employment. The Americans with Disabilities Act of 1990 provided significant protection for persons with disabilities. Since 1969, gay rights groups have become a significant political force, and social attitudes toward these groups are changing. Many states and cities now have laws specifically protecting the rights of gay men and lesbians. Whether same-sex couples should be allowed to marry is an issue that continues to divide society.

11 Affirmative action programs, because they involve special treatment of different groups of Americans, have always been controversial. Today, California and Washington have laws outlawing affirmative action programs in their states, and some programs have been deemed unconstitutional by the courts.

RESOURCES FOR FURTHER STUDY

Selected Readings

Anderson, Terry H. *The Pursuit of Fairness: A History of Affirmative Action.* New York: Oxford University Press, 2004. This history of affirmative action begins with the administration of Franklin D. Roosevelt in the 1940s and ends with the Supreme Court's 2003 decisions on the University of Michigan's affirmative action programs.

Brown, Dee. *Bury My Heart at Wounded Knee.* New York: Holt, Rinehart & Winston, 1971. This is an important examination of the treatment of Native Americans as the frontier pushed westward.

Freedman, Estelle B. *No Turning Back: The History of Feminism and the Future of Women.* New York: Ballantine Books, 2002.

This book summarizes the history of the women's movement using an interdisciplinary approach—examining the historical, economic, and cultural implications of feminism. The author employs a narrative style that makes this book highly readable.

Moats, David. *Civil Wars: A Battle for Gay Marriage.* New York: Harcourt, 2004. A noted journalist describes the struggle to legalize same-sex marriage in Vermont.

Woodward, C. Vann. *The Strange Career of Jim Crow.* New York: Oxford University Press, 1957. This is the classic study of segregation in the southern United States.

Politics on the Web

- Stanford University's Web site contains primary documents written by Martin Luther King, Jr., as well as secondary documents written about King. The URL for the "Martin Luther King Directory" is **http://www.stanford.edu/group/King**

- If you are interested in learning more about the Equal Employment Opportunity Commission (EEOC), the laws it enforces, how to file a charge with the EEOC, and general information about this agency, go to **http://www.eeoc.gov**

- The home page for the National Association for the Advancement of Colored People (NAACP), which contains extensive information about African American civil rights issues, is **http://www.naacp.org**

- For information on Hispanics in the United States, Latino Link is a good source. You can find it at **http://www.latinolink.org**

- The most visible and successful advocacy group for older Americans is the AARP (formerly known as the American Association of Retired Persons). Its home page contains helpful links and much information. Go to **http://www.aarp.org**

- The home page of the National Organization for Women (NOW) has links to numerous resources containing information on the rights and status of women both in the United States and around the world. You can find NOW's home page at **http://www.now.org**

- You can access the Web site of the Women's Web World, which focuses on equality for women, at **http://www.feminist.org**

- For information on the Americans with Disabilities Act (ADA), including the text of the act, go to **http://www.jan.wvu.edu/links/adalinks.htm**

- The Gay and Lesbian Alliance against Defamation has an online News Bureau. To find this organization's home page, go to **http://www.glaad.org**

Online Resources for This Chapter

This text's Companion Web Site, at **http://www.americaatodds.com**, offers links to numerous resources that you can utilize to learn more about the topics covered in this chapter. For a list describing these resources, see the inside front cover of this book.

chapter 6
interest groups

CHAPTER OBJECTIVES

After reading this chapter, you should be able to . . .

▶ Explain what an interest group is and how interest groups form.

▶ Indicate how interest groups function in American politics and how they differ from political parties.

▶ Identify various types of interest groups.

▶ Discuss how the activities of interest groups help to shape government policymaking.

▶ Describe how interest groups are regulated by government.

Should We Privatize Social Security?

Any proposal to change a major government program usually sends *interest groups,* the subject of this chapter, scrambling to lobby (attempt to influence) politicians on behalf of their constituents. One of the pressing questions Americans face today is how to fix Social Security, the federal pension program established in the midst of the Great Depression to protect elderly Americans from poverty.

Some analysts predict that Social Security will eventually go bankrupt unless major changes are made. President George W. Bush has proposed a partial privatization of the program that would give workers the option of investing a portion of their Social Security taxes in stocks or bonds. Many claim that Americans can generate more income for their retirement if they are allowed to personally invest those tax dollars—rather than simply handing the funds over to the government. Others believe that Bush's plans for privatization are dangerous and argue that the current system requires only minor changes.

Privatization Promotes an "Ownership Society"

Supporters of privatization believe that Social Security requires a major overhaul. Social Security is currently a "pay-as-you-go" system, meaning that today's taxpayers pay for today's retirees. Such a model becomes problematic when there are fewer workers to support a growing number of retirees—which is increasingly becoming the situation. Numerous analysts predict that by the year 2018, the Social Security Administration will be paying out more funds in benefits than it collects in taxes. These analysts argue that something must be done now to avert disastrous consequences in the future.

When President Bush discusses privatizing Social Security, he often speaks of creating an "ownership society." He wants to see a shift in the Social Security Administration's mission from "public entitlement" to "individual ownership." Essentially, supporters of privatization want to give Americans greater control over their future retirement. Society Security checks alone rarely provide enough income for seniors to live on. Privatization would give citizens an opportunity to increase their retirement income through their own investment decisions.

Supporters of privatization also contend that an influx of funds into the stock market will have the additional effect of creating more jobs and improving the economy. Wall Street brokers and the corporate sector are undoubtedly lobbying for partial privatization. The reforms could free substantial sums for private investment, and brokerage houses would stand to make greater profits.

The Existing System Needs Only Minor Changes

Others argue that the future of Social Security is far from doomed. The AARP (formerly the American Association of Retired Persons), a powerful interest group for older Americans, believes that only minor changes are required to shore up the existing system. Many economists share this view. They argue that even if no changes are made, the system should remain "solvent" until about 2042. Some analysts say that future problems can be avoided by imposing a small tax hike or by increasing the maximum income amount that is subject to Social Security taxes beyond the current limit of $90,000 per year.

Opponents of privatization argue that major reform would be dangerous. The initial changes alone could cost trillions of dollars. Furthermore, although the stock market may be the path to riches for some, it can also lead to financial ruin if the wrong investments are made. Most workers do not have enough time to research stocks thoroughly or to monitor the ups and downs of the stock market closely.

The most outspoken critics of privatization argue that Bush is pushing the program to further enrich wealthy Americans and fuel Wall Street at the expense of average Americans. They claim that Social Security provides a foundation for every American's retirement years. The system was intended to help citizens pay for their basic living expenses and to serve as one part of a "three-legged stool" for retirement—the other two "legs" being personal savings and private pensions.

Where Do You Stand?

1. If you could choose between privately investing part of your Social Security taxes and retaining the current system, which would you prefer? Why?

2. Do you believe that American workers can be trusted to make sound investment decisions with their personal retirement accounts? Why or why not?

Explore This Issue Online

- The Social Security Administration's official Web site contains extensive information regarding economic projections and the future of Social Security at **http://www.ssa.gov**.
- A more detailed explanation of partial privatization of Social Security and arguments in favor of Social Security reform can be found at the Cato Institute's Web site at **http://www.socialsecurity.org**.

Introduction

The groups supporting and opposing a partial privatization of Social Security provide but one example of how Americans form groups to pursue or protect their interests. All of us have interests that we would like to have represented in government: farmers want higher prices for their products, young people want good educational opportunities, environmentalists want clean air and water, and the homeless want programs that provide food and shelter.

The old adage that there is strength in numbers is certainly true in American politics. The right to organize groups is even protected by the Constitution, which guarantees people the right "peaceably to assemble, and to petition the Government for redress of grievances." The United States Supreme Court has defended this important right over the years.

Special interests significantly influence American government and politics. Indeed, some Americans think that this influence is so great that it jeopardizes representative democracy. Others maintain that interest groups are a natural consequence of democracy. After all, throughout our nation's history, people have organized into groups to protect special interests. Because of the important role played by interest groups in the American system of government, in this chapter we focus solely on such groups. We look at what they are, why they are formed, and how they influence policymaking.

Interest Groups and American Government

An **interest group** is an organization of people sharing common objectives who actively attempt to influence government policymakers through direct and indirect methods. Whatever their goals—more or fewer social services, higher or lower prices—interest groups pursue these goals on every level and in every branch of government.

On any given day in Washington, D.C., you can see national interest groups in action. If you eat breakfast in the Senate dining room, you might see congressional committee staffers reviewing testimony with representatives from women's groups. Later that morning, you might visit the Supreme Court and watch a civil rights lawyer arguing on behalf of a client in a discrimination suit. Lunch in a popular Washington restaurant might find you listening in on a conversation between an agricultural lobbyist and a congressional representative.

That afternoon you might visit an executive department, such as the Department of Labor, and watch bureaucrats working out rules and regulations with representatives from a business interest group. Then you might stroll past the headquarters of the National Rifle Association (NRA), the AARP, or the National Wildlife Federation.

interest group An organized group of individuals sharing common objectives who actively attempt to influence policymakers in all three branches of the government and at all levels.

Protesters against the privatization of Social Security demonstrate in San Francisco. They argued that privatization would saddle working Americans and the investing public with benefit cuts, greater risk, and economic instability due to increased government debt.

How Interest Groups Form

Interest groups form in response to change: a political or economic change, a dramatic shift in population or technology that affects how people live or work, or a change in social values or cultural norms. Some groups form to support the change or even speed it along, while others form to fight change. For example, during the economic boom of the 1990s, interest groups formed to support easing immigration restrictions on highly skilled workers who were in great demand in technology industries. After the terrorist attacks of September 11, 2001, however, other groups formed to support more restrictions on immigration.

As you will read shortly, there are many different types of interest groups—some represent the interests of a particular industry, while others lobby on behalf of employees. Some interest groups promote policies to protect the environment, and others seek to protect consumers. These types of groups may be interested in a broad array of issues. A consumer group may want to protect consumers from dangerous products as well as high prices. Other groups form in response to a single issue, such as a potential highway project. These groups are sometimes more successful than multi-issue groups.

AP Photo/Eric Risberg

Alexis de Tocqueville (1805–1859) was a well-known French political historian. His best-known work is *Democracy in America,* which was published in 1835. In that book, he stated, "If men are to remain civilized or to become civilized, the art of association must develop and improve among them at the same speed as equality of conditions spreads." (Vol. 2, Part II, Chapter 5)

patron An individual or organization that provides financial backing to an interest group.

free rider problem The difficulty faced by interest groups that lobby for a public good. Individuals can enjoy the outcome of the group's efforts without having to contribute, such as by becoming members of the group.

TABLE 6–1

Percentage of Americans Belonging to Various Groups

Health organizations	16%
Social clubs	17
Neighborhood groups	18
Hobby, garden, and computer clubs	19
PTA and school groups	21
Professional and trade associations	27
Health, sport, and country clubs	30
Religious groups	61

SOURCE: The AARP.

Financing   To have much success in gaining members and influencing policy, an interest group must have **patrons**—people or organizations willing to finance the group. Although groups usually collect fees or donations from their members, few can survive without large grants or donations. The level of financing required to form and expand an interest group successfully depends on the issues involved and the amount of lobbying the group needs to do. A group that pays professional lobbyists to meet with lawmakers in Washington, D.C., will require more funding than a group that operates with leaflets printed out from a Web site and distributed by volunteers.

As you can see in Figure 6–1 on page 133, the budgets of different interest groups can vary widely. The AARP's budget surpasses $770 million, while the League of Women Voters operates with only $5.3 million. Some interest groups can become very powerful very quickly if they have wealthy patrons. Other groups can raise money in a hurry if a particular event galvanizes public attention on an issue. For example, the devastating Indian Ocean tsunami brought in millions of dollars for international relief groups, such as the American Red Cross, in 2004 and 2005.

Incentives to Join a Group

The French political observer and traveler Alexis de Tocqueville wrote in 1835 that Americans have a tendency to form "associations" and have perfected "the art of pursuing in common the object of their common desires." "In no other country of the world," said Tocqueville, "has the principle of association been more successfully used or applied to a greater multitude of objectives than in America."[1] Of course, Tocqueville could not foresee the thousands of associations that now exist in this country. Surveys show that over 85 percent of Americans belong to at least one group. Table 6–1 shows the percentage of Americans who belong to various types of groups today.

This penchant for joining groups is just part of the story, however. Americans have other incentives for joining interest groups. Some people enjoy the camaraderie and sense of belonging that comes from associating with other people who share their interests and goals. Some groups offer their members material incentives for joining, such as discounts on products, subscriptions, or group insurance programs. But sometimes these incentives are not enough to persuade people to join.

The Free Rider Problem

A public good is something from which everybody benefits. People cannot be excluded from enjoying the good just because they didn't pay for it. If an interest group is successful in lobbying for laws that will improve air quality, for example, everyone who breathes that air will benefit, whether they paid for the lobbying effort or not. This is called the **free rider problem.** In some instances, the free rider problem can be overcome. For example, social pressure may persuade some people to join or donate to a group for fear of being ostracized. The government can also step in to ensure that the burden of lobbying for the public good is shared by all. When the government classifies interest groups as nonprofit organizations, it confers on them tax-exempt status. The groups' operating costs are reduced because they do not have to pay taxes, and the impact of the government's lost revenue is absorbed by all taxpayers.

How Interest Groups Function in American Politics

Despite the bad press that interest groups tend to get in the United States, they do serve several purposes in American politics:

- Interest groups help bridge the gap between citizens and government and enable citizens to explain their views on policies to public officials.
- Interest groups help raise public awareness and inspire action on various issues.
- Interest groups often provide public officials with specialized and detailed information that might be difficult to obtain otherwise. This information may be useful in making policy choices.
- Interest groups serve as another check on public officials to make sure that they are carrying out their duties responsibly.

Access to Government

In a sense, the American system of government invites the participation of interest groups by offering many points of access for groups wishing to influence policy. Consider the possibilities at just the federal level. An interest group can lobby members of Congress to act in the interests of the group. If the Senate passes a bill opposed by the group, the group's lobbying efforts can shift to the House of Representatives. If the House passes the bill, the group can try to influence the new law's application by lobbying the executive agency that is responsible for implementing the law. The group might even challenge the law in court, directly (by filing a lawsuit) or indirectly (by filing a brief as an *amicus curiae*,[2] or "friend of the court").

Pluralist Theory

The **pluralist theory** of American democracy focuses on the participation of groups in a decentralized structure of government that offers many points of access to policymakers. According to the pluralist theory, politics is a contest among various interest groups. These groups vie with each other—at all levels of government—to gain benefits for their members. Pluralists maintain that the influence of interest groups on government is not undemocratic because individual interests are indirectly represented in the policymaking process through these groups. Although not every American belongs to an interest group, inevitably some group will represent each individual's interests. Each interest is satisfied to some extent through the compromises made in settling conflicts among competing interest groups.[3]

Pluralists also contend that because of the extensive number of interest groups vying for political benefits, no one group can dominate the political process. Additionally, because most people have more than one interest, conflicts among groups do not divide the nation into hostile camps. Not all scholars agree that this is how interest groups function, however.

> **pluralist theory** A theory that views politics as a contest among various interest groups—at all levels of government—to gain benefits for their members.

AMERICA at odds

Can We Control the "Mischiefs of Factions"?

Interest groups were a cause of concern even before the Constitution was ratified. Recall from Chapter 2 that those opposed to the Constitution (the Anti-Federalists) claimed that a republican form of government could not work in a country this size because so many factions—interest groups—would be contending for power. The result would be anarchy and chaos.

James Madison attempted to allay these fears in *Federalist Paper* No. 10 (presented in Appendix F) by arguing that the "mischiefs of factions" could be controlled. Madison pointed out that factions would be inevitable in a democratic form of government. After all, different groups in society have different interests, and all citizens have the right to express their views and petition the government for redress. Yet precisely because of the large size of the United States, there would be so many diverse interests and factions that no one faction would be able to gain control of the government. Small factions could simply be outvoted, thus eliminating the possibility that they could impose the will of a minority on the majority. Large factions would be neutralized by other large factions, which would emerge in a large republic.

What Madison did not foresee is that small, intensely focused interest groups can indeed affect policymaking in the United States. The most powerful groups—those with the most resources and political influence—are primarily business, trade, or professional groups. Some of the most successful groups are those that focus on very specific issues—such as tobacco farming, funding of abortions, or handgun control. If very small groups of Americans can have such a profound influence on public policy, do we have a true democracy?

How Do Interest Groups Differ from Political Parties?

Although interest groups and political parties are both groups of people joined together for political purposes, they differ in several important ways. As you will read in Chapter 7, a political party is a group of individuals outside government who organize to win elections, operate the government, and determine policy. Interest groups, in contrast, do not seek to win elections or operate the government. Clearly, though, they do seek to influence policy. Interest groups also differ from political parties in other ways, including the following:

- Interest groups are often policy *specialists,* whereas political parties are policy *generalists.* Political parties are broad-based organizations that must attract the support of many opposing groups and consider a large number of issues. Interest groups, in contrast, have only a handful of key policies to push. An environmental group will not be as concerned about the economic status of Hispanics as it is about polluters. A manufacturing group is more involved with pushing for fewer regulations than it is with inner-city poverty.

- Interest groups are usually more tightly organized than political parties. They are often financed through contributions or dues-paying memberships. Organizers of interest groups communicate with members and potential members through conferences, mailings, newsletters, and electronic formats, such as e-mail.

- A political party's main sphere of influence is the electoral system; parties run candidates for political office. Interest groups try to influence the outcome of elections, but unlike parties, they do not compete for public office. Although a candidate for office may be sympathetic to—or even be a member of—a certain group, he or she does not run for election as a candidate of that group.

Different Types of Interest Groups

American democracy embraces almost every conceivable type of interest group, and the number is increasing rapidly. No one has ever compiled a *Who's Who* of interest groups, but you can get an idea of the number and variety by looking through the annually published *Encyclopedia of Associations.* Look at Figure 6–1 to see profiles of some selected important interest groups.

Some interest groups have large memberships. The AARP, for example, has over 35 million members. Others, such as the Tulip Growers Association, have as few as fourteen members. Some, such as the NRA, are household names and have been in existence for many years, while others crop up overnight. Some are highly structured and run by professional, full-time staffs, while others are loosely structured and informal.

The most common interest groups are those that promote private interests. These groups seek public policies that benefit the economic interests of their members and work against policies that threaten those interests. Other groups, sometimes called **public-interest groups,** are formed with the broader goal of working for the "public good"; the American Civil Liberties Union and Common Cause are examples.

Business Interest Groups

Business has long been well organized for effective action. Hundreds of business groups are now operating in Washington, D.C., in the fifty state capitals, and at the local level across the country. Two umbrella organizations that include small and large corporations and businesses are the U.S. Chamber of Commerce and the National Association of Manufacturers (NAM). In addition to representing about 3 million individual businesses, the Chamber has nearly 3,000 local, state, and regional affiliates. It has become a major voice for the nation's millions of small businesses. The NAM chiefly represents big business and has more than 13,000 members.

The hundreds of **trade organizations** are far less visible than the Chamber of Commerce and the NAM, but they are also important in seeking policy goals for their members. Trade organizations usually support policies that benefit specific industries. For example, people in the oil industry work for policies that favor the development of oil as an energy resource. Other business groups have worked for policies that favor the development of coal, solar power, and nuclear power. Trucking companies would work for policies that would result in more highways being built. Railroad companies would, of course, not want more highways built because that would hurt their business.

public-interest group An interest group formed for the purpose of working for the "public good"; examples of public-interest groups are the American Civil Liberties Union and Common Cause.

trade organization An association formed by members of a particular industry, such as the oil industry or the trucking industry, to develop common standards and goals for the industry. Trade organizations, as interest groups, lobby government for legislation or regulations that specifically benefit their groups.

These senior dancers were part of the AARP's festivities surrounding a recent rally in Nashville, Tennessee. Hundreds of AARP members flooded the city to urge lawmakers there to support tax reform and improve nursing-home care.

AP Photo/Eric Parsons/*The Tennessean*

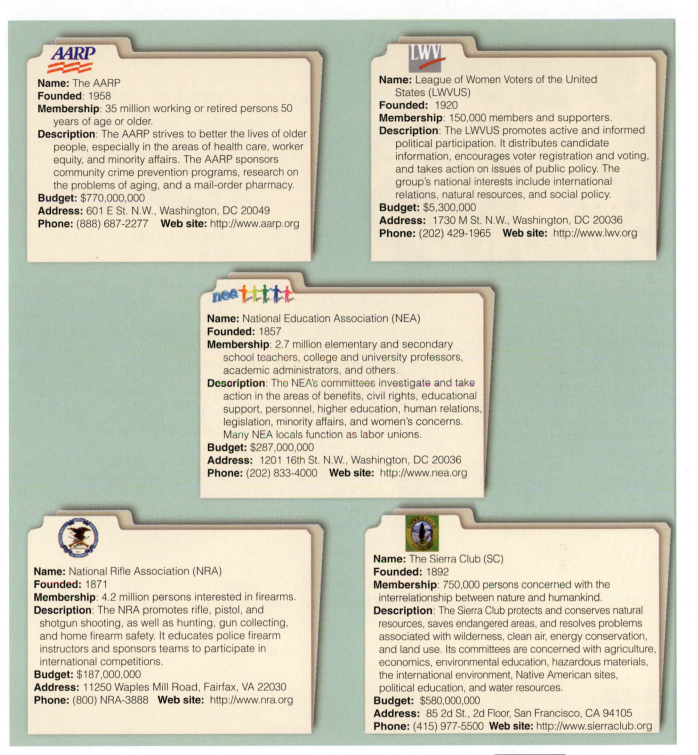

Name: The AARP
Founded: 1958
Membership: 35 million working or retired persons 50 years of age or older.
Description: The AARP strives to better the lives of older people, especially in the areas of health care, worker equity, and minority affairs. The AARP sponsors community crime prevention programs, research on the problems of aging, and a mail-order pharmacy.
Budget: $770,000,000
Address: 601 E St. N.W., Washington, DC 20049
Phone: (888) 687-2277 **Web site:** http://www.aarp.org

Name: League of Women Voters of the United States (LWVUS)
Founded: 1920
Membership: 150,000 members and supporters.
Description: The LWVUS promotes active and informed political participation. It distributes candidate information, encourages voter registration and voting, and takes action on issues of public policy. The group's national interests include international relations, natural resources, and social policy.
Budget: $5,300,000
Address: 1730 M St. N.W., Washington, DC 20036
Phone: (202) 429-1965 **Web site:** http://www.lwv.org

Name: National Education Association (NEA)
Founded: 1857
Membership: 2.7 million elementary and secondary school teachers, college and university professors, academic administrators, and others.
Description: The NEA's committees investigate and take action in the areas of benefits, civil rights, educational support, personnel, higher education, human relations, legislation, minority affairs, and women's concerns. Many NEA locals function as labor unions.
Budget: $287,000,000
Address: 1201 16th St. N.W., Washington, DC 20036
Phone: (202) 833-4000 **Web site:** http://www.nea.org

Name: National Rifle Association (NRA)
Founded: 1871
Membership: 4.2 million persons interested in firearms.
Description: The NRA promotes rifle, pistol, and shotgun shooting, as well as hunting, gun collecting, and home firearm safety. It educates police firearm instructors and sponsors teams to participate in international competitions.
Budget: $187,000,000
Address: 11250 Waples Mill Road, Fairfax, VA 22030
Phone: (800) NRA-3888 **Web site:** http://www.nra.org

Name: The Sierra Club (SC)
Founded: 1892
Membership: 750,000 persons concerned with the interrelationship between nature and humankind.
Description: The Sierra Club protects and conserves natural resources, saves endangered areas, and resolves problems associated with wilderness, clean air, energy conservation, and land use. Its committees are concerned with agriculture, economics, environmental education, hazardous materials, the international environment, Native American sites, political education, and water resources.
Budget: $580,000,000
Address: 85 2d St., 2d Floor, San Francisco, CA 94105
Phone: (415) 977-5500 **Web site:** http://www.sierraclub.org

FIGURE 6-1
Profiles of Selected Interest Groups

Traditionally, business interest groups have been viewed as staunch supporters of the Republican Party. This is because Republicans are more likely to promote a "hands-off" government policy toward business. Over the last decade, however, donations from corporations to the Democratic National Committee more than doubled. Why would business groups make contributions to the Democratic National Committee? Fred McChesney, a professor of law and business at Emory University's School of Law, offers an interesting answer to this question. He argues that campaign contributions are often made not for political favors but rather to avoid political disfavor. Just as government officials can take away wealth from citizens (in the form of taxes, for example), politicians can extort from private parties payments

Membership in a labor union allows employees to bargain collectively with their employer to obtain higher salaries, improved working conditions, and so on. Here, airline pilots exercise a union's ultimate right—the right to strike when labor-management negotiations fail to result in a satisfactory outcome.

labor force All of the people over the age of sixteen who are working or actively looking for jobs.

not to expropriate private wealth.[4] (For an example of the power of business interests, see this chapter's *The Politics of National Security* feature.)

Labor Interest Groups

Interest groups representing labor have been some of the most influential groups in our country's history. They date back to at least 1886, when the American Federation of Labor (AFL) was formed. The largest and most powerful labor interest group today is the AFL–CIO (the American Federation of Labor–Congress of Industrial Organizations), an organization that includes nearly ninety unions representing more than 13 million workers. Several million additional workers are members of other unions (not affiliated with the AFL–CIO), such as the United Electrical Workers.

Like labor unions everywhere, American labor unions press for policies to improve working conditions and ensure better pay for their members. On some issues, however, unions may take opposing sides. For example, separate unions of bricklayers and carpenters may try to change building codes to benefit their own members even though the changes may hurt other unions. Unions may also compete for new members. In many states, the National Education Association and the AFL–CIO's American Federation of Teachers compete fiercely for members. Also, organized labor represents less than 13 percent of the **labor force**—defined as all of the people over the age of sixteen who are working or actively looking for a job.

Although unions were highly influential in the late 1800s and the early 1900s, their strength and political power have waned in the last several decades, as you can see in Figure 6–2. In an attempt to reverse this general trend, two large industrial groups announced plans to merge in 2004. The United Steelworkers of America and the Paper, Allied Industrial, Chemical and Energy Workers International Union (PACE) believed that by combining their resources and influence, they could better represent their members' interests. While labor groups have generally experienced a decline in lobbying power, public employee unions have grown in both numbers and political clout in recent years. Public employees enjoy some of the nation's best health-care and retirement benefits because of the efforts of their labor groups.

Agricultural Interest Groups

Many groups work for general agricultural interests at all levels of government. Three broad-based agricultural groups represent millions of American farmers, from peanut farmers to dairy producers to tobacco growers. They are the American Farm Bureau Federation (Farm Bureau), the National Grange, and the National Farmers Union. The Farm Bureau, with over

FIGURE 6-2

Union Membership, 1952 to 2005

This figure shows the percentage of the workforce represented by unions from 1952 to 2005. As you can see, union membership has declined significantly over the past several decades.

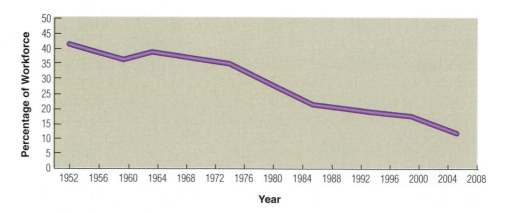

The Military-Industrial Complex

Given the lack of a military draft at the present time and the shortage of volunteers, the U.S. Army has been spread thin while fighting the war on terrorism. Needing more personnel, especially in Iraq, the Bush administration has turned to private contractors.

Although there is nothing new about private contractors playing a role in American war efforts, they are being used in Iraq on an unprecedented scale. By the beginning of 2005, approximately 10,000 private contractor workers were in Iraq. Indeed, U.S. civilian workers outnumbered the British troops (9,900) stationed in Iraq. Never before has the U.S. military relied so heavily on private contractors.

PRIVATE CONTRACTORS IN IRAQ

In Iraq, civilian workers are now providing services that traditionally have been provided by military personnel. These workers have been hired by companies that have won government contracts to carry out work that the military lacks adequate personnel to do alone. Civilian workers in Iraq have filled roles ranging from interrogators and prison guards to fuel-truck drivers and accountants. Many find themselves in grave danger on a daily basis, and a number of them have been victims of car bombings and guerrilla warfare. Because of the dangerous environment, many of the civilian workers in Iraq are former members of the armed services.

PRIVATE CONTRACTORS AND SPECIAL INTERESTS

The intertwining of the special interests of defense contractors with the war effort in Iraq has produced some possibly unsettling results. For example, Texas oil giant Halliburton Corporation was awarded multibillion-dollar contracts for handling fuel-related and infrastructure work in Iraq during the occupation and rebuilding process. Vice President Dick Cheney once headed Halliburton, and the company still pays him nearly $1 million annually as part of a severance contract.

Bechtel Corporation, a California-based firm, employs Jack Sheehan, who is a member of the government's Defense Policy Board (which advises Defense Secretary Donald Rumsfeld). Bechtel won a contract to improve Iraq's infrastructure. The contract bidding, however, was open only to six select companies, which had contributed a total of $3.6 million to reelect Republican politicians over the previous three years.

United Nations (UN) auditors have questioned the U.S. decision to award over $1 billion in reconstruction contracts to American companies without any competitive bidding

whatsoever. UN auditors have also complained that they cannot determine how private contractors are using government funds. The Bush administration has not been cooperative in providing access to accounting records for the U.S. government's Development Fund for Iraq.

EISENHOWER'S WARNING

President Dwight D. Eisenhower, during his 1961 farewell address, puzzled many Americans by warning that "we must guard against the acquisition of unwarranted influence, whether sought or unsought, by the military-industrial complex." Eisenhower was referring to the increasingly close relationship among the federal government, the U.S. military, and private defense contractors.

Eisenhower, who had been a general during World War II (1939–1945) and who served as president during the last year of the Korean War (1950–1953), had firsthand knowledge of the joining of interests that he called the military-industrial complex. According to Eisenhower, "The potential for the disastrous rise of misplaced power exists and will persist." With the growing reliance on private contractors, some contend that the United States may be drifting toward the "unwarranted influence" and "misplaced power" against which Eisenhower cautioned.

Are We Safer?

Does the use of private contractors to help conduct a war jeopardize our national security in any way? Why or why not?

AP Photo/John Moore

A private contractor looks down into a crater made from a suicide bomb attack in Baghdad, Iraq, in October 2004. The U.S. government hired large numbers of private contractors to perform operations in Iraq that traditionally would have been handled by military personnel.

PhotoDisc

A number of national interest groups protect the interests of farmers. Through their lobbying efforts and campaign contributions, these groups have wielded significant influence on congressional policymaking with respect to agricultural subsidies and other forms of assistance.

5 million members, is the largest and generally the most effective of the three. Founded in 1919, the Farm Bureau achieved one of its greatest early successes when it helped to obtain government guarantees of "fair" prices during the Great Depression of the 1930s.[5] The Grange, founded in 1867, is the oldest group. It has a membership of about 300,000 rural families. The National Farmers Union comprises approximately 250,000 farm and ranch families.

Like special interest labor groups, producers of various specific farm commodities, such as dairy products, soybeans, grain, fruit, corn, cotton, beef, sugar beets, and so on, have formed their own organizations. These specialized groups, such as the Associated Milk Producers, Inc., also have a strong influence on farm legislation. Like business and labor groups, farm organizations sometimes find themselves in competition. In some western states, for example, barley farmers, cattle ranchers, and orchard owners may compete to influence laws governing water rights. Different groups also often disagree over the extent to which the government should regulate farmers.

Consumer Interest Groups

Groups organized for the protection of consumer rights were very active in the 1960s and 1970s. Some are still active today. The best known and perhaps the most effective are the public-interest consumer groups organized under the leadership of consumer activist Ralph Nader. Another well-known consumer group is Consumers Union, a nonprofit organization started in 1936. In addition to publishing *Consumer Reports,* Consumers Union has been influential in pushing for the removal of phosphates from detergents, lead from gasoline, and pesticides from food. Consumers Union strongly criticizes government agencies when they act against consumer interests.

In each city, consumer groups have been organized to deal with such problems as poor housing, discrimination against minorities and women, discrimination in the granting of credit, and business inaction on consumer complaints.

AMERICA at odds

Taxing the Internet

Online shopping has become increasingly popular as more Americans connect their home computers to the Internet. Books, antiques, sporting equipment, and even cars can now be purchased from the comfort of home. For many consumers, online purchases often have the added benefit of being exempt from state sales taxes. Many brick-and-mortar retailers and state governments have lobbied against the ban on e-commerce taxes. Although the federal ban has been repeatedly renewed, the Internet tax issue continues to be hotly debated by a variety of interest groups.

Many Americans want to maintain existing laws prohibiting state sales taxes on Internet purchases. They point to the United States Supreme Court's decision to block states from taxing mail-order and catalogue purchases when the company does not have a physical presence in the state where the consumer resides. Citing the commerce clause of the U.S. Constitution, the Court ruled that such taxes were unconstitutional because only the federal government possesses the right to regulate interstate commerce.[6] Opponents of e-commerce taxes argue that Internet purchases should enjoy the same tax exemption as mail-order and catalogue purchases. In 1998, the U.S. Congress agreed with this view and passed the Internet Tax Freedom Act (ITFA), which has since been renewed several times. Many politicians and consumers now contend that the ITFA's ban on Internet taxation should become permanent.

Others contend that *all* purchases should be subject to existing state sales taxes. Many brick-and-mortar retailers complain that the current ban on e-commerce taxes gives an unfair advantage to Internet businesses. Consumers may choose to make purchases over the Internet simply to avoid sales taxes, they argue. In addition, the ban costs state and local governments billions of dollars in lost revenue annually. Those in favor of e-commerce taxes also claim that the ban has a disporportionate impact on poorer Americans because they are unlikely to have regular access to the Internet and thus must shop at traditional brick-and-mortar stores, where sales taxes apply in most states. Some economists argue that sales taxes are by nature *regressive*, meaning that they have greater impact on individuals in lower-income brackets than on wealthier consumers. According to these economists, banning taxes on e-commerce only increases the burden on the poor.

Many people now make purchases from out-of-state sellers via the Internet. State governments are banned from taxing such purchases, however.

Senior Citizen Interest Groups

While the population of the nation as a whole has tripled since 1900, the number of elderly has increased eightfold. Persons over the age of sixty-five now account for 13 percent of the population, and many of these people have united to call attention to their special needs and concerns. As you read in the chapter-opening *America at Odds* feature, senior citizens have a great deal at stake in the current debate over Social Security. Interest groups formed to promote the interests of the elderly have been very outspoken and persuasive. As pointed out before, the AARP has more than 35 million members and is a potent political force.

Environmental Interest Groups

With the current concern for the environment, the membership of established environmental groups has blossomed, and many new groups have formed. They are becoming some of the most powerful interest groups in Washington, D.C. The National Wildlife Federation has about 4.5 million members. Table 6–2 on the following page lists some of the major environmental groups and the number of members in each group.

Environmental groups have organized to support pollution controls, wilderness protection, and clean-air legislation. They have opposed strip-mining, nuclear power plants, logging activities, chemical waste dumps, and many other potential environmental hazards.

Senior Americans can access the AARP's Web site to learn how various policy proposals will affect them.

Professional Interest Groups

Most professions that require advanced education or specialized training have organizations to protect and promote their interests. These groups are concerned mainly with the standards of their professions, but they also work to influence government policy. Some also function as labor unions. Four major professional groups are the American Medical Association, representing physicians; the American Bar Association, representing lawyers; and the National Education Association and the American Federation of Teachers, both representing teachers. In addition, there are dozens of less well known and less politically active professional groups, such as the Screen Actors Guild, the National Association of Social Workers, and the American Political Science Association.

Single-Issue Interest Groups

Numerous interest groups focus on a single issue. For example, Mothers Against Drunk Driving (MADD) lobbies for stiffer penalties for drunk-driving

TABLE 6-2
Selected Environmental Interest Groups

Name of Group	Year Founded	Number of U.S. Members
Environmental Defense Fund	1967	400,000
Greenpeace USA	1971	250,000
Izaak Walton League of America	1922	50,000
League of Conservation Voters	1970	50,000
National Audubon Society	1905	500,000
National Wildlife Federation	1936	4,500,000
The Nature Conservancy	1951	1,000,000
The Sierra Club	1892	750,000
The Wilderness Society	1935	225,000
The World Wildlife Fund	1948	1,200,000

SOURCES: Foundation for Public Affairs, 1996; plus authors' updates.

convictions. Formed in 1980, MADD now boasts over 3 million members and supporters. The abortion debate has created various single-issue groups, such as the Right to Life organization (which opposes abortion) and NARAL Pro-Choice America (which supports it). Other examples of single-issue groups are the NRA and the American Israel Public Affairs Committee (a pro-Israel group).

Government Interest Groups

Efforts by state and local governments to lobby the federal government have escalated in recent years. With many states experiencing growing budget shortfalls, these governments have lobbied in Washington, D.C., for additional federal funds. The federal government has lobbied in individual states, too. During the 2004 elections, the U.S. Attorney General's office lobbied against medical marijuana in states that were considering ballot measures on the issue. Additionally, the Department of Education came under criticism for paying a prominent conservative talk-show host, Armstrong Williams, to promote the No Child Left Behind Act. Amidst that controversy, the Social Security Administration announced it would not use similar tactics to push President George W. Bush's partial privatization plan for Social Security.

How Interest Groups Shape Policy

Interest groups operate at all levels of government and use a variety of strategies to steer policies in ways beneficial to their interests. Sometimes they attempt to influence policymakers directly, but at other times they try to exert indirect influence on policymakers by shaping public opinion. The extent and nature of the groups' activities depend on their goals and their resources.

Direct Techniques

direct technique Any method used by an interest group to interact with government officials directly to further the group's goals.

lobbying All of the attempts by organizations or by individuals to influence the passage, defeat, or contents of legislation or to influence the administrative decisions of government.

lobbyist An individual who handles a particular interest group's lobbying efforts.

Lobbying and providing election support are two important **direct techniques** used by interest groups to influence government policy.

Lobbying   Today, **lobbying** refers to all of the attempts by organizations or individuals to influence the passage, defeat, or contents of legislation or to influence the administrative decisions of government. (The term *lobbying* arose because, traditionally, individuals and groups interested in influencing government policy would gather in the foyer, or lobby, of the legislature to corner legislators and express their concerns.) A **lobbyist** is an individual who handles a particular interest group's lobbying efforts. Most of the larger interest groups have lobbyists in Washington, D.C. These lobbyists often include former members of Congress or former employees of executive bureaucracies who are experienced in the methods of political influence and who "know people." Many lobbyists also work at state and local levels. In fact, lobbying at the state level has increased in recent years as states have begun to play a more significant role in policymaking. Table 6–3 summarizes some of the basic methods by which lobbyists directly influence legislators and government officials.

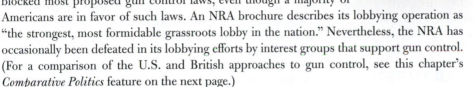

The Effectiveness of Lobbying   Lobbying is one of the most widely used and effective ways to influence legislative activity. For example, Mothers Against Drunk Driving has had many lobbying successes at both the state and federal levels. The NRA has successfully blocked most proposed gun control laws, even though a majority of Americans are in favor of such laws. An NRA brochure describes its lobbying operation as "the strongest, most formidable grassroots lobby in the nation." Nevertheless, the NRA has occasionally been defeated in its lobbying efforts by interest groups that support gun control. (For a comparison of the U.S. and British approaches to gun control, see this chapter's *Comparative Politics* feature on the next page.)

Lobbyists often line up in the "lobbies," or halls, of Congress while awaiting their turns to consult with members of Congress. The term *lobby* comes from the medieval Latin *lobia*, which referred to a monastic cloister. The word began to be used in U.S. politics in the 1830s, when agents gathered in the lobbies of both Congress and state legislatures to press their causes.

Paul Conklin/PhotoEdit

TABLE 6–3
Direct Lobbying Techniques

TECHNIQUE	DESCRIPTION
Making Personal Contacts with Key Legislators	A lobbyist's personal contacts with key legislators or other government officials—in their offices, in the halls of Congress, or on social occasions, such as dinners, boating expeditions, and the like—are one of the most effective direct lobbying techniques. The lobbyist provides the legislators with information on a particular issue in an attempt to convince them to support the interest group's goals.
Providing Expertise and Research Results for Legislators	Lobbyists often have knowledge and expertise that are useful in drafting legislation, and this expertise can be a major strength for an interest group. Because many harried members of Congress cannot possibly be experts on everything they vote on and therefore eagerly seek information to help them make up their minds, some lobbying groups conduct research and present their findings to those legislators.
Offering "Expert" Testimony before Congressional Committees	Lobbyists often provide "expert" testimony before congressional committees for or against proposed legislation. A bill to regulate firearms, for example, might concern several interest groups. The NRA would probably oppose the bill, and representatives from the interest group might be asked to testify. Groups that would probably support the bill, such as law enforcement personnel or wildlife conservationists, might also be asked to testify. Each side would offer as much evidence as possible to support its position.
Providing Legal Advice to Legislators	Many lobbyists assist legislators in drafting legislation or prospective regulations. Lobbyists are a source of ideas and sometimes offer legal advice on specific details.
Following Up on Legislation	Because executive agencies responsible for carrying out legislation can often increase or decrease the power of the new law, lobbyists may also try to influence the bureaucrats who implement the policy. For example, beginning in the early 1960s, regulations outlawing gender discrimination were broadly outlined by Congress. Both women's rights groups favoring the regulations and interest groups opposing the regulations lobbied for years to influence how those regulations were carried out.

Gun Control in Britain and the United States—A Tale of Two Lobbies

In March 1995, a former Boy Scout leader named Thomas Hamilton acquired four high-powered rifles and took them to a primary school in a peaceful Scottish village named Dunblane. There he methodically slaughtered sixteen small children and their teacher. Gun violence was no longer something the British could dismiss as a uniquely American problem.

Less than a year and a half later, the government in London responded by banning virtually all handguns except .22 caliber and smaller guns, which later were also banned. Under these laws, which are said to be among the toughest gun control laws in the world, British residents face the prospect of up to ten years in prison if they fail to give up their weapons.

TWO DIFFERENT GUN CULTURES

The United States has experienced many "slaughters" similar to the one in Dunblane, Scotland, and yet our gun control laws do not come close to those of Britain. As Table 6–4 shows, the United States and Britain also differ considerably in both the number of guns owned and the number of murders committed with guns.

TABLE 6–4
Ownership of Firearms and Number of Murders in the United States versus Britain

	UNITED STATES	BRITAIN
Total firearms	222,000,000	409,000
Firearms per capita	0.853	0.006
Total firearm murders per year	14,000	80
Firearm murders per year per 100,000 people	5.25	0.116

SOURCES: Bureau of Justice Statistics (United States); Home Office (Britain).

A DIFFERENT MENTALITY OR JUST DIFFERENT LOBBYING?

The British have had a long history of stringent gun control laws. In the past, anyone seeking a gun in Britain had to obtain a certificate from the police and demonstrate a need for the weapon. Whereas 50 percent of private citizens in the United States have guns in their homes, fewer than 5 percent of British citizens do.

Before the ban on guns in Britain, an opinion poll showed that British citizens favored such a ban by 81 percent to 15 percent.[7] Similarly, in the United States a majority of citizens would like stricter gun control laws; yet such laws have not been passed in this country. Why not?

The answer to this question, at least in part, is the effective lobbying efforts of the NRA, which strongly opposes any gun control legislation. One of the NRA's most effective techniques continues to be grassroots lobbying: encouraging members to get involved in the legislative process through letter writing, e-mails, and phone calls to legislators.

In contrast, the most important gun lobby in Britain is primarily concerned with protecting the group's interest in sport shooting. Sport shooting in Britain is associated with landowning. Joining a good shooting club gives rural residents a step up the social ladder in the British countryside. Those who shoot typically use shotguns, which have escaped bans in Britain. Thus, the gun lobby in Britain has been effective in protecting this niche interest in sport shooting, but it has expended much less effort than the NRA in mounting massive grassroots campaigns to protect gun ownership overall.

For Critical Analysis
At the time the British handgun ban was passed in 1996, opponents of the ban argued that 41 percent of homicides were from knives; 29 percent were from blunt objects, hitting, and kicking; and 18 percent were from strangulation. That left only 12 percent from guns.[8] Do these statistics represent a valid argument against the British handgun ban? Explain.

Lobbying can be directed at the legislative branch of government and also at administrative agencies and even at the courts. For example, individuals stricken with AIDS formed a strong lobby in the early 1990s to force the Food and Drug Administration to allow patients to use experimental drugs to treat AIDS before the drugs were fully tested. Lobbying can also be directed at changing international policies. For example, after political changes had opened up Eastern Europe to business in the late 1980s and early 1990s, intense lobbying by Western business groups helped persuade the United States and other industrial powers to reduce controls on the sale of high-technology products, such as personal computers, to Eastern European countries.

Providing Election Support   Interest groups often become directly involved in the election process. Many interest group members join and work with political parties to influence party platforms and the nomination of candidates. Interest groups provide campaign support for legislators who favor their policies and sometimes urge their own members to try to win posts in party organizations. Most important, interest groups urge their members to vote for candidates who support the views of the group. They can also threaten legislators with the withdrawal of votes. No candidate can expect to have support from *all* interest groups, but if the candidate is to win, she or he must have support (or little opposition) from the most powerful ones.

Since the 1970s, federal laws governing campaign financing have allowed corporations, labor unions, and special interest groups to raise funds and make campaign contributions through **political action committees (PACs).** Both the number of PACs and the amount of money they spend on elections have grown astronomically in recent years. There were about one thousand PACs in 1976; today, there are more than four thousand PACs. In 1973, total spending by PACs amounted to $19 million; in recent elections, total spending by PACs has reached nearly $600 million.[9] We discuss PACs in more detail in Chapter 9.

Although campaign contributions do not guarantee that officials will vote the way the groups wish, contributions usually do ensure that the groups will have the ear of the public officials they have helped to elect. PACs have also succeeded in bypassing campaign-contribution limits, thereby obtaining the same type of "vote-buying" privileges that wealthy individual contributors enjoyed in the past.

political action committee (PAC) A committee that is established by a corporation, labor union, or special interest group to raise funds and make contributions on the establishing organization's behalf.

Indirect Techniques

Interest groups also try to influence public policy indirectly through third parties or the general public. Such **indirect techniques** may appear to be spontaneous, but they are generally as well planned as the direct lobbying techniques just discussed. Indirect techniques can be particularly effective because public officials are often more impressed by contacts from voters than from lobbyists.

indirect technique Any method used by interest groups to influence government officials through third parties, such as voters.

Shaping Public Opinion
Public opinion weighs significantly in the policymaking process, so interest groups cultivate their public images carefully. If public opinion favors a certain group's interests, then public officials will be more ready to listen and more willing to pass legislation favoring that group. To cultivate public opinion, an interest group's efforts may include television publicity, newspaper and magazine advertisements, mass mailings, and the use of public relations techniques to improve the group's public image.

For example, environmental groups run television ads to dramatize threats to the environment. Oil companies respond to criticism about increased gasoline prices with advertising showing their concern for the public welfare. The goal of all these activities is to influence public opinion and bring grassroots pressure to bear on officials.

Some interest groups also try to influence legislators through **rating systems.** A group selects legislative issues that it feels are important to its goals and rates legislators according to the percentage of times they vote favorably on that legislation. For example, a score of 90 percent on the Americans for Democratic Action (ADA) rating scale means that the legislator supported that group's position to a high degree. Other groups tag members of Congress who support (or fail to support) their interests to a significant extent with telling labels. For instance, the Communications Workers of America refers to policymakers who take a position consistent with its members' own views as "Heroes" and those who take the opposite position as "Zeroes." Needless to say, such tactics can be an effective form of indirect lobbying, particularly with legislators who do not want to earn a low ADA score or be placed on the "Zeroes" list.

rating system A system by which a particular interest group evaluates (rates) the performance of legislators based on how often the legislators have voted with the group's position on particular issues.

Interest groups often use celebrities to help promote their causes to the public. Here, actor Will Smith helps the Ford Motor Company promote booster seats for children.

Ford Motor Company

Issue Ads and "527s"
One of the most powerful indirect techniques used by interest groups is the "issue ad"—a television or radio ad supporting or opposing a particular issue. The Supreme Court has made it clear that the First Amendment's guarantee of free speech protects interest groups' rights to set forth their positions on issues. Nevertheless, issue advocacy is controversial because the funds spent to air issue ads have had a clear effect on the outcome of elections.

Both parties have benefited from such interest group spending. In many instances, the sponsors of the ads are clearly identified, as required by the Federal Communications Commission. Some ads, however, have been aired by "front groups," which have been created to disguise the true identity of the sponsors. For example, prescription drug companies and pharmaceutical trade groups have created seemingly independent groups, such as the Citizens for Better Medicare and Citizens for the Right to Know, to promote their positions.[10]

The Bipartisan Campaign Reform Act of 2002 attempted to address the power of issue ads by banning unlimited donations to campaigns and political parties, called *soft money*. The reform would have severely curbed the use of issue ads, but partisan groups called "527s" (after the provision of the tax code that covers them) discovered a loophole in the law. Soft money could still be collected so long as 527s did not officially work with campaigns or candidates. Wealthy individuals, such as George Soros, were quick to donate large sums to 527s. By taking advantage of the finance loophole, 527 organizations—such as MoveOn.org, America Coming Together, and Swift Boat Veterans for Truth—played an influential role in the 2004 elections.

Mobilizing Constituents
Interest groups sometimes urge members and other constituents to contact government officials—by letter, e-mail, or telephone—to show their support for or opposition to a certain policy. Large interest groups can generate hundreds of thousands of letters, e-mail messages, and phone calls. Interest groups often provide form letters or postcards for constituents to fill out and mail. The NRA has successfully used this tactic to fight strict federal gun control legislation by delivering half a million letters to Congress within a few weeks. Policymakers recognize that the letters were initiated by an interest group, but they are still made aware that an issue is important to that group.

Going to Court
The legal system offers another avenue for interest groups to influence the political process. Civil rights groups paved the way for interest group litigation in the 1950s and 1960s with major victories in cases concerning equal housing, school desegregation, and employment discrimination. Environmental groups, such as the Sierra Club, have also successfully used litigation to protect their interests. For example, an environmental group might challenge in court an activity that threatens to pollute the environment or that will destroy the natural habitat of an endangered species. The legal challenge forces those engaging in the activity to bear the costs of defending themselves and possibly delays their project. In fact, much of the success of environmental groups has been linked to their use of lawsuits.

Interest groups can also influence the outcome of litigation without being a party to a lawsuit. As you read earlier in this chapter, interest groups often file *amicus curiae* ("friend of the court") briefs in appellate (reviewing) courts. These briefs state the group's legal argument in support of their desired outcome in a case. For example, in the case *Metro-Goldwyn-Mayer Studios, Inc. v. Grokster, Ltd.*[11]—involving the legality of file-sharing software—hundreds of *amicus* briefs were filed by various groups on behalf of the petitioners. Groups filing *amicus* briefs for the case, which was heard by the Supreme Court in 2005, included the National Basketball Association, the National Football League, the National Association of Broadcasters, the Association of American Publishers, and numerous state governments. Often, interest groups have statistics and research that support their position on a certain issue, and this research can have considerable influence on the justices deciding the case. Also, filing a brief in a case gives the group publicity, which aids in promoting its causes.

Demonstration Techniques
Some interest groups stage protests to make a statement in a dramatic way. The Boston Tea Party of 1773, in which American colonists dressed as Native Americans and threw tea into Boston Harbor to protest British taxes, is testimony to how long this tactic has been around. Over the years, many groups have organized protest marches and rallies to support or oppose such issues as legalized abortion, busing, gay and lesbian rights, government assistance to farmers, the treatment of Native Americans, restrictions on the use of federally owned lands in the West, trade relations with China, and the activities of global organizations, such as the World Trade Organization. Not all demonstration techniques are peaceful. Some environmental groups, for example, have used such

tactics as spiking trees and setting traps on logging roads that puncture truck tires. Pro-life groups have bombed clinics, and members of People for the Ethical Treatment of Animals (PETA) have broken into laboratories and freed animals being used for experimentation.

Today's Lobbying Establishment

Without a doubt, interest groups and their lobbyists have become a permanent feature in the landscape of American government. The major interest groups all have headquarters in Washington, D.C., close to the center of government. Professional lobbyists and staff members of various interest groups move freely between their groups' headquarters and congressional offices and committee rooms. Interest group representatives are routinely consulted when Congress drafts new legislation. As already mentioned, interest group representatives are frequently asked to testify before congressional committees or subcommittees on the effect or potential effect of particular legislation or regulations. In a word, interest groups have become an integral part of the American government system.

As interest groups have become a permanent feature of American government, lobbying has developed into a profession. A professional lobbyist—one who has mastered the techniques of lobbying discussed earlier in this chapter—is a valuable ally to any interest group seeking to influence government. Professional lobbyists can and often do move from one interest group to another.

The "Revolving Door" between Interest Groups and Government

In recent years, it has become increasingly common for those who leave positions with the federal government to become lobbyists or consultants for the private-interest groups they helped to regulate. Former government officials, particularly those who held key positions in Congress or the executive branch, have little difficulty finding work as lobbyists. For one thing, they often have inside information that can help an interest group's efforts. More important, they normally have an established network of personal contacts, which is a great political asset.

In spite of legislation and regulations that have been created in an attempt to reduce this "revolving door" syndrome, it is still functioning quite well. When Representative Sam Gibbons (D., Fla.) retired, he went to work as a lobbyist on the same tax and trade issues he had handled as a member of the House Ways and Means Committee. Representative Bill Brewster (D., Okla.) stated that when he retired, he planned to work on the same health-care and energy issues he worked on in Congress. Even though current law requires former lawmakers and aides to wait a year before directly lobbying their former colleagues, the restrictions have had little discernible effect. On average, about one in four former lawmakers becomes a lobbyist.

Why Do Interest Groups Get Bad Press?

Despite their importance to democratic government, interest groups, like political parties, are sometimes criticized by both the public and the press. Our image of interest groups and their special interests is not very favorable. You may have run across political cartoons depicting lobbyists standing in the hallways of Congress with briefcases stuffed with money, waiting to lure representatives into a waiting limousine.

These cartoons are not entirely factual, but they are not entirely fictitious either. President Richard Nixon (1969–1974) was revealed to have yielded to the campaign contributions of milk producers by later authorizing a windfall increase in milk subsidies. In 1977, "Koreagate," a scandal in which a South Korean businessman was accused of offering lavish "gifts" to several members of Congress, added to the view that politicians were too easily susceptible to the snares of special interests. In the early 1990s, it was revealed that a number of senators who received generous contributions from one particular savings and loan association subsequently supported a "hands-off" policy by savings and loan regulators. The savings and loan association in question later got into financial trouble, costing the taxpayers billions of dollars.

A lobbyist talks with a member of Congress outside the member's office. Interest groups often hire former members of Congress to serve as lobbyists, thus creating a "revolving door" between interest groups and government.

As you will read shortly, Congress has tried to impose stricter regulations on lobbyists. For example, after numerous scandals over the years, in 1996 both the House and the Senate passed a set of rules that prohibited members of Congress from accepting free trips, meals, and gifts from interest group lobbyists. The most important legislation regulating lobbyists was passed in 1946 and revised in 1995. The problem with stricter regulation is that it could abridge First Amendment rights. (For an example of how interest groups' influence over public policy can arouse public ire, see this chapter's *Perception versus Reality* feature.)

The Regulation of Interest Groups

In an attempt to control lobbying, Congress passed the Federal Regulation of Lobbying Act in 1946. The major provisions of the act are as follows:

- Any person or organization that receives money to be used principally to influence legislation before Congress must register with the clerk of the House and the secretary of the Senate.
- Any group or persons registering must identify their employer, salary, amount and purpose of expenses, and duration of employment.
- Every registered lobbyist must give quarterly reports on his or her activities, which are to be published in the *Congressional Quarterly*.
- Anyone failing to satisfy the specific provisions of this act can be fined up to $10,000 and be imprisoned for up to five years.

The act was very limited and did not succeed in regulating lobbying to any great degree for several reasons. First, the Supreme Court restricted the application of the law only to those lobbyists who seek to influence federal legislation directly.[12] Any lobbyist seeking to influence legislation indirectly through public opinion did not fall within the scope of the law. Second,

perception versus REALITY

Dishing Out the Pork

As you have read in this chapter, countless interest groups are vying for influence over politicians and public policy. Like it or not, many interest groups win support for their programs and ideas. Each year, the federal government adds billions of dollars to spending bills for special interest causes. This practice is commonly referred to as *pork barrel* spending. Who, you may ask, receives all of this *pork*?

THE PERCEPTION

Most Americans think that their federal tax dollars are, for the most part, divided equitably among the states. They believe that if the citizens of Maryland, for example, contribute $70 billion in federal taxes, then roughly the same amount returns to the state in various forms of federal spending. Many Americans also assume that their tax dollars go toward projects and programs—such as public education, roads, and national defense—that benefit a majority of citizens.

THE REALITY

In fact, congressional budgets tell quite a different story. Consider the 2005 congressional budget. North Dakota was given $335,000 to protect its sunflowers from blackbirds. Congress earmarked $443,000 to aid the development of salmon-fortified baby food in Alaska, and the Norwegian American Foundation in Seattle netted

$1 million. Indeed, Missouri corralled $50,000 in pork to combat wild hogs.

Such spending is nothing new. Men and women in Congress have long used pork to reward special interest groups that helped them win elections. Pork also allows members of Congress to prove to their home states that they are working on behalf of the people who sent them to Washington, D.C.

In addition, federal spending can be far from equitable. Senators and representatives with many years of experience in Congress tend to sit on important committees and have greater influence on how money is spent (you will read more about Congress in Chapter 11). For example, Senator Richard Shelby from Alabama, who serves on the powerful Senate Appropriations Committee, won enough special items for his state to fill twenty press releases in one month alone during 2005. From 1991 to 2001, Alabama obtained $100 billion more than its citizens paid in taxes. In contrast, California, New York, and Illinois each paid about $250 billion more than they received over that same period of time.[13]

What's Your Opinion?

Do you believe that pork barrel spending is undemocratic? Why or why not?

only persons or organizations whose principal purpose was to influence legislation were required to register. Many groups avoided registration by claiming that their principal function was something else. Third, the act did not cover lobbying directed at agencies in the executive branch or lobbyists who testified before congressional committees. Fourth, the public was almost totally unaware of the information in the quarterly reports, and Congress created no agency to oversee interest group activities. Not until 1995 did Congress finally address these loopholes by enacting new legislation.

The Lobbying Disclosure Act of 1995

In 1995, Congress passed new lobbying legislation that reformed the 1946 act in the following ways:

- Strict definitions now apply to determine who must register with the clerk of the House and the secretary of the Senate as a lobbyist. A lobbyist is anyone who either spends at least 20 percent of his or her time lobbying members of Congress, their staffs, or executive-branch officials, or is paid more than $5,000 in a six-month period for such work. Any organization that spends more than $20,000 in a six-month period conducting such lobbying activity must also register.
- Lobbyists must report their clients, the issues on which they lobbied, and the agency or house they contacted, although they do not need to disclose the names of individuals they contacted.

Tax-exempt organizations, such as religious groups, were exempted from these provisions, as were organizations that engage in grassroots lobbying, such as a media campaign that asks people to write or call their congressional representative. Nonetheless, the number of registered lobbyists nearly doubled in the first few years of the new legislation.

Interest Groups and Your Everyday Life

Interest groups exist in our political arena for only one reason: to influence political outcomes. The goal of interest groups is to inform the public and lobby the politicians about the good or bad aspects of some proposed policy. In addition, some interest groups may propose policies and then seek support from the public and politicians for those proposals. The success of interest groups is usually measured by the extent to which their members benefit from legislation. Realize, though, that any law passed by Congress affects not only the members of the interest group or groups that lobbied for the law's passage but all Americans.

Therefore, interest group activities very much affect your everyday life. At times, you might be among the Americans who benefit from a particular interest group's activities, even though you are not a member of that interest group. At other times, you may be affected adversely by legislation resulting from interest groups lobbying Congress. Consider some examples:

▶ The lobbying efforts of labor unions over the years have led to improved conditions in the workplace for all American workers, not just for union members. At the same time, labor interest groups have sometimes created severe barriers to entry in a given trade—the building trades, to cite just one example. Those who were able to get unionized jobs in the building trades benefited; others did not.

▶ For years, the American automobile industry successfully lobbied to have Congress and the president restrict imports of Japanese automobiles to protect American manufacturing interests. The same scenario has occurred at various times for steel products, citizen-band radios, chrome, and cheeses. While American companies producing these products benefited from restrictions on imports, the end result for you, as a consumer, is higher prices for cars, steel products, and so on because of less competition from imports.

▶ Public education interest groups have lobbied for benefits for teachers and the American public school system that employs them, yet these groups may also have restricted educational choices. Most families in America face a monopoly situation in K through 12 (kindergarten through high school) schooling.

That is to say, unless they have the resources to send their children to private schools, they must accept the public school that is closest to their house.

▶ Consumer groups have successfully lobbied for improved auto safety. As a result, cars now have padded dashboards, shoulder harnesses, air bags, high-impact bumpers, and the like. At the same time, these safety measures have driven up the prices of the cars we drive.

Taking Action

An obvious way to get involved in politics is to join an interest group whose goals you endorse, including one of the organizations on your campus. You can find lists of interest groups operating at the local, state, and national levels by simply going to a search engine online, such as Google, and keying in the words "interest groups." If you have a particular interest or goal that you would like to promote, consider forming your own group, as a group of Iowa students did when they formed a group called Students Toward Environmental Protection. In the photo alongside, a student of Grinnell College in Iowa holds a protest sign during a rally. The students wanted Iowa's lawmakers to issue tougher regulations governing factory farms and to expand the state's bottle deposit requirements.

AP Photo/Charlie Neibergall

Key Terms

direct technique 138	labor force 134	pluralist theory 131	rating system 141
free rider problem 130	lobbying 138	political action committee (PAC) 141	trade organization 132
indirect technique 141	lobbyist 138		
interest group 129	patron 130	public-interest group 132	

Chapter Summary

1 An interest group is an organization of people sharing common objectives who actively attempt to influence government policy-

makers through direct and indirect methods. Interest groups differ from political parties in that interest groups pursue specialized interests, are tightly organized, and do not compete for public office, as parties do.

2 Interest groups (a) help bridge the gap between citizens and government; (b) help raise public awareness and inspire action on various issues; (c) often provide public officials with specialized and detailed information, which helps officials to make informed public-policy choices; and (d) help to ensure that public officials are carrying out their duties responsibly. Pluralist theory explains American politics as a contest among various interest groups that compete at all levels of government to gain benefits for their members. Concerns over the potential harm that can be caused by interest groups, or factions, date back to the beginning of the nation.

3 The most common interest groups are private groups that seek government policies that will benefit (or at least, not harm) their members' interests. Many major interest groups are concerned with issues affecting the following areas or groups of persons: business, labor, agriculture, consumers, senior citizens, the environment, and professionals.

4 Direct techniques used by interest groups include lobbying and providing election support, particularly through the use of political action committees (PACs). Indirect techniques include advertising and other promotional efforts, mobilizing constituents, bringing lawsuits, and organizing demonstrations and protests. Regulating interest group contributions for "issue advocacy" presents a particularly thorny challenge because free speech issues are necessarily involved.

5 Interest group representatives serve as information sources for members of Congress. Government policymakers, in turn, often serve as political consultants or lobbyists for interest groups on leaving government office.

6 The Federal Regulation of Lobbying Act of 1946 attempted to regulate the activities of lobbyists, but it contained many loopholes. Lobbyists were able to continue influencing legislation with little government oversight or disclosure of their activities. In 1995, the Lobbying Disclosure Act created stricter definitions of who is a lobbyist, forcing many more lobbyists to register and report their activities to Congress.

RESOURCES FOR FURTHER STUDY

Selected Readings

Cigler, Allan J., and Burdett A. Loomis, eds. *Interest Group Politics,* 6th ed. Washington, D.C.: CQ Press, 2002. This sixth edition contains many new essays, including examinations of religious activists, environmental groups, and consumer groups. The editors assert that a new era of interest group politics is emerging.

Goldstein, Kenneth M. *Interest Groups, Lobbying, and Participation in America.* New York: Cambridge University Press, 2003. This book develops and tests a theory of how tactical choices in a grassroots campaign are made.

Herrnson, Paul S., Ronald G. Shaiko, and Clyde Wilcox, eds. *The Interest Group Connection: Electioneering, Lobbying, and Policymaking in Washington,* 2d ed. Washington, D.C.: CQ Press, 2004. This collection of new essays from leading scholars examines the theory and the reality of interest groups' influence on public policymaking.

Singer, P. W. *Corporate Warriors: The Rise of the Privatized Military Industry.* Ithaca, N.Y.: Cornell University Press, 2004. The author provides a comprehensive analysis of the private military industry, exploring the many implications of its rise.

Politics on the Web

- To find particular interest groups online, a good point of departure is the Internet Public Library Association, which provides links to hundreds of professional and trade associations. Go to **http://www.ipl.org/ref/AON**

- The Institute for Global Communications offers a host of lobbying and public-interest activities. Its home page can be accessed at **http://www.igc.apc.org**

- You can access the National Rifle Association online at **http://www.nra.org**

- The AARP's Web site can be found at **http://www.aarp.org**

- To learn about the activities of the National Education Association, go to **http://www.nea.org**

- You can find information on environmental issues and the activities of the National Resources Defense Council at **http://www.nrdc.org**

Online Resources for This Chapter

This text's Companion Web Site, at **http://www.americaatodds.com**, offers links to numerous resources that you can utilize to learn more about the topics covered in this chapter. For a list describing these resources, see the inside front cover of this book.

chapter 7
political parties

CHAPTER OBJECTIVES

After reading this chapter, you should be able to . . .

▶ Explain what a political party is and how parties function in American politics and government.

▶ Summarize the origins and development of the two-party system in the United States.

▶ Provide some of the reasons why the two-party system has endured.

▶ Describe the different types of third parties and how they function in the American political system.

▶ Discuss the structure of American political parties.

Do Colleges Shun Conservative Views?

American colleges pride themselves on their commitment to diversity. Many schools maintain that a well-rounded education comes, in part, from exposure to a variety of viewpoints and cultures. Academia, however, appears to many to be dominated by politically left-leaning individuals.

At esteemed Ivy League universities, such as Brown, Harvard, and Cornell, nearly 95 percent of the faculty members who are registered to vote belong to either the Democratic Party or the Green Party. Similarly, at leading public universities, such as Penn State University, the University of California at Los Angeles, and the University of Maryland, more than 85 percent of the faculty members have left-leaning political views. Some Americans believe that such a lack of political diversity degrades the quality of higher education and shows a bias in favor of hiring liberals. Others argue that political liberals are simply more inclined to pursue an academic career than conservatives and that party affiliation has nothing to do with the hiring process.

Colleges Are Hotbeds of Liberal Bias, Say Some

Academics have long denounced the U.S. military as a bastion of conservatism. Yet university faculties boast an almost unparalleled orthodoxy of political ideology and affiliation. Conservative commentator David Horowitz argues that the rise of a liberal majority at universities "has resulted in politicized hiring practices, systematic exclusion of dissenting voices, and an atmosphere of political intimidation."

In 2004, the Duke Conservative Union at Duke University ran an advertisement in the school's newspaper that called attention to the widely disproportionate number of liberals in many academic departments. Responding to the ad, Professor Robert Brandon remarked in the school's newspaper, "If, as John Stuart Mill said, 'stupid people are generally conservative,' then there are lots of conservatives we will never hire." Although Brandon and most academics deny any official hiring bias based on political views, such comments are difficult to ignore.

Some, including Horowitz, argue that the political bias curtails a free exchange of ideas on many campuses and creates an atmosphere more akin to indoctrination than education. Representative Jack Kingston (R., Ga.) adds another element to the debate on political bias, claiming that campus funding for organizations is distributed at a 50:1 ratio for groups with "leftist agendas" over conservative groups. Kingston, along with Representative Walter Jones (R., N.C.), is currently attempting to push an "Academic Bill of Rights" through Congress that, in theory, would promote pluralism, diversity, openness, and fairness on college campuses.

Political Bias Is a Myth, Say Others

Many college administrators and professors bristle at the idea that political discrimination exists either in the classroom or in the hiring of new faculty. They claim that studies showing the political affiliations of professors are misleading. Such studies, they argue, wrongly assume that professors seek to use their courses as a forum to politically indoctrinate students. Many professors intentionally argue viewpoints contrary to their own in the classroom setting, both to expose students to a variety of perspectives and to teach critical-thinking and analytical skills. Furthermore, many disciplines, such as math and chemistry, have no political component, so a professor's partisanship is completely irrelevant.

Some argue that making assumptions of bias based on party affiliation can be dangerous. Many are quick to point out that both parties contain a large number of political "moderates" who do not adhere to some of the more radical views of the party.

With respect to hiring, most academics claim that political ideology or affiliation does not surface when selecting the best candidate for a job. Usually, a new faculty member's political ideology does not become evident until he or she settles into the position, they argue. The decision to retain a faculty member or to grant tenure is based almost entirely on the quality of the individual's teaching and the strength of her or his publications and research.

Where Do You Stand?

1. In which types of courses, if any, would a professor's political views or party affiliation affect the way the class was taught? How? Why?

2. Some argue that faculties should have a more equal number of liberal and conservative professors. What do you think of such a proposal?

Explore This Issue Online

- The *Chronicle of Higher Education* has served as a forum for the debate over bias in the hiring and promotion process. To view the *Chronicle* online, go to **http://www.chronicle.com**.
- Students for Academic Freedom (SAF) is a group that has sprouted up on numerous campuses nationwide in response to the perceived liberal bias of college faculties. To access SAF's national Web site, go to **http://www.studentsforacademicfreedom.org**.

Introduction

Political ideology and party affiliation can spark heated debates between Americans, as you read in the chapter-opening *America at Odds* feature. A **political party** can be defined as a group of individuals *outside the government* who organize to win elections, operate the government, and determine policy. Political parties serve as major vehicles for citizen participation in our political system. It is hard to imagine democracy without political parties. Political parties provide a way for the public to choose who will serve in government and which policies will be carried out. Even citizens who do not identify with any political party or who choose not to participate in elections are affected by party activities and influence on government.

Political parties were an unforeseen development in American political history. The founders defined many other important institutions, such as the presidency and Congress, and described their functions in the Constitution. Political parties, however, are not even mentioned in the Constitution. In fact, the founders decried factions and parties. Thomas Jefferson probably best expressed the founders' antiparty sentiments when he declared, "If I could not go to heaven but with a party, I would not go there at all."[1]

If the founders did not want political parties, who was supposed to organize political campaigns and mobilize supporters of political candidates? Clearly, there was a practical need for some kind of organizing group to form a link between citizens and their government. Even our early national leaders, for all their antiparty feelings, realized this; several of them were active in establishing or organizing the first political parties.

A Short History of American Political Parties

Political parties have been a part of American politics since the early years of our nation. Throughout the course of our history, several parties have formed, and some have disappeared. Even today, although we have only two major political parties, numerous other parties are also contending for power, as will be discussed later in this chapter.

The First Political Parties

The founders reacted negatively to the idea of political parties because they thought the power struggles that would occur between small economic and political groups would eventually topple the balanced democracy they wanted to create. Nonetheless, two major political factions—the Federalists and Anti-Federalists—were formed even before the Constitution was ratified. Remember from Chapter 2 that the Federalists pushed for the ratification of the Constitution because they wanted a stronger national government than the one that had existed under the Articles of Confederation. The Anti-Federalists argued against ratification. They supported states' rights and feared a too-powerful central government.

These two national factions continued, in somewhat altered form, after the Constitution was ratified. Alexander Hamilton, the first secretary of the Treasury, became the leader of the Federalist Party, which supported a strong central government that would encourage the development of commerce and manufacturing. The Federalists generally thought that a democracy should be ruled by its wealthiest and best-educated citizens. Opponents of the Federalists and Hamilton's policies referred to themselves not as Anti-Federalists, but as Republicans. Today, they are often referred to as Democratic Republicans, or Jeffersonian Republicans, to distinguish this group from the later Republican Party. The Democratic Republicans were more sympathetic to the "common man" and favored a more limited role for government. They believed that the nation's welfare would be best served if the states had more power than the central government. In their view, Congress should dominate the government, and government policies should help the nation's shopkeepers, farmers, and laborers.

State University of New York trustee Candace de Russy works at her home. A conservative academic, de Russy's quill has skewered multiculturalism, radical feminism, some black studies programs, and anti-Americanism on campuses nationwide.

political party A group of individuals outside the government who organize to win elections, operate the government, and determine policy.

In 1796, John Adams (left), the Federalists' candidate to succeed George Washington as president, defeated Thomas Jefferson.

Library of Congress

From 1796 to 1860

The nation's first two parties clashed openly in the elections of 1796, in which John Adams, the Federalists' candidate to succeed George Washington as president, defeated Thomas Jefferson. Over the next four years, Jefferson and James Madison worked to extend the influence of the Democratic Republican Party. In the presidential elections of 1800 and 1804, Jefferson won the presidency under the Democratic Republican banner. His party also won control of Congress. The Federalists never returned to power and thus became the first (but not the last) American party to go out of existence. (See the time line of American political parties in Figure 7–1.)

The Democratic Republicans dominated American politics for the next twenty years. Jefferson was succeeded in the White House by two other Democratic Republicans—James Madison and James Monroe. In the mid-1820s, however, the Democratic Republicans split into two groups. Andrew Jackson, who was elected president in 1828, aligned himself with the group that called themselves the Democrats. The Democrats were mostly small farmers and debtors. The other group, the National Republicans (later the Whig Party), was led by the well-known John Quincy Adams and Henry Clay and the great orator Daniel Webster. It was a coalition of bankers, business owners, and southern planters.

Andrew Jackson (1767–1845) was the greatest military hero of his time and became associated with increased popular participation in government. The National Republican Party, a split-off from the Democratic Republican Party, was formed by John Q. Adams and Henry Clay to oppose Jackson's 1828 campaign for the presidency. Jackson won the election, nonetheless.

As the Whigs and Democrats competed for the White House throughout the 1840s and 1850s, the two-party system as we know it today emerged. Both parties were large, with well-known leaders and supporters across the nation. They both had grassroots organizations of party workers committed to winning as many political offices (at all levels of government) for the party as possible. Both the Whigs and the Democrats remained vague on the issue of slavery, and the Democrats were divided into northern and southern camps. By the mid-1850s, the Whig coalition fell apart, and most Whigs were absorbed into the new Republican Party, which opposed the extension of slavery into new territories. Campaigning on this platform, the Republicans succeeded in electing Abraham Lincoln as the first Republican president in 1860.

From the Civil War to the Great Depression

By the end of the Civil War in 1865, the Republicans and the Democrats were the most prominent political parties. From the election of Abraham Lincoln in 1860 until the election of Franklin Delano Roosevelt in 1932, the Republican Party, sometimes referred to as the Grand Old Party, or the GOP, remained the majority party in national politics, winning all but four presidential elections.

After the Great Depression

The social and economic impact of the Great Depression of the 1930s destroyed the majority support that the Republicans had enjoyed for so long and contributed to a realignment in the

Library of Congress

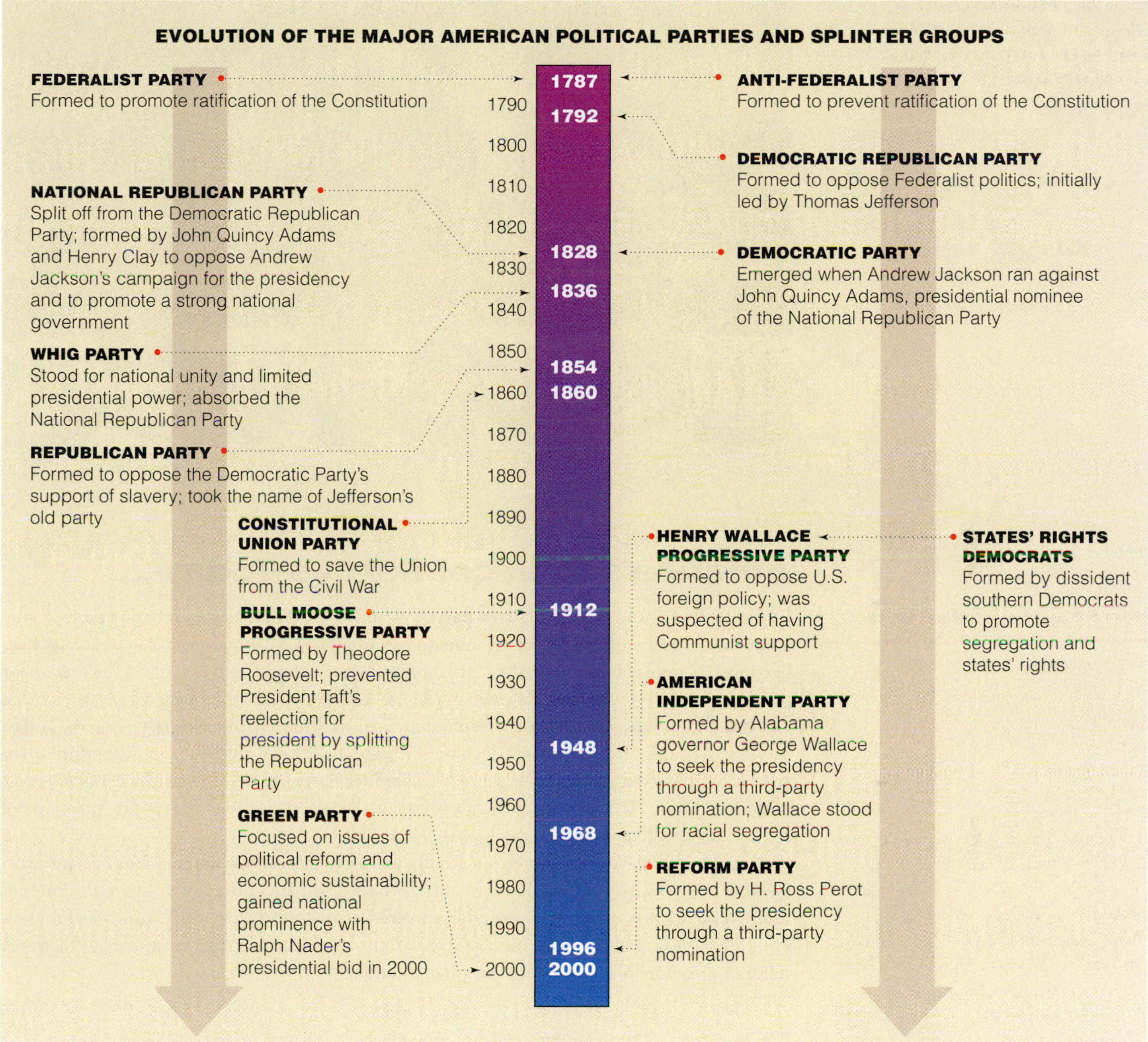

EVOLUTION OF THE MAJOR AMERICAN POLITICAL PARTIES AND SPLINTER GROUPS

FEDERALIST PARTY
Formed to promote ratification of the Constitution

ANTI-FEDERALIST PARTY
Formed to prevent ratification of the Constitution

NATIONAL REPUBLICAN PARTY
Split off from the Democratic Republican Party; formed by John Quincy Adams and Henry Clay to oppose Andrew Jackson's campaign for the presidency and to promote a strong national government

DEMOCRATIC REPUBLICAN PARTY
Formed to oppose Federalist politics; initially led by Thomas Jefferson

DEMOCRATIC PARTY
Emerged when Andrew Jackson ran against John Quincy Adams, presidential nominee of the National Republican Party

WHIG PARTY
Stood for national unity and limited presidential power; absorbed the National Republican Party

REPUBLICAN PARTY
Formed to oppose the Democratic Party's support of slavery; took the name of Jefferson's old party

CONSTITUTIONAL UNION PARTY
Formed to save the Union from the Civil War

BULL MOOSE PROGRESSIVE PARTY
Formed by Theodore Roosevelt; prevented President Taft's reelection for president by splitting the Republican Party

GREEN PARTY
Focused on issues of political reform and economic sustainability; gained national prominence with Ralph Nader's presidential bid in 2000

HENRY WALLACE PROGRESSIVE PARTY
Formed to oppose U.S. foreign policy; was suspected of having Communist support

AMERICAN INDEPENDENT PARTY
Formed by Alabama governor George Wallace to seek the presidency through a third-party nomination; Wallace stood for racial segregation

REFORM PARTY
Formed by H. Ross Perot to seek the presidency through a third-party nomination

STATES' RIGHTS DEMOCRATS
Formed by dissident southern Democrats to promote segregation and states' rights

Years: 1787, 1790, 1792, 1800, 1810, 1820, 1828, 1830, 1836, 1840, 1850, 1854, 1860, 1870, 1880, 1890, 1900, 1910, 1912, 1920, 1930, 1940, 1948, 1950, 1960, 1968, 1970, 1980, 1990, 1996, 2000

FIGURE 7-1
A Time Line of U.S. Political Parties

realigning election An election in which the popular support for and relative strength of the parties shift as the parties are reestablished with different coalitions of supporters.

two-party system. In a **realigning election,** the popular support for and relative strength of the parties shift. As a result, the minority (opposition) party may emerge as the majority party. (A realigning election can also reestablish the majority party in power, albeit with a different coalition of supporters.) The landmark realigning election of 1932 brought Franklin D. Roosevelt to the presidency and the Democrats back to power at the national level. Realigning elections also occurred in 1860, 1896, and arguably, 1968.

Roosevelt was reelected to the presidency in 1936, 1940, and 1944. When he died in office in 1945, his vice president, Harry Truman, assumed the presidential office. Truman ran for the presidency in 1948 and won the election. A Republican candidate, Dwight D. Eisenhower, won the presidential elections of 1952 and 1956. From 1960 through 1968, the Democrats, led by John F. Kennedy and Lyndon B. Johnson, respectively, held power. The Republicans came back into power in 1968 and, except for Jimmy Carter's one term (1977–1981), retained the presidency until Bill Clinton was elected in 1992. The Republicans regained the presidency in 2001, when George W. Bush became president.

In Congress, the Democrats were the dominant party from the Great Depression until 1994, when the Republicans gained control of both houses. They have held control of Congress ever since, except for two years when the Democrats controlled the Senate by one vote.

Chief Justice Charles Evans Hughes
administering the oath of office to
Franklin Delano Roosevelt on the
east portico of the U.S. Capitol,
March 4, 1933.

Library of Congress

America's Political Parties Today

two-party system A political system
in which two strong and established
parties compete for political offices.

In the United States, we have a **two-party system.** This means that two major parties—the
Democrats and the Republicans—dominate national politics. Why has the two-party system
become so firmly entrenched in the United States? According to some scholars, the first major
political division between the Federalists and the Anti-Federalists established a precedent that
continued over time and ultimately resulted in the domination of the two-party system. Today,
both the Republican Party and the Democratic Party tend to be moderate, middle-of-the-road
parties built on compromise. The parties' similarities have often led to criticism; their sternest
critics call them "Tweedledee" and "Tweedledum."[2] (We will discuss the policy positions of
the two parties in more detail later in this chapter.)

Recent polling data indicate that a sizable number of American voters (about 40 percent)
feel that the two-party system does not address issues that are important to them or represent
their views; 67 percent say they would like to see a strong third party run candidates for president, Congress, and state and local offices.[3] Yet the two-party system continues to thrive. A
number of factors help to explain this phenomenon.

The Self-Perpetuation of the Two-Party System

One of the major reasons for the perpetuation of the two-party system is simply that there is
no alternative. Minor parties, called *third parties,*[4] traditionally have found it extremely difficult to compete with the major parties for votes. As you will read later in this chapter, the reasons for this are multifold, including election laws and institutional barriers.

Election Laws Favoring Two Parties   American election laws tend to favor
the major parties. In many states, for example, the established major parties need relatively few
signatures to place their candidates on the ballot, whereas a third party must get many more
signatures. The criterion is often based on the total party vote in the last election, which penal-
izes a new party competing for the first time.

The rules governing campaign financing also favor the major parties. As you will read in
Chapter 9, both major parties receive federal funds for campaign expenses and for their
national conventions. Third parties, in contrast, receive federal funds only if they garner 5 percent of the vote, and they receive the funds only *after* the election.

Institutional Barriers to a Multiparty System   The structure of our insti-
tutions—from single-member congressional districts to the winner-take-all electoral system—

prevents third parties from enjoying electoral success. One of the major institutional barriers is the winner-take-all feature of the electoral college system for electing the president (discussed in more detail in Chapter 9). In a winner-take-all system, the winner of a state's popular vote gets all of that state's electoral votes. Thus, third-party candidates have little incentive to run for president because they are unlikely to get enough popular votes to receive any state's electoral votes. (Two states—Maine and Nebraska—also allocate their electoral votes proportionately.)

Another institutional barrier to a multiparty system is the single-member district. Today, all federal and most state legislative districts are single-member districts—that is, voters elect one member from their district to the House of Representatives and to their state legislature.[5] In most European countries, by contrast, districts are drawn as multimember districts and are represented by multiple elected officials from different parties, according to the proportion of the vote their party received.

Finally, third parties find it difficult to break through in an electoral system that perpetuates their own failure: because third parties normally do not win elections, Americans tend not to vote for them or to contribute to their campaigns, so they do not win elections. As long as Americans hold to the perception that third parties can never win big in an election, the current two-party system is likely to persist.

AMERICA at odds

Should Third-Party Candidates Debate?

Only twice since 1960, when the first presidential debate was held on television, have American TV viewers and radio listeners been able to hear the voice of a third-party candidate. The first third-party candidate to participate in a debate was John Anderson in 1980, and the second was H. Ross Perot in 1992. In 1996, the Commission for Presidential Debates (CPD) chose not to allow any third-party candidates on the air because they did not have a "realistic" chance of succeeding at the polls.[6] In the 2000 and 2004 elections, third-party candidates were again excluded from the debates. Under the CPD's criteria for participating in the 2004 debates, only candidates who had a level of support of at least 15 percent of the national electorate could participate.

Critics of the CPD's decisions point out that the founders had strong feelings about the right of the people to govern themselves through free elections. And free elections mean little if minor-party candidates do not have realistic access to public forums, such as televised debates. Furthermore, the CPD is not a government organization but a nonprofit corporation consisting of three Republicans and three Democrats and co-chaired by former heads of the Republican National Committee and the Democratic National Committee. Small wonder, say these critics, that third-party candidates are excluded from the debates.

Supporters of the CPD's position point out that opening up the presidential and vice presidential debates to third-party candidates could lead to chaos. Where would you draw the line? Should all third-party candidates be allowed to participate, even those who have virtually no electoral support? Standards of some kind are needed for deciding who can and who cannot participate. Furthermore, third parties have always been an unpredictable element in American politics. Allowing parties that have little national support to participate in the debates would only lead to political confusion.

Components of the Two Major American Parties

The two major American political parties are sometimes described as three-dimensional entities. This is because each party consists of three components: (1) the party in the electorate, (2) the party organization, and (3) the party in government.

The Party in the Electorate   The party in the **electorate** is the largest component, consisting of all of those people who describe themselves as Democrats or Republicans.

electorate All of the citizens eligible to vote in a given election.

There are no dues, no membership cards, and no obligatory duties. Members of the party in the electorate never need to work on a campaign or attend a party meeting. In most states, they may register as Democrats or Republicans, but registration is not legally binding and can be changed at will.

The Party Organization

Each major party has a national organization with national, state, and local offices. As will be discussed later in this chapter, the party organizations include several levels of people who maintain the party's strength between elections, make its rules, raise money, organize conventions, help with elections, and recruit candidates.

The Party in Government

The party in government consists of all of the candidates who have won elections and now hold public office. Even though members of Congress, state legislators, presidents, and all other officeholders almost always run for office as either Democrats or Republicans, the individual candidates do not always agree on government policy. The party in government helps to organize the government's agenda by coaxing and convincing its own party members to vote for its policies. If the party is to translate its promises into public policies, the job must be done by the party in government.

Where the Parties Stand on the Issues

party platform The document drawn up by each party at its national convention that outlines the policies and positions of the party.

Each of the two major political parties, as well as most of the minor parties, develops a **party platform,** or declaration of beliefs. The platform represents the official party position on various issues, although neither all party members nor all candidates running on the party's ticket share these positions exactly. The major parties usually revise their platforms every four years at the party's national convention, which is held to nominate a presidential and a vice presidential candidate. A new party agenda is also usually announced every two years as a new session of Congress gets under way. The party agendas of the Democrats and Republicans for the 109th Congress are shown in Table 7–1.

TABLE 7-1

Agendas of the Democratic and Republican Parties for the 109th Congress

DEMOCRATIC AGENDA	REPUBLICAN AGENDA
Homeland Security—To address existing vulnerabilities in our homeland security and authorize grants for first responders and state and local governments.	**Economic Growth**—To provide immediate job growth while laying the groundwork for long-term economic prosperity; to rally the stock market and energize the economy.
Medicare Prescription Drug Benefits—To legalize the safe importation of FDA-approved drugs from other industrialized countries.	**Federal Budget**—To craft a budget that funds important priorities, such as homeland security, defense, and other national needs.
Education Reform—To provide full funding for the No Child Left Behind Act of 2002 and to fully fund Head Start programs.	**National Security**—To fund the ongoing war on terrorism, including military efforts.
Pension Protection—To help American families prepare for retirement; to provide participants with better investment education, information, and advice; to protect Social Security benefits.	**Social Security Reform**—To ensure that Social Security remains a viable program for future generations; to explore the possibility of diverting a portion of Social Security taxes into individual accounts for investment purposes.
Health-Care Reform—To expand health coverage, improve the quality of care, and enact a Patients' Bill of Rights.	**Welfare Reform**—To extend welfare reform, strengthen work requirements, and promote marriage and abstinence programs.
Civil Rights—To expand protections against hate crimes and strengthen the enforcement of existing civil rights laws.	**Education Reform**—To monitor implementation of the No Child Left Behind Act of 2002.
Environment—To address global climate change and reduce greenhouse gas emissions.	**Tax Relief**—To make permanent the tax relief of 2001 and 2003, including repeal of the marriage penalty and the death tax.
Veterans' Benefits—To address health-care and death-benefit concerns of veterans.	**Medicare Prescription Drug Benefits**—To address current gaps in prescription drug coverage for seniors.
Crime—To protect Americans from crime and terrorism, assist victims, and improve the administration of justice.	**Liability Reform**—To limit frivolous lawsuits that hurt the economy.

Party platforms do not necessarily tell you what candidates are going to do when they take office, however. For example, although the Democratic Party is generally known as the party of the "little people" and generally favors social legislation to help the underclass in society, it was a Democratic president, Bill Clinton, who signed a major welfare reform bill in 1996, forcing many welfare recipients off the welfare rolls. The Democrats are also known to side with labor unions, yet President Clinton approved the North American Free Trade Agreement, despite bitter public denunciations by most of the nation's unions.

Moreover, a party's platform may not always be perfectly reflected in its congressional agenda. Republicans have often been known to oppose social legislation and welfare and to emphasize self-reliance, yet in an "Open Letter" that appeared in *USA Today* in 1999, Republicans Dennis Hastert (Speaker of the House of Representatives) and Trent Lott (then Senate majority leader) stated that it was time to "move on" to an agenda that would save Social Security, improve education, and ease the tax burden on "working people."[7] Thus, it may be that, as one veteran of American politics has stated, solutions to political issues are found not on the sides of the political spectrum but in the "sensible center."[8]

Events may dramatically alter the agendas of the two political parties. The terrorist attacks of September 11, 2001, thrust national security to the front of the political agendas of the two parties and played an important role in the outcome of the 2004 elections, as discussed in this chapter's *The Politics of National Security* feature on the next page.

Party Affiliation

What does it mean to belong to a political party? In many European countries, being a party member means that you actually join a political party. You get a membership card to carry around in your wallet, you pay dues, and you vote to select your local and national party leaders. In the United States, becoming a member of a political party is far less involved. To be a member of a political party, an American citizen has only to think of herself or himself as a Democrat or a Republican (or a member of a third party, such as the Green Party, the Libertarian Party, or the American Independent Party). Members of parties do not have to pay dues, work for the party, or attend party meetings. Nor must they support the party platform.[9]

Generally, the party in the electorate consists of **party identifiers** (those who identify themselves as being members of a particular party) and the **party elite**—active party members who choose to work for the party and even become candidates for office. Political parties need year-round support from the latter group to survive. During election campaigns in particular,

party identifier A person who identifies himself or herself as being a member of a particular political party.

party elite A loose-knit group of party activists who organize and oversee party functions and planning during and between campaigns.

President Bush shakes hands with Tom Ridge, the first secretary of homeland security, during a welcome ceremony held in 2003. The president's decisive response to the terrorist attacks of September 11, 2001, including the creation of a new cabinet department, strengthened support for his administration.

Reuters NewsMedia, Inc./Corbis

The POLITICS of national SECURITY

War and Party Politics

After September 11, 2001, President George W. Bush declared that the United States was at war with terrorists. Not only has that war continued, but there is no end in sight. In addition, as we all know, Americans actually went to war in both Afghanistan and Iraq. Although military problems in Afghanistan do not make the headlines so often anymore, those in Iraq certainly do. Iraqi insurgents continue to maim and kill men, women, and children, including members of the U.S. armed forces.

THE "WAR THEME" IN THE 2004 ELECTIONS

Both the war on terrorism and our continuing occupation of Iraq were major themes of the 2004 presidential elections. This is not surprising, given that terrorism and the situation in Iraq are still top priorities for Americans. In a February 2005 Gallup poll, 54 percent of Americans polled indicated that terrorism was "extremely important." Additionally, 53 percent said that the situation in Iraq was extremely important. Other issues including same-sex marriages, taxes, and Social Security were considered either less important or much less important.[10]

Not surprisingly—given the election results—the percentage of adults who said that terrorism and the situation in Iraq were "extremely important" differed between Republicans and Democrats. Among Republicans, 63 percent believed that terrorism was extremely important, and 56 percent felt the same about the situation in Iraq, compared to only 42 percent and 51 percent, respectively, of Democrats.

Some political commentators argue that Bush was able to capitalize on these concerns much better than Democratic Party candidate John Kerry during the heated campaign. Many analysts of voting patterns in the 2004 elections reached the same conclusion: the majority of Americans did not want to change the commander in chief during a time of covert and overt war. Ironically, Kerry was unable to successfully promote his military record in the Vietnam War. The fact that George W. Bush never served on active duty apparently did not bother voters who saw him as a strong commander in chief.

NOT ALL DEMOCRATS CRITICIZED THE WAR IN IRAQ

Many commentators continue to argue that the majority of Democrats oppose war and did not (and still do not) support the country's military activities in Iraq. Not all of the Democratic presidential hopefuls for 2008 share this view, however. Senator Hillary Rodham Clinton (D., N.Y.), wife of former president Bill Clinton, is viewed as one of the most likely Democratic presidential candidates

Reuters/Dusan Vranic/Pool/Landov

Senator Hillary Rodham Clinton (D., N.Y.) traveled to Iraq to visit U.S. troops in 2003 and again in 2005. Republicans and Democrats alike have realized they must address issues relating to foreign policy and terrorism because national security will continue to be a major election theme in the future.

in the 2008 presidential race. Senator Clinton has rarely explicitly criticized President Bush for his actions in Afghanistan and Iraq. She voted in favor of the U.S.-led invasion of Iraq in 2002 and has consistently stated that she stands by her decision to support Bush's call for military action.

Indeed, Senator Clinton made a point of visiting American troops in Iraq in 2003 and again in 2005. She has encouraged increasing the size of the U.S. Army and believes that more soldiers and military equipment should be committed to Iraq and Afghanistan. Moreover, on numerous occasions she has expressed support for the U.S. military and the "fine job that it has been doing."

Faced with the realities of a post–September 11 America, both parties have realized that they must address issues related to the nation's safety. National security, both at home and abroad, will surely continue to be a major election theme for years to come.

Are We Safer?

Do you believe that retaining the same commander in chief during a period of terrorism and foreign military engagements makes Americans safer? Why or why not?

candidates depend on active party members or volunteers to mail literature, answer phones, conduct door-to-door canvasses, organize speeches and appearances, and, of course, donate money. Between elections, parties also need active members to plan the upcoming elections, organize fund-raisers, and stay in touch with party leaders in other communities to keep the party strong. Generally, the major functions of American political parties are carried out by the party elite.

Why People Join Political Parties

Generally, in the United States people belong to a political party because they agree with many of its main ideas and support some of its candidates. In a few countries, such as the People's Republic of China, people belong to a political party because they are required to do so to get ahead in life, regardless of whether they agree with the party's ideas and candidates.

People join political parties for a multitude of reasons. One reason is that people wish to express their **solidarity,** or mutual agreement, with the views of friends, loved ones, and other like-minded people. People also join parties because they enjoy the excitement of politics. In addition, many believe they will benefit materially from joining a party through better employment or personal career advancement. The traditional institution of **patronage**—rewarding the party faithful with government jobs or contracts—lives on, even though it has been limited to prevent abuses.[11] Finally, some join political parties because they wish to actively promote a set of ideals and principles that they feel are important to American politics and society.

As a rule, people join political parties because of their overall agreement with what a particular party stands for. Thus, when interviewed, people may make the following remarks when asked why they support the Democratic Party: "It seems that the economy is better when the Democrats are in control." "The Democrats are for the working people." People might say about the Republican Party: "The Republicans help small businesses more than the Democrats." "The Republicans deal better with foreign policy issues."

solidarity Mutual agreement with others in a particular group.

patronage A system of rewarding the party faithful and workers with government jobs or contracts.

Demographic Factors and Party Identification

Regardless of how accurate or inaccurate these stereotypes are, individuals with similar characteristics do tend to align themselves more often with one or the other major party. Such factors as race, age, income, education, and marital status all influence party identification.

Normally, slightly more men than women identify with the Republican Party, and more women than men identify themselves as Democrats. While slightly more whites identify with the Republican Party, people in the other categories (nonwhite, black, and Hispanic) overwhelmingly classify themselves as Democrats. As to age, the most notable differences in party preferences are found in those over age sixty-five: a significantly larger number of people in this group identify themselves as Democrats than as Republicans. As mentioned, other factors, such as income, religion, and marital status, also seem to influence party preference. (For a discussion of geography as a factor in party identification and the 2004 elections, see this chapter's *Perception versus Reality* feature on the following page.)

Although there is clearly a link between these factors and party preference, each party encompasses diverse interests and activities. Both political parties welcome various groups and strive to attract as many members as possible.

What Do Political Parties Do?

As noted earlier, the Constitution does not mention political parties. Historically, though, political parties have played a vital role in our democratic system. Their main function has been to link the people's policy preferences to actual government policies. Political parties also perform many other functions.

Selecting Candidates

One of the most important functions of the two political parties is to recruit and nominate candidates for political office. This function simplifies voting choices for the electorate. Political parties take the large number of people who want to run for office and narrow the field to one candidate. They accomplish this by the use of the **primary,** which is a preliminary election to choose a party's final candidate. It is much easier for voters to choose between two candidates who have been selected by established political parties than to choose among many candidates.

primary A preliminary election held for the purpose of choosing a party's final candidate.

Red versus Blue America

Following the 2004 presidential elections, news organizations placed great emphasis on the electoral map. The map depicted states won by Democratic Party candidate John Kerry in blue, while the states won by Republican candidate President George W. Bush were in red. The visual evidence provided by these maps showed clusters of "blue states" on the West Coast, the upper Midwest, and the Northeast, while vast tracts in the southern and middle United States were bathed in red.

THE PERCEPTION

The sheer amount of land covered by "red states" on the electoral map is visually impressive. Many Americans looked at the map and assumed that Bush had won a stunning majority. Some commentators argued that the map showed a country deeply divided along geographic lines. These commentators used phrases like "red versus blue America," arguing that there was a growing political and cultural rift between regions of the United States. Red states were characterized as strongholds of evangelical Christians bent on imposing their "moral values" on all Americans. Blue states were said to be filled with liberals who passionately disliked President Bush and were ready to leave the country if he won reelection. One political cartoonist even labeled the blue states "The United States of Canada" and the red states "Jesusland."

THE REALITY

The 2004 presidential election results were far from a landslide, regardless of the visual impression given by the electoral map. President Bush won the elections by less than a 3 percent margin in the popular vote. Similarly, the electoral college count was one of the closest in American history (Bush won by a mere thirty-five electoral votes), with ultimate victory hinging on a narrow win in Ohio for Bush. Indeed, Bush's victory was far from lopsided.

The electoral map also overstated the perceived geographic divide plaguing the United States. Simply looking at red and blue states on a map fails to recognize that citizens within those states did not necessarily vote overwhelmingly in favor of one candidate or the other. In 2004, Bush won a greater percentage of the votes in fifteen of the twenty states that he had lost in the 2000 elections. In fact, only in twelve states did either candidate garner more than 60 percent of the vote. Furthermore, Bush or Kerry won every county of a state in only seven states. Broken down to the county and local levels, the states show patches of both red and blue.

What's Your Opinion?

Many claim that the United States is becoming more politically polarized. In what ways do you feel Americans are politically divided?

Dave Ruderman, buzzflash.com

Informing the Public

Political parties help educate the public about important current political issues. In recent years, these issues have included defense and environmental policies, our tax system, welfare reform, crime, education, and Social Security. Each party presents its view of these issues through television announcements, newspaper articles or ads, Web site materials, campaign speeches, rallies, debates, and pamphlets. These activities help citizens learn about the issues, consider proposed solutions, and form opinions.

Through these activities, political parties also help to stimulate citizens' interest and participation in public affairs. They seek people to work at party headquarters or to help with door-to-door canvasses, which involve distributing campaign literature and asking people to vote for the party's candidate. Political parties also ask volunteers to work at polling places where people cast their votes during elections and to drive voters to the polling places. Through such pursuits, citizens can participate in the political process.

"Someday, son, all this and more will be yours if you remember to always support the Republican party."

©Edward Frascino/Cartoon Bank

"I'd like to have myself frozen until the Democrats regain control of Congress."

©Mischa Richter/Cartoon Bank

Coordinating Policymaking

In our complex government, parties are essential for coordinating policy among the various branches of the government. The political party is usually the major institution through which the executive and legislative branches cooperate with each other. Each president, cabinet head, and member of Congress is normally a member of the Democratic or the Republican Party. The party with fewer members in the legislature is the **minority party.** The party with the most members is the **majority party.** The president works through party leaders in Congress to promote the administration's legislative program. Parties also act as the glue of our federal structure by connecting the various levels of government with a common bond. (For a more detailed discussion of the role played by political parties in Congress, see Chapter 11.)

minority party The political party that has fewer members in the legislature than the opposing party.

majority party The political party that has more members in the legislature than the opposing party.

Checking the Power of the Party in Government

The party that does not control Congress or a state legislature, or the presidency or a state governorship, also plays a vital function in American politics. The "out party" acts as a watchdog and keeps an eye on the activities of the party in power, thus providing a check on the party in government. Such monitoring by the loyal opposition encourages the party in power to heed the public's wishes and to remain responsive.

AMERICA at odds

Would Divided Government Be Better?

Since the 2002 midterm elections, the Republican Party has controlled both the White House and Congress. The Republicans added to their majorities in the Senate and House of Representatives in 2004. To be sure, a single party controlling both the executive and legislative branches of government is nothing new. Indeed, in the 1900s alone, the Democrats controlled both branches for thirty-six years, and the Republicans controlled both branches for twenty-two years. Some Americans believe that such single-party domination represents a mandate from the people to carry out that party's policies. Other Americans argue that government operates more fairly for all Americans when neither party controls both branches.

Majority Leader Tom DeLay (R., Tex.) is under investigation by officials in Texas for campaign-finance fraud. If indicted, he will not have to worry about losing his leadership position because his fellow Republicans—who controlled both chambers of Congress after the 2004 elections—voted in 2005 to change the rules to allow him to stay.

Reuters/Larry Downing/Landov

After the 2004 elections, the Republican Party embarked on an ambitious agenda. Following the lead of President George W. Bush, the Republican majority in Congress laid out plans to tackle a variety of domestic issues ranging from reforming the tax code to addressing the future of Social Security. Bush also renominated a number of controversial judges for seats on the federal courts. Any opposition mounted by the Democrats to these initiatives may be ineffective, given the Republicans' formidable majority in Congress. The Republicans and their supporters argue that their recent victories at the polls represent a mandate from the American people.

Those opposed to the idea of a single party controlling the White House and both chambers of Congress point to the arrogance exhibited by the Republican Party in recent years. To avoid losing House majority leader Tom DeLay, the Republicans have rewritten certain congressional ethics standards. DeLay is being investigated for campaign-finance irregularities in Texas. With their majority in the Senate, the Republicans have also threatened to change the filibuster rules that have allowed Democrats to block the confirmation of conservative judicial nominees. Many Americans fear that when either party has such a tight grip on government power, it can establish policies that, over time, may not be good for the country.

Balancing Competing Interests

coalition An alliance of individuals or groups with a variety of interests and opinions who join together to support all or part of a political party's platform.

Political parties are often described as vast umbrellas under which Americans with diverse interests can gather. Political parties are essentially **coalitions**—individuals and groups with a variety of interests and opinions who join together to support the party's platform, or parts of it.

The Republican Party, for example, includes a number of groups with many different views on the issue of abortion. The role of party leaders in this situation is to adopt a broad enough view on the issue so that the various groups will not be alienated. In this way, different groups can hold their individual views and still come together under the umbrella of the Republican Party. Leaders of both the Democratic Party and the Republican Party modify contending views and arrange compromises among different groups. In so doing, the parties help to unify, rather than divide, their members.

Running Campaigns

Through their national, state, and local organizations, parties coordinate campaigns. Political parties take care of a large number of small and routine tasks that are essential to the smooth functioning of the electoral process. For example, they work at getting party members registered and at conducting drives for new voters. Sometimes, party volunteers staff the polling places.

Third Parties and American Politics

Throughout American history, smaller minor parties, or **third parties,** have competed for power in the nation's two-party system. Indeed, as mentioned earlier, third parties have been represented in most of our national elections. Although third parties have found it difficult—if not impossible—to gain credibility within the two-party American system, they play an important role in our political life.

third party In the United States, any party other than one of the two major parties (Republican and Democratic).

The Many Kinds of Third Parties

Third parties are as varied as the causes they represent, but all of these parties have one thing in common: their members and leaders want to challenge the major parties because they believe that certain needs and values are not being properly addressed. Third parties name candidates who propose to remedy the situation.

Some third parties have tried to appeal to the entire nation; others have focused on particular regions of the country, states, or local areas. Most third parties have been short lived. A few, however, including the Socialist Labor Party (founded in 1891) and the Socialist Party (founded in 1901) lasted for a long time. The number and variety of third parties make them difficult to classify, but most fall into one of the general categories discussed in the following subsections.

Issue-Oriented Parties
An issue-oriented third party is formed to promote a particular cause or timely issue. For example, the Free Soil Party was organized in 1848 to oppose the expansion of slavery into the western territories. The Prohibition Party was formed in 1869 to advocate prohibiting the use and manufacture of alcoholic beverages. Most issue-oriented parties fade into history as the issue that brought them into existence fades from public attention, is taken up by a major party, or is resolved.

Some issue-oriented parties endure, however, when they expand their focus beyond a single area of concern. For example, the Green Party USA (the Green Party) was founded in 1972 to raise awareness of environmental issues, but it is no longer a single-issue party. Ralph Nader, the presidential candidate for the Green Party in 2000, campaigned against alleged corporate greed and the major parties' ostensible indifference to a number of issues, including universal health insurance, child poverty, the excesses of globalism, and the failure of the drug war. (For a discussion of the Green Party in the United States and Germany, see this chapter's *Comparative Politics* feature on the following page.)

Ideological Parties
As discussed in Chapter 1, an *ideology* is a comprehensive set of beliefs about human nature and government institutions. An ideological party supports a particular set of beliefs or political doctrine. For example, a party such as the Socialist Workers Party may believe that our free enterprise system should be replaced by one in which government or workers own all of the factories in the economy. The party's members may believe that competition should be replaced by cooperation and social responsibility so as to achieve an equitable distribution of income. In contrast, an ideological party such as the Libertarian Party may oppose virtually all forms of government interference with personal liberties and private enterprise.

Splinter or Personality Parties
A splinter party develops out of a split within a major party. Often, this split involves the formation of a party to elect a specific person. For example, when Theodore Roosevelt did not receive the Republican Party's nomination for president in 1912, he created the Bull Moose Party (also called the Progressive Party) to promote his platform. From the Democrats have come Henry Wallace's Progressive Party and the States' Rights (Dixiecrat) Party, both formed in 1948. In 1968, the American Independent Party was formed to support George Wallace's campaign for president.

Most splinter parties have been formed around a leader with a strong personality, which is why they are sometimes called personality parties. When that person steps aside, the party usually collapses. An example of a personality party is the Reform Party, which was formed in 1996 mainly to provide a campaign vehicle for H. Ross Perot.

When Theodore Roosevelt did not receive the Republican Party's presidential nomination in 1912, he created the Bull Moose Party (also called the Progressive Party) to promote his platform.

Library of Congress

comparative politics

The German Greens

Although the Green Party in the United States has only recently attracted national media attention, the Greens have been politically active in Europe for more than two decades. The German Green Party, known as *die Grünen,* was founded in 1979 when more than two hundred environmentalist groups merged to support limits on nuclear energy. They expanded their platform in the 1980s to include demilitarizing Europe and dismantling the North Atlantic Treaty Organization. In 1983, they won 5.6 percent of the vote, which, in Germany's system of proportional representation, was enough to gain seats in the Bundestag (Germany's legislature).

The German Greens have had to contend with ideological splits within the party. Under the leadership of Joschka Fischer, the German Greens moved more to the center in German politics. In 1998, the Greens won enough votes to be invited to form a coalition government with the Social Democrats. Fischer became Germany's foreign minister, a notion that is unthinkable in the winner-take-all system in the United States. In the September 2002 elections in Germany, the Greens garnered 8.6 percent of the vote, which translated into 55 seats in the 603-seat Bundestag.

In the United States, a few Green candidates for state offices in 2002 garnered as much as 35 percent of the vote, but that did not win them any seats in their state legislatures. The Green candidate for governor of Maine won 9.3 percent of the vote but was not asked to be part of the new governor's administration. Because Germany has a system of proportional representation, the Greens can win seats in government with a showing of as little as 5 percent at the polls. For the U.S. Green Party, 5 percent for Ralph Nader in 2000 would have resulted in a share of federal campaign funds for the 2004 elections, but nothing more.

AP Photo/Bernd Kammerer

Joschka Fischer, a prominent German Green Party leader, became the country's foreign minister after the party won enough votes in the 1998 elections to become a part of a coalition government with the ruling Social Democrats.

For Critical Analysis

Aside from the system of proportional representation in Germany, do you think there are other explanations for why the Green Party has been so much more successful there, and in other European countries, than it has been in the United States?

The Effect of Third Parties on American Politics

Although most Americans do not support third parties or vote for their candidates, third parties have influenced American politics in several ways, some of which we examine here.

Third Parties Bring Issues to the Public's Attention
Third parties have brought many political issues to the public's attention. They have exposed and focused on unpopular or highly debated issues that major parties have preferred to ignore. Third parties are in a position to take bold stands on issues that are avoided by major parties because third parties are not trying to be all things to all people. Progressive social reforms such as the minimum wage, women's right to vote, railroad and banking legislation, and old-age pensions were first proposed by third parties. The Free Soilers of the 1850s, for example, were the first true antislavery party, and the Populists and Progressives put many social reforms on the political agenda.

Some people have argued that third parties are often the unsung heroes of American politics, bringing new issues to the forefront of public debate. Some of the ideas proposed by third parties were never accepted, while others were taken up by the major parties as these ideas became increasingly popular.

Third Parties Can Affect the Vote
Third parties can influence not only voter turnout but also election outcomes. Third parties have occasionally taken victory from one major party and given it to another, thus playing the "spoiler" role.

For example, in 1912, when the Progressive Party split off from the Republican Party, the result was three major contenders for the presidency: Woodrow Wilson, the Democratic candidate; William Howard Taft, the regular Republican candidate; and Theodore Roosevelt, the Progressive candidate. The presence of the Progressive Party "spoiled" the Republicans' chances for victory and gave the election to Wilson, the Democrat. Without Roosevelt's third party, Taft might have won. Similarly, many commentators contended that Ralph Nader "spoiled" the chances of Democratic candidate Al Gore in the 2000 elections, because many of those who voted for Nader would have voted Democratic had Nader not been a candidate. In fact, to minimize Nader's impact on the vote for Gore, some "vote swapping" was done via the Internet. Voters in states that were solidly in the Gore camp reportedly agreed to vote for Nader, and, in exchange, Nader supporters in closely contested states agreed to cast their votes for Gore.

A significant showing by a minor party also reduces an incumbent party's chances of winning the election, as you can see in Figure 7–2. In 1992, for example, third-party candidate H. Ross Perot captured about 19 percent of the vote. Had those votes been distributed between the candidates of the major parties, incumbent George H. W. Bush and candidate Bill Clinton, the outcome of the election might have been different.

Third Parties Provide a Voice for Dissatisfied Americans Third parties also provide a voice for voters who are frustrated with and alienated from the Republican and Democratic parties. Americans who are unhappy with the two major political parties can still participate in American politics through third parties that reflect their opinions on political issues. Indeed, young Minnesota voters turned out in record numbers during the 1998 elections to vote for Jesse Ventura, a Reform Party candidate for governor in that state. Similarly, Ralph Nader was able to engage young Americans who might never have gone to the polls in 2000 if he had not been a candidate.

Andy King/Corbis Sygma

One of the most surprising results of the 1998 elections was Jesse Ventura's victory in the Minnesota gubernatorial race. Few thought that Reform Party candidate Ventura (a former professional wrestler) had even a slim chance to win the governorship.

FIGURE 7–2

The Effect of Third Parties on Vote Distribution, 1848–1992

In eight presidential elections, a third party's candidate received more than 10 percent of the popular vote—in six of those elections, the incumbent party lost. As shown here, only in 1856 and 1924 did the incumbent party manage to hold on to the White House in the face of a significant third-party showing.

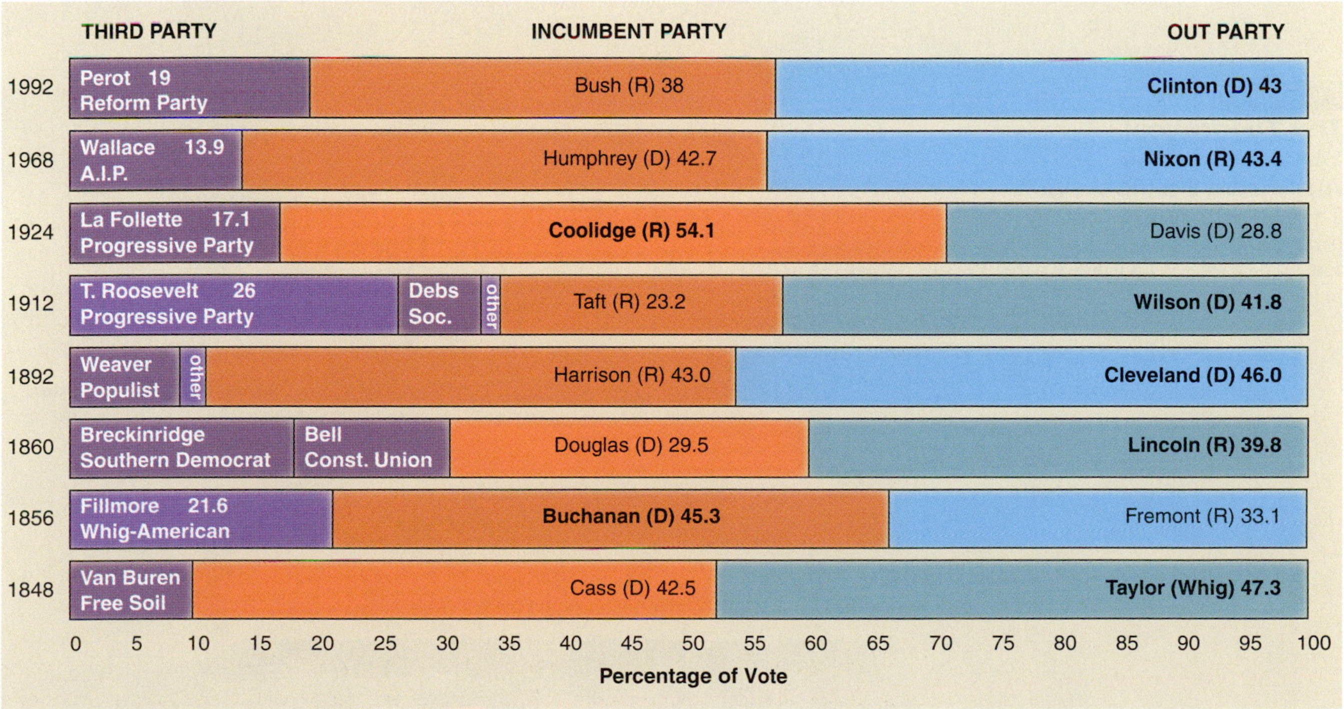

	THIRD PARTY	INCUMBENT PARTY	OUT PARTY
1992	Perot 19 Reform Party	Bush (R) 38	Clinton (D) 43
1968	Wallace 13.9 A.I.P.	Humphrey (D) 42.7	Nixon (R) 43.4
1924	La Follette 17.1 Progressive Party	Coolidge (R) 54.1	Davis (D) 28.8
1912	T. Roosevelt 26 Progressive Party / Debs Soc. / other	Taft (R) 23.2	Wilson (D) 41.8
1892	Weaver Populist / other	Harrison (R) 43.0	Cleveland (D) 46.0
1860	Breckinridge Southern Democrat / Bell Const. Union	Douglas (D) 29.5	Lincoln (R) 39.8
1856	Fillmore 21.6 Whig-American	Buchanan (D) 45.3	Fremont (R) 33.1
1848	Van Buren Free Soil	Cass (D) 42.5	Taylor (Whig) 47.3

Percentage of Vote
0 5 10 15 20 25 30 35 40 45 50 55 60 65 70 75 80 85 90 95 100

SOURCE: *Congressional Quarterly Weekly Report*, June 13, 1992, p. 1729.

How American Political Parties Are Structured

In theory, each of the major American political parties has a standard, pyramid-shaped organization (see Figure 7–3). This theoretical structure is much like that of a large company, in which the bosses are at the top and the employees are at various lower levels.

Actually, neither major party is a closely knit or highly organized structure. Both parties are fragmented and *decentralized,* which means there is no central power with a direct chain of command. If there were, the national chairperson of the party, along with the national committee, could simply dictate how the organization would be run, just as if it were Microsoft or General Electric. In reality, state party organizations are all very different and are only loosely tied to the party's national structure. Local party organizations are often quite independent from the state organization. There is no single individual or group who gives orders to all party members. Instead, a number of personalities, frequently at odds with one another, form loosely identifiable leadership groups.

State and Local Party Organizations

In both the Democratic and Republican parties, state and local party organizations are separate from the national party organizations. Most state and local parties work closely with their national organizations only during major elections.

State Organizations
The powers and duties of state party organizations differ from state to state. In general, the state party organization is built around a central committee and a chairperson. The committee works to raise funds, recruit new party members, maintain a strong party organization, and help members running for state offices.

The state chairperson is usually a powerful party member chosen by the committee. In some cases, however, the chairperson is selected by the governor or a senator from that state.

Local Organizations
Local party organizations differ greatly, but generally there is a party unit for each district in which elective offices are to be filled. These districts include congressional and legislative districts, counties, cities and towns, wards, and precincts.

A **ward** is a political division or district within a city. A **precinct** can be either a political district within a city, such as a block or a neighborhood, or a portion of a rural county. The

---

ward A local unit of a political party's organization, consisting of a division or district within a city.

precinct A political district within a city (such as a block or a neighborhood) or a portion of a rural county; the smallest voting district at the local level.

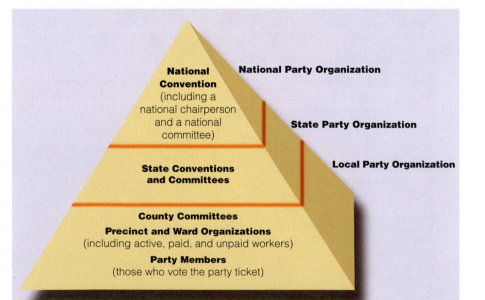

FIGURE 7–3

The Theoretical Structure of the American Political Party
The relationship between state and local parties varies from state to state. Further, some state parties resist national party policies.

local, grassroots foundations of politics are formed within voting precincts. Polling places are located within the precincts. Political parties elect or appoint precinct captains or chairpersons who organize the precinct, assist new members, register voters, and take care of party business.

The National Party Organization

On the national level, the party's presidential candidate is considered to be the leader of the party. In some cases, well-known members of Congress are viewed as national party leaders. In addition to the party leaders, the structure of both parties includes four major elements: the national convention, the national committee, the national chairperson, and the congressional campaign committees.

The National Convention

Most of the public attention that the party receives comes at the **national convention,** which is held every four years during the summer before the presidential election. The news media always cover these conventions, and as a result, they have become quite extravagant. They are often described as the party's national voice and are usually held in major cities.

The national conventions are attended by delegates chosen by the states in various ways. The delegates' most important job is to choose the party's presidential and vice presidential candidates, who together make up the **party ticket.** The delegates also write the party platform, which, as mentioned, sets forth the party's positions on national issues. Essentially, through its platform, the party promises to initiate certain policies if it wins the presidency. Despite the widespread perception that, once in office, candidates can and do ignore these promises, in fact, many of them become law.[12]

national convention The meeting held by each major party every four years to select presidential and vice presidential candidates, write a party platform, and conduct other party business.

party ticket A list of a political party's candidates for various offices.

Cheering delegates at the 2004 Democratic National Convention in Boston listened to top party leaders, such as former presidents Bill Clinton and Jimmy Carter, who outlined the themes of the presidential election. Delegates selected Senator John Kerry of Massachusetts as their presidential candidate.

Reuters/Rick Wilking/Landov

Delegates hold "W" signs at the 2004 Republican National Convention, which was held in New York City. The delegates were showing their support for George W. Bush, who won the party's nomination as its presidential candidate.

Reuters/Robert Galbraith/Landov

national party committee The political party leaders who direct party business during the four years between the national party conventions, organize the next national convention, and plan how to obtain a party victory in the next presidential election.

national party chairperson An individual who serves as a political party's administrative head at the national level and directs the work of the party's national committee.

The National Committee   Each state elects a number of delegates to the **national party committee.** The Republican National Committee and the Democratic National Committee direct the business of their respective parties during the four years between national conventions. The committees' most important duties, however, are to organize the next national convention and to plan how to obtain a party victory in the next presidential election.

The National Chairperson   The party's national committee elects a **national party chairperson** to serve as administrative head of the national party. The main duty of the national chairperson is to direct the work of the national committee from party headquarters in Washington, D.C. The chairperson is involved in raising funds, providing for publicity, promoting party unity, recruiting new voters, and other activities. In presidential election years, the chairperson's attention is focused on the national convention and the presidential campaign.

The Congressional Campaign Committees   Each party has a campaign committee, made up of senators and representatives, in each chamber of Congress. Members are chosen by their colleagues and serve for two-year terms. The committees work to help reelect party members to Congress.

why does it MATTER?

Political Parties and Your Everyday Life

In the past, the activities of political parties often had a very direct effect on citizens' everyday lives. In the 1930s, for example, strong party machines dominated local politics in many large cities. In some cities, such as Chicago, the party machine was almost omnipresent. Had you been living in such a city, the party machine would have affected your everyday life. Party machines then bestowed government contracts on loyal supporters. The machines often helped the poor and the unfortunate with gifts of food and clothing (particularly before an election).

Today, there are no real party machines. Nonetheless, political parties do affect your everyday life, if more indirectly. Consider that whichever party has the most members in Congress dominates that institution. Congressional leaders and committee chairs come from the dominant political party. Thus, a particular political party's success can often lead to new laws and regulations that affect your daily life. You may have to pay higher or lower taxes, face more or fewer employment opportunities, or experience changes in the social environment around you. Suppose, for example, that you live in a city with a relatively high and rising crime rate. If a political party that wants to spend more government resources on crime reduction wins a majority in Congress, your everyday life could be significantly affected.

Similarly, political parties play important roles in state legislatures and governorships. A state legislature controlled by Democrats will create and implement different policies than a legislature controlled by Republicans, and vice versa. These policies could affect the amount of tuition you pay, the amount of state taxes that are withheld from your paycheck, the speed limit

Photo by Alex Wong/Getty Images

Democratic presidential nominee Senator John Kerry visited many college campuses during his 2004 campaign.

on your state's highways, the job opportunities available to you, and so on.

Taking Action

Getting involved in political parties is as simple as going to the polls and casting your vote for the candidate of one of the major parties—or of a third party. If you want to go a step further, you can attend a speech given by a political candidate or even volunteer to assist a political party or specific candidates' campaign activities.

Key Terms

coalition 162	national party committee 168	political party 151	two-party system 154
electorate 155	party elite 157	precinct 166	ward 166
majority party 161	party identifier 157	primary 159	
minority party 161	party platform 156	realigning election 153	
national convention 167	party ticket 167	solidarity 159	
national party chairperson 168	patronage 159	third party 163	

Chapter Summary

1 A political party is a group of individuals outside the government who organize to win elections, operate the government, and determine policy.

2 In the early years of the nation, the Federalists and the Democratic Republicans vied for power and laid the groundwork for our two-party system. Since 1860, the Democrats and Republicans have been the major parties controlling American government.

3 In the United States, we have a two-party system in which two major parties, the Democrats and the Republicans, vie for control of the government. The two-party system has become entrenched in the United States for several reasons, including election laws and institutional barriers, which make it difficult for third parties to compete successfully against the major parties.

4 Each of the two major parties consists of three components: the party in the electorate, the party organization, and the party in government. Generally, the party organization takes positions on issues facing the nation and outlines them in the party platform. The party in government will attempt to enact policies consistent with the party platform, although this is not mandatory for candidates once they take office.

5 A large number of party members, known as party identifiers, are not actively involved in party politics. A smaller group of actively involved party members, the party elite, carry out the major functions of the party. People join political parties for a variety of reasons, including the desire to express their solidarity with the views of others, to benefit materially from party membership, and to promote political ideas and principles.

6 Political parties link the people's policy preferences to actual government policies, select candidates to run for political office, inform the public about important political issues, coordinate policymaking among the various branches and levels of government, check the power of the party in government (a function of the "out party"), balance competing interests and effect compromises, and run campaigns.

7 There are many different kinds of minor parties, or third parties. Some are issue oriented while others are based on ideology. Some third parties form as splinter parties as a result of a split within a major party. Third parties bring political issues to the public's attention, alter election outcomes by gaining votes that would otherwise go to one of the major parties, and provide a voice for dissatisfied voters.

8 In theory, both of the major political parties have a pyramid-shaped organization, with the national committee and national chairperson at the top of the organization and the local party units at the bottom. In practice, the parties are decentralized, and the state and local party organizations work closely with the national organization only during major elections.

9 At the national level, the most public event is the party's national convention, which is held every four years. Delegates from each state choose the party's presidential and vice presidential candidates and write the party platform.

RESOURCES FOR FURTHER STUDY

Selected Readings

Black, Earl, and Merle Black. *The Rise of Southern Republicans.* Cambridge, Mass.: Belknap Press of Harvard University Press, 2002. The authors study the transformation in southern politics since the 1960s. The conservative wing of the Democratic Party had held power in the South since Reconstruction. The election of Ronald Reagan as president in 1980, however, contributed to a political shift in the South and the rise of the Republican Party as representing white southern interests.

Chhibber, Pradeep K., and Ken Kollman. *The Formation of National Party Systems: Federalism and Party Competition in Canada, Great Britain, India, and the United States.* Princeton, N.J.: Princeton University Press, 2004. This book is the first to establish a link between federalism and the formation of national or regional party systems in a comparative context. The authors question the widespread notion that the United States has always had a two-party system.

Disch, Lisa Jane. *The Tyranny of the Two-Party System.* New York: Columbia University Press, 2002. The author argues that neither the Constitution nor the winner-take-all system need create a two-party system as we know it. Furthermore, the present system impairs democracy. She argues in favor of a system of "electoral fusion," popular in the nineteenth century, in which candidates run on the ballots of both the established party and a third party.

Green, John C., and Paul S. Herrnson, eds. *Responsible Partisanship? The Evolution of American Political Parties since 1950.* Lawrence, Kans.: University Press of Kansas, 2003. This collection of articles examines the role of political parties in government and in the electorate, as well as trends in voting behavior and party identification. It focuses on recent changes in laws governing parties and party finance.

Politics on the Web

- For a list of political Web sites available on the Internet, sorted by country and with links to parties, organizations, and governments throughout the world, go to **http://www. politicalresources.net**

- The Democratic Party is online at **http://www.democrats.org**

- The Republican National Committee is online at **http://www.rnc.org**

- The Libertarian Party has a Web site at **http://www.lp.org**

- The Socialist Party's Web site can be accessed at **http://sp-usa.org**

- The Green Party's Web site can be accessed by going to **http://www.greenparty.org**

- For information on the Reform Party, go to its Web site at **http://www.reformparty.org**

Online Resources for This Chapter

This text's Companion Web Site, at **http://www.americaatodds.com**, offers links to numerous resources that you can utilize to learn more about the topics covered in this chapter. For a list describing these resources, see the inside front cover of this book.

chapter **8**
public opinion and voting

CHAPTER OBJECTIVES

After reading this chapter, you should be able to . . .

▶ Explain what public opinion is and how it is measured.

▶ Describe the political socialization process.

▶ Summarize the history of polling in the United States, and explain how polls are conducted and how they are used in the political process.

▶ Indicate some of the factors that affect voter turnout.

▶ Discuss the different factors that affect voter choices.

Is Political Polling Good for Democracy?

Data culled from public opinion polls are used by a variety of groups in America and for a number of purposes. During political campaigns, opinion polls provide candidates with feedback on how well their images or stances on particular issues meet with public approval. Politicians in office often use surveys to learn the public's views on particular issues. Today, polls are part of our political life and are taken daily on virtually every imaginable issue or topic.

One of the issues over which Americans are at odds is whether our elected representatives should let public opinion dictate government policy. Some believe that government officials should listen closely to the people when forming policy. Others contend that public officials should use their own judgment and that allowing public opinion to determine policy issues would be bad for democracy.

Elected Officials Should Follow the Will of the People

Many Americans believe that our government representatives, when creating policies, should be guided by the public's views on the issues at hand. If members of Congress have to decide whether to declare war, for example, they should survey the public to see what the people want. After all, a democracy is, at least in theory, a government by the people. Indeed, according to Thomas Jefferson, "The will of the people is the only legitimate foundation of any government." Polls are powerful tools for soliciting information and obtaining feedback from the people.

The polls themselves indicate that Americans want to participate in policymaking. According to one poll, 94 percent of the respondents believed that the views of the majority of Americans should have a great deal or a fair amount of influence on the decisions of officials in Washington, D.C. More than half of the respondents thought that elected officials should even go against their own knowledge and judgment in favor of what the majority wants.[1]

Clearly, a direct democracy—a type of democracy in which the people participate directly (see Chapter 1)—is unthinkable in a country as large as the United States. Yet polls offer Americans the opportunity to communicate more directly with the president and members of Congress. Our elected representatives should use opinion polls to ensure that their decisions are consistent with the will of the citizenry.

Elected Officials Should Use Their Own Judgment

Other groups contend that elected officials should ignore public opinion polls—for a number of reasons. For one thing, when voters in a district elect a person to represent them in government, they expect that person to have some moral backbone and to make reasonable and sound judgments. They don't want a representative who blindly follows public opinion when making decisions. Clearly, public opinion is not always right or in the best interest of the nation. At one time, for example, polls showed that a majority of Americans supported racial segregation. Was segregation therefore a reasonable policy?

Consider also that people responding to questions in opinion polls often have little time to dwell on the questions. Thus, their responses can hardly reflect thoughtful, considered judgments. As one political scientist noted, "Modern polling can give us back only what citizens know the moment the phone rings."[2] Additionally, poll respondents often lack information on particular issues. To base policy decisions on the snap judgments of uninformed respondents would be a mistake.

There is another reason why polls should not drive policy decision making. Simply put, policy choices involve risks and consequences that are not addressed in polls. Any sound decision-making process requires careful evaluation of those risks and consequences. Opinion polls simply do not allow for this type of deliberation.

Where Do You Stand?

1. In your opinion, to what extent should government officials be guided by public opinion polls when forming policy?

2. "Polls are unlikely to be improved enough to help with policy choices." Do you agree with this statement? Why or why not?

Explore This Issue Online

- The Gallup Organization, one of the nation's oldest and most respected polling firms, can be visited online at **http://www.gallup.com**.
- The Public Broadcasting Service (PBS) offers advice on how to interpret public opinion polls at **http://www.pbs.org/elections/savvyvoter.html**.

Introduction

Many Americans are concerned about the low number of citizens who have turned out to vote during some elections, particularly those in the 1990s. After all, if people do not vote, how can their opinions affect public policy? In a democracy, at a minimum, members of the public must form opinions and openly express them to their elected public officials. Only when the opinions of Americans are communicated effectively to elected representatives can those opinions form the basis of government action. As President Franklin D. Roosevelt once said, "A government can be no better than the public opinion that sustains it."

What exactly is "public opinion"? How do we form our opinions on political issues? How can public opinion be measured accurately? What factors affect voter participation? Researchers and scholars have addressed these questions time and again. They are important questions because the backbone of our democracy has always been civic participation—taking part in the political life of the country. Civic participation means many things, but perhaps the most important way that Americans participate in their democracy is through voting—expressing their opinions in the polling places.

What Is Public Opinion?

People hold opinions—sometimes very strong ones—about a variety of issues, ranging from the ethics of capital punishment to the latest trends in fashion. In this chapter, however, we are concerned with only a portion of those opinions. For our purposes here, we define **public opinion** as the views of the citizenry on a particular issue. Public opinion is the sum total of a complex collection of opinions held by many people on issues in the public arena, such as taxes, health care, Social Security, clean-air legislation, unemployment, and so on.

When you hear a news report or read a magazine article stating that "a significant number of Americans" feel a certain way about an issue, you are probably hearing that a particular opinion is held by a large enough number of people to make government officials turn their heads and listen. For example, in 2004, as public opinion surveys showed that Americans were very concerned about the war in Iraq and national security, presidential candidates John Kerry and George W. Bush took strong public stances on the war on terrorism.

public opinion The views of the citizenry about politics, public issues, and public policies; a complex collection of opinions held by many people on issues in the public arena.

An NBC pollster conducts an interview. Public opinion polls allow us to measure public opinion on a given issue at a given point in time.

Billy E. Barnes/PhotoEdit

Political socialization starts at a very young age, usually within the family unit. Children also learn about politics and government through such school activities as reciting the Pledge of Allegiance and displaying the American flag.

Mary Kate Denny/PhotoEdit

How Do People Form Political Opinions?

When asked, most Americans are willing to express an opinion on political issues. Not one of us, however, was born with such opinions. Most people acquire their political attitudes, opinions, beliefs, and knowledge through a complex learning process called **political socialization.** This process begins early in childhood and continues throughout the person's life.

Most political socialization is informal, and it usually begins during early childhood, when the dominant influence on a child is the family. Although parents normally do not sit down and say to their children, "Let us explain to you the virtues of becoming a Democrat," their children nevertheless come to know the parents' feelings, beliefs, and attitudes. The strong early influence of the family later gives way to the multiple influences of school, peers, television, co-workers, and other groups. People and institutions that influence the political views of others are called **agents of political socialization.**

political socialization A learning process through which most people acquire their political attitudes, opinions, beliefs, and knowledge.

agents of political socialization People and institutions that influence the political views of others.

The Importance of Family

As just suggested, most parents or guardians do not deliberately set out to form their children's political ideas and beliefs. They are usually more concerned with the moral, religious, and ethical values of their offspring. Yet a child first sees the political world through the eyes of his or her family, which is perhaps the most important force in political socialization. Children do not "learn" political attitudes the same way they learn to master in-line skating. Rather, they learn by hearing their parents' everyday conversations and stories about politicians and issues and by observing their parents' actions. They also learn from watching and listening to their siblings, as well as from the kinds of situations in which their parents place them.

The family's influence is strongest when children clearly perceive their parents' attitudes. For example, in one study, more high school students could identify their parents' political party affiliation than their parents' other attitudes or beliefs. In many situations, the political party of the parents becomes the political party of the children, particularly if both parents belong to the same party.

The Schools and Educational Attainment

Education also strongly influences an individual's political attitudes. From their earliest days in school, children learn about the American political system. They say the Pledge of Allegiance and sing patriotic songs. They celebrate national holidays, such as Presidents' Day and Veterans' Day, and learn about the history and symbols associated with them. In the upper grades, young people acquire more knowledge about government and democratic procedures through civics classes and through student government and various clubs. They also learn citizenship skills through school rules and regulations. Generally, those with more education have more knowledge about politics and policy than those with less education. The level of education also influences a person's political values, as will be discussed later in this chapter.

Although the schools have always been important agents of political socialization, many Americans today believe that our schools are not fulfilling this mission. Too many students are graduating from high school with too little knowledge of the American system of government.

Students learn about the political process early on when they participate in class elections.

The Media

The **media**—newspapers, magazines, television, radio, and the Internet— also have an impact on political socialization. The most influential of these media is, of course, television. Television does not necessarily decrease the level of information about politics. It is the leading source of political and public affairs information for most people.

Some contend that the media's role in shaping public opinion is increasing to the point at which the media are as influential as the family, particularly among high school students. For example, in her analysis of the media's role in American politics, media scholar Doris A. Graber points out that high school students, when asked where they obtain the information on which they base their attitudes, mention the mass media far more than their families, friends, and teachers.[3]

Other studies have shown that the media's influence on people's opinions may not be as great as was once thought. Generally, people watch television and read articles with preconceived ideas about the issues. These preconceived ideas act as a kind of perceptual screen that blocks out information that is not consistent with those ideas. For example, if you are already firmly convinced that daily meditation is beneficial for your health, you probably will not change your mind if you watch a TV show that asserts that those who meditate live no longer on average than people who do not. Generally, the media tend to wield the most influence over the views of persons who have not yet formed opinions about certain issues or political candidates. (See Chapter 10 for a more detailed discussion of the media's role in American politics.)

media Newspapers, magazines, television, radio, the Internet, and any other printed or electronic means of communication.

Opinion Leaders

Every state or community has well-known citizens who are able to influence the opinions of their fellow citizens. These people may be public officials, religious leaders, teachers, or celebrities. They are the people to whom others listen and from whom others draw ideas and convictions about various issues of public concern. These opinion leaders play a significant role in the formation of public opinion. The Reverend Jesse Jackson, for example, has long been a powerful and outspoken opinion leader for civil rights.

Opinion leaders often include politicians. Certainly, Americans' attitudes are influenced by the public statements of important government leaders such as the president or secretary of state. Sometimes, however, opinion leaders can fall from grace when they express views radically different from what most Americans believe. For example, in 2002 Senate Republican leader Trent Lott (R., Miss.) expressed an opinion that seemed to approve of America's history of racial segregation. Within two weeks, public disapproval of this opinion forced Lott to resign from his position in the Republican Party leadership, although he continued to serve out his term as senator.

Major Life Events

Often, the political attitudes of an entire generation of Americans are influenced by a major event. For example, the Great Depression (1929–1939), the most severe economic depression

In a speech to religious and charitable leaders in 2002, President George W. Bush stated that then Senate Republican majority leader Trent Lott's comments about America's segregated past were offensive. Lott later resigned his Senate leadership position due to negative public opinion over those comments.

in modern U.S. history, persuaded many Americans who lived through it that the federal government should step in when the economy is in decline. Many observers then felt that increased federal spending and explicit job-creation programs contributed to the economic recovery. The generation that lived through World War II (1939–1945) tends to believe American intervention in foreign affairs is good. In contrast, the generation that came of age during the Vietnam War (1964–1975) is more skeptical of American interventionism. A national tragedy, such as the terrorist attacks of September 11, 2001, is also likely to influence the political attitudes of a generation of Americans, though in what way is as yet difficult to predict.

Peer Groups

peer group Associates, often those close in age to oneself; may include friends, classmates, co-workers, club members, or religious group members. Peer group influence is a significant factor in the political socialization process.

Once children enter school, the views of friends begin to influence their attitudes and beliefs. From junior high school on, the **peer group**—friends, classmates, co-workers, club members, or religious group members—becomes a significant factor in the political socialization process. Most of this socialization occurs when the peer group is intimately involved in political activities. For example, your political beliefs might be influenced by a peer group with which you are working on a common political cause, such as preventing the clear-cutting of old-growth forests or saving an endangered species. Your political beliefs probably would not be as strongly influenced by peers with whom you snowboard regularly or attend concerts.

Some Americans worry that peer influence, particularly at the high school level, may be a negative agent in the political socialization process because of the increasing hostility among teens to traditional American values and political culture. For example, a recent poll indicates that 35 percent of teens believe that they are under a "great deal" or "some" pressure from their peers to "break the rules." Additionally, 48 percent of teens say they "like to live dangerously"; 48 percent say they like to "shock people"; and 54 percent say that one usually cannot trust people who are in power.[4]

Polls also indicate that a significant number of high school students blame peer influence for the "bad things" that are happening in America, such as school killings. In a survey taken of views on the high school killings in Littleton, Colorado, for example, about 40 percent of the teenage respondents placed the blame on peer influence, and only 4 percent thought that parents or family were responsible for the violence. (Interestingly, 45 percent of the adults surveyed in the same poll felt that the responsibility for the shootings lay with the parents and family, and none of the parents considered peer influence to be a cause.[5])

Economic Status and Occupation

A person's economic status may influence her or his political views. For example, poorer people are more likely to favor government assistance programs. On an issue such as abortion, lower-income people are more likely to be conservative—that is, to be against abortion—than are higher-income groups (of course, there are many exceptions).

Where a person works will also affect her or his opinion. Individuals who spend a great deal of time working together tend to be influenced by their co-workers. For example, labor union members working together for a company will tend to have similar political opinions, at least on the issue of government involvement in labor. Individuals working for a non-profit agency that depends on government funds will tend to support government spending in that area. Business managers are more likely to favor tax laws helpful to businesses than are factory workers. People who work in factories are more likely to favor a government-sponsored, nationwide health-care program than are business executives.

Middle-class workers protest the Bush administration's tax cuts for wealthy Americans in 2003. People's economic status often influences their political opinion on a number of policies.

Measuring Public Opinion

If public opinion is to affect public policy, then public officials must be made aware of it. They must know which issues are of current concern to Americans and how strongly people feel about those issues. They must also know when public opinion changes. Of course, public officials most commonly learn about public opinion through election results, personal contacts, interest groups, and media reports. The only relatively precise way to measure public opinion, however, is through the use of public opinion polls.

A **public opinion poll** is a numerical survey of the public's opinion on a particular topic at a particular moment. The results of opinion polls are most often cast in terms of percentages: 62 percent feel this way, 27 percent do not, and 11 percent have no opinion. Of course, a poll cannot survey the entire U.S. population. Therefore, public opinion pollsters have devised scientific polling techniques for measuring public opinion through the use of **samples**—groups of people who are typical of the general population.

public opinion poll A numerical survey of the public's opinion on a particular topic at a particular moment.

sample In the context of opinion polling, a group of people selected to represent the population being studied.

Early Polling Efforts

Since the 1800s, magazines and newspapers have often spiced up their articles by conducting **straw polls,** or mail surveys, of readers' opinions. Straw polls try to read the public's collective mind by simply asking a large number of people the same question. Today, many newspapers and magazines still run "mail-in" polls. Increasingly, though, straw polls make use of telephone technology—encouraging people to call "900" numbers, for example—or the Internet. Visitors to a Web page can instantly register their opinion on an issue with the click of a mouse. The problem with straw polls is that the opinions expressed usually represent only a small subgroup of the population, or a **biased sample.** A survey of those who read the *Wall Street Journal* will most likely produce different results than a survey of those who read the *Reader's Digest*.

The most famous of all straw-polling errors was committed by the *Literary Digest* in 1936 when it tried to predict the presidential election's outcome. The *Digest* had accurately predicted the winning candidates in several earlier presidential elections, but in 1936 the *Digest* predicted that Alfred Landon would easily defeat incumbent Franklin D. Roosevelt. Instead, Roosevelt won by a landslide. The editors of the *Digest* had sent mail-in cards to citizens whose names appeared in telephone directories, to its own subscribers, and to automobile owners—in all, to a staggering 2,376,000 people. In the mid-Depression year of 1936, however, people who owned a car or a telephone or who subscribed to the *Digest* were certainly not representative of the majority of Americans. The vast majority of Americans were on the

straw poll A nonscientific poll; a poll in which there is no way to ensure that the opinions expressed are representative of the larger population.

biased sample A poll sample that does not accurately represent the population.

GALLUP POLL---SECRET BALLOT

Please Do Not Sign Your Name

. . .

Mark ⊠ before the man you prefer for President.

☐ **Dewey**   ☐ **Roosevelt**

☐ **Thomas**

© Bettmann/Corbis

A sample of a secret ballot used by the Gallup Organization in the 1944 presidential election. Today, Gallup polls still play an important role in determining public opinion on certain candidates, social issues, and policies.

random sample In the context of opinion polling, a sample in which each person within the entire population being polled has an equal chance of being chosen.

opposite end of the socioeconomic ladder. Despite the enormous number of people surveyed, the sample was unrepresentative and consequently inaccurate.

Several newcomers to the public opinion poll industry, however, did predict Roosevelt's landslide victory. Two of these organizations are still at the forefront of the polling industry today: the Gallup Organization, started by George Gallup; and Roper Associates, founded by Elmo Roper and now known as the Roper Center.

Polling Today

As you read in the chapter-opening *America at Odds* feature, polling is used extensively by political candidates and policymakers today. Politicians and the news media generally place a great deal of faith in the accuracy of poll results. Polls can be remarkably accurate when they are conducted properly. In the last fourteen presidential elections, Gallup polls conducted early in September predicted the eventual winners in eleven of the fourteen races. Even polls taken several months in advance have been able to predict the eventual winner quite well. This success is largely the result of careful sampling techniques.

Sampling   Today, most Gallup polls sample between 1,500 and 2,000 people. How can interviewing such a small group possibly indicate what millions of voters think? Clearly, to be representative of all the voters in the population, a sample must consist of a group of people who are typical of the general population. If the sample is properly selected, the opinions of those in the sample will be representative of the opinions held by the population as a whole. If the sample is not properly chosen, then the results of the poll may not reflect the ideas of the general population.

The most important principle in sampling is randomness. A **random sample** means that each person within the entire population being polled has an equal chance of being chosen. For example, if a poll is trying to measure how women feel about an issue, the sample should include respondents from all groups within the female population in proportion to their percentage of the entire population. A properly drawn random sample, therefore, would include appropriate numbers of women in terms of age, racial and ethnic characteristics, occupation, geography, household income level, and religious affiliation.

Bias   In addition to trying to secure a random sample, poll takers also want to ensure that there is no bias in their polling questions. How a question is phrased can significantly affect how people answer it. Consider a question about whether high-speed connections to the Internet should be added to the school library's computer center. One way to survey opinions on this issue is simply to ask, "Do you believe that the school district should provide high-speed connections to the Internet?" Another way to ask the same question is, "Are you willing to pay higher property taxes so that the school district can have high-speed connections to the Internet?" Undoubtedly, the poll results will differ depending on how the question is phrased.

Polling questions also sometimes reduce complex issues to questions that call for simply "yes" or "no" answers. For example, a survey question might ask respondents whether they favor giving aid to foreign countries. A respondent's opinion on the issue might vary, depending on the recipient country or the purpose and type of the aid. The poll would nonetheless force the respondent to give a "yes" or "no" answer that does not necessarily reflect his or her true opinion.

Respondents to such questions sometimes answer "I don't know" or "I don't have enough information to answer," even when the poll does not offer such answers. Interestingly, a study of how polling is conducted on the complex issue of school vouchers (see Chapter 4 for more on this issue) found that about 4 percent volunteered the answer "don't know" when asked if they favored or opposed vouchers. When respondents were offered the option of answering "I haven't heard or read enough to answer," however, the proportion choosing that answer jumped to 33 percent.[6]

Reliability of Polls

In addition to potential bias, poll takers must also be concerned about the general reliability of their polls. Those interviewed may be influenced by the interviewer's personality or tone of voice. They may answer without having any information on the issue, or they may give the answer that they think will please the interviewer. Additionally, any opinion poll contains a **sampling error,** which is the difference between what the sample results show and what the true results would have been had everybody in the relevant population been interviewed.

Opinion polls of voter preferences cannot reflect rapid shifts in public opinion unless they are taken frequently. During the 2004 presidential elections, polls showed George W. Bush ahead at times and John Kerry ahead at other times. The media reported extensively on the many polls conducted, with seemingly wild discrepancies. In the weeks prior to Election Day, a poll from Gallup, *USA Today,* and CNN showed Bush leading Kerry by a margin of eight points. Meanwhile, a poll by ABC News and the *Washington Post* showed Bush leading by a three-point margin. Yet another poll by the *New York Times* and CBS News showed the race as a tie.

Exit Polls

The reliability of polls was also called into question by the use of exit polls in the 2000 presidential elections. The Voter News Service (VNS)—a consortium of news networks—conducted polls of people exiting polling places on Election Day. These exit polls were used by the news networks to predict the winner of the Florida race—and they were wrong, not just once, but twice. First, they claimed that the Florida vote had gone to Al Gore. Then, a few hours later, they said it had gone to George W. Bush. Finally, they said the Florida race was too close to call.

These miscalls of the election outcome in Florida caused substantial confusion—and frustration—for the candidates as well as for the voters. They also led to a significant debate over exit polls: Should exit polls be banned, even though they provide valuable information on voter behavior and preferences?

One noticeable difference in the media coverage of the 2002 congressional elections was the lack of exit polls. On Election Day in 2002, the VNS announced that it would not release exit poll data, stating that it was "not satisfied with the accuracy" of its exit polls. Media outlets were forced to rely more heavily on returns from state election officials, and many close elections were not called until very late that night. In January 2003, the VNS went out of business.

Exit polls were also employed during the 2004 presidential elections. Again the results were disastrous, as you will read shortly.

sampling error In the context of opinion polling, the difference between what the sample results show and what the true results would have been had everybody in the relevant population been interviewed.

AMERICA at odds

Should Exit Polls Be Outlawed?

The 2004 presidential elections will go down in history as a low point in the accuracy of exit polls, but they were only the most recent in a series of elections in which flawed data have emerged. Many Americans would like to outlaw exit polls, but others are not so sure.

Exit polling can be construed as speech that is protected by the First Amendment to the U.S. Constitution. Supporters of exit polls maintain that it would be unconstitutional to outlaw such polls. During Election Day (and night), tens of millions of Americans stay tuned to their radios and TVs or keep checking the Internet for the latest election results. Would everyone be willing to simply go to bed and wait until the next morning to find out who won the presidency? Election results are political information, and every American has a right to as much political information as she or he wishes to obtain.

Those who want to ban exit polls point to the 2000 Florida fiasco and to the misleading exit poll results in 2004. During the early hours of the 2004 elections, exit polls caused the media to conclude that Democratic candidate John Kerry was leading in the race. Preliminary results

Supporters of Senator John Kerry react to exit polls on election night 2004. In a historically close election, exit poll results often fueled misleading reports on whether Kerry or George W. Bush was winning in a particular state.

UPI Photo/Michael Kleinfeld/Landov

of exit polls were leaked to the Internet by midafternoon. The word went out worldwide that Kerry was ahead of Bush and by a relatively large margin. After the votes were tallied, however, the exit poll results were shown to have inflated Kerry's support by 6.5 percent—the largest margin of error in decades. Critics of exit polls thus ask: What good is political information if it frequently turns out to be inaccurate or misinterpreted? The other issue is that even when exit polls are accurate, their existence may affect voter turnout in the western states. How many people will bother to vote for their preferred candidate if they already know who won the election based on exit polls in the eastern and central states?

Misuse of Polls

Today, a frequently heard complaint is that, instead of measuring public opinion, polls can end up creating it. For example, to gain popularity, a candidate might claim that all the polls show that he is ahead in the race. People who want to support the winning candidate (rather than the candidate of their choice) may support this candidate despite their true feelings. This is often called the "bandwagon" effect. Presidential approval ratings lend themselves to the bandwagon effect. For more on these types of polls, see this chapter's *The Politics of National Security* feature.

The media also sometimes misuse polls. Many journalists take the easy route during campaigns and base their political coverage almost exclusively on poll findings, with no mention of the chance for bias or the margin of error in the poll. A useful checklist for evaluating the quality of opinion polls is presented in Table 8–1 on page 182. An increasingly common misuse of polls by politicians is the *push poll,* discussed next.

Defining a Push Poll

A relatively recent tactic in political campaigns is to ask "fake" polling questions that are actually designed to "push" voters toward one candidate or another. The use of **push polls** has become so prevalent today that many states are taking steps to ban them. The problem with trying to ban push polls, or even to report accurately on which candidates are using them, is that defining a push poll can be difficult.

The National Council on Public Polls describes push polls as outright political manipulation, the spreading of rumors and lies by one candidate about another. For example, a push poll might ask, "Do you believe the rumor that Candidate A misused campaign funds to pay for a family vacation to Hawaii?" Push pollsters usually do not give their name or identify the poll's sponsor. The interviews last less than a minute, whereas legitimate pollsters typically

push poll A campaign tactic used to feed false or misleading information to potential voters, under the guise of taking an opinion poll, with the intent to "push" voters away from one candidate and toward another.

The "Perpetual War Campaign"

Pollsters routinely conduct surveys to gauge a sitting president's popularity among the public. How has President George W. Bush fared in this respect? When he first took office, some doubted that he would be a very popular president. After all, he had not won the popular vote in the 2000 presidential elections. Furthermore, although the Republicans held a slim majority in the House of Representatives, until 2002 the Senate was controlled by the opposition party—the Democrats.

Then came the terrorist attacks of September 11, 2001. The Bush administration declared a "war on terrorism" and provided the leadership the nation sought. Working closely with Congress, the president took steps to devise and implement homeland security strategies. He also launched a military attack against Afghanistan to replace the terrorist-friendly Taliban regime and to destroy al Qaeda terrorist camps. As a result of these actions, President Bush's approval ratings soared. Indeed, they climbed to 90 percent, the highest ratings ever reported in the history of the Gallup Organization.

WAR AND PRESIDENTIAL APPROVAL RATINGS

Traditionally, presidents have had widespread public support during times of war or national crises. During such periods, Americans tend to show their patriotism, put aside their political and ideological differences, and stand behind the nation's leader. This support typically has a short life, however. Once the national emergency is over, presidential ratings usually drop considerably.

Consider the first Gulf War in 1991. When Iraq invaded Kuwait, President George H. W. Bush sent U.S. troops to Saudi Arabia to thwart Saddam Hussein's aggression. Bush's approval ratings jumped significantly, ultimately reaching 89 percent. Within a year, however, his ratings fell to 50 percent, and the voters did not reelect him in 1992.

The younger Bush seemed to be suffering a similar fate by the spring of 2002, when his ratings began to drop. Bush's continued emphasis on the war on terrorism and the "national emergency" posed by terrorist threats, however, convinced the public that we remained a nation at war. The administration began to talk about a "preemptive" war against Iraq to quell the threat posed by that nation and its leader, Saddam Hussein. By the spring of 2003, when the second Gulf War was under way, Bush's approval ratings again climbed—to over 70 percent. Yet as the war in Iraq dragged on, Bush's approval rating periodically slipped below 50 percent during 2004 and 2005.

A WAR WITH NO END IN SIGHT

The war on terrorism is unlike any previous war in several respects. For one thing, it is a somewhat elusive war. As Robert Reich, secretary of labor during the Clinton administration, put it, America's goal of "rooting out terrorism on a global level" is not only "breathtaking in scope" but also vague. Who, exactly, are our enemies? Immediately after 9/11, the enemies appeared to be terrorists and

A Marine with the First Marine Division mans a post on a street in the center of Baghdad. Behind the Marine sit the remains of an icon of the fallen Iraqi regime, the pedestal from which a giant statue of Saddam Hussein was pulled down by Iraqi citizens and Marines. The First Marine Division and other elements of the First Marine Expeditionary Force secured the capital city less than three weeks into Operation Iraqi Freedom.

U.S. Marine photo by Sergeant Joseph R. Chenelly

the countries that harbored them. Before the second Gulf War in 2003, however, President Bush made it clear that our enemies also included any country caught producing weapons of mass destruction that could be used to terrorize the United States and other nations.

Even more notable is the fact that there is no obvious end to this war, which Reich has labeled a "permanent war."[7] In 2001, President Bush stated that the war against Afghanistan was "just the beginning" of the war on terrorism. Then came Iraq. What nations might be targeted next for regime change, by military force if need be? At what point can our leaders declare that this war has ended?

Scholars of American government, including Norman Ornstein, have often spoken of the "permanent political campaign." Before elections, candidates campaign for office; following elections, incumbents spend a major portion of their time campaigning to retain their offices.[8] Some observers contend that President George W. Bush's permanent political campaign consists of a "permanent war campaign." He has crafted his political image as a wartime president and will likely continue to foster that image through the remainder of his time in office.

Are We Safer?

During wartime, it is difficult to criticize a sitting president's policies or motives without sounding unpatriotic. How might the lack of any widespread criticism of President Bush's policies affect the security of U.S. citizens in the long run?

TABLE 8–1

Checklist for Evaluating Public Opinion Polls

Because public opinion polls are so widely used by the media and policymakers, and their reliability is so often called into question, several organizations have issued guidelines for evaluating polls. Below is a list of questions that you can ask to evaluate the quality and reliability of a poll.

1. Who conducted the poll, and who sponsored or paid for it?
2. How many people were interviewed for the survey, and what part of the population did they represent (for example, registered voters, likely voters, persons over age eighteen)?
3. How were these people chosen, and how random was the sample?
4. How were respondents contacted and interviewed (by telephone, by mail-in survey)?
5. Who should have been interviewed but was not (what was the "nonresponse" rate—people who should have been part of the random sample but who refused to be interviewed, do not have telephones, or do not have listed telephone numbers, for example)?
6. What is the margin of error for the poll? (The acceptable margin of error for national polls is usually plus or minus 4 percent.)
7. What questions did the poll ask?
8. In what order were the questions asked?
9. When was the poll conducted?
10. What other polls were conducted on this topic, and do they report similar findings?

interview a respondent for five to thirty minutes. Based on these characteristics, it can sometimes be easy to distinguish a push poll from a legitimate poll conducted by a respected research organization. The checklist in Table 8–1 can also help you distinguish between a legitimate poll and a push poll.

Some researchers argue that identifying a push poll is not that easy, however. Political analyst Charlie Cook points out that "there are legitimate polls that can ask push questions, which test potential arguments against a rival to ascertain how effective those arguments might be in future advertising. . . . These are not only legitimate tools of survey research, but any political pollster who did not use them would be doing his or her clients a real disservice."[9] Distinguishing between push polls and push questions, then, is sometimes difficult—which is usually the intent of the push pollsters. A candidate does not want to be accused of conducting push polls because the public considers them a "dirty trick" and may turn against the candidate who uses them. In several recent campaigns, candidates have accused each other of con-

FIGURE 8–1
Voter Turnout since 1964

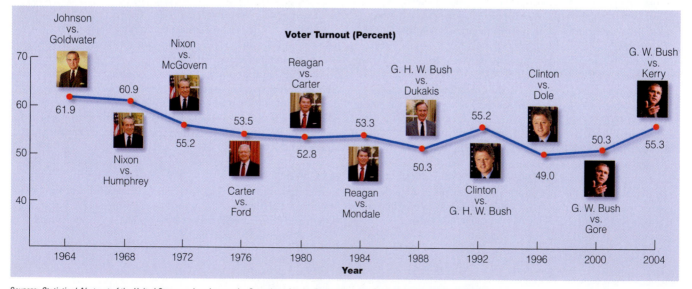

SOURCES: *Statistical Abstract of the United States,* various issues; the Committee for the Study of the American Electorate; authors' updates.

ducting push polls—accusations that could not always be proved or disproved. The result has been an increase in public cynicism about opinion polls and the political process in general.

Factors Affecting Voter Turnout

Voting is arguably the most important way in which citizens participate in the political process. Because we do not live in a direct democracy, Americans use the vote to elect politicians to represent their interests, values, and opinions in government. In many states, public-policy decisions—such as access to medical marijuana—are decided by voters. Americans' right to vote also helps keep elected officials accountable to campaign promises because they must face reelection. If voting is so important, then why do so few Americans exercise their right to vote?

The increasing public cynicism about the political process just described is one factor affecting voter turnout. In the past, legal restrictions based on income, gender, race, and other factors limited the number of people who could vote. Today, those restrictions have virtually disappeared, yet voter turnout remained around the 50 percent level in the 1996 and 2000 presidential elections, as you can see in Figure 8–1 on the facing page. The right to vote is available to more Americans than ever, yet relatively few people choose to exercise that right.

The Legal Right to Vote

In the United States today, all citizens who are at least eighteen years of age have the right to vote. This was not always true, however. Recall from Chapter 5 that restrictions on *suffrage*, the legal right to vote, have existed since the founding of our nation. Expanding the right to vote has been an important part of the gradual democratization of the American electoral process. Table 8–2 summarizes the major amendments, Supreme Court decisions, and laws that extended the right to vote to various American groups.

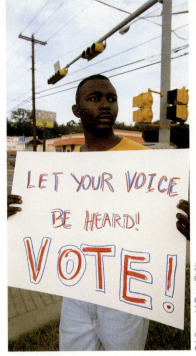

An African American does his part to "get out the vote" before an election. African Americans faced significant restrictions on voting until the 1950s and 1960s, when new laws and policies helped to end both formal and informal barriers to voting for this group. Today, although voter turnout among African Americans is increasing, they remain underrepresented at the polls.

TABLE 8-2
Extension of the Right to Vote

YEAR	ACTION	IMPACT
1870	Fifteenth Amendment	Discrimination based on race outlawed.
1920	Nineteenth Amendment	Discrimination based on gender outlawed.
1924	Congressional act	All Native Americans given citizenship.
1944	*Smith v. Allwright*	Supreme Court prohibits white primary.
1957	Civil Rights Act of 1957	Justice Department can sue to protect voting rights in various states.
1960	Civil Rights Act of 1960	Courts authorized to appoint referees to assist voter-registration procedures.
1961	Twenty-third Amendment	Residents of District of Columbia given right to vote for president and vice president.
1964	Twenty-fourth Amendment	Poll tax in national elections outlawed.
1965	Voting Rights Act of 1965	Literacy tests prohibited; federal voter registrars authorized in seven southern states.
1970	Voting Rights Act Amendments of 1970	Voting age for federal elections reduced to eighteen years; maximum thirty-day residency requirement for presidential elections; state literacy tests abolished.
1971	Twenty-sixth Amendment	Minimum voting age reduced to eighteen for all elections.
1975	Voting Rights Act Amendments of 1975	Federal voter registrars authorized in ten more states; bilingual ballots to be used in certain circumstances.
1982	Voting Rights Act Amendments of 1982	Extended provisions of Voting Rights Act amendments of 1970 and 1975; allows private parties to sue for violations.

Civil rights protesters, led by Martin Luther King, Jr., march on the road from Selma to Montgomery, Alabama, in March 1965. During the five-day, fifty-mile march, federal troops were stationed every one hundred yards along the route to protect the marchers from violent attacks by segregationists.

AP Photo/Matt Heron/Smithsonian

Historical Restrictions on Voting

Those who drafted the Constitution left the power to set suffrage qualifications to the individual states. Most states limited suffrage to adult white males who owned property, but these restrictions were challenged early on in the history of the republic. By 1810, religious restrictions on the right to vote were abolished in all states, and property ownership and tax-payment requirements gradually began to disappear as well. By 1850, all white males were allowed to vote. Restrictions based on race and gender continued, however.

The Fifteenth Amendment, ratified in 1870, guaranteed suffrage to African American males. Yet, for many decades, African Americans were effectively denied the ability to exercise their voting rights. Using methods ranging from mob violence to economic restrictions, groups of white southerners kept black Americans from voting. Some states required those who wished to vote to pass **literacy tests** and to answer complicated questions about government and history before they could register to vote. These tests, however, were not evenly applied to whites and African Americans. The **poll tax,** a fee of several dollars, was another device used to prevent African Americans from voting. At the time, this tax was a sizable burden, not only for most blacks but also for immigrants, small farmers, and the poor generally. Another popular restriction was the **grandfather clause,** which restricted the franchise (voting rights) to those whose grandfathers had voted.

Voting Rights Today

Today, these devices for restricting voting rights are explicitly outlawed by constitutional amendments and by the Voting Rights Act of 1965, as discussed in Chapter 5. Furthermore, the Nineteenth Amendment gave women the right to vote in 1920. In 1971, the Twenty-sixth Amendment reduced the voting age to eighteen.

Some restrictions on voting rights still exist. Every state except North Dakota requires voters to register with the appropriate state or local officials before voting. In the past, many states expected people to appear in person at an official building during normal working hours to register. In 1993, however, Congress passed the National Voter Registration Act (often referred to as the "Motor Voter Law"), which made registration easier. The act requires states to provide all eligible citizens with the opportunity to register to vote when they apply for or renew a driver's license. The law also requires that states allow mail-in registration, with forms given out at certain public-assistance agencies. Since the law took effect on January 1, 1995, it has facilitated millions of registrations.

Residency requirements are also usually imposed for voting. Since 1972, no state can impose a residency requirement of more than thirty days. Twenty-five states require that length of time, while the other twenty-five states require fewer or no days. Another voting

literacy test A test given to voters to ensure that they could read and write and thus evaluate political information; a technique used in many southern states to restrict African American participation in elections.

poll tax A fee of several dollars that had to be paid before a person could vote; a device used in some southern states to prevent African Americans from voting.

grandfather clause A clause in a state law that restricted the franchise (voting rights) to those whose grandfathers had voted; one of the techniques used in the South to prevent African Americans from exercising their right to vote.

Women suffragists protesting at the White House, circa 1917.

Corbis

requirement is citizenship. Aliens may not vote in any public election held anywhere in the United States. Most states also do not permit prison inmates, mentally ill people, convicted felons, or election-law violators to vote.

AMERICA at odds

A National Vote-by-Mail System

Voting by mail was first tried in Monterey, California, in 1977, and since then hundreds of elections have been handled via the U.S. mail. Oregon was a pioneer in the 1990s in opening up more and more elections to voting by mail. Since 1998, when 70 percent of Oregonians approved a vote-by-mail initiative, all elections in that state, including presidential elections, have been handled via the mail.

Those in favor of voting by mail point to the successes in Oregon. Not only has the state saved millions of dollars in voting costs, but voter participation has increased dramatically. In 2004, 2.1 million Oregonians registered to vote, more than ever before in that state's history, and 84 percent of those registered voters actually cast votes. Oregon now ranks among the three states with the highest voter participation, the other two being Minnesota and Wisconsin. Proponents of mail-in voting argue that it allows voters to make more deliberative choices because they have time to think between receiving their ballots in the mail and sending them in before Election Day. Additionally, because lists of registered voters must be kept up to date for mailing purposes, the count of eligible voters can be more accurate. Finally, there is no need to arrange for poll workers, distribute and retrieve election-day supplies, or make other preparations—and no confusion as to where people must go to vote.

Not everyone believes that a national mail-in system would be the best option for our democracy. Some argue that voting by mail isolates Americans from one another. They contend that going to a physical balloting place generates political energy and facilitates personal contact with other concerned citizens. Other critics maintain that employers, family, friends, and others might influence individuals to make ballot choices that they might not make if they were in the privacy of a voting booth. Still others claim that election fraud is also a possibility. Finally, with mail-in voting, voters lack the ability to change their minds at the last minute (especially if some new event or revelation occurs that affects a candidate's credibility) because most will have already sent in their ballots.

A worker moves bundled, vote-by-mail ballots in Portland, Oregon. Oregon, which is the only state in the country to conduct all elections exclusively by mail, now ranks among the top three states with the highest voter participation. Many credit the vote-by-mail system as the main reason for this ranking.

AP Photo/John Gress

Who Actually Votes

Just because an individual is eligible to vote does not necessarily mean that the person will actually go to the polls on Election Day and vote. Why do some eligible voters go to the polls while others do not? Although nobody can answer this question with absolute conviction, certain factors, including those discussed next, appear to affect voter turnout.

Educational Attainment   Among the factors affecting voter turnout, education appears to be the most important. The more education a person has, the more likely it is that she or he will be a regular voter. People who graduated from high school vote more regularly than those who dropped out, and college graduates vote more often than high school graduates.

Income Level and Age   Differences in income also lead to differences in voter turnout. Wealthy people tend to be overrepresented among regular voters. Generally, older voters turn out to vote more regularly than younger voters do, although participation tends to decline among the most elderly. Participation likely increases with age because older people tend to be more settled, are already registered, and have had more experience with voting.

Minority Status   Racial and ethnic minorities traditionally have been underrepresented among the ranks of voters. In several recent elections, however, participation by these groups, particularly African Americans and Hispanics, has increased.

Turnout among both African Americans and Hispanics rose significantly in the 1996 elections, but it did not show a further increase in 2000 or 2004. African American turnout in 2004 held steady at around 10 percent of overall turnout, which mirrors the 1996 percentage. Turnout among Hispanics, who constituted 6 percent of the voting electorate in 1996, even decreased somewhat in the 2004 elections—to roughly 4 percent. Of course, in absolute terms, the number of Hispanics in the United States has increased. In the years between 1996 and 2004, the majority of newly naturalized citizens in the United States were of Hispanic origin.

Why People Vote as They Do

What prompts some citizens to vote Republican and others to vote Democratic? What persuades voters to choose certain kinds of candidates? Obviously, more is involved than measuring one's own position against the candidates' positions and then voting accordingly. Voters choose candidates for many reasons, some of which are explored here. These questions cannot be answered with absolute certainty, but because of the technology of opinion polling, researchers have collected more information on voting than on any other form of political participation in the United States. These data shed some light on why people decide to vote for particular candidates.

Party Identification

Many voters have a standing allegiance to a political party, or a party identification, although the proportion of the population that does so is shrinking. For established voters, party identification is one of the most important and lasting predictors of how a person will vote. Party identification is an emotional attachment to a party that is influenced by family, age, peer groups, and other factors that play a role in the political socialization process discussed earlier.

Increasingly, there are indications that party identification has lost some of its impact. A growing number of voters now call themselves independents. Despite this label, many independents actually do support one or the other of the two major parties quite regularly. Figure 8–2 shows how those who identified themselves as Democrats, Republicans, and independents voted in the 2004 presidential elections.

Perception of the Candidates

Voters' choices also depend on their image of the candidates. Voters often base their decisions more on their *impressions* of the candidates than on the candidates' *actual* qualifications.

To some extent, voter attitudes toward candidates are based on emotions rather than on any judgment about experience or policy. In 2004, for example, voters' decisions in the presidential elections were largely guided by their perceptions of which candidate they could trust on matters of national security. President George W. Bush was more successful than his opponent, John Kerry, in convincing Americans that he had a plan for the war on terrorism—both at home and abroad. Bush pointed to his experience and leadership in the difficult years following the September 11 attacks. At the same time, many portrayed Kerry as indecisive and lacking a clear plan for the war on terrorism. Kerry failed to capitalize on the fact that he had been a decorated officer in Vietnam, while Bush had never served on active duty in the armed forces.

Policy Choices

When people vote for candidates who share their positions on particular issues, they are engaging in policy voting. If a candidate for senator in your state opposes gun control laws, for example, and you decide to vote for her for that reason, you have engaged in policy voting.

Historically, economic issues have had the strongest influence on voters' choices. When the economy is doing well, it is very difficult for a challenger, particularly at the presidential level,

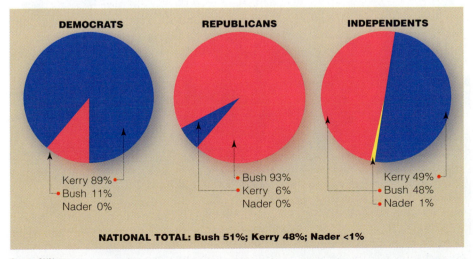

FIGURE 8–2

Party Identification and Voting Behavior in the 2004 Presidential Elections

DEMOCRATS

Kerry 89%
Bush 11%
Nader 0%

REPUBLICANS

Bush 93%
Kerry 6%
Nader 0%

INDEPENDENTS

Kerry 49%
Bush 48%
Nader 1%

NATIONAL TOTAL: Bush 51%; Kerry 48%; Nader <1%

SOURCE: CNN.com.

to defeat the incumbent. In contrast, when the country is experiencing increasing inflation, rising unemployment, or high interest rates, the incumbent will likely be at a disadvantage. Studies of how economic conditions affect voting choices differ in their conclusions, however. Some studies indicate that people vote on the basis of their personal economic well-being, whereas other studies seem to show that people vote on the basis of the nation's overall economic health.

Some of the most heated debates in American political campaigns involve social issues, such as abortion, gay and lesbian rights, the death penalty, and religion in the schools. In general, presidential candidates prefer to avoid taking a definite stand on these types of issues, because voters who have strong opinions about such issues are likely to be offended if a candidate does not share their views.

Socioeconomic Factors

Some of the factors that influence how people vote can be described as socioeconomic. These factors include a person's educational attainment, income level, age, gender, religion, and geographic location. Some of these factors have to do with the families and circumstances into which individuals are born; others have to do with choices made later in life. Figure 8–3 shows how various groups voted in the 2004 presidential elections.

Educational Attainment

As a general rule, people with more education are more likely to vote Republican, although at the upper levels of educational attainment this pattern breaks down. Typically, those with less education are more inclined to vote for the Democratic nominee. Educational attainment as a factor in voting can be linked to income level. One in seventeen Americans from families with a household income of $30,000 or less finishes college, while one in two of those from families making $80,000 or more completes a four-year degree.

Occupation and Income Level

Professionals and businesspersons tend to vote Republican. Manual laborers, factory workers, and especially union members are more likely to vote Democratic. In the past, the higher the income, the more likely it was that a person would vote Republican. Conversely, a much larger percentage of low-income individuals voted Democratic. But this pattern is also breaking down, and there are no hard-and-fast rules. Some very poor individuals are devoted Republicans, just as some extremely wealthy persons are supporters of the Democratic Party. (For a discussion of how income level factored into the 2004 presidential elections, see this chapter's *Perception versus Reality* feature on page 190.)

Older Americans generally turn out to vote in greater numbers than do younger Americans, in part because older people tend to be more settled, are already registered, and have had more experience with voting.

AP Photo/Charles Krupa

FIGURE 8-3
Voting by Groups in the 2004 Presidential Elections

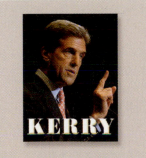

PERCENTAGE VOTING FOR KERRY

Gender
Male — 44
Female — 51

Race
Whites — 41
Blacks — 88
Hispanics — 53
Asians — 56

Education
College — 46
High school — 47
Grade school — 50

Household Income (thousands of dollars)
Under $30 — 59
$30–49.9 — 50
$50–74.9 — 43
$75 or more — 42

Age
Under 30 — 54
30–44 — 46
45–59 — 48
60 and older — 46

Religion
Protestants — 40
Catholics — 47
Jews — 74

Region
Northeast — 56
Midwest — 48
South — 42
West — 50

NATIONAL TOTAL FOR KERRY: 48%

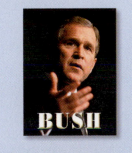

PERCENTAGE VOTING FOR BUSH

Gender
Male — 55
Female — 48

Race
Whites — 58
Blacks — 11
Hispanics — 44
Asians — 44

Education
College — 52
High school — 52
Grade school — 49

Household Income (thousands of dollars)
Under $30 — 40
$30–49.9 — 49
$50–74.9 — 56
$75 or more — 57

Age
Under 30 — 45
30–44 — 53
45–59 — 51
60 and older — 54

Religion
Protestants — 59
Catholics — 52
Jews — 25

Region
Northeast — 43
Midwest — 51
South — 58
West — 49

NATIONAL TOTAL FOR BUSH: 51%

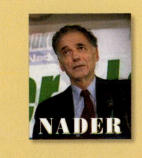

PERCENTAGE VOTING FOR NADER

Gender
Male — <1
Female — <1

Race
Whites — <1
Blacks — <1
Hispanics — 2
Asians — <1

Education
College — 1
High school — <1
Grade school — <1

Household Income (thousands of dollars)
Under $30 — <1
$30–49.9 — <1
$50–74.9 — <1
$75 or more — 1

Age
Under 30 — <1
30–44 — 1
45–59 — <1
60 and older — <1

Religion
Protestants — <1
Catholics — <1
Jews — <1

Region
Northeast — 1
Midwest — <1
South — <1
West — 1

NATIONAL TOTAL FOR NADER: <1%

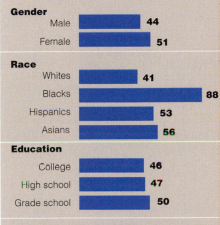
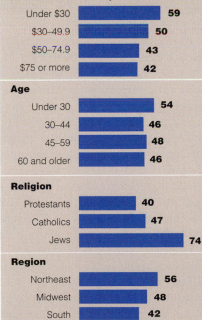
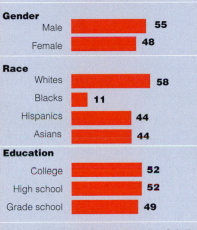

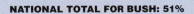

SOURCE: CNN.com.

Voting with One's Wallet

During any election, political candidates and their parties have to distinguish themselves from the opposition. For many years, candidates have attempted to entice voters to support them on the basis of the voters' economic interests.

THE PERCEPTION

During modern times, the economic interests of the "common person" have been associated with the Democratic Party. Democrats have almost universally been viewed as being in favor of policies that increase workers' rights and incomes. The Democratic Party has also been associated with progressive policies that provide a safety net for the poor and the less fortunate in our society. Democrats have traditionally advocated reducing taxes on the poor and the middle class and increasing them on the upper-income classes. The Republican Party, in contrast, has typically been viewed as favoring policies that will create an economic environment that benefits businesses, the rich, and the super rich.

THE REALITY

At least in the most recent presidential elections, the Republican Party seems to have appealed to the middle class and even the poor.[10] In 2004, of the twenty-eight states with the lowest per capita income, George W. Bush won twenty-six. One might say that an administration accused of protecting "the rich" was kept in office by the very people who, according to political analysts, would suffer

most by Bush's reelection. Thus, millions of factory workers, waiters and waitresses, and other working-class groups seemingly voted against their own economic interests when they cast their votes for Republican candidates.

This trend actually started in the 2000 presidential elections in which Bush and Democratic candidate Al Gore contested for the presidency. In that election, almost 40 percent of households that had incomes below $30,000 were residents of pro-Bush counties. Only about 7 percent of the voters in those counties had incomes of $100,000 or more.

Just as the Republicans drew support from lower-income voters, the Democrats found support among the rich. Six of the top ten contributors to Democratic candidate John Kerry's campaign were major brokerage and banking firms, such as Goldman Sachs and Citigroup, even though Kerry promised to raise their taxes. In just one day, Kerry received $3 million from owners of beach houses in the ritzy Hamptons area outside New York City. Kerry's campaign also benefited from contributions from the most aggressive election donors—lawyers. As a group, lawyers gave more than $150 million to 2004 political candidates, mainly to Democrats. Bush, in contrast, relied heavily on small donors.

What's Your Opinion?

What might cause individuals to vote against their own personal economic interests? (Hint: What other issues might be more important?)

Age   Although one might think that a person's chronological age would determine political preferences, apparently age does not matter very much. Some differences can be identified, however: young adults tend to be more liberal than older Americans on most issues, and young adults tend to hold more progressive views than older persons on such issues as racial and gender equality.

Although older Americans tend to be somewhat more conservative than younger groups, their greater conservatism may be explained simply by the fact that individuals maintain the values they learned when they first became politically aware. Forty years later, those values may be considered relatively conservative. Additionally, people's attitudes are sometimes shaped by the events that unfolded as they grew up. Individuals who grew up during an era of Democratic Party dominance will likely remain Democrats throughout their lives. The same will hold true for those who grew up during an era of Republican Party dominance.

In elections from 1952 through 1980, voters under the age of thirty clearly favored the Democratic presidential candidates. This trend reversed itself in 1984 when voters under age thirty voted heavily for Ronald Reagan. George H. W. Bush maintained that support in 1988. In 1992, however, Bill Clinton won back the young voters by 10 percentage points, a margin that expanded to 20 percentage points in 1996. In 2004, Democrat John Kerry won the youth vote over Republican George W. Bush by 9 percentage points.

Gender   Until relatively recently, there seemed to be no fixed pattern of voter preferences by gender in presidential elections. One year, more women than men would vote for the Democratic candidate; another year, more men than women would do so. Some political analysts believe that a **gender gap** became a major determinant of voter decision making in the 1980 presidential elections, however. In that year, Ronald Reagan outdrew Jimmy Carter by

gender gap A term used to describe the difference between the percentage of votes cast for a particular candidate by women and the percentage of votes cast for the same candidate by men.

16 percentage points among male voters, whereas women gave about an equal number of votes to each candidate. Although the gender gap has varied since 1980, it reappeared in force in 1996, when President Clinton received 54 percent of women's votes and only 43 percent of men's votes. The gender gap was also significant in 2000, with more women (54 percent) than men (42 percent) voting for Gore, and more men (53 percent) than women (43 percent) voting for Bush. The gender gap partially contracted in 2004, as John Kerry won only 51 percent of the female vote, compared to George W. Bush's 48 percent. The male vote remained strongly Republican, however, as Bush beat Kerry by 11 percentage points among men.

Religion and Ethnic Background

Traditionally, the majority of Protestants have voted Republican, while Catholics and Jews have tended to be Democrats. Voters of Italian, Irish, Polish, Eastern European, and Slavic descent have generally supported Democrats, while those of British, Scandinavian, and French descent have voted Republican.

African Americans vote principally for Democrats. They have given the Democratic presidential candidate a clear majority of their votes in every election since 1952, although this majority weakened in the 1980s. Democratic presidential candidates have received, on average, more than 80 percent of the African American vote since 1956. In 2004, the percentage reached 88 percent.

Geographic Region

Where a voter lives also influences his or her preferences. For more than one hundred years after the Civil War, most white southerners, regardless of background or socioeconomic status, were Democrats. In large part, this is because the Republicans were in power when the Civil War broke out, and many southerners thus blamed the Republicans for that conflict and its results for the South. Known as the **Solid South,** this strong coalition has recently crumbled in the presidential elections, although the rural vote in parts of the South still tends to be Democratic.

Solid South A term used to describe the tendency of the southern states to vote Democratic after the Civil War.

Although the Solid South is no more, it appears that something like a Solid Northeast may be emerging, with a strong Democratic majority. Republicans continue to draw much of their strength from the mountain and plains states in the West and from rural areas throughout the country (except in the South).

Ideology as an Indicator of Voting Behavior

A significant percentage of Americans today identify themselves as moderates. Recent polls indicate that 41 percent of Americans consider themselves to be moderates, 18 percent consider themselves liberals, and 41 percent identify themselves as conservatives. Additionally—and somewhat surprisingly— most Americans do not see a relationship between today's issues and political ideology. For example, polling data show that only a small fraction—about 2 percent—of Americans identify either side of the abortion debate with conservatism or liberalism.

For some Americans, then, where they fall in the political spectrum is a strong indicator of how they will vote: liberals vote for Democrats, Greens, or other liberal candidates, and conservatives vote for Republicans, Libertarians, or other conservative candidates. The large numbers of Americans who fall in the political center do not adhere strictly to an ideology. In most elections, the candidates compete aggressively for these voters because they know their "base"—on the left or right—is secure.

In 1949, historian Arthur Schlesinger, Jr., described the position between the political extremes as the **vital center.** The center is vital because, without it, reaching the compromises that are necessary to a political system's continuity may be difficult, if not impossible. Voter apathy and low voter turnout are found most commonly among those in the center. That means that the most motivated voters are the "ideologically zealous."[11] The declining number of political moderates in Congress in the mid-1990s seemed to be proof of this trend. President George W. Bush has looked to the vital center for support on many of his policies, but in doing so, as you will read in the next chapter, he did not alienate his base of support on the right as he won reelection in 2004.

vital center The center of the political spectrum, or those who hold moderate political views. The center is vital because without it, it may be difficult, if not impossible, to reach the compromises that are necessary to a political system's continuity.

why does it MATTER?

Voting and Your Everyday Life

For many of you, voting is a civic duty that you must undertake to be a responsible citizen. For others, voting seems to be a waste of time. After all, how much can one vote more or less really matter? Moreover, even if a vote would make a difference, does it matter who is in office?

On both counts, such a cavalier attitude toward voting is misguided. Each vote does count, particularly given the closeness of elections throughout our history. Recent elections have certainly proved that point. In 2000, the presidency was decided by just several hundred votes in the state of Florida. Similarly, the 2004 presidential election came down to a tight race in Ohio.

What a Difference a President Makes

Think about some of the political issues that affect you on a personal level.

▶ If you are living in a town that depends on logging or mining, and a president declares the surrounding region a national monument and thus out of bounds for such activities, your pocketbook may be affected.

▶ If you are working, you pay income taxes. In the 2004 campaign, John Kerry did not voice opposition to raising taxes. George W. Bush, in contrast, proposed making the aggressive tax cuts enacted in his first term permanent. Your after-tax income, and thus your standard of living, was directly affected by this tax cut and will continue to be affected by each and every presidential election.

▶ Most of us will eventually rely on Social Security as a significant source of retirement income. John Kerry campaigned to protect the benefits that Americans have come to expect for their elderly years. As you read in Chapter 6, President George W. Bush has proposed a partial privatization of Social Security. Many economists argue that Bush's proposal will create significant cuts in the benefits provided to retirees, while adding trillions of dollars in debt to the national deficit. Bush's reelection in 2004 could have a significant effect on our national pension system.

Taking Action

One of the lessons Americans learned from recent elections is that every vote counts. The 2004 Washington state gubernatorial race reaffirmed this fact. Perhaps the closest vote in recent memory, a mere 129 votes out of the total 2.9 million cast decided the race between Christine Gregoire and Dino Rossi. Three recounts, with the final count done by hand, were required before Gregoire was declared the new governor of Washington. Despite numerous close elections in recent years, U.S. voter turnout remains low compared to most other Western democracies. Nationwide, only 76 percent of eligible voters register, and roughly 50 percent actually vote. Those numbers are even lower for young voters: only about 45 percent of eligible voters between the ages of 18 and 24 years register, and only about 32 percent vote.

Many groups focus on registration and "get out the vote" efforts targeted at young voters. For example, "Rock the Vote" was formed for the purpose of getting young people involved in political issues. The organization holds concerts and sponsors other activities to "get out the youth vote" before elections. In the photo below, two volunteers register a voter during a "Rock the Vote" concert in Fresno, California, prior to a recent election.

AP Photo/Tomas Ovalle/The Fresno Bee

Key Terms

agents of political socialization 174	literacy test 184	public opinion 173	sampling error 179
biased sample 177	media 175	public opinion poll 177	Solid South 191
gender gap 190	peer group 176	push poll 180	straw poll 177
grandfather clause 184	political socialization 174	random sample 178	vital center 191
	poll tax 184	sample 177	

Chapter Summary

1 Public opinion is the views of the citizenry about politics, public issues, and public policies. Most people acquire their political views through a complex learning process called political socialization, which begins early in a person's childhood and continues throughout that person's life.

2 A public opinion poll is a numerical survey of the public's opinion on a particular topic at a particular moment. To achieve the most accurate results possible, pollsters use random samples, in which each person within the entire population being polled has an equal chance of being chosen. Nonetheless, there are many problems with polls.

3 One of the major problems with polls today is the way they are used by politicians and the media. The media frequently neglect to inform the public about a poll's possible bias or margin of error. Politicians use push polls as a campaign tactic to "push" voters toward one candidate and away from another. The public today tends to regard poll taking and poll results with some cynicism.

4 In the early days of this nation, an important factor affecting voter turnout was, of course, the existence of numerous restrictions on voting. These restrictions were based on property, race, gender, religious beliefs, and payment of taxes. Over time, these restrictions were removed (refer back to Table 8–2 on page 183).

5 There are still some voting restrictions in the form of registration, residency, and citizenship requirements. Even those who meet these requirements do not always turn out at the polls, however. Although the reasons why some people vote and others do not cannot be known with certainty, indications are that voter turnout is affected by specific factors, including educational attainment, income level, age, and minority status.

6 The following factors all influence voters' preferences: party identification, perception of the candidates, policy choices, and socioeconomic status.

RESOURCES FOR FURTHER STUDY

Selected Readings

Alvarez, R. Michael, and John Brehm. *Hard Choices, Easy Answers: Values, Information, and American Public Opinion.* Princeton, N.J.: Princeton University Press, 2002. The authors examine the process of opinion polling in the United States. In particular, they examine how such factors as a respondent's political knowledge and psychological predisposition affect survey responses. They conclude that most often respondents are simply uncertain about how their personal values translate into political opinions.

Baradat, Leon P. *Political Ideologies,* 8th ed. Upper Saddle River, N.J.: Prentice Hall, 2002. This book gives a broad but clear overview of political ideologies and how they change over time. It is an excellent introduction to the spectrum of political attitudes that have shaped world politics.

Frank, Thomas. *What's the Matter with Kansas? How Conservatives Won the Heart of America.* New York: Henry Holt & Company, 2004. The author looks at how the Republican Party gained its current dominance in the American heartland. Frank examines why so many Americans vote against their economic interests.

Newport, Frank. *Polling Matters: Why Leaders Must Listen to the Wisdom of the People.* New York: Warner Books, 2004. The author, who serves as the editor in chief of the *Gallup Poll,* argues that polls lie at the heart of a well-functioning free society.

Politics on the Web

■ Recent polls conducted and analyzed by the Roper Center for Public Opinion Research can be found at **http://www.ropercenter.uconn.edu**

■ According to its home page, the mission of the National Election Studies (NES) "is to produce high-quality data on voting, public opinion, and political participation that serves the research needs of social scientists, teachers, students, and policymakers concerned with understanding the theoretical and empirical foundations of mass politics in a democratic society." The NES is a good source of information on public opinion. To reach this site, go to **http://www.umich.edu/~nes**

■ At the Gallup Organization's Web site, you can find the results of recent polls as well as an archive of past polls and information on how polls are conducted. Go to **http://www.gallup.com**

■ You can find further links to poll data and other sources on public opinion at the following site: **http://www.publicagenda.org**

■ The Polling Report Web site provides polling results on a number of issues, organized by topics. The site is easy to use and up to date. Go to **http://www.pollingreport.com**

■ PBS features a section on its Web site titled "PBS by the People," which provides some good tips on how to analyze a poll. Go to **http://www.pbs.org/elections/savvyanalyze.html**

Online Resources for This Chapter

This text's Companion Web Site, at **http://www.americaatodds.com**, offers links to numerous resources that you can utilize to learn more about the topics covered in this chapter. For a list describing these resources, see the inside front cover of this book.

chapter 9

campaigns and elections

CHAPTER OBJECTIVES

After reading this chapter, you should be able to . . .

▶ Discuss how candidates are nominated.

▶ Indicate what is involved in launching a political campaign today.

▶ Describe the structure and functions of a campaign organization.

▶ Summarize the laws that regulate campaign financing and the role of money in modern political campaigns.

▶ Explain how elections are held and how the electoral college functions in presidential elections.

Why All the Negative Campaigning?

The 2000 and 2004 presidential elections featured extremely close, bitterly fought races. Some commentators have argued that American politics has become increasingly polarized in recent years, causing many citizens to harbor deep animosity toward those with different political views. Issues such as the war in Iraq, homeland security, same-sex marriage, and the economy have divided Americans.

Politicians often exploit these divisions through negative campaigning, defining their candidacy as much by what they oppose as by what they favor. Beyond the issues, political candidates often attack their opponents personally by publicly questioning their character, competence, or leadership ability. Americans often complain about "attack ads" and mudslinging, yet negative campaigning has seemingly been on the rise. Not surprisingly, there are differing viewpoints on the effectiveness of these tactics.

America Has a Tradition of Negative Campaigning

Some Americans believe that negative campaigning is a necessary, albeit not always desirable, part of elections. Voters must be made aware of a candidate's shortcomings, they argue. Character flaws, questionable ideas, and dubious policy decisions may not come to light if candidates refuse to "go negative."

Many claim that negative campaigning is sometimes the only method of informing voters of certain facts. Oftentimes, candidates will run advertisements that highlight controversial positions held by their opponents. For example, senior citizens would want to know if a candidate had plans to cut back on government-funded prescription drug benefits.

Furthermore, proponents argue, America has a long tradition of negative campaigning. By historical standards, today's mudslinging is quite tame compared to the negativity of campaigns in the early 1800s. For example, one newspaper claimed that Thomas Jefferson was a traitorous agent of the French government and labeled James Madison as nothing more than Jefferson's "political pimp." Other papers openly suggested that Alexander Hamilton was of mixed-race parentage and mocked him as a "common bastard." During this era, newspapers were often mouthpieces of political partisans. A newspaper's owner and editors would use the paper as a forum for supporting their party's candidates and platforms, while attacking those of the opposing party.

Some supporters of negative campaigning also point to its entertainment value and ability to mobilize otherwise apathetic voters. They argue that hard-fought elections such as the 2004 presidential race stir up emotions and create excitement.

Negativity Hurts the Democratic Process

Those who oppose negative campaigning argue that candidates attack their opponents instead of discussing their own views and agendas. Often, it is much easier to malign another candidate's ideas than to come up with a viable solution of one's own. Recently, political action committees and issue groups (such as 527s) have joined candidates in churning out negative information on opposing candidates.

Attack ads and negative campaigning often skew the facts or play on voters' fears, say opponents. Politicians have been known to take the words of an opponent out of context or mislead the public about her or his views. In the 2002 midterm elections, Senator Max Cleland (D., Ga.) became the target of a misleading campaign by Republican challenger Saxby Chambliss. Chambliss accused Cleland of being weak on national security because he had not supported President Bush's legislation to create the Department of Homeland Security. Cleland, a veteran who had lost both legs and an arm in the Vietnam War, had opposed Bush's plan because he supported an alternative homeland security bill. His position was complex and thus difficult to explain in short sound bites. As a result, Chambliss won the election largely by using attack ads that went as far as including Osama bin Laden and Saddam Hussein in the background.

Many Americans believe that negative campaigning creates a hostile political environment. Some potential voters become so disheartened by the negativity that they cease paying attention to politics and stay away from the polls on Election Day, they claim.

Where Do You Stand?

1. Do you believe that attack ads have informative value? Why or why not?

2. Is negative campaigning more or less likely to encourage you to turn out and vote? Explain.

Explore This Issue Online

- Source Watch, a project of the Center for Media and Democracy, offers an informative look into attack ads. Go to **http://www.sourcewatch.org/wiki.phtml?title= Attack_ads**.
- A good place to check claims made by candidates in debates or ads is **http://www.vote-smart.org**. You can search by issue or politician.

Introduction

During elections, candidates vie to become representatives of the people—in both national and state offices. The population of the United States is now close to 295 million. Clearly, all voting-age citizens cannot gather in one place to make laws and run the government. We have to choose representatives to govern the nation and act on behalf of our interests. We accomplish this through popular elections.

Campaigning for election has become an arduous task for every politician. As you will see in this chapter, American campaigns are long, complicated, and very expensive undertakings. They can also be wearing on the citizens who are not running for office. Yet they are an important component of our political process because it is through campaigns that citizens learn about the candidates and decide how they will cast their votes. As you read in the chapter-opening *America at Odds* feature, Americans are divided as to whether negative campaigning adds to their knowledge about the candidates or is so misleading and unfair that it discourages people from voting.

How We Nominate Candidates

The first step on the long road to winning an election is the nomination process. Nominations narrow the field of possible candidates and limit each political party's choice to one person. In the past, self-nomination was the most common way to become a candidate, and this method is still used in small towns and rural sections of the country. A self-proclaimed candidate usually files a petition to be listed on the ballot. Each state has laws that specify how many signatures a candidate must obtain to show that he or she has some public support. An alternative is to be a write-in candidate—voters write the candidate's name on the ballot on Election Day.

Serious candidates for most offices are rarely nominated in these ways, however. As you read in Chapter 7, most candidates for high office are nominated by a political party and receive considerable support from party activists throughout their campaigns.

Party Control over Nominations

George Washington was essentially unopposed in the first U.S. elections in 1789—no other candidate was seriously considered in any state. But many of the Constitution's framers wondered how candidates would be nominated after Washington. Most envisioned that candidates would simply "stand" for election, rather than actively run for office. Instead of shaking hands and making speeches, they would stay on their farms and wait for the people's call, as Washington did. Some framers believed that the electors of the electoral college would put forward candidates' names.

By the end of Washington's eight years in office, however, political divisions among the nation's leaders had solidified into political parties, the Federalists and the Democratic Republicans (see Chapter 7). Party leaders recognized that the ability to choose nominees was essential to their political power. Beginning in 1797, they began to hold congressional conferences, later called **caucuses,**[1] to nominate candidates in secret. The voters at large played no part in choosing nominees.

caucus A meeting held by party leaders to choose political candidates. The caucus system of nominating candidates was eventually replaced by nominating conventions and, later, by direct primaries.

Negative ads were featured prominently during the 2004 presidential campaigns. In the top photo, a campaign ad for President George W. Bush criticized the Democratic presidential nominee, Senator John Kerry of Massachusetts. In the bottom photo, a Kerry campaign ad emphasizes that even a Republican senator, John McCain of Arizona, thought that an ad by Bush supporters that questioned Kerry's military record went "beyond the pale."

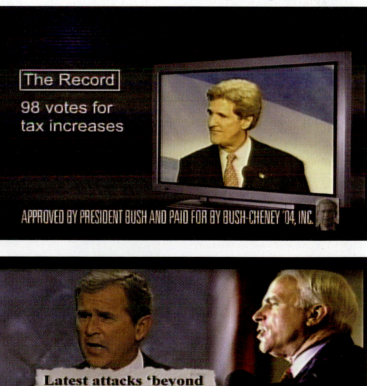

The Record
98 votes for tax increases

APPROVED BY PRESIDENT BUSH AND PAID FOR BY BUSH-CHENEY '04, INC.

AP Photo/Bush-Cheney 2004

Latest attacks 'beyond the pale' - John McCain
Houston Chronicle - 2/5/00

AP Photo/Kerry-Edwards 2004

By the presidential race of 1824, the caucus method of nomination had become a controversial issue. Andrew Jackson and other presidential candidates who felt that the caucus was undemocratic derisively referred to the system as "King Caucus." Faced with rising opposition, party leaders were forced to find other methods of nominating candidates. As the caucus system faded away in presidential politics, its use diminished at the state and local levels as well. Today, only a few states continue to use caucuses in their electoral politics.

The Party Nominating Convention

nominating convention An official meeting of a political party to choose its candidates. Nominating conventions at the state and local levels also select delegates to represent the people of their geographic areas at a higher-level party convention.

delegate A person selected to represent the people of one geographic area at a party convention.

As the use of the caucus method diminished around the country, it was replaced in many states by party conventions. A **nominating convention** is an official meeting of a political party to choose its candidates and to select **delegates**—persons sent to a higher-level party convention to represent the people of one geographic area. For example, delegates at a local party convention would nominate candidates for local office and would also choose delegates to represent the party at the state convention. By 1840, the convention system had become the most common way of nominating candidates for government offices at every level.

Little by little, criticism of corruption in nominating conventions at the state level caused state legislatures to disband most of them. They are still used in some states, including Connecticut, Delaware, Michigan, and Utah, to nominate candidates for some state offices. At the national level, the convention is still used to select presidential and vice-presidential candidates.

The Direct Primary and Loss of Party Control

direct primary An election held within each of the two major parties—Democratic and Republican—to choose the party's candidates for the general election.

In most states, direct primaries gradually replaced nominating conventions. A **direct primary** is an election held within each of the two major parties—Democratic and Republican—to pick its candidates for the general election. This is the method most commonly used today to nominate candidates for office.

Most states require the major parties to use a primary to choose their candidates for the U.S. Senate and the House of Representatives, for the governorship and all other state offices, and for most local offices as well. A few states, however, use different combinations of nominating conventions and primaries to pick candidates for the top offices. Although the primaries are *party* nominating elections, they are closely regulated by the states. The states set the dates and conduct the primaries. The states also provide polling places, election officials, registration lists, and ballots, in addition to counting the votes.

These boxes are full of voter-information booklets that were prepared for the March 5, 2002, Los Angeles County primary election. There were several hundred different versions of the pamphlet, which was used by voters in different parties and geographic areas.

AP Photo/Reed Saxon

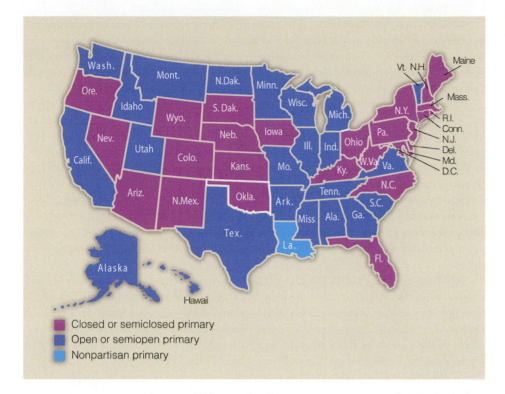

FIGURE 9–1
Types of Direct Primaries

Closed or semiclosed primary
Open or semiopen primary
Nonpartisan primary

The advent of the direct primary has meant some loss of party control over the nominating process. As you will read shortly, state laws have created different types of primaries across the country, though they generally fall into two broad categories: closed primaries and open primaries. Open primaries allow voters to vote for a party's candidates even if they do not belong to that party. As open primaries have become more common, the nominating process has become less party centered and more candidate centered. Louisiana is unique in that all candidates run in the same, nonpartisan primary election. Figure 9–1 shows which states have closed (or semiclosed), open (or semiopen), or nonpartisan primaries.

Closed Primaries   In a **closed primary,** only party members can vote to choose that party's candidates, and they may vote only in the primary of their own party. Thus, only registered Democrats can vote in the Democratic primary to select candidates of the Democratic Party. Only registered Republicans can vote for the Republican candidates. A person usually establishes party membership when she or he registers to vote. Some states have a *semiclosed* primary, which allows voters to register with a party or change their party affiliations on Election Day. Regular party workers favor the closed primary because it promotes party loyalty. Independent voters oppose it because it excludes them from the nominating process.

closed primary A primary in which only party members can vote to choose that party's candidates.

Open Primaries   An **open primary** is a direct primary in which voters can vote for a party's candidates regardless of whether they belong to the party. In most open primaries, all voters receive both a Republican ballot and a Democratic ballot. Voters then choose either the Democratic or the Republican ballot in the privacy of the voting booth. In a *semiopen* primary, voters request the ballot for the party of their choice.

open primary A primary in which voters can vote for a party's candidates regardless of whether they belong to the party.

Nominating Presidential Candidates

In some respects, being nominated for president is more difficult than being elected. The nominating process narrows a very large number of hopefuls down to a single candidate from each party. Choosing a presidential candidate is unlike nominating candidates for any other office. One reason for this is that the nomination process combines several different methods.

Presidential Primaries

The majority of the states hold presidential primaries, beginning early in the election year. For a candidate, a good showing in the early primaries results in plenty of media attention as television networks and newspaper reporters play up the results. Subsequent state primaries tend to serve as contests to eliminate unlikely candidates.

State legislatures and state parties make the laws that determine how the primaries are set up, who may enter them, and who may vote in them. Several different methods of voting are used in presidential primaries. In some states, for example, primary voters only select delegates to a party's national convention and do not know which candidates the delegates intend to vote for at the convention. In other states, the voters cast ballots for candidates, and the delegates must vote for the winning candidate at the national convention.

In some states, delegates to the national convention are chosen through caucuses or conventions instead of through presidential primaries. Iowa, for example, holds caucuses to choose delegates to local conventions. These delegates, in turn, choose those who will attend the state and national conventions. Other states use a combination of caucuses and primaries.

Primaries—The Rush to Be First

In an effort to make their primaries prominent in the media and influential in the political process, many states have moved the date of their primary to earlier in the year. This "front-loading" of the primaries started after the 1968 Democratic National Convention in Chicago, which appeared to be ruled by a few groups. Then, in 1988, southern states created "Super Tuesday" by holding most of their primaries on the same day in early March. Recently, many states in the Midwest, New England, and the Pacific West (including California) have moved their primaries to an earlier date, too. If this trend continues, we may eventually have a one-day national primary.

The practice of front-loading primaries gained a momentum of its own in the last decade. The states with later primary dates found that most nominations were decided early in the season, leaving their voters out of the action. As more states moved their primary dates up, however, the more important the early primaries became. Sometimes, the political parties try to manipulate primary dates to maximize their candidates' media attention. The order and timing of primary dates also influence the candidates' fund-raising.

Some Americans worry that with a shortened primary season, long-shot candidates will no longer be able to propel themselves into serious contention by doing well in small, early-voting states, such as New Hampshire or Iowa. Traditionally, for example, a candidate who had a successful showing in the New Hampshire primary had time to obtain enough financial backing to continue in the race. The candidate also had time to become known to the voters through political advertising, TV appearances, and campaign speeches along the campaign trail. With the shortened primary season, the winners will be those candidates who can start their fund-raising early and load up on national TV spots. The fear is that an accelerated schedule of presidential primaries will likely favor the richest candidates.

National Party Conventions

Born in the 1830s, the American national political convention is unique in Western democracies. Elsewhere, candidates for prime minister or chancellor are chosen within the confines of party councils. That is actually the way the framers wanted it done—the Constitution does not mention a nominating convention. Indeed, Thomas Jefferson loathed the idea. He feared that if the presidential race became a popularity contest, it would develop into "mobocracy."

At one time, the conventions were indeed giant free-for-alls. It wasn't clear who the winning presidential and vice-presidential candidates would be until the delegates voted. As more states opted to hold primaries in which candidates ran and delegates were selected, the drama of national conventions diminished. Today, the conventions have been described as massive pep rallies. Nonetheless, each convention's task remains a serious one. In late summer or early fall, two to three thousand delegates gather at each convention to represent the wishes of the voters and political leaders of their home states. They adopt the official party platform and declare their support for the party's presidential and vice-presidential candidates.

On the first day of the convention, delegates hear the reports of the **Credentials Committee,** which inspects each prospective delegate's claim to be seated as a legitimate representative of

Credentials Committee A committee of each national political party that evaluates the claims of national party convention delegates to be the legitimate representatives of their states.

her or his state. When the eligibility of delegates is in question, the committee decides who will be seated. In the evening, there is usually a keynote speaker to whip up enthusiasm among the delegates. The second day includes committee reports and debates on the party platform. The third day is devoted to nominations and voting. Balloting begins with an alphabetical roll call in which states and territories announce their votes. By midnight, the convention's real work is over and the presidential candidate has been selected. The vice-presidential nomination and the acceptance speeches occupy the fourth day.

Many Americans complain that recent conventions have been little more than prolonged infomercials. Convention activities are highly staged events. Even so-called impromptu moments seem to have been well prepared. Furthermore, the major news networks have cut their convention coverage dramatically since the 1980s. In view of these developments, some Americans question whether the conventions serve any purpose at all.

AMERICA at odds

Do National Conventions Serve Any Purpose Today?

In 2004, the Republican National Convention in New York City cost $154 million to stage, making it the most expensive party convention in the nation's history. The $154 million paid for a wide range of expenses, including $301,460 for limousine services and $281,000 to build the circular stage that President George W. Bush used to make his acceptance speech on the last night of the convention. The Democratic National Convention in Boston cost less—just under $100 million.[2] Are the conventions worth such staggering costs? Do they serve any real purpose today?

Yes, according to some. For example, political commentator George Will once argued that a well-scripted political convention is "the meticulous expression of the party's thinking" and an important part of the process of persuading voters to support the party's candidates.[3] Former CNN chair Tom Johnson makes a similar argument. Johnson contends that even though the conventions are largely contrived, they offer a valuable perspective on the parties, the policies they represent, and their candidates—all important information for the voters. Furthermore, consider what is at stake in selecting a president. The winner will have the power to launch nuclear weapons, make decisions that influence war and peace, and shape policy through presidential appointments, such as to the Supreme Court.[4]

Others argue that the conventions today are simply fund-raising stunts, giving the major political parties a chance to reward contributors and ask for more money. Interest groups—corporations and lobbyists—are the first ones asked to pay the high price tag of the convention. Interest groups thus increase their access to the candidates and their influence on the party's platform. Everything that goes on at the conventions is considered "party building" and is therefore exempt from campaign-financing regulations (these regulations will be discussed shortly). In the future, the question of whether national party conventions serve any meaningful purpose for voters will likely be raised again.

The Modern Political Campaign

Once nominated, candidates focus on their campaigns. The term *campaign* originated in the military context. Generals mounted campaigns, using their scarce resources (soldiers and materials) to achieve military objectives. Using the term in a political context is apt. In a political campaign, candidates also use scarce resources (time and money) in an attempt to defeat their adversaries in the battle to win votes.

To run a successful campaign, the candidate's campaign staff must be able to raise funds for the effort, get media coverage, produce and pay for political ads, schedule the candidate's time effectively with constituent groups and potential supporters, convey the candidate's position on the issues, conduct research on the opposing candidate, and get the voters to go to the polls. When party identification was stronger and TV campaigning was still in its infancy, a strong party organization on the local, state, or national level could furnish most of the services and expertise that the candidate needed. Less effort was spent on advertising a single candidate's position and character because the party label communicated that information to many of the voters.

Today, party labels are no longer as important as they once were. In part, this is because fewer people identify with the major parties, as evidenced by the rising number of independent voters. Instead of relying so extensively on political parties, candidates now turn to professionals to manage their campaigns.

The Professional Campaign Organization

political consultant A professional political adviser who, for a large fee, works on an area of a candidate's campaign. Political consultants include campaign managers, pollsters, media advisers, and "get out the vote" organizers.

campaign strategy The comprehensive plan for winning an election developed by a candidate and his or her advisers. The strategy includes the candidate's position on issues, slogan, advertising plan, press events, personal appearances, and other aspects of the campaign.

With the rise of candidate-centered campaigns in the past two decades, the role of the political party in managing campaigns has declined. Professional **political consultants** now manage nearly all aspects of a presidential candidate's campaign. Indeed, President George W. Bush stated that his longtime political adviser Karl Rove was the "architect" of his reelection victory in 2004. Most candidates for governor, the House, and the Senate also rely on consultants. Political consultants generally specialize in a particular area of the campaign, such as researching the opposition, conducting polls, developing the candidate's advertising, or organizing "get out the vote" efforts. Nonetheless, most candidates have a campaign manager who coordinates and plans the **campaign strategy.** Figure 9–2 shows a typical presidential campaign organization. As this figure also indicates, the political party continues to play an important role in recruiting volunteers and getting out the vote.

A major development in contemporary American politics is the focus on reaching voters through effective use of the media, particularly television. Much of President Bush's 2004 campaign, for example, centered on his plans for fighting the war on terrorism and creating a democracy in Iraq. He used television advertisements extensively to promote his stances on foreign policy. (The rebuilding of Iraq and its 2005 elections are discussed in this chapter's *The Politics of National Security* feature on page 204.) At least half of the budget for a major political campaign is consumed by television advertising. The media consultant is therefore a

President George W. Bush and his longtime political consultant and senior adviser Karl Rove leave the White House together.

AP Photo/Ron Edmonds

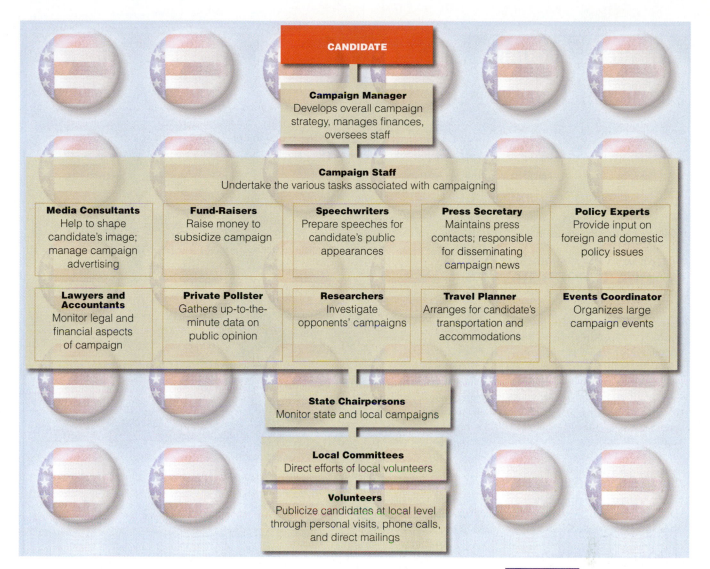

CANDIDATE

Campaign Manager
Develops overall campaign strategy, manages finances, oversees staff

Campaign Staff
Undertake the various tasks associated with campaigning

Media Consultants Help to shape candidate's image; manage campaign advertising	**Fund-Raisers** Raise money to subsidize campaign	**Speechwriters** Prepare speeches for candidate's public appearances	**Press Secretary** Maintains press contacts; responsible for disseminating campaign news	**Policy Experts** Provide input on foreign and domestic policy issues
Lawyers and Accountants Monitor legal and financial aspects of campaign	**Private Pollster** Gathers up-to-the-minute data on public opinion	**Researchers** Investigate opponents' campaigns	**Travel Planner** Arranges for candidate's transportation and accommodations	**Events Coordinator** Organizes large campaign events

State Chairpersons
Monitor state and local campaigns

Local Committees
Direct efforts of local volunteers

Volunteers
Publicize candidates at local level through personal visits, phone calls, and direct mailings

FIGURE 9-2

A Typical Presidential Campaign Organization
Most aspects of a candidate's campaign are managed by professional political consultants, as this figure illustrates.

pivotal member of the campaign staff. The nature of political advertising is discussed in more detail in Chapter 10. How candidates obtain the money needed to pay for advertising, consultants, and other campaign costs is discussed next.

What It Costs to Win

The modern political campaign is an expensive undertaking. Huge sums must be spent for professional campaign managers and consultants, television and radio ads, the printing of campaign literature, travel, office rent, equipment, and other necessities. To get an idea of the cost of waging a campaign for Congress today, consider that candidates for the House of Representatives spent a total of more than $640 million on their campaigns in 2004, and candidates for the Senate spent a total of $490 million. Indeed, the South Dakota Senate race between Democratic incumbent Tom Daschle and Republican challenger John Thune cost $36 million alone. Thune emerged victorious over Daschle despite spending $5 million less than the former Senate minority leader.[5]

Presidential campaigns are even more costly. In 1992, Americans were stunned to learn that about $550 million had been spent in the presidential campaigns. In 1996, presidential campaign expenditures rose even higher, to about $600 million. In 2004, they climbed to nearly $830 million, making the 2004 presidential campaigns the most expensive in history.

Clearly, money matters in determining success at the polls. In the 2004 elections, for example, candidates who outspent their opponents generally emerged victorious in the House and Senate races.[6]

The POLITICS of national SECURITY

You are here

Elections in Iraq and Nation Building

After ousting Saddam Hussein's authoritarian regime in Iraq, the United States faced the difficult prospect of nation building. President George W. Bush, as you have previously read, has repeatedly stated his desire to export democracy to Middle Eastern nations. A "free and democratic" Iraq, he argued, would benefit the Iraqi people and improve American national security. One of the first steps in bringing about a democracy in Iraq, administration officials claimed, would be holding free elections.

HIGH VOTER TURNOUT DESPITE TERROR THREATS

On January 30, 2005, Iraqi citizens went to the polls in droves, marking the nation's first free elections in half a century. Women, long denied the right to vote, participated in great numbers and proudly posed for media photographers. Initial reports claimed a 72 percent voter turnout, but later estimates showed that the number was closer to 60 percent. Still, even that figure would be 5 percentage points higher than the turnout in the 2004 presidential elections in the United States.

Participation in the Iraqi elections was high despite threats of terrorism by Iraqi militants. Fears of shootings and car bombings were very real in a nation torn by internal warfare since the U.S. invasion and subsequent occupation. Close to fifty people died in suicide and mortar attacks on polling stations.

As a key first step in the Bush administration's plans for nation building, the elections will be followed by the creation of a constitution by newly elected representatives. Many fear that the boycott of the election by Sunni Iraqis, the nation's minority Muslim sect, may negatively affect the perceived legitimacy of the new government, however.

Reuters/Azad Lashkari/Landov

An Iraqi man carried his elderly mother to a ballot box so she could cast her vote during the historic democratic elections held in January 2005. Millions of Iraqis flocked to the polling places in defiance of insurgent groups that killed twenty-five people in bloody attacks in an attempt to derail the voting process.

ANOTHER VIETNAM?

Similar issues of nation building came up during America's involvement in the Vietnam War (1964–1975). The United States expressed optimism following the successful 1967 elections in Vietnam. Officials claimed an 83 percent voter turnout despite threats of Vietcong terror. Then president Lyndon B. Johnson believed, like Bush, that free elections were an important stepping-stone to creating a democratic form of government. Yet, despite American efforts to create a self-sufficient democracy in South Vietnam, the nation was overrun by Communist North Vietnamese forces shortly after the U.S. military pulled out of the country.

Many foreign policy analysts today wonder if Iraq will also collapse once the U.S. military departs. Any new government in Iraq

will be fragile because of the nation's numerous ethnic and religious groups. Each group has a distinctly different view of what the "new Iraq" should look like. A civil war could erupt in Iraq if the Shiite religious majority emerges from the elections with enough power to impose an Iran-style theocracy (as discussed in the *Comparative Politics* feature in Chapter 1). Such a government would undoubtedly spur open hostility from the Sunni and Kurdish minorities.

Are We Safer?

Assuming that a democratic Iraq is important to American national security, what measures should the United States take to ensure the new government's long-term survival?

The connection between money and campaigns gives rise to some of the most difficult challenges in American politics. The biggest fear is that campaign contributors may be able to influence people running for office by giving large gifts or loans. Another possibility is that some special interest groups will try to buy favored treatment from those who are elected to office. In an attempt to prevent these abuses, the government regulates campaign financing.

The Federal Election Campaign Act

Congress passed the Federal Election Campaign Act (FECA) of 1971[7] in an effort to curb irregularities and abuses in the ways political campaigns were financed. The 1971 act placed no limit on overall spending but restricted the amount that could be spent on mass media advertising, including television. It limited the amount that candidates and their families could contribute to their own campaigns and required disclosure of all contributions and expenditures in excess of $100. In principle, the 1971 act limited the role of labor unions and corporations in political campaigns. Also in 1971, Congress passed a law that provided for a $1 checkoff on federal income tax returns for general campaign funds to be used by major-party presidential candidates. This law was first applied in the 1976 campaign. (Since then, the amount of the checkoff has been raised to $3.)

Amendments in 1974
The 1971 act did not go far enough, however. Amendments to the act passed in 1974 essentially did the following:

- *Created the Federal Election Commission (FEC) to administer and enforce the act's provisions.*
- *Provided public financing for presidential primaries and general elections.* Presidential candidates who raise some money on their own in at least twenty states can get funds from the U.S. Treasury to help pay for primary campaigns. For the general election campaign, presidential candidates receive federal funding for almost all of their expenses if they are willing to accept campaign-spending limits.
- *Limited presidential campaign spending.* Any candidate accepting federal support must agree to limit expenditures to amounts set by federal law.
- *Required disclosure.* Candidates must file periodic reports with the FEC that list the contributors to the campaign and indicate how the contributed money was spent.
- *Limited contributions.* Individuals could contribute up to $1,000 to each candidate in each federal election or primary. The total limit for any individual in one year was $25,000. Groups could contribute a maximum of $5,000 to a candidate in any election.

Buckley v. Valeo
In a significant 1976 case, *Buckley v. Valeo,*[8] the Supreme Court declared unconstitutional the provision in the 1971 act that limited the amount each individual could spend on his or her own campaign. The Court held that a "candidate, no less than any other person, has a First Amendment right to engage in the discussion of public issues and vigorously and tirelessly to advocate his own election."

The Rise of PACs
The FECA allows corporations, labor unions, and special interest groups to set up *political action committees* (PACs) to raise money for candidates. For a PAC to be legitimate, the money must be raised from at least fifty volunteer donors and must be given to at least five candidates in the national elections. PACs can contribute up to $5,000 per candidate in each election, but there is no limit on the total amount of PAC contributions during an election cycle. As discussed in Chapter 6, the number of PACs has grown significantly since the 1970s, as have their campaign contributions. In the 2004 election cycle, about 36 percent of campaign funds spent on House races came from PACs.[9]

Skirting the Campaign-Financing Rules

The money spent on campaigns has been rising steadily for decades. Spending during the 2004 campaigns, though, marked a major leap—it was more than twice what it had been in 1996. Where does all this money come from? The answer is that individuals and corporations have found **loopholes**—legal ways of evading certain legal requirements—in the federal laws limiting campaign contributions.

loophole A legal way of evading a certain legal requirement.

Soft Money
The biggest loophole in the FECA and its amendments was that they did not prohibit individuals or corporations from contributing to political *parties.* Many contributors would make donations to the national parties to cover the costs of such activities as registering voters, printing brochures and fliers, advertising in the media (which often means running candidate-oriented ads), developing campaigns to "get out the vote," and holding fund-raising events. Contributions to political parties, instead of to particular candidates, are called **soft money** because, as one observer said, they are "so squishy." Although soft money clearly was used to support the candidates, it was difficult to track exactly where the money was going.

soft money Campaign contributions that are made to political parties, instead of to particular candidates.

Although this loophole had existed since the passage of a 1979 amendment to the federal election laws, it was little known or used until the 1990s. By 2000, though, the use of soft money had become standard operating procedure, and the parties raised nearly $463 million through soft money contributions. Soft dollars became the main source of campaign money in the presidential race, far outpacing PAC contributions and federal campaign funds. In both 1996 and 2000, the political parties and their interest group allies went to great lengths to skirt the laws that were put on the books in the 1970s.

Independent Expenditures Another major loophole in campaign-financing laws was that they did not prohibit corporations, labor unions, and special interest groups from making **independent expenditures** in an election campaign. Independent expenditures, as the term implies, are expenditures for activities that are independent from (not coordinated with) those of the candidate or a political party. In other words, interest groups can wage their own "issue" campaigns as long as they do not go so far as to say "Vote for Candidate X." The problem is, where do you draw the line between advocating a position on a particular issue, such as abortion (which a group has a right to do under the First Amendment's guarantee of freedom of speech), and contributing to the campaign of a candidate who endorses that position? In addressing this thorny issue, the United States Supreme Court has developed two determinative tests. Under the first test, a group's speech is a campaign "expenditure" only if it explicitly calls for the election of a particular candidate. Using this test, the courts repeatedly have held that interest groups have the right to advocate their positions. For example, the Christian Coalition has the right to publish voter guides informing voters of candidates' positions. The second test applies when a group or organization has made expenditures explicitly for the purpose of endorsing a candidate. Such expenditures are permissible unless they were made in "coordination" with a campaign. According to the Supreme Court, an issue-oriented group has a First Amendment right to advocate the election of its preferred candidates as long as it acts independently.

In 1996, the Supreme Court held that these guidelines apply to expenditures by political parties as well. Parties may spend money on behalf of candidates if they do so independently—that is, if they do not let the candidates know how, when, or for what the money was spent.[10] As critics of this decision have pointed out, parties generally work closely with candidates, so establishing the "independence" of such expenditures is problematic.

independent expenditure An expenditure for activities that are independent from (not coordinated with) those of a political candidate or a political party.

The Bipartisan Campaign Reform Act of 2002

Demand for further campaign-finance reform had been growing for several years, but in 2000 a Republican presidential candidate, John McCain, made it one of the cornerstones of his campaign. McCain competed aggressively against George W. Bush in the Republican presidential primaries, and his continued popularity after he lost the Republican nomination forced Congress to address the issue in 2001. A series of corporate scandals, including the bankruptcies of Enron and WorldCom, both of which had been large campaign contributors, also kept campaign-finance reform in the public eye.

Forcing incumbent political leaders to address campaign-finance reform is one of the most difficult tasks in government. Most elected officials came to power under the existing laws. They recognize that setting tighter limits and closing loopholes could hurt their reelection bids in the future. Nonetheless, in 2002, Congress passed and the president signed the Bipartisan Campaign Reform Act.

Changes under the New Law The most significant change imposed by the 2002 law was to ban the large, unlimited contributions to national political parties known as soft money. The law also regulates the use of campaign ads paid for by interest groups. Such issue advocacy is now prohibited within thirty days of a primary election or sixty days of a general election.

The 2002 act increased the amount an individual can contribute to a federal candidate from $1,000 to $2,000. The amount that an individual can give to all federal candidates was raised from $25,000 per year to $95,000 over a two-year election cycle. Individuals can still contribute to state and local parties, so long as the contributions do not exceed $10,000 per year per individual. The new law went into effect on November 6, 2002.

Constitutional Challenges to the New Law   Soon after the 2002 act was passed, several groups filed lawsuits challenging the constitutionality of its provisions. Supporters of the restrictions on campaign ads by special interest groups argued that the large amounts of funds spent on these ads create an appearance of corruption in the political process. In contrast, an attorney for the National Rifle Association (NRA), one of the plaintiffs claiming that the provision unconstitutionally restricts free speech, argued that because the NRA represents "millions of Americans speaking in unison . . . [it] is not a *corruption* of the democratic political process; it *is* the democratic political process."[11]

Those who drafted the law anticipated the constitutional challenges and included a provision in the law to expedite the legal process. The lawsuits went first to a three-judge panel of the U.S. District Court for the District of Columbia and then directly to the United States Supreme Court. In December 2003, the Supreme Court upheld nearly all of the clauses of the act in *McConnell v. Federal Election Commission.*[12]

As you read in Chapter 6, "issue advocacy" groups such as 527s have attempted to exploit soft money loopholes in the Bipartisan Campaign Reform Act of 2002. Because 527s technically do not endorse a particular candidate, they do not fall under the same campaign-financing restrictions as political parties and PACs. In the 2004 election cycle, 527s spent more than $550 million to "advocate positions" (see Figure 9–3).[13]

With spending reaching new heights in the 2004 elections, campaign-finance reform efforts have yet to make a noticeable impact. Numerous proponents of reform, however, have already targeted the loopholes that still allow expenditures by issue advocacy groups, such as 527s.

Campaign Contributions and Policy Decisions

Considering the passion on both sides of the debate about campaign-finance reform, one might wonder how much campaign contributions actually influence policy decisions. Table 9–1 on the next page lists the top twenty industries and other groups contributing to both parties in the 2004 election cycle. These contributors must want something in return for their dollars, but what, exactly, does the money buy? Do these donations influence government policymaking?

Clearly, there is no reason to conclude that a member of Congress who received financial contributions from certain groups while campaigning for Congress will vote differently on policy issues than she or he would otherwise vote. After all, many groups make contributions not so much to influence a candidate's views as to ensure that a candidate whose views the group supports will win the elections.

Many groups routinely donate to candidates from both parties so that, regardless of who wins, the groups will have access to the officeholder. Note that some of the groups listed in Table 9–1 contributed to both parties. Not surprisingly, campaign contributors find it much easier than other constituents to get in to see politicians or get them to return phone calls. Because politicians are more likely to be influenced by those with whom they have personal contacts, access is important for those who want to influence policymaking. The real question is whether money also buys votes.

AMERICA at odds

Does Money Buy Votes?

Several "watchdog" groups are devoted to discovering whether campaign contributions directly affect how legislators vote. The Center for Responsive Politics (**http://www.opensecrets.org**) is one such group. In a special section of its Web site entitled "Tracking the Payback," the center examines key legislation before Congress, the groups and industries that stand to benefit from it, the congressional committees overseeing it, and the campaign contributors to those committees'

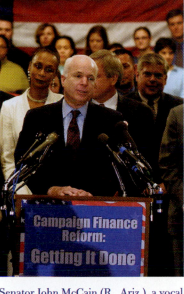

Senator John McCain (R., Ariz.), a vocal proponent of campaign-finance reform, played a vital role in bringing this issue before the public and Congress. In 2002, Congress passed, and President Bush signed, the Bipartisan Campaign Reform Act.

FIGURE 9-3
Expenditures by 527s

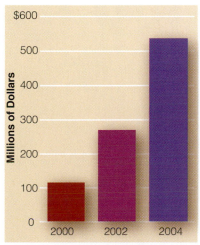

SOURCE: Center for Public Integrity analysis of Internal Revenue Service reports.

members. The Center focuses primarily on research and statistics rather than conclusions, however.

Charles Lewis, a former journalist, concludes that Congress has been "bought" by special interests. He supports his conclusions with hundreds of examples, from gun control legislation to prescription drug laws.[14] Another journalist, Jeffrey H. Birnbaum, opens his recent book with the following statement: "Almost everyone who works in official Washington eventually has what can be described as the Moment: that instant when they finally realize that money plays too big a role in politics, way too big." Birnbaum then explains how money is the grease that keeps the wheels of D.C. politics in motion. The relationship between campaign donors and politicians, says Birnbaum, is part of "a deeply ingrained system that's as difficult to fix as it is horrific to behold."[15]

Political scientists and academicians tend to make fewer generalizations, however. Political scientist Jeff Fox points out that, by and large, members of Congress vote along party lines. Additionally, public opinion plays an important role in many policy debates, and few politicians will defy public opinion and lose potential voters to accommodate a campaign donor's wishes. Also, politicians often receive donations from different groups, making it difficult to please all groups if their wishes happen to conflict. According to Fox, money is most likely to influence policymaking decisions when the public is inattentive to an issue, when there is little competition from opposing groups, when the politician personally benefits from a contribution, and in some other particular circumstances. Generally, while not discounting the importance of money in the nation's capital, Fox believes that votes are influenced by contributions far less often than Americans think.[16]

TABLE 9-1

Top Industries and Other Groups Contributing Funds in the 2004 Election Cycle

This table lists the top twenty contributors during the 2004 election cycle.

RANK	INDUSTRY/GROUP	AMOUNT	TO DEMOCRATS	TO REPUBLICANS
1	Retired People	$168,657,391	45%	55%
2	Lawyers/Law Firms	166,904,190	74	26
3	Real Estate	87,754,428	41	59
4	Securities/Investments	81,864,589	47	53
5	Health Professionals	67,463,548	37	62
6	Candidate Committees	64,776,591	61	39
7	Business Services	37,482,610	54	45
8	Insurance	34,312,720	32	68
9	Education	32,635,424	77	22
10	Leadership PACs	29,479,947	28	72
11	Commercial Banks	29,417,337	35	64
12	TV/Movies/Music	28,861,668	68	31
13	Computers/Internet	25,895,899	53	46
14	General Contractors	23,965,639	24	76
15	Lobbyists	23,833,436	48	52
16	Misc. Mfg./Distrib.	22,607,568	27	73
17	Oil & Gas	22,525,240	19	81
18	Automotive	18,545,416	22	78
19	Civil Servants	18,230,186	57	43
20	Pharm./Health Products	16,576,483	33	67

SOURCE: Center for Responsive Politics, 2005.

How We Elect Candidates

The drama surrounding both the 2000 and 2004 presidential elections probably caused Americans to learn more than they ever wanted to know about the election process in this country. The focus on the Florida vote in 2000 and the Ohio vote in 2004 taught citizens about the significance of balloting procedures, types of voting equipment, county election boards, state election laws, and state officials in the elective process. In 2000, even the courts became involved, and ultimately the U.S. Supreme Court cast the deciding "vote" on who would be our next president.

Types of Elections

The ultimate goal of the political campaign and the associated fund-raising efforts is, of course, winning the election. The most familiar kind of election is the **general election,** which is a regularly scheduled election held in even-numbered years on the first Tuesday after the first Monday in November. During general elections, the voters decide who will be the U.S. president, vice president, and senators and representatives in Congress. The president and vice president are elected every four years, senators every six years, and representatives every two years. General elections are also held to choose state and local government officials, often at the same time as those for national offices. A **special election** is held at the state or local level when the voters must decide an issue before the next general election or when vacancies occur by reason of death or resignation.

Types of Ballots

Since 1888, all states in the United States have used the **Australian ballot**—a secret ballot that is prepared, distributed, and counted by government officials at public expense. Two variations of the Australian ballot are used today. Most states use the **party-column ballot** (also called the Indiana ballot), which lists all of a party's candidates together in a single column under the party label. In some states, the party-column ballot allows voters to vote for all of a party's candidates for local, state, and national offices by registering a single vote. The major parties favor this ballot form because it encourages straight-ticket voting.

Other states use the **office-block ballot,** which lists together all of the candidates for each office. Politicians tend to dislike the office-block ballot because it places more emphasis on the office than on the party and thus encourages split-ticket voting.

Conducting Elections and Counting the Votes

Recall from Chapter 8 that local units of government, such as cities, are divided into smaller voting districts, or precincts. State laws usually restrict the size of precincts, and local officials set their boundaries. Within each precinct, voters cast their ballots at one polling place.

A precinct election board supervises the polling place and the voting process in each precinct. The board sets hours for the polls to be open according to the laws of the state and sees that ballots or voting machines are available. In most states, the board provides the list of registered voters and makes certain that only qualified voters cast ballots in that precinct. When the polls close, the board counts the votes and reports the results, usually to the county clerk or the board of elections. Representatives from each party, called **poll watchers,** are allowed at each polling place to make sure the election is run fairly and to avoid fraud. (For a recent example of a hotly contested foreign election, see this chapter's *Comparative Politics* feature on the following page.)

Presidential Elections and the Electoral College

As you read in the *America at Odds* feature in Chapter 2, when voters vote for president and vice president, they are not voting directly for the candidates. Instead, they are voting for **electors** who will cast their ballots in the **electoral college.** The electors are selected during

---

general election A regularly scheduled election to elect the U.S. president, vice president, and representatives and senators in Congress. General elections are held in even-numbered years on the first Tuesday after the first Monday in November.

special election An election that is held at the state or local level when the voters must decide an issue before the next general election or when vacancies occur by reason of death or resignation.

Australian ballot A secret ballot that is prepared, distributed, and counted by government officials at public expense; used by all states in the United States since 1888.

party-column ballot A ballot (also called the Indiana ballot) that lists all of a party's candidates under the party label. Voters can vote for all of a party's candidates for local, state, and national offices by making a single "X" or pulling a single lever.

office-block ballot A ballot that lists together all of the candidates for each office.

poll watcher A representative from one of the two major political parties who is allowed to monitor a polling place to make sure that the election is run fairly and to avoid fraud.

elector A member of the electoral college.

electoral college The group of electors who are selected by the voters in each state to officially elect the president and vice president. The number of electors in each state is equal to the number of that state's representatives in both chambers of Congress.

comparative politics

The "Orange Revolution" in Ukraine

Ukraine, an Eastern European nation of nearly 48 million people, captured the world's attention for more than a month in 2004 with a stunning demonstration of democratic spirit. After Ukrainian prime minister Viktor Yanukovich claimed victory over reformist candidate Viktor Yushchenko in the November presidential elections, many Ukrainians immediately questioned the outcome. Indeed, the presidential elections were marred by rampant voting fraud and allegations of Russian meddling. The fraudulent elections led to a massive peaceful protest, as Ukrainians gathered in the nation's capital of Kiev and called for new elections. Adopting the campaign color of Yushchenko's reform party, the protesters staged what would become known as the "Orange Revolution."

DEMOCRACY TAKES ROOT IN THE FORMER SOVIET BLOC

After seventy years within the former Soviet Union, Ukraine broke away from Moscow in 1991 as the Communist regime collapsed. Although Ukraine set up a democratic republic following its independence, the nation largely remained within the authoritarian Russian sphere of influence.

The 2004 presidential elections, however, represented a historic shift away from Russia's orbit. Yanukovich, a firmly pro-Russian candidate, initially claimed victory and was quickly congratulated by Russian president Vladimir Putin. Yet supporters of the pro-West reformist candidate, Yushchenko, soon pointed to massive violations in the vote-counting process. When the evidence of tampering came to light, tens of thousands of Ukrainians took to the streets and demanded new elections. For weeks, protesters braved freezing weather to camp outside the nation's capitol building in Kiev. Their democratic spirit was rewarded in December, when new elections produced a Yushchenko victory.

YOUNGER UKRAINIANS LEAD THE WAY

Much of the Orange Revolution's success has been credited to the Ukrainian youth. Students from universities across the nation left

EPA/Sergei Chirikov/Landov

When opposition leader Viktor Yushchenko lost the November 2004 presidential elections in Ukraine to then prime minister Viktor Yanukovich, Yushchenko's supporters took to the streets in a peaceful protest, demanding a new election. As the country's new Supreme Court heard arguments over the election's validity, young protestors braved freezing temperatures for weeks and captured the world's attention.

their studies and flocked to Kiev to join the protests. Bands played live concerts to help keep the protesters' spirits high. Such tight bonds were formed among the demonstrators that many young people married during their weeks outside the capitol building. Younger Ukrainians were a key group that rallied around Yushchenko's promises to break with a past marked by government corruption. "Today we are turning a page of lies, censorship, and violence," Yushchenko announced to the crowds after his victory. Ahead, he said, lay a "new epoch of great democracy."

For Critical Analysis
Why might Yushchenko's promises of reform have resonated with so many young people?

---

each presidential election year by the states' political parties, subject to the laws of the state. Each state has as many electoral votes as it has U.S. senators and representatives (see Figure 9–4). In addition, there are three electors from the District of Columbia. The electoral college system is a **winner-take-all system,** in which the candidate who receives the largest popular vote in a state is credited with all that state's electoral votes. The only exceptions are Maine and Nebraska, which apportion their electoral votes to the percentage of the popular vote won by candidates.

winner-take-all system In most states, the system that awards all of the state's electoral votes to the candidate who receives the most popular votes in that state.

Electoral College Voting In December, after the general election, electors (either Democrats or Republicans, depending on which candidate won the state's popular vote) meet in their state capitals to cast their votes for president and vice president. When the Constitution was drafted, the framers intended that the electors would use their own discretion in deciding who would make the best president. Today, however, the electors usually vote for the candidates who won popular support in their states. The electoral college ballots are then sent to the Senate, which counts and certifies them before a joint session of Congress held early in January. The

Contested ballots are reviewed in
Florida after the November 2000
elections.

AP Photo/Victor R. Caivano

candidates who receive a majority of the electoral votes are officially declared president and vice
president. To be elected, a candidate must receive more than half of the 538 electoral votes available. Thus, a candidate needs 270 votes to win. If no presidential candidate gets an electoral college majority (which has happened twice—in 1800 and 1824), the House of Representatives
votes on the candidates, with each state delegation casting only a single vote. The vice president
is then chosen by the Senate, with each senator casting one vote.

Were the 2000 Elections an Anomaly?   The events surrounding the 2000
presidential elections are still fresh in the minds of some Americans. It was the first time since

FIGURE 9-4

**State Electoral
Votes in 2004**
The map of the United States shown
here is distorted to show the relative
weight of the states in terms of the
electoral votes in 2004, following the
changes required by the 2000 census.
A candidate must win 270 electoral
votes to be elected president.

Reuters/Jason Reed/Landov

Representative Stephanie Tubbs Jones (D., Ohio) walked away from other members of Congress on the floor of the House of Representatives as the proceedings of the Joint Session of Congress to verify the official count of electoral votes after the 2004 presidential elections resumed. Earlier, Tubbs Jones had protested the results of the official electoral votes from Ohio, which had interrupted the proceedings.

1888 that the electoral college system gave Americans a president who had not won the popular vote.[17] The events of the 2000 elections will undoubtedly be recounted in history books, but was the outcome an anomaly? Can we expect the winner of the popular vote also to win the electoral vote for the next 112 years? Or will presidential elections continue to be close in the near future, even as close as the 2000 elections?

In 2000, then vice president Al Gore won the popular vote by 540,000 votes. Nonetheless, on election night, the outcome in Florida, which would have given Gore the winning votes in the electoral college, was deemed "too close to call." Initially, George W. Bush was leading Al Gore by only 1,700 votes, out of 6 million cast in that state. An initial recount in Florida reduced Bush's lead to just over 300 votes. Controversy erupted over the types of ballots used, however, and some counties in Florida began recounting ballots by hand. This was the issue that ultimately came before the United States Supreme Court: Did manual recounts of some ballots but not others violate the Constitution's equal protection clause? On December 12, five weeks after the election, the Supreme Court finally ruled against the manual recounts. The final vote tally in Florida gave Bush a 537-vote lead, all of Florida's twenty-five electoral votes, and the presidency.[18]

Other recent presidential elections have been extremely close. In 1960, John F. Kennedy defeated Richard Nixon by less than 120,000 votes, out of 70 million cast, although Kennedy had a sizable victory in the electoral college. In 1968, a shift of only 60,000 votes to third-party candidate George C. Wallace would have thrown the race into the House of Representatives. Again in 1976, a shift of only a few thousand votes would have produced an electoral victory for Gerald Ford despite a popular vote win for Jimmy Carter.

The 2004 Elections

The 2004 presidential elections produced another close race, with President Bush edging Democratic challenger John Kerry by a mere thirty-five electors. Unlike 2000, Bush won the popular vote in 2004, defeating Kerry by a 3 percentage point margin. Many commentators argued that the elections were decided by the closely contested vote in Ohio. A repeat of the 2000 fiasco in Florida was averted, however.

From early in the 2004 election cycle, Ohio had been viewed as a *battleground state*—a state where voters were not clearly leaning toward a particular candidate leading up to the elections. Some political analysts and news media outlets placed a great deal of emphasis on the so-called battleground states, arguing that these states could potentially decide the outcome with their electoral votes.

Future Elections Are Not Easy to Predict

Some scholars have suggested that we simply know too little about elections to make any predictions about the future. Polls are not as accurate as we hope. Voters are not as predictable as we think. Finally, variables such as third-party candidates and voter turnout will continue to affect future elections.

Campaigns and Your Everyday Life

Campaigns certainly do affect your everyday life whenever election time comes around. In the months before an election, it seems that everywhere you look, you see signs urging voters to select one candidate or another. When you turn on the TV, you hear campaign ads praising the virtues of one of the candidates or lamenting the shortcomings of his or her opponent. News channels have an ongoing stream of announcements about the candidates' issue positions or about which candidate is ahead in the race. If you open a newspaper or go to a news Web site, you are bombarded with campaign news. You may even get phone calls asking you to vote for a particular candidate.

To be sure, this barrage of campaign information can affect your everyday life, but campaigns are important to you for another reason as well: they offer you the chance to become familiar with the candidates for office. You learn about their personalities, their views on issues, and the promises they make. During campaigns, you have an opportunity to compare the contestants for office and, ultimately, decide how you will cast your vote.

Campaigns are important to your everyday life for another reason: the winning candidates will hold government offices. Winning congressional candidates may pass new laws or change old ones, and you may or may not benefit from the results. The winning candidate in the presidential campaigns will have significant influence over what laws and policies will be adopted in the future—and many of these may directly affect your life. (For some examples, refer back to the *Why Does It Matter?* feature in Chapter 8.)

Taking Action

As you have read in this chapter, many groups have worked toward reforming the way campaign funds are raised and spent in politics today. One nonprofit, nonpartisan, grassroots organization that lobbies for campaign-finance reform is Common Cause. In the photo below, a participant in Colorado Common Cause's effort to reform campaign financing holds up a mock-up of a TV remote control with a large mute button at a news conference. The group was asking voters to "mute" attack ads directed against a Colorado initiative to amend the state constitution to limit campaign financing and set contribution limits.

AP Photo/Ed Andrieski

Key Terms

Chapter Summary

1 Today, candidates are nominated for political offices by either a state convention system (in a few states) or by a direct primary. The direct primary is a statewide election held within each party to pick its candidates for the general election.

2 The majority of the states hold presidential primaries to elect delegates to the parties' national conventions. The primary campaign recently has been shortened to the first few months of the year. In late summer or early fall, each political party holds a national convention during which the convention delegates, among other things, adopt the official party platform and decide who will be the party's presidential and vice-presidential candidates.

3 American political campaigns are lengthy and extremely expensive. In recent years, they have become more candidate centered than party centered in response to technological innovations and declining party identification among the voters. Candidates rely less on the party and more on paid professional campaign managers and political consultants.

4 The amount of money spent in financing campaigns increased dramatically in the 2000 and 2004 elections. Federal legislation instituted major reforms in the 1970s by limiting spending and contributions, but the parties have skirted the federal campaign regulations via loopholes. In 2002, Congress passed the Bipartisan Campaign Reform Act, which aims to curb the use of soft money and independent expenditures in elections.

5 General elections are regularly scheduled elections held in even-numbered years on the first Tuesday after the first Monday in November. During general elections, the voters decide who will be the U.S. president, vice president, and senators and representatives in Congress. State general elections, which may occur at the same time, are held to elect state and local government officials.

Since 1888, all states in the United States have used the Australian ballot—a secret ballot that is prepared, distributed, and counted by government officials at public expense.

6 Elections are held in voting precincts (districts within each local government unit). Precinct officials supervise the polling place and the voting process. Poll watchers from each of the two major parties typically monitor the polling place as well to ensure that the election is conducted fairly and to prevent voting fraud.

7 In the presidential elections, citizens do not vote directly for the president and vice president; instead, they vote for electors who will cast their ballots in the electoral college. Each state has as many electoral votes as it has U.S. senators and representatives; there are also three electors from the District of Columbia. The electoral college is a winner-take-all system because, in nearly all states, the candidate who receives the most popular votes in a state wins all of that state's electoral votes.

RESOURCES FOR FURTHER STUDY

Selected Readings

Abramson, Paul R., John H. Aldrich, and David W. Rohde. *Change and Continuity in the 2000 and 2002 Elections.* Washington, D.C.: CQ Press, 2003. This book offers a thorough analysis and comparison of the 2000 presidential elections and the 2002 midterm elections.

Burton, Michael J., and Daniel M. Shea. *Campaign Mode: Strategy, Leadership, and Successful Elections.* Lanham, Md.: Rowman & Littlefield, 2002. The authors, both of whom have served as political consultants to major political candidates, offer first-hand observations on campaign strategy and what they call the "campaign mode"—a state of mind in which strategic thinking is combined with political ambition.

Ceaser, James W., and Andrew E. Busch. *Red over Blue: The 2004 Elections and American Politics.* Lanham, Md.: Rowman & Littlefield, 2005. Building on their studies of the previous three presidential elections, the authors explore the events, outcomes, and effects of the 2004 elections.

Moore, James C., and Wayne Slater. *Bush's Brain: How Karl Rove Made George W. Bush President.* New York: John Wiley & Sons, 2003. The authors take a close-up look at Karl Rove, President George W. Bush's longtime political consultant.

Politics on the Web

■ You can find out exactly what the letter of the law is with respect to campaign financing by accessing the Federal Election Commission's Web site. The commission has provided an online "Citizen's Guide" that spells out exactly what is and is not legal. You can also download actual data on campaign donations from the site. Go to **http://www.fec.gov**

■ To look at the data available from the Federal Election Commission in a more user-friendly way, you can access the following nonpartisan independent site that allows you to type in an elected official's name and receive large amounts of information on contributions to that official. Go to **http://www.FECInfo.com**

■ Another excellent source for information on campaign financing, including who's contributing what amounts to which candidates, is the Center for Responsive Politics. You can access its Web site at **http://www.opensecrets.org**

■ Common Cause offers similar information on its Web site at **http://www.commoncause.org**

■ Project Vote Smart offers information on campaign financing, as well as voting, on its Web site at **http://www.vote-smart.org**

Online Resources for This Chapter

This text's Companion Web Site, at **http://www.americaatodds.com**, offers links to numerous resources that you can utilize to learn more about the topics covered in this chapter. For a list describing these resources, see the inside front cover of this book.

chapter **10**
politics and the media

CHAPTER OBJECTIVES

After reading this chapter, you should be able to . . .

▸ Explain the role of a free press in a democracy.

▸ Define the different types of media and indicate which one is the primary news source for most Americans.

▸ Summarize how television influences the conduct of political campaigns.

▸ Describe types of media bias and explain how such bias affects the political process.

▸ Describe the extent to which the Internet is reshaping political campaigns.

Do Media Monopolies Threaten a Free Press?

The First Amendment to the U.S. Constitution guarantees freedom of the press. Unlike the governments in many countries, our government does not own or control the news media. As citizens of a democratic republic, we rely on the media to provide the information we need to be informed citizens and voters. Our elected officials are held accountable for their policies and actions in large part because professional journalists play a "watchdog" role.

Yet the media are not without bias. Large corporations own the news media, and these corporations ultimately decide what information reaches the public. In recent years, federal lawmakers have passed legislation that has led to increased monopolization of television, radio, and the print media. With fewer corporations owning a greater number of media outlets, many Americans fear that media monopolies could threaten our democracy. Other Americans are not so sure, arguing that free market competition will ensure that the media include a variety of voices and perspectives.

Consolidation of Media Undermines Democracy

Many Americans are disturbed by the current trend toward media monopolies. In numerous geographical markets, the same corporation owns both a daily newspaper and a local television station. A conglomerate such as Time Warner, for example, may own a broad variety of media, including an Internet service, multiple cable television stations, and periodicals. Today's media companies are more concentrated than at any time during the past forty years.

A consistent loosening of ownership regulations in recent years has allowed a smaller number of news outlets to control the information marketplace. In 1990, for example, the major television networks (ABC, CBS, NBC, and Fox) owned a mere 12.5 percent of the new series they aired. By 2002, the same networks owned 77.5 percent of their recent series, and the ownership percentage keeps climbing.[1] In addition, new laws have made it difficult for new companies to break into the existing marketplace. Ted Turner, the founder of part of what is now Time Warner, has repeatedly complained that he would never have been able to launch TBS and CNN in today's climate.

Some Americans argue that recent legislation has abandoned the Federal Communications Commission's commitment to encouraging a diversity of views and perspectives in the media. If fewer companies own an increasing number of outlets, the American people will not have access to the information they need to sustain our democracy. Having fewer voices means that corporate interests will have more control over information, they argue.

Free Market Competition Ensures Variety

Others are not so sure that increasing consolidation of the media threatens the free exchange of information and ideas. These Americans argue that money drives the media, and if there is a demand for a type of programming or a certain perspective, some company will supply that demand.

Proponents of media consolidation assert that the media already offer a wide variety of viewpoints, allowing Americans to choose from more sources of information than ever before. Fox News, for example, has a distinctly different perspective from that offered by ABC, CBS, or NBC News. Those with cable or satellite television can also access the different perspectives found on CNN, or even international channels such as Deutsche Welle. Individuals who prefer radio can now listen to Sirius Satellite Radio, which has emerged as a serious competitor to traditional radio programming. An example of Sirius's challenge to current radio monopolies came when it recently pried popular radio-show host Howard Stern away from Clear Channel, offering him a lucrative $500 million five-year contract. In addition, a number of independent media outlets exist, such as National Public Radio, Public Broadcasting Service, and the *Nation*.

Those who doubt that media monopolies will undermine democracy also point to the Internet. Web logs, or blogs, have become an increasingly popular source of information for Americans, and blogs span the ideological spectrum. Furthermore, blogs are emerging as a "watchdog" force and have even uncovered mistakes made by television and print media.

Where Do You Stand?

1. Do you feel that today's media offer an adequate number of perspectives? Why or why not?
2. To what extent should the government regulate media ownership?

Explore This Issue Online

- Take Back the Media is a group dedicated to combating corporate bias in the media. Visit its site at **http://www.takebackthemedia.com**.
- The *Columbia Journalism Review* offers a comprehensive list of who owns which media outlets. To visit one of the nation's premier media monitors, go to **http://www.cjr.org/tools/owners/index.asp**.

Introduction

The debate over media monopolies underscores the importance of the media in American politics. Strictly defined, the term *media* means communication channels. It is the plural form of *medium of communication.* In this strict sense, any method used by people to communicate—including the telephone—is a communication medium. In this chapter, though, we look at the **mass media**—channels through which people can communicate to mass audiences. These channels include the **print media** (newspapers and magazines) and the **electronic media** (radio, television, and, to an increasing extent, the Internet).

The media are a dominant presence in our lives largely because they provide entertainment. Americans today enjoy more leisure time than at any time in history, and we fill it up with books, movies, and television—a huge amount of television. But the media play a vital role in our political lives as well. The media have a wide-ranging influence on American politics, particularly during campaigns and elections. Politicians and political candidates have learned—often the hard way—that positive media exposure and news coverage are essential to winning votes.

mass media Communication channels, such as newspapers and radio and television broadcasts, through which people can communicate to mass audiences.

print media Communication channels that consist of printed materials, such as newspapers and magazines.

electronic media Communication channels that involve electronic transmissions, such as radio, television, and, to an extent, the Internet.

The Role of the Media in a Democracy

As you read in Chapter 4, one of the most important civil liberties protected in the Bill of Rights is freedom of the press. Like free speech, a free press is considered a vital tool of the democratic process. If people are to cast informed votes, they must have access to a forum in which they can discuss public affairs fully and assess the conduct and competency of their officials. The media provide this forum.

The framers knew firsthand the power of mass media. In the 1700s, political ideas were disseminated through newspapers and pamphlets, which could be just as powerful as radio and television are today. Thomas Paine's *Common Sense* was a fifty-page pamphlet that could be printed and distributed quickly and cheaply. In a few months, it sold 500,000 copies (the equivalent of about 8 or 9 million copies with today's population) and helped to persuade the colonial masses of the need for independence from Britain. The *Federalist Papers,* which argued in favor of the U.S. Constitution, were first published in New York newspapers, as were many of the arguments of the Anti-Federalists.

The exact nature of the media's influence on the political process today is difficult to characterize. Clearly, what the media say and do has an impact on what Americans think about

AP Photo/Richard Drew

In January 2001, Time Warner and America Online (AOL), in an unprecedented combination of old and new media, overcame their last regulatory hurdle and joined forces. Officials from both companies and the New York Stock Exchange applauded the exchange's opening bell on the day they closed the deal.

Thomas Paine

political issues. But just as clearly, the media also *reflect* what Americans think about politics. Some scholars argue that the media is the fourth "check" in our political system—checking and balancing the power of the president, the Congress, and the courts. The power of the media today is enormous, but how the media use their power is an issue about which Americans are often at odds.

The Agenda-Setting Function of the Media

One of the criticisms often levied against the media is that they play too large a role in determining the issues, events, and personalities that are in the public eye. When people hear the evening's top news stories, they usually assume automatically that these stories concern the most important issues facing the nation. In actuality, the media decide the relative importance of issues by publicizing some issues and ignoring others, and by giving some stories high priority and others low priority. By helping to determine what people will talk and think about, the media set the *political agenda*—the issues that politicians will address. In other words, to borrow from Bernard Cohen's classic statement on the media and public opinion, the media may *not* be successful in telling people what to think, but they are "stunningly successful in telling their audience what to think about."[2]

For example, television played a significant role in shaping public opinion concerning the Vietnam War (1964–1975), which has been called the first "television war." Part of the public opposition to the war in the late 1960s came about as a result of the daily portrayal of the war's horrors on TV news programs. Film footage and narrative accounts of the destruction, death, and suffering in Vietnam brought the war into living rooms across the United States. (The current events in Iraq have also been the subject of constant news coverage. For a discussion of the media's role in wartime, see this chapter's *The Politics of National Security* feature on the facing page.)

The degree to which the media influence public opinion is not always clear, however. As you read in Chapter 8, some studies show that people filter the information they receive from the media through their own preconceived ideas about issues. Scholars who try to analyze the relationship between American politics and the media inevitably confront the chicken-and-egg conundrum: Do the media cause the public to hold certain views, or do the media merely reflect views that are formed independently of the media's influence?

Beginning with the Vietnam War, the media have brought close-up war coverage into the living rooms of virtually all Americans. Here, a retired banker—who was held by Iraqi forces in the first Gulf War in 1991 as a "human shield"—watches MSNBC News to stay abreast of recent events unfolding in Iraq.

What Is the Media's Role in Wartime?

Not surprisingly, on September 11, 2001, Americans were glued to their television sets and radios to learn more about the events unfolding in New York, Washington, D.C., and Pennsylvania. Americans continued to stay tuned in during the weeks following the terrorist attacks. According to the Pew Research Center, 78 percent of those surveyed in mid-October 2001 reported that they were still paying "very close" attention to news about the attacks.[3]

Such intense public interest in the news coverage of the terrorist attacks, the investigation of the perpetrators, and the ensuing war on terrorism gives the media significant influence over public opinion. When the United States went to war in Afghanistan and then Iraq, the public continued to rely on the media for its information. Americans view these events through the media's "lens"—seeing and hearing what the media choose to report.

WHAT AMERICANS DID NOT HEAR

The American press tends to temper its coverage when civilian deaths are involved. Compared to coverage in the foreign press, the American press showed few graphic scenes of the dead and dying on September 11. Details of civilian casualties from American bombing campaigns in Afghanistan and Iraq were also limited. For example, in December 2001, some U.S. bombs that had been aimed at an al Qaeda stronghold in Afghanistan went astray and destroyed a village. The *New York Times* reported simply that bombs "also hit civilian targets." The *Independent* of London, in contrast, gave a detailed account of the freshly dug graves at the village, the blasted houses and rubble, and, rather sarcastically, a report from the U.S. Defense Department saying that the bombing had never happened.[4]

A study by the Project for Excellence in Journalism found that the American press rarely dissented from the Bush administration's viewpoint on the terrorist attacks. In the three months after the September 11 attacks, the study found that at most only 10 percent of news stories could be perceived as critical of the official U.S. point of view.[5] The public clearly approved of this pro-American reporting. In November 2001, 77 percent of those surveyed rated the media's performance as "excellent" or "good." Sixty-nine percent of Americans thought news organizations should "stand up for America."[6]

GUIDELINES FOR WAR REPORTING

Only relatively recently have foreign correspondents been able to report from "behind enemy lines." American reporters were not stationed in Berlin during World War II (1939–1945), but they were in Baghdad during the first Gulf War (1990–1991). Going a step fur-

Members of the press raise their hands to avoid getting shot as they make their way down a street in Najaf, Iraq.

ther, "embedded" reporters have been allowed to accompany U.S. military units during the most recent conflicts in Afghanistan and Iraq. This change in war reporting has forced reporters to ask, in the words of historian and journalist Harold Evans, "Is the first duty of the correspondent to truth or to his [or her] country?"[7] Reporters may learn details about military strategy, civilian casualties, or "friendly fire" incidents that could aid the enemy or hinder the allies. Should they report everything they learn?

By the same token, should the media report stories critical of the president in a time of war? Most Americans approve of some military censorship to protect national security. They also believe, however, that the press should report all points of view, including those critical of the United States, and that reporters should investigate stories fully rather than rely on information from government or military officials. Clearly, the role of the media in time of war is an issue that Americans will debate as the war on terrorism continues.

Are We Safer?

To what extent should the media be allowed to report on U.S. military involvement overseas? Are we safer if we are fully informed, or is it better for our national security if news stories critical of government actions during wartime are censored?

The Medium Does Affect the Message

Of all the media, television has the greatest impact. Television reaches into almost every home in the United States. Virtually all homes have televisions. Even outside their homes, Americans can watch television—in airports, shopping malls, golf clubhouses, and medical offices. Today, television is the primary news source for more than 65 percent of Americans. Figure 10–1 on the next page shows the clear prominence of television among the media.

As you will read shortly, politicians take maximum advantage of the power and influence of television. But does the television medium alter the presentation of political information in any way?

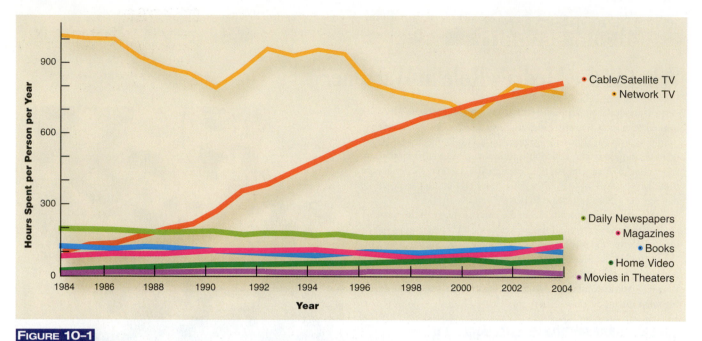

FIGURE 10-1

**Media Usage by
Consumers, 1984–2004**

SOURCES: U.S. Department of Commerce, *Statistical Abstract of the United States, 2002* (Washington, D.C.: U.S. Government Printing Office, 2002), p. 698; and authors' updates.

sound bite In televised news reporting, a brief comment, lasting for only a few seconds, that captures a thought or a perspective and has an immediate impact on the viewers.

If you compare the coverage given to an important political issue by the print media and by the TV networks, you will note some striking differences. For one thing, the print media (particularly leading newspapers such as the *Washington Post,* the *New York Times,* and the *Wall Street Journal*) treat an important issue in much more detail. In addition to news stories based on reporters' research, you will find editorials taking positions on the issue and arguments supporting those positions. Television news, in contrast, is often criticized as being too brief and too superficial.

Time Constraints The medium of television necessarily imposes constraints, particularly with respect to time, on how political issues are presented. News stories must be reported quickly, in only a few minutes or occasionally in only a **sound bite,** a brief comment lasting for just a few seconds that captures a thought or a perspective and has an immediate impact on the viewers.

A Visual Medium Television reporting also relies extensively on visual elements, rather than words, to capture the viewers' attention. Inevitably, the photos or videos selected to depict a particular political event have exaggerated importance. The visual aspect of television contributes to its power, but it also creates a potential bias. Those watching the news presentation do not know what portions of a video being shown have been deleted, what other photos may have been taken, or whether other records of the event exist. This kind of "selection bias" will be discussed in more detail later in this chapter.

Television Is "Big Business" Today's TV networks compete aggressively with each other to air "breaking news" and to produce quality news programs. Competition in the television industry understandably has had an effect on how the news is presented. To make profits, or even stay in business, TV stations need viewers. And to attract viewers, the news industry has turned to "infotainment"—programs that inform and entertain at the same time. Slick sets, attractive reporters, and animated graphics that dance across the television screen are now commonplace on most news programs, particularly on the cable news channels.

TV networks also compete with each other for advertising income. Although the media in the United States are among the freest in the world, their programming nonetheless remains vulnerable to the influence of the political bias of their advertising sponsors.

The Candidates and Television

Given the TV-saturated environment in which we live, it should come as no surprise that candidates spend a great deal of time—and money—obtaining TV coverage through political ads, debates, and general news coverage. Candidates and their campaign managers realize that the time and money are well spent because television has an important impact on the way people see the candidates, understand the issues, and cast their votes.

Political Advertising

Today, televised **political advertising** consumes at least half of the total budget for a major political campaign. In the 2000 election cycle, $665 million was spent for political advertising on broadcast TV. In the 2004 election cycle, the amount of funds spent on television advertising reached $1.5 billion. As you can see in Figure 10–2, this is five times the amount spent in the 1992 election cycle. Furthermore, television advertising battles did not cease after the 2004 elections, as issue advocacy and interest groups began spending millions more on political ads regarding Social Security reform in 2005.

The Emergence of Televised Political Advertising

Political advertising first appeared on television during the 1952 presidential campaign. At that time, there were only about 15 million television sets; today, there are well over 100 million. Initially, political TV commercials were more or less like any other type of advertising. Instead of focusing on the positive qualities of a product, thirty-second or sixty-second ads focused on the positive qualities of a political candidate. Within the decade, however, **negative political advertising** began to appear in the TV medium.

Negative Political Ads Despite the barrage of criticism levied against the candidates' use of negative political ads during recent election cycles, such ads are not new. Indeed, **attack ads**—advertising that attacks the character of an opposing candidate—have a long tradition in this country. In 1800, an article in the *Federalist Gazette of the United States* described Thomas Jefferson as having a "weakness of nerves, want of fortitude, and total imbecility of character."

Candidates also use **issue ads**—ads that focus on flaws in the opponents' positions on issues. For example, in the 2004 presidential campaigns, rarely did the candidates attack each other personally. Rather, they leveled criticisms at each other's stated positions on various issues, such as the war in Iraq and Social Security, and previous actions with respect to those issues. Candidates also try to undermine their opponents' credibility by pointing to discrepancies between what the opponents say in their campaign speeches and their political records,

FIGURE 10–2

Political Ad Spending on Broadcast TV, 1992–2004

As you can see in this figure, spending for political advertising has increased steadily over the last six elections.

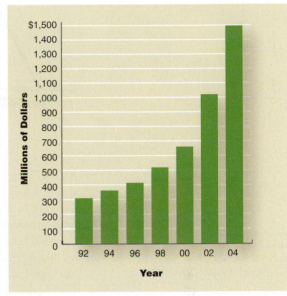

SOURCES: Television Bureau of Advertising, as presented in Lorraine Woellert and Tom Lowry, "A Political Nightmare: Not Enough Airtime," *Business Week*, November 23, 2000, p. 111; and authors' updates.

political advertising Advertising undertaken by or on behalf of a political candidate to familiarize voters with the candidate and his or her views on campaign issues; also advertising for or against policy issues.

negative political advertising Political advertising undertaken for the purpose of discrediting an opposing candidate in the eyes of the voters. Attack ads and issue ads are forms of negative political advertising.

attack ad A negative political advertisement that attacks the character of an opposing candidate.

issue ad A negative political advertisement that focuses on flaws in an opposing candidate's position on a particular issue.

AARP chief executive officer William D. Novelli campaigns against President George W. Bush's plan for allowing younger workers to divert a portion of their Social Security payroll taxes into private investments.

*"The thing to do now, Senator, is to
hit back with some negative advertising of our own."*

such as voting records, which are available to the public and thus can easily be verified. As noted in Chapters 6 and 9, issue ads are also used by interest groups to gather support for candidates who endorse the groups' causes.

Issue ads can be even more devastating than personal attacks—as Barry Goldwater learned in 1964 when his opponent in the presidential race, President Lyndon Johnson, aired the "daisy girl" ad. This ad, which set new boundaries for political advertising, showed a little girl standing quietly in a field of daisies. She held a daisy and pulled off the petals, counting to herself. Suddenly, a deep voice was heard counting: "10, 9, 8, 7, 6 . . . ." When the countdown hit zero, the unmistakable mushroom cloud of an atomic bomb filled the screen. Then President Johnson's voice was heard saying, "These are the stakes: to make a world in which all of God's children can live, or to go into the dark. We must either love each other or we must die." A message on the screen then read: "Vote for President Johnson on November 3." The implication, of course, was that Goldwater would lead the country into a nuclear war.[8]

Public Relations Contracts
In recent years, politicians have also used public relations firms to promote their ideas and agendas—using tax dollars. During his first term in office, President George W. Bush handed out $250 million in public relations contracts. Although the practice of spending government funds on public relations is not without precedent, the Bush administration spent twice as much on outside contracts with public relations firms as the Clinton administration. The public relations firms used some of the money to hire journalists. For example, conservative commentator Armstrong Williams was awarded a $240,000 contract to promote Bush's No Child Left Behind Act.

Additionally, the Bush administration produced television ads designed to look like news broadcasts. Called Video News Releases (VNRs), these ads focused on subjects such as airport security and Medicare reform and reported favorably on administration policies and actions. Although the ads were paid for with government funds, they did not disclose that government

The "daisy" commercial (left) was used by President Lyndon B. Johnson in 1964. A remake (right) targeted Democratic candidate Al Gore in the 2000 election. The ad contended that because the Clinton/Gore administration "sold" the nation's security "to Communist Red China in exchange for campaign contributions," China has "the ability to threaten our homes with long-range nuclear warheads." It then showed a girl, counting down as she plucked daisy petals. Her counting was then replaced by a countdown of a missile, which was followed by a nuclear bomb explosion. "Don't take a chance. Please vote Republican" then appeared on the screen. The ad proved so controversial that it was pulled shortly after it began airing on television.

agencies produced them and that no professional journalists were involved. They were distributed to local television news stations, many of which included the VNRs in their news programs.

Television Debates

Televised debates have been a feature of presidential campaigns since 1960, when presidential candidates Republican Richard M. Nixon and Democrat John F. Kennedy squared off in the first great TV debate. Television debates provide an opportunity for voters to find out how candidates differ on issues. They also allow candidates to capitalize on the power of television to improve their images or point out the failings of their opponents.

The presidential debates of 1992 included a third-party candidate, H. Ross Perot, along with the candidates from the two major parties, Republican George H. W. Bush, the incumbent president, and Democrat Bill Clinton. In 1996, two third-party candidates, H. Ross Perot and John Hagelin, sought to participate in the TV debates but were prevented from doing so by the Commission for Presidential Debates.[9]

In 2000, the commission similarly excluded Ralph Nader and Pat Buchanan from the debates. (For a further discussion of third-party candidates and presidential debates, see Chapter 7.) In 2000, there were three presidential debates, each using a different format, between George W. Bush and Al Gore and one vice-presidential debate between their respective running mates, Dick Cheney and Joe Lieberman.

The 2004 debates followed the practice of excluding third-party candidates, once again denying independent Ralph Nader the opportunity to participate. Nevertheless, George W. Bush and John Kerry engaged in some spirited exchanges, filled with attacks on each other's viewpoints and stances. As in 2000, there were three presidential debates along with a vice-presidential debate between Dick Cheney and John Edwards. Much of the four debates' content focused on the war in Iraq, the threat of terrorism, health care, and the economy.

Many contend that the presidential debates offer a significant opportunity for voters to assess the personalities and issue positions of the candidates. Thus, the debates help to shape the outcome of the elections. Others doubt that these televised debates—or the "spins" put on them by political commentators immediately after they are over—have ever been taken very seriously by voters.

News Coverage

Whereas political ads are expensive, coverage by the news media is free. Accordingly, the candidates try to take advantage of the media's interest in campaigns to increase the quantity and

The Bush administration awarded Armstrong Williams, a nationally syndicated radio, print, and television personality, a $240,000 public relations contract to promote the president's No Child Left Behind Act on his shows and in his commentaries.

The 1960 presidential debate between Republican Vice President Richard M. Nixon (left) and Senator John F. Kennedy, the Democratic presidential nominee (right), was viewed by many as helping Kennedy win at the polls.

quality of news coverage. This is not always easy. Generally, the media devote the lion's share of their coverage to polls showing who is ahead in the race.

In recent years, candidates' campaign managers and political consultants have shown increasing sophistication in creating newsworthy events for journalists and TV camera crews to cover, an effort commonly referred to as **managed news coverage.** As one scholar points out, "To keep a favorable image of their candidates in front of the public, campaign managers arrange newsworthy events to familiarize potential voters with their candidates' best aspects."[10] (For a discussion of how other nations "manage" news coverage through censorship or media control, see this chapter's *Comparative Politics* feature.)

Besides becoming aware of how camera angles and lighting affect a candidate's appearance, the political consultant plans political events to accommodate the press. The campaign staff attempts to make what the candidate is doing appear interesting. The staff also knows that journalists and political reporters compete for stories and that they can be manipulated by granting favors, such as an exclusive personal interview with the candidate. Each candidate's press advisers, often called **spin doctors,** also try to convince reporters to give the story or event a **spin,** or interpretation, that is favorable to the candidate.

managed news coverage News coverage that is manipulated (managed) by a campaign manager or political consultant to gain media exposure for a political candidate.

spin doctor A political candidate's press adviser who tries to convince reporters to give a story or event concerning the candidate a particular "spin" (interpretation, or slant).

spin A reporter's slant on, or interpretation of, a particular event or action.

comparative politics

When the State Controls the Media

During a 2005 visit to Europe, President George W. Bush criticized Russian president Vladimir Putin for what Bush believed was a weakening commitment to the expansion of democracy in Russia. Bush noted that one area in particular need of reform was the Russian media. After his election to office in 2000, Putin immediately tightened the government's grip on the Russian media. Putin sought to defuse any political dissent or criticism of the government, forcing media moguls with critical views to surrender their ownership of media outlets to the government. He described his media policies as an attempt to create a "manageable democracy." In other words, Putin's regime wanted to manage the information Russians received.

The majority of the Russian people, however, do not seem to be bothered by Putin's efforts to bring the media under government control. Outside Moscow and St. Petersburg, the nation's two largest cities, people tend to be distrustful of private initiative generally and of the private media in particular. For example, surveys have consistently shown that residents of rural Russia trust state-controlled newspapers more than private ones. Putin's approval ratings have frequently been higher than 80 percent throughout his time in office. Such ratings are astounding compared to Bush's ratings in the United States, which have often dropped below 50 percent. At least one factor in this difference is the lack of criticism of Putin in the Russian press. Bush, in contrast, faces daily critiques from television, newspaper, and radio commentators.

Some Americans take freedom of the press for granted, but in addition to Russia, numerous nations across the globe either censor

Shortly after his election in 2000, Russian president Vladimir Putin, second right, immediately tightened the government's grip on the Russian media. Putin sought to defuse any political dissent or criticism of the government by forcing media moguls with critical views to surrender their ownership of media outlets to the government.

the media or control them altogether. In China, for example, many teenagers and college students have been arrested for sending e-mails that criticized government policies. The Chinese government has strict censorship laws restricting political speech. Iranians have been jailed in recent years for accessing Web sites that were banned by the ruling theocracy. In Cuba, Fidel Castro's Communist government has long controlled and censored the media.

For Critical Analysis
Why do you think that many Russians do not object to state control over the media?

AMERICA at odds

Who Are the Real "Winners" in Expensive Campaigns?

In Chapter 9, we discussed the recent efforts to limit the amount of funds raised and spent in political campaigns. Campaign-finance reformers have had to fight incumbent politicians who see themselves as the beneficiaries of the old laws. But the other "winners" in expensive political campaigns are TV stations.

Indeed, the National Association of Broadcasters spends millions of dollars on lobbying efforts to squelch reform that would allow free political TV airtime. On average, a candidate has to pay about $3,000 to purchase a thirty-second spot for a political ad. For an ad broadcast during a popular show with high viewer ratings, the price goes up—to $5,000 or more. A local TV station can make even more from campaign ads for ballot initiatives than from candidate ads. For example, in 2002, local television and radio stations in Arizona made an estimated $30 million from a flurry of last-minute ads for ballot initiatives in that state.[11] The campaigns have only so many days until the election, and the stations have only so many advertising spots to sell, so the price of each spot goes up with the demand.

The public has decried the negative, tasteless, and relentless political ads that appear every campaign season. Americans generally blame the politicians, their media consultants, and the system of campaign financing. Reformers have focused on how much money candidates can raise from individuals and groups. Yet limits on contributions do little to reform the system when broadcasters continue to charge top dollar to air campaign ads. The law of the free market dictates that broadcasters will continue to air these ads as long as political campaigns pay for them.

"Popular" Television

Although not normally regarded as a forum for political debate, television programs such as dramas, sitcoms, and late-night comedy shows often use political themes. For example, the popular courtroom drama *Law and Order* regularly broaches controversial topics such as the death penalty, the USA Patriot Act, and the rights of the accused. The sitcom *Will and Grace* consistently brings to light issues regarding gay and lesbian rights. As for the late-night shows, movie star and current governor of California Arnold Schwarzenegger originally announced his candidacy in the 2003 gubernatorial race on the *Tonight Show with Jay Leno*.

Talk Radio—The Wild West of the Media

Ever since Franklin D. Roosevelt held his first "fireside chats" on radio, politicians have realized the power of radio. Today, talk radio is a political force to be reckoned with. In 1988, there were 200 talk-show radio stations. Today, there are over 1,200, and that number is growing. According to the most recent estimates, one in six Americans listens to talk radio regularly.

Talk radio is sometimes characterized as the Wild West of the media. Journalistic conventions do not exist. Political ranting and raving are common. Many popular talk shows do seem to have a conservative bent, but their supporters argue that talk radio has been a good way to counter the liberal bias in the print and TV media (we discuss bias in the media in the following section).

Some people are uneasy because talk shows empower fringe groups, perhaps magnifying their rage. Clearly, a talk show is not necessarily a democratic forum in which all views are aired. Talk-show hosts such as Rush Limbaugh do not attempt to hide their political biases; if anything, they exaggerate them for effect. Supporters of the sometimes outrageous, sometimes reactionary remarks broadcast during talk-radio shows reply that such shows are simply a response to consumer demand. Furthermore, those who think that talk radio is good for the country argue that talk shows, taken together, provide a great populist forum for political

President Franklin D. Roosevelt (1933–1945) was the first president to use radio broadcasts to send messages to the American people. Roosevelt gave twenty-eight "fireside chats," the first of which—on the bank crisis—was transmitted on March 12, 1933. He transmitted his last fireside chat on June 12, 1944.

Library of Congress

debate. They maintain that in a sense, talk radio has become an equalizer because it is relatively inexpensive to start up a rival talk show.

Those who claim that talk-show hosts go too far in their rantings and ravings ultimately have to deal with the constitutional issue of free speech. After all, as First Amendment scholars point out, there is little the government can do about the forces that shape the media. The courts have always protected freedom of expression to the fullest extent possible, although, for many reasons, the government has been able to exercise some control over the electronic media—see the discussion of freedom of the press in Chapter 4.

The Question of Media Bias

Since the media first appeared on the American political landscape, they have been criticized by one group or another as being biased. The many studies that have been undertaken on the subject of media bias, however, have reached different conclusions.

Conservative radio talk-show host Rush Limbaugh puffs on his cigar while waiting to tee off at the Pebble Beach Golf Links. Limbaugh began his syndicated radio talk show in 1988, and today, his show continues to rank as one of the top-rated talk shows in America.

AP Photo/Eric Risberg

Studies on Media Bias

For years, conservatives have contended that there is a liberal bias in the media. Indeed, some evidence seems to support this. For example, in a significant study conducted in the 1980s, the researchers found that the media producers, editors, and reporters (the "media elite") showed a notably liberal bias in their news coverage.[12] Surveys over the past three decades have also consistently shown that national, Washington-based reporters are more likely to describe themselves as liberals than conservatives. Surveys also show that a majority of these reporters have voted Democratic for quite some time.

Yet other research data suggest that even if reporters hold liberal views, these views are not reflected in their reporting. Based on an analysis of media coverage of presidential campaigns, Kathleen Hall Jamieson, director of the Annenberg Public Policy Center at the University of Pennsylvania, concludes that there is no systematic liberal, Democratic bias in news coverage.[13] A poll of voters on the question of media bias during the 2004 presidential campaigns revealed that 53 percent of those surveyed thought that the media "often" let political views influence coverage. Yet, overall, the voters believed that the media had been fair to both presidential candidates.[14]

Calvin Exoo, in his study of the media and politics, suggests that journalists have neither a liberal nor a conservative bias. Rather, they are constrained by both the pro-American bias of media ownership and the journalists' own code of objectivity. Most are more interested in improving their career prospects than in discussing public policies.[15] Other scholars, including political scientist Thomas Patterson, agree that news reporting is largely apolitical. Media bias exists, but it is toward bad news and cynicism and is not partisan in nature.

The Bias against Losers

Kathleen Hall Jamieson believes that media bias plays a significant role in shaping presidential campaigns and elections, but she argues that it is not a partisan bias. Rather, it is a bias against losers. A candidate who falls behind in the race is immediately labeled a "loser," making it even more difficult for the candidate to regain favor in the voters' eyes.[16]

Jamieson argues that the media use the winner-loser paradigm to describe events throughout the campaigns. Even a presidential debate is regarded as a "sporting match" that results in a winner and a loser. Before the 2004 debates, reporters focused on what each candidate had to do to "win" the debate. When the debate was over, reporters immediately speculated about who had "won" as they waited for postdebate polls to answer that question. According to Jamieson, this approach "squanders the opportunity to reinforce learning." The debates are an important source of political information for the voters, and this fact is eclipsed by the media's win-lose focus.

"Selection Bias"

As mentioned earlier, television is big business, and maximizing profits from advertising is a major consideration in what television stations choose to air. After all, a station or network that incurs losses will eventually go bankrupt. The expansion of the media universe to include cable channels and the Internet has also increased the competition among news sources. As a result, news directors select programming they believe will attract the largest audiences and garner the highest advertising revenues. Furthermore, most Americans have a remote control in hand while watching TV and quickly click to another channel if they lose interest in one particular station's programming.[17] Consequently, even when an in-depth political discussion is available on television, viewership may be abysmal.

Self-Censorship In 2000, the Pew Research Center released a survey that studied how journalists choose news stories and why they pursue some stories but not others. More than half of the journalists surveyed reported that they sometimes avoid newsworthy stories because their audiences might find them too complex or dull.[18] Roughly the same number said that newsworthy stories are "often or sometimes ignored" to protect the corporate interests of the news organization. The pressure to avoid a story is sometimes subtle, however. The journalists in the survey reported that they choose not to pursue a story when they "get signals" or "anticipate negative responses" from superiors in their news organizations. In general, the journalists surveyed were pessimistic about their profession, with a majority saying that the media do only a "fair" job of telling the public what it wants and needs to know.[19]

TV News Magazines and Commentary

In the battle to increase ratings and decrease costs, many news directors have opted to use the TV "news magazine" format. These programs, such as *The O'Reilly Factor* on Fox and *Larry King Live* on CNN, are popular with viewers and relatively inexpensive to produce. Journalists themselves lament the effect that these programs are having on the delivery of the news.

In another cost-cutting measure, news networks have reduced the number of news correspondents. As a result, talk *about* news is replacing news—viewers receive commentary rather than information. Every viewpoint gets aired, whether or not there is research to back it up. Some media researchers believe that what we are now hearing and viewing is simply cocktail party conversation that is falsely labeled journalism.

A Changing News Culture

A large majority of news professionals also believe that the culture of news is changing. The traditional respect for facts and factual verification is giving way to a news culture characterized by argument, opinion, haste, and news as entertainment. According to the survey, 69 percent of journalists believe that the distinction between reporting and commentary has been seriously eroded.

The American public agrees with journalists that news coverage is less accurate today than it was in the past. Confidence in the media's credibility has eroded steadily over the past twenty years. As Figure 10–3 shows, the percentage of Americans who are skeptical of the media increased substantially during that period.

FIGURE 10–3

Public Skepticism of the Media, 1985 and 2004

Public mistrust of the media has increased significantly over the past twenty years. This graphic shows the percentage of respondents to polls in 1985 and 2004 who stated that they believed "next to nothing" reported by the media outlets listed.

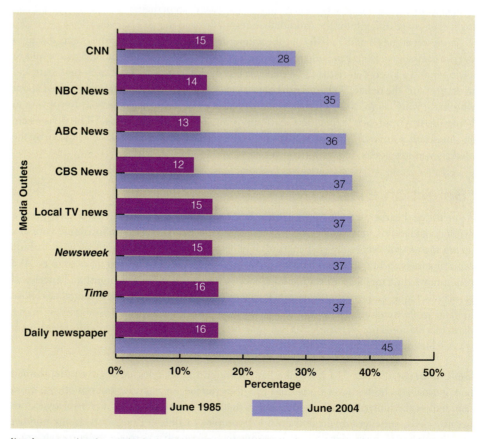

NOTE: Answers are based on people who say they are able to rate the media.
SOURCE: Pew Research Center for the People and the Press, June 2004.

Racial Bias in the Media?

Another type of media bias that recent studies have identified is racial bias. As you read in Chapter 5, Americans and political leaders are concerned about the practice of "racial profiling" by law enforcement officers. Racial profiling is a denigrating form of discrimination that occurs when, for example, a police officer pulls over a disproportionate number of drivers from a particular minority group. In recent years, some researchers have noticed another, far more subtle type of discrimination based on skin color: racial profiling in the media.

News Reporting on Crime and Drugs

In 2000, political scientists Franklin Gilliam and Shanto Iyengar published the results of a study they had conducted on the effects of news reporting on attitudes toward African Americans.[20] These scholars found that stories about crime dominate local news programming because crime stories satisfy viewers' demands for "action news." The prevalence of this kind of reporting, they claim, has led to a crime narrative ("script") that includes two core elements: (1) crime is violent, and (2) perpetrators of crime are nonwhite males. This crime script has a significant impact on the viewing public because local television news is the public's primary source of information on public affairs.

Gilliam and Iyengar's central finding was that the racial element of the crime script promotes negative attitudes about African Americans among white viewers (but not among African American viewers). One result is increased support among the public for more punitive approaches to crime.

Some scholars contend that the media also create misperceptions about drug users. A medical study on the effects of U.S. drug policy showed that the majority of Americans have little firsthand experience with the problems associated with drug use. What they know about this issue comes largely from the news media, particularly television. That Americans are getting the wrong picture is confirmed by another study of drug policy conducted by a prominent group of physicians, the Physician Leadership on National Drug Policy (PLNDP). The PLNDP found that more than half of those who admit to using cocaine and heroin are white and that over 67 percent of regular marijuana users are white; less than 17 percent are African Americans.[21]

"Racializing" Welfare

Yale University political scientist Martin Gilens contends that racial profiling in the media has also promoted negative attitudes toward welfare. Based on a detailed analysis of surveys and other sources, Gilens believes that TV programs and news magazines misrepresent the racial composition of America's poor people by calling up old stereotypes—such as African Americans as "lazy"—when visually portraying poverty. Gilens concludes that this "racialization" of welfare is responsible for a contradictory belief held by many Americans: welfare should be ended, and at the same time, the government should be spending more to help poor people trying to support themselves.[22]

Media Blackface

According to Mikal Muharrar, the problem of racial profiling can best be understood as the "politically acceptable and very American practice of defining a social problem in 'blackface'—that is, in racial terms—through indirect association." Issues defined in blackface, he contends, include the black drug dealer, the black criminal, and the lazy black welfare recipient. Defining issues in this way allows "the issue—be it crime, welfare, drug abuse, or what have you—[to be] seen by many as a real issue that is only *coincidentally* about race." This is brilliant, he claims, because the media can thus deny responsibility for any punitive public policies that result from such media profiles.[23]

Political News on the Web

The Internet has become, in a very brief span of time, a significant medium for the delivery of political news. Today, at least two-thirds of Americans have Internet access. If you count those who have access outside their homes, such as at school or work, an even higher number of Americans are Internet users. Around 50,000 more Americans are connected to the Internet each day. About two-thirds of Internet users now consider the Internet to be an important source of news.

Matt Drudge carries a laptop computer as he walks up the stairs in Los Angeles. The *Drudge Report,* the daily barrage of breaking news, gossip, and politics that he e-mails to some 65,000 subscribers, is hotter than hot.

Certainly, news now abounds on the Web. Almost every major news provider, both print and broadcast, has deployed a Web site. Although there are a few Internet-only news outlets, most news sites on the Web are maintained by already well established newspapers, magazines, and TV broadcasters. Has the growth of the Internet as a source for news been responsible for a decline in the use of traditional news sources? For a discussion of this question, see this chapter's *Perception versus Reality* feature.

Tabloid Journalism on the Internet

Matt Drudge, creator of the Web's *Drudge Report,* has become widely known for his tabloid-type journalism. Critics refer to him as a "cybergossip" who is not all that concerned about distinguishing between fact and fiction in his "news" reports. For example, in January 1998, he "reported" that then president Bill Clinton had had an affair with White House intern Monica Lewinsky. The allegation was unsubstantiated and apparently had been taken from a *Newsweek* article that was never printed. Nonetheless, it set the media wheels in motion. Within days, the *Washington Post* had investigated the allegation and published an article based on documented facts. The other major media quickly followed suit, and the details of the "Lewinsky scandal" unfolded before the American public.

In one sense, what happened here was not really new. After all, printed tabloids have often been the first to mention breaking scandals or other news items, which then find their way into the more "respectable" news media. What is striking about the events following the *Drudge Report*'s story about Monica Lewinsky is how quickly the story was investigated and reported on by the leading print and electronic news sources. Indeed, some journalists claim that the Internet has not only increased the amount of tabloid "reporting" but has also accelerated the pace of publication. Thus, online tabloids could dramatically increase the potential impact of tabloid journalism on mainstream journalism. Indeed, Drudge himself has become somewhat mainstream. He has a radio show that is carried on some of the biggest stations in the country.

The accelerated pace of publication has also had another effect: an increased pressure on news publishers to compete for top stories within a short period. Even respected, mainstream news organizations have occasionally posted inaccurate stories on their Web sites.[24]

"Narrowcasting" the News

Technology is quickening the pace at which the "one size fits all" news standard is being replaced by highly specialized "packets." The Internet is the ultimate vehicle for what is known as "narrowcasting"—tailoring media programming to the specialized tastes and pref-

perception versus REALITY

Does Online Information Mean the Death of Traditional News?

News on the Web is, in fact, itself news. Numerous articles appear in the traditional press discussing how much news is being transmitted on the Internet.

THE PERCEPTION

A broad sampling of traditional news articles about online information sources gives the impression that people are turning to their information appliance—the personal computer—when they need news. Because this perception is becoming increasingly widespread, the traditional news media, including TV networks, are devoting substantial resources to establishing a "presence" on the Internet.

THE REALITY

Clearly, the number of Americans who go online to obtain news is rising rapidly. Recent studies suggest, though, that those who obtain news online are also those who view news programs on TV and read daily newspapers. In other words, there is no evidence that going online for news leads to less reading or viewing of more traditional news sources. In fact, one recent survey indicated that Internet users and nonusers alike ranked printed books and magazines higher than television as important news sources.[25]

What's Your Opinion?

Do you believe that the Internet will ever replace traditional news sources, such as television broadcast news, newspapers, and news magazines? Why or why not?

erences of targeted audiences. If you are interested in UFOs, you can direct the Internet to give you just news on UFOs.

The latest in news systems further enhances the narrowcasting of news. Using so-called **push technology,** Web users can totally customize their daily supply of information. The best-known providers of this type of service are CNN/PointCast Network and Infogate. You decide which type of news you want, and the provider will "push" this news through your Internet hookup. How do you decide what type of news you really want? You first select one of the thousand or more search engines available. Then you start "surfing" the Web to find the sites that you like most. Then you tell the "push" software which sites to go to and how many times a day. One of the problems with such narrowcasting is that users do not get different views on a particular subject.

push technology Software that enables Internet users to customize the type of information they receive from Web sources. The information is "pushed" to the user automatically as it is put on the Web.

The Emergence of Blogs

Internet Web logs, or *blogs,* have become increasingly popular in the cybercommunity. Blogs serve as forums for debate and sources of information on a variety of political topics. In numerous instances during the 2004 elections, blogs were the first source to discredit false, misleading, or biased statements by candidates, interest groups, and even members of the mainstream media. Members of the mainstream media have criticized blogs, questioning their accuracy and credibility. Still, blogs continue to expand their readership and participation.

Cyberspace and Political Campaigns

Today's political parties and candidates not only realize the benefits of using computers and computer databases to communicate with voters but also understand that the Internet can be used to conduct online campaigns and raise funds. Voters also are increasingly using the Web to access information about parties and candidates, promote political goals, and obtain political news.

In a sense, the use of the Internet is the least costly way for candidates to contact, recruit, and mobilize supporters, as well as disseminate information on their positions on issues. In effect, the Internet can replace brochures, letters, and position papers. Individual voters or political-party supporters can use the Internet to avoid having to go to special meetings or to a campaign site to do volunteer work or obtain information on a candidate's position.

That the Internet is now a viable medium for communicating political information and interacting with voters was made clear in the 2004 presidential election cycle. According to a postelection Pew Research Center survey, 29 percent of Americans said that they went online for election news, up from 4 percent who did so in the 1996 campaign. Nearly seven in ten of this group went online to seek information on the candidates' positions. Moreover, 43 percent of this group claimed that the information they found online affected their voting decisions.[26]

Online Fund-Raising

Today's political candidates are realizing that the Internet can be an effective—and inexpensive—way to raise campaign funds. The leading candidates in the 2004 presidential race all engaged in online fund-raising, as did the national committees of the Republican and Democratic parties.

Fund-raising on the Internet by presidential candidates became widespread after the Federal Election Commission decided, in June 1999, that the federal government could distribute matching funds for credit-card donations received by candidates via the Internet. In 2003, Democratic presidential hopeful Howard Dean showed the fund-raising power of the Internet by raising more than $20 million online. Political analysts marveled at Dean's success, especially in shifting the focus of campaign finance from a few large donors to countless small donors.

These important new Internet strategies were then adopted by the presidential campaigns of John Kerry and George W. Bush in 2004. The Democratic and Republican National Committees followed suit, as did candidates on the state and local levels. After witnessing Dean's success with online fund-raising, Kerry's campaign used similar strategies and raised nearly $82 million in online contributions. Bush's campaign, which used its Web site mainly to organize and communicate with supporters, collected only about $14 million online. Thus, Kerry's

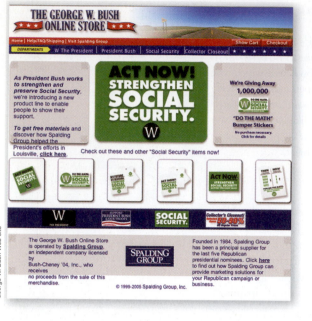

George W. Bush Web site

www.georgebushstore.com

John Kerry Web site

www.johnkerry.com

online fund-raising efforts enabled him to compete with Bush financially. The success of fund-raising via the Internet, and particularly the ability of candidates to extend their appeals to "low-dollar" donors online, led one campaign analyst to conclude that the Internet is "the ultimate grassroots fund-raising mechanism."[27]

Of course, voters can also go online to find out who is contributing to which candidates. In addition to the Federal Election Commission's online database of campaign contributors, numerous public-interest Web sites can be accessed by voters interested in learning where the money is coming from. Common Cause, the Center for Responsive Politics, and Vote Smart are just a few of the Web sites that offer this information (for the Web sites of these organizations, see the *Politics on the Web* feature at the end of Chapter 9).

The Rise of the Internet Campaign Strategy

Increasingly, candidates are facing the need for professionals who can create well-designed, informative, and user-friendly campaign Web sites to attract viewers, hold their attention, manage their e-mail, and track credit-card contributions from supporters. Politicians now hire Internet campaign strategists, professional consultants who manage a candidate's Web site. Democratic presidential candidate Howard Dean assembled a tech-savvy campaign staff. His campaign manager, Joe Trippi, relied heavily on the Internet, making it the centerpiece of the Dean campaign. In addition to establishing Dean's personal Web site, Trippi and his staff used sites such as meetup.com and MoveOn.org to identify and bring together potential supporters.

AMERICA at odds

Will the Internet Change Political Campaigning as We Know It?

Although some observers claim that the Internet will fundamentally change the way political candidates conduct their campaigns, others are not yet convinced. To be sure, the Internet is playing an increasingly important role in political campaigns. Many candidates have proved that the Internet can be a powerful fund-raising tool. Others, however, hesitate to rely too much on this still-emerging medium.

Especially to Democrats, Howard Dean personifies the importance of the Internet in today's political campaigns. Although his run for the presidency in 2004 was short lived, Dean showed how a Web site can be used both to raise funds and to communicate with supporters. In addition to attracting contributions, Dean's Web site, and in particular its blog, provided his supporters with a forum where they could discuss issues. To participate in the blog, Dean required that individuals register on the Web site with their contact information. The registration requirement gave Dean an effective direct-mailing tool, allowing him to send e-mails to supporters on a regular basis. Numerous politicians have mimicked Dean's approach, believing that the Internet will revolutionize political campaigning as we know it.

Others remain skeptical of the Internet's current effectiveness in political campaigns. For one thing, to reach out to large numbers of voters, candidates need a mass medium, such as television, and the Internet is not that kind of medium—at least, not yet. Many poor Americans still lack consistent access to the Internet, not to mention the skills required to navigate it. While acknowledging the increasing success of fund-raising on the Internet, some analysts have claimed that cyberbased groups actually brought new levels of partisanship and negativity to the 2004 elections. Online issue advocacy groups ran intensely negative campaigns on behalf of their preferred candidates, making little effort to hide their deep-seated animosity for the other party's policies and viewpoints. Such a culture of negative campaigning may ultimately end up alienating political moderates from the Internet's political landscape.

AP Photo/Randy Siner

During the 2004 presidential primary elections, Howard Dean (D., Vt.) demonstrated to the rest of the country how the Internet could boost a political campaign. Through his Web site, Dean not only raised funds for his campaign, he gleaned contact information that allowed him to communicate one on one with voters.

Politics, the Media, and Your Everyday Life

The relationship between politics and the media influences your everyday life no matter who you are. Why? The reason is that, especially during elections, the media present political stories, issues, and debates virtually every day twenty-four hours a day.

The point is that you will never be able to avoid political information. No matter what magazine or newspaper you read, you cannot avoid the political discussions that are regular features in the print media. If you watch the news on TV, there are political stories every single day. If you listen to commercial FM or AM radio, you will hear political news at least once an hour. During campaigns, you will hear paid political announcements on a regular basis.

Because political news dominates much of the media, you have three choices: (1) you can simply "tune out" the political information you encounter; (2) you can "stay tuned," but assimilate the information superficially because you are not very knowledgeable about politics; or (3) you can fully enjoy and utilize all of the political information to which you are exposed by gaining a better, deeper, and more analytical understanding of American politics and government.

Political news will always be part of your life. Therefore, simply for your own enjoyment, you have an incentive to gain a better grasp of politics.

Taking Action

Remember, too, that you can use the media to express your views—by writing letters to newspaper editors or calling a radio

talk show, for example. Radio talk-show hosts routinely invite listeners to call their stations and share their thoughts on political issues. Additionally, many political leaders have call-in radio shows during which voters can ask questions or voice their concerns on specific topics. The photo below shows Donald DiFrancesco answering a New Jersey resident's question on a radio program. DiFrancesco was acting governor of New Jersey during 2001 and 2002.

AP Photo/Daniel Hulshizer

Key Terms

attack ad   221

electronic media   217

issue ad   221

managed news
   coverage   224

mass media   217

negative political
   advertising   221

political advertising   221

print media   217

push technology   231

sound bite   220

spin   224

spin doctor   224

Chapter Summary

1 The mass media include the print media (newspapers and magazines) and electronic media (radio, television, and the Web). The media have long played a vital role in the democratic process, both reflecting and influencing what Americans think about politics. The media can also influence what issues are on the political agenda.

2 Television is the primary news source for most Americans, but the limitations of the TV medium significantly affect the scope and depth of news coverage. Candidates for political office spend a great deal of time and money obtaining TV exposure through

political ads, debates, and general news coverage. Candidates and their political consultants have become increasingly sophisticated in creating newsworthy events for the media to cover.

3 Talk radio has been characterized as the Wild West of the media, where the usual journalistic conventions do not apply. Political ranting and raving are common.

4 The media are frequently accused of bias toward one group or another. Studies have examined whether the media show a liberal bias, commercial bias, or racial bias. The expanding media universe, which now includes cable news channels twenty-four hours a day and the Internet, has changed the nature of news coverage.

5 An increasing number of Americans are turning to Web sites for political news. Almost all major newspapers and magazines now have online versions, and the major TV news sources also have Web sites.

6 The Internet provides an inexpensive way for candidates to contact, recruit, and mobilize supporters; to disseminate information on the issues; and to raise funds. A problem with using the Internet for campaigning is that it cannot yet reach mass audiences, as TV can. Voters can go to various Web sites to learn who is contributing to a particular candidate's campaign.

RESOURCES FOR FURTHER STUDY

Selected Readings

Cook, Timothy. *Governing with the News: The News Media as a Political Institution.* Chicago: University of Chicago Press, 2005. The author not only questions the objectivity of the media, but argues that the media are in fact political institutions integral to the day-to-day operations of the three branches of our government.

Croteau, David, and William Hoynes. *Media/Society: Industries, Images, and Audiences.* Thousand Oaks, Calif.: Pine Forge Press, 2002. This insightful exploration of the media from their beginnings to the leap into cyberspace shows the complex interactions between the media and society and emphasizes how economics drives news coverage.

Herman, Edward S., and Noam Chomsky. *Manufacturing Consent: The Political Economy of the Mass Media.* New York: Pantheon Books, 2002. The authors argue that media bias inevitably results from such factors as media ownership and advertising.

Solomon, Norman. *War Made Easy: How Presidents and Pundits Keep Spinning Us to Death.* New York: John Wiley & Sons, 2005. The author explores what he describes as a pro-war bias and the media's role in reporting on armed conflicts.

Politics on the Web

- Literally thousands of news sources, including newspapers, news magazines, and television and radio stations, are now online. TotalNEWS offers a directory of more than a thousand news sources, including Fox News, MSNBC, CBS, ABC, and *USA Today.* To find TotalNEWS, go to **http://totalnews.com**

- If you are interested in news stories covered by ABC, CBS, and NBC television since 1968, you can find abstracts of these stories at Vanderbilt University's Television News Archive, which is online at **http://tvnews. vanderbilt.edu**

- Newspapers.com features links to more than ten thousand newspapers nationwide. You can also search by categories such as business, college newspapers, and industry. Go to **http://www.newspapers.com**

- The Claremont Institute is an interactive community that aims to bring Internet users together with public-policy organizations under "the broad umbrella of 'conservative' thoughts, ideas, and actions." It can be found at **http:// www.townhall.com**

- The Polling Report Web site provides polling results on a number of issues, organized by topics. The site is easy to use and up to date. Go to **http://www.pollingreport.com**

- The Public Broadcasting Service (PBS) features a section on its Web site titled "PBS by the People," which provides some good tips on how to analyze a poll. Go to: **http://www.pbs. org/elections/savvyanalyze.html**

Online Resources for This Chapter

This text's Companion Web Site, at **http://www.americaatodds.com**, offers links to numerous resources that you can utilize to learn more about the topics covered in this chapter. For a list describing these resources, see the inside front cover of this book.

chapter **11**

congress

CHAPTER OBJECTIVES

After reading this chapter, you should be able to . . .

▶ Explain how seats in the House of Representatives are apportioned among the states.

▶ Understand the power of incumbency and the arguments for and against term limits.

▶ Identify the key leadership positions in Congress.

▶ State some important differences between the House of Representatives and the Senate.

▶ Summarize the specific steps in the lawmaking process.

▶ Indicate Congress's oversight functions and explain how Congress fulfills them.

▶ Describe the congressional budgeting process.

Does Congress Have to Look Like America to Represent It?

The 109th Congress that began its term in January 2005 is, as Congress has always been, a predominantly white male institution. Of the 535 members of Congress (435 in the House and 100 in the Senate), 15.0 percent are women, 7.7 percent are African American, and 5.2 percent are Hispanic. In contrast, in the general population of the United States, 51 percent are women, 12.5 percent are Hispanic, and 12.3 percent are African American. Clearly, in terms of race and gender, Congress does not look like America. Does this matter?

In 1776, John Adams wrote of representative assemblies, "[They] should be in miniature an exact portrait of the people at large." James Wilson repeated the sentiment at the Constitutional Convention in 1787 when he said, "The legislature ought to be the most exact transcript of the whole society, . . . the faithful echo of the voices of the people." The theory of representation to which the founders subscribed dictates that the competing interests in society should be represented in Congress. Are race and gender among these "interests"? Can a man represent a woman's interests? Can a white person represent the interests of African Americans?

Demographic Balance Matters

Demographic balance in Congress matters because the experiences of different groups can lead to different perceptions, interests, and desires. Female legislators might be more interested in or sensitive to women's health issues or sexual harassment, for example. African Americans or Hispanics in Congress may be more concerned about the erosion of civil liberties than other members of Congress are. Can the interests of all Americans be adequately represented by white men?

Furthermore, about 30 percent of the members of Congress are millionaires, compared to only 1 percent of Americans. Many members of the House and Senate are lawyers. A large number also have significant investments in U.S. corporations. Several members take pay cuts when they come to the House of Representatives, where the annual salary is only $162,000. Of course, this is a very comfortable salary when compared to the median household income in the United States of about $43,000 per year.

The notion that our legislators should mirror their constituents in terms of race or gender, or even income or age, is called "descriptive representation" by political scientists. It has sometimes been dismissed by those outside academia as mere "political correctness" rather than genuine political reform. Still, proponents argue that descriptive representation is vital to overcoming the political marginalization of minorities and women in our society.

Legislators Are the Trustees of Society

No one disputes that a member of Congress has an obligation to his or her constituents. Less clear is the extent to which broad national interests should play a role in congressional representation. The "trustee" view of representation holds that legislators should act as the trustees of the broad interests of the entire society. If legislators believe that a national need outweighs the narrow interests of their constituents, they should vote their conscience. If legislators are trustees, then there is no reason why white males cannot represent the interests of women and minorities as well as any other group of legislators. For example, for decades, Ted Kennedy (D., Mass.), a white senator, has been well known for championing the cause of civil rights in Congress.

As you will read later in this chapter, one of the objections to racial gerrymandering—in which congressional districts are redrawn to maximize the number of minority group members within district boundaries—is that it assumes that people of a particular race, merely because of their race, think alike. Opponents of "descriptive representation" argue that there is no reason to assume that a black member of Congress can represent the interests of black people better than a white member of Congress. African Americans hold a broad range of views on the issues facing our nation, as do women, Hispanics, and Asians. As long as our views are represented, it does not matter whether our race or gender is represented.

Where Do You Stand?

1. Do you think that Congress needs to look like America to represent it?
2. Do you feel that your views and needs are adequately represented in Congress now?

Explore This Issue Online

- Women's Policy, Inc., provides information on the history, accomplishments, and current members of the Congressional Caucus for Women's Issues. You can access this site at **http://www.womenspolicy.org/caucus**.

- Ethnic Majority offers an interesting site that includes biographies of minority members of Congress, as well as demographic and civil rights information. Go to **http://www.ethnicmajority.com/congress.htm**.

Introduction

Congress is the lawmaking branch of government. When someone says, "There ought to be a law," at the federal level it is Congress that will make that law. The framers had a strong suspicion of a powerful executive authority. Consequently, they made Congress—not the executive branch (the presidency)—the central institution of American government. Yet, as noted in Chapter 2, the founders created a system of checks and balances to ensure that no branch of the federal government, including Congress, could exercise too much power.

Many Americans view Congress as a largely faceless, anonymous legislative body that is quite distant and removed from their everyday lives. Yet, as you read in the chapter-opening *America at Odds* feature, the people you elect to Congress represent and advocate your interests at the very highest level of power. Furthermore, the laws created by the men and women in the U.S. Congress affect the daily lives of every American in one way or another. Getting to know your congressional representatives and how they are voting in Congress on issues that concern you is an important step toward becoming an informed voter.

The Structure and Make-up of Congress

The framers agreed that the Congress should be the "first branch of the government," as James Madison said, but they did not agree on its organization. Ultimately, they decided on a bicameral legislature—a Congress consisting of two chambers. This was part of the Great Compromise, which you read about in Chapter 2. The framers favored a bicameral legislature so that the two chambers, the House and the Senate, might serve as checks on each other's power and activity. The House was to represent the people as a whole, or the majority. The Senate was to represent the states and would protect the interests of small states by giving them the same number of senators (two per state) as the larger states. (For a discussion of the differences between the U.S. Congress and the British Parliament, see this chapter's *Comparative Politics* feature.)

comparative politics

How the British Parliament Differs from the U.S. Congress

The framers of the U.S. Constitution, for the most part, were used to the British form of government in which the central institution is the national legislature, known as Parliament. Like our own Congress, Parliament is a bicameral body: it is made up of the House of Commons and the House of Lords. Unlike Congress, however, the British Parliament (as in all parliamentary systems) is based on the *fusion* of powers rather than the *separation* of powers. It manages both the legislative and the executive powers of the nation. Parliament's legislative powers include passing and changing laws; its executive powers include choosing the prime minister, who is the leader of the majority party in the House of Commons, and the cabinet (the heads of executive agencies) that will serve the prime minister.

THE HOUSE OF COMMONS

The House of Commons is the legislative branch and currently consists of 659 elected officials. This lower house, known as "the Commons," is the more powerful of the two houses. Its members, known as Members of Parliament, or MPs, are popularly elected from geographic districts. Any MP is allowed to introduce legislation, but most measures are introduced by the government, which is made up of the prime minister and the cabinet collectively. The bill is then debated and sent to one of the eight standing committees that review bills and prepare them for final consideration by the full chamber. Unlike congressional committees, which specialize in areas such as agriculture or the armed forces, committees in the House of Commons are general committees that consider bills on a wide variety of subjects.

THE HOUSE OF LORDS

The upper chamber of Parliament is known as the House of Lords. In the past, the House of Lords included 750 hereditary peers (members of the nobility who became so by birth) with such titles as *baron, viscount, earl,* and *duke.* Due to recent reforms, only 92 hereditary peers now sit in the House of Lords. The other members of the House of Lords include 544 persons who are appointed as peers for life by the queen and 26 bishops of the Church of England.

The House of Lords was once a powerful branch of the British government, but today it has little real authority over legislation. If the House of Lords defeats a bill passed in the Commons, the Commons need only pass it a second time in the next session to make the bill become law. The House of Lords may amend legislation, but any changes it makes can be canceled by the Commons.

For Critical Analysis

What is one of the key differences between the upper chamber of the British Parliament and the U.S. Senate?

Republican congressional candidate Rebecca Armendariz Klein met with some senior voters during the 2004 elections. Klein lost her bid for the U.S. House of Representatives to incumbent U.S. Rep. Lloyd Doggett (D., Tex.).

Apportionment of House Seats

apportionment The distribution of House seats among the states on the basis of their respective populations.

The Constitution provides for the **apportionment** (distribution) of House seats among the states on the basis of their respective populations. States with larger populations, such as California, have many more representatives than states with smaller populations, such as Wyoming. California, for example, currently has fifty-three representatives in the House; Wyoming has only one.

Every ten years, House seats are reapportioned based on the outcome of the decennial (ten-year) census conducted by the U.S. Census Bureau. Figure 11–1 indicates the states that gained and lost seats based on population changes noted in the 2000 census. This redistribution of seats took effect with the 108th Congress elected in 2002.

FIGURE 11–1

Reapportionment of House Seats following the 2000 Census

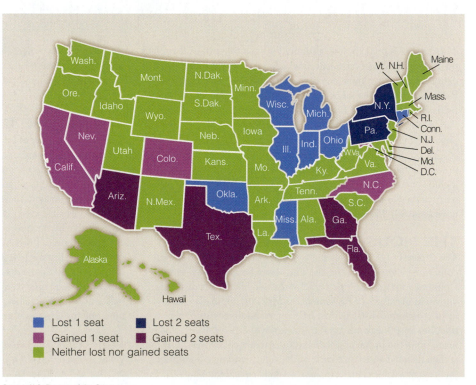

SOURCE: U.S. Bureau of the Census.

Each state is guaranteed at least one seat, no matter what its population. Today, seven states have only one representative.[1] The District of Columbia, American Samoa, Guam, and the U.S. Virgin Islands all send nonvoting delegates to the House. Puerto Rico, a self-governing possession of the United States, is represented by a nonvoting resident commissioner.

Congressional Districts

Whereas senators are elected to represent all of the people in the state, representatives are elected by the voters of a particular area known as a **congressional district.** The Constitution makes no provisions for congressional districts, and in the early 1800s each state was given the right to decide whether to have districts at all. Most states set up single-member districts, in which voters in each district elected one of the state's representatives. In states that chose not to have districts, representatives were chosen at large, from the state as a whole. In 1842, however, Congress passed an act that required all states to send representatives to Congress from single-member districts, as you read in Chapter 7.

In the early 1900s, the number of House members increased as the population expanded. In 1929, however, a federal law fixed House membership at 435 members. Today, the 435 members of the House are chosen by the voters in 435 separate congressional districts across the country. If a state's population allows it to have only one representative, as is the situation in a few states, the entire state is one congressional district. In contrast, states with large populations have numerous districts. California, for example, because its population entitles it to send fifty-three representatives to the House, has fifty-three congressional districts.

The lines of the congressional districts are drawn by the authority of state legislatures. States must meet certain requirements, though, in drawing district boundaries. To ensure equal representation in the House, districts must contain, as nearly as possible, an equal number of people. Additionally, each district must have contiguous boundaries and must be "geographically compact."

The Requirement of Equal Representation

If congressional districts are not made up of equal populations, the value of people's votes is not the same. In the past, state legislatures often used this knowledge to their advantage. For example, traditionally, many state legislatures were controlled by rural areas. By drawing districts that were not equal in population, rural leaders attempted to curb the number of representatives from growing urban centers. At one point in the 1960s, in many states the largest district had twice the population of the smallest district. In effect, this meant that a person's vote in the largest district had only half the value of a person's vote in the smallest district.

For some time, the Supreme Court refused to address this problem. In 1962, however, in *Baker v. Carr,*[2] the Court ruled that the Tennessee state legislature's **malapportionment** was an issue that could be heard in the federal courts because it affected the constitutional requirement of equal protection under the law. Two years later, in *Wesberry v. Sanders,*[3] the Supreme Court held that congressional districts must have equal populations. This principle has come to be known as the **"one person, one vote" rule.** In other words, one person's vote has to count as much as another's vote.

Gerrymandering

Although the Supreme Court, in the 1960s, ruled that congressional districts must be equal in population, it continued to be silent on the issue of gerrymandered districts. **Gerrymandering** occurs when a district's boundaries are drawn to maximize the influence of a certain group or political party. Where a party's voters are scarce, the boundaries can be drawn to include as many of the party's voters as possible. Where the party is strong, the lines are drawn so that the opponent's supporters are spread across two or more districts, thus diluting the opponent's strength. (The term *gerrymandering* was originally used in reference to the district lines drawn to favor the party of Governor Elbridge Gerry of Massachusetts prior to the 1812 election—see Figure 11–2 on the next page.)

congressional district The geographic area that is served by one member in the House of Representatives.

malapportionment A condition that results when, based on population and representation, the voting power of citizens in one district becomes more influential than the voting power of citizens in another district.

"one person, one vote" rule A rule, or principle, requiring that congressional districts have equal populations so that one person's vote counts as much as another's vote.

gerrymandering The drawing of a legislative district's boundaries in such a way as to maximize the influence of a certain group or political party.

Elbridge Gerry, governor of Massachusetts, 1810–1812.

Library of Congress

FIGURE 11-2
The First "Gerrymander"
Prior to the 1812 elections, the
Massachusetts legislature divided up
Essex County in a way that favored
Governor Elbridge Gerry's party; the
result was a district that looked like a
salamander. A newspaper editor of the
time referred to it as a "gerrymander,"
and the name stuck.

Although there have been constitutional challenges to political gerrymandering,[4] the practice continues. It was certainly evident following the 2000 census. Sophisticated computer programs can now analyze the partisan leanings of individual neighborhoods and city blocks. District lines are drawn to "pack" the opposing party's voters into the smallest number of districts or "crack" the opposing party's voters into several different districts. "Packing and cracking" makes congressional races less competitive. In 2003, for example, Texas adopted a controversial redistricting plan that was spearheaded by House Majority Leader Tom DeLay (R., Tex.). DeLay and Texas Republicans used "pack and crack" tactics to redraw districts that had formerly leaned toward Democratic candidates. The plan effectively cost four Democratic representatives their seats in the 2004 elections. Subsequently, DeLay faced charges for ethics violations, stemming in part from his role in the political gerrymandering.

AMERICA at odds

Redistricting for Competitive Elections

In 2005, California governor Arnold Schwarzenegger touched off a heated debate over congressional redistricting when he proposed that the responsibility for drawing congressional district lines be taken away from politicians and given to a panel of nonpartisan retired judges. Schwarzenegger suggested the change because a majority of congressional and state legislative elections have been noncompetitive in recent years. In the 2004 elections, only 23 of the 435 congressional districts nationwide were decided by 10 percentage points or less. Many Americans have voiced support for Schwarzenegger's proposal, but others are skeptical that such changes will serve the people's best interests.

Americans who support redistricting reform claim that the current lack of competitive elections hurts democracy. Politicians draw district lines to protect incumbents or to preserve seats in Congress for particular parties, they argue. This practice takes choice away from the voters and promotes political "careerism." The people cannot hold their representatives accountable if elections are rigged in favor of entrenched politicians. In California, for example, none of the state's fifty-three seats in the U.S. House of Representatives changed party hands. "What kind of democracy is that?" Schwarzenegger asked. The state of Iowa, in contrast, decided to turn over its district boundary decisions to a bureaucratic agency, which is directed by law to create

AP Photo/Damian Dovarganes

In 2005, California governor Arnold Schwarzenegger met with local residents and business owners in Long Beach. He was pushing his proposal for a constitutional amendment that would take away the legislature's power to redraw the state's legislative and congressional district boundaries and give that duty to a panel of retired judges.

compact and contiguous districts irrespective of partisan implications. Iowa's congressional races are consistently more competitive than those in most other states, and voter participation rates are much higher.

Other Americans are not convinced that redistricting reform will be in the best interests of the people. They argue that many districts are drawn to ensure that a maximum number of people in a particular district will have similar views to those of their representative. Less politically homogeneous districts could result in many bitter, divisive elections. Redrawing districts so that they are evenly split between the parties could erase the common interest that currently exists between citizens of a district and their representative. For example, a district in which 65 percent of the registered voters are affiliated with a single party likely elects a representative who satisfies two-thirds of that district. In contrast, an evenly divided district would likely elect a representative who displeases almost half of the people.

Racial Gerrymandering   Although political gerrymandering has a long history in this country, racial gerrymandering is a relatively new phenomenon. In the early 1990s, the U.S. Department of Justice instructed state legislatures to draw district lines to maximize the voting power of minority groups. As a result, several so-called **minority-majority districts** were created, many of which took on bizarre shapes. For example, North Carolina's newly drawn Twelfth Congressional District was 165 miles long—a narrow strip that, for the most part, followed Interstate 85. Georgia's new Eleventh District stretched from Atlanta to the Atlantic, splitting eight counties and five municipalities. The practice of racial gerrymandering has generated heated argument on both sides of the issue.

Some groups contend that minority-majority districts are necessary to ensure equal representation of minority groups, as mandated by the Voting Rights Act of 1965. They further contend that these districts have been instrumental in increasing the number of African Americans holding political office. Minority-majority districts in the South contain, on average, 45 percent nonblack voters, whereas before 1990 redistricting plans in the South created segregated, white-majority districts.[5] Opponents of racial gerrymandering argue that such race-based districting is unconstitutional because it violates the equal protection clause. In a series of cases in the 1990s, the Supreme Court agreed and held that when race is the dominant factor in the drawing of congressional district lines, the districts are unconstitutional and must be redrawn.[6]

In 2001, however, the Supreme Court issued a ruling that seemed—at least to some observers—to be out of step with its earlier rulings. North Carolina's Twelfth District, which

minority-majority district A district whose boundaries are drawn so as to maximize the voting power of minority groups.

had been redrawn in 1997, was again challenged in court as unconstitutional, and a lower court agreed. When the case reached the Supreme Court, however, the justices concluded that there was insufficient evidence that race had been the dominant factor in redrawing the district's boundaries.[7] Clearly, the controversy over racial gerrymandering will continue for some time to come.

The Representation Function of Congress

Of the three branches of government, Congress has the closest ties to the American people. Members of Congress represent the interests and wishes of the constituents in their home states. At the same time, they must also consider larger national issues such as international trade and the environment. Oftentimes, legislators find that the interests of their constituents are at odds with the demands of national policy. For example, stricter regulations on air pollution would benefit the health of all Americans. Yet members of Congress who come from states where industry and mining are important might be afraid that new laws would hurt the local economy and cause companies to lay off workers. All members of Congress face difficult votes that set representational interests against lawmaking realities. There are several views on how legislators should fulfill their representation function.

trustee A view of the representation function that holds that representatives should serve the broad interests of the entire society, and not just the narrow interests of their constituents.

The Trustee View of Representation
Some believe that representatives should act as **trustees** of the broad interests of the entire society rather than serving only the narrow interests of their constituents. Under the trustee view, a legislator should act according to her or his conscience and perception of national needs. For example, a senator from North Carolina might support laws regulating the tobacco industry even though the state's economy could be negatively affected.

instructed delegate A view of the representation function that holds that representatives should mirror the views of the majority of their constituents.

The Instructed-Delegate View of Representation
In contrast, others believe that members of Congress should behave as **instructed delegates.** The instructed-delegate view requires representatives to mirror the views of their constituents. Under this view, a senator from Nebraska would strive to obtain farm subsidies for corn growers, and a representative from the Detroit area would seek to protect the interests of the automobile industry.

The Partisan View of Representation
Because the political parties often take different positions on legislative issues, there are times when members of Congress are most attentive to the wishes of the party leadership. Especially on matters that are controversial, the Republican members of Congress will be more likely to vote in favor of policies endorsed by George W. Bush, a Republican president, while Democrats will be more likely to oppose them.

The Politico Style
Typically, however, members of Congress combine these approaches in what is often called the "politico" style. Most representatives often find themselves in difficult positions that require them to weigh the broad interests of the entire society against the interests of their own constituents as well as their party. Legislators may take a trustee approach on some issues, adhere to the instructed-delegate view on other matters, and follow the party line on still others.

Congressional Elections

The U.S. Constitution requires that congressional representatives be elected every second year by popular vote. Senators are elected every six years, also (since the ratification of the Seventeenth Amendment) by popular vote. Under Article I, Section 4, of the Constitution, state legislatures control the "Times, Places and Manner of holding Elections for Senators and Representatives." Congress, however, "may at any time by Law make or alter such Regulations." As you read in Chapter 9, control over the process of nominating congressional candidates has shifted from party conventions to direct primaries in which the party identifiers in the electorate select the candidates who will carry that party's endorsement into the actual election.[8]

Who Can Be a Member of Congress?

The Constitution sets forth only a few qualifications that those running for Congress must meet. To be a member of the House, a person must be a citizen of the United States for at least seven years prior to his or her election, a legal resident of the state from which he or she is to be elected, and at least twenty-five years of age. To be elected to the Senate, a person must be a citizen for at least nine years, a legal resident of the state from which she or he is to be elected, and at least thirty years of age. The Supreme Court has ruled that neither the Congress nor the states can add to these three qualifications.[9]

Once elected to Congress, a senator or representative receives an annual salary from the government. He or she also enjoys certain perks and privileges. Additionally, if a member of Congress wants to run for reelection in the next congressional elections, that person's chances are greatly enhanced by the power that incumbency brings to a reelection campaign.

The Power of Incumbency

The power of incumbency has long been noted in American politics. Today, incumbents win so often and by such large margins that political scientist Ross K. Baker has compared our electoral system to a kind of "hereditary entitlement."[10] As you can see in Table 11–1, most incumbents in Congress are reelected at election time.

Incumbent politicians enjoy several advantages over their opponents. A key advantage is their fund-raising ability. Most incumbent members of Congress have a much larger network of contacts, donors, and lobbyists than their opponents. Incumbents raise, on average, twice as much in campaign funds as their challengers. Other advantages that incumbents can put to work at election time include:

- *Congressional franking privileges*—members of Congress can mail newsletters and other correspondence to their constituents at the taxpayer's expense.
- *Professional staffs*—members have large administrative staffs both in Washington, D.C., and in their home districts.
- *Lawmaking power*—members of Congress can back legislation that will benefit their states or districts, and then campaign on that legislative record in the next election.
- *Access to the media*—because they are elected officials, members have many opportunities to stage events for the press and thereby obtain free publicity.
- *Name recognition*—incumbent members are far better known to the voters than challengers are.

TABLE 11–1
The Power of Incumbency

	PRESIDENTIAL-YEAR ELECTIONS							MIDTERM ELECTIONS						
	1980	1984	1988	1992	1996	2000	2004	1978	1982	1986	1990	1994	1998	2002
House														
Number of incumbent candidates	398	411	409	368	384	403	404	382	393	394	406	387	402	393
Reelected	361	392	402	325	361	394	400	358	354	385	390	349	395	383
Percentage of total	90.7	95.4	98.3	88.3	94.0	97.8	99.0	93.7	90.1	97.7	96.0	90.2	98.3	97.5
Defeated	37	19	7	43	23	9	4	24	39	9	16	38	7	10
Senate														
Number of incumbent candidates	29	29	27	28	21	29	26	25	30	28	32	26	29	28
Reelected	16	26	23	23	19	23	25	15	28	21	31	24	26	24
Percentage of total	55.2	89.6	85.2	82.1	90.5	79.3	96.2	60.0	93.3	75.0	96.9	92.3	89.7	85.7
Defeated	13	3	4	5	2	6	1	10	2	7	1	2	3	4

SOURCES: Norman Ornstein, Thomas E. Mann, and Michael J. Malbin, *Vital Statistics on Congress, 2001–2002*, (Washington, D.C.: The AEI Press, 2002); and authors' updates.

Critics of the advantage enjoyed by incumbents argue that it reduces the competition necessary for a healthy democracy. It also suppresses voter turnout. Voters are less likely to turn out when an incumbent candidate is virtually guaranteed reelection. The solution often proposed to eliminate the power of incumbency is term limits. Persuading incumbent politicians to vote for term limits, however, is nearly impossible.

Congressional Terms and Term Limits

As you read earlier, members of the House of Representatives serve two-year terms, and senators serve six-year terms. This means that every two years, we hold congressional elections: the entire House of Representatives and a third of the Senate are up for election. In January of every odd-numbered year, a "new" Congress convenes (of course, two-thirds of the senators are not new, and most incumbents are reelected, so they are not new to Congress, either). Each Congress has been numbered consecutively, dating back to 1789. The Congress that convened in 2005 is the 109th.

Each congressional term is divided into two regular sessions, or meetings—one for each year. Until about 1940, Congress remained in session for only four or five months, but the complicated rush of legislation and increased demand for services from the public in recent years have forced Congress to remain in session through most of each year.[11] Both chambers, however, schedule short recesses, or breaks, for holidays and vacations. The president may call a *special session* during a recess, but because Congress now meets on nearly a year-round basis, such sessions are rare.

As you will read in Chapter 12, the president can serve for no more than two terms in office, thanks to the Twenty-second Amendment. There is no limit on the number of terms a senator or representative can serve, however. Indeed, Strom Thurmond (R., S.C.) served eight terms in the U.S. Senate, from 1955 until he retired, at the age of one hundred, in 2003.

Term limits have stirred controversy at all levels of government. Here, Maryland politician Robin Ficker expresses his views on term limits from atop a stepladder during rush-hour traffic in Bethesda, Maryland. A "Yes" vote on Question C, a question on the ballot for an upcoming election, would establish term limits for certain county officeholders.

AP Photo/Leslie E. Kossoff

Efforts to pass a constitutional amendment that would impose term limits on members of Congress have had little success. Most recently, the House of Representatives failed to pass a term-limits constitutional amendment in 1995. Nonetheless, the notion of imposing congressional term limits remains an issue for debate and discussion.

AMERICA at odds

Are Term Limits the Cure for Congressional Careerism?

In contrast to congressional representatives and senators in the past, today's legislators often view holding congressional office as a career in itself. As a result, the argument goes, our political leaders make decisions less on the basis of any perceived national interest than on how their decisions will affect their chances for reelection. One of the arguments in favor of term limits is that they would remove the element of careerism from politics. Term limits would allow legislators to exercise independent judgment, and Congress could assume the role of a deliberative body whose foremost concern is to maintain a carefully crafted balance of power among competing interests.

Although polls show that a majority of Americans support term limits, it may be difficult—if not impossible—to enact them. Incumbents, once in power, rarely vote to force themselves out. In the years when the Democrats controlled Congress, they tended to oppose term limits, and the Republicans favored them. Since 1994, when the Republicans came to power, Republican members have been abandoning the push for term limits. Indeed, several members of Congress who pledged voluntarily to serve no more than two or three terms have reneged on their promises.

There is another explanation for the weakening support for term limits among many Republicans, however. David Broder, columnist for the *Washington Post,* argues that there is "an acknowledgment on the part of Republicans that running government is a serious business where experience counts."[12] Members of Congress who oppose term limits may simply be acknowledging that governing this country is a task best left to experienced politicians.

Congressional Leadership

How each chamber of Congress is organized is largely a function of the two major political parties. The majority party in each chamber chooses the major officers of that chamber, controls debate on the floor, selects all committee chairpersons, and has a majority on all committees.

House Leadership

Both the House and the Senate have systems of leadership. Before Congress begins work, members of each party in each chamber meet to choose their leaders. The Constitution provides for the presiding officers of the House and Senate; Congress may choose what other leaders it feels it needs.

Speaker of the House Chief among the leaders in the House of Representatives is the **Speaker of the House.** This office is mandated by the Constitution and is filled by a vote taken at the beginning of each congressional term. The Speaker has traditionally been a long-time member of the majority party who has risen in rank and influence through years of service in the House. The candidate for Speaker is selected by the majority-party caucus; the House as a whole then approves the selection.

As the presiding officer of the House and the leader of the majority party, the Speaker has a great deal of power. In the nineteenth century, the Speaker had even more power and was known as the "king of the congressional mountain." Speakers known by such names as "Uncle

Speaker of the House The presiding officer in the House of Representatives. The Speaker has traditionally been a longtime member of the majority party and is often the most powerful and influential member of the House.

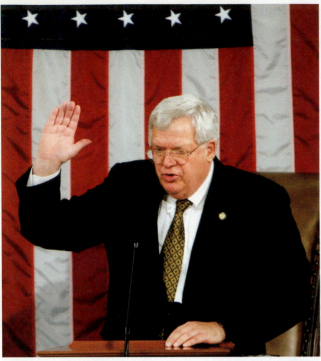

Reuters/Larry Downing/Landov

During the opening session of the 109th Congress in January 2005, Dennis Hastert (R., Ill.) was sworn in as the Speaker of the House of the U.S. House of Representatives. The House members select the speaker by conducting a vote within the House chambers.

majority leader The party leader elected by the majority party in the House or in the Senate.

minority leader The party leader elected by the minority party in the House or in the Senate.

whip A member of Congress who assists the majority or minority leader in the House or in the Senate in managing the party's legislative preferences.

Joe Cannon" and "Czar Reed" ruled the House with almost exclusive power. A revolt in 1910 reduced the Speaker's powers and gave some of those powers to various committees. Today, the Speaker still has many important powers, including the following:

- The Speaker has substantial control over what bills get assigned to which committees.
- The Speaker presides over the sessions of the House, recognizing or ignoring members who wish to speak.
- The Speaker votes in the event of a tie, interprets and applies House rules, rules on points of order (questions about procedures asked by members), puts questions to a vote, and interprets the outcome of most of the votes taken.
- The Speaker plays a major role in making important committee assignments, which all members desire.
- The Speaker schedules bills for action.

The Speaker may choose whether to vote on any measure. If the Speaker chooses to vote, he or she appoints a temporary presiding officer (called a Speaker *pro tempore*), who then occupies the Speaker's chair. Under the House rules, the only time the Speaker *must* vote is to break a tie, because otherwise a tie automatically defeats a bill. The Speaker does not often vote, but by choosing to vote in some cases, the Speaker can actually cause a tie and defeat a proposal that is unpopular with the majority party.

Majority Leader   The **majority leader** of the House is elected by the caucus of party members to act as spokesperson for the party and to keep the party together. The majority leader's job is to help plan the party's legislative program, organize other party members to support legislation favored by the party, and make sure the chairpersons on the many committees finish work on bills that are important to the party. The House majority leader makes speeches on important bills, stating the majority party's position.

Minority Leader   The House **minority leader** is the leader of the minority party. Although not as powerful as the majority leader, the minority leader has similar responsibilities. The primary duty of the minority leader is to maintain cohesion within the party. The minority leader persuades influential members of the party to follow its position and organizes fellow party members in criticism of the majority party's policies and programs.

Whips   The leadership of each party includes assistants to the majority and minority leaders known as **whips.** Whips originated in the British House of Commons, where they were named after the "whipper in," the rider who keeps the hounds together in a fox hunt. The term was applied to assistant party leaders because of the pressure that they place on party members to follow the party's positions. Whips try to determine how each member is going to vote on certain issues and then advise the party leaders on the strength of party support. Whips also try to see that members are present when important votes are to be taken and that they vote with the party leadership. For example, if the Republican Party strongly supports a tax-cut bill, the Republican Party whip might meet with other Republican Party members in the House to try to persuade them to vote with the party.

Senate Leadership

The Constitution makes the vice president of the United States the president of the Senate. As presiding officer, the vice president may call on members to speak and put questions to a vote. The vice president is not an elected member of the Senate, however, and may not take part in Senate debates. The vice president may cast a vote in the Senate only in the event of a tie.

AP Photo/Eric Risberg

AP Photo/Eric Lyle Kayne/*The Facts*

The current House minority leader is Nancy Pelosi (D., Calif.), shown on the left. The current House majority leader is Tom DeLay (R., Tex.), shown on the right.

President Pro Tempore Because vice presidents are rarely available to preside over the Senate, senators elect another presiding officer, the president pro tempore ("pro tem"), who serves in the absence of the vice president. The president pro tem is elected by the whole Senate and is ordinarily the member of the majority party with the longest continuous term of service in the Senate. In the absence of both the president pro tem and the vice president, a temporary presiding officer is selected from the ranks of the Senate, usually a junior member of the majority party.

Party Leaders The real power in the Senate is held by the majority leader, the minority leader, and their whips. The majority leader is the most powerful individual and chief spokesperson of the majority party. The majority leader directs the legislative program and

AP Photo/Doug Mills/File

UPI Photo/Michael Kleinfeld/Landov

Bill Frist (R., Tenn.), left, is the Senate majority leader, and Harry Reid (D., Nev.), right, is the Senate minority leader.

party strategy. The minority leader commands the minority party's opposition to the policies of the majority party and directs the legislative strategy of the minority party.

Congressional Committees

Thousands of bills are introduced during every session of Congress, and no single member can possibly be adequately informed on all the issues that arise. The committee system is a way to provide for specialization, or a division of the legislative labor. Members of a committee can concentrate on just one area or topic—such as agriculture or transportation—and develop sufficient expertise to draft appropriate legislation when needed. The flow of legislation through both the House and the Senate is determined largely by the speed with which the members of these committees act on bills and resolutions. The permanent and most powerful committees of Congress are called **standing committees;** their names are listed in Table 11–2.

Before any bill can be considered by the entire House or Senate, it must be approved by a majority vote in the standing committee to which it was assigned. As mentioned, standing committees are controlled by the majority party in each chamber. Committee membership is generally divided between the parties according to the number of members in each chamber. In both the House and the Senate, committee *seniority*—the length of continuous service on a particular committee—typically plays a role in determining the committee chairpersons.

Most House and Senate committees are also divided into **subcommittees,** which have limited areas of jurisdiction. Today, there are more than two hundred subcommittees. There are also other types of committees in Congress. Special, or select, committees, which may be either permanent or temporary, are formed to study specific problems or issues. Joint committees are formed by the concurrent action of both chambers of Congress and consist of members from each chamber. Joint committees have dealt with the economy, taxation, and the Library of Congress. There are also conference committees, which include members from both the House and the Senate. They are formed for the purpose of achieving agreement between the House and the Senate on the exact wording of legislative acts when the two chambers pass legislative proposals in different forms. No bill can be sent to the White House to be signed into law unless it first passes both chambers in identical form.

Most of the actual work of legislating is performed by the committees and subcommittees (the "little legislatures"[13]) within Congress. In creating or amending laws, committee members work closely with relevant interest groups and administrative agency personnel. (For more details on the interaction among these groups, see the discussion of "iron triangles" in Chapter 13.)

standing committee A permanent committee in Congress that deals with legislation concerning a particular area, such as agriculture or foreign relations.

subcommittee A division of a larger committee that deals with a particular part of the committee's policy area. Most of the standing committees in Congress have several subcommittees.

Senators Hillary Rodham Clinton (D., N.Y.) and Joseph Lieberman (D., Conn.), both members of the Senate Subcommittee on Clean Air, Wetlands, and Climate Change, listen to testimony during a 2002 hearing that examined the possible health hazards stemming from the fires and dusts at the site of the World Trade Center terrorist attacks. The senators heard testimony on disaster management, health monitoring, and the effects of pollution on residents and rescue workers.

AP Photo/Jeff Zelevansky

TABLE 11-2

Standing Committees in the 109th Congress, 2005–2007

HOUSE COMMITTEES	SENATE COMMITTEES
Agriculture	Agriculture, Nutrition, and Forestry
Appropriations	Appropriations
Armed Services	Armed Services
Budget	Banking, Housing, and Urban Affairs
Education and the Workforce	Budget
Energy and Commerce	Commerce, Science, and Transportation
Financial Services	Energy and Natural Resources
Government Reform	Environment and Public Works
Homeland Security	Finance
House Administration	Foreign Relations
International Relations	Health, Education, Labor, and Pensions
Judiciary	Homeland Security and Governmental Affairs
Resources	Judiciary
Rules	Rules and Administration
Science	Small Business and Entrepreneurship
Small Business	Veterans' Affairs
Standards of Official Conduct	
Transportation and Infrastructure	
Veterans' Affairs	
Ways and Means	

The Differences between the House and the Senate

The major differences between the House and the Senate are listed in Table 11–3 on the next page. To understand what goes on in the chambers of Congress, we need to look at the effects of bicameralism. Each chamber of Congress has developed certain distinct features.

Size Matters

Obviously, with 435 members, the House cannot operate the same way that the Senate can with only 100 members. (There are also nonvoting delegates from the District of Columbia, Guam, American Samoa, Puerto Rico, and the U.S. Virgin Islands in the House.) With its larger size, the House needs both more rules and more formal rules; otherwise no work would ever get done. The most obvious formal rules that are required have to do with debate on the floor.

The Senate normally permits extended debate on all issues that arise before it. In contrast, the House uses an elaborate system: the House **Rules Committee** normally proposes time limitations on debate for any bill, which are accepted or modified by the House. Despite its greater size, as a consequence of its stricter time limits on debate, the House is often able to act on legislation more quickly than the Senate.

Rules Committee A standing committee in the House of Representatives that provides special rules governing how particular bills will be considered and debated by the House. The Rules Committee normally proposes time limitations on debate for any bill, which are accepted or modified by the House.

In the Senate, Debate Can Just Keep Going and Going

At one time, both the House and the Senate allowed unlimited debates, but the House ended this practice in 1811. When unlimited debate in the Senate is used to obstruct legislation, it is called **filibustering.** The longest filibuster was waged by Senator Strom Thurmond of South Carolina, who held forth on the Senate floor for twenty-four hours and eighteen minutes in an attempt to thwart the passage of the 1957 Civil Rights Act.

filibustering The Senate tradition of unlimited debate, undertaken for the purpose of preventing action on a bill.

TABLE 11-3

Major Differences between the House and the Senate

HOUSE*	SENATE*
Members chosen from local districts	Members chosen from an entire state
Two-year term	Six-year term
Always elected by voters	Originally (until 1913) elected by state legislatures
May impeach (accuse, indict) federal officials	May convict federal officials of impeachable offenses
Larger (435 voting members)	Smaller (100 members)
More formal rules	Fewer rules and restrictions
Debate limited	Debate extended
Floor action controlled	Unanimous consent rules
Less prestige and less individual notice	More prestige and media attention
Originates bills for raising revenues	Power of "advice and consent" on presidential appointments and treaties
Local or narrow leadership	National leadership

*Some of these differences, such as term of office, are provided for in the Constitution, while others, such as debate rules, are not.

cloture A method of ending debate in the Senate and bringing the matter under consideration to a vote by the entire chamber.

Today, under Senate Rule 22, debate may be ended by invoking **cloture**—a method of closing debate and bringing the matter under consideration to a vote in the Senate. Sixteen senators must sign a petition requesting cloture, and then, after two days have elapsed, three-fifths of the entire membership must vote for cloture. Once cloture is invoked, each senator may speak on a bill for no more than one hour before a vote is taken. Additionally, a final vote must take place within one hundred hours after cloture has been invoked.

The Senate Wins the Prestige Race, Hands Down

Because of the large number of representatives, few can garner the prestige that a senator enjoys. Senators have relatively little difficulty in gaining access to the media. Members of the House, who run for reelection every two years, have to survive many reelection campaigns before they can obtain recognition for their activities. Usually, a representative has to become an important committee leader before she or he can enjoy the consistent attention of the national news media.

Democratic Minority Leader Harry Reid (D., Nev.), center, stood with fellow Democrats on the steps of the U.S. Capitol in 2005. Reid made a statement that the Democrats would forcefully oppose any Republican plans to limit the use of filibustering.

EPA/Mike Theiler/Landov

The Legislative Process

Look at Figure 11–3 on the following page, which shows the basic elements of the process through which a bill becomes law at the national level. Not all of the complexities of the process are shown, to be sure. For example, the schematic does not indicate the extensive lobbying and media politics that are often involved in the legislative process. There is also no mention of the informal negotiations and "horse trading" that go on to get a bill passed.

The basic steps in the process are as follows:

1. *Introduction of legislation.* Most bills are proposed by the executive branch, although individual members of Congress or its staff can come up with ideas for new legislation; so, too, can private citizens or lobbying groups. Only a member of Congress can formally introduce legislation, however. In reality, an increasing number of bills are proposed, developed, and often written by the White House or an executive agency. Then a "friendly" senator or representative introduces the bill in Congress. Such bills are rarely ignored entirely, although they are often amended or defeated.

2. *Referral to committees.* As soon as a bill is introduced and assigned a number, it is sent to the appropriate standing committee. In the House, the Speaker assigns the bill to the appropriate committee. In the Senate, the presiding officer assigns bills to the proper committees. For example, a farm bill in the House would be sent to the Agriculture Committee; a gun control bill would be sent to the Judiciary Committee. A committee chairperson will typically send the bill on to a subcommittee. For example, a Senate bill concerning additional involvement in NATO (North Atlantic Treaty Organization) in Europe would be sent to the Senate Foreign Relations Subcommittee on European Affairs. Alternatively, the chairperson may decide to put the bill aside and ignore it. Most bills that are pigeonholed in this manner receive no further action.

   If a bill is not pigeonholed, committee staff members go to work researching the bill. The committee may hold public hearings during which people who support or oppose the bill may express their views. Committees also have the power to order witnesses to testify at public hearings. Witnesses may be executive agency officials, experts on the subject, or representatives of interest groups concerned about the bill.

   The subcommittee must meet to approve the bill as it is, add new amendments, or draft a new bill. This meeting is known as the **markup session.** If members cannot agree on changes, a vote is taken. When a subcommittee completes its work, the bill goes to the full standing committee, which then meets for its own markup session. The committee may hold its own hearings, amend the subcommittee's version, or simply approve the subcommittee's recommendations.

3. *Reports on a bill.* Finally, the committee will report the bill back to the full chamber. It can report the bill favorably, report the bill with amendments, or report a newly written bill. It can also report a bill unfavorably, but usually such a bill will have been pigeonholed earlier instead. Along with the bill, the committee will send to the House or Senate a written report that explains the committee's actions, describes the bill, lists the major changes made by the committee, and gives opinions on the bill.

4. *The Rules Committee and scheduling.* Scheduling is an extremely important part of getting a bill enacted into law. A bill must be put on a calendar. Typically, the House Rules Committee plays a major role in the scheduling process. This committee, along with the House leaders, regulates the flow of the bills through the House. The Rules Committee will also specify the amount of time to be spent on debate and whether amendments can be made by a floor vote.

   In the Senate, a few leading members control the flow of bills. The Senate brings a bill to the floor by "unanimous consent," a motion by which all members present on the floor set aside the formal Senate rules and consider a bill. In contrast to the procedure in the House, individual senators have the power to disrupt work on legislation.

5. *Floor debate.* Because of its large size, the House imposes severe limits on floor debate. The Speaker recognizes those who may speak and can force any member who does not "stick to the subject" to give up the floor. Normally, the chairperson of the standing committee reporting the bill will take charge of the session during which it is debated. You can often watch such debates on C-SPAN.

markup session A meeting held by a congressional committee or subcommittee to approve, amend, or redraft a bill.

FIGURE 11-3
How a Bill Becomes a Law
This illustration shows the most typical way in which proposed legislation is enacted into law. The process is illustrated with two hypothetical bills, House bill No. 100 (HR 100) and Senate bill No. 200 (S 200). Bills must be passed by both chambers in identical form before they can be sent to the president. The path of HR 100 is traced by an orange line, and that of S 200 by a purple line. In practice, most bills begin as similar proposals in both chambers.

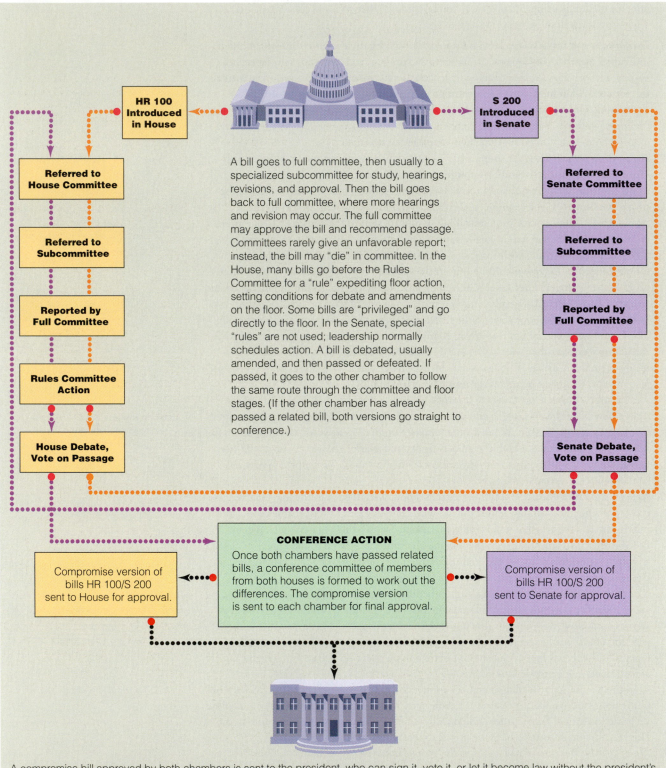

A compromise bill approved by both chambers is sent to the president, who can sign it, veto it, or let it become law without the president's signature. Congress may override a veto by a two-thirds majority vote in each chamber.

Only on rare occasions does a floor debate change anybody's mind. The written record of the floor debate completes the legislative history of the proposed bill in the event that the courts have to interpret it later on. Floor debates also give the full House or Senate the opportunity to consider amendments to the original version of the bill.

6. *Vote.* In both the House and the Senate, the members present generally vote for or against the bill. There are several methods of voting, including voice votes, standing votes, and recorded votes (also called roll-call votes). Since 1973, the House has had electronic voting. The Senate does not have electronic voting, however.

7. *Conference committee.* To become a law, a bill must be passed in identical form by both chambers. When the two chambers pass separate versions of the same bill, the measure is turned over to a special committee called a **conference committee**—a temporary committee with members from the two chambers.

Most members of the committee are drawn from the standing committees that handled the bill in both chambers. In theory, the conference committee can consider only those points in a bill on which the two chambers disagree; no proposals are supposed to be added. In reality, however, the conference committee sometimes makes important changes in the bill or adds new provisions.

Once the conference committee members agree on the final compromise bill, a **conference report** is submitted to each house. The bill must be accepted or rejected by both houses as it was written by the committee, with no further amendments made. If the bill is approved by both chambers, it is ready for action by the president.

8. *Presidential action.* All bills passed by Congress have to be submitted to the president for approval. The president has ten days to decide whether to sign the bill or veto it. If the president does nothing, the bill goes into effect unless Congress has adjourned before the ten-day period expires. In that case, the bill dies in what is called a **pocket veto.**

9. *Overriding a veto.* If the president decides to veto a bill, Congress can still get the bill enacted into law. With a two-thirds majority vote in both chambers, Congress can override the president's veto.

Investigation and Oversight

Steps 8 and 9 of the legislative process just described illustrate the integral role that both the executive and the legislative branches play in making laws. The relationship between Congress and the president is at the core of our system of government, although, to be sure, the judicial branch plays a vital role as well (see Chapter 14). One of the most important functions of Congress is its oversight of the executive branch and its many federal departments and agencies. The executive bureaucracy, which includes the president's cabinet departments, wields

conference committee A temporary committee that is formed when the two chambers of Congress pass separate versions of the same bill. The conference committee, which consists of members from both the House and the Senate, works out a compromise form of the bill.

conference report A report submitted by a congressional conference committee after it has drafted a single version of a bill.

pocket veto A special type of veto power used by the chief executive after the legislature has adjourned. Bills that are not signed by the president die after a specified period of time and must be reintroduced if Congress wishes to reconsider them.

During the Clinton administration, House Speaker Dennis Hastert of Illinois, center, pointed to a mock coffin filled with tax regulations during a Capitol Hill news conference. Hastert and other lawmakers urged Congress to override President Bill Clinton's veto of a bill that would have eliminated the inheritance tax. A congressional attempt to override the veto failed.

AP Photo/Dennis Cook

tremendous power, as you will read in Chapters 12 and 13. Congress can rein in that power by choosing not to provide the funds necessary for the bureaucracy to function (the budgeting process is discussed later in this chapter).

The Investigative Function

Congress also has the authority to investigate the actions of the executive branch, the need for certain legislation, and even the actions of its own members. The Congressional Research Service and the Congressional Budget Office, for example, both provide members of Congress with vital information about policies and economic projections. The numerous congressional committees and subcommittees regularly hold hearings to investigate the actions of the executive branch. Congressional committees receive opinions, reports, and assessments on a broad range of issues, from the state of the world economy to the loss of the space shuttle *Columbia* in 2003.

Impeachment Power

Congress also has the power to impeach and remove from office the president, vice president, and other "civil officers," such as federal judges. To impeach means to accuse or charge a public official with improper conduct in office. The House of Representatives is vested with this power and has exercised it twice against the president; the House voted to impeach Andrew Johnson in 1868 and Bill Clinton in 1998. After a vote to impeach in the full House, the president is then tried in the Senate. If convicted by a two-thirds vote, the president is removed from office. Both Johnson and Clinton were acquitted by the Senate. A vote to impeach President Richard Nixon was pending before the full House of Representatives in 1974 when Nixon chose to resign. Nixon is the only president ever to resign from office.

Congress can also take action to remove other officials. The House of Representatives voted to impeach Judge Alcee Hastings in 1988, and the Senate removed him from the bench (he was later elected to the House in 1992). Only one United States Supreme Court justice has ever been impeached; the House impeached Samuel Chase in 1804, although he was later acquitted by the Senate.

The House Judiciary Committee, shown here, approved three articles of impeachment against President Richard M. Nixon in late July 1974. The articles charged Nixon with obstruction of justice, abuse of power, and contempt of Congress. Nixon resigned on August 9, 1974, before the full House of Representatives voted on the articles.

Senate Confirmation

Article II, Section 2, of the Constitution states that the president may appoint ambassadors, justices of the Supreme Court, and other officers of the United States "with the Advice and Consent of the Senate." The Constitution leaves the precise nature of how the Senate will give this "advice and consent" up to the lawmakers. In practice, the Senate confirms the president's nominees for the Supreme Court, other federal judgeships, and members of the president's cabinet. Nominees appear first before the appropriate Senate committee—the Judiciary Committee for

AP Photo

UPI Photo/Michael Kleinfeld/Landov

In January 2005, then nominee for secretary of state Condoleezza Rice testified before the Senate Foreign Relations Committee at her nomination hearing. The hearing was often marked by bitter debate over the war in Iraq. A week later, however, Rice won Senate confirmation.

federal judges, or the Foreign Relations Committee for the secretary of state, for example. If the individual committee approves of the nominee, the full Senate will vote on the nomination.

As you will read further in Chapters 12 and 14, Senate confirmation hearings have been very politicized at times. Judicial appointments often receive the most intense scrutiny by the Senate because the judges serve on the bench for life. The president has a somewhat freer hand with cabinet appointments because the heads of executive departments are expected to be fiercely loyal to the president. Nonetheless, Senate confirmation remains an important check on the president's power. We will discuss the relationship between Congress and the president in more detail in Chapter 12.

The Budgeting Process

The Constitution makes it very clear that Congress has the power of the purse. Only Congress can impose taxes, and only Congress can authorize expenditures. To be sure, the president submits a budget, but all final decisions are up to Congress.

The congressional budget is, of course, one of the most important determinants of what policies will or will not be implemented. For example, the president might order executive agencies under presidential control to undertake specific programs, but these orders are meaningless if there is no money to pay for their execution. It is Congress, after all, that has the power of the "purse strings," and this power is significant. Congress can easily nullify a president's ambitious program by simply refusing to allocate the necessary funds to executive agencies to implement it.

Thus, although the congressional budgeting process may seem abstract and unimportant to our everyday lives, it is in fact relevant. Also, tracking the various legislative acts and the amendments that are "tacked on" to various budget bills that are sure to pass can be an informative experience for any American concerned about how government policies are established and implemented.

Authorization and Appropriation

The budgeting process involves a two-part procedure. **Authorization** is the first part. It involves the creation of the legal basis for government programs. In this phase, Congress passes authorization bills outlining the rules governing the expenditure of funds. Limits may be placed on how much money can be spent and for what period of time.

Appropriation is the second part of the budgeting process. In this phase, Congress determines how many dollars will actually be spent in a given year on a particular set of government

authorization A part of the congressional budgeting process that involves the creation of the legal basis for government programs.

appropriation A part of the congressional budgeting process that involves determining how many dollars will be spent in a given year on a particular set of government activities.

entitlement program A government program (such as Social Security) that allows, or entitles, a certain class of people (such as the elderly) to receive special benefits. Entitlement programs operate under open-ended budget authorizations that, in effect, place no limits on how much can be spent.

activities. Appropriations must never exceed the authorized amounts, but they can be less. (For a discussion of how congressional spending has affected the public debt, see this chapter's *Perception versus Reality* feature.)

Many **entitlement programs** operate under open-ended authorizations that, in effect, place no limits on how much can be spent. The government is obligated to provide benefits, such as Social Security benefits, veterans' benefits, and the like, to persons who qualify under entitlement laws. The remaining federal programs are subject to discretionary spending and can be altered at will by Congress. National defense is the most important item in the discretionary-spending part of the budget.

perception versus REALITY

Is Our Public Debt a Problem?

As you have read in this chapter, Congress possesses the "power of the purse." After boasting a balanced budget between 1998 and 2001, Congress has overseen a significant increase in *deficit spending* in recent years. Each year that the government spends more than it collects in revenues, it runs a deficit. Any deficit spending is added to the *public debt,* which is often called the "national debt." Numerous economists have predicted that the United States could be headed toward an economic crisis if the public debt is not reduced.

THE PERCEPTION

Many Americans believe that the public debt has grown to unprecedented amounts in recent years. The *gross,* or overall total, public debt is roughly $8 trillion. This amount routinely increases by millions, and sometimes billions, of dollars on a daily basis.[14] Foreigners—banks, corporations, individuals, and governments—hold a significant portion of the U.S. public debt, around 40 percent. Some fear that foreigners may "call in" their investments, causing a financial crisis in the United States as the government struggles to pay its debtors.

THE REALITY

In reality, the gross public debt is a misleading figure. The gross public debt includes government holdings of bonds issued by government agencies. These, of course, are simply reshufflings of IOUs within the U.S. government. For example, Congress has frequently authorized the use of money from the Social Security trust fund to pay for other government programs.

The more important figure when assessing the nation's financial liability is the *net* public debt, which is the gross public debt minus intragovernmental borrowing. The net public debt is the amount that the government owes to everyone else, and it is about $4.75 trillion. Although this is still quite a large figure, it is much less daunting than the frequently cited $8 trillion.

Furthermore, the idea that the public debt has reached unprecedented levels is similarly misleading. The primary method of gauging the burden of the public debt is to view it in relation to the country's gross domestic product (GDP). GDP is the total market value of all *final* goods and services produced within the country's borders; it is a standard measure of economic well-being and strength. By the beginning of 2005, the net public debt was about 35 percent of the nation's GDP. This percentage is relatively low compared to the late 1940s, when the net public debt exceeded 100 percent of the nation's GDP (see Figure 11–4).

What's Your Opinion?

Should current deficit spending be curbed to avoid passing massive debts to future generations of taxpayers? Why or why not?

FIGURE 11–4

Net U.S. Public Debt as a Percentage of GDP
During World War II (1939–1945), the net public debt grew dramatically. It fell until the 1970s, rose again until the early 1990s, and declined until the early 2000s.

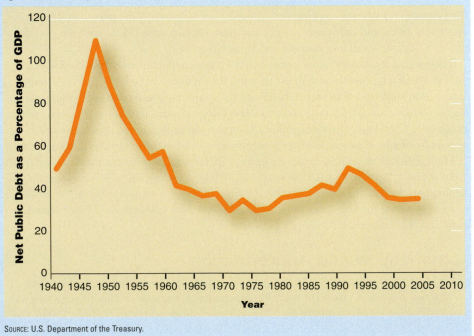

SOURCE: U.S. Department of the Treasury.

President George W. Bush speaks to reporters during a bipartisan budget meeting with members of Congress. Congress's power to control the "purse strings" of government is one of its most significant powers.

AP Photo/Ron Edmonds

The Actual Budgeting Process

Look at Figure 11–5, which is a schematic outlining the lengthy budgeting process. The process runs from January, when the president submits a proposed federal budget for the next **fiscal year,** to the start of that fiscal year on October 1. In actuality, about eighteen months prior to October 1, the executive agencies submit their requests to the Office of Management and Budget (OMB), and the OMB outlines a proposed budget. If the president approves it, the budget is officially submitted to Congress.

The legislative budgeting process begins eight to nine months before the start of the fiscal year. The **first budget resolution** is supposed to be passed in May. It sets overall revenue goals and spending targets and, by definition, the size of the federal budget deficit or surplus. The **second budget resolution,** which sets "binding" limits on taxes and spending, is supposed to be passed in September, prior to the beginning of the fiscal year on October 1. Whenever

fiscal year A twelve-month period that is established for bookkeeping or accounting purposes. The government's fiscal year runs from October 1 through September 30.

first budget resolution A budget resolution, which is supposed to be passed in May, that sets overall revenue goals and spending targets for the next fiscal year, which begins on October 1.

second budget resolution A budget resolution, which is supposed to be passed in September, that sets "binding" limits on taxes and spending for the next fiscal year.

FIGURE 11–5
The Budgeting Process

EXECUTIVE BUDGETING PROCESS		Executive agency requests: about 1 to 1½ years prior to start of fiscal year, or in March to September	OMB review and presidential approval: 9 months to 1 year before start of fiscal year, or in September to December
LEGISLATIVE BUDGETING PROCESS	Second budget resolution: by October 1	First budget resolution in May	Executive branch submittal of budget to Congress: 8 to 9 months before start of fiscal year, at end of January
EXECUTION	Start of fiscal year: October 1	Outlays and obligations: October 1 to September 30	Audit of fiscal year outlays on a selective basis by Government Accountability Office (GAO)

Is the Big Spending Really to Fight Terrorists?

The Congressional Budget Office predicted that the government would run a deficit (in which the government spends more than it raises in revenues in a particular year) of $300 billion to $400 billion in fiscal year 2005. Nonetheless, in December 2004, Congress passed an omnibus discretionary spending package for $388 billion. President George W. Bush commended the bill's passage, claiming that the budget would provide valuable resources for priorities such as homeland security, military operations, and education. One could reasonably (but incorrectly) argue that since September 11, 2001, the federal government has had to spend more on antiterrorism measures, which have increased spending and driven up the federal deficit. Of the $388 billion of discretionary funds appropriated in December 2004, however, only about 5 percent was related to homeland security.

IT ISN'T ALL DUE TO SEPTEMBER 11

Spending on homeland security and national defense has been a small blip on the radar screen of total increases in federal spending in the past eight years. Roughly $30 billion was spent on homeland security and national defense programs in the months following September 11. Of this amount, $10 billion went to fighting in Afghanistan and about $20 billion to improving transportation security and rebuilding New York City. But in fiscal year 2002, Congress voted an additional $90 billion of new discretionary spending, only a small amount of which was related to increased security either at home or abroad. This spending included funds for medical research and highway construction.[15]

What has been true, and will continue to be true into the foreseeable future, is that numerous expenditures that have absolutely nothing to do with countering terrorism will be approved in the name of the fight against terrorism. Consider the latest set of "gifts" to agribusiness, an example of how old-fashioned special interest subsidies can be hidden under the cover of the war on terrorism. Since 1978, farmers have received subsidies of over $300 billion from the federal government. With the Farm Security and Rural Investment Act of 2002, new subsidies, combined with existing federal subsidies, will cost American taxpayers about $180 billion over ten years. An attempt was made to link the 2002 farm bill to national security needs by, among other things, including the word *security* in the act's title, but few observers were convinced that the bill had much to do with national security (see Chapter 13 for a further discussion of this legislation).

THE NEW DEPARTMENT OF HOMELAND SECURITY

When President Bush proposed the new Department of Homeland Security (DHS), he argued that it would not make government larger. In principle, the DHS has simply combined twenty-two agencies and 170,000 workers to create a more efficient way to protect Americans at home. Realize, though, that this department is the most massive new bureaucracy since the Department of Defense (DOD)

AP Photo/Susan Walsh

Government Printing Office employees stand behind copies of President George W. Bush's federal budget for fiscal year 2004. President Bush had sent Congress a $2.23 trillion spending plan that would accelerate tax cuts to bolster the weak economy, overhaul some of the government's biggest social programs, and shower billions of additional dollars on defense and homeland security.

was created in 1947. The likelihood of the DHS remaining even close to its original size is small. Many DHS activities, like DOD activities, are secret. This reduces the chances that spending on them will be carefully scrutinized. Furthermore, DHS activities, like DOD activities, are complex and far-reaching. It is easy to claim—and difficult to refute—that a cut in spending on one project will have spillover effects that will irreparably damage many other projects.

The result with the DOD has been a budget that seems immune to shrinkage. And, of course, plenty of private-sector firms have an incentive to keep that budget big because they are doing business with the department. Hence, they lobby for additional funding so that they, too, can get some of those extra federal dollars. It is likely that these types of incentives will work their magic with the DHS budget. Indeed, since the DHS asked private corporations to make proposals about new technologies to fight terrorism, some 1,500 companies have pitched their ideas. Again, it is easy to imagine spending on projects barely related to homeland security.

Are We Safer?

Few government agencies achieve the most efficient spending as they try to fulfill the nation's goals. Can homeland security be undertaken only by government? To what extent can the private sector help protect Americans from terrorist acts?

Congress is unable to pass a complete budget by October 1, it passes **continuing resolutions,** which enable the executive agencies to keep on doing whatever they were doing the previous year with the same amount of funding. Even continuing resolutions have not always been passed on time.

continuing resolution A temporary resolution passed by Congress when an appropriations bill has not been passed by the beginning of the new fiscal year.

The budget process involves making predictions about the state of the U.S. economy for years to come. This process is necessarily very imprecise. Since 1996, both Congress and the president have attempted to make ten-year projections for income (from taxes) and spending, but no one can know what the financial picture of the United States will look like in ten years.[16] The workforce could grow or shrink, which would drastically alter government revenue from taxes. Any number of emergencies could arise that would require increased government spending—from going to war against terrorists to inoculating federal employees against smallpox. How the government goes about planning for and funding such contingencies is discussed in this chapter's *The Politics of National Security* feature on the facing page.

why does it MATTER?

Congress and Your Everyday Life

It is almost a cliché to say that Congress affects your everyday life. After all, Congress has passed laws that affect virtually every aspect of your everyday life, from establishing safety standards for your job to declaring when daylight saving time starts and ends to deciding whether there should be a military draft. Perhaps more important, Congress decides how much the federal government will spend each year. But how much the federal government will spend is also tied to possibly the most important congressional action with respect to your everyday life: how the federal government taxes you.

Federal Income Taxes— They Haven't Always Been There

If we were writing this text in 1900, we would have nothing to say about Congress and income taxes. Not until February 3, 1913, when the Sixteenth Amendment to the Constitution was ratified, did Congress actually start to require U.S. residents to pay federal income taxes. That amendment reads:

> The Congress shall have power to lay and collect taxes on incomes, from whatever source derived, without apportionment among the several States, and without regard to any census or enumeration.

Today, about 22 percent of all total national income each year goes to the federal government as taxes. This is the highest percentage in the history of the United States, matching the level reached during World War II. Because you can spend only the income left after you pay taxes, the level at which Congress chooses to tax you is indeed important to your everyday life.

AP Photo/John Russell

Taking Action

Several individuals and groups have tried since 1913 to reform or eliminate the income tax system in the United States. Other individuals and groups have taken action in response to state or local tax proposals. For example, in the photo above, two citizens who both supported a proposed Tennessee state tax reform made up their own radio station in Nashville to mock local radio personalities who were opposed to the reform. Lining the street nearby are other supporters of the tax reform.

Key Terms

apportionment 240

appropriation 257

authorization 257

cloture 252

conference
    committee 255

conference report 255

congressional
    district 241

continuing
    resolution 261

entitlement
    program 258

filibustering 251

first budget
    resolution 259

fiscal year 259

gerrymandering 241

instructed delegate 244

majority leader 248

malapportionment 241

markup session 253

minority leader 248

minority-majority
    district 243

"one person, one vote"
    rule 241

pocket veto 255

Rules Committee 251

second budget
    resolution 259

Speaker of the
    House 247

standing committee 250

subcommittee 250

trustee 244

whip 248

Chapter Summary

1 The U.S. Constitution established a bicameral legislature—a Congress consisting of two chambers, the House and the Senate.

2 Each representative to the House is elected by voters in a specific area, or congressional district. The lines of congressional districts are drawn by the authority of state legislatures, and in the past, districts of unequal population and the practice of gerrymandering (drawing district lines to maximize the control of a particular party or group) were common. As a result of a series of Supreme Court decisions, state legislatures are required to ensure that voting districts have equal populations.

3 The U.S. Constitution requires that congressional representatives be elected every second year by popular vote. Senators are elected every six years, also (since the ratification of the Seventeenth Amendment) by popular vote. State legislatures control the times, places, and manner of holding congressional elections.

4 To be a member of Congress, only a few qualifications—relating to citizenship, residency, and age—must be met. Nonetheless, incumbent legislators have proved to have an advantage over their opponents at reelection time. Americans have been at odds over congressional "careerism" and the issue of term limits.

5 The majority party in each chamber of Congress chooses the major officers of that chamber, controls debate on the floor, selects committee chairpersons, and has a majority on all committees. The Speaker of the House is the chief leader in the House of Representatives. Other significant leaders in the House are the majority leader, the minority leader, and the whips.

6 The Constitution makes the vice president the president of the Senate, but in practice the vice president is rarely present in the Senate. The president "pro tem" (pro tempore), an alternate presiding officer elected by the senators, serves in the absence of the vice president. The real power in the Senate is held by the majority leader, the minority leader, and their respective whips.

7 Most of the actual work of Congress is handled by committees and subcommittees. The permanent and most powerful committees are called standing committees. Before any bill can be considered by the entire House or Senate, it must be approved by a majority vote in the standing committee to which it was assigned.

8 Many of the differences between the House and the Senate are due to their different sizes. With its larger size, the House requires more formal rules, particularly with respect to debate on the floor. In the House, the Rules Committee places time limitations on debate for most bills. In the Senate, in contrast, the tradition of unlimited debate continues. Members of the Senate generally enjoy more prestige due to their positions than do members of the House.

9 There are several steps in the legislative process—the process by which a bill becomes a law. To become law, a bill must be passed in identical form by both chambers. If the bill is approved by both houses, it is submitted to the president, who can sign the bill, veto it, or do nothing (in which case the bill becomes law within ten days unless Congress adjourns before that ten-day period expires; in that event, the president has effected a pocket veto).

10 Congress is charged with certain powers to oversee and investigate other branches of government, including the executive and judicial branches. The House of Representatives has the power to impeach the president, vice president, and federal judges. The Senate can refuse to confirm certain officers of government, including the president's cabinet members and Supreme Court justices. Congress can also refuse to fund certain government programs.

11 The Constitution provides that only Congress can impose taxes and authorize expenditures. The congressional budgeting process involves authorization and appropriation. Whenever Congress is unable to pass a complete budget by the beginning of the new fiscal year on October 1, it operates on the basis of continuing resolutions, which enable the executive agencies to keep on doing whatever they were doing the previous year with the same amount of funding.

RESOURCES FOR FURTHER STUDY

Selected Readings

Hamilton, Lee H. *How Congress Works and Why You Should Care.* Bloomington, Ind.: Indiana University Press, 2004. The author, a former member of Congress, provides an inside look at the way the legislative branch works and affects the lives of all Americans.

Jacobson, Gary C. *The Politics of Congressional Elections,* 6th ed. New York: Longman Publishers, 2003. Now in its sixth edition, this book provides a comprehensive view of congressional elections, including gerrymandering, the incumbency factor, fund-raising, and campaign strategy. It also provides an excellent general overview of congressional and national politics.

Oleszek, Walter J. *Congressional Procedures and the Policy Process,* 6th ed. Washington, D.C.: CQ Press, 2004. This book pro-

vides a comprehensive overview of how Congress functions, including House and Senate rules, the budgeting process, new developments in how the two chambers resolve differences, and new trends in legislative oversight. It has even been assigned to new congressional staff members.

Sidlow, Edward I. *Challenging the Incumbent: An Underdog's Undertaking.* Washington, D.C.: CQ Press, 2004. The author recounts Lance Pressl's 2000 campaign to unseat long-term Illinois congressman Phil Crane. The narrative vividly illustrates the power of incumbency.

Politics on the Web

- There is an abundance of online information relating to Congress and congressional activities. The THOMAS site (named for Thomas Jefferson), maintained by the Library of Congress, provides a record of all bills introduced into Congress, information about each member of Congress and how he or she voted on specific bills, and other data. Go to **http://thomas.loc.gov**

- The U.S. Government Printing Office (GPO) Access on the Web offers information on Congress in session, bills pending and passed, and a history of the bills at **http://www.gpoaccess.gov/index.html**

- To learn more about how a bill becomes a law, go to **http://www.vote-smart.org**

  Click on "Political Resources" and scroll down to "Vote Smart Classroom." Select "An Introduction to the U.S. Government," and then choose "How a Bill Becomes Law."

- You can find e-mail addresses and home pages for members of the House of Representatives at **http://www.house.gov**

- For e-mail addresses and home pages for members of the Senate, go to **http://www.senate.gov**

Online Resources for This Chapter

This text's Companion Web Site, at **http://www.americaatodds.com,** offers links to numerous resources that you can utilize to learn more about the topics covered in this chapter. For a list describing these resources, see the inside front cover of this book.

chapter **12**
the presidency

CHAPTER OBJECTIVES

After reading this chapter, you should be able to . . .

▶ List the constitutional requirements for becoming president.

▶ Explain the roles that a president performs while in office.

▶ Indicate the scope of presidential powers.

▶ Describe key areas where Congress and the president have advantages in their institutional relationship.

▶ Discuss the role of cabinet members in presidential administrations.

Should Presidents Be Able to Go to War on Their Own?

When the framers wrote the provisions for the office of the presidency, they did so with George Washington in mind. He was the general who had led the colonies to victory in the Revolutionary War, and he had the respect and admiration of the nation. His ability to lead the armed forces as "commander in chief" was unquestioned, and so the framers gave the president that explicit authority.

As commander in chief, the president has the power to defend the nation and to repel sudden attacks by foreign powers. In an offensive war, however, only Congress has the constitutional authority to declare war. Congress has declared war against other nations, but not since 1941 when it declared war on Japan. The United Nations (UN) charter, which the United States signed in 1945, makes war illegal except in cases of self-defense—when the president can act without Congress. This has led some scholars to argue that Congress's authority to "declare war" is meaningless today. So, should presidents be able to commit U.S. troops to war on their own?

Presidents Must Have a Free Hand to Act

The War Powers Resolution of 1973, discussed in more detail later in this chapter, requires the president to inform Congress within forty-eight hours after American forces have been deployed. Thus, the resolution gives the president the opportunity to act first and ask Congress later. When a president acts, as commander in chief, to place troops in harm's way, Congress cannot simply reverse the order and bring them home. Even debating the issue could undermine the troops' effectiveness and destroy their morale.

Furthermore, those who favor giving the president a free hand point out that, in modern warfare, the enemy is likely to exploit congressional indecision over troop deployments. For example, in October 2002, Congress passed a resolution authorizing President George W. Bush to use military force against Iraq if the latter did not comply with the UN's demand to disarm. By March 2003, however, many of the signers of that resolution had changed their minds and publicly said that President Bush should wait for the UN to authorize an offensive attack against Iraq.

Congress's commitment to a military campaign could easily weaken in the face of a terrorist attack on U.S. troops overseas or decreasing support from U.S. allies. Presidents, in contrast, have demonstrated the ability to harden themselves against such blows to the national will. As political scientist Harold Laski once wrote, "Great power makes great leadership possible." The president's war powers today are tremendous, and presidents will rise to the occasion and exhibit great leadership.

Congress Must Check the President's War Powers

The framers recognized that Congress's size and complex decision-making processes would make it a more deliberative and divided institution than the presidency. They expected Congress to hold public debates about the most monumental choice of any nation: whether or not to go to war. Even among scholars today who believe that the president should have expansive war powers, some make a distinction between air strikes and ground troops. When thousands of American men and women are asked to risk their lives in a ground assault, these scholars say, the decision should be debated in Congress first.

Even if Congress is not asked for a declaration of war, it has other means to check the president's war powers, and it should use them. First, Congress can deny the president the funds to wage war. Second, Congress can use its persuasive powers to rein in the president, sway public opinion, and limit the length and breadth of a war.

Some scholars argue that if fulfilling U.S. treaty obligations involves committing U.S. troops, the president can do so without authorization from Congress. Others dismiss this argument. In fact, in 1995 the Senate passed a unanimous resolution that holds that a UN Security Council resolution is not a substitute for congressional authorization of military action. The Supreme Court has also upheld this view: although a treaty obligation is a legal commitment, Congress can compel the president to violate it.[1]

Where Do You Stand?

1. Do you think that presidents should have the right to go to war on their own, without seeking authorization from Congress?

2. Do you think that some aspects of modern warfare require more independent action by the president than the framers of the Constitution envisioned when they gave the power to declare war to Congress alone?

Explore This Issue Online

- The *Modern Tribune* offers a detailed discussion of the War Powers Resolution as it applied to the Iraq War in 2003. You can find this article and links to other issues related to the War Powers Resolution at **http://www.themoderntribune.com/united_states_supreme_court_war_powers_act.htm**.

- For a conservative interpretation of the president's ability to go to war, visit **http://www.proconservative.net/WarAmericaContents.shtml**.

Introduction

President Lyndon B. Johnson (1963–1969) stated in his autobiography[2] that "[o]f all the 1,886 nights I was President, there were not many when I got to sleep before 1 or 2 A.M., and there were few mornings when I didn't wake up by 6 or 6:30." President Harry Truman (1945–1953) once observed that no one can really understand what it is like to be president: there is no end to "the chain of responsibility that binds him," and he is "never allowed to forget that he is president." These responsibilities are, for the most part, unremitting. Unlike Congress, the president never adjourns.

Given the demands of the presidency, why would anyone seek the office? There are some very special perks associated with the presidency. The president enjoys, among other things, the use of the White House. The White House has 132 rooms located on 18.3 acres of land in the heart of the nation's capital. At the White House, the president in residence has a staff of more than eighty persons, including chefs, gardeners, maids, butlers, and a personal tailor. Amenities also include a tennis court, a swimming pool, bowling lanes, and a private movie theater. Additionally, the president has at his disposal a fleet of automobiles, helicopters, and jets (including *Air Force One,* which costs $30,000 an hour to run). For relaxation, the presidential family can go to Camp David, a resort hideaway in the Catoctin Mountains of Maryland. Other perks include free dental and medical care.

These amenities are only a minor motivation for wanting to be president of the United States, however. A greater motivation is that the presidency is at the apex of the political ladder. It is the most powerful and influential political office that any one individual can hold. Presidents can help to shape not only domestic policy but also global developments. With the demise of the Soviet Union and its satellite Communist countries in the early 1990s, the president of the United States is regarded by many as the leader of the most powerful nation on earth. The president heads the greatest military force anywhere. It is not surprising, therefore, that many Americans aspire to attain this office. Beyond power, many presidential aspirants desire a place in history. Scholars and ordinary Americans alike have long debated presidential "greatness." To review the results of three different polls on presidential greatness, see Table 12–1.

Who Can Become President?

The notion that anybody can become president of this country has always been a part of the American dream. Certainly, the requirements for becoming president set forth in Article II, Section 1, of the Constitution are not difficult to meet:

TABLE 12–1

Who Is the Greatest President?

RANK	C-SPAN	*WALL STREET JOURNAL*	GALLUP
1	Abraham Lincoln	George Washington	Ronald Reagan
2	Franklin D. Roosevelt	Abraham Lincoln	Bill Clinton
3	George Washington	Franklin D. Roosevelt	Abraham Lincoln
4	Theodore Roosevelt	Thomas Jefferson	Franklin D. Roosevelt
5	Harry Truman	Theodore Roosevelt	John F. Kennedy
6	Woodrow Wilson	Andrew Jackson	George W. Bush
7	Thomas Jefferson	Harry Truman	George Washington
8	John F. Kennedy	Ronald Reagan	Jimmy Carter
9	Dwight D. Eisenhower	Dwight D. Eisenhower	Harry Truman
10	Lyndon B. Johnson	James Polk	Theodore Roosevelt

SOURCES: C-SPAN survey of American historians, 1999; *The Wall Street Journal* survey of historians, political scientists, and law professors, 2000; Gallup poll, February 18, 2005.

> No Person except a natural born Citizen, or a Citizen of the United States, at the time of the Adoption of this Constitution, shall be eligible to the Office of President; neither shall any Person be eligible to that Office who shall not have attained to the Age of thirty-five Years, and been fourteen Years a Resident within the United States.

It is true that modern presidents have included a haberdasher (Harry Truman), a peanut farmer (Jimmy Carter), and an actor (Ronald Reagan), although all of these men also had significant political experience before assuming the presidency. If you look at Appendix E, though, you will see that the most common previous occupation of U.S. presidents has been the legal profession. Out of forty-three presidents, twenty-six have been lawyers, and many presidents have been wealthy. Additionally, although the Constitution states that anyone who is thirty-five years of age or older can become president, the average age at inauguration has been fifty-four. The youngest person elected president was John F. Kennedy (1961–1963), who assumed the presidency at the age of forty-three (the youngest person to hold the office was Theodore Roosevelt, who was forty-two when he became president after the assassination of William McKinley); the oldest was Ronald Reagan (1981–1989), who was sixty-nine years old when he became president. Even the requirement that the president be a natural-born citizen has been questioned recently.

AMERICA at odds

A Foreign-Born President?

As you just read, Article II of the Constitution states that "[n]o Person except a natural born Citizen . . . shall be eligible to the Office of President." This restriction is now being challenged, however. Supporters of the popular governor of California, Arnold Schwarzenegger, want the Austrian-born former film star to run for president in 2008. Many Americans are calling for an "Arnold amendment." Others argue that the constitutional requirement that the president be a natural-born citizen should stand.

America is a nation of immigrants, so it strikes some as odd that a foreigner would be barred from aspiring to the presidency. More than 13 million of today's Americans were born outside the United States. The constitutional ban against foreign-born individuals becoming president is discriminatory, many argue. Moreover, they claim that the clause is outdated. Indeed, it was originally intended to keep European princes from attempting to partition the country in the late 1700s. Throughout its history, America has been enriched by immigrants to these shores. Immigrants have held important national positions, such as secretary of state, on numerous occasions. Schwarzenegger's supporters argue that it is time we allow a foreign-born citizen to become president.

Other Americans believe that the constitutional ban should remain. They argue that national security could be compromised by a foreign-born president. With the immense power that the president wields, especially in the realm of foreign policy, loyalty is of the utmost concern. The current war on terrorism only heightens the need to assure that the president does not have divided loyalties. In addition, the Constitution is quite difficult to amend, requiring support from two-thirds of both chambers of Congress and ratification by three-fourths of the fifty states. The need for an amendment that would allow Schwarzenegger and other immigrants to run for president is hardly as pressing as the need for past antidiscrimination amendments such as those abolishing slavery and giving women the right to vote, opponents argue.

To date, all U.S. presidents have been male, white, and (with the exception of John F. Kennedy, who was a Roman Catholic) from the Protestant tradition. Polls indicate, though, that many Americans expect to see a woman or an African American assume the office in the not-too-distant future. A 2005 poll conducted by Siena College Research Institute found that 81 percent of people surveyed would vote for a woman for president. Another recent poll, conducted by the Gallup Organization, reported that 92 percent of respondents would vote for an African American candidate.[3]

President George W. Bush, right, speaks to his staff inside the private dining room at the White House before his address to the nation on September 11, 2001.

The President's Many Roles

As will be discussed shortly, the president has the authority to exercise a variety of powers; some of these are explicitly outlined in the Constitution, and some are simply required by the office—such as the power to persuade. In the course of exercising these powers, the president performs a variety of roles. For example, as commander in chief of the armed services, the president can exercise significant military powers. Which roles a president executes successfully usually depends on what is happening domestically and internationally, as well as on the president's personality. Some presidents, including Bill Clinton during his first term, have shown much more interest in domestic policy than in foreign policy. Others, such as George H. W. Bush (1989–1993), were more interested in foreign affairs than in domestic policies.

Table 12–2 on the next page summarizes the major roles of the president. An important role is, of course, that of chief executive. Other roles include those of commander in chief, chief of state, chief diplomat, chief legislator, and political party leader.

Chief Executive

According to Article II of the Constitution,

> The executive Power shall be vested in a President of the United States of America. . . . [H]e may require the Opinion, in writing, of the principal Officer in each of the executive Departments, upon any Subject relating to the Duties of their respective Offices . . . and he shall nominate, and by and with the Advice and Consent of the Senate, shall appoint . . . Officers of the United States . . . . [H]e shall take Care that the Laws be faithfully executed.

This constitutional provision makes the president of the United States the nation's **chief executive,** or the head of the executive branch of the federal government. When the framers created the office of the president, they created a uniquely American institution. Nowhere else in the world at that time was there a democratically elected chief executive. The executive branch is also unique among the branches of government because it is headed by a single individual—the president.

chief executive The head of the executive branch of government. In the United States, the president is the head of the executive branch of the federal government.

Commander in Chief

The Constitution states that the president "shall be Commander in Chief of the Army and Navy of the United States, and of the Militia of the several States, when called into the actual Service of the United States." As **commander in chief** of the nation's armed forces, the president exercises tremendous power.

commander in chief The supreme commander of the military forces of the United States.

TABLE 12-2
Roles of the President

ROLE	DESCRIPTION	EXAMPLES
Chief executive	Enforces laws and federal court decisions, along with treaties signed by the United States	■ Can appoint, with Senate approval, and remove high-ranking officers of the federal government ■ Can grant reprieves, pardons, and amnesty ■ Can handle national emergencies during peacetime, such as riots or natural disasters
Commander in chief	Leads the nation's armed forces	■ Can commit troops for up to ninety days in response to a military threat (War Powers Resolution) ■ Can make secret agreements with other countries ■ Can set up military governments in conquered lands ■ Can end fighting by calling a cease-fire (armistice)
Chief of state	Performs certain ceremonial roles as personal symbol of the nation	■ Decorates war heroes ■ Dedicates parks and post offices ■ Throws out first pitch of baseball season ■ Lights national Christmas tree
Chief diplomat	Directs U.S. foreign policy and is the nation's most important representative in dealing with foreign countries	■ Can negotiate and sign treaties with other nations, with Senate approval ■ Can make pacts (executive agreements) with other heads of state, without Senate approval ■ Can accept the legal existence of another country's government (power of recognition) ■ Receives foreign chiefs of state
Chief legislator	Informs Congress about the condition of the country and recommends legislative measures	■ Proposes legislative program to Congress in traditional State of the Union address ■ Suggests budget to Congress and submits annual economic report ■ Can veto a bill passed by Congress ■ Can call special sessions of Congress
Political party leader	Heads political party	■ Chooses a vice president ■ Makes several thousand top government appointments, often to party faithful (patronage) ■ Tries to execute the party's platform ■ May attend party fund-raisers ■ May help reelect party members running for office as mayors, governors, or members of Congress

Unlike many who preceded him in the presidential office, President George W. Bush has publicly emphasized his role as commander in chief. Here, the president shakes hands with a group of Weapons Ordnance Mates in May 2003 on the deck of the aircraft carrier USS *Abraham Lincoln* as it steams toward San Diego.

AP Photo/Damian Dovarganes

As you read in the chapter-opening *America at Odds* feature, under the Constitution, war powers are divided between Congress and the president. Congress was given the power to declare war and the power to raise and maintain the country's armed forces. The president, as commander in chief, was given the power to deploy the armed forces. The president's role as commander in chief has evolved over the last century. We examine this shared power between the president and Congress in more detail later in this chapter.

Chief of State

Traditionally, a country's monarch has performed the function of chief of state—the country's representative to the rest of the world. The United States, of course, has no king or queen to act as **chief of state.** Thus, the president of the United States fulfills this role. The president engages in many symbolic or ceremonial activities, such as throwing out the first pitch to open the baseball season and turning on the lights of the national Christmas tree. The president also decorates war heroes, dedicates parks and post offices, receives visiting chiefs of state at the White House, and goes on official state visits to other countries. Some argue that presidents should not perform such ceremonial duties because they take time that the president should be spending on "real work." (See this chapter's *Comparative Politics* feature on the following page for more information on how other countries handle this issue.)

chief of state The person who serves as the ceremonial head of a country's government and represents that country to the rest of the world.

Chief Diplomat

A **diplomat** is a person who represents one country in dealing with representatives of another country. In the United States, the president is the nation's **chief diplomat.** The Constitution did not explicitly reserve this role to the president, but since the beginning of this nation, presidents have assumed the role based on their explicit constitutional powers to recognize foreign governments and, with the advice and consent of the Senate, to appoint ambassadors and make treaties. As chief diplomat, the president directs the foreign policy of the United States and is its most important representative.

diplomat A person who represents one country in dealing with representatives of another country.

chief diplomat The role of the president in recognizing and interacting with foreign governments.

Chief Legislator

Nowhere in the Constitution do the words *chief legislator* appear. The Constitution, however, does require that the president "from time to time give to the Congress Information of the State of the Union, and recommend to their Consideration such Measures as he shall judge necessary and expedient." The president has, in fact, become a major player in shaping the congressional agenda—the set of measures that actually get discussed and acted on. This was not always the case. In the nineteenth century, some presidents preferred to let Congress lead the way in proposing and implementing policy. Since the administration of Theodore

President Woodrow Wilson throwing out the first pitch on the opening day of the baseball season in 1916.

National Photo Company Collection/Library of Congress

Having a Separate Chief of State

In the seven Western European countries headed by royalty, the monarch is considered the chief of state and plays a ceremonial role. In the United Kingdom, for example, Queen Elizabeth II represents the state when she performs ceremonial duties, such as opening sessions of Parliament, christening ships, and holding receptions for foreign ambassadors.

In the monarchies of the Netherlands and Norway, the king or queen initiates the process of forming a government after national elections by determining which parties can combine to rule in a coalition. This process really depends on the results of the election and the desires of the political parties—yet the monarch must certify the results.

The majority of European states are not monarchies, but they nonetheless split the

Queen Elizabeth II of the United Kingdom

duties of government between a prime minister and a president. In Switzerland, for example, the president is elected indirectly by the legislature and assumes purely ceremonial duties.

Throughout Western Europe, the pattern is the same: presidents have ceremonial powers only. The single exception to this rule occurs in France, which has a presidential system in which the head of state has real political power, particularly in foreign affairs.

For Critical Analysis

What are the benefits of having a single person perform only chief-of-state activities? Are there any benefits to the American system, in which the functions of chief executive and chief of state are combined?

Roosevelt (1901–1909), however, presidents have taken an activist approach. Presidents are now expected to develop a legislative program and propose a budget to Congress every year. This shared power often puts Congress and the president at odds—as you will read shortly.

Political Party Leader

The president of the United States is also the leader of his or her political party. The Constitution, of course, does not mention this role because, in the eyes of the founders, presidents (and other political representatives) were not to be influenced by "factional" (partisan) interests.

As party leader, the president exercises substantial powers. For example, the president chooses the chairperson of the party's national committee. The president can also exert political power within the party by using presidential appointment and removal powers. Naturally, presidents are beholden to the party members who put them in office, and usually they indulge in the practice of **patronage**—appointing individuals to government or public jobs—to reward those who helped them win the presidential contest. The president may also reward party members with fund-raising assistance (campaign financing is discussed in Chapter 9). The president is, in a sense, "fund-raiser in chief" for his or her party. Understandably, the use of patronage within the party system gives the president singular powers.

patronage The practice of giving government jobs to individuals belonging to the winning political party.

The President's Constitutional Powers

As you have read, the constitutional source for the president's authority is found in Article II of the Constitution, which states, "The executive Power shall be vested in a President of the United States of America." The Constitution then sets forth the president's relatively limited constitutional responsibilities. Just how much power should be entrusted to the president was debated at length by the framers of the Constitution. On the one hand, they did not want a king. On the other hand, they believed that a strong executive was necessary if the republic was to survive. The result of their debates was an executive who was granted enough powers in the Constitution to balance those of Congress.[4]

Article II grants the president broad but vaguely described powers. From the very beginning, there were different views as to what exactly the "executive Power" clause enabled the president to do. Nonetheless, Sections 2 and 3 of Article II list the following specific presidential powers:

- To serve as commander in chief of the armed forces and the state militias.
- To appoint, with the Senate's consent, the heads of the executive departments, ambassadors, justices of the Supreme Court, and other top officials.
- To grant reprieves and pardons, except in cases of impeachment.
- To make treaties, with the advice and consent of the Senate.
- To deliver the annual State of the Union address to Congress and to send other messages to Congress from time to time.
- To call either house or both houses of Congress into special sessions.
- To receive ambassadors and other representatives from foreign countries.
- To commission all officers of the United States.
- To ensure that the laws passed by Congress "be faithfully executed."

In addition, Article I, Section 7, gives the president the power to veto legislation. We discuss some of these powers in more detail below. As you will see, many of these powers are balanced by the powers of Congress. We address the complex relationship between the president and Congress in a later section of this chapter.

Proposal and Ratification of Treaties

A **treaty** is a formal agreement between two or more sovereign states. The president has the sole power to negotiate and sign treaties with other countries. The Senate, however, must approve the treaty by a two-thirds vote of the members present before it becomes effective. If the treaty is approved by the Senate and signed by the president, it becomes law.

Presidents have not always succeeded in winning the Senate's approval for treaties. Woodrow Wilson (1913–1921) lost his effort to persuade the Senate to approve the Treaty of Versailles,[5] the peace treaty that ended World War I in 1918. Among other things, the treaty would have made the United States a member of the League of Nations. In contrast, Jimmy Carter (1977–1981) convinced the Senate to approve a treaty returning the Panama Canal to Panama by the year 2000 (over such objections as that of Senator S. I. Hayakawa, a Republican from California, who said, "We stole it fair and square"). The treaty was approved by a margin of a single vote.

Here, President Bush announces that he will endorse a constitutional amendment that would ban gay marriage. The president often influences the legislative agenda in Congress.

treaty A formal agreement between the governments of two or more countries.

One of the significant powers of the president is the power to negotiate and sign treaties. Here, President Jimmy Carter, left, and other officials watch as Panama's president, General Omar Torrijos, signs the Panama Canal Treaty on September 7, 1977.

President Gerald Ford reads a proclamation in the White House on September 9, 1974, granting former president Richard Nixon "a full, free and absolute pardon" for all "offenses against the United States" during the period of his presidency.

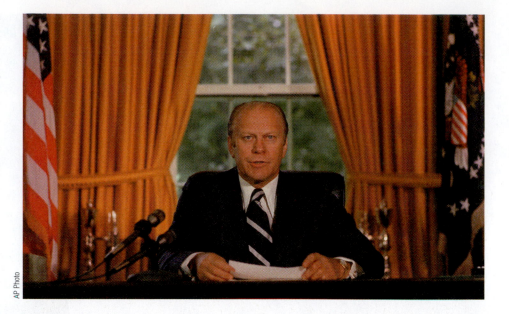

AP Photo

The Power to Grant Reprieves and Pardons

The president's power to grant a pardon serves as a check on judicial power. A *pardon* is a release from punishment or the legal consequences of a crime; it restores a person to the full rights and privileges of citizenship. In 1925, the Supreme Court upheld an expansive interpretation of the president's pardon power in a case involving an individual convicted for contempt of court. The Court held that the power covers all offenses "either before trial, during trial, or after trial, by individuals, or by classes, conditionally or absolutely, and this without modification or regulation by Congress."[6] The president can grant a pardon for any federal offense, except in cases of impeachment. One of the most controversial pardons was that granted by President Gerald Ford (1974–1977) to former president Richard Nixon (1969–1974) after the Watergate affair, before any formal charges were brought in court. Sometimes pardons are granted to a class of individuals, as a general amnesty. For example, President Jimmy Carter (1977–1981) granted amnesty to approximately 10,000 people who had resisted the draft during the Vietnam War.

The President's Veto Power

veto A Latin word meaning "I forbid"; the refusal by an official, such as the president of the United States or a state governor, to sign a bill into law.

As noted in Chapter 11, the president can **veto** a bill passed by Congress. Congress can override the veto with a two-thirds vote by the members present in each chamber. The result of an overridden veto is that the bill becomes law against the wishes of the president. If the president does not send a bill back to Congress after ten congressional working days, the bill becomes law without the president's signature. If the president refuses to sign the bill and Congress adjourns within ten working days after the bill has been submitted to the president, the bill is killed for that session of Congress. As mentioned in Chapter 11, this is called a *pocket veto*.

Presidents used the veto power sparingly until the administration of Andrew Johnson (1865–1869). Johnson vetoed twenty-one bills, and his successor, Ulysses Grant (1869–1877), vetoed forty-five. Franklin D. Roosevelt (1933–1945) vetoed more bills by far than any of his predecessors or successors in the presidency. During his administration, there were 372 regular vetoes, 9 of which were overridden by Congress, and 263 pocket vetoes. By the end of his presidency in 2001, President Clinton had vetoed thirty-seven bills.

Many presidents have complained that they cannot control "pork barrel" legislation—federal expenditures tacked onto bills to "bring home the bacon" to a particular congressional member's district. For example, expenditures on a specific sports stadium might be added to a bill involving crime. The reason is simple: without a line-item veto (the ability to veto just one item in a bill), to eliminate the "pork" in proposed legislation, the president would have to veto the entire bill—and that might not be feasible politically. Congress passed and President Clinton signed a line-item veto bill in 1996. The Supreme Court concluded in 1998 that it was unconstitutional, however.[7]

President Bill Clinton used line-item veto powers to eliminate nearly forty construction projects worth $287 million from the military construction bill during a ceremony in the Oval Office in the fall of 1997. "The use of the line-item veto saves taxpayers nearly $290 million and makes clear the old rules have in fact changed," Clinton declared during the ceremony. The line-item veto legislation, passed in 1996, was ruled unconstitutional by the United States Supreme Court in 1998.

AP Photo/Greg Gibson

The President's Inherent Powers

In addition to the powers explicitly granted by the Constitution, the president also has inherent powers—powers that are necessary to carry out the specific responsibilities of the president as set forth in the Constitution. The presidency is, of course, an institution of government, but it is also an institution that consists, at any one moment in time, of one individual. That means that the lines between the presidential office and the person who holds that office often become blurred. Certain presidential powers that are today considered part of the rights of the office were simply assumed by strong presidents to be inherent powers of the presidency, and their successors then continued to exercise these powers.

President Woodrow Wilson clearly indicated this interplay between presidential personality and presidential powers in the following statement:

> The President is at liberty, both in law and conscience to be as big a man as he can. His capacity will set the limit; and if Congress be overborne by him, it will be no fault of the makers of the Constitution—it will be from no lack of constitutional powers on his part, but only because the President has the nation behind him, and Congress has not.[8]

In other words, because the Constitution is vague as to the actual carrying out of presidential powers, presidents are left to define the limits of their authority—subject, of course, to the other branches of government.

As you will read in this chapter, Congress has sometimes allowed the president to exercise certain powers and has sometimes limited presidential powers. Additionally, the Supreme Court, as the head of the judicial branch of the government and the final arbiter of the Constitution, can check the president's powers. The Court, through its power of judicial review, can determine whether the president, by taking a certain action, has exceeded the powers granted by the Constitution.

The Expansion of Presidential Powers

The Constitution defines presidential powers in very general language, and even the founders were uncertain just how the president would perform the various functions. Only experience would tell. Thus, over the past two centuries, the powers of the president have been defined and expanded by the personalities and policies of various White House occupants.

For example, George Washington removed officials from office, interpreting the constitutional power to appoint officials as implying a power to remove them as well.[9] He established

As commander in chief, George Washington used troops to put down a rebellion in Pennsylvania, and as chief diplomat, he made foreign policy without consulting Congress. This latter action laid the groundwork for the president's active role in the area of foreign policy.

By the time Abraham Lincoln gave his Inauguration Day speech, seven southern states had already seceded from the Union. Four more states seceded after he issued a summons to the militia. In 1863, during the Civil War, Lincoln issued the Emancipation Proclamation. Some scholars believe that his skillful and vigorous handling of the Civil War increased the power and prestige of the presidency.

When Franklin D. Roosevelt assumed the presidency in 1933, he launched his "Hundred Days" of legislation in an attempt to counter the effects of the Great Depression. Roosevelt's administration not only extended the role of the national government in regulating the nation's economic life but also further increased the power of the president.

the practice of meeting regularly with the heads of the three departments that then existed and of turning to them for political advice. He set a precedent of the president acting as chief legislator by submitting proposed legislation to Congress. Abraham Lincoln (1861–1865), confronting the problems of the Civil War during the 1860s, took several important actions while Congress was not in session. He suspended certain constitutional liberties, spent funds that Congress had not appropriated, blockaded southern ports, and banned "treasonable correspondence" from the U.S. mails. All of these actions were carried out in the name of his power as commander in chief and his constitutional responsibility to "take Care that the Laws be faithfully executed."

Other presidents, including Thomas Jefferson, Andrew Jackson, Woodrow Wilson, and Franklin D. Roosevelt, have also greatly expanded the powers of the president. The power of the president continues to evolve, depending on the person holding the office, the relative power of Congress, and events at home and abroad.

The Expansion of the President's Legislative Powers

Congress has come to expect the president to develop a legislative program. From time to time the president submits special messages on certain subjects. These messages call on Congress to enact laws that the president thinks are necessary. The president also works closely with members of Congress to persuade them to support particular programs. The president writes, telephones, and meets with various congressional leaders to discuss pending bills. The president also sends aides to lobby on Capitol Hill. One study of the legislative process found that "no other single actor in the political system has quite the capability of the president to set agendas in given policy areas." As one lobbyist told a researcher, "Obviously, when a president sends up a bill [to Congress], it takes first place in the queue. All other bills take second place."

The Power to Persuade

The president's political skills and ability to persuade others play a large role in determining the administration's success. According to Richard Neustadt, in his classic work entitled *Presidential Power,* "Presidential power is the power to persuade."[10] For all of the resources at the president's disposal, the president still must rely on the cooperation of others if the administration's goals are to be accomplished. After three years in office, President Harry Truman made this remark about the powers of the president:

> The president may have a great many powers given to him in the Constitution and may have certain powers under certain laws which are given to him by the Congress of the United States; but the principal power that the president has is to bring people in and try to persuade them to do what they ought to do without persuasion. That's what the powers of the president amount to.[11]

For example, President George W. Bush embarked on an ambitious legislative agenda following his reelection in 2004. His ability to win congressional support for his plans depended largely on his persuasive power. Persuasive powers are particularly important when divided government exists. If a president from one political party faces a Congress dominated by the other party, the president must overcome more opposition than usual to get legislation passed.

Going Public

The president may also use a strategy known as "going public"[12]—that is, using press conferences, public appearances, and televised events to arouse public opinion in favor of certain legislative programs. The public may then pressure legislators to support the administration's programs. A president who has the support of the public can wield significant persuasive powers over Congress. Presidents who are voted into office through "landslide" elections have increased bargaining power because of their widespread popularity (see this chapter's *Perception versus Reality* feature on page 279). Those with less popular support have less bargaining leverage.

AMERICA at odds

The President and Moral Politics

Franklin D. Roosevelt once said, "The presidency is not merely an administrative office. That is the least of it. It is preeminently a place of moral leadership."[13] George W. Bush has not hesitated to apply his moral and religious values to his role as president. Many of his staunchest supporters are evangelical Christians who voted for him in the hope that he would champion moral causes, such as curtailing abortion rights, banning gay marriage, and endorsing "faith-based" services. Bush has not failed to "go public" on such issues, openly promoting a moral agenda to the American people.

Many people have supported Bush's public promotion of moral and religious views. In 2005, for example, Bush willingly supported emergency legislation passed by Congress to keep Terri Schiavo alive. Schiavo had been in a persistent vegetative state for many years and her husband, Michael Schiavo, repeatedly insisted on having her feeding tube removed. The husband claimed that Terri had told him that she would not want to be kept alive by artificial means. Terri's parents fought this decision in the Florida courts, but ultimately the Florida Supreme Court held that Terri's husband, as her legal guardian, had the right to make the decision. Claiming that they were promoting "a culture of life," members of Congress enacted a law allowing Terri's case to be heard by a federal court. The federal trial and appellate courts, however, agreed with the Florida Supreme Court, and the United States Supreme Court refused to review the case. Bush's collaboration with Congress in the Schiavo case won strong approval from many Christian and pro-life Americans, who applauded his moral leadership.

Other Americans say that the president should not be using the presidency as a pulpit for moral politics. They argue that the president should respect the constitutionally mandated separation of church and state and the right of Americans to believe as they will. Furthermore, they maintain that the federal government's involvement in the Schiavo case blatantly violated the constitutionally established division of powers in our federal system. According to these critics, the federal government had no constitutional authority to intervene in the Schiavo case after the

In 2005, Terri Schiavo, a woman who had been in a persistent vegetative state since 1991, had her feeding tube removed after courts ruled that her husband had the right to do so. President Bush, who sided with the Schiavo supporters shown here, signed emergency legislation aimed at prolonging her life. The courts' rulings prevailed, however. Schiavo died soon after.

Carlos Barria/Reuters/Landov

executive order A presidential order to carry out a policy or policies described in a law passed by Congress.

President Bush hosted a conversation about Social Security in Montgomery, Alabama, in 2005. Bush was promoting his proposals to reform Social Security.

Reuters/Kevin Lamarque/Landov

highest Florida state court rendered its decision. As you will read in Chapter 14, the Constitution limits federal court jurisdiction (the authority to hear and decide cases) to cases involving a federal question (a question involving a treaty, the Constitution, or a federal law) or cases involving citizens from different states. Neither of these bases for federal jurisdiction existed in the Schiavo case.

The Power to Influence the Economy Some of the greatest expansion of presidential power occurred during Franklin D. Roosevelt's administration. Roosevelt claimed the presidential power to regulate the economy during the Great Depression in the 1930s. Since that time, Americans have expected the president to be actively involved in economic matters and social programs. Today, Congress annually receives from the president a suggested budget and the *Economic Report of the President*. The budget message suggests what amounts of money the government will need for its programs. The *Economic Report of the President* presents the state of the nation's economy and recommends ways to improve it.

The Legislative Success of Various Presidents Look at Figure 12–1, which shows the success record of presidents in getting their legislation passed. Success is defined as how often the president won his way on roll-call votes on which he took a clear position. As you can see, typically a president's success record is very high when he first takes office and then gradually declines. This is sometimes attributed to the president's "honeymoon period," when the Congress may be most likely to work with the president to achieve his legislative agenda. The media often put a great deal of emphasis on the president's success during his "first hundred days" in office. Ironically, this is also the period when the president is least experienced in the "ways" of the White House, particularly if the president was a Washington outsider, such as a state governor, before becoming president.

The Increasing Use of Executive Orders

As the nation's chief executive, the president is considered to have the inherent power to issue **executive orders,** which are presidential orders to carry out policies described in laws that have been passed by Congress. These orders have the force of law. Presidents have issued executive orders for a variety of purposes, including to establish procedures for appointing noncareer administrators, restructure the

Presidents and the "Popular Vote"

Every four years, American citizens go to the polls to cast their votes for the presidential candidate of their choice. Some presidential contests are very close, such as the 2000 race between Al Gore and George W. Bush and the 2004 race between John Kerry and Bush. Others are less so, such as the one between Lyndon Johnson and Barry Goldwater in 1964. When a presidential candidate wins the race by a wide margin, we may hear the result referred to as a *landslide election* or a *landslide victory* for the winning candidate.

THE PERCEPTION

The traditional perception has been that, in general, our presidents are elected by a majority of eligible American voters. As the people's choice, the president is beholden to the wishes of the broad American electorate that voted him into office. A president who has been swept into office by a so-called landslide victory may claim to have received a "mandate from the people" to govern the nation. A president may assert that a certain policy or program he endorsed in campaign speeches is backed by popular support simply because he was elected to office by a majority of the voters.

THE REALITY

In reality, the "popular vote" is not all that popular, in the sense of representing the wishes of a majority of American citizens who are eligible to vote. In fact, the president of the United States has never received the votes of a majority of all adults of voting age. Lyndon Johnson, in 1964, came the closest of any president in history to gaining the votes of a majority of the voting-age public, and even he

won the votes of less than 40 percent of those who were old enough to cast a ballot.

The hotly contested presidential elections of 2000 and 2004 were divisive, leaving the millions of Americans who had voted for the losing candidate unhappy with the results. In neither 2000 nor 2004 did a candidate win a significant number of states by more than 20 percent of the vote. Indeed, in winning the elections of 2000 and 2004, Bush received the votes of a mere 24.5 percent and 27.6 percent of the voting-age population, respectively. Nonetheless, Bush claimed that his 2004 victory represented a "mandate" from the American people, saying: "I have earned capital in the campaign, political capital, and now I intend to spend it." Bush assumed that his reelection was a signal from the American people to push his controversial domestic ideas, such as Social Security reform, as well as an endorsement of his foreign policy and the war on terrorism. Yet 72.4 percent of the voting-age population did not vote for him.

It is useful to keep these figures in mind whenever a president claims to have received a mandate from the people. The truth is, no president has ever been elected with sufficient popular backing to make this a serious claim.

What's Your Opinion?

Does it matter whether a presidential candidate, once elected, received a relatively high (or low) percentage of the popular votes cast?

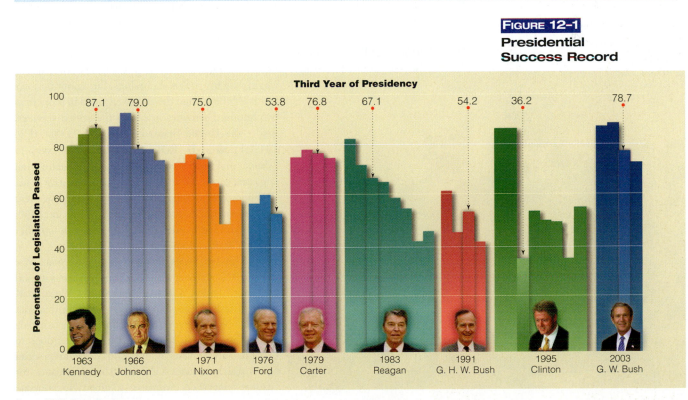

FIGURE 12-1
Presidential Success Record

Third Year of Presidency

| | 87.1 | 79.0 | 75.0 | 53.8 | 76.8 | 67.1 | 54.2 | 36.2 | 78.7 |

Percentage of Legislation Passed

| 1963 Kennedy | 1966 Johnson | 1971 Nixon | 1976 Ford | 1979 Carter | 1983 Reagan | 1991 G. H. W. Bush | 1995 Clinton | 2003 G. W. Bush |

White House bureaucracy, ration consumer goods and administer wage and price controls under emergency conditions, classify government information as secret, implement affirmative action policies, and regulate the export of certain items. Presidents issue executive orders frequently, sometimes as many as one hundred a year.

Evolving Presidential Power in Foreign Affairs

As you read in the chapter-opening *America at Odds* feature, the precise extent of the president's power in foreign affairs is constantly evolving. The president is commander in chief and chief diplomat, but only Congress has the power to formally declare war, and the Senate must ratify any treaty that the president has negotiated with other nations. George Washington laid the groundwork for our long history of the president's active role in foreign policy. For example, when war broke out between Britain and France in 1793, Washington chose to disregard a treaty of alliance with France and to pursue a course of strict neutrality. Since that time, presidents have taken military actions and made foreign policy on many occasions without consulting Congress.

executive agreement A binding international agreement, or pact, that is made between the president and another head of state and that does not require Senate approval.

The Power to Make Executive Agreements
Presidential power in foreign affairs is enhanced by the ability to make **executive agreements,** which are pacts between the president and other heads of state. Executive agreements do not require Senate approval (even though Congress may refuse to appropriate the necessary funds to carry out the agreements), but they have the same legal status as treaties.

Presidents form executive agreements for a wide range of purposes. Some involve routine matters, such as promises of trade or assistance to other countries. Others concern matters of great importance. In 1940, for example, President Franklin D. Roosevelt formed an important executive agreement with Prime Minister Winston Churchill of Great Britain. The agreement provided that the United States would lend American destroyers to Britain to help protect that nation's land and shipping during World War II. In return, the British allowed the United States to use military and naval bases on British territories in the Western Hemisphere.

To prevent presidential abuse of the power to make executive agreements, Congress passed a law in 1972 that requires the president to inform Congress within sixty days of making any executive agreement. The law did not limit the president's power to make executive agreements, however, and they continue to be used far more than treaties in making foreign policy.

Franklin D. Roosevelt and Winston Churchill discuss matters relating to World War II aboard a British battleship in August 1941.

Presidential Military Actions
As you have read, the U.S. Constitution gives Congress the power to declare war. Consider, however, that although Congress has declared war in only five different conflicts during our nation's history,[14] the United States has engaged in more than two hundred activities involving the armed services. Before the United States entered World War II in 1941, Franklin D. Roosevelt ordered the Navy to "shoot on sight" any German submarine that appeared in the Western Hemisphere security zone. Without a congressional declaration of war, President Truman sent U.S. armed forces to Korea in 1950, thus involving American troops in the conflict between North and South Korea.

The United States also entered the Vietnam War (1964–1975) without a congressional declaration, and President Lyndon B. Johnson personally selected targets and ordered bombing missions during that war. President Nixon personally made the decision to invade Cambodia in 1970. President Reagan sent troops to Lebanon and Grenada in 1983 and ordered American fighter planes to attack Libya in 1986 in retaliation for terrorist attacks on American soldiers. No congres-

Bettmann/Corbis

sional vote was taken before President George H. W. Bush sent troops into Panama in 1989. Bush did, however, obtain congressional approval to use American troops to force Iraq to withdraw from Kuwait in 1991. President Bill Clinton made the decision to send troops to Haiti in 1994 and to Bosnia in 1995, and to bomb Iraq in 1998. In 1999, he also decided to send U.S. forces, under the command of NATO (the North Atlantic Treaty Organization), to bomb Yugoslavia.

The War Powers Resolution As commander in chief, the president can respond quickly to a military threat without waiting for congressional action. This power to commit troops and to involve the nation in a war upset many members of Congress as the undeclared war in Vietnam dragged on for years into the 1970s. Criticism of the president's role in the Vietnam conflict led to the passage of the War Powers Resolution of 1973, which limits the president's war-making powers. The law, which was passed over Nixon's veto, requires the president to notify Congress within forty-eight hours of deploying troops. It also prevents the president from sending troops abroad for more than sixty days (or ninety days, if more time is needed for a successful withdrawal). If Congress does not authorize a longer period, the troops must be removed.

The War on Terrorism President George W. Bush did not obtain a declaration of war from Congress for the war against terrorism that began on September 11, 2001. Instead, Congress invoked the War Powers Resolution and passed a joint resolution authorizing the president to use "all necessary and appropriate force against those nations, organizations, or persons he determines planned, authorized, committed, or aided the terrorist attacks that occurred on September 11, 2001." The resolution set no date for Bush to halt military operations, and, as a consequence, the president has invoked certain emergency wartime measures. For example, through executive order the president created military tribunals for trying terrorist suspects. The president has also held American citizens as "enemy combatants," denying them access to their attorneys (see Chapter 5 for a discussion of this issue).

Nuclear Weapons Since 1945, the president, as commander in chief, has been responsible for the most difficult of all military decisions—if and when to use nuclear weapons. In 1945, Harry Truman made the awesome decision to drop atomic bombs on the Japanese cities of Hiroshima and Nagasaki. "The final decision," he said, "on where and when to use the atomic bomb was up to me. Let there be no mistake about it." Today, the president travels at all times with the "football"—the briefcase containing the codes used to launch a nuclear attack.

President Bush speaks at the U.S. Coast Guard installation in Philadelphia in March 2003. Bush, linking war in Iraq to his global antiterrorism campaign, warned that Saddam Hussein or his terrorist allies might try to strike America in retaliation for the U.S.-led fighting.

Congressional and Presidential Relations

Despite the seemingly immense powers at the president's disposal, the president is limited in what he or she can accomplish, or even attempt. In our system of checks and balances, the president must share some powers with the legislative and judicial branches of government. And the president's power is checked not only by these institutions, but also by the media, public opinion, and the voters. The founders hoped that this system of shared power would lessen the chance of tyranny. The consequence, however, has sometimes been an inability by the president to exercise decisive leadership. William Cohen, secretary of defense in the Clinton administration, once said about the American system of checks and balances: "The difficulty with this diffusion of power . . . is that everyone is in check, but no one is in charge."[15]

Some scholars believe the relationship between Congress and the president is the most important one in the American system of government.[16] Congress has the upper hand in relation to the president in some distinct areas, primarily in passing legislation. In some other areas, though, particularly in foreign affairs, the president can exert tremendous power that Congress is virtually unable to check.

Advantage: Congress

Congress has the advantage over the president in the areas of legislative authorization, the regulation of foreign and interstate commerce, and some budgetary matters. Of course, as you have already read, the president today proposes a legislative agenda and a budget to Congress every year. Nonetheless, only Congress has the power to pass the legislation and appropriate the funds. The most the president can do constitutionally is veto an entire bill if it contains something that the president does not like.

As you have read, presidential popularity is considered to be a source of power for the president in relation to Congress. Presidents spend a great deal of time courting public opinion, eyeing the "presidential approval ratings," and meeting with the press. Much of this activity is for the purpose of gaining leverage with Congress. The president can put all of his or her persuasive powers to work in achieving a legislative agenda, but Congress retains the ultimate lawmaking authority.

Divided Government   When government is divided—with at least one house of Congress controlled by a different party than the White House—the president can have diffi-

President Bush is surrounded by members of Congress in April 2001, in the Rose Garden of the White House. Bush invited the lawmakers to the White House for a luncheon to mark the president's first one hundred days in office and to promote bipartisanship.

AP Photo/Ron Edmonds

culty getting a legislative agenda to the floor for a vote. President Bill Clinton found this to be the case after the congressional elections of 1994 brought the Republicans to power in Congress. Clinton's success rate in implementing his legislative agenda dropped to 36.2 percent in 1995, after a high of 86.4 the previous year (see Figure 12–1 on page 279).

Different Constituencies   Congress and the president have different constituencies, and this fact influences their relationship. Members of Congress represent a state or a local district, and this gives them a particularly regional focus. As we discussed in Chapter 11, members of Congress like to have legislative successes of their own to bring home to their constituents—military bases that remain open, public-works projects that create local jobs, or trade rules that benefit a big, local employer. Ideally, the president's focus should be on the nation as a whole: national defense, homeland security, the national economy. At times, this can put the president at odds even with members of his or her own party in Congress.

Furthermore, members of Congress and the president face different election cycles (every two years in the House, every six years in the Senate, and every four years for the president), and the president is limited to two terms in office. Consequently, the president and Congress sometimes feel a different sense of urgency about implementing legislation. For example, the president often feels the need to demonstrate legislative success during the first year in office, when the excitement over the elections is still fresh in the minds of politicians and the public.

Advantage: The President

The president has the advantage over Congress in dealing with a national crisis, in setting foreign policy, and in influencing public opinion. In times of crisis, the presidency is arguably the most crucial institution in government because, when necessary, the president can act quickly, speak with one voice, and represent the nation to the world. George W. Bush's presidency was unquestionably changed by the terrorist attacks of September 11, 2001. He represented the United States as it was under attack from foreign enemies and reeling from shock and horror. The president swiftly announced his resolve to respond to the terrorist attacks. No member of Congress could wield the kind of personal power that accrues to a president in a time of national crisis. (See this chapter's *The Politics of National Security* feature on the next page for more on presidential power during national emergencies.)

The framers of the Constitution recognized the need for individual leadership in foreign affairs. They gave the president the power to negotiate treaties and lead the armed forces. Some scholars have argued that recent presidents have abused the powers of the presidency by committing U.S. troops to undeclared wars and by negotiating secret agreements without consulting Congress. For example, Arthur M. Schlesinger, Jr., wrote in 1972 of an "imperial presidency," referring in particular to the extensive war powers used by Lyndon Johnson and Richard Nixon in conducting the Vietnam War. For example, in 1970 Nixon ordered secret bombing raids of Cambodia and Laos, Vietnam's neighbors, thereby expanding the war.

Others have argued that there is an unwritten "doctrine of necessity" under which presidential powers can and should be expanded during a crisis. When this has happened in the past, however, Congress has always retaken some control when the crisis was over, in a natural process of institutional give-and-take.

Executive Privilege

As you read in Chapter 11, Congress has the authority to investigate and oversee the activities of other branches of government. Nonetheless, both Congress and the public have accepted that a certain degree of secrecy by the executive branch is necessary to protect national security. Some presidents have claimed an inherent executive power to withhold information from, or to refuse to appear before, Congress or the courts. This is called **executive privilege,** and it has been invoked by presidents from George Washington to George W. Bush.

One of the problems with executive privilege is that it has been used for more purposes than simply to safeguard national security secrets. President Nixon invoked executive privilege in an attempt to avoid handing over taped White House conversations to Congress during the

executive privilege An inherent executive power claimed by presidents to withhold information from, or to refuse to appear before, Congress or the courts. The president can also accord the privilege to other executive officials.

Presidential Power in a Time of Crisis

Thomas Cronin and Michael Genovese, in their work on the American presidency, point out that there are cycles in politics over which the president has little control. Yet these cycles influence presidential power. "There are times when, and conditions under which, presidents are afforded considerable leverage and power. There are also times when presidents are kept on a short leash."[17] When George W. Bush became president, many observers assumed that he would be one of those presidents who are granted limited power to influence the domestic agenda or foreign policy. September 11, 2001, changed that perception entirely. In some circles, Bush is now regarded as one of the most powerful presidents in decades.

LEADERSHIP STYLE

George W. Bush became president under inauspicious circumstances: he lost the popular vote to his opponent, Al Gore, and he won the electoral college only after the Supreme Court intervened in the ballot counting in Florida. Even subsequent to the leap in Bush's approval ratings after September 11, 2001, from 51 percent the week before the attacks to 90 percent two weeks after the attacks, there were doubts about his leadership. Many in the news media suggested that he was not prepared for the task of leading the nation to war. Bush came to the presidency with little experience in foreign policy. He prefers to delegate the more mundane aspects of the day-to-day operations of his office. Some scholars have pointed out that he does not possess a "deliberative" leadership style and lacks an understanding of the broader implications of his decisions.[18]

SOURCES OF BUSH'S POWER

Despite these shortcomings, Bush has proved to be confident, outgoing, and adept at rallying public support. By taking an active role in the congressional elections of 2002, he managed to secure something of the "mandate" he lacked after his own election in 2000. Bush campaigned aggressively for Republican candidates, making the congressional elections about national issues such as homeland security and a potential war in Iraq. Republicans regained control of the Senate and increased their majority in the House. In 2004, Bush's efforts on behalf of congressional candidates helped the Republicans increase their majorities in both chambers.

The successes on Election Day in 2002 and 2004 are just one source of Bush's power. In 2002, he persuaded Congress to vote overwhelmingly in favor of a war in Iraq if Iraqi president Saddam Hussein failed to appropriately disarm. Then he achieved a resounding success at the United Nations by securing a unanimous vote from the Security Council to challenge Saddam Hussein and reinstate weapons inspections. As columnist James Klurfeld pointed out at the end of 2002, Bush "has support to start a war against Iraq any time he wants, . . . and at a time when there is no challenger to United States military power."[19]

In early 2003, Bush faced increasingly vocal opposition to war in Iraq from the public and some members of Congress, as well as challenges from France and Germany to his policy in Iraq. In March 2003, however, Bush opted to invade Iraq despite this opposition. The nation remains divided on U.S. foreign policy in Iraq.

AP Photo/Doug Mills

President Bush talks with then Senate Majority Leader Tom Daschle (D., S.Dak.), left, as Vice President Dick Cheney and Speaker of the House of Representatives Dennis Hastert (R., Ill.), second from left, join in during a meeting with congressional leaders in the White House Oval Office in September 2002.

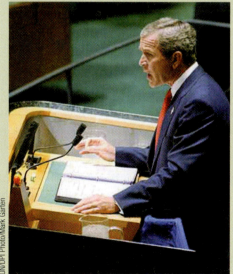

UN/DPI Photo/Mark Garten

President Bush addresses the United Nations General Assembly.

Are We Safer?

Do you think that the president should be given emergency powers in a time of crisis, even if this risks upsetting the system of checks and balances established by the Constitution?

Watergate scandal. President Clinton invoked the privilege in an attempt to keep details of his sexual relationship with Monica Lewinsky a secret. President George W. Bush claimed executive privilege to keep Tom Ridge, when he was director of the Office of Homeland Security, from testifying before Congress. Some scholars have argued that invoking executive privilege has impeded legitimate congressional investigations and that Congress should pass a law to ban its use or that the Supreme Court should find it unconstitutional.

Since the war on terrorism began, the Bush administration has maintained that it has been compelled—for our safety—to keep more information secret than ever before. Information about homeland security measures and protection of vital infrastructure, such as nuclear power facilities, has been kept secret. In 2002, then attorney general John Ashcroft even instructed federal agencies to remove previously public information from Web sites.[20] Executive privilege was challenged by the 9/11 Commission in July 2004, however. This was a bipartisan congressional panel formed to investigate how the government handled intelligence leading up to the September 11 attacks. The 9/11 Commission ultimately gained access to the president's daily intelligence briefings. These highly classified briefings had previously been considered privileged material accessible only to the president and top administration officials.

The Organization of the Executive Branch

In the early days of this nation, presidents answered their own mail, as George Washington did. Only in 1857 did Congress authorize a private secretary for the president, to be paid by the federal government. Even Woodrow Wilson typed most of his correspondence, although by that time several secretaries were assigned to the president. When Franklin D. Roosevelt became president in 1933, the entire staff consisted of thirty-seven employees. Only after Roosevelt's New Deal and World War II did the presidential staff become a sizable organization.

The President's Cabinet

The Constitution does not specifically mention presidential assistants and advisers. The Constitution states only that the president "may require the Opinion, in writing, of the principal Officer in each of the executive Departments." Since the time of our first president, presidents have had an advisory group, or **cabinet,** to turn to for counsel. Originally, the cabinet consisted of only four officials—the secretaries of state, treasury, and war and the attorney general. Today, the cabinet includes fourteen secretaries and the attorney general (see Table 12–3 on the next page for the names of cabinet members as of 2005).

Because the Constitution does not require the president to consult with the cabinet, its use is purely discretionary. Some presidents have relied on the counsel of their cabinets. Other presidents solicited the opinions of their cabinets and then did what they wanted to do anyway. After a cabinet meeting in which a vote was seven nays against his one aye, President Lincoln supposedly said, "Seven nays and one aye, the ayes have it."[21] Still other presidents have sought counsel from so-called **kitchen cabinets.** A kitchen cabinet is a very informal group of persons, such as Ronald Reagan's trusted California coterie, to whom the president turns for advice. The term *kitchen cabinet* originated during the presidency of Andrew Jackson, who relied on the counsel of close friends who often met with him in the kitchen of the White House.

In general, few presidents have relied heavily on the advice of the formal cabinet, and often presidents meet with their cabinet heads only reluctantly. To a certain extent, the growth of other components of the executive branch has rendered the formal cabinet less significant as an advisory board to the president. Additionally, the department heads are at times more responsive to the wishes of their own staffs or to their own political ambitions than they are to the president. They may be more concerned with obtaining resources for their departments than with helping presidents achieve their goals. As a result, there is often a conflict of interest between presidents and their cabinet members. It is likely that formal cabinet meetings are held more out of respect for the cabinet tradition than for their problem-solving value.

Watergate scandal A scandal involving an illegal break-in at the Democratic National Committee offices in 1972 by members of President Nixon's reelection campaign staff. Before Congress could vote to impeach Nixon for his participation in covering up the break-in, Nixon resigned from the presidency.

cabinet An advisory group selected by the president to assist with decision making. Traditionally, the cabinet has consisted of the heads of the executive departments and other officers whom the president may choose to appoint.

kitchen cabinet The name given to a president's unofficial advisers. The term was coined during Andrew Jackson's presidency.

TABLE 12-3

The Cabinet as of 2005

Executive Office of the President (EOP) A group of staff agencies that assist the president in carrying out major duties. Franklin D. Roosevelt established the EOP in 1939 to cope with the increased responsibilities brought on by the Great Depression.

White House Office The personal office of the president. White House Office personnel handle the president's political needs and manage the media.

chief of staff The person who directs the operations of the White House Office and who advises the president on important matters.

press secretary A member of the White House staff who holds news conferences for reporters and makes public statements for the president.

The Executive Office of the President

In 1939, President Franklin D. Roosevelt set up the **Executive Office of the President (EOP)** to cope with the increased responsibilities brought on by the Great Depression. Since then, the EOP has grown significantly to accommodate the expansive role played by the national government, including the executive branch, in the nation's economic and social life.

The EOP is made up of the top advisers and assistants who help the president carry out major duties. The EOP also includes the staff of the First Lady. First Ladies have at times taken important, independent roles within the White House. For example, Eleanor Roosevelt wrote a newspaper column entitled "My Day" and advocated women's and civil rights. Hillary Rodham Clinton attempted to rally support for a national health-care system and won a seat in the U.S. Senate following her husband's tenure in the White House. Many speculate that she will eventually run for president.

Over the years, the EOP has changed according to the needs and leadership style of each president. It has become an increasingly influential and important part of the executive branch. Table 12–4 lists various offices within the EOP. We look at some of the key offices of the EOP in the following subsections.

The White House Office   Of all of the executive staff agencies, the **White House Office** has the most direct contact with the president. The White House Office is headed by the **chief of staff,** who advises the president on important matters and directs the operations of the presidential staff. The chief of staff, who is often a close, personal friend of the president, has been one of the most influential of the presidential aides in recent years. A number of other top officials, assistants, and special assistants to the president also aid him in such areas as national security, the economy, and political affairs. A **press secretary** meets with reporters and makes public statements for the president. The counsel to the president serves as the White House lawyer and handles the president's legal matters. The White House staff also includes speechwriters, researchers, the president's physician, the director of the staff for the First Lady, and a correspondence secretary. Altogether, the White House Office has more than four hundred employees.

The White House staff has several duties. First, the staff investigates and analyzes problems that require the president's attention. Staff members who are specialists in certain areas, such as diplomatic relations or foreign trade, gather information for the president and suggest solutions. White House staff members also screen the questions, issues, and problems that people present to the president, so matters that can be handled by other officials do not reach the president's desk. Additionally, the staff provides public relations support. For example, the press staff handles the president's relations with the White House press corps and schedules news conferences. Finally, the White House staff ensures that the president's initiatives are effectively transmitted to the relevant government personnel. Several staff members are usually assigned to work directly with members of Congress for this purpose.

The Office of Management and Budget

The **Office of Management and Budget (OMB)** was originally the Bureau of the Budget. Under recent presidents, the OMB has become an important and influential unit of the Executive Office of the President. The main function of the OMB is to assist the president in preparing the proposed annual budget, which the president must submit to Congress in January of each year (see Chapter 11 for details on preparing the annual budget). The federal budget lists the revenues and expenditures expected for the coming year. It indicates which programs the federal government will pay for and how much they will cost. Thus, the budget is an annual statement of the public policies of the United States translated into dollars and cents. Making changes in the budget is a key way for presidents to try to influence the direction and policies of the federal government.

The president appoints the director of the OMB with the consent of the Senate. The director of the OMB has become at least as important as the cabinet members and is often included in cabinet meetings. She or he oversees the OMB's work and argues the administration's position before Congress. The director also lobbies members of Congress to support the president's budget or to accept key features of it. Once the budget is approved by Congress, the OMB has the responsibility of putting it into practice. The OMB oversees the execution of the budget, checking the federal agencies to ensure that they use funds efficiently.

Beyond its budget duties, the OMB also reviews new bills prepared by the executive branch. It checks all legislative matters to be certain that they agree with the president's own position.

Office of Management and Budget (OMB) An agency in the Executive Office of the President that assists the president in preparing and supervising the administration of the federal budget.

TABLE 12–4
The Executive Office of the President

DEPARTMENT	YEAR ESTABLISHED
White House Office	1939
Office of the Vice President of the United States	1939
Council of Economic Advisers	1946
National Security Council	1947
Office of the U.S. Trade Representative	1963
Council on Environmental Quality	1969
Office of Management and Budget	1970
Office of Science and Technology Policy	1976
Office of Administration	1977
Office of Policy Development	1977
—Domestic Policy Council	1993
—National Economic Council	1993
Office of National Drug Control Policy	1989

SOURCE: *United States Government Manual, 2004/05* (Washington, D.C.: U.S. Government Printing Office, 2004).

Council of Economic Advisers (CEA)
A three-member council created in 1946 to advise the president on economic matters.

National Security Council (NSC) A council that advises the president on domestic and foreign matters concerning the safety and defense of the nation; established in 1947.

The Council of Economic Advisers   The Employment Act of 1946 established a **Council of Economic Advisers (CEA),** consisting of three members, to advise the president on economic matters. For the most part, the function of the CEA has been to prepare the annual economic report to Congress. Each of the three members is appointed by the president and can be removed at will.

The National Security Council   The **National Security Council (NSC)** was established in 1947 to manage the defense and foreign policy of the United States. Its members are the president, the vice president, and the secretaries of state and defense; it also has several informal advisers. The NSC is the president's link to his key foreign and military advisers. The president's special assistant for national security affairs heads the NSC staff.

The Vice Presidency and Presidential Succession

As a rule, presidential nominees choose running mates who balance the ticket or whose appointment rewards or appeases party factions. For example, a presidential candidate from the South may solicit a running mate from the West. President Clinton ignored this tradition when he selected Senator Al Gore of Tennessee as his running mate in 1992 and in 1996. Gore, close in age and ideology to Clinton, also came from the mid-South. Despite these similarities, Clinton gained two advantages by choosing Gore: Gore's appeal to environmentalists and Gore's compatibility with Clinton.

George W. Bush picked Dick Cheney, a well-known Republican with extensive political experience in Washington, D.C. Among other things, Cheney had held the post of secretary of defense in the administration of Bush's father (1989–1993). The appointment of Cheney helped Bush gather support from those who thought his lack of national political experience and familiarity with Washington politics would be a handicap.

The Role of Vice Presidents   Vice presidents play a unique role in the American political system. On the one hand, they are usually regarded as appendages to the presidency and can wield little power on their own. For much of our history, the vice president has had almost no responsibilities. (In recent years, however, vice presidents, including Al Gore and Dick Cheney, have been important presidential advisers.) On the other hand, the vice president is in a position to become the nation's chief executive should the president die, be impeached, or resign the presidential office. Eight vice presidents have become president because of the death of the president.

President Bush meets with members of his Cabinet at the White House in 2005.

EPA/Win McNamee/Pool/Landov

Presidential Succession One of the questions left unanswered by the Constitution was what the vice president should do if the president becomes incapable of carrying out necessary duties while in office. The Twenty-fifth Amendment to the Constitution, ratified in 1967, filled this gap. The amendment states that when the president believes that he is incapable of performing the duties of his office, he must inform Congress in writing of this fact. Then the vice president serves as acting president until the president can resume his normal duties. For example, President George W. Bush invoked the Twenty-fifth Amendment in 2002 before undergoing a colonoscopy.

When the president is unable to communicate, a majority of the cabinet, including the vice president, can declare that fact to Congress. Then the vice president serves as acting president until the president resumes normal duties. If a dispute arises over the return of the president's ability to discharge the normal functions of the presidential office, a two-thirds vote of Congress is required to decide whether the vice president shall remain acting president or whether the president shall resume these duties.

The Twenty-fifth Amendment also addresses the question of how the president should fill a vacant vice presidency. Section 2 of the amendment states, "Whenever there is a vacancy in the office of the Vice President, the President shall nominate a Vice President who shall take office upon confirmation by a majority vote of both Houses of Congress."

In 1973, Gerald Ford became the first appointed vice president of the United States after Spiro Agnew was forced to resign. One year later, President Richard Nixon resigned, and Ford advanced to the office of president. President Ford named Nelson Rockefeller as his vice president. For the first time in U.S. history, neither the president nor the vice president was elected to his position.

What if both the president and the vice president die, resign, or are disabled? According to the Succession Act of 1947, then the Speaker of the House of Representatives will act as president on his resignation as Speaker and as representative. If the Speaker is unavailable, next in line is the president pro tem of the Senate, followed by members of the president's cabinet in the order of the creation of their departments (see Table 12–5).

Vice President Dick Cheney addresses a town meeting held at La Roche College near Pittsburgh, Pennsylvania, on the subject of Social Security in 2005.

UPI/Archie Carpenter/Landov

TABLE 12–5

The Line of Succession to the U.S. Presidency

1	Vice president
2	Speaker of the House of Representatives
3	President pro tem of the Senate
4	Secretary of the Department of State
5	Secretary of the Department of the Treasury
6	Secretary of the Department of Defense
7	Attorney general
8	Secretary of the Department of the Interior
9	Secretary of the Department of Agriculture
10	Secretary of the Department of Commerce
11	Secretary of the Department of Labor
12	Secretary of the Department of Health and Human Services
13	Secretary of the Department of Housing and Urban Development
14	Secretary of the Department of Transportation
15	Secretary of the Department of Energy
16	Secretary of the Department of Education
17	Secretary of the Department of Veterans Affairs
18	Secretary of the Department of Homeland Security

The Presidency and Your Everyday Life

Certainly, the presidency affects your everyday life in the sense that the media treat you to a daily dose of every activity the president engages in, whether it be taking a jog, acquiring a new dog, or attending church. Everyone accepts the daily entertainment value of examining the current president through a microscope. More important to your daily life, though, are the vast powers the president can wield. As one example, the president's ability, through executive order, to declare large areas of American land as national monuments can affect your life.

AP Photo/Nick Ut

Executive Orders and More

Because the president is our chief executive, presidential executive orders have the force of law. In principle, executive orders are issued to carry out policies that have been described in laws that have been passed by Congress. In reality, some presidents have used executive orders extensively, perhaps even illegally. In 1971, for example, President Richard M. Nixon issued an executive order establishing wage and price controls for the entire United States. The effect on each American's everyday life was profound. The order led to shortages of gasoline and a number of other problems in the marketplace. In all, by the time George W. Bush assumed the presidency, his forty-two predecessors in that office had issued 13,500 executive orders.

In addition to issuing executive orders, presidents can affect your everyday life in other ways. For example, the president proposes most major legislation, even though all legislation must be introduced by members of Congress. Had President Bill Clinton's proposed overhaul of our nation's health-care system been successful in the last decade, your everyday life with respect to medical care would have been dramatically changed. Although Congress decides how much is actually spent, it is now the president's Office of Management and Budget that prepares the budget each year.

Taking Action

If you believe that the president now in office should (or should not) take a particular action, you can get involved. One way to do this is by contacting your political representatives to voice your views. For example, in 2003, supporters of the "Win without War" campaign organized a "virtual" march on Washington. The actors shown in the photo to the left (including Tyne Daly in the foreground) contacted participants in the campaign and asked them all to phone, fax, or e-mail their representatives in Congress about their opposition to a war with Iraq.

Key Terms

cabinet 285

chief diplomat 271

chief executive 269

chief of staff 286

chief of state 271

commander in chief 269

Council of Economic
 Advisers (CEA) 288

diplomat 271

executive
 agreement 280

Executive Office of the
 President (EOP) 286

executive order 278

executive privilege 283

kitchen cabinet 285

National Security Council
 (NSC) 288

Office of Management
 and Budget
 (OMB) 287

patronage 272

press secretary 286

treaty 273

veto 274

Watergate scandal 285

White House Office 286

Chapter Summary

1 The Constitution sets forth relatively few requirements for becoming president. To be eligible for the presidency, a person must be a natural-born citizen, at least thirty-five years of age, and a U.S. resident for fourteen years. Most presidents have been well educated, and many have been wealthy. The average age of presidents at the time of their inauguration has been fifty-four. To date, all U.S. presidents have been male, white, and (with the exception of John F. Kennedy, who was a Roman Catholic) from the Protestant tradition.

2 Article II of the Constitution makes the president the nation's chief executive, commander in chief, and chief of state. Over time, the president has also assumed other roles, such as chief diplomat and chief legislator. The president is also the leader of his political party.

3 The Constitution gives the president explicit powers, such as the power to propose and ratify treaties, to grant reprieves and pardons, and to veto acts of Congress. Over time, the scope of the president's power has expanded beyond these explicit powers. For example, the president also has certain inherent powers—powers necessary to fulfill the presidential responsibilities explicitly mentioned in the Constitution. The president's powers to persuade and to conduct foreign affairs are also significant.

4 The relationship between the president and Congress is arguably one of the most important institutional relationships in American government. Congress has the advantage in this relationship in certain areas, such as legislative authorization, the regulation of foreign and interstate commerce, and some budgetary matters. The president has the advantage in other areas, such as in dealing with a national crisis, setting foreign policy, and influencing public opinion.

5 The cabinet—advisers to the president—consists of the heads of the fifteen executive departments. Some presidents have preferred to rely on the counsel of close friends and associates (sometimes called a "kitchen cabinet").

6 The president also receives advice from the members of the Executive Office of the President (including the White House Office, the Office of Management and Budget, the Council of Economic Advisers, and the National Security Council).

7 The vice president is next in line for the presidency if the president should die, be impeached, resign from office, or become incapacitated. The Twenty-fifth Amendment sets out procedures to be followed in the event the president becomes incapacitated. The Succession Act of 1947 established the line of succession to the presidency in the event that both the president and the vice president die or become unable to fulfill their responsibilities (see Table 12–5 on page 289).

RESOURCES FOR FURTHER STUDY

Selected Readings

Adler, David Gray, and Michael A. Genovese, eds. *The Presidency and the Law: The Clinton Legacy.* Lawrence, Kans.: University of Kansas Press, 2002. This book assesses the change in our constitutional and legal understanding of the American presidency, exploring such topics as war power, executive privilege, impeachment, and pardon power.

Barber, James David. *Presidential Character: Predicting Performance in the White House,* 4th ed. Englewood Cliffs, N.J.: Prentice Hall, 1992. Now in its fourth edition, this book is a classic study of political psychology. Barber identifies four presidential personality types and argues that one can use these types to predict how presidential candidates will perform once in office.

Cronin, Thomas E., and Michael A. Genovese. *The Paradoxes of the American Presidency.* New York: Oxford University Press, 1998. This book examines the unique paradox in American government of democratic leadership—the vesting in one person of power that, by definition, is held by the people. It is an excellent examination of the vagaries of presidential power.

Thurber, James A., ed. *Rivals for Power: Presidential-Congressional Relations,* 2d ed. Lanham, Md.: Rowman & Littlefield, 2002. Legal scholars, political scientists, former White House staff, and former members of Congress all contribute to this examination of the rivalry between the president and Congress.

Walters, Ronald. *Freedom Is Not Enough: Black Voters, Black Candidates, and American Presidential Politics.* Lanham, Md.: Rowman & Littlefield, 2005. The author demonstrates why passing a law is not the same as ensuring the law's enforcement and legitimacy.

Politics on the Web

■ The White House home page offers links to numerous sources of information on the presidency. You can access this site at **http://www. whitehouse.gov**

■ For a variety of links on selected presidential writings and articles, go to the Library of Congress's "American Memory" Web page at **http://memory.loc.gov/ammen**

Click on "Presidents" and scroll down the list of links. (Note that one of the links provides a portrait of each president and First Lady.)

■ If you are interested in reading the inaugural addresses of American presidents from George Washington to George W. Bush, go to **http://www.bartleby.com/124**

In addition to the full text of the inaugural addresses, this site provides biographical information on the presidents.

■ If you would like to research documents and academic resources concerning the presidency, a good Internet site to consult is that provided by the University of Virginia's Miller Center of Public Affairs at **http://www. americanpresident.org**

■ To access the various presidential libraries, visit the National Archives site at **http://www.archives.gov/presidential_ libraries/index.html**

Online Resources for This Chapter

This text's Companion Web Site, at **http://www.americaatodds.com**, offers links to numerous resources that you can utilize to learn more about the topics covered in this chapter. For a list describing these resources, see the inside front cover of this book.

chapter **13**
the bureaucracy

CHAPTER OBJECTIVES

After reading this chapter, you should be able to . . .

▸ Describe the size and functions of the U.S. bureaucracy.

▸ Discuss the structure and basic components of the federal bureaucracy.

▸ Indicate when the federal civil service was established and explain how bureaucrats get their jobs.

▸ Explain how regulatory agencies make rules and the significance of agencies' rulemaking powers for American government.

▸ Identify the key players in "iron triangles" and explain how they affect policymaking in government.

293

Should the Federal Bureaucracy Be Privatized?

The president of the United States, as the head of the executive branch of the government, is the nation's chief administrator. Helping the president are the fifteen cabinet departments, hundreds of federal agencies, and some 2.7 million federal employees in the executive branch. This is what is meant by the federal bureaucracy. The cost of maintaining this bureaucracy is staggering—as you will read in this chapter.

To curb costs and increase efficiency, governments around the world have been experimenting with privatizing certain services traditionally performed by government. *Privatization* involves contracting with firms or individuals in the private sector to perform specific types of government services. Within the United States, state and local governments have privatized many of their services. To a limited extent, the federal government has also privatized some of its work. President George W. Bush has announced plans to go further in this direction and privatize some 850,000 federal jobs in the near future. Of course, certain types of government work that are inherently governmental in nature, such as intelligence gathering, cannot be contracted out to the private sector.

Is privatization the solution to the problems of bureaucratic waste and inflexibility? Americans are at odds over this issue. While some say yes, others are not so sure.

We Should Create a "Market-Based" Government

Those in favor of privatization argue that the private sector would deliver services more efficiently and at lower cost. This group contends that tax dollars should not be used to support services that could be better delivered by private firms. Private organizations that submit bids for government work must find ways to lower the cost of providing the services if they are to compete successfully with other bidders. Thus, if government programs were turned over to the marketplace, the inefficiencies characteristic of government-run operations would disappear.

Consider just one example—the National Railroad Passenger Corporation (Amtrak). Although its passengers pay a higher fare per mile than the average airline or bus passenger, Amtrak has trouble meeting its operating costs. Indeed, keeping Amtrak afloat has cost the taxpayers more than $25 billion since its creation in 1970.[1] Proponents of privatization claim that if Amtrak were privatized, Americans would have better rail service at lower cost.

Some have suggested a type of privatization called "managed competition," in which government agencies compete with private organizations for the job of providing specific services. If a government agency could perform the work at a lower cost, then the agency would retain the job. Forcing the bureaucracy to compete with the private sector could help to create a more efficient government.

We Should Not Put Government Services Up for Sale

Other Americans are less optimistic about the outcome of privatizing the work of the bureaucracy. Among the strongest opponents of privatization are the labor unions that protect the rights of government workers. For example, the American Federation of State, County, and Municipal Employees (AFSCME) contends not only that the benefits of contracting out government services are elusive but also that employee welfare would suffer—because employees in the private sector usually have fewer rights than government employees enjoy.

The AFSCME also points out that when state and local governments have experimented with privatization, the public sector has frequently outperformed the private sector. Furthermore, contracting out has led to some giant boondoggles. In New Jersey, for example, a privately run vehicle inspection program cost taxpayers $247 million more than it would have cost if run by the state.[2]

Generally, those who oppose privatization believe that the quality of government services deteriorates when profit making becomes a factor in the delivery of services. Additionally, the private sector is less sensitive to the needs of minority and disadvantaged groups than government agencies traditionally have been. Finally, opponents feel that the expertise of government bureaucrats is especially necessary today, when we face the threat of terrorist attacks and need to respond effectively.

Where Do You Stand?

1. In your opinion, which kinds of government work could be handled just as well, if not better, by the private sector? Why?
2. The argument for privatization is based on the idea that competition for government work will increase efficiency and lower costs. Do you agree? Why or why not?

Explore This Issue Online

- Reason Foundation runs a Web site devoted to providing information on privatization and government reform. Go to **http://www.privatization.org**.
- The AFSCME offers arguments against government privatization at **http://www.afscme.org/private/**.

Introduction

Did you eat breakfast this morning? If you did, **bureaucrats**—individuals who work in the offices of government—had a lot to do with that breakfast. If you had bacon, the meat was inspected by federal agents. If you drank milk, the price was affected by rules and regulations of the Department of Agriculture. If you looked at a cereal box, you saw fine print about minerals and vitamins, which was the result of regulations made by several other federal agencies, including the Food and Drug Administration. If you ate leftover pizza for breakfast, bureaucrats made sure that the kitchen of the pizza house was sanitary and safe and that the employees who put together (and perhaps delivered) the pizza were protected against discrimination in the workplace.

Today, the word *bureaucracy* often evokes a negative reaction. For some, it conjures up visions of depersonalized automatons performing their chores without any sensitivity toward the needs of those they serve. For others, it is synonymous with government "red tape." A **bureaucracy,** however, is simply a large, complex administrative organization that is structured hierarchically in a pyramid-like fashion.[3] Government bureaucrats carry out the policies of elected government officials. Bureaucrats deliver our mail, clean our streets, teach in our public schools, and run our national parks. Life as we know it would be impossible without government bureaucrats to keep our governments—federal, state, and local—in operation.

Some critics think that the bureaucracy has grown too big and is too costly to maintain. For some, privatization of the federal bureaucracy, or at least a sizable chunk of it, is one way to downsize the bureaucracy and save taxpayers' dollars—an issue discussed in this chapter's opening *America at Odds* feature. Before we examine the growth of the bureaucracy, though, we need first to look at its nature.

bureaucrat An individual who works in a bureaucracy. As generally used, the term refers to a government employee.

bureaucracy A large, complex, hierarchically structured administrative organization that carries out specific functions.

The Nature and Size of the Bureaucracy

The concept of a bureaucracy is not confined to the federal government. Any large organization has to have a bureaucracy. In each bureaucracy, everybody (except the head of the bureaucracy) reports to at least one other person. For the federal government, the head of the bureaucracy is the president of the United States, and the bureaucracy is part of the executive branch.[4]

The government, through its bureaucracy, extensively regulates American social and economic life. Here, employees of the Environmental Protection Agency run tests at a toxic waste clean-up site in Denver.

A. Ramey/PhotoEdit

A bureaucratic form of organization allows each person to concentrate on her or his area of knowledge and expertise. In your college or university, for example, you do not expect the basketball coach to solve the problems of the finance department. The reason the bureaucracy exists is that Congress, over time, has delegated certain tasks to specialists. For example, in 1914, Congress passed the Federal Trade Commission Act, which established the Federal Trade Commission to regulate deceptive and unfair trade practices. Those appointed to the commission were specialists in this area. Similarly, in 1972, Congress passed the Consumer Product Safety Act, which established the Consumer Product Safety Commission to investigate the safety of consumer products placed on the market. The commission is one of many federal administrative agencies.

Another key aspect of any bureaucracy is that the power to act resides in the *position* rather than in the *person.* In your college or university, the person who is currently president has more or less the same authority as any previous president. Additionally, bureaucracies usually entail standard operating procedures—directives on what procedures should be followed in specific circumstances. Bureaucracies normally also have a merit system, meaning that people are hired and promoted on the basis of demonstrated skills and achievements.

The Growth of Bureaucracy

The federal government that existed in 1789 was small. It had three departments, each with only a few employees: (1) the Department of State (nine employees); (2) the Department of War (two employees); and (3) the Department of the Treasury (thirty-nine employees). By 1798, the federal bureaucracy was still quite small. The secretary of state had seven clerks. His total expenditures on stationery and printing amounted to $500, or about $6,100 in 2005 dollars. The Department of War spent, on average, a grand total of $1.4 million each year, or about $17.1 million in 2003 dollars.

Times have changed. Figure 13–1 shows the growth in the number of government employees since 1975. Most growth has been at the state and local levels. All in all, the three levels of government employ about 15 percent of the civilian labor force. Currently, more Americans are employed by government (at all three levels) than by the entire manufacturing sector of the U.S. economy.

During election campaigns, politicians throughout the nation claim they will "cut big government and red tape" and "get rid of overlapping and wasteful bureaucracies." For the last several decades, virtually every president has campaigned on a platform calling for a reduction in the size of the federal bureaucracy. Yet, at the same time, candidates promise to establish programs that require new employees—even if they are "consultants" who are not officially counted as part of the bureaucracy.

FIGURE 13–1
Government Employment at Federal, State, and Local Levels

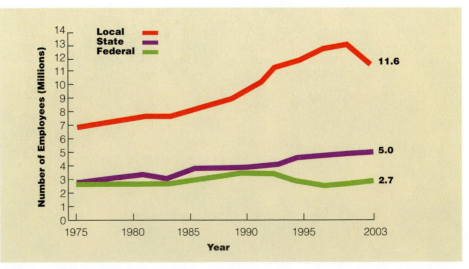

SOURCE: U.S. Department of Commerce, Bureau of the Census, 2005.

The Costs of Maintaining the Government

The costs of maintaining the government are high and growing. In 1929, government at all levels accounted for about 8.5 percent of the total national income in the United States. Today, that figure exceeds 30 percent of the nation's gross domestic product. The average citizen pays a similar portion of his or her income to federal, state, and local governments. You do this by paying income taxes, sales taxes, property taxes, and many other types of taxes and fees. To fully understand the amount of money spent by federal, state, and local governments each year, consider that the same sum of money could be used to purchase all of the farmland in the United States plus all of the assets of the one hundred largest American corporations.

The government is costly, to be sure, but it also provides numerous services for Americans. Cutting back on the size of government inevitably means a reduction in those services.

How the Federal Bureaucracy Is Organized

A complete organization chart of the federal government would cover an entire wall. A simplified version is provided in Figure 13–2. The executive branch consists of a number of

FIGURE 13-2

The Organization of the Federal Government

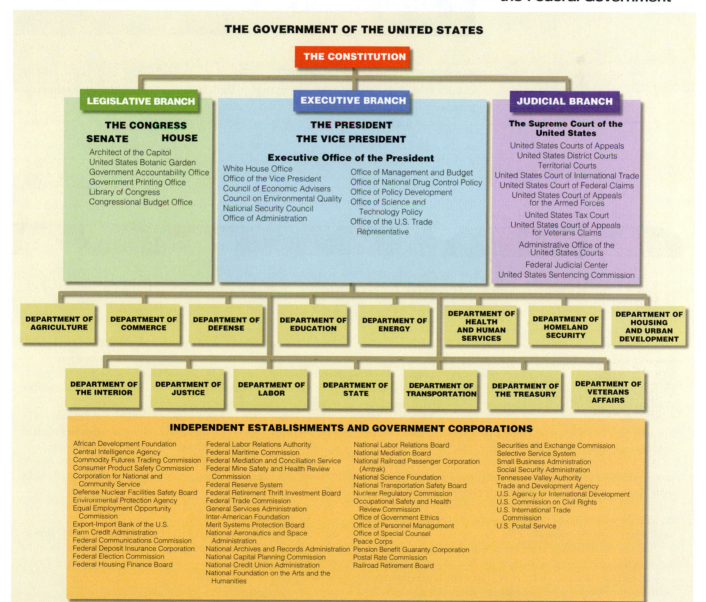

SOURCE: *United States Government Manual, 2004/05* (Washington, D.C.: U.S. Government Printing Office, 2004), p. 21.

Every day, hundreds of thousands of government employees report to work at various federal buildings across the country. In spite of recent attempts to downsize the bureaucracy, the total number of people working for all levels of government continues to rise.

Mark Richards/PhotoEdit

bureaucracies that provide services to Congress, to the federal courts, and to the president directly. (For a comparison of the organization of the U.S. bureaucracy with that of other countries, see this chapter's *Comparative Politics* feature.)

The executive branch of the federal government includes four major types of structures:

- Executive departments.
- Independent executive agencies.
- Independent regulatory agencies.
- Government corporations.

Each type of structure has its own relationship to the president and its own internal workings.

The U.S. Bureaucracy Really Is Special

Americans like to think that they are different, and with respect to the federal bureaucracy, they have a lot of facts to back them up. Consider that in the United States, the federal bureaucracy is controlled by several institutions. The president and Congress can exercise control over any agency. If you ever get appointed to a senior position in the federal bureaucracy, you will have to deal with two masters: the one who appointed you (the executive branch) and the one who pays you (Congress). Several congressional committees or subcommittees may also be able to nose around in your affairs.

Not so in Great Britain. In that country and in most parliamentary systems, the prime minister controls the cabinet ministers (the equivalent of our "secretaries") who appoint the bureaucrats. Most British and French bureaucrats, for example, have little or nothing to do with Parliament. Rather, they take orders only from the ministers in charge of their departments.

Because the U.S. political system is federal, as opposed to unitary (see Chapter 3), most agencies in the federal bureaucracy have counterparts at the state or local level. The federal agencies often work together with state and local agencies in performing certain

government functions. Consider the Department of Health and Human Services. It is involved with numerous state and local government agencies, and it often reimburses state and local governments for money spent on health care for the nation's underclass. The Department of Labor provides funds to state and local agencies to help pay for job-training programs.

In contrast, in any unitary system, by definition the number of subnational agencies is very limited. Local governments in France at the *département* (a unit of government somewhat like our county) and municipal levels have limited control over housing, education, or health and employment programs. Those programs are all run by the central government.

For Critical Analysis

Would a bureaucracy in a unitary system be more "efficient" than a bureaucracy in a federal system, such as the United States? Would a unitary or a federal system promote more responsiveness to citizens' needs?

AP Photo/Rick Bowmer

President Bush stands in front of the new employees of the Department of Homeland Security. The federal government marked a historic day on March 1, 2003, when over 170,000 employees from more than twenty different agencies officially became part of the new cabinet department.

The Executive Departments

You were introduced to the various executive departments in Chapter 12, when you read about how the president works with the cabinet and other close advisers. The fifteen executive departments (also referred to as cabinet departments), which are directly accountable to the president, are the major service organizations of the federal government. They are responsible for performing government functions, such as training troops (Department of Defense), printing money (Department of the Treasury), and enforcing federal laws setting minimum safety and health standards for workers (Department of Labor).

Each department was created by Congress as the perceived need for it arose, and each department manages a specific policy area. In 2002, for example, Congress created the Department of Homeland Security to deal with the threat of terrorism. Following the terrorist attacks of September 11, 2001, President George W. Bush established a special office, called the Office of Homeland Security, within the Executive Office of the President. Because of the importance of this policy area, Bush soon agreed that Congress should create a new cabinet department to combine the expertise of groups that previously had been scattered among several departments and agencies. The creation of the new cabinet department elevated the status of homeland security to a major administrative level in the executive branch of the federal government.

The head of each department is known as the secretary, except for the Department of Justice, which is headed by the attorney general. Each department head is appointed by the president and confirmed by the Senate. Table 13–1 on the next two pages provides an overview of each of the departments within the executive branch.

A Typical Departmental Structure

Cabinet departments consist of the various heads of the department (the secretary of the department, deputy secretary, undersecretaries, and so on), plus a number of agencies. For example, the National Park Service is an agency within the Department of the Interior. The Drug Enforcement Administration is an agency within the Department of Justice.

Although there are organizational differences among the departments, each department generally follows a typical bureaucratic structure. The Department of Agriculture provides a model for how an executive department is organized (see Figure 13–3 on page 302).

TABLE 13–1

Executive Departments

DEPARTMENT (Year Established)	PRINCIPAL DUTIES	SELECTED SUBAGENCIES
State (1789)	Negotiates treaties; develops our foreign policy; protects citizens abroad.	Passport Agency; Bureau of Diplomatic Security; Foreign Service; Bureau of Human Rights and Humanitarian Affairs; Bureau of Consular Affairs.
Treasury (1789)	Pays all federal bills; borrows money; collects federal taxes; mints coins and prints paper currency; supervises national banks.	Internal Revenue Service; U.S. Mint.
Interior (1849)	Supervises federally owned lands and parks; operates federal hydroelectric power facilities; supervises Native American affairs.	U.S. Fish and Wildlife Service; National Park Service; Bureau of Indian Affairs; Bureau of Land Management.
Justice (1870)	Furnishes legal advice to the president; enforces federal criminal laws; supervises the federal corrections system (prisons).	Federal Bureau of Investigation; Drug Enforcement Administration; Bureau of Prisons; U.S. Marshals Service.
Agriculture (1889)	Provides assistance to farmers and ranchers; conducts research to improve agricultural activity and to prevent plant disease; works to protect forests from fires and disease.	Soil Conservation Service; Agricultural Research Service; Food and Safety Inspection Service; Federal Crop Insurance Corporation; Farmers Home Administration.
Commerce (1903)	Grants patents and trademarks; conducts national census; monitors the weather; protects the interests of businesses.	Bureau of the Census; Bureau of Economic Analysis; Minority Business Development Agency; Patent and Trademark Office; National Oceanic and Atmospheric Administration.
Labor (1913)	Administers federal labor laws; promotes the interests of workers.	Occupational Safety and Health Administration; Bureau of Labor Statistics; Employment Standards Administration; Office of Labor-Management Standards.

TABLE 13–1

Executive Departments (Continued)

DEPARTMENT (Year Established)	PRINCIPAL DUTIES	SELECTED SUBAGENCIES
Defense (1949)*	Manages the armed forces (Army, Navy, Air Force, Marines); operates military bases.	National Security Agency; Joint Chiefs of Staff; Departments of the Air Force, Navy, Army.
Health and Human Services (1979)†	Promotes public health; enforces pure food and drug laws; is involved in health-related research.	Food and Drug Administration; Public Health Service, including the Centers for Disease Control; Administration for Children and Families; Health Care Financing Administration.
Housing and Urban Development (1965)	Concerned with the nation's housing needs; develops and rehabilitates urban communities; promotes improvements in city streets and parks.	Office of Block Grant Assistance; Emergency Shelter Grants Program; Office of Urban Development Action Grants; Office of Fair Housing and Equal Opportunity.
Transportation (1967)	Finances improvements in mass transit; develops and administers programs for highways, railroads, and aviation.	Federal Aviation Administration; Federal Highway Administration; National Highway Traffic Safety Administration; Federal Transit Administration.
Energy (1977)	Involved in conservation of energy and resources; analyzes energy data; conducts research and development.	Office of Civilian Radioactive Waste Management; Office of Nuclear Energy; Energy Information Administration.
Education (1979)†	Coordinates federal programs and policies for education; administers aid to education; promotes educational research.	Office of Special Education and Rehabilitation Services; Office of Elementary and Secondary Education; Office of Postsecondary Education; Office of Vocational and Adult Education.
Veterans Affairs (1989)	Promotes the welfare of veterans of the U.S. armed forces.	Veterans Health Administration; Veterans Benefits Administration; National Cemetery System.
Homeland Security (2002)	Works to prevent terrorist attacks within the United States, reduce America's vulnerability to terrorism, and minimize the damage from potential attacks and natural disasters.	U.S. Customs Service; Bureau of Citizenship and Immigration Services; Bureau of Immigration and Customs Enforcement; Bureau of Customs and Border Patrol; U.S. Coast Guard; Secret Service; Federal Emergency Management Agency.

* Formed from the Department of War (1789) and the Department of the Navy (1798).
† Formed from the Department of Health, Education, and Welfare (1953).

One aspect of the secretary of agriculture's job is to carry out the president's agricultural policies. Another aspect, however, is to promote and protect the department. The secretary spends time ensuring that Congress allocates enough money for the department to work effectively. The secretary also makes sure that constituents, or the people the department serves—usually owners of major farming corporations—are happy. In general, the secretary tries to maintain or improve the status of the department with respect to all of the other departments and units of the federal bureaucracy.

The secretary of agriculture is assisted by a deputy secretary and several assistant secretaries and undersecretaries, all of whom are nominated by the president and put into office with Senate approval. The secretary and each assistant secretary have staff who help with all sorts of jobs, such as hiring new people and generating positive public relations for the Department of Agriculture.

Independent Executive Agencies

independent executive agency A federal agency that is not located within a cabinet department.

Independent executive agencies are federal bureaucratic organizations that have a single function. They are independent in the sense that they are not located within a department; rather, independent executive agency heads report directly to the president who has appointed them. A new federal independent executive agency can be created only through joint cooperation between the president and Congress.

Prior to the twentieth century, the federal government did almost all of its work through the executive departments. In the twentieth century, in contrast, presidents asked for certain executive agencies to be kept separate, or independent, from existing departments. Today, there are more than two hundred independent executive agencies.

FIGURE 13-3

The Organization of the Department of Agriculture

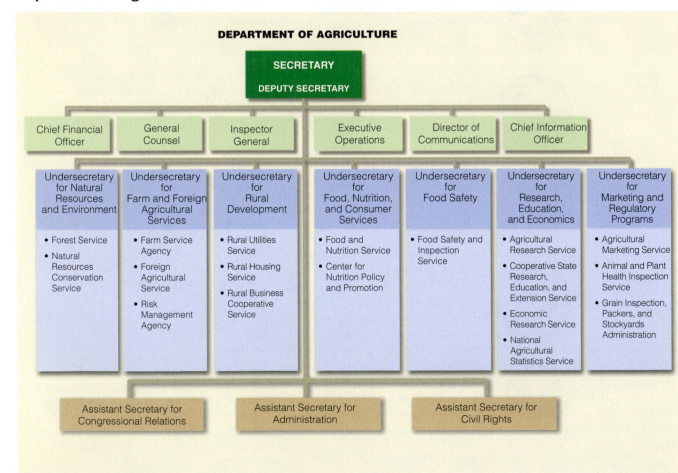

SOURCE: *United States Government Manual, 2004/05* (Washington, D.C.: U.S. Government Printing Office, 2004), p. 106.

TABLE 13–2

Selected Independent Executive Agencies

NAME	DATE FORMED	PRINCIPAL DUTIES
Central Intelligence Agency (CIA)	1947	Gathers and analyzes political and military information about foreign countries so that the United States can improve its own political and military status; conducts covert activities outside the United States.
General Services Administration (GSA)	1949	Purchases and manages all property of the federal government; acts as the business arm of the federal government, overseeing federal government spending projects; discovers overcharges in government programs.
National Science Foundation (NSF)	1950	Promotes scientific research; provides grants to all levels of schools for instructional programs in the sciences.
Small Business Administration (SBA)	1953	Promotes the interests of small businesses; provides low-cost loans and management information to small businesses.
National Aeronautics and Space Administration (NASA)	1958	Responsible for U.S. space program, including building, testing, and operating space vehicles.

Sometimes, agencies are kept independent because of the sensitive nature of their functions; at other times, Congress has created independent agencies to protect them from **partisan politics**—politics in support of a particular party. The Civil Rights Commission, which was created in 1957, is a case in point. Congress wanted to protect the work of the Civil Rights Commission from the influences not only of its own political interest groups but also of the president. The Central Intelligence Agency (CIA), which was formed in 1947, is another good example. Both Congress and the president know that the intelligence activities of the CIA could be abused if it were not independent. Finally, the General Services Administration (GSA) was created as an independent executive agency in 1949 to monitor federal government spending. To perform its function of overseeing congressional spending, it has to be an independent agency.

Among the more than two hundred independent executive agencies, a few stand out in importance either because of the mission they were established to accomplish or because of their large size. We list selected independent executive agencies in Table 13–2.

partisan politics Political actions or decisions that benefit a particular party.

AMERICA at odds

Is the Civil Rights Commission Outdated?

The Civil Rights Commission, as you just read, is an independent executive agency. The commission was founded to study and collect information relating to discrimination and report its findings to the president and Congress. In the late 1950s and 1960s, the commission played a vital role in the civil rights movement, and over the past half century, it has continued to secure voting rights and equal protection under the law for previously mistreated groups. Americans are at odds, however, over whether the commission's work remains relevant today.

Some Americans argue that the Civil Rights Commission is no longer necessary because the civil rights battle has already been won. In a recent column, conservative commentator George Will argued that the time has come to retire the Civil Rights Commission and its multimillion-dollar annual budget. According to Will, "civil rights rhetoric has become a crashing bore and, worse, a cause of confusion: Almost everything designated as a 'civil rights' problem isn't."[5] Many Americans believe that "civil rights" claims have become little more than demands for "special rights." Moreover, the commission has been prone to extremist pronouncements, such as former chair Mary Frances Berry's unsubstantiated charges that some Florida voters from certain ethnic minorities were "disenfranchised" in 2000. The commission may have been an integral part of the civil rights movement, this group claims, but it is no longer relevant or necessary.

Others strongly believe that discrimination still exists and that the commission's work remains relevant. The Civil Rights Commission continues to ensure that all Americans receive

Mary Frances Berry, former chairperson of the Civil Rights Commission, reports before the Senate Rules and Administration Committee. The committee was investigating claims of disenfranchisement of ethnic minority voters in the 2000 presidential elections.

Mike Theiler/Getty Images

equal protection under the law. Its continued relevance has come into question, supporters believe, only because of the appointment of a new chair, Gerald Reynolds, who openly admits that he is "skeptical" of most discrimination claims. In recent years, the commission has championed such causes as the rights of the disabled and the improvement of health care for Native Americans. Although laws have been passed to guarantee equality, much work remains to be done in enforcing those laws. Supporters argue that the commission serves a watchdog role, holding the president and Congress accountable for protecting the civil rights of all Americans.

Independent Regulatory Agencies

independent regulatory agency A federal organization that is responsible for creating and implementing rules that regulate private activity and protect the public interest in a particular sector of the economy.

Independent regulatory agencies are responsible for a specific type of public policy. Their function is to create and implement rules that regulate private activity and protect the public interest in a particular sector of the economy. They are sometimes called the "alphabet soup" of government, because most such agencies are known in Washington by their initials.

One of the earliest independent regulatory agencies was the Interstate Commerce Commission (ICC), established in 1887. (This agency was abolished in 1995.) After the ICC was formed, other agencies were created to regulate aviation (the Civil Aeronautics Board, or CAB, which was abolished in 1985), communication (the Federal Communications Commission, or FCC), the stock market (the Securities and Exchange Commission, or SEC), and many other areas of business. Table 13–3 lists some major independent regulatory agencies.

Government Corporations

government corporation An agency of the government that is run as a business enterprise. Such agencies engage in primarily commercial activities, produce revenues, and require greater flexibility than that permitted in most government agencies.

The newest form of federal bureaucratic organization is the **government corporation,** a business that is owned by the government. Government corporations are not exactly like corporations in which you buy stock, become a shareholder, and share in the profits by collecting dividends. The U.S. Postal Service is a government corporation, but it does not sell shares. If a government corporation loses money in the course of doing business, taxpayers, not shareholders, foot the bill.

Government corporations are like private corporations in that they provide a service that could be handled by the private sector. They are also like private corporations in that they charge for their services, though sometimes they charge less than what a consumer would pay

TABLE 13-3
Selected Independent Regulatory Agencies

NAME	DATE FORMED	PRINCIPAL DUTIES
Federal Reserve System Board of Governors (Fed)	1913	Determines policy with respect to interest rates, credit availability, and the money supply.
Federal Trade Commission (FTC)	1914	Works to prevent businesses from engaging in unfair trade practices and to stop the formation of monopolies in the business sector; protects consumers' rights.
Securities and Exchange Commission (SEC)	1934	Regulates the nation's stock exchanges, where shares of stocks are bought and sold; requires full disclosure of the financial profiles of companies that wish to sell stocks and bonds to the public.
Federal Communications Commission (FCC)	1934	Regulates all communications by telegraph, cable, telephone, radio, and television.
National Labor Relations Board (NLRB)	1935	Protects employees' rights to join unions and to bargain collectively with employers; attempts to prevent unfair labor practices by both employers and unions.
Equal Employment Opportunity Commission (EEOC)	1964	Works to eliminate discrimination that is based on religion, gender, race, color, national origin, age, or disability; examines claims of discrimination.
Environmental Protection Agency (EPA)	1970	Undertakes programs aimed at reducing air and water pollution; works with state and local agencies to help fight environmental hazards.
Nuclear Regulatory Commission (NRC)	1974	Ensures that electricity-generating nuclear reactors in the United States are built and operated safely; regularly inspects operations of such reactors.

for similar services provided by private-sector corporations. Table 13–4 on the next page lists selected government corporations.

How Bureaucrats Get Their Jobs

As already noted, federal bureaucrats holding top-level positions are appointed by the president and confirmed by the Senate. These bureaucrats include department and agency heads, their deputy and assistant secretaries, and so on. The list of positions that are filled by appointments is published after each presidential election in a document called *Policy and Supporting Positions.* The booklet is more commonly known as the "Plum Book," because the eight thousand jobs it summarizes are known as "political plums." Normally, these jobs go to those who supported the winning presidential candidate—in other words, the patronage system is alive and well but on a limited basis.[6]

The rank-and-file bureaucrats—the rest of the federal bureaucracy—are part of the **civil service** (nonmilitary employment in government). They obtain their jobs through the Office of Personnel Management (OPM), an agency established by the Civil Service Reform Act of 1978. The OPM recruits, interviews, and tests potential government workers and determines who should be hired. The OPM makes recommendations to the individual agencies as to which persons meet the standards (typically, the top three applicants for a position), and the agencies generally decide whom to hire. The 1978 act also created the Merit Systems Protection Board (MSPB) to oversee promotions, employees' rights, and other employment matters. The MSPB evaluates charges of wrongdoing, hears employee appeals from agency decisions, and can order corrective action against agencies and employees.

civil service Nonmilitary government employment.

The idea that the civil service should be based on a merit system dates back more than a century. The Civil Service Reform Act of 1883 established the principle of government employment on the basis of merit through open, competitive examinations. Initially, only about 10 percent of federal employees were covered by the merit system. Today, more than 90 percent of the federal civil service is recruited on the basis of merit.

The Web site maintained by the Office of Personnel Management provides employment information.

legislative rule An administrative agency rule that carries the same weight as a statute enacted by a legislature.

enabling legislation A law enacted by a legislature to establish an administrative agency. Enabling legislation normally specifies the name, purpose, composition, and powers of the agency being created.

Regulatory Agencies: Are They the Fourth Branch of Government?

In Chapter 2, we considered the system of checks and balances among the three branches of the U.S. government—executive, legislative, and judicial. Recent history, however, shows that it may be time to regard the regulatory agencies as a fourth branch of the government. Although the U.S. Constitution does not mention regulatory agencies, they can and do make **legislative rules** that are as legally binding as laws passed by Congress. With such powers, this administrative branch has an influence on the nation's businesses that rivals that of the president, Congress, and the courts. Indeed, most Americans do not realize how much of our "law" is created by regulatory agencies, as we indicate in this chapter's *Perception versus Reality* feature.

Regulatory agencies have been on the American political scene since the nineteenth century, but their golden age came during the regulatory explosion of the 1960s and 1970s. Congress itself could not have overseen the actual implementation of all of the laws that it was enacting at the time to control pollution and deal with other social problems. It therefore chose (and still chooses) to delegate to administrative agencies the tasks involved in implementing its laws. By delegating some of its authority to an administrative agency, Congress may indirectly monitor a particular area in which it has passed legislation without becoming bogged down in the details relating to the enforcement of that legislation—details that are often best left to specialists. In recent years, the government has been hiring increasing numbers of specialists to oversee its regulatory work.

Agency Creation

To create an administrative agency, Congress passes **enabling legislation,** which specifies the name, purpose, composition, and powers of the agency being created. The Federal Trade Commission (FTC), for example, was created in 1914 by the Federal Trade Commission Act, as mentioned earlier. The act prohibits unfair and deceptive trade practices. The act also describes the procedures that the agency must follow to charge persons or organizations with violations of the act, and it provides for judicial review of agency orders.

Other portions of the act grant the agency powers to "make rules and regulations for the purpose of carrying out the Act," to conduct investigations of business practices, to obtain reports on business practices from interstate corporations, to investigate possible violations of

TABLE 13-4
Selected Government Corporations

NAME	DATE FORMED	PRINCIPAL DUTIES
Tennessee Valley Authority (TVA)	1933	Operates a Tennessee River control system and generates power for a seven-state region and for U.S. aeronautics and space programs; promotes the economic development of the Tennessee Valley region; controls floods and promotes the navigability of the Tennessee River.
Federal Deposit Insurance Corporation (FDIC)	1933	Insures individuals' bank deposits up to $100,000; oversees the business activities of banks.
Export/Import Bank of the United States (Ex/Im Bank)	1933	Promotes American-made goods abroad; grants loans to foreign purchasers of American products.
National Railroad Passenger Corporation (Amtrak)	1970	Provides a national and intercity rail passenger service network; controls over 23,000 miles of track with about 505 stations.
U.S. Postal Service (formed from the old U.S. Post Office Department—the Post Office itself is older than the Constitution)	1971	Delivers mail throughout the United States and its territories; is the largest government corporation.

Who Makes the Law?

The Constitution is clear. In Article I, Section 1, it states as follows:

All legislative Powers herein granted shall be vested in a Congress of the United States, ...

Further, the Constitution, in Article II, Section 3, indicates that the president "shall take Care that the Laws be faithfully executed."

THE PERCEPTION

Not surprisingly, most Americans assume that Congress makes the laws at the federal level because the Constitution authorized only Congress to do so. Indeed, all federal statutes must be enacted by Congress. Americans normally also assume that the regulatory agencies simply administer the laws' provisions—no more, no less. That perception is simple and straightforward—but incomplete.

THE REALITY

Through their rulemaking functions, regulatory agencies staffed by bureaucrats, not Congress, make much of the "law" in the United States. Some even claim that administrative agency rulemaking has created a "new executive state," in which the executive branch has assumed functions that the founders intended Congress to have.[7]

Indeed, much of the body of environmental law consists of regulations issued by the Environmental Protection Agency. Some federal agencies have even levied taxes, which is a power that supposedly only Congress can exercise. For example, the Federal Communications Commission has imposed a tax on long-distance telephone services to help fund the provision of Internet services to schools.

State agencies have also established much of the law governing states. Consider just one state—Oregon. The Oregon Health Plan pays for physician-assisted suicide as a result of an agency rule, not legislation passed by state legislators. Development on Oregon beaches is restricted by rule, not legislation. Logging on private land is regulated by rule. The way books are chosen for public and school libraries is decided by rule. Library Internet access policies are decided by rule.

In short, Congress and the state legislatures do not make all of the laws in our land.

What's Your Opinion?

Why would Congress willingly give up its legislative powers to administrative agencies?

---

federal antitrust statutes, to publish findings of its investigations, and to recommend new legislation. The act also empowers the FTC to hold trial-like hearings and to **adjudicate** (formally resolve) certain kinds of trade disputes that involve FTC regulations or federal antitrust laws. When adjudication takes place, within the FTC or any other regulatory agency, an administrative law judge (ALJ) conducts the hearing and, after weighing the evidence presented, issues an *order*. Unless it is overturned on appeal, the ALJ's order becomes final.

Enabling legislation makes the regulatory agency a potent organization. For example, the Securities and Exchange Commission (SEC) imposes rules regarding the disclosures a company must make to those who purchase its stock. Under its enforcement authority, the SEC also investigates and prosecutes alleged violations of these regulations. Finally, the SEC sits as judge and jury in deciding whether its rules have been violated and, if so, what punishment should be imposed on the offender (although the judgment may be appealed to a federal court).

adjudicate To render a judicial decision. In regard to administrative law, the process in which an administrative law judge hears and decides issues that arise when an agency charges a person or firm with violating a law or regulation enforced by the agency.

Rulemaking

A major function of a regulatory agency is **rulemaking**—the formulation of new regulations. The power that an agency has to make rules is conferred on it by Congress in the agency's enabling legislation. For example, the Occupational Safety and Health Administration (OSHA) was authorized by the Occupational Safety and Health Act of 1970 to develop and issue rules governing safety in the workplace. Under this authority, OSHA has issued various safety standards. For example, OSHA deemed it in the public interest to issue a rule regulating the health-care industry to prevent the spread of certain diseases, including acquired immune deficiency syndrome (AIDS). The rule specified various standards—on how contaminated instruments should be handled, for instance—with which employers in that industry must comply. Agencies cannot just make a rule whenever they wish, however. Rather, they must follow certain procedural requirements, particularly those set forth in the Administrative Procedure Act of 1946.

Agencies must also make sure that their rules are based on substantial evidence and are not "arbitrary and capricious." Therefore, before proposing a new rule, an agency may engage in

rulemaking The process undertaken by an administrative agency when formally proposing, evaluating, and adopting a new regulation.

extensive investigation (through research, on-site inspections of the affected industry, surveys, and so on) to obtain data on the problem to be addressed by the rule. Based on this information, the agency may undertake a cost-benefit analysis of a new rule to determine whether its benefits outweigh its costs. For example, when issuing new rules governing electrical equipment, OSHA predicted that they would cost business $21.7 billion annually but would save 60 lives and eliminate 1,600 worker injuries a year. The agency also estimated that its safety equipment regulations for manufacturing workers would cost $52.4 billion, save 4 lives, and prevent 712,000 lost workdays because of injuries each year.

Don't get the idea that rulemaking is isolated from politics. Indeed, as you will read shortly, bureaucrats work closely with members of Congress as well as interest groups when making rules.

AMERICA at odds

Should Agencies Give More Weight to Compliance Costs?

As already mentioned, the number of regulatory rules generated by federal agencies has climbed steadily over the years, as have the costs of administering those rules. Not surprisingly, the costs of complying with agency rules have also risen. For every dollar spent on regulation, the public now spends $45 in compliance costs—twice as much as twenty-five years ago. According to one author, the total cost of compliance with regulatory rules today is close to $1 trillion, which equates to one-tenth of the U.S. economy.[8]

Some Americans, and particularly businesses, believe that agencies should not have such a free hand in devising rules that are extremely costly to implement. They argue that federal agencies should give more weight to compliance costs when issuing new regulatory rules. Consider just one example. In 1996, the Environmental Protection Agency (EPA) issued new rules establishing more rigorous standards for particulate matter and ozone. (Ozone, which is the basic ingredient of smog, is formed when sunlight combines with pollutants from cars and other sources.) At the time, business groups estimated that the cost of complying with these new rules could amount to over $100 billion per year. These groups contended that the EPA should have been required to take these calculations into account when issuing the new rules.

Others contend that agencies should not be concerned with compliance costs but should focus only on fulfilling their regulatory purpose. For the EPA, this means preserving and improving the quality of our environmental resources, such as air and water, and protecting against the adverse effects of pollution. Indeed, the EPA pointed out that the rules would save 15,000 lives. Given that the EPA values a human life at $5 million, the agency felt that its rules were more than justified.[9]

Policymaking and the Iron Triangle

neutral competency The application of technical skills to jobs without regard to political issues.

Federal bureaucrats are expected to exhibit **neutral competency,** which means that they are supposed to apply their technical skills to their jobs without regard to political issues. In principle, they should not be swayed by the thought of personal or political gain. In reality, each independent agency and each executive department is interested in its own survival and expansion. Each is constantly battling the others for a larger share of the budget. All agencies and departments wish to retain or expand their functions and staffs; to do this, they must gain the goodwill of both the White House and Congress.

Although administrative agencies of the federal government are prohibited from directly lobbying Congress, departments and agencies have developed techniques to help them gain congressional support. Each organization maintains a congressional information office, which specializes in helping members of Congress by supplying any requested information and solving casework problems. For example, if a member of the House of Representatives receives a complaint from a constituent that his Social Security checks are not arriving on time, that member of Congress may go to the Social Security Administration and ask that something be done. Typically, requests from members of Congress receive immediate attention.

Analysts have determined that one way to understand the bureaucracy's role in policy-making is to examine the **iron triangle,** which is the three-way alliance among legislators (members of Congress), bureaucrats, and interest groups. (Iron triangles are also referred to as subgovernments.) Presumably, the laws that are passed and the policies that are established benefit the interests of all three sides of the iron triangle.

iron triangle A three-way alliance among legislators, bureaucrats, and interest groups to make or preserve policies that benefit their respective interests.

Agriculture as an Example

Consider the bureaucracy within the Department of Agriculture. It consists of about 100,000 individuals working directly for the federal government and thousands of other individuals who work indirectly for the department as contractors, subcontractors, or consultants. Now consider that various interest groups or client groups are concerned with what certain bureaus or agencies in the Agriculture Department do for agribusinesses. Some of these groups are the American Farm Bureau Federation, the National Cattleman's Association, the National Milk Producers Association, the Corn Growers Association, and the Citrus Growers Association.

Finally, take a close look at Congress and you will see that two major committees are concerned with agriculture: the House Committee on Agriculture and the Senate Committee on Agriculture, Nutrition, and Forestry. Each committee has several specialized subcommittees. The triangle is an alliance of bureaucrats, interest groups, and legislators who cooperate to create mutually beneficial regulations or legislation. Iron triangles, or policy communities, are well established in almost every part of the bureaucracy.

Congress's Role

The secretary of agriculture is nominated by the president (and confirmed by the Senate) and is the head of the Department of Agriculture. But that secretary cannot even buy a desk lamp if Congress does not approve the appropriations for the department's budget. Within Congress, the responsibility for considering the Department of Agriculture's request for funding belongs first to the House and Senate appropriations committees and then to the agriculture subcommittees under them. The members of those subcommittees, most of whom represent agricultural states, have been around a long time and have their own ideas about what is appropriate for the Agriculture Department's budget. They carefully scrutinize the ideas of the president and the secretary of agriculture.

The Influence of Interest Groups

Finally, the various interest groups—including producers of farm chemicals and farm machinery, agricultural cooperatives, grain dealers, and exporters—have vested interests in whatever the Department of Agriculture does and in whatever Congress lets the department do. Those interests are well represented by the lobbyists who crowd the halls of Congress. Many lobbyists have been working for agricultural interest groups for decades. They know the congressional committee members and Agriculture Department staff extremely well and routinely meet with them.

The Success of the Iron Triangle in Agriculture

For whatever reason, our nation's farmers have benefited greatly from the iron triangle in agriculture. Indeed, according to the Organization for Economic Cooperation and Development, U.S. taxpayers paid more than $400 billion to farmers between 1986 and 1995.[10] In 1996, Congress decided to change course and passed the Freedom to Farm Act. The purpose of the legislation was to gradually wean farmers from subsidies and let the market dictate prices for farm goods.

In 2002, however, Congress passed the Farm Security and Rural Investment Act. The act called for an 80 percent increase in agricultural subsidies (guaranteeing prices for certain agricultural products), for a total handout to farmers of up to $190 billion over a ten-year period. The bill even included *new* subsidies for some products, including milk, peanuts, lentils, chickpeas, honey, wool, and mohair.

Issue Networks

The iron triangle relationship does not apply to all policy domains, however. When making policy decisions on environmental and welfare issues, for example, many members of Congress and agency officials rely heavily on "experts." Legislators and agency heads tend to depend on their staff members for specialized knowledge of rules, regulations, and legislation. These experts have frequently served variously as interest group lobbyists and as public-sector staff members during their careers, creating a revolving-door effect. They often have strong opinions and interests regarding the direction of policy and are thus able to exert a great deal of influence on legislators and bureaucratic agencies. The relationships among these experts, which are less structured than iron triangles, are often referred to as **issue networks.** Like iron triangles, issue networks are made up of people with similar policy concerns. Issue networks are less interdependent and unified than iron triangles, however, and often include more players, such as media outlets.

issue networks Groups of individuals or organizations—which consist of legislators and legislative staff members, interest group leaders, bureaucrats, the media, scholars, and other experts—that support particular policy positions on a given issue.

Curbing Waste and Improving Efficiency

There is no doubt that our bureaucracy is costly. There is also little doubt that at times it can be wasteful and inefficient. Each year it is possible to cull through the budgets of the various federal agencies and discover quite outrageous examples of government waste. Here are some recent ones:

■ More than $11 million paid to psychics by the Pentagon and the Central Intelligence Agency to discover whether the psychics would offer insights about foreign threats to the United States.

President Bush talks with Representative Eva Clayton (D., N.C.), right, as he signs a ten-year, $190 billion farm bill in 2002. The bill expanded subsidies to growers, and even some fellow Republicans called the measure a budget-busting step backward in agriculture planning.

AP Photo/Ron Edmonds

- Payments of more than $20 million a year to thousands of prison inmates through the Social Security Administration's Supplemental Income Program.
- A total of $10 million per year paid by the Department of Energy to its employees to encourage them to lose weight.
- More than $30 million paid over two years by the Internal Revenue Service to tax filers claiming nonexistent slavery tax credits.
- A total of $1.1 million spent for a program that informed tenants of public housing about the types of gemstones, incense, and clothing colors that would best improve their self-esteem.

According to researcher Robert Tollison, "You could multiply the famous examples by a factor of one-thousand and still not cover the wasteful and redundant government programs."[11]

The government has made several attempts to reduce waste, inefficiency, and wrongdoing. For example, over the years both the federal government and state governments have passed laws requiring more openness in government. Further attempts at bureaucratic reform have included, among other things, encouraging government employees to report to appropriate government officials any waste and wrongdoing that they observe.

Coleen Rowley, an agent for the Federal Bureau of Investigation (FBI), testifies before the Senate Judiciary Committee in 2002. The committee was investigating oversight on counterterrorism. Rowley had earlier accused FBI headquarters of putting roadblocks in the way of Minneapolis field agents during an investigation of a terrorist suspect.

Helping Out the Whistleblowers

The term **whistleblower,** as applied to the federal bureaucracy, has a special meaning: it is someone who blows the whistle, or reports, on gross governmental inefficiency, illegal action, or other wrongdoing. Federal employees are often reluctant to blow the whistle on their superiors, however, for fear of reprisals.

To encourage federal employees to report government wrongdoing, Congress has passed laws to protect whistleblowers. The 1978 Civil Service Reform Act included some protection for whistleblowers by prohibiting reprisals against whistleblowers by their superiors. The act also set up the Merit Systems Protection Board as part of this protection. The Whistle-Blower Protection Act of 1989 provided further protection for whistleblowers. That act authorized the Office of Special Counsel (OSC), an independent agency, to investigate complaints of reprisals against whistleblowers. Many federal agencies also have toll-free hot lines that employees can use to anonymously report bureaucratic waste and inappropriate behavior.

In spite of these laws, there is little evidence that whistleblowers are adequately protected against retaliation. According to a study conducted by the Government Accountability Office, 41 percent of the whistleblowers who turned to the OSC for protection during a recent three-year period reported that they were no longer employed by the agencies on which they blew the whistle. Many other federal employees who have blown the whistle say that they would not do so again because it was so difficult to get help, and even when they did, the experience was a stressful ordeal. Creating more effective protection for whistleblowers remains an ongoing goal of the government. The basic problem, though, is that most organizations, including federal government agencies, do not like to have their wrongdoings and failings exposed, especially by insiders.

whistleblower In the context of government employment, someone who "blows the whistle" (reports to authorities) on gross governmental inefficiency, illegal action, or other wrongdoing.

Improving Efficiency and Getting Results

The Government Performance and Results Act, which went into effect in 1997, has forced the federal government to change the way it does business. In pilot programs throughout the federal government, agencies have experienced a shakedown. Since 1997, virtually every agency (except the intelligence agencies) has had to describe its new goals and a method for evaluating how well those goals are met. A results-oriented goal of an agency could be as broad as lowering the number of highway traffic deaths or as narrow as trying to reduce the number of times an agency's phone rings before it is answered.

As one example, consider the National Oceanic and Atmospheric Adminstration. It improved the effectiveness of its short-term forecasting services, particularly in issuing warnings of tornadoes. The warning time has increased from seven to nine minutes. This may seem insignificant, but it provides additional critical time for those in the path of a tornado.

President George W. Bush's "performance-based budgeting" further extends this idea of focusing on results. Performance-based budgeting is designed to increase overall agency performance and accountability by linking the funding of federal agencies to their actual performance. Numerous federal programs now have to meet specific performance criteria. If they do, they will receive more funds. If they do not, their funding will be reduced or removed entirely. To determine the extent to which performance criteria have been met, the Office of Management and Budget now "grades" each agency on how well it manages its operations, and these grades are considered during the budgeting process.

Another Approach—Pay-for-Performance Plans

For some time, the private sector has used pay-for-performance plans as a means to increase employee productivity and efficiency. About one-third of the major firms in this country use some kind of alternative pay system such as team-based pay, skill-based pay, profit-sharing plans, or individual bonuses. In contrast, workers for the federal government traditionally have received fixed salaries; promotions, salary increases, and the like are given on the basis of seniority, not output.

The federal government has also been experimenting with pay-for-performance systems. For example, the U.S. Postal Service has implemented an Economic Value Added program, which ties bonuses to performance. As part of a five-year test of a new pay system, three thousand scientists working in Air Force laboratories received salaries based on actual results. Also, the Department of Veterans Affairs launched a skill-based pay project at its New York regional office.

Many hope that by offering such incentives, the government will be able to compete more effectively with the private sector for skilled and talented employees. Additionally, according to some, pay-for-performance plans will go a long way toward countering the entitlement mentality that has traditionally characterized employment within the bureaucracy.

Privatization

privatization The transfer of the task of providing services traditionally provided by government to the private sector.

Another alternative for reforming the federal bureaucracy is **privatization,** which means turning over certain types of government work to the private sector. As you read in this chapter's opening *America at Odds* feature, privatization can take place by contracting out (outsourcing)

These U.S. Forest Service employees standing in front of the regional headquarters in Missoula, Montana, were the first victims of the Bush administration's program seeking to cut costs by privatizing government work in 2003.

AP Photo/Chad Harder

work to the private sector or by "managed competition" in which the task of providing public services is opened up to competition. In managed competition, both the relevant government agency and private firms can compete for the work. Vouchers are another way in which certain services traditionally provided by government, such as education, can be provided on the open market. The government pays for the vouchers, but the services are provided by the private sector.

State and local governments have been experimenting with privatization for some time. Virtually all of the states have privatized at least a few of their services, and some states, including California, Colorado, and Florida, have privatized over one hundred activities formerly undertaken by government. In Scottsdale, Arizona, the city contracts for fire protection. In Baltimore, Maryland, nine of the city's schools are outsourced to private entities. In other cities, services ranging from janitorial work to recreational facilities are handled by the private sector.

As mentioned earlier, the Bush administration intends to follow the states' lead and privatize work now undertaken by some 850,000 federal workers. Whether airport traffic control, military support services, and a host of other federal services should also be privatized is currently being debated in think tanks and, to some extent, by policymakers. One issue that has been of foremost concern to Americans is whether Social Security should be partially privatized.

Is It Possible to Reform the Bureaucracy?

Some claim that the bureaucracy is so massive, unwieldy, and self-perpetuating that it is impossible to reform. Attempts at reform, including those just discussed, can, at most, barely touch the surface of the problem. (For a recent example of bureaucratic reform, see this chapter's *The Politics of National Security* feature on the following page.)

In large part, this is because the positions over which the president has direct or indirect control, through the appointment process, amount to less than 1 percent of the 2.7 million civilian employees who work for the executive branch. The bureaucracy is also deeply entrenched and is often characterized by inertia and by slow-moving responses to demands for change. As Laurence J. Peter, of "Peter Principle" fame, once said, a "bureaucracy defends the status quo long past the time when the quo has lost its status." It should come as no surprise, then, that virtually every president in modern times has found it difficult to exercise much control over the bureaucracy.

Complicating the problem is the fact that political appointees often know little about the work of the agency to which they are appointed and are rarely trained specifically in the areas that they supervise. Typically, they must look for assistance to the rank-and-file staff, whose jobs do not come and go with each administration. Furthermore, federal employees have significant rights. Once a federal worker is hired, firing him or her is extremely difficult, regardless of job performance. Similarly, once a federal agency is created, it takes on a life of its own and tends to become permanent. Indeed, President Ronald Reagan (1981–1989) once commented that "a government bureau is the nearest thing to eternal life we'll ever see on this earth."[12]

Government in the Sunshine

The past four decades saw a trend toward more openness in government. The theory was that because Americans pay for the government, they own it—and they have a right to know what the government is doing with the taxpayers' dollars.

In response to pressure for more government openness and disclosure, Congress passed the Freedom of Information Act in 1966. This act required federal agencies to disclose any information in agency files, with some exceptions, to any persons requesting it. Since the 1970s, "sunshine laws," which require government meetings to be open to the public, have been enacted at all levels of American government. During the Clinton administration (1993–2001), Americans gained even greater access to government information as federal and state agencies went online.

The trend toward greater openness in government came to an abrupt halt on September 11, 2001. In the wake of the terrorist attacks on the World Trade Center and the Pentagon, the

The POLITICS of national SECURITY   You are here   chemical attack

Reforming U.S. Intelligence Agencies

In the aftermath of the terrorist attacks of September 11, 2001, many Americans wondered how terrorists were able to execute their plans successfully on our soil. Most Americans consider U.S. intelligence agencies to be the finest in the world, but a breakdown had obviously occurred. Few disputed that intelligence reform would be needed if we were to avoid future terrorist attacks.

THE 9/11 COMMISSION

The 9/11 Commission, a bipartisan panel made up of ten members, conducted a nineteen-month investigation of the attacks. The commission then submitted a detailed report of its findings to Congress, essentially revising the history of September 11. Along with piecing together the events of September 11, the report provided a time line of intelligence blunders in the months and years before the terrorist attacks. The commission also offered recommendations for reforming the structure of the U.S. intelligence agencies.

One of the primary findings of the 9/11 Commission was that the various intelligence agencies, including the Central Intelligence Agency, the National Security Council, and the Federal Bureau of Investigation, had engaged in turf battles, rather than coordinating their efforts. This lack of cooperation ultimately compromised national security, the commission asserted, because these agencies failed to share vital information.

CONGRESS PASSES INTELLIGENCE REFORM

Following the lead of the 9/11 Commission, in 2004 Congress passed legislation that created a National Counterterrorism Center to coordinate terrorism intelligence gathering and sharing throughout the government. Congress also created the new position of national intelligence director to oversee the existing agencies, along with the government's estimated $40 billion annual intelligence budget. The director reports directly to the White House.

The intelligence reform bill generally followed the major recommendations of the 9/11 Commission. Among its numerous provisions, the bill called for new electronic surveillance powers for law enforcement agencies, thousands of additional federal agents to patrol U.S. borders, and uniform national standards for issuing driver's licenses. Some civil liberties groups voiced concern that the reforms would erode the privacy rights of Americans. In an attempt to quiet such critics, Congress established an independent civil liberties board to review the government's privacy policies.

UPI Photo/Michael Kleinfeld/Landov

9/11 Commissioner Lee Hamilton stands in front of a chart during a news conference regarding the bill that eventually became the Intelligence Reform and Terrorism Prevention Act of 2004. The act reorganized the U.S. intelligence community by creating a National Counterterrorism Center and a national intelligence director to streamline operations.

CALLS FOR FURTHER REFORM

Most members of Congress claimed that the intelligence reform bill would make the nation more secure. Representative F. James Sensenbrenner (R., Wisc.), however, described the reforms as "woefully incomplete." He and numerous other Republicans in the House of Representatives called for additional law enforcement and immigration provisions. For example, he wanted to bar illegal immigrants from obtaining driver's licenses and other forms of identification. Some states have provided identification to noncitizens, and many of the September 11 hijackers had obtained valid driver's licenses or identification cards. "Good intelligence is useless without good homeland security," Sensenbrenner said, claiming that some of the reform provisions that dealt with immigration control were "worse than the current law." Supporters of Sensenbrenner in the House have vowed to attempt additional reforms in the future.

Are We Safer?

Do you believe that additional reforms are necessary to improve our national security? Why or why not?

government began tightening its grip on information. In the months following the attacks, hundreds of thousands of documents were removed from government Web sites. No longer can the public access plans of nuclear power plants, descriptions of airline security violations, or maps of pipeline routes. Agencies were instructed to be more cautious about releasing information in their files and were given new guidelines on what should be considered public information. State and local agencies followed the federal government's lead. Some states barred access to such information as emergency preparedness evacuation plans. Others established commissions or panels whose activities are exempt from state sunshine laws.

The Federal Bureaucracy and Your Everyday Life

Taken as a whole, the spending and actions of bureaucrats affect just about everything you can or cannot do. Just consider some of the fifteen executive departments and how their actions affect your everyday life. The Department of Transportation develops and administers programs for the highways on which you travel. The Department of Agriculture provides assistance to farmers, affecting the prices that you pay for food. The Department of Treasury includes the U.S. Mint, which determines the kinds of money you use in your daily activities. The Department of Homeland Security coordinates efforts to protect your safety in the event of terrorist attacks.

AP Photo/Lennox McLendon

Taking Action

Although this chapter's focus is on the federal bureaucracy, realize that all levels of government require bureaucracies to implement their goals. In virtually every community, however, there are needs that government agencies cannot meet. Often, agencies simply lack the funds to hire more personnel or to provide assistance to those in need. To help address these needs, many Americans do volunteer work. If you want to take action in this way,

check with your local government offices and find out which agencies or offices have volunteer programs. In the photo shown here, volunteers are answering "hot lines" that teenagers can call when they need help. Many volunteers at such "hot line" services have found this type of work especially rewarding.

Key Terms

adjudicate   307

bureaucracy   295

bureaucrat   295

civil service   305

enabling legislation   306

government corporation   304

independent executive agency   302

independent regulatory agency   304

iron triangle   309

issue networks   310

legislative rule   306

neutral competency   308

partisan politics   303

privatization   312

rulemaking   307

whistleblower   311

Chapter Summary

1 A bureaucracy is a large, complex administrative organization that is structured hierarchically in a pyramid-like fashion. The federal bureaucracy is an administrative organization that carries out the policies of elected government officials.

2 In 1789, the federal bureaucracy had only about fifty civilian employees. Today, the federal government has about 2.7 million employees. Together, the three levels of government employ about 15 percent of the civilian labor force.

3 There are four major types of bureaucratic structures within the executive branch of the federal government. These structures include executive departments, independent executive agencies, independent regulatory agencies, and government corporations.

4 Bureaucrats holding the top positions in the federal government are appointed by the president and confirmed by the Senate.

Rank-and-file employees obtain their jobs through the Office of Personnel Management (OPM), which was created by the Civil Service Reform Act of 1978. The 1978 act also created the Merit Systems Protection Board to protect employees' rights. The civil service is based on the merit system, which was initiated in 1883 by the Civil Service Reform Act of that year.

5 Administrative agencies are sometimes regarded as the fourth branch of government because of the powers they wield. They can make legislative rules that are as legally binding as the laws passed by Congress.

6 Iron triangles are at work throughout the bureaucracy. An iron triangle consists of legislators, bureaucrats, and interest groups that work together to create mutually beneficial legislation in a specific policy area, such as agriculture.

7 Over the years, Congress has made several attempts to curb bureaucratic waste and inefficiency by creating protections for whistleblowers and providing incentives to federal workers to improve their efficiency. The need to reform the bureaucracy is widely recognized, but some claim that it may be impossible to do so effectively.

RESOURCES FOR FURTHER STUDY

Selected Readings

Behn, Robert D. *Rethinking Democratic Accountability.* Washington, D.C.: The Brookings Institution, 2001. The author looks closely at an ongoing question: How can the American bureaucracy be made more accountable to society?

Gronlund, Ake, ed. *Electronic Government: Design, Applications, and Management.* Hershey, Pa.: Idea Group Publishing, 2002. This collection of essays focuses on how electronic government might make government services better and more effective while at the same time including citizens in democratic processes.

Light, Paul C. *Government's Greatest Achievements: From Civil Rights to Homeland Security.* Washington, D.C.: The Brookings Institution, 2002. At a time when the U.S. government and bureaucracy are increasingly targeted for criticism, this book reminds us of the government's many achievements over the past half century.

Suleiman, Ezra N. *Dismantling Democratic States.* Princeton, N.J.: Princeton University Press, 2005. The author challenges the notion that bureaucracy is the source of democracy's ills.

Politics on the Web

■ For information on the government, including the Web sites for federal agencies, go to the federal government's "gateway" Web site at **http://www. firstgov.gov**

■ The Web site of the Office of Management and Budget offers information ranging from new developments in administrative policy, to the costs of the bureaucracy, to paperwork-reduction efforts. You can access the OMB directly at **http://www.whitehouse.gov/omb**

■ To learn more about the mission of the General Services Administration (GSA) and its role in managing the federal bureaucracy, go to **http://www.gsa.gov**

■ Federal World is a government site that contains links to numerous federal agencies and government information. You can find this site at **http://www.fedworld.gov**

■ If you want to get an idea of what federal agencies are putting on the Web, you can go to the Department of Commerce's Web site at **http://www.doc.gov**

■ The *Federal Register* is the official publication for executive-branch documents. This publication, which includes the orders, notices, and rules of all federal administrative agencies, is online at **http://www.access.gpo.gov/**

From this home page, click on "A to Z Resource List," which is listed in the "Online Federal Information" section. Scroll down until you see *Federal Register.*

■ The *United States Government Manual* contains information on the functions, organization, and administrators of every federal department. You can now access the most recent edition of the manual online at **http://www.access.gpo.gov/**

From this home page, click on "A to Z Resource List," which is listed in the "Online Federal Information" section. Scroll down until you see *United States Government Manual.*

Online Resources for This Chapter

This text's Companion Web Site, at **http://www.americaatodds.com**, offers links to numerous resources that you can utilize to learn more about the topics covered in this chapter. For a list describing these resources, see the inside front cover of this book.

chapter **14**
the judiciary

CHAPTER OBJECTIVES

After reading this chapter, you should be able to . . .

▶ Summarize the origins of the American legal system and the basic sources of American law.

▶ Delineate the structure of the federal court system.

▶ Indicate how federal judges are appointed.

▶ Explain how the federal courts make policy.

▶ Describe the role of ideology and judicial philosophies in judicial decision making.

Supreme Court Appointees: Does Partisan Ideology Matter?

The United States Supreme Court is not often an issue in presidential campaigns. In 2000 and again in 2004, however, the Supreme Court became an issue. During both campaigns, news commentators pointed out that several of the justices on the Court were nearing retirement. If one or more of the justices were to retire in the four years following the presidential elections, whoever became president would be able to nominate a replacement to the high court—and thus "make a difference" in national politics for many years to come.

President George W. Bush did not have the opportunity to appoint any new justices to the Supreme Court during his first term. Chief Justice William Rehnquist, who announced in late 2004 that he has thyroid cancer, may have already stepped down by the time you read this text. The prospect of a Supreme Court nomination has rekindled a long-standing debate on the following question: Are the liberal or conservative leanings of Supreme Court nominees really as significant as they are often made out to be? Some believe that the ideology of Supreme Court nominees does matter. Others are not so sure.

Ideology of Nominees Does Matter

Those who argue that the ideology of Supreme Court nominees does matter believe that the next set of Supreme Court justices will be critical. Suppose, for example, that in addition to Chief Justice Rehnquist's likely retirement, Justice John Paul Stevens also decides to leave the bench. While Rehnquist has led the Court in a conservative direction during his long tenure as chief justice since 1986, Stevens has been a staunch liberal. If both of these justices were replaced by justices with conservative leanings, the Court would move even further to the right ideologically.

Consider how a more conservative Supreme Court might affect our national life and policies. The current Supreme Court has issued very close decisions (voting five to four) on a number of controversial issues. For example, after the 2000 presidential elections, the Supreme Court voted five to four not to allow the Florida votes to be recounted. If only one additional justice had voted in favor of recounting those votes, the outcome of the elections might have been different. In other words, Democratic candidate Al Gore might have become president instead of Republican George W. Bush.

The Court has also been strongly divided on the constitutionality of new or old laws relating to abortion, gay rights, states' rights versus federal regulatory powers, gun control, the separation of church and state, and other significant issues. The next one or two Supreme Court justices will make a difference. We could end up with a strongly conservative Court making the final decisions on constitutional questions affecting our rights and liberties. Ideology does matter.

Ideology Is Only One Facet

Others argue that one factor looms large in the debate over judicial appointments, and that factor is the U.S. Senate. A president can *nominate* a justice to the Court, but the Senate must *confirm* the nomination. In other words, without the Senate's approval, no justice can sit on the high court.

Furthermore, history tells us that justices do not always conform to the wishes of their nominating presidents once they are on the bench. Consider just one example. Republican president George H. W. Bush (1989–1993) appointed David Souter to the Court with the expectation that Souter would take a conservative approach on the bench. Souter has, however, been a leading counterforce to the Court's conservatives—more evidence that justices can confound the expectations of the presidents who appoint them.

Finally, some scholars argue that the partisan labels *liberal* and *conservative* do not adequately describe the range of views on today's Supreme Court. These scholars note that the current dividing lines on the Court have less to do with partisanship than with other issues. An important division on the Court today has to do with the justices' perception of how the Court should approach its work. Should the Court establish "rules" for the lower courts to follow, or should it take a more "pragmatic" approach and establish flexible "standards" to guide the lower courts? Neither approach in this debate carries an ideological guarantee with respect to the outcome of a specific case.

Where Do You Stand?

1. Is it possible for a justice to separate his or her personal philosophical and ideological convictions from the judicial decision-making process? Explain.

2. When interpreting a law and applying it to a specific case, should Supreme Court justices take into account such factors as the circumstances that existed at the time of the law's creation, and whether those circumstances have changed? Why or why not?

Explore This Issue Online

- For an article on how the outcome of the 2004 presidential elections could affect the ideological complexion of the Supreme Court in the future, through possible new appointments, go to **http://www.cnn.com/2004/ ALLPOLITICS/10/20/scotus.sidebar/index.html**.

- You can find data correlating the policy of presidents with the ideological behavior of the justices that they appoint to the Supreme Court at the following page: **http://www. sunysb.edu/polsci/jsegal/data/pressc_main.htm**.

Introduction

When the United States Supreme Court renders an opinion on how the Constitution is to be interpreted, it is, necessarily, making policy on a national level. The exercise of policymaking powers always generates controversy, and this is certainly true with respect to today's Court, as you read in the chapter-opening feature. To understand the nature of this controversy, however, you need to first understand how the **judiciary** (the courts) functions in this country. We begin by looking at the origins and sources of American law. We then examine the federal (national) court system, at the apex of which is the United States Supreme Court.

> **judiciary** The courts; one of the three branches of the federal government in the United States.

The Origins and Sources of American Law

The American colonists brought with them the legal system that had developed in England over hundreds of years. Thus, to understand how the American legal system operates, we need to go back in time to the early English courts and the traditions they established.

The Common Law Tradition

After the Normans conquered England in 1066, William the Conqueror and his successors began the process of unifying the country under their rule. One of the means they used to this end was the establishment of the "king's courts," or *curiae regis.* Before the Norman Conquest, disputes had been settled according to the local legal customs and traditions in various regions of the country. The law developed in the king's courts applied to the country as a whole. What evolved in these courts was the beginning of the **common law**—a body of general rules prescribing social conduct that was applied throughout the entire English realm.

> **common law** The body of law developed from judicial decisions in English and U.S. courts, not attributable to a legislature.

The Rule of Precedent The early English courts developed the common law rules from the principles underlying judges' decisions in actual legal controversies. Judges attempted to be consistent, and whenever possible, they based their decisions on the principles applied in earlier cases. They sought to decide similar cases in a similar way and considered new cases with care, because they knew that their decisions would make new law. Each interpretation became part of the law on the subject and served as a legal **precedent**—that is, a decision that furnished an example or authority for deciding subsequent cases involving similar legal principles or facts.

> **precedent** A court decision that furnishes an example or authority for deciding subsequent cases involving identical or similar facts and legal issues.

> *stare decisis* A common law doctrine under which judges normally are obligated to follow the precedents established by prior court decisions.

The practice of deciding new cases with reference to former decisions, or precedents, eventually became a cornerstone of the English and American judicial systems. The practice forms a doctrine called *stare decisis*[1] ("to stand on decided cases"). Under this doctrine, judges are obligated to follow the precedents established in their jurisdictions. For example, if the Supreme Court of Georgia holds that a state law requiring political candidates to pass drug tests is unconstitutional, that decision will control the outcome of future cases on that issue brought before the state courts in Georgia. Similarly, a decision on a given issue by the United States Supreme Court (the nation's highest court) is binding on all inferior (lower) courts. For example, if the Georgia case on drug testing is appealed to the United States Supreme Court and the Court agrees that the Georgia law is unconstitutional, the high court's ruling will be binding on *all* courts in the United States. In other words, similar drug-testing laws in other states would be invalid and unenforceable.

A fourteenth-century depiction of the Battle of Hastings. In the lower right, William the Conqueror is shown killing the English King Harold.

Smithsonian Photo

Departures from Precedent Sometimes a court will depart from the rule of precedent if it decides that a precedent is simply incorrect or that technological or social changes have rendered the precedent inapplicable. Cases that overturn precedent often receive a great deal of publicity. For example, in 1954, in *Brown v. Board of Education of Topeka,*[2] the United States Supreme Court expressly overturned precedent when it concluded that separate educational facilities for African Americans, which had been upheld as constitutional in numerous prior cases under the "separate-but-equal" doctrine[3] (see Chapter 5), were inherently unequal and violated the equal protection clause. The Supreme Court's departure from precedent in *Brown* received a tremendous amount of publicity as people began to realize the political and social ramifications of this change in the law.

More recently, the Supreme Court departed from precedent when it held in a 2003 case, *Lawrence v. Texas*,[4] that a Texas sodomy law (see Chapter 5) violated the U.S. Constitution. In that case, the Court concluded that consensual sexual conduct, including homosexual conduct, was part of the liberty protected by the due process clause of the Constitution. This decision overturned the Court's established precedent on such laws—specifically, its ruling in *Bowers v. Hardwick*,[5] a 1986 case in which the Court upheld a Georgia sodomy statute.

Sources of American Law

In any governmental system, the primary function of the courts is to interpret and apply the law. In the United States, the courts interpret and apply numerous sources of law when deciding cases. We look here only at the **primary sources of law**—that is, sources that *establish* the law—and the relative priority of these sources when particular laws come into conflict.

primary source of law A source of law that establishes the law. Primary sources of law include constitutions, statutes, administrative agency rules and regulations, and decisions rendered by the courts.

Constitutional Law
The U.S. government and each of the fifty states have separate written constitutions that set forth the general organization, powers, and limits of their respective governments. **Constitutional law** consists of the rights and duties set forth in these constitutions.

constitutional law Law based on the U.S. Constitution and the constitutions of the various states.

The U.S. Constitution is the supreme law of the land. As such, it is the basis of all law in the United States. Any law that violates the Constitution is invalid and unenforceable. Because of its paramount importance in the American legal system, the complete text of the U.S. Constitution is found in Appendix A.

The Tenth Amendment to the U.S. Constitution reserves to the states and to the people all powers not granted to the federal government. Each state in the union has its own constitution. Unless they conflict with the U.S. Constitution or a federal law, state constitutions are supreme within the borders of their respective states.

Statutory Law
Statutes enacted by legislative bodies at any level of government make up another source of law, which is generally referred to as **statutory law.** Federal statutes—laws enacted by the U.S. Congress—apply to all of the states. State statutes—laws enacted by state legislatures—apply only within the state that enacted the law. Any state statute that conflicts with the U.S. Constitution, with federal laws enacted by Congress, or with the state's constitution will be deemed invalid and will not be enforced. Statutory law also includes the ordinances (such as local zoning or housing-construction laws) passed by cities and counties, none of which can violate the U.S. Constitution, the relevant state constitution, or any existing federal or state laws.

statutory law The body of law enacted by legislatures (as opposed to constitutional law, administrative law, or case law).

Administrative Law
Another important source of American law consists of **administrative law**—the rules, orders, and decisions of administrative agencies. As you read in Chapter 13, at the federal level, Congress creates executive agencies, such as the Food and Drug Administration or the Environmental Protection Agency, to perform specific functions. Typically, when Congress establishes an agency, it authorizes the agency to create rules that have the force of law and to enforce those rules by bringing legal actions against violators. Rules issued by various government agencies now affect virtually every aspect of our economy. For example, almost all of a business's operations, including the firm's capital structure and financing, its hiring and firing procedures, its relations with employees and unions, and the way it manufactures and markets its products, are subject to government regulation.

administrative law The body of law created by administrative agencies (in the form of rules, regulations, orders, and decisions) in order to carry out their duties and responsibilities.

Government agencies exist at the state and local levels as well. States commonly create agencies that parallel federal agencies. Just as federal statutes take precedence over conflicting state statutes, federal agency regulations take precedence over conflicting state regulations.

Case Law
As is evident from the discussion of the common law tradition, another basic source of American law consists of the rules of law announced in court decisions, or **case law.** These rules of law include interpretations of constitutional provisions, of statutes enacted by

case law The rules of law announced in court decisions. Case law includes the aggregate of reported cases that interpret judicial precedents, statutes, regulations, and constitutional provisions.

legislatures, and of regulations issued by administrative agencies. Thus, even though a legislature passes a law to govern a certain area, how that law is interpreted and applied depends on the courts. The importance of case law, or judge-made law, is one of the distinguishing characteristics of the common law tradition. (See this chapter's *Comparative Politics* feature for a discussion of another type of legal system that is used in many other countries.)

Civil Law and Criminal Law

All of the sources of law just discussed can be classified in other ways as well. One of the most significant classification systems divides all law into two categories: civil law and criminal law. **Civil law** spells out the duties that individuals in society owe to other persons or to their governments, excluding the duty not to commit crimes. Typically, in a civil case, a private party sues another private party (although the government can also sue a party for a civil law violation). The object of a civil lawsuit is to make the defendant—the person being sued—comply with a legal duty (such as a contractual promise) or pay money damages for failing to comply with that duty.

civil law The branch of law that spells out the duties that individuals in society owe to other persons or to their governments, excluding the duty not to commit crimes.

---

comparative politics

Legal Systems of the World

Legal systems, of course, vary from country to country because each country's law reflects the interests, customs, activities, and values that are unique to that nation's culture. Even though the laws and legal systems of various countries differ substantially, broad similarities do exist.

TWO TYPES OF LEGAL SYSTEMS

Basically, there are two types of legal systems in today's world. One is the common law system of England and the United States, which we have already discussed. The other type of system is based on Roman civil law, or "code law." The term *civil law,* as used here, refers not to civil as opposed to criminal law but to codified law—an ordered grouping of legal principles enacted into law by a legislature or governing body. In a *civil law system,* the primary source of law is a statutory code, and case precedents are not judicially binding, as they normally are in a common law system. Although judges in a civil law system routinely refer to previous decisions as sources of legal guidance, they are not bound by precedent; in other words, the doctrine of *stare decisis* does not apply.

Generally, those countries that were once colonies of Great Britain retained their English common law heritage after they achieved their independence. Similarly, the civil law system, which is followed in most of the continental European countries, was retained in the Latin American, African, and Asian countries that were once colonies of the continental European nations. Japan and South Africa also have civil law systems. In the United States, the state of Louisiana, because of its historical ties to France, has in part a civil law system. The legal systems of Puerto Rico, Québec, and Scotland are similarly characterized as having elements of the civil law system.

LEGAL SYSTEMS COMPARED

Common law and civil law systems are not wholly distinct. For example, although the United States has a common law system,

crimes are defined by statute as in civil law systems. Civil law systems may also allow considerable room for judges to develop law. There is also some variation within common law and civil law systems. The judges of different common law nations have produced differing common law principles. Although the United States and India both derived their legal traditions from England, the common law principles governing certain areas of the law vary in some respects between the two countries.

Similarly, the laws of nations that have civil law systems differ considerably. For example, the French code tends to set forth general principles of law, while the German code is far more specific and runs to thousands of sections.

In many Muslim countries in the Middle East and elsewhere, law codes are grounded in the religious law of Islam, as noted in Chapter 1. This is a basic difference between civil law codes and traditional Islamic law. Traditional Islamic law, known as *sharia,*[6] is a comprehensive code of laws that is based on the belief that the law should provide everything necessary to a person's well-being, both spiritually and physically. Note, though, that the relevance and applicability of *sharia* in today's Muslim world vary from country to country. Some Muslim nations, such as Turkey, are largely governed by secular constitutions and laws. Other predominantly Muslim nations, including Iran and Saudi Arabia, have only religious *(sharia)* courts. Still other Muslim countries have a dual system of courts—some secular and some religious.

For Critical Analysis

Would the judicial branch exercise more power and influence in a common law system than in a civil law system? Why or why not?

criminal law The branch of law that defines and governs actions that constitute crimes. Generally, criminal law has to do with wrongful actions committed against society for which society demands redress.

Criminal law, in contrast, has to do with wrongs committed against the public as a whole. Criminal acts are prohibited by local, state, or federal government statutes. Thus, criminal defendants are prosecuted by public officials, such as a district attorney (D.A.), on behalf of the government, not by their victims or other private parties. In a criminal case, the government seeks to impose a penalty (a fine and/or imprisonment) on a person who has violated a criminal law. When someone robs a convenience store, that person has committed a crime and, if caught and proved guilty, will normally be in prison for some period of time.

Basic Judicial Requirements

A court cannot decide just any issue at any time. Before any court can hear and decide a case, specific requirements must be met. To a certain extent, these requirements act as restraints on the judiciary because they limit the types of cases that courts can hear and decide. Courts also have procedural requirements that frame the judicial process.

jurisdiction The authority of a court to hear and decide a particular case.

Jurisdiction
In Latin, *juris* means "law," and *diction* means "to speak." Therefore, **jurisdiction** literally refers to the power "to speak the law." Jurisdiction applies either to the geographic area in which a court has the right and power to decide cases, or to the right and power of a court to decide matters concerning certain persons, property, or subject matter. Before any court can hear a case, it must have jurisdiction over the person against whom the suit is brought, the property involved in the suit, and the subject matter.

trial court A court in which trials are held and testimony taken.

A state trial court (a **trial court** is, as the term implies, a court in which a trial is held and testimony taken), for example, usually has jurisdictional authority over the residents of a particular area of the state, such as a county or district. A state's highest court (often called the state supreme court)[7] has jurisdictional authority over all residents within the state. In some cases, if an individual has committed an offense such as injuring someone in an automobile accident or selling defective goods within the state, the court can exercise jurisdiction even if the individual is a resident of another state. State courts can also exercise jurisdiction over people who do business within the state. A New York company that distributes its products in California, for example, can be sued by a California resident in a California state court.

Because the federal (national) government is a government of limited powers, the jurisdiction of the federal courts is limited. Article III, Section 2, of the Constitution states that the federal courts can exercise jurisdiction over all cases "arising under this Constitution, the Laws of the United States, and Treaties made, or which shall be made, under their Authority." Whenever a case involves a claim based, at least in part, on the U.S. Constitution, a treaty, or a federal law, a federal question arises. Any lawsuit involving a **federal question** can originate in a federal court.

federal question A question that pertains to the U.S. Constitution, acts of Congress, or treaties. A federal question provides a basis for federal court jurisdiction.

diversity of citizenship A basis for federal court jurisdiction over a lawsuit that arises when (1) the parties in the lawsuit live in different states or when one of the parties is a foreign government or a foreign citizen, and (2) the amount in controversy is more than $75,000.

Federal courts can also exercise jurisdiction over cases involving **diversity of citizenship.** Such cases may arise when the parties in a lawsuit live in different states or when one of the parties is a foreign government or a foreign citizen. Before a federal court can take jurisdiction in a diversity case, the amount in controversy must be more than $75,000.

standing to sue The requirement that an individual must have a sufficient stake in a controversy before he or she can bring a lawsuit. The party bringing the suit must demonstrate that he or she has either been harmed or been threatened with a harm.

Standing to Sue
To bring a lawsuit before a court, a person must have **standing to sue,** or a sufficient "stake" in the matter to justify bringing a suit. Thus, the party bringing the suit must have suffered a harm or been threatened with a harm by the action at issue, and the issue must be justiciable. A **justiciable**[8] **controversy** is one that is real and substantial, as opposed to hypothetical or academic.

The requirement of standing clearly limits the issues that can be decided by the courts. For example, suppose that an environmental interest group sues a company for polluting a local stream in violation of federal law. Even if the company is, in fact, violating federal law, the group cannot sue the firm unless it can produce evidence that its members have actually been harmed, or are about to be harmed, by the polluting activity.

justiciable controversy A controversy that is not hypothetical or academic but real and substantial; a requirement that must be satisfied before a court will hear a case.

As another example, consider a case that came before the United States Supreme Court in 2004. In this case, which was mentioned in Chapter 4, Michael Newdow challenged the constitutionality of a public school district's policy of a teacher-led recitation of the Pledge of Allegiance, which contains the words "under God." Newdow claimed that his daughter had to

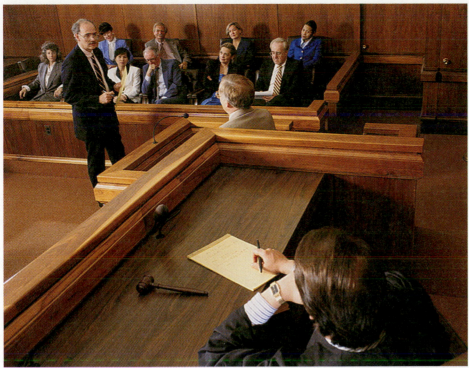

Most cases start in some type of trial court, where testimony is taken and other evidence evaluated. Trial courts exist in all of the fifty state court systems. In the federal court system, trial courts are called district courts.

© John Neubauer/PhotoEdit

"watch and listen" in her classroom during what Newdow maintained was "a ritual proclaiming that there is a God." Although a federal appellate court agreed with Newdow and held that the words "under God" violated the First Amendment's establishment clause, the United States Supreme Court dismissed the case. According to the high court, Newdow, who was divorced, did not have sufficient custody rights over his daughter to allow him to sue on her behalf. In other words, he did not have a sufficient "stake" in the controversy and thus lacked standing to sue.[9]

Court Procedures   Both the federal and the state courts have established procedural rules that apply in all cases. These procedures are designed to protect the rights and interests of the parties, ensure that the litigation proceeds in a fair and orderly manner, and identify the issues that must be decided by the court—thus saving court time and costs. Different procedural rules apply in criminal and civil cases. Generally, criminal procedural rules attempt to ensure that defendants are not deprived of their constitutional rights.

Parties involved in civil or criminal cases must comply with court procedural rules or risk being held in contempt of court. A party who is held in contempt of court can be fined, taken into custody, or both. A court must take care to ensure that the parties—and the court itself—comply with procedural requirements. Procedural errors often serve as grounds for a mistrial or for appealing the court's decision to a higher tribunal.

The Federal Court System

The federal court system is a three-tiered model consisting of U.S. district courts (trial courts), U.S. courts of appeals, and the United States Supreme Court. Figure 14–1 on the next page shows the organization of the federal court system.

Bear in mind that the federal courts constitute only one of the fifty-two court systems in the United States. Each of the fifty states has its own court system, as does the District of Columbia. No two state court systems are exactly the same, but generally each state has different levels, or tiers, of courts, just as the federal system does. Generally, state courts deal with questions of state law, and the decisions of a state's highest court on matters of state law are normally final. If a federal question is involved, however, a decision of a state supreme court may be appealed to the United States Supreme Court.

FIGURE 14–1
The Organization of the
Federal Court System

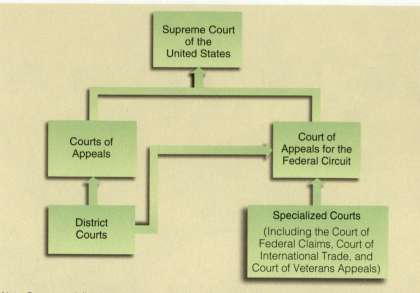

Note: Some specialized courts, such as the Tax Court, are not included in this figure.

U.S. District Courts

On the lowest tier of the federal court system are the U.S. district courts, or federal trial courts. These are the courts in which cases involving federal laws begin, and the cases are decided by a judge or a jury (if it is a jury trial). There is at least one federal district court in every state, and there is one in the District of Columbia. The number of judicial districts varies over time, primarily owing to population changes and corresponding caseloads. Currently, there are ninety-four judicial districts; Figure 14–2 shows their geographic boundaries. The federal system also includes other trial courts, such as the Court of International Trade and others shown in Figure 14–1. These courts have limited, or specialized, subject-matter jurisdiction; that is, they can exercise authority only over certain subjects.

U.S. Courts of Appeals

appellate court A court having appellate jurisdiction that normally does not hear evidence or testimony but reviews the transcript of the trial court's proceedings, other records relating to the case, and the attorneys' respective arguments as to why the trial court's decision should or should not stand.

On the middle tier of the federal court system are the U.S. courts of appeals. Courts of appeals, or **appellate courts,** do not hear evidence or testimony. Rather, an appellate court reviews the transcript of the trial court's proceedings, other records relating to the case, and the attorneys' respective arguments as to why the trial court's decision should or should not stand. In contrast to a trial court, where normally a single judge presides, an appellate court consists of a panel of three or more judges. The task of the appellate court is to determine whether the trial court erred in applying the law to the facts and issues involved in a particular case.

There are thirteen U.S. courts of appeals in the United States. The courts of appeals for twelve of the circuits, including the Court of Appeals for the D.C. Circuit, hear appeals from the U.S. district courts located within their respective judicial circuits (see Figure 14–2). Appeals from decisions made by federal administrative agencies, such as the Federal Trade Commission, may also be made to the U.S. courts of appeals. The Court of Appeals for the Federal Circuit has national jurisdiction over certain types of cases, such as those concerning patent law and some claims against the national government.

The decisions of the federal appellate courts may be appealed to the United States Supreme Court. If a decision is not appealed, or if the high court declines to review the case, the appellate court's decision is final.

The United States Supreme Court

The highest level of the three-tiered model of the federal court system is the United States Supreme Court. According to Article III of the U.S. Constitution, there is only one national

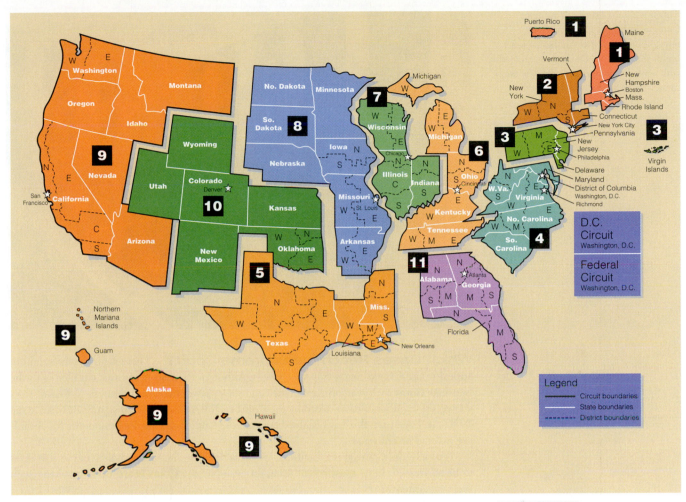

SOURCE: Administrative Office of the United States Courts.

FIGURE 14–2
U.S. Courts of Appeals
and U.S. District Courts

Supreme Court. Congress is empowered to create additional ("inferior") courts as it deems necessary. The inferior courts that Congress has created include the second tier in our model—the U.S. courts of appeals—as well as the district courts and any other courts of limited, or specialized, jurisdiction.

The United States Supreme Court consists of nine justices—a chief justice and eight associate justices—although that number is not mandated by the Constitution. The Supreme Court has original, or trial, jurisdiction only in rare instances (set forth in Article III, Section 2). In other words, only rarely does a case originate at the Supreme Court level. Most of the Court's work is as an appellate court. The Supreme Court has appellate authority over cases decided by the U.S. courts of appeals, as well as over some cases decided in the state courts when federal questions are at issue.

The Writ of *Certiorari*

To bring a case before the Supreme Court, a party may request that the Court issue a **writ of *certiorari*,**[10] popularly called "cert.," which is an order that the Supreme Court issues to a lower court requesting the latter to send it the record of the case in question. Parties can petition the Supreme Court to issue a writ of *certiorari,* but whether the Court will do so is entirely within its discretion. The Court will not issue a writ unless at least four of the nine justices approve. In no instance is the Court required to issue a writ of *certiorari.*[11]

Most petitions for writs of *certiorari* are denied. A denial is not a decision on the merits of a case, nor does it indicate that the Court agrees with a lower court's opinion. Furthermore, the denial of a writ has no value as a precedent. A denial simply means that the decision of the lower court remains the law within that court's jurisdiction.

writ of *certiorari* An order from a higher court asking a lower court for the record of a case.

This is a photo of the U.S. Supreme Court chamber. In 1935, the Court moved from its quarters in the Capitol building to its own building, constructed with white Vermont marble. No television cameras have been allowed inside the chamber during the presentation of an actual case.

Paul Conklin/PhotoEdit

Which Cases Reach the Supreme Court?

There is no absolute right to appeal to the United States Supreme Court. Although thousands of cases are filed with the Supreme Court each year, on average the Court hears fewer than one hundred. As Figure 14–3 shows, the number of cases heard by the Court each year has declined significantly since the 1980s. In large part, this has occurred because the Court has raised its standards for accepting cases in recent years.

Typically, the Court grants petitions for cases that raise important policy issues that need to be addressed. In its most recent term, for example, the Court heard cases involving such pressing issues as:

- Whether the downloading and exchanging of copyrighted musical works by computer users violates federal copyright law.
- Whether the death penalty should be imposed on those who were under the age of eighteen when they committed their crimes.
- Whether local governments can seize private property and turn it over to other private parties to be used for tax-producing projects such as shopping malls and sports arenas.
- Whether terrorist suspects held at the U.S. Naval Base in Guantánamo Bay, Cuba, should have the right to due process of law.

If the lower courts have rendered conflicting opinions on an important issue, the Supreme Court may review a case involving that issue to define the law on the matter. For example, in

FIGURE 14-3

The Number of Supreme Court Opinions

During the 1952 term (the term beginning in October 1952 and ending in June 1953), the Supreme Court issued 65 written opinions. The number of opinions peaked at 151 in the 1982 term and has been more or less declining steadily ever since. During the 2003 term (ending in June 2004), the Court issued 73 written opinions.

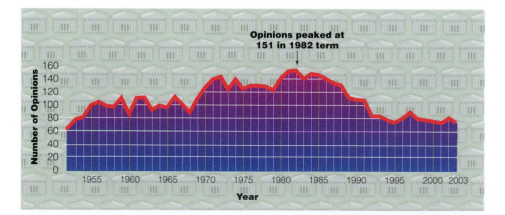

2002 the Court agreed to review two cases raising the issue of whether affirmative action programs (see Chapter 5) violate the equal protection clause of the Constitution. Different federal appellate courts had reached conflicting opinions on this issue.

Supreme Court Opinions   Like all appellate courts, the United States Supreme Court normally does not hear any evidence. The Court's decision in a particular case is based on the written record of the case and the written arguments (legal briefs) that the attorneys submit. The attorneys also present **oral arguments**—arguments presented in person rather than on paper—to the Court, after which the justices discuss the case in **conference.** The conference is strictly private—only the justices are allowed in the room.

When the Court has reached a decision, the chief justice, if in the majority, assigns the task of writing the Court's **opinion** to one of the justices. When the chief justice is not in the majority, the most senior justice voting with the majority assigns the writing of the Court's opinion. The opinion outlines the reasons for the Court's decision, the rules of law that apply, and the judgment.

Often, one or more justices who agree with the Court's decision may do so for different reasons than those outlined in the majority opinion. These justices may write **concurring opinions,** setting forth their own legal reasoning on the issue. Frequently, one or more justices disagree with the Court's conclusion. These justices may write **dissenting opinions,** outlining the reasons why they feel the majority erred in arriving at its decision. Although a dissenting opinion does not affect the outcome of the case before the Court, it may be important later. In a subsequent case concerning the same issue, a jurist or attorney may use the legal reasoning in the dissenting opinion as the basis for an argument to reverse the previous decision and establish a new precedent.

Federal Judicial Appointments

Unlike state court judges, who are often elected, all federal judges are appointed. Article II, Section 2, of the Constitution authorizes the president to appoint the justices of the Supreme Court with the advice and consent of the Senate. Laws enacted by Congress provide that the same procedure be used for appointing judges to the lower federal courts as well.

Federal judges receive lifetime appointments (because under Article III of the Constitution they "hold their Offices during good Behaviour"). Federal judges may be removed from office through the impeachment process, but such proceedings are extremely rare and are usually undertaken only if a judge engages in blatantly illegal conduct, such as bribery. In the history of this nation, only thirteen federal judges have been impeached, seven of whom were removed from office. Normally, federal judges serve until they resign, retire, or die.

Although the Constitution sets no specific qualifications for those who serve on the Supreme Court, all who have done so share one characteristic: all have been attorneys. The backgrounds of the Supreme Court justices have been far from typical of the characteristics of the American public as a whole. Table 14–1 on the following page summarizes the backgrounds of all of the 108 Supreme Court justices to 2005.

The Nomination Process

The president receives suggestions and recommendations as to potential nominees for Supreme Court positions from various sources, including the Justice Department, senators, other judges, the candidates themselves, state political leaders, bar associations, and other interest groups. After selecting a nominee, the president submits her or his name to the Senate for approval. The Senate Judiciary Committee then holds hearings and makes its recommendation to the Senate, where it takes a majority vote to confirm the nomination.

When judges are nominated to the district courts (and, to a lesser extent, the U.S. courts of appeals), a senator of the president's political party from the state where there is a vacancy traditionally has been allowed to veto the president's choice. This practice is known as **senatorial courtesy.** At one time, senatorial courtesy sometimes even permitted senators from the opposing party to veto presidential choices. Because of senatorial courtesy, home-state senators of the president's party may also be able to influence the choice of the nominee.

oral argument An argument presented to a judge in person by an attorney on behalf of her or his client.

conference In regard to the Supreme Court, a private meeting of the justices in which they present their arguments with respect to a case under consideration.

opinion A written statement by a court expressing the reasons for its decision in a case.

concurring opinion A statement written by a judge or justice who agrees (concurs) with the court's decision, but for reasons different from those in the majority opinion.

dissenting opinion A statement written by a judge or justice who disagrees with the majority opinion.

senatorial courtesy A practice that allows a senator of the president's party to veto the president's nominee to a federal court judgeship within the senator's state.

TABLE 14–1
Backgrounds of Supreme Court Justices to 2005*

	NUMBER OF JUSTICES (108 = TOTAL)
Occupational Position before Appointment	
Private legal practice	25
State judgeship	21
Federal judgeship	28
U.S. attorney general	7
Deputy or assistant U.S. attorney general	2
U.S. solicitor general	2
U.S. senator	6
U.S. representative	2
State governor	3
Federal executive post	9
Other	3
Religious Affiliation	
Protestant	83
Roman Catholic	11
Jewish	6
Unitarian	7
No religious affiliation	1
Age on Appointment	
Under 40	5
41–50	31
51–60	58
61–70	14
Political Party Affiliation	
Federalist (to 1835)	13
Jeffersonian Republican (to 1828)	7
Whig (to 1861)	1
Democrat	44
Republican	42
Independent	1
Education	
College graduate	92
Not a college graduate	16
Gender	
Male	106
Female	2
Race	
Caucasian	106
African American	2

*This table reflects the backgrounds of the justices until mid-2005.

SOURCES: Congressional Quarterly, *Congressional Quarterly's Guide to the U.S. Supreme Court* (Washington, D.C.: Congressional Quarterly Press, 1997); and authors' update.

It should come as no surprise that partisanship plays a significant role in the president's selection of nominees to the federal bench, particularly to the Supreme Court, the crown jewel of the federal judiciary. Traditionally, presidents have attempted to strengthen their legacies by appointing federal judges with similar political and philosophical views. (For a further discussion of judicial appointments and presidential legacies, see this chapter's *Perception versus Reality* feature.) In the history of the Supreme Court, fewer than 13 percent of the justices nominated by a president have been from an opposing political party.

Appointments to the U.S. courts of appeals can also have a lasting impact. Recall that these courts occupy the level just below the Supreme Court in the federal court system. Also recall that the decisions rendered by these courts—about 60,000 per year—are final unless overturned by the Supreme Court. Given that the Supreme Court renders opinions in fewer than one hundred cases a year, the decisions of the federal appellate courts have a wide-reaching impact on American society. For example, a decision interpreting the federal Constitution by the U.S. Court of Appeals for the Ninth Circuit, if not overruled by the Supreme Court, establishes a precedent that will be followed in the states of Alaska, Arizona, California, Hawaii, Idaho, Montana, Nevada, Oregon, and Washington.

Confirmation or Rejection by the Senate

The president's nominations are not always confirmed. In fact, almost 20 percent of presidential nominations for the Supreme Court have been either rejected or not acted on by the Senate. The process of nominating and confirming federal judges, especially Supreme Court justices, often involves political debate and controversy. Many bitter battles over Supreme Court appointments have ensued when the Senate and the president have disagreed on political issues.

From 1893 until 1968, the Senate rejected only three Court nominees. From 1968 through 1986, however, two presidential nominees to the highest court were rejected, and two more nominations, both by President Ronald Reagan, failed in 1987. First, the Senate rejected Robert Bork, who faced sometimes hostile questioning about his views on the Constitution during the confirmation hearings. Next, Reagan nominated Douglas Ginsburg, who ultimately withdrew his nomination when the press leaked information about his alleged use of marijuana during the 1970s. Finally, the Senate approved Reagan's third choice, Anthony Kennedy. Although both of President George H. W. Bush's nominees to the Supreme Court—David Souter and Clarence Thomas—were confirmed by the Senate, Thomas's nomination aroused considerable controversy. Thomas's confirmation hearings were extremely volatile and received widespread publicity on national television. The nation watched as Anita Hill, a former aide, leveled charges of sexual harassment at Thomas.

In 1993, President Bill Clinton had little trouble gaining approval for his nominee to fill the seat left vacant by Justice Byron White. Ruth Bader Ginsburg became the second female Supreme Court justice, the first being Sandra Day O'Connor, who was appointed by President Reagan in 1981. When Justice Harry Blackmun retired in 1994, Clinton nominated Stephen Breyer to fill Blackmun's seat. Breyer was confirmed without significant opposition.

Judicial Appointments and the Bush Administration

As discussed in the chapter-opening *America at Odds* feature, prior to both the 2000 and 2004 presidential elections, there was much conjecture about how the election outcomes might affect the federal judiciary—particularly, the make-up of the United States Supreme Court. No justice retired from the Supreme Court during George W. Bush's first term as president. As mentioned earlier, however, Chief Justice Rehnquist may have already stepped down by the time you read this text. Rehnquist's departure will give Bush his first opportunity to nominate a justice to the Supreme Court. Should other Supreme Court justices retire during Bush's second term, he will have further opportunities to make appointments to the high court.

Nonetheless, when Bush assumed the presidency, there were numerous vacancies to be filled on the lower courts, including vacancies on the benches of the U.S. courts of appeals. For the most part, Bush's nominations to the lower courts during his first term were confirmed. By

Judicial Appointments and Presidential Legacies

It is not unusual for a U.S. president to want to create a legacy— a long-lasting imprint on American politics. In principle, a sitting president can make a mark on the future by appointing (always with the consent of the Senate) federal court judges who share the president's political philosophy. Every year, there are numerous vacancies within the federal judiciary, and occasionally a vacancy occurs on the Supreme Court.

THE PERCEPTION

It is commonly perceived that a president will naturally nominate federal judges who share the president's political and philosophical views. Certainly, this was a widely shared assumption when Bill Clinton became president in 1992. Prior to his election, Clinton campaigned in favor of what are generally considered liberal causes—abortion rights, gay rights, and more aggressive enforcement of environmental laws. He also promised to appoint more minorities and women to federal court benches. Consequently, the public's initial perception of Clinton was that he was going to appoint liberal-leaning individuals to the federal judiciary.

THE REALITY

In reality, presidential appointments do not always fulfill the expectations of the president's party. Certainly, this was true with respect to Clinton's appointments. To be sure, during his first years in office, Clinton appointed more women and minorities to the federal bench than his predecessors had. Nonetheless, Clinton spurned activists and ideologues in his court appointments, choosing instead cautious moderates, such as respected state jurists and partners in large law firms. Prospective nominees were never asked their views on abortion, and even some pro-lifers were appointed. His Supreme Court nominees—Ruth Bader Ginsburg and Stephen Breyer—were clear moderates who were easily confirmed. Indeed, the moderation and compromise that marked the Clinton administration's judicial appointments caused some Democrats to view the Clinton years as a lost opportunity to pursue a liberal policy agenda.

Keep in mind that often an important consideration in nominating a particular judicial candidate to a federal court bench is whether the candidate is likely to be confirmed by the Senate. Although President George W. Bush will likely leave a lasting imprint on the make-up of the federal judiciary, whether he will succeed in appointing one or more Supreme Court justices with ideological views that mirror his own remains to be seen. As you will read later in this chapter, during Bush's first term as president the Democrats in the Senate blocked the confirmation of judicial nominees to the federal appellate courts who were known to hold extremely conservative views.

What's Your Opinion?

What are some of the pros and cons of the constitutional requirement that the Senate confirm presidential appointments to the federal judiciary? Would the nation be better off if the Constitution were amended to drop this requirement? Why or why not?

Rob Crandall/Stock, Boston

The Senate has the ultimate say over who becomes a justice of the United States Supreme Court. Here, Ruth Bader Ginsburg faces questioning by members of the Senate Judiciary Committee. On August 10, 1993, she became the 107th justice of the Supreme Court—and one of only two women ever to be appointed to that tribunal.

mid-2005, Republican appointees made up 60 percent of all of the active judges on the U.S. courts of appeals. If all of Bush's pending nominees win confirmation, that number will rise to 85 percent.[12] Very likely, though, not all of these nominees will be confirmed.

For example, during Bush's first term, the Democrats (and some Republicans) had serious objections to ten of Bush's fifty-two nominations to the U.S. courts of appeals. Believing that these nominees were too extreme in their conservative ideology, the Democrats blocked a full Senate vote on them by using filibusters. (Recall from Chapter 11 that the *filibuster* allows senators to debate as long as they wish, thereby effectively stalling a vote that they know they will lose.) The filibusters succeeded because the Republican leadership in the Senate was unable to garner the sixty votes necessary to invoke cloture and end the filibusters.

The Democrats' refusal to allow a vote on these candidates led to acrimonious exchanges between the Republicans and the Democrats in the Senate. At the beginning of Bush's second term, the Democrats urged the White House to come up with a list of nominees who would be acceptable to both parties. The Bush administration refused to negotiate, however, and Bush even took the unusual step of renominating several of the same candidates who had been blocked by the Democrats' filibusters. When the Democrats declared that they would continue to use filibusters to block these nominations, the Republicans countered by threatening to change the Senate rules to prohibit the use of filibusters to block judicial appointments. The Democrats responded that if the Republicans changed the rules on filibustering, they would bring the Senate—or at least all but its most essential functions—to a standstill. How this controversy will be resolved remains to be seen.

AMERICA at odds

Should Filibusters on Judicial Nominees Be Banned?

Democrats refer to the proposal to change the Senate rules to prohibit filibusters on judicial appointments as the "nuclear option." As the term indicates, changing the rules on filibustering simply to keep Democrats from blocking the confirmation of some of Bush's judicial nominees strikes some people as an extreme approach to resolving the problem.

Those who support the idea of banning filibusters on judicial nominees (mostly Republicans, including the Republican leadership in the Senate) argue that this move would be a "constitutional option," not a "nuclear option." According to this group, the Democrats' filibusters have essentially created a "supermajority" (60 percent) requirement for judicial confirmations. This, they claim, is not what the nation's founders intended when they drafted the Constitution. Furthermore, all of Bush's nominees were chosen for their ability to apply the law. The partisan or ideological preferences of the judges should not be an issue. If the Democrats continue the filibusters, this group claims, the Republicans will have little choice but to change the rules if judicial vacancies are to be filled.

Those opposed to banning the use of filibusters to block judicial confirmations (mostly Democrats, but some moderate Republicans as well) say that resorting to such a ban is an extreme and unnecessary measure. After all, the vast majority of Bush's judicial nominees (more than two hundred district and appellate court judges) were confirmed during his first term. The filibuster serves to protect the rights of the minority group in the Senate to object to nominees who, if confirmed, would hold lifetime positions on federal benches and influence national policy for decades to come. In a two-party system such as in the United States, this is an important right. Furthermore, this group claims, banning filibusters to block judicial nominees would change the fundamental character of the Senate as that body was envisioned by the nation's founders. The problem, they say, lies less with the Democrats than with the

President George W. Bush has maligned Democrats in Congress for blocking a number of his judicial nominees who are of Hispanic heritage. Here, Representative Charlie Gonzalez (D., Tex.) speaks against the nomination of Miguel Estrada to a federal appeals court in 2003.

AP Photo/Charles Dharapak

Republicans, who have abandoned the long-standing tradition of consulting with the minority party on controversial judicial choices.

The Courts as Policymakers

In a common law system, such as that of the United States, judges and justices play a major role in government. In part, this is because of the doctrine of *stare decisis,* which theoretically obligates judges to follow precedents. Additionally, unlike judges in some other countries, U.S. judges have the power to decide on the constitutionality of laws or actions undertaken by the other branches of government.

Clearly, the function of the courts is to interpret and apply the law, not to make law—that is the function of the legislative branch of government. Yet judges can and do "make law"; indeed, they cannot avoid making law in some cases because the law does not always provide clear answers to questions that come before the courts. The text of the U.S. Constitution, for example, is set forth in broad terms. When a court interprets a constitutional provision and applies that interpretation to a specific set of circumstances, the court is essentially "making the law" on that issue. Examples of how the courts, and especially the United States Supreme Court, make law abound. Consider privacy rights, which we discussed in Chapter 4. Nothing in the Constitution or its amendments specifically states that we have a right to privacy. Yet the Supreme Court, through various decisions, has established such a right by deciding that it is implied by several constitutional amendments. The Court has also held that this right to privacy includes a number of specific rights, such as the right to have an abortion.

Statutory provisions and other legal rules also tend to be expressed in general terms, and the courts must decide how those general provisions and rules apply to specific cases. Consider the Americans with Disabilities Act of 1990. The act requires employers to reasonably accommodate the needs of employees with disabilities. But the act does not say exactly what employers must do to "reasonably accommodate" such persons. Thus, the courts must decide, on a case-by-case basis, what this phrase means. Additionally, in some cases there is no relevant law or precedent to follow. In recent years, for example, courts have been struggling with new kinds of legal issues stemming from new communications technology, including the Internet. Until legislative bodies establish laws governing these issues, it is up to the courts to fashion the law that will apply—and thus make policy.

The Impact of Court Decisions

As already mentioned, how the courts interpret particular laws can have a widespread impact on society. For example, in 1996, in *Hopwood v. Texas,*[13] the U.S. Court of Appeals for the Fifth Circuit held that an affirmative action program implemented by the University of Texas School of Law in Austin was unconstitutional. The program allowed admissions officials to take race and other factors into consideration when determining which students would be admitted. The court stated that the program violated the equal protection clause because it discriminated in favor of minority applicants. The court further held that the use of race even as a means to achieve diversity on college campuses violated the Constitution's equal protection mandate. The court's decision in *Hopwood* set a precedent for all federal courts within the Fifth Circuit's jurisdiction (which covers Texas, Louisiana, and Mississippi). Thus, whenever similar affirmative action programs in those states were challenged, the federal courts hearing the cases had to apply the law as interpreted by the Court of Appeals for the Fifth Circuit.

Decisions rendered by the United States Supreme Court, of course, have an even broader impact on American society, because all courts in the nation are obligated to follow precedents set by the high court. For example, in 2003 the Supreme Court issued a ruling on affirmative action programs at the University of Michigan. Unlike the appeals court in the *Hopwood* case, the Supreme Court held that diversity on college campuses was a legitimate goal and that affirmative action programs that took race into consideration as part of an examination of each applicant's background did not necessarily violate the equal protection clause of the Constitution. This decision rendered any contrary ruling, including the ruling by the court in the *Hopwood* case, invalid.

Thus, when the Supreme Court interprets laws, it establishes national policy. If the Court deems that a law passed by Congress or a state legislature violates the Constitution, for example, that law will be void and unenforceable in any court within the United States.

The Power of Judicial Review

Recall from Chapter 2 that the U.S. Constitution divides government powers among the executive, legislative, and judicial branches. This division of powers is part of our checks and balances system. Essentially, the founders gave each branch of government the constitutional authority to check the other two branches. The federal judiciary can exercise a check on the actions of either of the other branches through its power of **judicial review.** (For a discussion of a significant question raised by the war on terrorism—whether the judicial branch should check the actions and decisions of a "wartime" president—see this chapter's *The Politics of National Security* feature.)

The Constitution does not actually mention judicial review. Rather, the Supreme Court claimed the power for itself in *Marbury v. Madison*.[14] In that case, which was decided by the Court in 1803, Chief Justice John Marshall held that a provision of a 1789 law affecting the Supreme Court's jurisdiction violated the Constitution and was thus void. Marshall declared, "It is emphatically the province and duty of the judicial department [the courts] to say what the law is. . . . If two laws conflict with each other, the courts must decide on the operation of

judicial review The power of the courts to decide on the constitutionality of legislative enactments and of actions taken by the executive branch.

The POLITICS of national SECURITY

Judicial Checks on a Wartime President

Wartime presidents often exercise their constitutional powers as the head of the executive branch of government and commander in chief to make urgent decisions regarding our national security. Certainly, President George W. Bush has done so during the war on terrorism. Shortly after the terrorist attacks of September 11, 2001, Congress passed a joint resolution giving the president further authority. The resolution authorized President Bush "to use all necessary and appropriate force against those nations, organizations, or persons he determines planned, authorized, committed, or aided the terrorist attacks . . . , or harbored such organizations or persons."

Having obtained this authorization, in 2001 Bush ordered military operations in Afghanistan against the terrorist network al Qaeda and the Taliban regime that harbored the organization. During the military operations, U.S. forces took custody of many individuals who were fighting against the allied forces, as well as suspected terrorists in other countries, including the United States. The president then unilaterally designated these individuals as "enemy combatants" and held them in detention at the U.S. Naval Base in Guantánamo Bay, Cuba. According to the Bush administration, any person who is designated as an enemy combatant is not entitled to the constitutional liberties and procedures that are normally afforded to criminal suspects in U.S. courts. Such persons can be held indefinitely until either the war on terrorism is over or the military determines that they do not pose a threat to the security of the United States.

Traditionally, the courts have given heightened deference to actions taken by a wartime president. But concerns over the rights of the detainees at Guantánamo Bay have led some courts to place limits on the executive branch's actions.

CHECKS ON THE EXECUTIVE BRANCH

The first significant check on the Bush administration's treatment of enemy combatants came in 2004. In the case of *Hamdi v. Rumsfeld*[15]

(discussed in Chapter 5), the United States Supreme Court held that "due process demands that . . . an enemy combatant be given a meaningful opportunity to contest the factual basis for that detention before a neutral decisionmaker." The Court stated that the military could not just declare fighters enemy combatants and detain them at Guantánamo without first holding hearings to find out if such persons were "unlawful combatants"—and thus properly detained.

In response to the Supreme Court's ruling, the U.S. Defense Department established military review tribunals to determine the legal status of the detainees. These tribunals, which have been criticized by some liberal groups as little more than "kangaroo courts," have since come under review by several lower courts. In early 2005, federal district court judge Joyce Hens Green openly challenged the legality of the tribunals in *In re Guantánamo Detainees Cases*.[16] The judge concluded that the way in which the tribunal proceedings were conducted violated both the U.S. Constitution and international law. Among other things, the detainees were neither represented by attorneys nor told of some of the evidence against them. According to Judge Green, the president's need to protect the nation against unprecedented threats "cannot negate the existence of the most basic fundamental rights for which the people of this country have fought and died for well over 200 years."

WHO QUALIFIES AS AN "ENEMY COMBATANT"?

Judge Green also challenged the Bush administration's broad definition of the term *enemy combatant*. To narrow the definition, she posed a series of hypotheticals, including the following scenario: Would "a little old lady in Switzerland who writes checks to what she thinks is a charity that helps orphans in Afghanistan but [that] really is a front to finance al Qaeda activities" fit the government's definition of an enemy combatant? The government said yes, also each. . . . So if a law be in opposition to the constitution . . . the court must determine which of these conflicting rules governs the case. This is the very essence of judicial duty."

Although the Constitution did not explicitly provide for judicial review, most constitutional scholars believe that the framers intended that the federal courts should have this power. In *Federalist Paper* No. 78, Alexander Hamilton clearly espoused the doctrine of judicial review. Hamilton stressed the importance of the "complete independence" of federal judges and their special duty to "invalidate all acts contrary to the manifest tenor of the Constitution." Without judicial review by impartial courts, there would be nothing to ensure that the other branches of government stayed within constitutional limits when exercising their powers, and "all the reservations of particular rights or privileges would amount to nothing." Chief Justice Marshall shared Hamilton's views and adopted Hamilton's reasoning in *Marbury v. Madison*.

Judicial Activism versus Judicial Restraint

As already noted, making policy is not the primary function of the federal courts. Yet it is unavoidable that courts do, in fact, influence or even establish policy when they interpret and apply the law. Further, the power of judicial review gives the courts, and particularly the Supreme Court, an important policymaking tool. When the Supreme Court upholds or invalidates a state or federal statute, the consequences for the nation can be profound.

The POLITICS of national SECURITY You are here

Judicial Checks on a Wartime President (Continued)

arguing that the president has the authority to detain such a person until the end of the war on terrorism.

WHEN WILL THIS WAR END?

Various laws and policies that have been created since September 11, 2001, have caused many Americans to worry about the future of their civil liberties. The treatment of enemy combatants is of particular concern because the right to due process of law and other constitutional protections goes to the heart of our democracy. The problem is particularly thorny because of the unusual nature of the war in which we are engaged.

When President Bush declared a war on terrorism following the September 11 terrorist attacks, he took an unprecedented step. He did not declare war on a nation with geographic limits; rather, he declared war on a *category* of crime—terrorism. This is not a war that can be won quickly or even in a few years. Indeed, by its own admission, the government anticipates that the war could last for "several generations." Essentially, this means that we are now living in a permanent wartime state, and the executive branch of our government is headed by a permanent wartime president. It also means that enemy combatants, if they can be detained until the war ends, could be detained for the rest of their lives.

Are We Safer?

How might designating individuals suspected of having terrorist connections as "enemy combatants" and detaining them indefinitely help to prevent future terrorist attacks? Is it conceivable that such detentions might help to instigate future terrorist actions against the United States?

AP Photo/Evan Vucci

Attorney Jenny Martinez, who represents José Padilla, stands outside the U.S. Supreme Court building. Padilla, a U.S. citizen, has been detained as an "enemy combatant" without trial. Martinez argued that President Bush overstepped his authority by jailing Padilla because of his suspected links to terrorism and denying him access to a lawyer and the court system.

John Marshall (1755–1835) served as chief justice of the Supreme Court from 1801 to 1835.

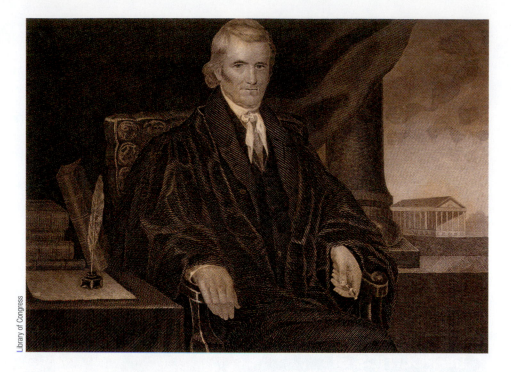

Library of Congress

One issue that is often debated is how the federal courts should wield their policymaking power, particularly the power of judicial review. Often, this debate is couched in terms of judicial activism versus judicial restraint.

Chief Justice Earl Warren (1897–1974) presided over the U.S. Supreme Court from 1953 to 1969. The Warren Court played a significant role in furthering the civil rights of African Americans and other minorities.

Activist versus Restraintist Justices

Although the terms *judicial activism* and *judicial restraint* lack any precise meaning, generally an activist judge or justice believes that the courts should actively use their powers to check the actions of the legislative and executive branches to ensure that they do not exceed their authority. A restraintist judge or justice, in contrast, generally assumes that the courts should defer to the decisions of the legislative and executive branches, because members of Congress and the president are elected by the people whereas federal court judges are not. In other words, the courts should not thwart the implementation of legislative acts unless they are clearly unconstitutional.

Political Ideology and Judicial Activism/Restraint

One of the Supreme Court's most activist eras occurred during the period from 1953 to 1969 under the leadership of Chief Justice Earl Warren. The Warren Court propelled the civil rights movement forward by holding, among other things, that laws permitting racial segregation violated the equal protection clause (see Chapter 5).

Because of the activism of the Warren Court, the term *judicial activism* has often been linked with liberalism. Indeed, many liberals are in favor of an activist federal judiciary because they believe that the judiciary can "right" the "wrongs" that result from unfair laws or from "antiquated" legislation at the state and local levels. Neither judicial activism nor judicial restraint is necessarily linked to a particular political ideology, however. In fact, many observers now claim that the Supreme Court is actively pursuing a conservative agenda.

Library of Congress

Ideology and the Courts

The policymaking role of the courts gives rise to an important question: To what extent do ideology and personal policy preferences affect judicial decision making? Numerous scholars have attempted to answer this question, especially with respect to Supreme Court justices.

Ideology and Supreme Court Decisions

In one study, judicial scholars Jeffrey Segal and Harold Spaeth concluded that "the Supreme Court decides disputes in light of the facts of the case vis-à-vis the ideological attitudes and values of the justices. Simply put, Rehnquist votes the way he does because he is extremely conservative."[17] The authors maintain that the Supreme Court justices base their decisions on policy preferences simply because they are free to do so—they are not accountable to the electorate because they are not elected to their positions. The desire to attain higher office is also not a factor in the Court's decision making because the justices are at the apex of the judicial career ladder.

Few doubt that ideology affects judicial decision making, although, of course, other factors play a role as well. Different courts (such as a trial court and an appellate court) can look at the same case and draw different conclusions as to what law is applicable and how it should be applied. Certainly, there are numerous examples of how ideology affects Supreme Court decisions. As new justices replace old ones and new ideological alignments are formed, the Court's decisions are affected. Yet many scholars argue that there is no real evidence indicating that personal preferences influence Supreme Court decisions to an *unacceptable* extent.

Keep in mind that judicial decision making, particularly at the Supreme Court level, can be very complex. When deciding cases, the Supreme Court often must consider any number of sources, including constitutions, statutes, and administrative agency regulations—as well as cases interpreting relevant portions of those sources. At times, the Court also takes foreign laws and international opinion into account when deciding an issue—although whether the Court should give significant weight to such sources is subject to controversy.

AMERICA at odds

Should the Supreme Court Look to Foreign Laws for Guidance?

On a few occasions in the last several years, the United States Supreme Court has referred to decisions of foreign courts and international human rights laws when rendering its decisions. For example, in two cases decided in 2003, *Lawrence v. Texas*[18] and *Grutter v. Bollinger,*[19] the Court compared other nations' laws and international human rights law with U.S. laws concerning gay rights and affirmative action, respectively. In a 2005 case, *Roper v. Simmons,*[20] the Court again looked to foreign laws and international opinion for guidance when deciding whether individuals who were juveniles (under the age of eighteen) when they committed their crimes should be subject to the death penalty. These actions by the Court sparked a significant debate over whether foreign sources should ever guide the decisions of this country's highest court on matters of national importance.

Some jurists, politicians, and other Americans believe that it is inappropriate for our nation's highest court to look to any laws other than U.S. laws for guidance. This group also believes that measuring the constitutionality of U.S. policies against the yardstick of foreign practices poses a threat to our national sovereignty. Indeed, after the Supreme Court's 2003 decisions mentioned above, some seventy Republicans in the House of Representatives cosponsored a joint resolution that, had it been adopted, would have placed what some have called a "gag order" on the federal courts. The resolution, titled the "Reaffirmation of American Independence Resolution," directed federal judges to disregard international law when interpreting the U.S. Constitution. Perhaps one of the harshest critics of the Supreme Court's willingness to consider international law and practices is Supreme Court justice Antonin Scalia. In his dissent to the majority opinion in the *Roper v. Simmons* case, he sharply criticized what he called the basic premise of the Court's argument—"that American law should conform to the laws of the rest of the world"—and said that the idea "ought to be rejected out of hand." Ultimately, claimed Scalia, looking to foreign laws results in very subjective decision making. Selecting which of the countless conflicting foreign laws to emphasize inevitably reflects the justices' personal beliefs concerning fairness and justice.

A number of other Americans—including Supreme Court justices Sandra Day O'Connor, Anthony Kennedy, Ruth Bader Ginsburg, and Stephen Breyer—argue that we should not ignore the opinions of the rest of the world. In our increasingly global community, it is vitally important to try to attain a deeper understanding of human rights on a worldwide level. Many in this group also maintain that those in Congress who would prevent U.S. courts from looking to foreign laws have overreached their authority by attempting to influence judicial decision making. Such attempts, they claim, would not only bar the Court from considering a whole range of valuable ideas but also strike at the heart of an independent judiciary. Some in this group believe that the United States has, in fact, lagged behind the community of nations in its judicial decision making. The highest courts in several other nations, including Canada, India, and Israel, frequently look to United States Supreme Court decisions for guidance on similar issues that come before their courts. Why shouldn't U.S. courts do likewise?

Approaches to Legal Interpretation

In contrast to the liberal Supreme Court under Earl Warren (1953–1969) and to a lesser extent under Warren Burger (1969–1986), today's Court is generally conservative. The Court began its rightward shift after President Ronald Reagan (1981–1989) appointed conservative William Rehnquist as chief justice in 1986, and the Court moved further to the right as other conservative appointments to the bench were made by Reagan and George H. W. Bush (1989–1993).

As mentioned in the chapter-opening *America at Odds* feature, however, it would be a mistake to look at the judicial philosophy of today's Supreme Court solely in terms of the political ideologies of liberalism and conservatism. In fact, some Supreme Court scholars have suggested that the justices' judicial philosophies with respect to how the law should be interpreted and their perception of the Supreme Court's role in the federal judiciary are more important in understanding why they decide as they do.

Strict versus Broad Construction
Legal scholars have often used the terms *strict* and *broad* construction to describe how judges and justices interpret the law. Generally, strict constructionists look to the letter of the law as written when trying to decipher its meaning, whereas broad constructionists look more to the purpose and context of the law. Strict constructionists believe that the letter of the law should guide the courts' decisions. Broad constructionists believe that the law is an evolving set of standards and is not fixed in concrete. Generally, broad constructionists are more willing to "read between the lines" of a law to serve what they perceive to be the law's intent and purpose.

Strict construction of the law is often linked with conservative views, and broad construction with liberal views. The conservative justices on today's Supreme Court are often labeled strict constructionists because they give great weight to the text of the law.

The Role of the Supreme Court
How justices view the role of the Supreme Court in the federal judiciary also affects their decision making. Two of the Court's justices—Antonin Scalia and Stephen Breyer—have made public their different visions of the Court's role. For Justice Scalia, a conservative voice on the Court, the Court should establish clear rules for the lower courts to follow when they apply the law. For Justice Breyer, who holds moderate-to-liberal views, the Court's role should be to establish flexible standards for the lower courts to apply on a case-by-case basis. This rules-versus-standards debate is reflected in the justices' opinions.

In one case, for example, Breyer, who wrote the majority opinion, concluded that a seniority system in the workplace should "ordinarily" take priority over a disabled worker's right to "reasonable accommodation" under the Americans with Disabilities Act (ADA) of 1990—see

Chapter 5. Yet, stated Breyer, there might be special circumstances that would make a disabled worker's reassignment to another position "reasonable" even though an employee with more seniority also had a right to the position. In other words, Breyer left the door open for the lower courts to deal with the question on a case-by-case basis, in light of the surrounding circumstances. Justice Scalia, in his dissent, concluded that a seniority system should always prevail. Saying that it should "ordinarily" prevail did not give any clear guidance to the lower courts and turned the "reasonable accommodation" provision in the ADA into a "standardless grab bag."[21]

These two positions reflect totally different concepts of the Court's role. For Scalia, it would be irresponsible to leave the law in such an indeterminate state. Therefore, the justices must provide strong guidance for the lower courts. For Breyer, an absolutist approach is unworkable. In a "participatory democracy," claims Breyer, the Court should not stand in the way of a new understanding of the law that "bubbles up from below."[22]

Constitutional Interpretation: Original Intent versus Modernism

The terms *strict construction* and *broad construction* describe different approaches to interpreting the law generally. These approaches may be used when determining the meaning of any law, whether it be a statutory provision, a specific regulation, or a constitutional clause. When discussing *constitutional* interpretation, however, the terms *original intent* and *modernism* are often used to describe the differences in Supreme Court justices' reasoning.

Original Intent Some of the justices believe that to determine the meaning of a particular constitutional phrase, the Court should look to the intentions of the founders. What did the framers of the Constitution themselves intend when they included the phrase in the document? In other words, what was the "original intent" of the phrase? To discern the intent of the founders, the justices should look to sources that shed light on the founders' views. These sources include contemporary writings by the founders, newspaper articles, the *Federalist Papers,* and notes taken during the Constitutional Convention. Justice Antonin Scalia, one of the Court's most conservative justices, gives some insight into this approach to constitutional interpretation in his book, *A Matter of Interpretation.*[23] In response to those who maintain that the Constitution is a "living Constitution" and should be interpreted in light of society's needs and practices today, Scalia contends that constitutional principles are fixed, not evolving: "The Constitution that I interpret and apply is not living, but dead."

Modernism Other justices, sometimes referred to as "modernists," believe that the Constitution is indeed a "living" document that evolves to meet changing times and new social needs. Otherwise, how could the Constitution even be relevant to today's society? How could the opinions of a small group of white men who drafted the document more than two hundred years ago possibly apply to today's large and diverse population? Moreover, the founders themselves often disagreed on what the Constitution should specify. Additionally, if original intent is the goal, what about the intentions of those who ratified the Constitution? Shouldn't they be taken into consideration also? The modernist approach to constitutional interpretation thus looks at the Constitution in the context of today's society and considers how today's life affects the words in the document. Modernists also defend their approach by stating that the founders intentionally left many constitutional provisions vague so that future generations could interpret the document in a manner that would meet the needs of a growing nation.

Assessing the Role of Federal Courts

The federal courts have often come under attack, particularly in the last decade or so, for many reasons. This should come as no surprise in view of the policymaking power of the courts. Because of our common law tradition, the federal judiciary in the United States has always played a far more significant role in politics and government than do the judiciaries in countries that do not have a common law system. After all, just one Supreme Court decision can establish what national policy will be on such issues as abortion, racial segregation, or online pornography.

Criticisms of the Federal Courts

Certainly, policymaking by unelected judges and justices in the federal courts has serious implications in a democracy. Some Americans, including a number of socially conservative members of the House of Representatives, contend that making policy from the bench has upset the balance of powers envisioned by the framers of the Constitution. They cite Thomas Jefferson, who once said, "It is a very dangerous doctrine to consider the judges as the ultimate arbiters of all constitutional questions." This group believes that we should rein in the power of the federal courts, and particularly judicial activism. Indeed, since the mid-1990s, when the Republicans took control of Congress, a number of bills to restrain the power of the federal judiciary have been introduced in Congress. Among other things, it has been proposed that Congress, not the Supreme Court, have the ultimate say in determining the meaning of the Constitution; that judges who ignore the will of Congress or follow foreign laws be impeached; that federal courts not be allowed to decide certain types of cases, such as those involving abortion or the place of religion in public life; and that Congress should be empowered to use its control over the judiciary to punish judges who overstep their authority.

The Case for the Courts

On the other side of the debate over the courts are those who claim that a strong case can be made for leaving the courts alone. Several federal court judges, including Chief Justice William Rehnquist and a member of the federal appeals court that heard the Terri Schiavo case (see Chapter 12), have sharply criticized congressional efforts to interfere with their authority. They claim that such efforts violate the Constitution's separation of powers. Other critics of Congress's attacks on the federal judiciary include Senator James M. Jeffords, an independent senator from Vermont, who likened the federal court system to a referee: "The first lesson we teach children when they enter competitive sports is to respect the referee, even if we think he [or she] might have made the wrong call. If our children can understand this, why can't our political leaders?"[24]

Others argue that there are already sufficient checks on the courts, some of which we look at next. Additionally, Americans traditionally have held the federal courts, and particularly the Supreme Court, in high regard.

Judicial Traditions and Doctrines

One check on the courts is judicial restraint. Supreme Court justices traditionally have exercised a great deal of self-restraint. Justices sometimes admit to making decisions that fly in the face of their personal values and policy preferences, simply because they feel obligated to do so in view of existing law. Self-restraint is also mandated by various judicially established traditions and doctrines, including the doctrine of *stare decisis,* which theoretically obligates the Supreme Court to follow its own precedents. Furthermore, the Supreme Court will not hear a meritless appeal just so it can rule on the issue. Finally, more often than not, the justices narrow their rulings to focus on just one aspect of an issue, even though there may be nothing to stop them from broadening their focus and thus widening the impact of their decisions.

Other Checks

The judiciary is subject to other checks as well. Courts may make rulings, but they cannot force federal and state legislatures to appropriate the funds necessary to carry out those rulings. For example, if the Supreme Court decides that prison conditions must be improved, a legislature has to find the funds to carry out the ruling. Additionally, legislatures can rewrite (amend) old laws or pass new ones to negate courts' rulings. This may happen when a court interprets a statute in a way that Congress had not intended. Congress may also propose amendments to the Constitution to reverse Supreme Court rulings, and Congress has the authority to limit or otherwise alter the jurisdiction of the lower federal courts. Finally, although it is most unlikely, Congress could even change the number of justices on the Supreme Court, in an attempt to change the ideological balance on the Court.

The Public's Regard for the Supreme Court As mentioned, some have proposed that Congress, not the Supreme Court, be the final arbiter of the Constitution. In debates on this topic, one factor is often overlooked: the American public's high regard for the Supreme Court and the federal courts generally. The Court continues to be respected as a fair arbiter of conflicting interests and the protector of constitutional rights and liberties. Even when the Court issued its decision to halt the manual recount of votes in Florida following the 2000 elections, Americans respected the Court's decision-making authority—even though many disagreed with the Court's decision. Polls continue to show that Americans have more trust and confidence in the Supreme Court than they do in Congress. In the eyes of many Americans, the Supreme Court stands in sharp contrast to a Congress that seems incapable of rising above the partisan bickering of Washington politics.

why does it MATTER?

The Judiciary and Your Everyday Life

"The Judicial Department comes home in its effects to every man's fireside: it passes on his property, his reputation, his life, his all." So stated John Marshall, chief justice of the United States Supreme Court from 1801 to 1835. If you reflect a moment on these words, you will realize their truth. A single Supreme Court decision can affect the lives of millions of Americans. Consider just a few examples:

AP Photo/Gary C. Knapp

- In 1942, the Supreme Court held that wheat produced by an individual farmer for consumption on his own farm was subject to federal regulation, even though the commerce clause of the Constitution states that the national government can regulate only *interstate* commerce. The Court's reasoning was ingenious: when farmers consume their own wheat, less wheat is put into the interstate marketplace; therefore, the farmer's home consumption affects the overall price of wheat in the nation. This decision was one of a number of decisions that upheld Congress's authority to regulate commercial activities—even activities occurring solely within state borders. As a result, today the federal government regulates virtually every aspect of business life in this country. Thus, we now have minimum-wage laws, uniform workplace standards, and literally thousands of other federal regulations.
- In 1954, the Supreme Court held that state laws upholding racial segregation in public schools violated the Fourteenth Amendment to the Constitution and were thus invalid. This decision has affected the lives of millions of Americans.
- Beginning in 1978, the Supreme Court has also upheld the constitutionality of many affirmative action programs designed to "level the playing field" for African Americans, other minorities, and women—groups that had become disadvantaged due to past discriminatory treatment. Although affirmative action has come under attack in the last decade, these programs continue to exist and affect how businesses hire and fire employees, how universities make admissions decisions, and how government agencies decide who should benefit from government contracts.

- In 1973, the Supreme Court held that the constitutional right to privacy included the right to have an abortion. This controversial decision has also affected the lives of millions of Americans.
- Over time, the Supreme Court has issued many decisions concerning the rights of accused persons. If you are ever stopped by a police officer, you will be entitled to exercise these rights. You do not have to worry about being thrown into jail arbitrarily or about not being able to have legal assistance when you need it.

Taking Action

In this chapter, you have learned about the role played by the judiciary in our system of government. If you feel strongly about a particular judicial nominee, contact the U.S. senators from your state and voice your opinion. To get a better understanding of court procedures, consider visiting your local county court when a trial is in session (check with the clerk of the court before entering the trial room, though). If you have an opportunity to participate in a mock trial at your school, consider doing so. In the photo above, a College of William and Mary law student stands at the podium, left, and makes opening remarks to a jury during a mock trial of a terrorist. The mock trial relied heavily on computer technology and the Internet to bring together the witnesses, lawyers, judge, and jury.

Key Terms

administrative law   320

appellate court   324

case law   320

civil law   321

common law   319

concurring opinion   327

conference   327

constitutional law   320

criminal law   322

dissenting opinion   327

diversity of
   citizenship   322

federal question   322

judicial review   332

judiciary   319

jurisdiction   322

justiciable
   controversy   322

opinion   327

oral argument   327

precedent   319

primary source of
   law   320

senatorial courtesy   327

standing to sue   322

stare decisis   319

statutory law   320

trial court   322

writ of *certiorari*   325

Chapter Summary

1 The American legal system is an offshoot of the common law tradition that developed in England over hundreds of years. The cornerstone of the English and American legal systems is the doctrine of *stare decisis,* which theoretically obligates judges to follow precedents (previous court decisions in their jurisdiction) when interpreting the law.

2 Primary sources of American law include constitutional law, statutory law, administrative law, and case law. Law can also be classified in other ways. An important classification divides all law into civil law or criminal law.

3 Certain judicial requirements limit the types of cases courts can hear and decide. Before a court can hear a case, it must have jurisdiction over the person against whom the case is brought, the property involved, and the subject matter. The party bringing the case must also have standing to sue—that is, the party must have a definable stake in the controversy at hand and the issue must be real and definite, not hypothetical or abstract. Additionally, both the federal and state courts have established procedural rules that apply in judicial proceedings.

4 The federal court system is a three-tiered model consisting of U.S. district (trial) courts, U.S. courts of appeals, and the United States Supreme Court. There is no absolute right of appeal to the Supreme Court.

5 All federal judges are appointed by the president and confirmed by the Senate. Presidents have attempted to strengthen their legacies by appointing federal judges with similar political, ideological, and philosophical views.

6 Judges play an important policymaking role in the United States because of our common law system, the doctrine of *stare decisis,*

and the power of judicial review. Judges can decide on the constitutionality of laws or actions undertaken by the other branches of government. The extent to which ideology affects judicial decision making in the federal courts has led to substantial controversy because federal judges are appointed and are not accountable to the electorate.

7 Judicial activism has also led to controversy. Activist judges believe that the courts should actively check the actions of the other two branches of government to ensure that they do not exceed their authority. Restraintist judges tend to show more deference to the decisions of the other branches because they are elected by the people whereas federal judges are not. Although activism is often associated with the liberalism of the Warren Court, today judicial activism is increasingly associated with conservative judges.

8 The extent to which ideology affects the Supreme Court's decision making has often been explored, with differing conclusions. Some scholars have recently suggested that other factors—such as how the justices interpret the law or their perception of the role of the Supreme Court in the federal judiciary—may be more important than conservative or liberal political ideology in understanding why the justices decide as they do.

9 Although the courts are often criticized for allowing personal preferences and philosophies to influence their decision making, in fact there are many checks on the courts. The courts are restrained by judicial traditions and doctrines, their lack of enforcement powers, and potential congressional actions in response to court decisions.

RESOURCES FOR FURTHER STUDY

Selected Readings

Comiskey, Michael. *The Judging of Supreme Court Nominees.* Lawrence, Kans.: University of Kansas Press, 2004. The author counters criticisms of the confirmation process for judicial nominees, arguing that, in fact, the process works well. By improving the level of scrutiny of prospective judges, the confirmation process has resulted in court vacancies being filled with capable jurists.

Keck, Thomas M. *The Most Activist Supreme Court in History.* Chicago: University of Chicago Press, 2004. As the title of this book suggests, the author maintains that the modern Supreme Court actively exercises its powers, in both conservative and liberal directions. The Court, despite its traditional conservative commitment to restraint, has settled political conflicts on abortion, gay rights, affirmative action, presidential elections, and a host of other divisive issues.

Marmour, Andrei. *Interpretation and Legal Theory,* 2d ed. Portland, Ore.: Hart Publications, 2005. The author, a professor at the University of Southern California Law School, argues for a modernist approach to constitutional interpretation. He contends that constitutional interpretation should be guided by moral reasoning and should be detached from any need to consult the framers' intentions.

Raskin, Jamin B. *We the Students: Supreme Court Cases for and about Students,* 2d ed. Washington, D.C.: CQ Press, 2003. The author, using an interactive approach, focuses on a number of Supreme Court cases dealing with issues of high interest to students.

Politics on the Web

■ An excellent Web site for information on the justices of the United States Supreme Court is http://www.oyez.org

This site offers biographies of the justices, links to opinions they have written, and, for justices who have served after 1920, video and audio materials. Oral arguments before the Supreme Court are also posted on this site.

■ Another helpful Web site is http://supct.law.cornell.edu/supct/

This is the index of the United States Supreme Court. It has recent Court decisions by year and name of party, and it also has selected historic decisions rendered by the Court.

■ The Supreme Court makes its opinions available online at its official Web site. Go to http://supremecourtus.gov

■ FindLaw offers a free searchable database of Supreme Court decisions since 1907 at http://www.findlaw.com

■ Increasingly, decisions of the state courts are also becoming available online. You can search through the texts of state cases that are on the Internet, as well as federal cases and state and federal laws, by accessing WashLaw at http://www.washlaw.edu

■ To learn more about the federal court system, go to http://www.uscourts.gov

This is the home page for the federal courts. Among other things, you can follow the "path" a case takes as it moves through the federal court system.

Online Resources for This Chapter

This text's Companion Web Site, at http://www.americaatodds.com, offers links to numerous resources that you can utilize to learn more about the topics covered in this chapter. For a list describing these resources, see the inside front cover of this book.

the constitution of the united states

Preamble

We the People of the United States, in Order to form a more perfect Union, establish Justice, insure domestic Tranquility, provide for the common defence, promote the general Welfare, and secure the Blessings of Liberty to ourselves and our Posterity, do ordain and establish this Constitution for the United States of America.

Article I

Section 1. All legislative Powers herein granted shall be vested in a Congress of the United States, which shall consist of a Senate and House of Representatives.

Section 2. The House of Representatives shall be composed of Members chosen every second Year by the People of the several States, and the Electors in each State shall have the Qualifications requisite for Electors of the most numerous Branch of the State Legislature.

No Person shall be a Representative who shall not have attained to the Age of twenty five Years, and been seven Years a Citizen of the United States, and who shall not, when elected, be an Inhabitant of that State in which he shall be chosen.

Representatives and direct Taxes shall be apportioned among the several States which may be included within this Union, according to their respective Numbers, which shall be determined by adding to the whole Number of free Persons, including those bound to Service for a Term of Years, and excluding Indians not taxed, three fifths of all other Persons. The actual Enumeration shall be made within three Years after the first Meeting of the Congress of the United States, and within every subsequent Term of ten Years, in such Manner as they shall by Law direct. The Number of Representatives shall not exceed one for every thirty Thousand, but each State shall have at Least one Representative; and until such enumeration shall be made, the State of New Hampshire shall be entitled to chuse three, Massachusetts eight, Rhode Island and Providence Plantations one, Connecticut five, New York six, New Jersey four, Pennsylvania eight, Delaware one, Maryland six, Virginia ten, North Carolina five, South Carolina five, and Georgia three.

When vacancies happen in the Representation from any State, the Executive Authority thereof shall issue Writs of Election to fill such Vacancies.

The House of Representatives shall chuse their Speaker and other Officers; and shall have the sole Power of Impeachment.

Section 3. The Senate of the United States shall be composed of two Senators from each State, chosen by the Legislature thereof, for six Years; and each Senator shall have one Vote.

Immediately after they shall be assembled in Consequence of the first Election, they shall be divided as equally as may be into three Classes. The Seats of the Senators of the first Class shall be vacated at the Expiration of the second Year, of the second Class at the Expiration of the fourth Year, and of the third Class at the Expiration of the sixth Year, so that one third may be chosen every second Year; and if Vacancies happen by Resignation, or otherwise, during the Recess of the Legislature of any State, the Executive thereof may make temporary Appointments until the next Meeting of the Legislature, which shall then fill such Vacancies.

No Person shall be a Senator who shall not have attained to the Age of thirty Years, and been nine Years a Citizen of the United States, and who shall not, when elected, be an Inhabitant of that State for which he shall be chosen.

The Vice President of the United States shall be President of the Senate, but shall have no Vote, unless they be equally divided.

The Senate shall chuse their other Officers, and also a President pro tempore, in the Absence of the Vice President, or when he shall exercise the Office of President of the United States.

The Senate shall have the sole Power to try all Impeachments. When sitting for that Purpose, they shall be on Oath or Affirmation. When the President of the United States is tried, the Chief Justice shall preside: And no Person shall be convicted without the Concurrence of two thirds of the Members present.

Judgment in Cases of Impeachment shall not extend further than to removal from Office, and disqualification to hold and enjoy any Office of honor, Trust, or Profit under the United States: but the Party convicted shall nevertheless be liable and subject to Indictment, Trial, Judgment, and Punishment, according to Law.

Section 4. The Times, Places and Manner of holding Elections for Senators and Representatives, shall be prescribed in each State by the Legislature thereof; but the Congress may at any time by Law make or alter such Regulations, except as to the Places of chusing Senators.

The Congress shall assemble at least once in every Year, and such Meeting shall be on the first Monday in December, unless they shall by Law appoint a different Day.

Section 5.   Each House shall be the Judge of the Elections, Returns, and Qualifications of its own Members, and a Majority of each shall constitute a Quorum to do Business; but a smaller Number may adjourn from day to day, and may be authorized to compel the Attendance of absent Members, in such Manner, and under such Penalties as each House may provide.

Each House may determine the Rules of its Proceedings, punish its Members for disorderly Behavior, and, with the Concurrence of two thirds, expel a Member.

Each House shall keep a Journal of its Proceedings, and from time to time publish the same, excepting such Parts as may in their Judgment require Secrecy; and the Yeas and Nays of the Members of either House on any question shall, at the Desire of one fifth of those Present, be entered on the Journal.

Neither House, during the Session of Congress, shall, without the Consent of the other, adjourn for more than three days, nor to any other Place than that in which the two Houses shall be sitting.

Section 6.   The Senators and Representatives shall receive a Compensation for their Services, to be ascertained by Law, and paid out of the Treasury of the United States. They shall in all Cases, except Treason, Felony and Breach of the Peace, be privileged from Arrest during their Attendance at the Session of their respective Houses, and in going to and returning from the same; and for any Speech or Debate in either House, they shall not be questioned in any other Place.

No Senator or Representative shall, during the Time for which he was elected, be appointed to any civil Office under the Authority of the United States, which shall have been created, or the Emoluments whereof shall have been increased during such time; and no Person holding any Office under the United States, shall be a Member of either House during his Continuance in Office.

Section 7.   All Bills for raising Revenue shall originate in the House of Representatives; but the Senate may propose or concur with Amendments as on other Bills.

Every Bill which shall have passed the House of Representatives and the Senate, shall, before it become a Law, be presented to the President of the United States; If he approve he shall sign it, but if not he shall return it, with his Objections to the House in which it shall have originated, who shall enter the Objections at large on their Journal, and proceed to reconsider it. If after such Reconsideration two thirds of that House shall agree to pass the Bill, it shall be sent together with the Objections, to the other House, by which it shall likewise be reconsidered, and if approved by two thirds of that House, it shall become a Law. But in all such Cases the Votes of both Houses shall be determined by Yeas and Nays, and the Names of the Persons voting for and against the Bill shall be entered on the Journal of each House respectively. If any Bill shall not be returned by the President within ten Days (Sundays excepted) after it shall have been presented to him, the Same shall be a Law, in like Manner as if he had signed it, unless the Congress by their Adjournment prevent its Return in which Case it shall not be a Law.

Every Order, Resolution, or Vote, to which the Concurrence of the Senate and House of Representatives may be necessary (except on a question of Adjournment) shall be presented to the President of the United States; and before the Same shall take Effect, shall be approved by him, or being disapproved by him, shall be repassed by two thirds of the Senate and House of Representatives, according to the Rules and Limitations prescribed in the Case of a Bill.

Section 8.   The Congress shall have Power To lay and collect Taxes, Duties, Imposts and Excises, to pay the Debts and provide for the common Defence and general Welfare of the United States; but all Duties, Imposts and Excises shall be uniform throughout the United States;

To borrow Money on the credit of the United States;

To regulate Commerce with foreign Nations, and among the several States, and with the Indian Tribes;

To establish an uniform Rule of Naturalization, and uniform Laws on the subject of Bankruptcies throughout the United States;

To coin Money, regulate the Value thereof, and of foreign Coin, and fix the Standard of Weights and Measures;

To provide for the Punishment of counterfeiting the Securities and current Coin of the United States;

To establish Post Offices and post Roads;

To promote the Progress of Science and useful Arts, by securing for limited Times to Authors and Inventors the exclusive Right to their respective Writings and Discoveries;

To constitute Tribunals inferior to the supreme Court;

To define and punish Piracies and Felonies committed on the high Seas, and Offenses against the Law of Nations;

To declare War, grant Letters of Marque and Reprisal, and make Rules concerning Captures on Land and Water;

To raise and support Armies, but no Appropriation of Money to that Use shall be for a longer Term than two Years;

To provide and maintain a Navy;

To make Rules for the Government and Regulation of the land and naval Forces;

To provide for calling forth the Militia to execute the Laws of the Union, suppress Insurrections and repel Invasions;

To provide for organizing, arming, and disciplining, the Militia, and for governing such Part of them as may be employed in the Service of the United States, reserving to the States respectively, the Appointment of the Officers, and the Authority of training the Militia according to the discipline prescribed by Congress;

To exercise exclusive Legislation in all Cases whatsoever, over such District (not exceeding ten Miles square) as may, by Cession of particular States, and the Acceptance of Congress, become the Seat of the Government of the United States, and to exercise like Authority over all Places purchased by the Consent of the Legislature of the State in which the Same shall be, for the Erection of Forts, Magazines, Arsenals, dock-Yards, and other needful Buildings;—And

To make all Laws which shall be necessary and proper for carrying into Execution the foregoing Powers, and all other Powers vested by this Constitution in the Government of the United States, or in any Department or Officer thereof.

Section 9.   The Migration or Importation of such Persons as any of the States now existing shall think proper to admit, shall not be prohibited by the Congress prior to the Year one thousand eight hundred and eight, but a Tax or duty may be imposed on such Importation, not exceeding ten dollars for each Person.

The privilege of the Writ of Habeas Corpus shall not be suspended, unless when in Cases of Rebellion or Invasion the public Safety may require it.

No Bill of Attainder or ex post facto Law shall be passed.

No Capitation, or other direct, Tax shall be laid, unless in Proportion to the Census or Enumeration herein before directed to be taken.

No Tax or Duty shall be laid on Articles exported from any State.

No Preference shall be given by any Regulation of Commerce or Revenue to the Ports of one State over those of another: nor shall Vessels bound to, or from, one State be obliged to enter, clear, or pay Duties in another.

No Money shall be drawn from the Treasury, but in Consequence of Appropriations made by Law; and a regular Statement and Account of the Receipts and Expenditures of all public Money shall be published from time to time.

No Title of Nobility shall be granted by the United States: And no Person holding any Office of Profit or Trust under them, shall, without the Consent of the Congress, accept of any present, Emolument, Office, or Title, of any kind whatever, from any King, Prince, or foreign State.

Section 10.   No State shall enter into any Treaty, Alliance, or Confederation; grant Letters of Marque and Reprisal; coin Money; emit Bills of Credit; make any Thing but gold and silver Coin a Tender in Payment of Debts; pass any Bill of Attainder, ex post facto Law, or Law impairing the Obligation of Contracts, or grant any Title of Nobility.

No State shall, without the Consent of the Congress, lay any Imposts or Duties on Imports or Exports, except what may be absolutely necessary for executing its inspection Laws: and the net Produce of all Duties and Imposts, laid by any State on Imports or Exports, shall be for the Use of the Treasury of the United States; and all such Laws shall be subject to the Revision and Controul of the Congress.

No State shall, without the Consent of Congress, lay any Duty of Tonnage, keep Troops, or Ships of War in time of Peace, enter into any Agreement or Compact with another State, or with a foreign Power, or engage in War, unless actually invaded, or in such imminent Danger as will not admit of delay.

Article II

Section 1.   The executive Power shall be vested in a President of the United States of America. He shall hold his Office during the Term of four Years, and, together with the Vice President, chosen for the same Term, be elected, as follows:

Each State shall appoint, in such Manner as the Legislature thereof may direct, a Number of Electors, equal to the whole Number of Senators and Representatives to which the State may be entitled in the Congress; but no Senator or Representative, or Person holding an Office of Trust or Profit under the United States, shall be appointed an Elector.

The Electors shall meet in their respective States, and vote by Ballot for two Persons, of whom one at least shall not be an Inhabitant of the same State with themselves. And they shall make a List of all the Persons voted for, and of the Number of Votes for each; which List they shall sign and certify, and transmit sealed to the Seat of the Government of the United States, directed to the President of the Senate. The President of the Senate shall, in the Presence of the Senate and House of Representatives, open all the Certificates, and the Votes shall then be counted. The Person having the greatest Number of Votes shall be the President, if such Number be a Majority of the whole Number of Electors appointed; and if there be more than one who have such Majority, and have an equal Number of Votes, then the House of Representatives shall immediately chuse by Ballot one of them for President; and if no Person have a Majority, then from the five highest on the List the said House shall in like Manner chuse the President. But in chusing the President, the Votes shall be taken by States, the Representation from each State having one Vote; A quorum for this Purpose shall consist of a Member or Members from two thirds of the States, and a Majority of all the States shall be necessary to a Choice. In every Case, after the Choice of the President, the Person having the greater Number of Votes of the Electors shall be the Vice President. But if there should remain two or more who have equal Votes, the Senate shall chuse from them by Ballot the Vice President.

The Congress may determine the Time of chusing the Electors, and the Day on which they shall give their Votes; which Day shall be the same throughout the United States.

No person except a natural born Citizen, or a Citizen of the United States, at the time of the Adoption of this Constitution, shall be eligible to the Office of President; neither shall any Person be eligible to that Office who shall not have attained to the Age of thirty five Years, and been fourteen Years a Resident within the United States.

In Case of the Removal of the President from Office, or of his Death, Resignation or Inability to discharge the Powers and Duties of the said Office, the same shall devolve on the Vice President, and the Congress may by Law provide for the Case of Removal, Death, Resignation or Inability, both of the President and Vice President, declaring what Officer shall then act as President, and such Officer shall act accordingly, until the Disability be removed, or a President shall be elected.

The President shall, at stated Times, receive for his Services, a Compensation, which shall neither be increased nor diminished during the Period for which he shall have been elected, and he shall not receive within that Period any other Emolument from the United States, or any of them.

Before he enter on the Execution of his Office, he shall take the following Oath or Affirmation: "I do solemnly swear (or affirm) that I will faithfully execute the Office of President of the United States, and will to the best of my Ability, preserve, protect and defend the Constitution of the United States."

Section 2.   The President shall be Commander in Chief of the Army and Navy of the United States, and of the Militia of the several States, when called into the actual Service of the United States; he may require the Opinion, in writing, of the principal Officer in each of the executive Departments, upon any Subject relating to the Duties of their respective Offices, and he shall have Power to grant Reprieves and Pardons for Offenses against the United States, except in Cases of Impeachment.

He shall have Power, by and with the Advice and Consent of the Senate to make Treaties, provided two thirds of the Senators present concur; and he shall nominate, and by and with the Advice and Consent of the Senate, shall appoint Ambassadors, other public Ministers and Consuls, Judges of the supreme Court, and all other Officers of the United States, whose Appointments are not herein otherwise provided for, and which shall be established by Law; but the Congress may by Law vest the Appointment of such inferior Officers, as they think proper, in the President alone, in the Courts of Law, or in the Heads of Departments.

The President shall have Power to fill up all Vacancies that may happen during the Recess of the Senate, by granting Commissions which shall expire at the End of their next Session.

Section 3.   He shall from time to time give to the Congress Information of the State of the Union, and recommend to their Consideration such Measures as he shall judge necessary and expedient; he may, on extraordinary Occasions, convene both Houses, or either of them, and in Case of Disagreement between them, with Respect to the Time of Adjournment, he may adjourn them to such Time as he shall think proper; he shall receive Ambassadors and other public Ministers; he shall take Care that the Laws be faithfully executed, and shall Commission all the Officers of the United States.

Section 4.   The President, Vice President and all civil Officers of the United States, shall be removed from Office on Impeachment for, and Conviction of, Treason, Bribery, or other high Crimes and Misdemeanors.

Article III

Section 1.   The judicial Power of the United States, shall be vested in one supreme Court, and in such inferior Courts as the Congress may from time to time ordain and establish. The Judges, both of the supreme and inferior Courts, shall hold their Offices during good Behaviour, and shall, at stated Times, receive for their Services a Compensation, which shall not be diminished during their Continuance in Office.

Section 2.   The judicial Power shall extend to all Cases, in Law and Equity, arising under this Constitution, the Laws of the United States, and Treaties made, or which shall be made, under their Authority;—to all Cases affecting Ambassadors, other public Ministers and Consuls;—to all Cases of admiralty and maritime Jurisdiction;—to Controversies to which the United States shall be a Party;—to Controversies between two or more States;—between a State and Citizens of another State;—between Citizens of different States;—between Citizens of the same State claiming Lands under Grants of different States, and between a State, or the Citizens thereof, and foreign States, Citizens or Subjects.

In all Cases affecting Ambassadors, other public Ministers and Consuls, and those in which a State shall be a Party, the supreme Court shall have original Jurisdiction. In all the other Cases before mentioned, the supreme Court shall have appellate Jurisdiction, both as to Law and Fact, with such Exceptions, and under such Regulations as the Congress shall make.

The Trial of all Crimes, except in Cases of Impeachment, shall be by Jury; and such Trial shall be held in the State where the said Crimes shall have been committed; but when not committed within any State, the Trial shall be at such Place or Places as the Congress may by Law have directed.

Section 3.   Treason against the United States, shall consist only in levying War against them, or, in adhering to their Enemies, giving them Aid and Comfort. No Person shall be convicted of Treason unless on the Testimony of two Witnesses to the same overt Act, or on Confession in open Court.

The Congress shall have Power to declare the Punishment of Treason, but no Attainder of Treason shall work Corruption of Blood, or Forfeiture except during the Life of the Person attainted.

Article IV

Section 1.   Full Faith and Credit shall be given in each State to the public Acts, Records, and judicial Proceedings of every other State. And the Congress may by general Laws prescribe the Manner in which such Acts, Records and Proceedings shall be proved, and the Effect thereof.

Section 2.   The Citizens of each State shall be entitled to all Privileges and Immunities of Citizens in the several States.

A Person charged in any State with Treason, Felony, or other Crime, who shall flee from Justice, and be found in another State, shall on Demand of the executive Authority of the State from which he fled, be delivered up, to be removed to the State having Jurisdiction of the Crime.

No Person held to Service or Labour in one State, under the Laws thereof, escaping into another, shall, in Consequence of any Law or Regulation therein, be discharged from such Service or Labour, but shall be delivered up on Claim of the Party to whom such Service or Labour may be due.

Section 3.   New States may be admitted by the Congress into this Union; but no new State shall be formed or erected within the Jurisdiction of any other State; nor any State be formed by the Junction of two or more States, or Parts of States, without the Consent of the Legislatures of the States concerned as well as of the Congress.

The Congress shall have Power to dispose of and make all needful Rules and Regulations respecting the Territory or other Property belonging to the United States; and nothing in this Constitution shall be so construed as to Prejudice any Claims of the United States, or of any particular State.

Section 4.   The United States shall guarantee to every State in this Union a Republican Form of Government, and shall protect each of them against Invasion; and on Application of the Legislature, or of the Executive (when the Legislature cannot be convened) against domestic Violence.

Article V

The Congress, whenever two thirds of both Houses shall deem it necessary, shall propose Amendments to this Constitution, or, on the Application of the Legislatures of two thirds of the several States, shall call a Convention for proposing Amendments, which, in either Case, shall be valid to all Intents and Purposes, as part of this Constitution, when ratified by the Legislatures of three fourths of the several States, or by Conventions in three fourths thereof, as the one or the other Mode of Ratification may be proposed by the Congress; Provided that no Amendment which may be made prior to the Year One thousand eight hundred and eight shall in any Manner affect the first and fourth Clauses in the Ninth Section of the first Article; and that no State, without its Consent, shall be deprived of its equal Suffrage in the Senate.

Article VI

All Debts contracted and Engagements entered into, before the Adoption of this Constitution shall be as valid against the United States under this Constitution, as under the Confederation.

This Constitution, and the Laws of the United States which shall be made in Pursuance thereof; and all Treaties made, or which shall be made, under the Authority of the United States, shall be the supreme Law of the Land; and the Judges in every State shall be bound thereby, any Thing in the Constitution or Laws of any State to the Contrary notwithstanding.

The Senators and Representatives before mentioned, and the Members of the several State Legislatures, and all executive and judicial Officers, both of the United States and of the several States, shall be bound by Oath or Affirmation, to support this Constitution; but no religious Test shall ever be required as a Qualification to any Office or public Trust under the United States.

Article VII

The Ratification of the Conventions of nine States shall be sufficient for the Establishment of this Constitution between the States so ratifying the Same.

Amendment I [1791]

Congress shall make no law respecting an establishment of religion, or prohibiting the free exercise thereof; or abridging the freedom of speech, or of the press; or the right of the people peaceably to assemble, and to petition the Government for a redress of grievances.

Amendment II [1791]

A well regulated Militia, being necessary to the security of a free State, the right of the people to keep and bear Arms, shall not be infringed.

Amendment III [1791]

No Soldier shall, in time of peace be quartered in any house, without the consent of the Owner, nor in time of war, but in a manner to be prescribed by law.

Amendment IV [1791]

The right of the people to be secure in their persons, houses, papers, and effects, against unreasonable searches and seizures, shall not be violated, and no Warrants shall issue, but upon probable cause, supported by Oath or affirmation, and particularly describing the place to be searched, and the persons or things to be seized.

Amendment V [1791]

No person shall be held to answer for a capital, or otherwise infamous crime, unless on a presentment or indictment of a Grand Jury, except in cases arising in the land or naval forces, or in the Militia, when in actual service in time of War or public danger; nor shall any person be subject for the same offense to be twice put in jeopardy of life or limb; nor shall be compelled in any criminal case to be a witness against himself, nor be deprived of life, liberty, or property, without due process of law; nor shall private property be taken for public use, without just compensation.

Amendment VI [1791]

In all criminal prosecutions, the accused shall enjoy the right to a speedy and public trial, by an impartial jury of the State and district wherein the crime shall have been committed, which district shall have been previously ascertained by law, and to be informed of the nature and cause of the accusation; to be confronted with the witnesses against him; to have compulsory process for obtaining witnesses in his favor, and to have the Assistance of Counsel for his defence.

Amendment VII [1791]

In Suits at common law, where the value in controversy shall exceed twenty dollars, the right of trial by jury shall be preserved, and no fact tried by a jury, shall be otherwise re-examined in any Court of the United States, than according to the rules of the common law.

Amendment VIII [1791]

Excessive bail shall not be required, nor excessive fines imposed, nor cruel and unusual punishments inflicted.

Amendment IX [1791]

The enumeration in the Constitution, of certain rights, shall not be construed to deny or disparage others retained by the people.

Amendment X [1791]

The powers not delegated to the United States by the Constitution, nor prohibited by it to the States, are reserved to the States respectively, or to the people.

Amendment XI [1798]

The Judicial power of the United States shall not be construed to extend to any suit in law or equity, commenced or prosecuted against one of the United States by Citizens of another State, or by Citizens or Subjects of any Foreign State.

Amendment XII [1804]

The Electors shall meet in their respective states, and vote by ballot for President and Vice-President, one of whom, at least, shall not be an inhabitant of the same state with themselves; they shall name in their ballots the person voted for as President, and in distinct ballots the person voted for as Vice-President, and they shall make distinct lists of all persons voted for as President, and of all persons voted for as Vice-President, and of the number of votes for each, which lists they shall sign and certify, and transmit sealed to the seat of the government of the United States, directed to the President of the Senate;—The President of the Senate shall, in the presence of the Senate and House of Representatives, open all the certificates and the votes shall then be counted;—The person having the greatest number of votes for President, shall be the President, if such number be a majority of the whole number of Electors appointed; and if no person have such majority, then from the persons having the highest numbers not exceeding three on the list of those voted for as President, the House of Representatives shall choose immediately, by ballot, the President. But in choosing the President, the votes shall be taken by states, the representation from each state having one vote; a quorum for this purpose shall consist of a member or members from two-thirds of the states, and a majority of all states shall be necessary to a choice. And if the House of Representatives shall not choose a President whenever the right of choice shall devolve upon them, before the fourth day of March next following, then the Vice-President shall act as President, as in the case of the death or other constitutional disability of the President.—The person having the greatest number of votes as Vice-President, shall be the Vice-President, if such number be a majority of the whole number of Electors appointed, and if no person have a majority, then from the two highest numbers on the list, the Senate shall choose the Vice-President; a quorum for the purpose shall consist of two-thirds of the whole number of Senators, and a majority of the whole number shall be necessary to a choice. But no person constitutionally ineligible to the office of President shall be eligible to that of Vice-President of the United States.

Amendment XIII [1865]

Section 1.   Neither slavery nor involuntary servitude, except as a punishment for crime whereof the party shall have been duly convicted, shall exist within the United States, or any place subject to their jurisdiction.

Section 2.   Congress shall have power to enforce this article by appropriate legislation.

Amendment XIV [1868]

Section 1.   All persons born or naturalized in the United States, and subject to the jurisdiction thereof, are citizens of the United States and of the State wherein they reside. No State shall make or enforce any law which shall abridge the privileges or immunities of citizens of the United States; nor shall any State deprive any person of life, liberty, or property, without due process of law; nor deny to any person within its jurisdiction the equal protection of the laws.

Section 2.   Representatives shall be apportioned among the several States according to their respective numbers, counting the whole number of persons in each State, excluding Indians not taxed. But when the right to vote at any election for the choice of electors for President and Vice President of the United States, Representatives in Congress, the Executive and Judicial officers of a State, or the members of the Legislature thereof, is denied to any of the male inhabitants of such State, being twenty-one years of age, and citizens of the United States, or in any way abridged, except for participation in rebellion, or other crime, the basis of representation therein shall be reduced in the proportion which the number of such male citizens shall bear to the whole number of male citizens twenty-one years of age in such State.

Section 3.   No person shall be a Senator or Representative in Congress, or elector of President and Vice President, or hold any office, civil or military, under the United States, or under any State, who having previously taken an oath, as a member of Congress, or as an officer of the United States, or as a member of any State legislature, or as an executive or judicial officer of any State, to support the Constitution of the United States, shall have engaged in insurrection or rebellion against the same, or given aid or comfort to the enemies thereof. But Congress may by a vote of two-thirds of each House, remove such disability.

Section 4.   The validity of the public debt of the United States, authorized by law, including debts incurred for payment of pensions and bounties for services in suppressing insurrection or rebellion, shall not be questioned. But neither the United States nor any State shall assume or pay any debt or obligation incurred in aid of insurrection or rebellion against the United States, or any claim for the loss or emancipation of any slave; but all such debts, obligations and claims shall be held illegal and void.

Section 5.   The Congress shall have power to enforce, by appropriate legislation, the provisions of this article.

Amendment XV [1870]

Section 1.   The right of citizens of the United States to vote shall not be denied or abridged by the United States or by any State on account of race, color, or previous condition of servitude.

Section 2.   The Congress shall have power to enforce this article by appropriate legislation.

Amendment XVI [1913]

The Congress shall have power to lay and collect taxes on incomes, from whatever source derived, without apportionment among the several States, and without regard to any census or enumeration.

Amendment XVII [1913]

Section 1.   The Senate of the United States shall be composed of two Senators from each State, elected by the people thereof, for six years; and each Senator shall have one vote. The electors in each State shall have the qualifications requisite for electors of the most numerous branch of the State legislatures.

Section 2.   When vacancies happen in the representation of any State in the Senate, the executive authority of such State shall issue writs of election to fill such vacancies: Provided, That the legislature of any State may empower the executive thereof to make temporary appointments until the people fill the vacancies by election as the legislature may direct.

Section 3.   This amendment shall not be so construed as to affect the election or term of any Senator chosen before it becomes valid as part of the Constitution.

Amendment XVIII [1919]

Section 1.   After one year from the ratification of this article the manufacture, sale, or transportation of intoxicating liquors within, the importation thereof into, or the exportation thereof from the United States and all territory subject to the jurisdiction thereof for beverage purposes is hereby prohibited.

Section 2.   The Congress and the several States shall have concurrent power to enforce this article by appropriate legislation.

Section 3.   This article shall be inoperative unless it shall have been ratified as an amendment to the Constitution by the legislatures of the several States, as provided in the Constitution, within seven years from the date of the submission hereof to the States by the Congress.

Amendment XIX [1920]

Section 1.   The right of citizens of the United States to vote shall not be denied or abridged by the United States or by any State on account of sex.

Section 2.   Congress shall have power to enforce this article by appropriate legislation.

Amendment XX [1933]

Section 1.   The terms of the President and Vice President shall end at noon on the 20th day of January, and the terms of Senators and Representatives at noon on the 3d day of January, of the years in which such terms would have ended if this article had not been ratified; and the terms of their successors shall then begin.

Section 2. The Congress shall assemble at least once in every year, and such meeting shall begin at noon on the 3d day of January, unless they shall by law appoint a different day.

Section 3. If, at the time fixed for the beginning of the term of the President, the President elect shall have died, the Vice President elect shall become President. If the President shall not have been chosen before the time fixed for the beginning of his term, or if the President elect shall have failed to qualify, then the Vice President elect shall act as President until a President shall have qualified; and the Congress may by law provide for the case wherein neither a President elect nor a Vice President elect shall have qualified, declaring who shall then act as President, or the manner in which one who is to act shall be selected, and such person shall act accordingly until a President or Vice President shall have qualified.

Section 4. The Congress may by law provide for the case of the death of any of the persons from whom the House of Representatives may choose a President whenever the right of choice shall have devolved upon them, and for the case of the death of any of the persons from whom the Senate may choose a Vice President whenever the right of choice shall have devolved upon them.

Section 5. Sections 1 and 2 shall take effect on the 15th day of October following the ratification of this article.

Section 6. This article shall be inoperative unless it shall have been ratified as an amendment to the Constitution by the legislatures of three-fourths of the several States within seven years from the date of its submission.

Amendment XXI [1933]

Section 1. The eighteenth article of amendment to the Constitution of the United States is hereby repealed.

Section 2. The transportation or importation into any State, Territory, or possession of the United States for delivery or use therein of intoxicating liquors, in violation of the laws thereof, is hereby prohibited.

Section 3. This article shall be inoperative unless it shall have been ratified as an amendment to the Constitution by conventions in the several States, as provided in the Constitution, within seven years from the date of the submission hereof to the States by the Congress.

Amendment XXII [1951]

Section 1. No person shall be elected to the office of the President more than twice, and no person who has held the office of President, or acted as President, for more than two years of a term to which some other person was elected President shall be elected to the office of President more than once. But this Article shall not apply to any person holding the office of President when this Article was proposed by the Congress, and shall not prevent any person who may be holding the office of President, or acting as President, during the term within which this Article becomes operative from holding the office of President or acting as President during the remainder of such term.

Section 2. This article shall be inoperative unless it shall have been ratified as an amendment to the Constitution by the legislatures of three-fourths of the several States within seven years from the date of its submission to the States by the Congress.

Amendment XXIII [1961]

Section 1. The District constituting the seat of Government of the United States shall appoint in such manner as the Congress may direct:

A number of electors of President and Vice President equal to the whole number of Senators and Representatives in Congress to which the District would be entitled if it were a State, but in no event more than the least populous state; they shall be in addition to those appointed by the states, but they shall be considered, for the purposes of the election of President and Vice President, to be electors appointed by a state; and they shall meet in the District and perform such duties as provided by the twelfth article of amendment.

Section 2. The Congress shall have power to enforce this article by appropriate legislation.

Amendment XXIV [1964]

Section 1. The right of citizens of the United States to vote in any primary or other election for President or Vice President, for electors for President or Vice President, or for Senator or Representative in Congress, shall not be denied or abridged by the United States, or any State by reason of failure to pay any poll tax or other tax.

Section 2. The Congress shall have power to enforce this article by appropriate legislation.

Amendment XXV [1967]

Section 1. In case of the removal of the President from office or of his death or resignation, the Vice President shall become President.

Section 2. Whenever there is a vacancy in the office of the Vice President, the President shall nominate a Vice President who shall take office upon confirmation by a majority vote of both Houses of Congress.

Section 3. Whenever the President transmits to the President pro tempore of the Senate and the Speaker of the House of Representatives his written declaration that he is unable to discharge the powers and duties of his office, and until he transmits to them a written declaration to the contrary, such powers and duties shall be discharged by the Vice President as Acting President.

Section 4. Whenever the Vice President and a majority of either the principal officers of the executive departments or of such other body as Congress may by law provide, transmit to the President pro tempore of the Senate and the Speaker of the House of Representatives their written declaration that the President is unable to discharge the powers and duties of his office, the Vice President shall immediately assume the powers and duties of the office as Acting President.

Thereafter, when the President transmits to the President pro tempore of the Senate and the Speaker of the House of Representatives his written declaration that no inability exists, he shall resume the powers and duties of his office unless the Vice President and a majority of either the principal officers of the executive department or of such other body as Congress may by law provide, transmit within four days to the President pro tempore of the Senate and the Speaker of the House of Representatives their written declaration that the President is unable to discharge the powers and duties of his office. Thereupon Congress shall decide the issue, assembling within forty-eight hours for that purpose if not in session. If the Congress, within twenty-one days after receipt of the latter written declaration, or, if Congress is not in session, within twenty-one days after Congress is required to assemble, determines by two-thirds vote of both Houses that the President is unable to discharge the powers and duties of his office, the Vice President shall continue to discharge the same as Acting President; otherwise, the President shall resume the powers and duties of his office.

Amendment XXVI [1971]

Section 1.   The right of citizens of the United States, who are eighteen years of age or older, to vote shall not be denied or abridged by the United States or by any State on account of age.

Section 2.   The Congress shall have power to enforce this article by appropriate legislation.

Amendment XXVII [1992]

No law, varying the compensation for the services of the Senators and Representatives, shall take effect, until an election of Representatives shall have intervened.

IN CONGRESS, JULY 4, 1776

A Declaration by the Representatives of the United States of America, in General Congress assembled. When in the Course of human Events, it becomes necessary for one People to dissolve the Political Bands which have connected them with another, and to assume among the Powers of the Earth, the separate and equal Station to which the Laws of Nature and of Nature's God entitle them, a decent Respect to the Opinions of Mankind requires that they should declare the causes which impel them to the Separation.

We hold these Truths to be self-evident, that all Men are created equal, that they are endowed by their Creator with certain unalienable Rights, that among these are Life, Liberty, and the Pursuit of Happiness—That to secure these Rights, Governments are instituted among Men, deriving their just Powers from the Consent of the Governed, that whenever any Form of Government becomes destructive of these Ends, it is the Right of the People to alter or to abolish it, and to institute new Government, laying its Foundation on such Principles, and organizing its Powers in such Forms, as to them shall seem most likely to effect their Safety and Happiness. Prudence, indeed, will dictate that Governments long established should not be changed for light and transient Causes; and accordingly all Experience hath shewn, that Mankind are more disposed to suffer, while Evils are sufferable, than to right themselves by abolishing the Forms to which they are accustomed. But when a long Train of Abuses and Usurpations, pursuing invariably the same Object, evinces a Design to reduce them under absolute Despotism, it is their Right, it is their Duty, to throw off such Government, and to provide new Guards for their future Security. Such has been the patient Sufferance of these Colonies; and such is now the Necessity which constrains them to alter their former Systems of Government. The History of the present King of Great-Britain is a History of repeated Injuries and Usurpations, all having in direct Object the Establishment of an absolute Tyranny over these States. To prove this, let Facts be submitted to a candid World.

He has refused his Assent to Laws, the most wholesome and necessary for the public Good.

He has forbidden his Governors to pass Laws of immediate and pressing Importance, unless suspended in their Operation till his Assent should be obtained; and when so suspended, he has utterly neglected to attend to them.

He has refused to pass other Laws for the Accommodation of large Districts of People, unless those People would relinquish the Right of Representation in the Legislature, a Right inestimable to them, and formidable to Tyrants only.

He has called together Legislative Bodies at Places unusual, uncomfortable, and distant from the Depository of their Public Records, for the sole Purpose of fatiguing them into Compliance with his Measures.

He has dissolved Representative Houses repeatedly, for opposing with manly Firmness his Invasions on the Rights of the People.

He has refused for a long Time, after such Dissolutions, to cause others to be elected; whereby the Legislative Powers, incapable of Annihilation, have returned to the People at large for their exercise; the State remaining in the mean time exposed to all the Dangers of Invasion from without, and Convulsions within.

He has endeavoured to prevent the Population of these States; for that Purpose obstructing the Laws for Naturalization of Foreigners; refusing to pass others to encourage their Migrations hither, and raising the Conditions of new Appropriations of Lands.

He has obstructed the Administration of Justice, by refusing his Assent to Laws for establishing Judiciary Powers.

He has made Judges dependent on his Will alone, for the Tenure of their offices, and the Amount and payment of their Salaries.

He has erected a Multitude of new Offices, and sent hither Swarms of Officers to harrass our People, and eat out their Substance.

He has kept among us, in Times of Peace, Standing Armies, without the consent of our Legislatures.

He has affected to render the Military independent of, and superior to the Civil Power.

He has combined with others to subject us to a Jurisdiction foreign to our Constitution, and unacknowledged by our Laws; giving his Assent to their Acts of pretended Legislation:

For quartering large Bodies of Armed Troops among us:

For protecting them, by a mock Trial, from Punishment for any Murders which they should commit on the Inhabitants of these States:

For cutting off our Trade with all Parts of the World:

For imposing Taxes on us without our Consent:

For depriving us, in many cases, of the Benefits of Trial by Jury:

For transporting us beyond Seas to be tried for pretended Offences:

For abolishing the free System of English Laws in a neighbouring Province, establishing therein an arbitrary Government, and enlarging its Boundaries, so as to render it at once an Example and fit Instrument for introducing the same absolute Rule into these Colonies:

For taking away our Charters, abolishing our most valuable Laws, and altering fundamentally the Forms of our Governments:

For suspending our own Legislatures, and declaring themselves invested with Power to legislate for us in all Cases whatsoever.

He has abdicated Government here, by declaring us out of his Protection and waging War against us.

He has plundered our Seas, ravaged our Coasts, burnt our towns, and destroyed the Lives of our People.

He is, at this Time, transporting large Armies of foreign Mercenaries to compleat the works of Death, Desolation, and Tyranny, already begun with circumstances of Cruelty and Perfidy, scarcely paralleled in the most barbarous Ages, and totally unworthy the Head of a civilized Nation.

He has constrained our fellow Citizens taken Captive on the high Seas to bear Arms against their Country, to become the Executioners of their Friends and Brethren, or to fall themselves by their Hands.

He has excited domestic Insurrections amongst us, and has endeavoured to bring on the Inhabitants of our Frontiers, the merciless Indian Savages, whose known Rule of Warfare, is an undistinguished Destruction, of all Ages, Sexes and Conditions.

In every state of these Oppressions we have Petitioned for Redress in the most humble Terms: Our repeated Petitions have been answered only by repeated Injury. A Prince, whose Character is thus marked by every act which may define a Tyrant, is unfit to be the Ruler of a free People.

Nor have we been wanting in Attentions to our British Brethren. We have warned them from Time to Time of Attempts by their Legislature to extend an unwarrantable Jurisdiction over us. We have reminded them of the Circumstances of our Emigration and Settlement here. We have appealed to their native Justice and Magnanimity, and we have conjured them by the Ties of our common Kindred to disavow these Usurpations, which, would inevitably interrupt our Connections and Correspondence. They too have been deaf to the Voice of Justice and of Consanguinity. We must, therefore, acquiesce in the Necessity, which denounces our Separation, and hold them, as we hold the rest of Mankind, Enemies in War, in Peace, Friends.

We, therefore, the Representatives of the UNITED STATES OF AMERICA, in General Congress Assembled, appealing to the Supreme Judge of the World for the Rectitude of our Intentions, do, in the Name, and by the Authority of the good People of these Colonies, solemnly Publish and Declare, That these United Colonies are, and of Right ought to be, Free and Independent States; that they are absolved from all Allegiance to the British Crown, and that all political Connection between them and the State of Great-Britain, is and ought to be totally dissolved; and that as Free and Independent States, they have full Power to levy War, conclude Peace, contract Alliances, establish Commerce, and to do all other Acts and Things which Independent States may of right do. And for the support of this declaration, with a firm Reliance on the Protection of divine Providence, we mutually pledge to each other our lives, our Fortunes, and our sacred Honor.

supreme court justices since 1900

Chief Justices

NAME	YEARS OF SERVICE	STATE APP'D FROM	APPOINTING PRESIDENT	AGE APP'D	POLITICAL AFFILIATION	EDUCATIONAL BACKGROUND*
Fuller, Melville Weston	1888–1910	Illinois	Cleveland	55	Democrat	Bowdoin College; studied at Harvard Law School
White, Edward Douglass	1910–1921	Louisiana	Taft	65	Democrat	Mount St. Mary's College; Georgetown College (now University)
Taft, William Howard	1921–1930	Connecticut	Harding	64	Republican	Yale; Cincinnati Law School
Hughes, Charles Evans	1930–1941	New York	Hoover	68	Republican	Colgate University; Brown; Columbia Law School
Stone, Harlan Fiske	1941–1946	New York	Roosevelt, F.	69	Republican	Amherst College; Columbia
Vinson, Frederick Moore	1946–1953	Kentucky	Truman	56	Democrat	Centre College
Warren, Earl	1953–1969	California	Eisenhower	62	Republican	University of California, Berkeley
Burger, Warren Earl	1969–1986	Virginia	Nixon	62	Republican	University of Minnesota; St. Paul College of Law (Mitchell College)
Rehnquist, William Hubbs	1986–	Virginia	Reagan	62	Republican	Stanford; Harvard; Stanford University Law School

*SOURCE: Educational background information derived from Elder Witt, *Guide to the U.S. Supreme Court,* 2d ed. (Washington, D.C.: Congressional Quarterly Press, Inc., 1990). Reprinted with the permission of the publisher.

Associate Justices

NAME	YEARS OF SERVICE	STATE APP'D FROM	APPOINTING PRESIDENT	AGE APP'D	POLITICAL AFFILIATION	EDUCATIONAL BACKGROUND
Harlan, John Marshall	1877–1911	Kentucky	Hayes	61	Republican	Centre College; studied law at Transylvania University
Gray, Horace	1882–1902	Massachusetts	Arthur	54	Republican	Harvard College; Harvard Law School
Brewer, David Josiah	1890–1910	Kansas	Harrison	53	Republican	Wesleyan University; Yale; Albany Law School
Brown, Henry Billings	1891–1906	Michigan	Harrison	55	Republican	Yale; studied at Yale Law School and Harvard Law School
Shiras, George, Jr.	1892–1903	Pennsylvania	Harrison	61	Republican	Ohio University; Yale; studied law at Yale and privately
White, Edward Douglass	1894–1910	Louisiana	Cleveland	49	Democrat	Mount St. Mary's College; Georgetown College (now University)

Associate Justices (continued)

NAME	YEARS OF SERVICE	STATE APP'D FROM	APPOINTING PRESIDENT	AGE APP'D	POLITICAL AFFILIATION	EDUCATIONAL BACKGROUND
Peckham, Rufus Wheeler	1896–1909	New York	Cleveland	58	Democrat	Read law in father's firm
McKenna, Joseph	1898–1925	California	McKinley	55	Republican	Benicia Collegiate Institute, Law Dept.
Holmes, Oliver Wendell, Jr.	1902–1932	Massachusetts	Roosevelt, T.	61	Republican	Harvard College; studied law at Harvard Law School
Day, William Rufus	1903–1922	Ohio	Roosevelt, T.	54	Republican	University of Michigan; University of Michigan Law School
Moody, William Henry	1906–1910	Massachusetts	Roosevelt, T.	53	Republican	Harvard; Harvard Law School
Lurton, Horace Harmon	1910–1914	Tennessee	Taft	66	Democrat	University of Chicago; Cumberland Law School
Hughes, Charles Evans	1910–1916	New York	Taft	48	Republican	Colgate University; Brown University; Columbia Law School
Van Devanter, Willis	1911–1937	Wyoming	Taft	52	Republican	Indiana Asbury University; University of Cincinnati Law School
Lamar, Joseph Rucker	1911–1916	Georgia	Taft	54	Democrat	University of Georgia; Bethany College; Washington and Lee University
Pitney, Mahlon	1912–1922	New Jersey	Taft	54	Republican	College of New Jersey (Princeton); read law under father
McReynolds, James Clark	1914–1941	Tennessee	Wilson	52	Democrat	Vanderbilt University; University of Virginia
Brandeis, Louis Dembitz	1916–1939	Massachusetts	Wilson	60	Democrat	Harvard Law School
Clarke, John Hessin	1916–1922	Ohio	Wilson	59	Democrat	Western Reserve University; read law under father
Sutherland, George	1922–1938	Utah	Harding	60	Republican	Brigham Young Academy; one year at University of Michigan Law School
Butler, Pierce	1923–1939	Minnesota	Harding	57	Democrat	Carleton College
Sanford, Edward Terry	1923–1930	Tennessee	Harding	58	Republican	University of Tennessee; Harvard; Harvard Law School
Stone, Harlan Fiske	1925–1941	New York	Coolidge	53	Republican	Amherst College; Columbia University Law School
Roberts, Owen Josephus	1930–1945	Pennsylvania	Hoover	55	Republican	University of Pennsylvania; University of Pennsylvania Law School
Cardozo, Benjamin Nathan	1932–1938	New York	Hoover	62	Democrat	Columbia University; two years at Columbia Law School
Black, Hugo Lafayette	1937–1971	Alabama	Roosevelt, F.	51	Democrat	Birmingham Medical College; University of Alabama Law School
Reed, Stanley Forman	1938–1957	Kentucky	Roosevelt, F.	54	Democrat	Kentucky Wesleyan University; Foreman Yale; studied law at University of Virginia and Columbia University; University of Paris
Frankfurter, Felix	1939–1962	Massachusetts	Roosevelt, F.	57	Independent	College of the City of New York; Harvard Law School
Douglas, William Orville	1939–1975	Connecticut	Roosevelt, F.	41	Democrat	Whitman College; Columbia University Law School
Murphy, Frank	1940–1949	Michigan	Roosevelt, F.	50	Democrat	University of Michigan; Lincoln's Inn, London; Trinity College
Byrnes, James Francis	1941–1942	South Carolina	Roosevelt, F.	62	Democrat	Read law privately
Jackson, Robert Houghwout	1941–1954	New York	Roosevelt, F.	49	Democrat	Albany Law School

Associate Justices (continued)

NAME	YEARS OF SERVICE	STATE APP'D FROM	APPOINTING PRESIDENT	AGE APP'D	POLITICAL AFFILIATION	EDUCATIONAL BACKGROUND
Rutledge, Wiley Blount	1943–1949	Iowa	Roosevelt, F.	49	Democrat	University of Wisconsin; University of Colorado
Burton, Harold Hitz	1945–1958	Ohio	Truman	57	Republican	Bowdoin College; Harvard University Law School
Clark, Thomas Campbell	1949–1967	Texas	Truman	50	Democrat	University of Texas
Minton, Sherman	1949–1956	Indiana	Truman	59	Democrat	Indiana University College of Law; Yale Law School
Harlan, John Marshall	1955–1971	New York	Eisenhower	56	Republican	Princeton; Oxford University; New York Law School
Brennan, William J., Jr.	1956–1990	New Jersey	Eisenhower	50	Democrat	University of Pennsylvania; Harvard Law School
Whittaker, Charles Evans	1957–1962	Missouri	Eisenhower	56	Republican	University of Kansas City Law School
Stewart, Potter	1958–1981	Ohio	Eisenhower	43	Republican	Yale; Yale Law School
White, Byron Raymond	1962–1993	Colorado	Kennedy	45	Democrat	University of Colorado; Oxford University; Yale Law School
Goldberg, Arthur Joseph	1962–1965	Illinois	Kennedy	54	Democrat	Northwestern University
Fortas, Abe	1965–1969	Tennessee	Johnson, L.	55	Democrat	Southwestern College; Yale Law School
Marshall, Thurgood	1967–1991	New York	Johnson, L.	59	Democrat	Lincoln University; Howard University Law School
Blackmun, Harry A.	1970–1994	Minnesota	Nixon	62	Republican	Harvard; Harvard Law School
Powell, Lewis F., Jr.	1972–1987	Virginia	Nixon	65	Democrat	Washington and Lee University; Washington and Lee University Law School; Harvard Law School
Rehnquist, William H.	1972–1986	Arizona	Nixon	48	Republican	Stanford; Harvard; Stanford University Law School
Stevens, John Paul	1975–	Illinois	Ford	55	Republican	University of Colorado; Northwestern University Law School
O'Connor, Sandra Day	1981–	Arizona	Reagan	51	Republican	Stanford; Stanford University Law School
Scalia, Antonin	1986–	Virginia	Reagan	50	Republican	Georgetown University; Harvard Law School
Kennedy, Anthony M.	1988–	California	Reagan	52	Republican	Stanford; London School of Economics; Harvard Law School
Souter, David Hackett	1990–	New Hampshire	Bush, G. H. W.	51	Republican	Harvard; Oxford University
Thomas, Clarence	1991–	District of Columbia	Bush, G. H. W.	43	Republican	Holy Cross College; Yale Law School
Ginsburg, Ruth Bader	1993–	District of Columbia	Clinton	60	Democrat	Cornell University; Columbia Law School
Breyer, Stephen G.	1994–	Massachusetts	Clinton	55	Democrat	Stanford; Oxford University; Harvard Law School

party control of congress since 1900

CONGRESS	YEARS	PRESIDENT	MAJORITY PARTY IN HOUSE	MAJORITY PARTY IN SENATE
57th	1901–1903	T. Roosevelt	Republican	Republican
58th	1903–1905	T. Roosevelt	Republican	Republican
59th	1905–1907	T. Roosevelt	Republican	Republican
60th	1907–1909	T. Roosevelt	Republican	Republican
61st	1909–1911	Taft	Republican	Republican
62d	1911–1913	Taft	Democratic	Republican
63d	1913–1915	Wilson	Democratic	Democratic
64th	1915–1917	Wilson	Democratic	Democratic
65th	1917–1919	Wilson	Democratic	Democratic
66th	1919–1921	Wilson	Republican	Republican
67th	1921–1923	Harding	Republican	Republican
68th	1923–1925	Coolidge	Republican	Republican
69th	1925–1927	Coolidge	Republican	Republican
70th	1927–1929	Coolidge	Republican	Republican
71st	1929–1931	Hoover	Republican	Republican
72d	1931–1933	Hoover	Democratic	Republican
73d	1933–1935	F. Roosevelt	Democratic	Democratic
74th	1935–1937	F. Roosevelt	Democratic	Democratic
75th	1937–1939	F. Roosevelt	Democratic	Democratic
76th	1939–1941	F. Roosevelt	Democratic	Democratic
77th	1941–1943	F. Roosevelt	Democratic	Democratic
78th	1943–1945	F. Roosevelt	Democratic	Democratic
79th	1945–1947	Truman	Democratic	Democratic
80th	1947–1949	Truman	Republican	Democratic
81st	1949–1951	Truman	Democratic	Democratic
82d	1951–1953	Truman	Democratic	Democratic
83d	1953–1955	Eisenhower	Republican	Republican
84th	1955–1957	Eisenhower	Democratic	Democratic
85th	1957–1959	Eisenhower	Democratic	Democratic
86th	1959–1961	Eisenhower	Democratic	Democratic
87th	1961–1963	Kennedy	Democratic	Democratic
88th	1963–1965	Kennedy/Johnson	Democratic	Democratic
89th	1965–1967	Johnson	Democratic	Democratic
90th	1967–1969	Johnson	Democratic	Democratic
91st	1969–1971	Nixon	Democratic	Democratic
92d	1971–1973	Nixon	Democratic	Democratic
93d	1973–1975	Nixon/Ford	Democratic	Democratic
94th	1975–1977	Ford	Democratic	Democratic
95th	1977–1979	Carter	Democratic	Democratic
96th	1979–1981	Carter	Democratic	Democratic
97th	1981–1983	Reagan	Democratic	Republican
98th	1983–1985	Reagan	Democratic	Republican
99th	1985–1987	Reagan	Democratic	Republican
100th	1987–1989	Reagan	Democratic	Democratic
101st	1989–1991	G. H. W. Bush	Democratic	Democratic
102d	1991–1993	G. H. W. Bush	Democratic	Democratic
103d	1993–1995	Clinton	Democratic	Democratic
104th	1995–1997	Clinton	Republican	Republican
105th	1997–1999	Clinton	Republican	Republican
106th	1999–2001	Clinton	Republican	Republican
107th	2002–2003	G. W. Bush	Republican	Democratic
108th	2003–2005	G. W. Bush	Republican	Republican
109th	2005–2007	G. W. Bush	Republican	Republican

information on u.s. presidents

	TERM OF SERVICE	AGE AT INAUGURATION	PARTY AFFILIATION	COLLEGE OR UNIVERSITY	OCCUPATION OR PROFESSION
1. George Washington	1789–1797	57	None		Planter
2. John Adams	1797–1801	61	Federalist	Harvard	Lawyer
3. Thomas Jefferson	1801–1809	57	Democratic-Republican	William and Mary	Planter, Lawyer
4. James Madison	1809–1817	57	Democratic-Republican	Princeton	Lawyer
5. James Monroe	1817–1825	58	Democratic-Republican	William and Mary	Lawyer
6. John Quincy Adams	1825–1829	57	Democratic-Republican	Harvard	Lawyer
7. Andrew Jackson	1829–1837	61	Democrat		Lawyer
8. Martin Van Buren	1837–1841	54	Democrat		Lawyer
9. William H. Harrison	1841	68	Whig	Hampden-Sydney	Soldier
10. John Tyler	1841–1845	51	Whig	William and Mary	Lawyer
11. James K. Polk	1845–1849	49	Democrat	U. of N. Carolina	Lawyer
12. Zachary Taylor	1849–1850	64	Whig		Soldier
13. Millard Fillmore	1850–1853	50	Whig		Lawyer
14. Franklin Pierce	1853–1857	48	Democrat	Bowdoin	Lawyer
15. James Buchanan	1857–1861	65	Democrat	Dickinson	Lawyer
16. Abraham Lincoln	1861–1865	52	Republican		Lawyer
17. Andrew Johnson	1865–1869	56	National Union†		Tailor
18. Ulysses S. Grant	1869–1877	46	Republican	U.S. Mil. Academy	Soldier
19. Rutherford B. Hayes	1877–1881	54	Republican	Kenyon	Lawyer
20. James A. Garfield	1881	49	Republican	Williams	Lawyer
21. Chester A. Arthur	1881–1885	51	Republican	Union	Lawyer
22. Grover Cleveland	1885–1889	47	Democrat		Lawyer
23. Benjamin Harrison	1889–1893	55	Republican	Miami	Lawyer
24. Grover Cleveland	1893–1897	55	Democrat		Lawyer
25. William McKinley	1897–1901	54	Republican	Allegheny College	Lawyer
26. Theodore Roosevelt	1901–1909	42	Republican	Harvard	Author
27. William H. Taft	1909–1913	51	Republican	Yale	Lawyer
28. Woodrow Wilson	1913–1921	56	Democrat	Princeton	Educator
29. Warren G. Harding	1921–1923	55	Republican		Editor
30. Calvin Coolidge	1923–1929	51	Republican	Amherst	Lawyer
31. Herbert C. Hoover	1929–1933	54	Republican	Stanford	Engineer
32. Franklin D. Roosevelt	1933–1945	51	Democrat	Harvard	Lawyer
33. Harry S Truman	1945–1953	60	Democrat		Businessman
34. Dwight D. Eisenhower	1953–1961	62	Republican	U.S. Mil. Academy	Soldier
35. John F. Kennedy	1961–1963	43	Democrat	Harvard	Author
36. Lyndon B. Johnson	1963–1969	55	Democrat	Southwest Texas State	Teacher
37. Richard M. Nixon	1969–1974	56	Republican	Whittier	Lawyer
38. Gerald R. Ford‡	1974–1977	61	Republican	Michigan	Lawyer
39. James E. Carter, Jr.	1977–1981	52	Democrat	U.S. Naval Academy	Businessman
40. Ronald W. Reagan	1981–1989	69	Republican	Eureka College	Actor
41. George H. W. Bush	1989–1993	64	Republican	Yale	Businessman
42. William J. Clinton	1993–2001	46	Democrat	Georgetown	Lawyer
43. George W. Bush	2001–	54	Republican	Yale	Businessman

*Church preference; never joined any church.

†The National Union Party consisted of Republicans and War Democrats. Johnson was a Democrat.

**Inaugurated Dec. 6, 1973, to replace Agnew, who resigned Oct. 10, 1973.

‡Inaugurated Aug. 9, 1974, to replace Nixon, who resigned that same day.

§Inaugurated Dec. 19, 1974, to replace Ford, who became president Aug. 9, 1974.

	RELIGION	BORN	DIED	AGE AT DEATH	VICE PRESIDENT	
1.	Episcopalian	Feb. 22, 1732	Dec. 14, 1799	67	John Adams	(1789–1797)
2.	Unitarian	Oct. 30, 1735	July 4, 1826	90	Thomas Jefferson	(1797–1801)
3.	Unitarian*	Apr. 13, 1743	July 4, 1826	83	Aaron Burr	(1801–1805)
					George Clinton	(1805–1809)
4.	Episcopalian	Mar. 16, 1751	June 28, 1836	85	George Clinton	(1809–1812)
					Elbridge Gerry	(1813–1814)
5.	Episcopalian	Apr. 28, 1758	July 4, 1831	73	Daniel D. Tompkins	(1817–1825)
6.	Unitarian	July 11, 1767	Feb. 23, 1848	80	John C. Calhoun	(1825–1829)
7.	Presbyterian	Mar. 15, 1767	June 8, 1845	78	John C. Calhoun	(1829–1832)
					Martin Van Buren	(1833–1837)
8.	Dutch Reformed	Dec. 5, 1782	July 24, 1862	79	Richard M. Johnson	(1837–1841)
9.	Episcopalian	Feb. 9, 1773	Apr. 4, 1841	68	John Tyler	(1841)
10.	Episcopalian	Mar. 29, 1790	Jan. 18, 1862	71		
11.	Methodist	Nov. 2, 1795	June 15, 1849	53	George M. Dallas	(1845–1849)
12.	Episcopalian	Nov. 24, 1784	July 9, 1850	65	Millard Fillmore	(1849–1850)
13.	Unitarian	Jan. 7, 1800	Mar. 8, 1874	74		
14.	Episcopalian	Nov. 23, 1804	Oct. 8, 1869	64	William R. King	(1853)
15.	Presbyterian	Apr. 23, 1791	June 1, 1868	77	John C. Breckinridge	(1857–1861)
16.	Presbyterian*	Feb. 12, 1809	Apr. 15, 1865	56	Hannibal Hamlin	(1861–1865)
					Andrew Johnson	(1865)
17.	Methodist*	Dec. 29, 1808	July 31, 1875	66		
18.	Methodist	Apr. 27, 1822	July 23, 1885	63	Schuyler Colfax	(1869–1873)
					Henry Wilson	(1873–1875)
19.	Methodist*	Oct. 4, 1822	Jan. 17, 1893	70	William A. Wheeler	(1877–1881)
20.	Disciples of Christ	Nov. 19, 1831	Sept. 19, 1881	49	Chester A. Arthur	(1881)
21.	Episcopalian	Oct. 5, 1829	Nov. 18, 1886	57		
22.	Presbyterian	Mar. 18, 1837	June 24, 1908	71	Thomas A. Hendricks	(1885)
23.	Presbyterian	Aug. 20, 1833	Mar. 13, 1901	67	Levi P. Morton	(1889–1893)
24.	Presbyterian	Mar. 18, 1837	June 24, 1908	71	Adlai E. Stevenson	(1893–1897)
25.	Methodist	Jan. 29, 1843	Sept. 14, 1901	58	Garret A. Hobart	(1897–1899)
					Theodore Roosevelt	(1901)
26.	Dutch Reformed	Oct. 27, 1858	Jan. 6, 1919	60	Charles W. Fairbanks	(1905–1909)
27.	Unitarian	Sept. 15, 1857	Mar. 8, 1930	72	James S. Sherman	(1909–1912)
28.	Presbyterian	Dec. 29, 1856	Feb. 3, 1924	67	Thomas R. Marshall	(1913–1921)
29.	Baptist	Nov. 2, 1865	Aug. 2, 1923	57	Calvin Coolidge	(1921–1923)
30.	Congregationalist	July 4, 1872	Jan. 5, 1933	60	Charles G. Dawes	(1925–1929)
31.	Friend (Quaker)	Aug. 10, 1874	Oct. 20, 1964	90	Charles Curtis	(1929–1933)
32.	Episcopalian	Jan. 30, 1882	Apr. 12, 1945	63	John N. Garner	(1933–1941)
					Henry A. Wallace	(1941–1945)
					Harry S Truman	(1945)
33.	Baptist	May 8, 1884	Dec. 26, 1972	88	Alben W. Barkley	(1949–1953)
34.	Presbyterian	Oct. 14, 1890	Mar. 28, 1969	78	Richard M. Nixon	(1953–1961)
35.	Roman Catholic	May 29, 1917	Nov. 22, 1963	46	Lyndon B. Johnson	(1961–1963)
36.	Disciples of Christ	Aug. 27, 1908	Jan. 22, 1973	64	Hubert H. Humphrey	(1965–1969)
37.	Friend (Quaker)	Jan. 9, 1913	Apr. 22, 1994	81	Spiro T. Agnew	(1969–1973)
					Gerald R. Ford**	(1973–1974)
38.	Episcopalian	July 14, 1913			Nelson A. Rockefeller§	(1974–1977)
39.	Baptist	Oct. 1, 1924			Walter F. Mondale	(1977–1981)
40.	Disciples of Christ	Feb. 6, 1911	June 5, 2004	93	George H. W. Bush	(1981–1989)
41.	Episcopalian	June 12, 1924			J. Danforth Quayle	(1989–1993)
42.	Baptist	Aug. 19, 1946			Albert A. Gore	(1993–2001)
43.	Methodist	July 6, 1946			Dick Cheney	(2001–)

federalist papers no. 10 and no. 51

The founders completed drafting the U.S. Constitution in 1787. It was then submitted to the thirteen states for ratification, and a major debate ensued. As you read in Chapter 2, on the one side of this debate were the Federalists, who urged that the new Constitution be adopted. On the other side of the debate were the Anti-Federalists, who argued against ratification.

During the course of this debate, three men well known for their Federalist views—Alexander Hamilton, James Madison, and John Jay—wrote a series of essays in which they argued for immediate ratification of the Constitution. The essays appeared in the New York City Independent Journal *in October 1787, just a little over a month after the Constitutional Convention adjourned. Later, Hamilton arranged to have the essays collected and published in book form. The articles filled two volumes, both of which were published by May 1788. The essays are often referred to collectively as the* Federalist Papers.

Scholars disagree as to whether the Federalist Papers *had a significant impact on the decision of the states to ratify the Constitution. Nonetheless, many of the essays are masterpieces of political reasoning and have left a lasting imprint on American politics and government. Above all, the* Federalist Papers *shed an important light on what the founders intended when they drafted various constitutional provisions.*

Here we present just two of these essays, Federalist Paper *No. 10 and* Federalist Paper *No. 51. Each essay was written by James Madison, who referred to himself as "Publius." We have annotated each document to clarify the meaning of particular passages. The annotations are set in italics to distinguish them from the original text of the documents.*

#10

Federalist Paper No. 10 is a classic document that is often referred to by teachers of American government. Authored by James Madison, it sets forth Madison's views on factions in politics. The essay was written, in large part, to counter the arguments put forth by the Anti-Federalists that small factions might take control of the government, thus destroying the representative nature of the republican form of government established by the Constitution. The essay opens with a discussion of the "dangerous vice" of factions and the importance of devising a form of government in which this vice will be controlled.

Among the numerous advantages promised by a well-constructed Union, none deserves to be more accurately developed than its tendency to break and control the violence of faction. The friend of popular governments never finds himself so much alarmed for their character and fate as when he contemplates their propensity to this dangerous vice. He will not fail, therefore, to set a due value on any plan which, without violating the principles to which he is attached, provides a proper cure for it. The instability, injustice, and confusion introduced into the public councils have, in truth, been the mortal diseases under which popular governments have everywhere perished, as they continue to be the favorite and fruitful topics from which the adversaries to liberty derive their most specious declamations. The valuable improvements made by the American constitutions on the popular models, both ancient and modern, cannot certainly be too much admired; but it would be an unwarrantable partiality to contend that they have as effectually obviated the danger on this side, as was wished and expected. Complaints are everywhere heard from our most considerate and virtuous citizens, equally the friends of public and private faith and of public and personal liberty, that our governments are too unstable, that the public good is disregarded in the conflicts of rival parties, and that measures are too often decided, not according to the rules of justice and the rights of the minor party, but by the superior force of an interested and overbearing majority. However anxiously we may wish that these complaints had no foundation, the evidence of known facts will not permit us to deny that they are in some degree true. It will be found, indeed, on a candid review of our situation, that some of the distresses under which we labor have been erroneously charged on the operation of our governments; but it will be found, at the same time, that other causes will not alone account for many of our heaviest misfortunes; and, particularly, for that prevailing and increasing distrust of public engagements and alarm for private rights which are echoed from one end of the continent to the other. These must be chiefly, if not wholly, effects of the unsteadiness and injustice with which a factious spirit has tainted our public administration.

In the following paragraph, Madison clarifies for his readers his understanding of what the term faction *means.*

By a faction I understand a number of citizens, whether amounting to a majority or minority of the whole, who are united and actuated by some common impulse of passion, or of interest, adverse to the rights of other citizens, or the permanent and aggregate interests of the community.

In the following passages, Madison looks at the two methods of curing the "mischiefs of factions." One of these methods is removing the causes of faction. The other is to control the effects of factions.

There are two methods of curing the mischiefs of faction: the one, by removing its causes; the other, by controlling its effects.

There are again two methods of removing the causes of faction: the one, by destroying the liberty which is essential to its existence; the other, by giving to every citizen the same opinions, the same passions, and the same interests.

It could never be more truly said than of the first remedy that it was worse than the disease. Liberty is to faction what air is to fire, an aliment without which it instantly expires. But it could not be a less folly to abolish liberty, which is essential to political life, because it nourishes faction than it would be to wish the annihilation of air, which is essential to animal life, because it imparts to fire its destructive agency.

The second expedient is as impracticable as the first would be unwise. As long as the reason of man continues fallible, and his is at liberty to exercise it, different opinions will be formed. As long as the connection subsists between his reason and his self-love, his opinions and his passions will have a reciprocal influence on each other; and the former will be objects to which the latter will attach themselves. The diversity in the faculties of men, from which the rights of property originate, is not less an insuperable obstacle to a uniformity of interests. The protection of these faculties is the first object of government. From the protection of different and unequal faculties of acquiring property, the possession of different degrees and kinds of property immediately results; and from the influence of these on the sentiments and views of the respective proprietors ensues a division of the society into different interests and parties.

The latent causes of faction are thus sown in the nature of man; and we see them everywhere brought into different degrees of activity, according to the different circumstances of civil society. A zeal for different opinions concerning religion, concerning government, and many other points, as well of speculation as of practice; an attachment to different leaders ambitiously contending for pre-eminence and power; or to persons of other descriptions whose fortunes have been interesting to the human passions, have, in turn, divided mankind into parties, inflamed them with mutual animosity, and rendered them much more disposed to vex and oppress each other than to co-operate for their common good. So strong is this propensity of mankind to fall into mutual animosities that where no substantial occasion presents itself the most frivolous and fanciful distinctions have been sufficient to kindle their unfriendly passions and excite their most violent conflicts. But the most common and durable source of factions has been the various and unequal distribution of property. Those who hold and those who are without property have ever formed distinct interests in society. Those who are creditors, and those who are debtors, fall under a like discrimination. A landed interest, a manufacturing interest, a mercantile interest, a moneyed interest, with many lesser interests, grow up of necessity in civilized nations, and divide them into different classes, actuated by different sentiments and views. The regulation of these various and interfering interests forms the principal task of modern legislation and involves the spirit of party and faction in the necessary and ordinary operations of government.

No man is allowed to be a judge in his own cause, because his interest would certainly bias his judgment, and, not improbably, corrupt his integrity. With equal, nay with greater reason, a body of men are unfit to be both judges and parties at the same time; yet what are many of the most important acts of legislation but so many judicial determinations, not indeed concerning the rights of single persons, but concerning the rights of large bodies of citizens? And what are the different classes of legislators but advocates and parties to the causes which they determine? Is a law proposed concerning private debts? It is a question to which the creditors are parties on one side and the debtors on the other. Justice ought to hold the balance between them. Yet the parties are, and must be, themselves the judges; and the most numerous party, or in other words, the most powerful faction must be expected to prevail. Shall domestic manufacturers be encouraged, and in what degree, by restrictions on foreign manufacturers? Are questions which would be differently decided by the landed and the manufacturing classes, and probably by neither with a sole regard to justice and the public good. The apportionment of taxes on the various descriptions of property is an act which seems to require the most exact impartiality; yet there is, perhaps, no legislative act in which greater opportunity and temptation are given to a predominant party to trample on the rules of justice. Every shilling with which they overburden the inferior number is a shilling saved to their own pockets.

It is in vain to say that enlightened statesmen will be able to adjust these clashing interests and render them all subservient to the public good. Enlightened statesmen will not always be at the helm. Nor, in many cases, can such an adjustment be made at all without taking into view indirect and remote considerations, which will rarely prevail over the immediate interest which one party may find in disregarding the rights of another or the good of the whole.

The inference to which we are brought is that the causes of faction cannot be removed and that relief is only to be sought in the means of controlling its effects.

In the preceding passages, Madison has explored the causes of factions and has concluded that they cannot "be removed" without removing liberty itself, which is one of the causes, or altering human nature. He now turns to a discussion of how the effects of factions might be controlled.

If a faction consists of less than a majority, relief is supplied by the republican principle, which enables the majority to defeat its sinister views by regular vote. It may clog the administration, it may convulse the society; but it will be unable to execute and mask its violence under the forms of the Constitution. When a majority is included in a faction, the form of popular government, on the other hand, enables it to sacrifice to its ruling passion or interest both the public good and the rights of other citizens. To secure the public good and private rights against the danger of such a faction, and at the same time to preserve the spirit and the form of popular government, is then the great object to which our inquiries are directed. Let me add that it is the great desideratum by which alone this form of government can be rescued from the opprobrium under which it has so long labored and be recommended to the esteem and adoption of mankind.

According to Madison, one way of controlling the effects of factions is to make sure that the majority is not able to act in "concert," or jointly, to "carry into effect schemes of oppression."

By what means is this object attainable? Evidently by one of two only. Either the existence of the same passion or interest in a majority at the same time must be prevented, or the majority, having such coexistent passion or interest, must be rendered, by their number and local situation, unable to concert and carry into effect schemes of oppression. If the impulse and the opportunity be suffered to coincide, we well know that neither moral nor religious motives can be relied on as an adequate control. They are not found to be such on the injustice and violence of individuals, and lose their efficacy in proportion to the number combined together, that is, in proportion as their efficacy becomes needful.

From this view of the subject it may be concluded that a pure democracy, by which I mean a society consisting of a small number of citizens, who assemble and administer the government in person, can admit of no cure for the mischiefs of faction. A common passion or interest will, in almost every case, be felt by a majority of the whole; a communication and concert results from the form of government itself; and there is nothing to check the inducements to sacrifice the weaker party or an obnoxious individual. Hence it is that such democracies have ever been spectacles of turbulence and contention; have ever been found incompatible with personal security or the rights of property; and have in general been as short in their lives as they have been violent in their deaths. Theoretic politicians, who have patronized this species of government, have erroneously supposed that by reducing mankind to a perfect equality in their political rights, they would at the same time be perfectly equalized and assimilated in their possessions, their opinions, and their passions.

In the following six paragraphs, Madison sets forth some of the reasons why a republican form of government promises a "cure" for the mischiefs of factions. He begins by clarifying the difference between a republic and a democracy. He then describes how in a large republic, the elected representatives of the people will be large enough in number to guard against factions—the "cabals," or concerted actions, of "a few." On the one hand, representatives will not be so removed from their local districts as to be unacquainted with their constituents' needs. On the other hand, they will not be "unduly attached" to local interests and unfit to understand "great and national objects." Madison concludes that the Constitution "forms a happy combination in this respect."

A republic, by which I mean a government in which the scheme of representation takes place, opens a different prospect and promises the cure for which we are seeking. Let us examine the points in which it varies from pure democracy, and we shall comprehend both the nature of the cure and the efficacy which it must derive from the Union.

The two great points of difference between a democracy and a republic are: first, the delegation of the government, in the latter, to a small number of citizens elected by the rest; secondly, the greater number of citizens and greater sphere of country over which the latter may be extended.

The effect of the first difference is, on the one hand, to refine and enlarge the public views by passing them through the medium of a chosen body of citizens, whose wisdom may best discern the true interest of their country and whose patriotism and love of justice will be least likely to sacrifice it to temporary or partial considerations. Under such a regulation it may well happen that the public voice, pronounced by the representatives of the people, will be more consonant to the public good than if pronounced by the people themselves, convened for the purpose. On the other hand, the effect may be inverted. Men of factious tempers, of local prejudices, or of sinister designs, may, by intrigue, by corruption, or by other means, first obtain the suffrages, and then betray the interests of the people. The question resulting is, whether small or extensive republics are most favorable to the election of proper guardians of the public weal; and it is clearly decided in favor of the latter by two obvious considerations.

In the first place it is to be remarked that however small the republic may be the representatives must be raised to a certain number in order to guard against the cabals of a few; and that however large it may be they must be limited to a certain number in order to guard against the confusion of a multitude. Hence, the number of representatives in the two cases not being in proportion to that of the constituents, and being proportionally greatest in the small republic, it follows that if the proportion of fit characters be not less in the large than in the small republic, the former will present a greater option, and consequently a greater probability of a fit choice.

In the next place, as each representative will be chosen by a greater number of citizens in the large than in the small republic, it will be more difficult for unworthy candidates to practice with success the vicious arts by which elections are too often carried; and the suffrages of the people being more free, will be more likely to center on men who possess the most attractive merit and the most diffusive and established characters.

It must be confessed that in this, as in most other cases, there is a mean, on both sides of which inconveniencies will be found to lie. By enlarging too much the number of electors, you render the representative too little acquainted with all their local circumstances and lesser interests; as by reducing it too much, you render him unduly attached to these, and too little fit to comprehend and pursue great and national objects. The federal Constitution forms a happy combination in this respect; the great and aggregate interests being referred to the national, the local and particular to the State legislatures.

In the remaining passages of this essay, Madison looks at another "point of difference" between a republic and a democracy. Specifically, a republic can encompass a larger territory and a greater number of citizens than a democracy can. This fact, too, argues Madison, will help to control the influence of factions because the interests that draw people together to act in concert are typically at the local level and would be unlikely to affect or dominate the national government. As Madison states, "The influence of factious leaders may kindle a flame within their particular States but will be unable to spread a general conflagration through the other States." Generally, in a large republic, there will be numerous factions, and no particular faction will be able to "pervade the whole body of the Union."

The other point of difference is the greater number of citizens and extent of territory which may be brought within the compass of republican than of democratic government; and it is this circumstance principally which renders factious combinations less to be dreaded in the former than in the latter. The smaller the society, the fewer probably will be the distinct parties and interests composing it; the fewer the distinct parties and interests, the more frequently will a majority be found of the same party; and the smaller the number of individuals composing a majority, and the smaller the compass within which they are placed, the more easily will they concert and execute their plans of oppression. Extend the sphere and you take in a greater variety of parties and interests; you make it less probable that a majority of the whole will have a common motive to invade the rights of other citizens; or if such a common motive exists, it will be more difficult for all who feel it to discover their own strength and to act in unison with each other. Besides other impediments, it may be remarked that, where there is a consciousness of unjust or dishonorable purposes, communication is always checked by distrust in proportion to the number whose concurrence is necessary.

Hence, it clearly appears that the same advantage which a republic has over a democracy in controlling the effects of faction is enjoyed by a large over a small republic—is enjoyed by the Union over the States composing it. Does this advantage consist in the substitution of representatives whose enlightened views and virtuous sentiments render them superior to local prejudices and to schemes of injustice? It will not be denied that the representation of the Union will be most likely to possess these requisite endowments. Does it consist in the greater security afforded by a greater variety of parties, against the event of any one party being able to outnumber and oppress the rest? In an equal degree does the increased variety of parties comprised within the Union increase this security. Does it, in fine, consist in the greater obstacles opposed to the concert and accomplishment of the secret wishes of an unjust and interested majority? Here again the extent of the Union gives it the most palpable advantage.

The influence of factious leaders may kindle a flame within their particular States but will be unable to spread a general conflagration through the other States. A religious sect may degenerate into a political faction in a part of the Confederacy; but the variety of sects dispersed over the entire face of it must secure the national councils against any danger from that source. A rage for paper money, for an abolition of debts, for an equal division of property, or for any other improper or wicked project, will be less apt to pervade the whole body of the Union than a particular member of it, in the same proportion as such a malady is more likely to taint a particular county or district than an entire State.

In the extent and proper structure of the Union, therefore, we behold a republican remedy for the diseases most incident to republican government. And according to the degree of pleasure and pride we feel in being republicans ought to be our zeal in cherishing the spirit and supporting the character of federalists.

Publius
(James Madison)

#51

Federalist Paper *No. 51, which was also authored by James Madison, is one of the classics in American political theory. Recall from Chapter 2*

that a major concern of the founders was to create a relatively strong national government but one that would not be capable of tyrannizing over the populace. In the following essay, Madison sets forth the theory of "checks and balances." He explains that the new Constitution, by dividing the national government into three branches (executive, legislative, and judicial), offers protection against tyranny.

To what expedient, then, shall we finally resort, for maintaining in practice the necessary partition of power among the several departments as laid down in the Constitution? The only answer that can be given is that as all these exterior provisions are found to be inadequate the defect must be supplied, by so contriving the interior structure of the government as that its several constituent parts may, by their mutual relations, be the means of keeping each other in their proper places. Without presuming to undertake a full development of this important idea I will hazard a few general observations which may perhaps place it in a clearer light, and enable us to form a more correct judgment of the principles and structure of the government planned by the convention.

In the following two paragraphs, Madison explains that to ensure that the powers of government are genuinely separated, it is important that each of the three branches of government (executive, legislative, and judicial) should have a "will of its own." Among other things, this means that persons in one branch should not depend on persons in another branch for the "emoluments annexed to their offices" (pay, perks, and privileges). If they did, then the branches would not be truly independent of one another.

In order to lay a due foundation for that separate and distinct exercise of the different powers of government, which to a certain extent is admitted on all hands to be essential to the preservation of liberty, it is evident that each department should have a will of its own; and consequently should be so constituted that the members of each should have as little agency as possible in the appointment of the members of the others. Were this principle rigorously adhered to, it would require that all the appointments for the supreme executive, legislative, and judiciary magistracies should be drawn from the same fountain of authority, the people, through channels having no communication whatever with one another. Perhaps such a plan of constructing the several departments would be less difficult in practice than it may in contemplation appear. Some difficulties, however, and some additional expense would attend the execution of it. Some deviations, therefore, from the principle must be admitted. In the constitution of the judiciary department in particular, it might be inexpedient to insist rigorously on the principle: first, because peculiar qualifications being essential in the members, the primary consideration ought to be to select that mode of choice which best secures these qualifications; second, because the permanent tenure by which the appointments are held in that department must soon destroy all sense of dependence on the authority conferring them.

It is equally evident that the members of each department should be as little dependent as possible on those of the others for the emoluments annexed to their offices. Were the executive magistrate, or the judges, not independent of the legislature in this particular, their independence in every other would be merely nominal.

One of the striking qualities of the theory of checks and balances as posited by Madison is that it assumes that persons are not angels but driven by personal interests and motives. In the following two paragraphs, which are among the most widely quoted of Madison's writings, he stresses that the division of the government into three branches helps to check personal ambitions. Personal ambitions will naturally arise, but they will be linked to the constitutional powers of each branch. In effect, they will help to keep the three branches separate and thus serve the public interest.

But the great security against a gradual concentration of the several powers in the same department consists in giving to those who administer each department the necessary constitutional means and personal motives to resist encroachments of the others. The provision for defense must in this, as in all other cases, be made commensurate to the danger of attack. Ambition must be made to counteract ambition. The interest of the man must be connected with the constitutional rights of the place. It may be a reflection on human nature that such devices should be necessary to control the abuses of government. But what is government itself but the greatest of all reflections on human nature? If men were angels, no government would be necessary. If angels were to govern men, neither external nor internal controls on government would be necessary. In framing a government which is to be administered by men over men, the great difficulty lies in this: you must first enable the government to control the governed; and in the next place oblige it to control itself. A dependence on the people is, no doubt, the primary control on the government; but experience has taught mankind the necessity of auxiliary precautions.

This policy of supplying, by opposite and rival interests, the defect of better motives, might be traced through the whole system of human affairs, private as well as public. We see it particularly displayed in all the subordinate distributions of power, where the constant aim is to divide and arrange the several offices in such a manner as that each may be a check on the other—that the private interest of every individual may be a sentinel over the public rights. These inventions of prudence cannot be less requisite in the distribution of the supreme powers of the State.

In the next two paragraphs, Madison first points out that the "legislative authority necessarily predominates" in a republican form of government. The "remedy" for this lack of balance with the other branches of government is to divide the legislative branch into two chambers with "different modes of election and different principles of action."

But it is not possible to give to each department an equal power of self-defense. In republican government, the legislative authority necessarily predominates. The remedy for this inconveniency is to divide the legislature into different branches; and to render them, by different modes of election and different principles of action, as little connected with each other as the nature of their common functions and their common dependence on the society will admit. It may even be necessary to guard against dangerous encroachments by still further precautions. As the weight of the legislative authority requires that it should be thus divided, the weakness of the executive may require, on the other hand, that it should be fortified. An absolute negative on the legislature appears, at first view, to be the natural defense with which the executive magistrate should be armed. But perhaps it would be neither altogether safe nor alone sufficient. On ordinary occasions it might not be exerted with the requisite firmness, and on extraordinary

occasions it might be perfidiously abused. May not this defect of an absolute negative be supplied by some qualified connection between this weaker department and the weaker branch of the stronger department, by which the latter may be led to support the constitutional rights of the former, without being too much detached from the rights of its own department?

If the principles on which these observations are founded be just, as I persuade myself they are, and they be applied as a criterion to the several State constitutions, and to the federal Constitution, it will be found that if the latter does not perfectly correspond with them, the former are infinitely less able to bear such a test.

In the remaining passages of this essay, Madison discusses the importance of the division of government powers between the states and the national government. This division of powers, by providing additional checks and balances, offers a "double security" against tyranny.

There are, moreover, two considerations particularly applicable to the federal system of America, which place that system in a very interesting point of view.

First. In a single republic, all the power surrendered by the people is submitted to the administration of a single government; and the usurpations are guarded against by a division of the government into distinct and separate departments. In the compound republic of America, the power surrendered by the people is first divided between two distinct governments, and then the portion allotted to each subdivided among distinct and separate departments. Hence a double security arises to the rights of the people. The different governments will control each other, at the same time that each will be controlled by itself.

Second. It is of great importance in a republic not only to guard the society against the oppression of its rulers, but to guard one part of the society against the injustice of the other part. Different interests necessarily exist in different classes of citizens. If a majority be united by a common interest, the rights of the minority will be insecure. There are but two methods of providing against this evil: the one by creating a will in the community independent of the majority—that is, of the society itself; the other, by comprehending in the society so many separate descriptions of citizens as will render an unjust combination of a majority of the whole very improbable, if not impracticable. The first method prevails in all governments possessing an hereditary or self-appointed authority. This, at best, is but a precarious security; because a power independent of the society may as well espouse the unjust views of the major as the rightful interests of the minor party, and may possibly be turned against both parties. The second method will be exemplified in the federal republic of the United States. Whilst all authority in it will be derived from and dependent on the society, the society itself will be broken into so many parts, interests and classes of citizens, that the rights of individuals, or of the minority, will be in little danger from interested combinations of the majority. In a free government the security for civil rights must be the same as that for religious rights. It consists in the one case in the multiplicity of interests, and in the other in the multiplicity of sects. The degree of security in both cases will depend on the number of interests and sects; and this may be presumed to depend on the extent of country and number of people comprehended under the same government. This view of the subject must particularly recommend a proper federal system to all the sincere and considerate friends of republican government, since it shows that in exact proportion as the territory of the Union may be formed into more circumscribed Confederacies, or States, oppressive combinations of a majority will be facilitated; the best security, under the republican forms, for the rights of every class of citizen, will be diminished; and consequently the stability and independence of some member of the government, the only other security, must be proportionally increased. Justice is the end of government. It is the end of civil society. It ever has been and ever will be pursued until it be obtained, or until liberty be lost in the pursuit. In a society under the forms of which the stronger faction can readily unite and oppress the weaker, anarchy may as truly be said to reign as in a state of nature, where the weaker individual is not secured against the violence of the stronger; and as, in the latter state, even the stronger individuals are prompted, by the uncertainty of their condition, to submit to a government which may protect the weak as well as themselves; so, in the former state, will the more powerful factions or parties be gradually induced, by a like motive, to wish for a government which will protect all parties, the weaker as well as the more powerful. It can be little doubted that if the State of Rhode Island was separated from the Confederacy and left to itself, the insecurity of rights under the popular form of government within such narrow limits would be displayed by such reiterated oppressions of factious majorities that some power altogether independent of the people would soon be called for by the voice of the very factions whose misrule had proved the necessity of it. In the extended republic of the United States, and among the great variety of interests, parties, and sects which it embraces, a coalition of a majority of the whole society could seldom take place on any other principles than those of justice and the general good; whilst there being thus less danger to a minor from the will of a major party, there must be less pretext, also, to provide for the security of the former, by introducing into the government a will not dependent on the latter, or, in other words, a will independent of the society itself. It is no less certain than it is important, notwithstanding the contrary opinions which have been entertained, that the larger the society, provided it lie within a practicable sphere, the more duly capable it will be of self-government. And happily for the *republican cause,* the practicable sphere may be carried to a very great extent by a judicious modification and mixture of the *federal principle.*

Publius
(James Madison)

how to read case citations and find court decisions

Many important court cases are discussed in references in endnotes throughout this book. Court decisions are recorded and published. When a court case is mentioned, the notation that is used to refer to, or to cite, the case denotes where the published decision can be found.

State courts of appeals decisions are usually published in two places, the state reports of that particular state and the more widely used *National Reporter System* published by West Publishing Company. Some states no longer publish their own reports. The *National Reporter System* divides the states into the following geographic areas: Atlantic (A. or A.2d, where *2d* refers to *Second Series*), South Eastern (S.E. or S.E.2d), South Western (S.W., S.W.2d, or S.W.3d), North Western (N.W. or N.W.2d), North Eastern (N.E. or N.E.2d), Southern (So. or So.2d), and Pacific (P., P.2d, or P.3d).

Federal trial court decisions are published unofficially in West's *Federal Supplement* (F.Supp. or F.Supp.2d), and opinions from the circuit courts of appeals are reported unofficially in West's *Federal Reporter* (F., F.2d, or F.3d). Opinions from the United States Supreme Court are reported in the *United States Reports* (U.S.), the *Lawyers' Edition of the Supreme Court Reports* (L.Ed.), West's *Supreme Court Reporter* (S.Ct.), and other publications. The *United States Reports* is the official publication of United States Supreme Court decisions. It is published by the federal government. Many early decisions are missing from these volumes. The citations of the early volumes of the *U.S. Reports* include the names of the actual reporters, such as Dallas, Cranch, or Wheaton. *McCulloch v. Maryland,* for example, is cited as

17 U.S. (4 Wheat.) 316. Only after 1874 did the present citation system, in which cases are cited based solely on their volume and page numbers in the *United States Reports,* come into being. The *Lawyers' Edition of the Supreme Court Reports* is an unofficial and more complete edition of Supreme Court decisions. West's *Supreme Court Reporter* is an unofficial edition of decisions dating from October 1882. These volumes contain headnotes and numerous brief editorial statements of the law involved in the case.

State courts of appeals decisions are cited by giving the name of the case; the volume, name, and page number of the state's official report (if the state publishes its own reports); the volume, unit, and page number of the *National Reporter;* and the volume, name, and page number of any other selected reporter. Federal court citations are also listed by giving the name of the case and the volume, name, and page number of the reports. In addition to the citation, this textbook lists the year of the decision in parentheses. Consider, for example, the case *United States v. Curtiss-Wright Export Co.,* 299 U.S. 304 (1936). The Supreme Court's decision of this case may be found in volume 299 of the *United States Reports* on page 304. The case was decided in 1936.

Today, many courts, including the United States Supreme Court, publish their opinions online. This makes it much easier for students to find and read cases, or summaries of cases, that have significant consequences for American government and politics. To access cases via the Internet, use the URLs given in the *Politics on the Web* section at the end of Chapter 14.

spanish equivalents for important political terms

A

Acid Rain: Lluvia Acida

Acquisitive Model: Modelo Adquisitivo

Actionable: Procesable, Enjuiciable

Action-Reaction Syndrome: Sídrome de Acción y Reacción

Actual Malice: Malicia Expresa

Administrative Agency: Agencia Administrativa

Advice and Consent: Consejo y Consentimiento

Affirm: Afirmar

Affirmative Action: Acción Afirmativa

Agenda Setting: Agenda Establecida

Aid to Families with Dependent Children (AFDC): Ayuda para Familias con Niños Dependientes

Amicus Curiae Brief: Tercer persona o grupo no involucrado en el caso, admitido en un juicio para hacer valer el intéres público o el de un grupo social importante.

Anarchy: Anarquía

Anti-Federalists: Anti-Federalistas

Appellate Court: Corte de Apelación

Appointment Power: Poder de Apuntamiento

Appropriation: Apropiación

Aristocracy: Aristocracia

Attentive Public: Público Atento

Australian Ballot: Voto Australiano

Authority: Autoridad

Authorization: Autorización

B

Bad-Tendency Rule: Regla de Tendencia-mala

"Beauty Contest": Concurso de Belleza

Bicameralism: Bicameralismo

Bicameral Legislature: Legislatura Bicameral

Bill of Rights: Declaración de Derechos

Blanket Primary: Primaria Comprensiva

Block Grants: Concesiones de Bloque

Bureaucracy: Burocracia

Busing: Transporte Público

C

Cabinet: Gabinete, Consejo de Ministros

Cabinet Department: Departamento del Gabinete

Cadre: El núcleo de activistas de partidos políticos encargados de cumplir las funciones importantes de los partidos políticos americanos.

Canvassing Board: Consejo encargado con la encuesta de una violación.

Capture: Captura, Toma

Casework: Trabajo de Caso

Categorical Grants-in-Aid: Concesiones Categóricas de Ayuda

Caucus: Reunión de Dirigentes

Challenge: Reto

Checks and Balances: Chequeos y Equilibrio

Chief Diplomat: Jefe Diplomático

Chief Executive: Jefe Ejecutivo

Chief Legislator: Jefe Legislador

Chief of Staff: Jefe de Personal

Chief of State: Jefe de Estado

Civil Law: Derecho Civil

Civil Liberties: Libertades Civiles

Civil Rights: Derechos Civiles

Civil Service: Servicio Civil

Civil Service Commission: Comisión de Servicio Civil

Class-Action Suit: Demanda en representación de un grupo o clase.

Class Politics: Política de Clase

Clear and Present Danger Test: Prueba de Peligro Claro y Presente

Climate Control: Control de Clima

Closed Primary: Primaria Cerrada

Cloture: Cierre al Voto

Coattail Effect: Effecto de Cola de Chaqueta

Cold War: Guerra Fría

Commander in Chief: Comandante en Jefe

Commerce Clause: Clausula de Comercio

Commercial Speech: Discurso Comercial

Common Law: Ley Común, Derecho Consuetudinario

Comparable Worth: Valor Comparable

Compliance: De Acuerdo

Concurrent Majority: Mayoría Concurrente

Concurring Opinion: Opinión Concurrente

Confederal System: Sistema Confederal

Confederation: Confederación

Conference Committee: Comité de Conferencia

Consensus: Concenso

Consent of the People: Consentimiento de la Gente

Conservatism: Calidad de Conservador

Conservative Coalition: Coalición Conservadora

Consolidation: Consolidación

Constant Dollars: Dólares Constantes

Constitutional Initiative: Iniciativa Constitucional

Constitutional Power: Poder Constitucional

Containment: Contenimiento

Continuing Resolution: Resolució Contínua

Cooley's Rule: Régla de Cooley

Cooperative Federalism: Federalismo Cooperativo

Corrupt Practices Acts: Leyes Contra Acciones Corruptas

Council of Economic Advisers (CEA): Consejo de Asesores Económicos

Council of Government (COG): Consejo de Gobierno

County: Condado

Credentials Committee: Comité de Credenciales

Criminal Law: Ley Criminal

D

De Facto **Segregation:** Segregación de Hecho

De Jure **Segregation:** Segregación Cotidiana

Defamation of Character: Defamación de Carácter

Democracy: Democracia

Democratic Party: Partido Democratico

Détente: No Spanish equivalent.

Dillon's Rule: Régla de Dillon

Diplomacy: Diplomácia

Direct Democracy: Democracia Directa

Direct Primary: Primaria Directa

Direct Technique: Técnica Directa

Discharge Petition: Petición de Descargo

Dissenting Opinion: Opinión Disidente

Divisive Opinion: Opinión Divisiva

Domestic Policy: Principio Político Doméstico

Dual Citizenship: Ciudadanía Dual

Dual Federalism: Federalismo Dual

E

Economic Aid: Ayuda Económica

Economic Regulation: Regulación Económica

Elastic Clause, or Necessary and Proper Clause: Cláusula Flexible o Cláusula Propia Necesaria

Elector: Elector

Electoral College: Colegio Electoral

Electronic Media: Media Electronica

Elite: Elite (el Selecto)

Elite Theory: Teoría Elitista (de lo Selecto)

Emergency Power: Poder de Emergencia

Enumerated Power: Poder Enumerado

Environmental Impact Statement (EIS): Afirmación de Impacto Ambiental

Equal Employment Opportunity Commission (EEOC): Comisión de Igualdad de Oportunidad en el Empleo

Equality: Igualdad

Equalization: Igualación

Era of Good Feeling: Era de Buen Sentimiento

Era of Personal Politics: Era de Política Personal

Establishment Clause: Cláusula de Establecimiento

Euthanasia: Eutanasia

Exclusionary Rule: Régla de Exclusión

Executive Agreement: Acuerdo Ejecutivo

Executive Budget: Presupuesto Ejecutivo

Executive Office of the President (EOP): Oficina Ejecutiva del Presidente

Executive Order: Orden Ejecutivo

Executive Privilege: Privilegio Ejecutivo

Expressed Power: Poder Expresado

Extradite: Entregar por Extradición

F

Faction: Facción

Fairness Doctrine: Doctrina de Justicia

Fall Review: Revision de Otoño

Federal Mandate: Mandato Federal

Federal Open Market Committee (FOMC): Comité Federal de Libre Mercado

Federal Register: Registro Federal

Federal System: Sistema Federal

Federalists: Federalistas

Fighting Words: Palabras de Provocación

Filibuster: Obstrucción de Iniciativas de Ley

Fireside Chat: Charla de Hogar

First Budget Resolution: Resolució Primera Presupuesta

First Continental Congress: Primér Congreso Continental

Fiscal Policy: Político Fiscal

Fiscal Year (FY): Año Fiscal

Fluidity: Fluidez

Food Stamps: Estampillas para Comida

Foreign Policy: Política Extranjera

Foreign Policy Process: Proceso de Política Extranjera

Franking: Franqueando

Fraternity: Fraternidad

Free Exercise Clause: Cláusula de Ejercicio Libre

Full Faith and Credit Clause: Cláusula de Completa Fé y Crédito

Functional Consolidation: Consolidación Funcional

G

Gag Order: Orden de Silencio

Garbage Can Model: Modelo Bote de Basura

Gender Gap: Brecha de Género

General Law City: Régla General Urbana

General Sales Tax: Impuesto General de Ventas

Generational Effect: Efecto Generacional

Gerrymandering: División arbitraria de los distritos electorales con fines políticos.

Government: Gobierno

Government Corporation: Corporación Gubernamental

Government in the Sunshine Act: Gobierno en la Acta: Luz del Sol

Grandfather Clause: Cláusula del Abuelo

Grand Jury: Gran Jurado

Great Compromise: Grán Acuerdo de Negociación

H

Hatch Act (Political Activities Act): Acta Hatch (Acta de Actividades Políticas)

Hecklers' Veto: Veto de Abuchamiento

Home Rule City: Régla Urbana

Horizontal Federalism: Federalismo Horizontal

Hyperpluralism: Hiperpluralismo

I

Ideologue: Ideólogo

Ideology: Ideología

Image Building: Construcción de Imágen

Impeachment: Acción Penal Contra un Funcionario Público

Inalienable Rights: Derechos Inalienables
Income Transfer: Transferencia de Ingresos
Incorporation Theory: Teoría de Incorporación
Independent: Independiente
Independent Candidate: Candidato Independiente
Independent Executive Agency: Agencia Ejecutiva Independiente
Independent Regulatory Agency: Agencia Regulatoria Independiente
Indirect Technique: Técnica Indirecta
Inherent Power: Poder Inherente
Initiative: Iniciativa
Injunction: Injunción, Prohibición Judicial
In-Kind Subsidy: Subsidio de Clase
Institution: Institución
Instructed Delegate: Delegado con Instrucciones
Intelligence Community: Comunidad de Inteligencia
Intensity: Intensidad
Interest Group: Grupo de Interés
Interposition: Interposición
Interstate Compact: Compacto Interestatal
Iron Curtain: Cortina de Acero
Iron Triangle: Triágulo de Acero
Isolationist Foreign Policy: Política Extranjera de Aislamiento
Issue Voting: Voto Temático
Item Veto: Artículo de Veto

J

Jim Crow Laws: No Spanish equivalent.
Joint Committee: Comité Mancomunado
Judicial Activism: Activismo Judicial
Judicial Implementation: Implementación Judicial
Judicial Restraint: Restricción Judicial
Judicial Review: Revisión Judicial
Jurisdiction: Jurisdicción
Justiciable Dispute: Disputa Judiciaria
Justiciable Question: Pregunta Justiciable

K

Keynesian Economics: Economía Keynesiana
Kitchen Cabinet: Gabinete de Cocina

L

Labor Movement: Movimiento Laboral
Latent Public Opinion: Opinión Pública Latente

Lawmaking: Hacedores de Ley
Legislative History: Historia Legislativa
Legislative Initiative: Iniciativa de Legislación
Legislative Veto: Veto Legislativo
Legislature: Legislatura
Legitimacy: Legitimidad
Libel: Libelo, Difamación Escrita
Liberalism: Liberalismo
Liberty: Libertad
Limited Government: Gobierno Limitado
Line Organization: Organización de Linea
Literacy Test: Exámen de Alfabetización
Litigate: Litigar
Lobbying: Cabildeo
Logrolling: Práctica legislativa que consiste en incluir en un mismo proyecto de ley temas de diversa ídole.
Loophole: Hueco Legal, Escapatoria

M

Madisonian Model: Modelo Madisónico
Majority: Mayoría
Majority Floor Leader: Líder Mayoritario de Piso
Majority Leader of the House: Líder Mayoritario de la Casa
Majority Opinion: Opinión Mayoritaria
Majority Rule: Régla de Mayoría
Managed News: Noticias Manipuladas
Mandatory Retirement: Retiro Mandatario
Matching Funds: Fondos Combinados
Material Incentive: Incentivo Material
Media: Media
Media Access: Acceso de Media
Merit System: Sistema de Mérito
Military-Industrial Complex: Complejo Industriomilitar
Minority Floor Leader: Líder Minoritario de Piso
Minority Leader of the House: Líder Minorial del Cuerpo Legislativo
Monetary Policy: Política Monetaria
Monopolistic Model: Modelo Monopólico
Monroe Doctrine: Doctrina Monroe
Moral Idealism: Idealismo Moral
Municipal Home Rule: Régla Municipal

N

Narrow Casting: Mensaje Dirigído
National Committee: Comité Nacional

National Convention: Convención Nacional
National Politics: Política Nacional
National Security Council (NSC): Concilio de Seguridad Nacional
National Security Policy: Política de Seguridad Nacional
Natural Aristocracy: Aristocracia Natural
Natural Rights: Derechos Naturales
Necessaries: Necesidades
Negative Constituents: Constituyentes Negativos
New England Town: Pueblo de Nueva Inglaterra
New Federalism: Federalismo Nuevo
Nullification: Nulidad, Anulación

O

Office-Block, or Massachusetts, Ballot: Cuadro-Oficina, o Massachusetts, Voto
Office of Management and Budget (OMB): Oficina de Administració y Presupuesto
Oligarchy: Oligarquía
Ombudsman: Funcionario que representa al ciudadano ante el gobierno.
Open Primary: Primaria Abierta
Opinion: Opinión
Opinion Leader: Líder de Opinión
Opinion Poll: Encuesta, Conjunto de Opinión
Oral Arguments: Argumentos Orales
Oversight: Inadvertencia, Omisión

P

Paid-for Political Announcement: Anuncios Políticos Pagados
Pardon: Perdón
Party-Column, or Indiana, Ballot: Partido-Columna, o Indiana, Voto
Party Identification: Identificación de Partido
Party Identifier: Identificador de Partido
Party-in-Electorate: Partido Electoral
Party-in-Government: Partido en Gobierno
Party Organization: Organización de Partido
Party Platform: Plataforma de Partido
Patronage: Patrocinio
Peer Group: Grupo de Contemporáneos
Pendleton Act (Civil Service Reform Act): Acta Pendleton (Acta de Reforma al Servicio Civil)

Personal Attack Rule: Regla de Ataque Personal

Petit Jury: Jurado Ordinario

Pluralism: Pluralismo

Plurality: Pluralidad

Pocket Veto: Veto de Bolsillo

Police Power: Poder Policiaco

Policy Trade-Offs: Intercambio de Políticas

Political Action Committee (PAC): Comité de Acción Política

Political Consultant: Consultante Político

Political Culture: Cultura Política

Political Party: Partido Político

Political Question: Pregunta Política

Political Realism: Realismo Político

Political Socialization: Socialización Política

Political Tolerance: Tolerancia Política

Political Trust: Confianza Política

Politico: Político

Politics: Política

Poll Tax: Impuesto Sobre el Sufragio

Poll Watcher: Observador de Encuesta

Popular Sovereignty: Soberanía Popular

Power: Poder

Precedent: Precedente

Preferred-Position Test: Prueba de Posición Preferida

Presidential Primary: Primaria Presidencial

President Pro Tempore: Presidente Provisoriamente

Press Secretary: Secretaría de Prensa

Prior Restraint: Restricción Anterior

Privileges and Immunities: Privilégios e Imunidades

Privatization, or Contracting Out: Privatización

Property: Propiedad

Property Tax: Impuesto de Propiedad

Public Agenda: Agenda Pública

Public Debt Financing: Financiamiento de Deuda Pública

Public Debt, or National Debt: Deuda Pública o Nacional

Public Interest: Interes Público

Public Opinion: Opinión Pública

Purposive Incentive: Incentivo de Propósito

R

Ratification: Ratificación

Rational Ignorance Effect: Effecto de Ignorancia Racional

Reapportionment: Redistribución

Recall: Suspender

Recognition Power: Poder de Reconocimiento

Recycling: Reciclaje

Redistricting: Redistrictificación

Referendum: Referédum

Registration: Registración

Regressive Tax: Impuestos Regresivos

Relevance: Pertinencia

Remand: Reenviar

Representation: Representación

Representative Assembly: Asamblea Representativa

Representative Democracy: Democracia Representativa

Reprieve: Trequa, Suspensión

Republic: República

Republican Party: Partido Republicano

Resulting Powers: Poderes Resultados

Reverse: Cambiarse a lo Contrario

Reverse Discrimination: Discriminación Reversiva

Rule of Four: Régla de Cuatro

Rules Committee: Comité Regulador

Run-off Primary: Primaria Residual

S

Safe Seat: Asiento Seguro

Sampling Error: Error de Encuesta

Secession: Secesión

Second Budget Resolution: Resolución Segunda Presupuestal

Second Continental Congress: Segundo Congreso Continental

Sectional Politics: Política Seccional

Segregation: Segregación

Select Committee: Comité Selecto

Selectperson: Persona Selecta

Senatorial Courtesy: Cortesia Senatorial

Seniority System: Sistema Señorial

Separate-but-Equal Doctrine: Separados pero Iguales

Separation of Powers: Separación de Poderes

Service Sector: Sector de Servicio

Sex Discrimination: Discriminación Sexual

Sexual Harassment: Acosamiento Sexual

Slander: Difamación Oral, Calumnia

Sliding-Scale Test: Prueba Escalonada

Social Movement: Movimiento Social

Social Security: Seguridad Social

Socioeconomic Status: Estado Socioeconómico

Solidary Incentive: Incentivo de Solideridad

Solid South: Súr Sólido

Sound Bite: Mordida de Sonido

Soviet Bloc: Bloque Soviético

Speaker of the House: Vocero de la Casa

Spin: Girar/Giro

Spin Doctor: Doctor en Giro

Spin-Off Party: Partido Estático

Spoils System: Sistema de Despojos

Spring Review: Revisión de Primavera

Stability: Estabilidad

Standing Committee: Comité de Sostenimiento

Stare Decisis: El principio característico del ley comú por el cual los precedentes jurisprudenciales tienen fuerza obligatoria, no sólo entre las partes, sino tambien para casos sucesivos análogos.

State: Estado

State Central Committee: Comité Central del Estado

State of the Union Message: Mensaje Sobre el Estado de la Unión

Statutory Power: Poder Estatorial

Strategic Arms Limitation Treaty (SALT I): Tratado de Limitación de Armas Estratégicas

Subpoena: Orden de Testificación

Subsidy: Subsidio

Suffrage: Sufrágio

Sunset Legislation: Legislación Sunset

Superdelegate: Líder de partido o oficial elegido quien tiene el derecho de votar.

Supplemental Security Income (SSI): Ingresos de Seguridad Suplementaria

Supremacy Clause: Cláusula de Supremacia

Supremacy Doctrine: Doctrina de Supremacia

Symbolic Speech: Discurso Simbólico

T

Technical Assistance: Asistencia Técnica

Third Party: Tercer Partido

Third-Party Candidate: Candidato de Tercer Partido

Ticket Splitting: División de Boletos

Totalitarian Regime: Régimen Totalitario

Town Manager System: Sistema de Administrador Municipal

Town Meeting: Junta Municipal

Township: Municipio

Tracking Poll: Seguimiento de Encuesta

Trial Court: Tribunal de Primera

Truman Doctrine: Doctrina Truman

Trustee: Depositario

Twelfth Amendment: Doceava Enmienda

Twenty-fifth Amendment: Veinticincoava Enmienda

Two-Party System: Sistema de Dos Partidos

U

Unanimous Opinion: Opinión Unánime

Underground Economy: Economía Subterráea

Unicameral Legislature: Legislatura Unicameral

Unincorporated Area: Area no Incorporada

Unitary System: Sistema Unitario

Unit Rule: Régla de Unidad

Universal Suffrage: Sufragio Universal

U.S. Treasury Bond: Bono de la Tesoreria de E.U.A.

V

Veto Message: Comunicado de Veto

Voter Turnout: Renaimiento de Votantes

W

War Powers Act: Acta de Poderes de Guerra

Washington Community: Comunidad de Washington

Weberian Model: Modelo Weberiano

Whip: Látigo

Whistleblower: Privatización o Contratista

White House Office: Oficina de la Casa Blanca

White House Press Corps: Cuerpo de Prensa de la Casa Blanca

White Primary: Sufragio en Elección Primaria/Blancos Solamente

Writ of *Certiorari*: Prueba de certeza; orden emitida por el tribunal de apelaciones para que el tribunal inferior dé lugar a la apelación.

Writ of *Habeas Corpus:* Prueba de Evidencia Concreta

Writ of *Mandamus:* Un mandato por la corte para que un acto se lleve a cabo.

Y

Yellow Journalism: Amarillismo Periodístico

Notes

Chapter 1

1. Harold Lasswell, *Politics: Who Gets What, When, and How* (New York: McGraw-Hill, 1936).
2. Charles Lewis, *The Buying of Congress* (New York: Avon Books, 1998), p. 346.
3. See, for example, Thomas Sowell, *The Quest for Cosmic Justice* (Riverside, N.J.: Free Press, 1999).
4. *Kelo v. City of New London, Connecticut,* 125 S.Ct. 27 (2004).
5. Samuel P. Huntington, *Who Are We? The Challenges to America's National Identity* (New York: Simon & Schuster, 2004).
6. See, for example, a study conducted by Public Agenda, a nonpartisan research group in New York. This study, as well as a number of other recent surveys, can be accessed at Public Agenda's Web site at **http://www.publicagenda.org**.

Chapter 2

1. Today, there are 100 senators in the Senate and 435 members of the House of Representatives. In addition, the District of Columbia has 3 electoral votes.
2. The first *European* settlement in North America was St. Augustine, Florida (a city that still exists), which was founded on September 8, 1565, by the Spaniard Pedro Menéndez de Ávilés.
3. Archaeologists have recently discovered the remains of a colony at Popham Beach, on the southern coast of what is now Maine, that was established at the same time as the colony at Jamestown. The Popham colony disbanded after thirteen months, however, when the leader, after learning that he had inherited property back home, returned—with the other colonists—to England.
4. John Camp, *Out of the Wilderness: The Emergence of an American Identity in Colonial New England* (Middleton, Conn.: Wesleyan University Press, 1990).
5. Jon Butler, *Becoming America: The Revolution before 1776* (Cambridge, Mass.: Harvard University Press, 2000).
6. Paul S. Boyer *et al., The Enduring Vision: A History of the American People* (Lexington, Mass.: D. C. Heath, 1996).
7. Corsets are close-fitting undergarments that were worn at the time by both men and women to give the appearance of having a smaller waist. Whalebone was inserted in the corsets to make them stiff, and lacing was used to tighten them around the body.
8. Much of the colonists' fury over British policies was directed personally at King George III, who had ascended the British throne in 1760 at the age of twenty-two, rather than at Britain or British rule *per se.* If you look at the Declaration of Independence in Appendix B, you will note that much of that document focuses on what "He" (George III) has or has not done. George III's lack of political experience, his personality, and his temperament all combined to lend instability to the British government at this crucial point in history.
9. *The Political Writings of Thomas Paine,* Vol. 1 (Boston: J. P. Mendum Investigator Office, 1870), p. 46.
10. The equivalent in today's publishing world would be a book that sells between eight and ten million copies in its first year of publication.
11. As quoted in Winthrop D. Jordan *et al., The United States,* 6th ed. (Englewood Cliffs, N.J.: Prentice Hall, 1987).
12. Some scholars feel that Locke's influence on the colonists, including Thomas Jefferson, has been exaggerated. For example, Jay Fliegelman states that Jefferson's fascination with the ideas of Homer, Ossian, and Patrick Henry "is of greater significance than his indebtedness to Locke." Jay Fliegelman, *Declaring Independence: Jefferson, Natural Language, and the Culture of Performance* (Stanford, Calif.: Stanford University Press, 1993).
13. See, for example, Robert A. Dahl, "Liberal Democracy in the United States," in *A Prospect of Liberal Democracy*, ed. William Livingston (Austin, Tex.: University of Texas Press, 1979).
14. Well before the Articles were ratified, many of them had, in fact, already been implemented. The Second Continental Congress and the thirteen states conducted American military, economic, and political affairs according to the standards and form specified later in the Articles of Confederation. See Robert W. Hoffert, *A Politics of Tensions: The Articles of Confederation and American Political Ideas* (Niwot, Colo.: University Press of Colorado, 1992).
15. Contrary to the standard argument that patriotism and civic duty encouraged state cooperation, some scholars have claimed that material gain and local interests held the union together under the Articles of Confederation. Keith L. Dougherty, *Collective Action under the Articles of Confederation* (New York: Cambridge University Press, 2001).
16. Shays' Rebellion was not merely a small group of poor farmers. The participants and their supporters represented whole communities, including some of the wealthiest and most influential families of Massachusetts. Leonard L. Richards, *Shays' Rebellion: The American Revolution's Final Battle* (Philadelphia: University of Pennsylvania Press, 2003).
17. Madison was much more "republican" in his views than Hamilton. See Lance Banning, *The Sacred Fire of Liberty: James Madison and the Founding of the Federal Republic* (Ithaca, N.Y.: Cornell University Press, 1995).
18. The State House was later named Independence Hall. This was the same room in which the Declaration of Independence had been signed eleven years earlier.
19. Charles A. Beard, *An Economic Interpretation of the Constitution of the United States* (New York: Macmillan, 1913; New York: Free Press, 1986).
20. Morris was partly of French descent, which is why his first name may seem unusual. Note that naming one's child *Gouverneur* was not common at the time in any language, even French.
21. As quoted in Wendy McElroy, "Constitutional Intentions," *Ideas on Liberty,* June 2000, p. 15.
22. Some scholarship suggests that the *Federalist Papers* did not play a significant role in bringing about the ratification of the Constitution. Nonetheless, the papers have lasting value as an authoritative explanation of the Constitution.
23. The papers written by the Anti-Federalists are now online (see the *Politics on the Web* section at the end of Chapter 2 for the Web URL). For essays on the positions, arranged in topical order, of both the Federalists and the Anti-Federalists in the ratification debate, see John P. Kaminski and Richard Leffler, *Federalists and Antifederalists: The Debate over the Ratification of the Constitution,* 2d ed. (Madison, Wisc.: Madison House, 1998).
24. The concept of the separation of powers is generally credited to the French political philosopher Montesquieu (1689–1755), who included it in his monumental two-volume work entitled *The Spirit of Laws,* published in 1748.
25. The Constitution does not explicitly mention the power of judicial review, but the delegates at the Constitutional Convention probably assumed that the courts would have this power. Indeed, Alexander Hamilton, in *Federalist Paper* No. 78, explicitly outlined the concept of judicial review. In any event, whether the founders intended for the courts to exercise this power is a moot point, because in an 1803 decision, *Marbury v. Madison,* the Supreme Court claimed this power for the courts—see Chapter 14.
26. Eventually, Supreme Court decisions led to legislative reforms relating to apportionment. The amendment concerning compensation of members of Congress became the Twenty-seventh Amendment to the Constitution when it was ratified 203 years later, in 1992.

Chapter 3

1. *Raich v. Ashcroft,* 352 F.3d 1222 (2003).
2. The federal models used by the German and Canadian governments provide interesting comparisons with the U.S. system. See Arthur B. Gunlicks, *Laender and German Federalism* (Manchester, U.K.: Manchester University Press, 2003); and Jennifer Smith, *Federalism* (Vancouver: University of British Columbia Press, 2004).
3. Text of an address by the president to the National Conference of State Legislatures, Atlanta, Georgia (Washington, D.C.: The White House, Office of the Press Secretary, July 30, 1981).
4. An excellent illustration of this principle was President Dwight Eisenhower's disciplining of Arkansas governor Orval Faubus when he refused to allow a Little Rock high school to be desegregated in 1957. Eisenhower federalized the National Guard to enforce the court-ordered desegregation of the school.
5. 5 U.S. 137 (1803).
6. 4 Wheaton 316 (1819).
7. 9 Wheaton 1 (1824).
8. *Hammer v. Dagenhart,* 247 U.S. 251 (1918). This decision was overruled in *United States v. Darby,* 312 U.S. 100 (1941).
9. *Wickard v. Filburn,* 317 U.S. 111 (1942).

10. *McLain v. Real Estate Board of New Orleans, Inc.,* 444 U.S. 232 (1980).
11. Just as this book went to press, the U.S. Supreme Court handed down a decision that resolved this controversy in the case *Granholm v. Heald,* ___ U.S. ___ (2005). The Court held that a state law prohibiting out-of-state wineries from shipping wine directly to in-state consumers, but permitting in-state wineries to do so if licensed, discriminated against interstate commerce. The Court concluded that such discrimination was not excused by the Twenty-First Amendment.
12. 514 U.S. 549 (1995).
13. *Printz v. United States,* 521 U.S. 898 (1997).
14. *United States v. Morrison,* 529 U.S. 598 (2000).
15. National Governors Association statement on "Federalism, Preemption, and Regulatory Reform," December 2, 2002. You can view this and other statements by the National Governors Association at its Web site, **http://www.nga.org**.
16. Albert H. Cantril and Susan Davis Cantril, *Reading Mixed Signals: Ambivalence in American Public Opinion about Government* (Washington, D.C.: Woodrow Wilson Center Press, 1999).
17. Although Louisiana prohibited minors from purchasing alcohol, it did not prohibit bars and alcohol retailers from selling alcohol to minors. Not until 1996, when President Bill Clinton threatened to withhold federal highway funds from Louisiana, did that state fully comply with the drinking-age requirement.

Chapter 4

1. *Weems v. United States,* 217 U.S. 349 (1910).
2. 7 Peters 243 (1833).
3. 330 U.S. 1 (1947).
4. 370 U.S. 421 (1962).
5. 449 U.S. 39 (1980).
6. The hostages were eventually released, and the French law banning head scarves was not repealed.
7. *Wallace v. Jaffree,* 472 U.S. 38 (1985).
8. See, for example, *Brown v. Gwinnett County School District,* 112 F.3d 1464 (1997).
9. *Santa Fe Independent School District v. Doe,* 530 U.S. 290 (2000).
10. 393 U.S. 97 (1968).
11. *Edwards v. Aguillard,* 482 U.S. 578 (1987).
12. 403 U.S. 602 (1971).
13. *Mitchell v. Helms,* 530 U.S. 793 (2000).
14. *Simmons-Harris v. Zelman,* 234 F.3d 945 (6th Cir. 2000).
15. *Zelman v. Simmons-Harris,* 536 U.S. 639 (2002).
16. *Holmes v. Bush* (Fla.Cir.Ct. 2002). For details about this case, see David Royse, "Judge Rules School Voucher Law Violates Florida Constitution," *USA Today,* August 6, 2002, p. 7D.
17. *Newdow v. U.S. Congress,* 292 F.3d 597 (2002).
18. See Marie Failinger, "Indivisible Day and the Pledge of Allegiance: One Nation under God?" *Journal of Lutheran Ethics,* July 10, 2002.
19. See Howard Fineman, "One Nation, under . . . Who?" *Newsweek,* July 8, 2002, p. 20.
20. *Elk Grove School District v. Newdow,* 124 S.Ct. 2301 (2004).
21. 98 U.S. 145 (1878).
22. For more information on this case, see Bill Miller, "Firefighters Win Ruling in D.C. Grooming Dispute," *The Washington Post,* June 23, 2001, p. B01.
23. *Schenck v. United States,* 249 U.S. 47 (1919).
24. 341 U.S. 494 (1951).
25. *Brandenburg v. Ohio,* 395 U.S. 444 (1969).
26. *Liquormart v. Rhode Island,* 517 U.S. 484 (1996).
27. For more information on this case, see Samuel Maull, "Judges Rule against 2 Accused of Praising Sept. 11 Attacks," *The Washington Post,* March 31, 2002, p. A6.
28. 413 U.S. 15 (1973).
29. *Reno v. American Civil Liberties Union,* 521 U.S. 844 (1997).
30. *American Civil Liberties Union v. Reno,* 217 F.3d 160 (2000).
31. *United States v. American Library Association,* 539 U.S. 194 (2003).
32. *Ashcroft v. Free Speech Coalition,* 535 U.S. 234 (2002).
33. "Meeting Minutes of the Wesleyan Student Assembly Meeting, 2002–2003," October 2, 2002, p. 10.
34. 249 U.S. 47 (1919).
35. 268 U.S. 652 (1925).
36. 484 U.S. 260 (1988).
37. *Smith v. Collin,* 439 U.S. 916 (1978).
38. *City of Chicago v. Morales,* 527 U.S. 41 (1999).
39. *Gallo v. Acuna,* 14 Cal.4th 1090 (1997).
40. Brandeis made this statement in a dissenting opinion in *Olmstead v. United States,* 277 U.S. 438 (1928).
41. 381 U.S. 479 (1965).
42. The state of South Carolina challenged the constitutionality of this act, claiming that the law violated states' rights under the Tenth Amendment. The Supreme Court, however, held that Congress had the authority, under its commerce power, to pass the act because drivers' personal information had become articles of interstate commerce. *Reno v. Condon,* 528 U.S. 141 (2000).
43. 410 U.S. 113 (1973). Jane Roe was not the real name of the woman in this case. It is a common legal pseudonym used to protect a party's privacy.
44. See, for example, the Supreme Court's decision in *Lambert v. Wicklund,* 520 U.S. 1169 (1997). The Court held that a Montana law requiring a minor to notify one of her parents before getting an abortion was constitutional.
45. *Schenck v. ProChoice Network,* 519 U.S. 357 (1997); and *Hill v. Colorado,* 530 U.S. 703 (2000).
46. *Stenberg v. Carhart,* 530 U.S. 914 (2000).
47. *Carhart v. Ashcroft,* 331 F.Supp.2d 805 (D. Neb. 2004).
48. *Washington v. Glucksberg,* 521 U.S. 702 (1997).
49. This report, titled "Surveying the Digital Future" and based on an extensive study of attitudes concerning Internet use, was published in 2000 by the UCLA Center for Communication Policy. This 2000 report, as well as more recent Internet Reports, is available online at **http://ccp.ucla.edu/pages/ internet-report.asp**.
50. For more on the American Civil Liberties Union's position on privacy and technology, visit its Web site at **http://www.aclu.org/Privacy/PrivacyMain.cfm**.
51. 372 U.S. 335 (1963).
52. *Mapp v. Ohio,* 367 U.S. 643 (1961).
53. 384 U.S. 436 (1966).
54. *Moran v. Burbine,* 475 U.S. 412 (1986).
55. *Arizona v. Fulminante,* 499 U.S. 279 (1991).
56. *Davis v. United States,* 512 U.S. 452 (1994).
57. *Dickerson v. United States,* 530 U.S. 428 (2000).

Chapter 5

1. *Michael M. v. Superior Court,* 450 U.S. 464 (1981).
2. See, for example, *Craig v. Boren,* 429 U.S. 190 (1976).
3. *Orr v. Orr,* 440 U.S. 268 (1979).
4. *Mississippi University for Women v. Hogan,* 458 U.S. 718 (1982).
5. 518 U.S. 515 (1996).
6. 163 U.S. 537 (1896).
7. 347 U.S. 483 (1954).
8. 349 U.S. 294 (1955).
9. *Swann v. Charlotte-Mecklenburg Board of Education,* 402 U.S. 1 (1971).
10. *Keyes v. School District No. 1,* 413 U.S. 189 (1973).
11. *Milliken v. Bradley,* 418 U.S. 717 (1974).
12. *Riddick v. School Board of City of Norfolk,* 627 F.Supp. 814 (E.D.Va. 1984).
13. 515 U.S. 70 (1995).
14. See *Meritor Savings Bank, FSB v. Vinson,* 477 U.S. 57 (1986); and *Harris v. Forklift Systems, Inc.,* 510 U.S. 17 (1993).
15. *Oncale v. Sundowner Offshore Services,* 523 U.S. 75 (1998).
16. *Faragher v. City of Boca Raton,* 524 U.S. 775 (1998).
17. The Supreme Court upheld these actions in *Hirabayashi v. United States,* 320 U.S. 81 (1943); and *Korematsu v. United States,* 323 U.S. 214 (1944).
18. 414 U.S. 563 (1974).
19. On December 16, 2002, citizens and nationals of Libya, Iran, Iraq, Sudan, and Syria were required to register. On January 10, 2003, the program was expanded to include citizens or nationals of Afghanistan, Algeria, Bahrain, Eritrea, Lebanon, Morocco, North Korea, Oman, Qatar, Somalia, Tunisia, Yemen, and the United Arab Emirates. The program was expanded again on January 16, 2003, to include citizens or nationals of Bangladesh, Egypt, Indonesia, Kuwait, and Jordan.
20. *Hamdi v. Rumsfeld,* 124 S.Ct. 2633 (2004).

21. This siege was the subject of Dee Brown's best-selling book, *Bury My Heart at Wounded Knee* (New York: Holt, Rinehart & Winston, 1971).
22. *County of Oneida, New York v. Oneida Indian Nation,* 470 U.S. 226 (1985).
23. *Kimel v. Florida Board of Regents,* 528 U.S. 62 (2000).
24. *Board of Trustees of the University of Alabama v. Garrett,* 531 U.S. 356 (2001).
25. 539 U.S. 558 (2003).
26. 517 U.S. 620 (1996).
27. 438 U.S. 265 (1978).
28. 515 U.S. 200 (1995).
29. 84 F.3d 720 (5th Cir. 1996).
30. 539 U.S. 244 (2003).
31. 539 U.S. 306 (2003).

Chapter 6

1. *Democracy in America,* Vol. 1, ed. by Phillip Bradley (New York: Knopf, 1980), p. 191.
2. Pronounced ah-*mee*-kus *kure*-ee-eye.
3. David Truman, *The Governmental Process* (New York: Knopf, 1951); and Robert Dahl, *Who Governs?* (New Haven, Conn.: Yale University Press, 1961).
4. Fred McChesney, *Money for Nothing: Politicians, Rent Extraction and Political Extortion* (Cambridge, Mass.: Harvard University Press, 1997).
5. The Agricultural Adjustment Act of 1933 (declared unconstitutional) was replaced by the 1937 Agricultural Adjustment Act, which later was changed and amended several times.
6. *Quill Corp. v. North Dakota,* 504 U.S. 298 (1992).
7. "A Tale of Two Lobbies," *The Economist,* October 19, 1996, p. 20.
8. "Overboard on Gun Control," *The Wall Street Journal Europe,* October 23, 1996, p. 6.
9. Data on PAC contributions can be accessed at the Web site of the Federal Election Commission at **http://www.fec.gov**.
10. Jeff Gerth and Sheryl Gay Stolberg, "Medicine Merchants Cultivating Alliances: With Quiet, Unseen Ties, Drug Makers Sway Debate," *The New York Times,* October 5, 2000.
11. 380 F.3d 1154 (9th Cir. 2004); *cert* granted, 125 S.Ct. 686 (2004).
12. *United States v. Harriss,* 347 U.S. 612 (1954).
13. Matt Miller, "This Land Is Red Land, Paid for by Blue Land," *Fortune,* November 29, 2004, p. 76.

Chapter 7

1. Letter to Francis Hopkinson written from Paris while Jefferson was minister to France, as cited in John P. Foley, ed., *The Jeffersonian Cyclopedia* (New York: Russell & Russell, 1967), p. 677.
2. From the names of the twins in Lewis Carroll's *Through the Looking Glass and What Alice Found There,* first published in London in 1862–1863.
3. "A Notable Minority Challenges the System," *Public Perspective,* September/October 2000, p. 27; Gallup/CNN/*USA Today* poll conducted in July 1999.
4. The term *third party,* although inaccurate (because sometimes there have been fourth parties, fifth parties, and so on), is commonly used to refer to a minor party.
5. Today, twelve states have multimember districts for their state houses, and a handful also have multimember districts for their state senates.
6. H. Ross Perot and John Hagelin of the Natural Law Party challenged the decision in court, without success. *Perot v. Federal Election Commission,* 97 F.3d 553 (D.C.Cir. 1996).
7. *USA Today,* February 23, 1999, p. 6A. See also Albert R. Hunt, "The Me-Too—Or Yes-But—Republicans," *The Wall Street Journal,* February 25, 1999, p. A19.
8. Richard Darman, *Who's in Control? Polar Politics and the Sensible Center* (New York: Simon & Schuster, 1996).
9. In most states, a person must declare a preference for a particular party before voting in that state's primary election (discussed in Chapter 9). This declaration is usually part of the voter-registration process.
10. Gallup poll, February 4–6, 2005.
11. For an interesting discussion of the pros and cons of patronage from a constitutional perspective, see the majority opinion versus the dissent in the Supreme Court case *Board of County Commissioners v. Umbehr,* 518 U.S. 668 (1996).
12. Kathleen Hall Jamieson, *Everything You Think You Know about Politics . . . and Why You're Wrong* (New York: Basic Books, 2000).

Chapter 8

1. As reported in *Public Perspective,* July/August 2001, p. 11.
2. Robert Weissberg, *Why Politicians Should Ignore Public Opinion Polls,* policy analysis dated May 29, 2001, the Cato Institute, Washington, D.C.
3. Doris A. Graber, *Mass Media and American Politics,* 6th ed. (Chicago: University of Chicago Press, 2001).
4. *The Gallup Report,* April 28, 1999.
5. *The Gallup Report,* May 21, 1999.
6. John M. Benson, "When Is an Opinion Really an Opinion?" *Public Perspective,* September/October 2001, pp. 40–41.
7. Robert B. Reich, "The Unending War," *The American Prospect,* December 17, 2001.
8. Norman Ornstein, *The Permanent Campaign and Its Future* (Washington, D.C.: AEI Press, 2000).
9. As quoted in Karl G. Feld, "When Push Comes to Shove: A Polling Industry Call to Arms," *Public Perspective,* September/October 2001, p. 38.
10. See, for example, Thomas Frank, *What's the Matter with Kansas? How Conservatives Won the Heart of America* (New York: Henry Holt & Company, 2004).
11. As quoted in Owen Ullman, "Why Voter Apathy Will Make a Strong Showing," *BusinessWeek,* November 4, 1996.

Chapter 9

1. The word *caucus* apparently was first used in the name of a men's club, the Caucus Club of colonial Boston, sometime between 1755 and 1765. (Many early political and government meetings took place in pubs.) The origin of the word is unknown, but some scholars have concluded it is of Algonquin origin.
2. Michael Slackman, "GOP Convention Cost $154 Million," *The New York Times,* October 14, 2004.
3. George F. Will, "Conventional Journalism," *Newsweek,* September 2, 1996.
4. Tom Johnson, "Do Conventions Still Rate Big TV Coverage?" *USA Today,* July 31, 2000, p. 17A.
5. Center for Responsive Politics, 2005. Data showing the relationship between spending and winning, as well as other information on campaign expenditures, are available at the center's Web site at **http://www.opensecrets.org**.
6. *Ibid.*
7. This act is sometimes referred to as the Federal Election Campaign Act of 1972 because it became effective in that year. The official date of the act, however, is 1971.
8. 424 U.S. 1 (1976).
9. Center for Responsive Politics, 2005.
10. *Colorado Republican Federal Campaign Committee v. Federal Election Commission,* 518 U.S. 604 (1996).
11. Quoted in George Will, "The First Amendment on Trial," *The Washington Post,* December 1, 2002, p. B07.
12. 124 S.Ct. 619 (2003).
13. A political watchdog group, the Center for Public Integrity, has extensive information about 527 organizations at **http://www.publicintegrity.org**.
14. Charles Lewis, *The Buying of the Congress: How Special Interests Have Stolen Your Right to Life, Liberty, and the Pursuit of Happiness* (New York: Avon Books, 1998).
15. Jeffrey H. Birnbaum, *The Money Men: The Real Story of Fund-Raising's Influence on Political Power in America* (New York: Crown Publishers, 2000), pp. 3–4.
16. Fox expressed these views in an article that is available online at **http://www.thisnation.com/question/036.html**.
17. In 1824, no candidate received a majority of electoral votes; John Quincy Adams was elected president by the House of Representatives. Rutherford B. Hayes lost the popular vote in 1876, but after the resolution of an electoral dispute, he ultimately won a majority of electoral votes. In 1888, Benjamin Harrison lost the popular vote, but won a majority of electoral votes.
18. For a more detailed account of the 2000 presidential elections, see *36 Days: The Complete Chronicle of the 2000 Presidential Election Crisis* (New York: Times Books, 2001), by correspondents of *The New York Times.*

Chapter 10

1. Ted Turner, "My Beef with Big Media," *Washington Monthly,* July/August 2004.
2. Bernard Cohen, *The Press and Foreign Policy* (Princeton, N.J.: Princeton University Press, 1963), p. 81.

3. "Terrorism Transforms News Interest," *Pew Research Center for the People and the Press Survey Reports,* December 18, 2001. You can view this report and others at the Pew Research Center's Web site at **http://people-press.org**.

4. George Kennedy, "Perspectives on War: The British See Things Differently," *Columbia Journalism Review,* March/April 2002.

5. "Return to Normalcy? How the Media Have Covered the War on Terrorism," *Project for Excellence in Journalism Reports and Surveys,* January 28, 2002. You can view this report and others at the Web site of the Project for Excellence in Journalism and the Committee of Concerned Journalists, **http://www.journalism.org**.

6. "Terror Coverage Boosts News Media's Images," *Pew Research Center for the People and the Press Survey Reports,* November 28, 2001.

7. Harold Evans, "Reporting in the Time of Conflict," essay presented as part of the Newseum War Stories Exhibit, May 18–September 30, 2001. Also available online at **http://www.newseum.org/warstories/essay/warcorrespondent.htm**.

8. Interestingly, in the 2000 campaigns, a Texas group supporting George W. Bush's candidacy paid for a remake of the "daisy" commercial, but the target in the new ad was Al Gore—see the photo caption on page 222.

9. The commission's action was upheld by a federal court. See *Perot v. Federal Election Commission,* 97 F.3d 553 (D.C.Cir. 1996).

10. Doris Graber, *Mass Media and American Politics,* 5th ed. (Washington, D.C.: Congressional Quarterly Press, 1997), p. 59.

11. Kerry Fehr-Snyder, "TV, Radio Win Big on Proposition Ads," *The Arizona Republic,* October 29, 2002.

12. S. Robert Lichter, Stanley Rothman, and Linda S. Lichter, *The Media Elite* (New York: Adler & Adler, 1986).

13. Kathleen Hall Jamieson, *Everything You Think You Know about Politics . . . and Why You're Wrong* (New York: Basic Books, 2000), pp. 187–195.

14. Survey conducted by the Pew Research Center for the People and the Press, 2005.

15. Calvin F. Exoo, *The Politics of the Mass Media* (St. Paul: West Publishing Co., 1994), pp. 49–50.

16. Jamieson, *Everything You Think You Know about Politics,* pp. xiii–xiv.

17. According to a survey conducted by the Pew Research Center for the People and the Press from April 24 to May 11, 1998.

18. "Self-Censorship: How Often and Why," *Pew Research Center for the People and the Press Survey Reports,* April 30, 2000.

19. *Ibid.*

20. Franklin D. Gilliam, Jr., and Shanto Iyengar, "Prime Suspects: The Influence of Local Television News on the Viewing Public," *American Journal of Political Science,* Vol. 44 (July 2000).

21. These studies are discussed in Mikal Muharrar, "Media Blackface: 'Racial Profiling' in News Reporting," *Extra!,* September/October 1998.

22. Martin Gilens, *Why Americans Hate Welfare: Race, Media, and the Politics of Antipoverty Policy* (Chicago: University of Chicago Press, 1999).

23. Muharrar, "Media Blackface."

24. Brigid McMenamin, "Humbled by the Internet," *Forbes,* July 27, 1998.

25. University of California at Los Angeles Internet Report, October 2000. This report is online at **http://www.college.ucla.edu/InternetReport**.

26. A summary of this report is available online at **http://people-press.org**.

27. N. Rebecca Donatelli, as quoted in *BusinessWeek,* August 30, 1999, p. 54.

Chapter 11

1. These states are Alaska, Delaware, Montana, North Dakota, South Dakota, Vermont, and Wyoming.

2. 369 U.S. 186 (1962).

3. 376 U.S. 1 (1964).

4. See, for example, *Davis v. Bandemer,* 478 U.S. 109 (1986).

5. *Amicus curiae* brief filed by the American Civil Liberties Union (ACLU) in support of the appellants in *Easley v. Cromartie,* 532 U.S. 234 (2001).

6. See, for example, *Shaw v. Reno,* 509 U.S. 630 (1993); *Miller v. Johnson,* 515 U.S. 900 (1995); *Shaw v. Hunt,* 517 U.S. 899 (1996); and *Bush v. Vera,* 517 U.S. 952 (1996).

7. *Easley v. Cromartie,* 532 U.S. 234 (2001).

8. For a discussion of the role of political parties in the selection of congressional candidates, see Gary Jacobson, *The Politics of Congressional Elections,* 6th ed. (New York: Longman Publishers, 2003).

9. *Powell v. McCormack,* 395 U.S. 486 (1969).

10. Quoted in John Samples and Patrick Basham, "Election 2002 and the Problems of American Democracy," *Policy Analysis,* September 5, 2002.

11. Some observers maintain that another reason Congress *can* stay in session longer is the invention of air-conditioning. Until the advent of air-conditioning, no member of Congress wanted to stay in session during the hot and sticky late spring, summer, and early fall months.

12. David Broder, "The New GOP Take on Term Limits," *The Washington Post,* January 5, 2003, p. B-7.

13. A term used by Woodrow Wilson in *Congressional Government* (New York: Meridian Books, 1956 [first published in 1885]).

14. To see the latest figures on the public debt, visit the Bureau of the Public Debt at **http://www.publicdebt.treas.gov**.

15. Jeffrey H. Birnbaum, "The Return of Big Government: Federal Spending Is Skyrocketing, but Shockingly Little of It Is Related to September 11," *Fortune,* September 16, 2002, p. 112.

16. In 2005, President Bush's budget projections extended only five years, as had been the practice before 1996.

Chapter 12

1. Several Supreme Court cases have addressed whether the federal government can enter into treaties that contain provisions that violate the restrictions or requirements of the Constitution. See, for example, *Geofroy v. Riggs,* 133 U.S. 258 (1890); *U.S. v. Wong Kim Ark,* 169 U.S. 649 (1898); *Asakura v. City of Seattle,* 265 U.S. 332 (1924); *Reid v. Covert,* 354 U.S. 1 (1957); and *Boos v. Barry,* 485 U.S. 312 (1988).

2. Lyndon B. Johnson, *The Vantage Point: Perspectives of the Presidency, 1963–1969* (New York: Henry Holt & Co., 1971).

3. Siena College Research Institute poll, February 2005; Gallup poll, June 2003.

4. Forrest McDonald, *The American Presidency: An Intellectual History* (Lawrence, Kans.: University Press of Kansas, 1994), p. 179.

5. Versailles, located about twenty miles from Paris, is the name of the palace built by King Louis XIV of France. It served as the royal palace until 1793 and was then converted into a national historical museum, which it remains today. The preliminary treaty ending the American Revolution was signed by the United States and Great Britain at Versailles in 1783.

6. *Ex parte Grossman,* 267 U.S. 87 (1925).

7. *Clinton v. City of New York,* 524 U.S. 417 (1998).

8. As cited in Lewis D. Eigen and Jonathan P. Siegel, *The Macmillan Dictionary of Political Quotations* (New York: Macmillan, 1993), p. 565.

9. The Constitution does not grant the president explicit power to remove from office officials who are not performing satisfactorily or who do not agree with the president. In 1926, however, the Supreme Court prevented Congress from interfering with the president's ability to fire those executive-branch officials whom he had appointed with Senate approval. See *Myers v. United States,* 272 U.S. 52 (1926).

10. Richard E. Neustadt, *Presidential Power: The Politics of Leadership* (New York: John Wiley, 1980), p. 10.

11. As quoted in Richard M. Pious, *The American Presidency* (New York: Basic Books, 1979), pp. 51–52.

12. A phrase coined by Samuel Kernell in *Going Public: New Strategies of Presidential Leadership,* 2d ed. (Washington, D.C.: Congressional Quarterly Press, 1992).

13. Franklin D. Roosevelt, as quoted in *The New York Times,* November 13, 1932.

14. Congress used its power to declare war in the War of 1812, the Mexican War (1846–1848), the Spanish-American War (1898), and World War I (U.S. involvement lasted from 1916 until 1918) and on six different occasions during World War II (U.S. involvement lasted from 1941 until 1945).

15. William S. Cohen, "Why I Am Leaving," *The Washington Post National Weekly Edition,* January 28–February 4, 1996, p. 29.

16. See, for example, Thomas E. Cronin and Michael A. Genovese, *The Paradoxes of the American Presidency* (New York: Oxford University Press, 1998).

17. *Ibid.,* p. 108.

18. See the writings of Aubrey Immelman, a political psychologist and associate professor of psychology at the College of St. Benedict and St. John's University, at **http://www.csbsju.edu/uspp/Publications&Citations/Publications.html**.

19. James Klurfeld, "The Really Big Story: Bush's Awesome Power," *Newsday,* December 26, 2002.
20. "U.S. Places New Curbs on Weapons Data; Secrecy Watchdogs Warn of Rule's Broader Uses," *The Washington Post,* March 22, 2002, p. A3.
21. As quoted in Thomas E. Cronin, *The State of the Presidency,* 2d ed. (Boston: Little, Brown, 1980), p. 11.

Chapter 13

1. Geoffrey F. Segal, *Cato Handbook for Congress: Policy Recommendations for the 108th Congress* (Washington, D.C.: The Cato Institute, January 22, 2003), p. 327.
2. For further information on the AFSCME's position on privatization, go to **http://www.afscme.org/private**.
3. This definition follows the classical model of bureaucracy put forth by German sociologist Max Weber. See Max Weber, *Theory of Social and Economic Organization,* ed. Talcott Parsons (New York: Oxford University Press, 1974).
4. It should be noted that although the president is technically the head of the bureaucracy, the president cannot always control the bureaucracy—as you will read later in this chapter.
5. George Will, "Race and 'Rights,'" *The Washington Post,* March 11, 2005, p. A23.
6. "The Political Hacks' Ultimate Fantasy Book," *Fortune,* March 3, 1997, p. 46.
7. Christopher C. DeMuth, "After the Ascent: Politics and Government in the Super-Affluent Society," Francis Boyer lecture, American Enterprise Institute, Washington, D.C., February 15, 2000.
8. George Melloan, "Disturbing Trends for America's Rule of Law," *The Wall Street Journal,* November 5, 2002, p. A11.
9. Trucking associations and other business groups sued the EPA, claiming, among other things, that the EPA had to take economic costs into account when issuing new rules. Ultimately, the case reached the United States Supreme Court, which held that the EPA did not have to take such costs into consideration when creating new rules. *Whitman v. American Trucking Associations,* 531 U.S. 457 (2000).
10. Anne B. Fisher, "One Welfare Program That Won't Die," *Fortune,* November 27, 1995, p. 40.
11. As quoted in Bob Norton, "Why Federal Programs Won't Die," *Fortune,* August 21, 1995, p. 35.
12. As quoted in George Melloan, "Bush's Toughest Struggle Is with His Own Bureaucracy," *The Wall Street Journal,* June 25, 2002, p. A13.

Chapter 14

1. Pronounced *ster*-ay dih-*si*-sis.
2. 347 U.S. 483 (1954).
3. See *Plessy v. Ferguson,* 163 U.S. 537 (1896).
4. 539 U.S. 558 (2003).
5. 478 U.S. 186 (1986).
6. Pronounced shah-*ree*-uh.
7. Although a state's highest court is often referred to as the state supreme court, there are exceptions. In the New York court system, for example, the supreme court is a trial court, and the highest court is called the New York Court of Appeals.
8. Pronounced jus-*tish*-a-bul.
9. *Elk Grove Unified School District v. Newdow,* 124 S.Ct. 2301 (2004).
10. Pronounced sur-shee-uh-*rah*-ree.
11. Between 1790 and 1891, Congress allowed the Supreme Court almost no discretion over which cases to decide. After 1925, in almost 95 percent of appealed cases the Court could choose whether to hear arguments and issue an opinion. Beginning with the term in October 1988, mandatory review was virtually eliminated.
12. Pamela MacLean, "Bush's Nominees Likely to Put Stamp on Circuits," *The National Law Journal,* March 28, 2005, pp. 1–2.
13. 84 F.3d 720 (5th Cir. 1996).
14. 5 U.S. (1 Cranch) 137 (1803). The Supreme Court had considered the constitutionality of an act of Congress in *Hylton v. United States,* 3 U.S. 171 (1796), in which Congress's power to levy certain taxes was challenged. That particular act was ruled constitutional, rather than unconstitutional, however, so this first federal exercise of judicial review was not clearly recognized as such. Also, during the decade before the adoption of the federal Constitution, courts in at least eight states had exercised the power of judicial review.
15. 124 S.Ct. 2633 (2004).
16. 355 F.Supp.2d 443 (D.C. 2005).
17. Jeffrey A. Segal and Harold J. Spaeth, *The Supreme Court and the Attitudinal Model* (New York: Cambridge University Press, 1993), p. 65.
18. 539 U.S. 558 (2003)—this case was cited earlier in this chapter.
19. 539 U.S. 306 (2003).
20. 125 S.Ct. 1183 (2005).
21. *U.S. Airways v. Barnett,* 535 U.S. 391 (2002).
22. As cited in Linda Greenhouse, "The Competing Visions of the Role of the Court," *The New York Times,* July 7, 2002, p. 3.
23. Antonin Scalia, *A Matter of Interpretation* (Ewing, N.J.: Princeton University Press, 1997).
24. As cited in Carl Hulse and David D. Kirkpatrick, "DeLay Says Federal Judiciary Has 'Run Amok,' Adding Congress Is Partly to Blame," *The New York Times,* April 8, 2005, p. 5.

GLOSSARY

A

action-reaction syndrome For every government action, there will be a reaction by the public. The government then takes a further action to counter the public's reaction—and the cycle begins again.

adjudicate To render a judicial decision. In regard to administrative law, the process in which an administrative law judge hears and decides issues that arise when an agency charges a person or firm with violating a law or regulation enforced by the agency.

administrative law The body of law created by administrative agencies (in the form of rules, regulations, orders, and decisions) in order to carry out their duties and responsibilities.

affirmative action A policy calling for the establishment of programs that involve giving preference, in jobs and college admissions, to members of groups that have been discriminated against in the past.

agenda setting Part of the first stage of the policymaking process, which consists of getting an issue on the political agenda to be addressed by Congress.

agents of political socialization People and institutions that influence the political views of others.

Anti-Federalists A political group that opposed the adoption of the Constitution because of the document's centralist tendencies and because it did not include a bill of rights.

antitrust law The body of law that attempts to support free competition in the marketplace by curbing monopolistic and unfair trade practices.

appellate court A court having appellate jurisdiction that normally does not hear evidence or testimony but reviews the transcript of the trial court's proceedings, other records relating to the case, and the attorneys' respective arguments as to why the trial court's decision should or should not stand.

apportionment The distribution of House seats among the states on the basis of their respective populations.

appropriation A part of the congressional budgeting process that involves determining how many dollars will be spent in a given year on a particular set of government activities.

Articles of Confederation The nation's first national constitution, which established a national form of government following the American Revolution. The Articles provided for a confederal form of government in which the central government had few powers.

attack ad A negative political advertisement that attacks the character of an opposing candidate.

Australian ballot A secret ballot that is prepared, distributed, and counted by government officials at public expense; used by all states in the United States since 1888.

authority The ability to exercise power, such as the power to make and enforce laws, legitimately.

authorization A part of the congressional budgeting process that involves the creation of the legal basis for government programs.

autocracy A form of government in which the power and authority of the government are in the hands of a single person.

B

biased sample A poll sample that does not accurately represent the population.

bicameral legislature A legislature made up of two chambers, or parts. The United States has a bicameral legislature, composed of the House of Representatives and the Senate.

bill of attainder A legislative act that inflicts punishment on particular persons or groups without granting them the right to a trial.

Bill of Rights The first ten amendments to the U.S. Constitution. They list the freedoms—such as the freedoms of speech, press, and religion—that a person enjoys and that cannot be infringed on by the government.

block grant A federal grant given to a state for a broad area, such as criminal justice or mental-health programs.

bureaucracy A large, complex, hierarchically structured administrative organization that carries out specific functions.

bureaucrat An individual who works in a bureaucracy; as generally used, the term refers to a government employee.

busing The transportation of public school students by bus to schools physically outside their neighborhoods to eliminate school segregation based on residential patterns.

C

cabinet An advisory group selected by the president to assist with decision making. Traditionally, the cabinet has consisted of the heads of the executive departments and other officers whom the president may choose to appoint.

campaign strategy The comprehensive plan for winning an election developed by a candidate and his or her advisers. The strategy includes the candidate's position on issues, slogan, advertising plan, press events, personal appearances, and other aspects of the campaign.

case law The rules of law announced in court decisions. Case law includes the aggregate of reported cases that interpret judicial precedents, statutes, regulations, and constitutional provisions.

categorical grant A federal grant targeted for a specific purpose as defined by federal law.

caucus A meeting held by party leaders to choose political candidates. The caucus system of nominating candidates was eventually replaced by nominating conventions and, later, by direct primaries.

checks and balances A major principle of American government in which each of the three branches is given the means to check (to restrain or balance) the actions of the others.

chief diplomat The role of the president in recognizing and interacting with foreign governments.

chief executive The head of the executive branch of government. In the United States, the president is the head of the executive branch of the federal government.

chief of staff The person who directs the operations of the White House Office and who advises the president on important matters.

chief of state The person who serves as the ceremonial head of a country's government and represents that country to the rest of the world.

civil disobedience The deliberate and public act of refusing to obey laws thought to be unjust.

civil law The branch of law that spells out the duties that individuals in society owe to other persons or to their governments, excluding the duty not to commit crimes.

civil liberties Individual rights protected by the Constitution against the powers of the government.

civil rights The rights of all Americans to equal treatment under the law, as provided for by the Fourteenth Amendment to the Constitution.

civil rights movement The movement in the 1950s and 1960s, by minorities and concerned whites, to end racial segregation.

civil service Nonmilitary government employment.

closed primary A primary in which only party members can vote to choose that party's candidates.

cloture A method of ending debate in the Senate and bringing the matter under consideration to a vote by the entire chamber.

coalition An alliance of individuals or groups with a variety of interests and opinions who join together to support all or part of a political party's platform.

Cold War The war of words, warnings, and ideologies between the Soviet Union and the United States that lasted from the late 1940s through the early 1990s.

colonial empire A group of colonized nations that are under the rule of a single imperial power.

commander in chief The supreme commander of the military forces of the United States.

commerce clause The clause in Article I, Section 8, of the Constitution that gives Congress the power to regulate interstate commerce (commerce involving more than one state).

commercial speech Advertising statements that describe products. Commercial speech receives less protection under the First Amendment than ordinary speech.

common law The body of law developed from judicial decisions in English and U.S. courts, not attributable to a legislature.

Communist bloc The group of Eastern European nations that fell under the control of the Soviet Union following World War II.

competitive federalism A model of federalism devised by Thomas R. Dye in which state and local governments compete for businesses and citizens, who in effect "vote with their feet" by moving to jurisdictions that offer a competitive advantage.

concurrent powers Powers held by both the federal and state governments in a federal system.

concurring opinion A statement written by a judge or justice who agrees (concurs) with the court's decision, but for reasons different from those in the majority opinion.

confederal system A league of independent sovereign states, joined together by a central government that has only limited powers over them.

confederation A league of independent states that are united only for the purpose of achieving common goals.

conference In regard to the Supreme Court, a private meeting of the justices in which they present their arguments with respect to a case under consideration.

conference committee A temporary committee that is formed when the two chambers of Congress pass separate versions of the same bill. The conference committee, which consists of members from both the House and the Senate, works out a compromise form of the bill.

conference report A report submitted by a congressional conference committee after it has drafted a single version of a bill.

congressional district The geographic area that is served by one member in the House of Representatives.

consensus A general agreement among the citizenry (often defined as an agreement among 75 percent or more of the people) on matters of public policy.

conservatism A set of beliefs that includes a limited role for the national government in helping individuals, support for traditional values and lifestyles, and a cautious response to change.

conservative One who subscribes to a set of political beliefs that includes a limited role for government, support for traditional values, and a preference for the status quo.

Constitutional Convention The convention (meeting) of delegates from the states that was held in Philadelphia in 1787 for the purpose of amending the Articles of Confederation. In fact, the delegates wrote a new constitution (the U.S. Constitution) that established a federal form of government to replace the governmental system that had been created by the Articles of Confederation.

constitutional law Law based on the U.S. Constitution and the constitutions of the various states.

constitutional monarchy A form of monarchy in which the monarch shares governmental power with elected lawmakers; the monarch's power is limited, or checked, by other government leaders and perhaps by a constitution or a bill of rights.

consumption tax A tax on spending, or on the difference between what people earn and what they save, regardless of how much they earn.

containment A U.S. policy designed to contain the spread of communism by offering military and economic aid to threatened nations.

continuing resolution A resolution, which Congress passes when it is unable to pass a complete budget by October 1, that enables the executive agencies to keep on doing whatever they were doing the previous year with the same amount of funding.

cooperative federalism The theory that the states and the federal government should cooperate in solving problems.

Council of Economic Advisers (CEA) A three-member council created in 1946 to advise the president on economic matters.

Credentials Committee A committee of each national political party that evaluates the claims of national party convention delegates to be the legitimate representatives of their states.

criminal law The branch of law that defines and governs actions that constitute crimes. Generally, criminal law has to do with wrongful actions committed against society for which society demands redress.

Cuban missile crisis A nuclear standoff that occurred in 1962 when the United States learned that the Soviet Union had placed nuclear warheads in Cuba, an island ninety miles off the U.S. coast. The crisis was defused diplomatically, but it is generally considered the closest the two Cold War superpowers came to a nuclear confrontation.

D

de facto segregation Racial segregation that occurs not as a result of deliberate intentions but because of past social and economic conditions and residential patterns.

de jure segregation Racial segregation that is legally sanctioned—that is, segregation that occurs because of laws or decisions by government agencies.

delegate A person selected to represent the people of one geographic area at a party convention.

democracy A system of government in which the people have ultimate political authority. The word is derived from the Greek *demos* (people) and *kratia* (rule).

détente A French word meaning a "relaxation of tensions." Détente characterized the relationship between the United States and the Soviet Union in the 1970s, as the two Cold War rivals attempted to pursue cooperative dealings and arms control.

deterrence A policy of building up military strength for the purpose of discouraging (deterring) military attacks by other nations; the policy of "building weapons for peace" that supported the arms race between the United States and the Soviet Union during the Cold War.

devolution In the context of American politics, the transfer to the states of some of the responsibilities assumed by the national government since the 1930s.

dictatorship A form of government in which absolute power is exercised by a single person who has usually obtained his or her power by the use of force.

diplomat In regard to international relations, a person who represents one country in dealing with representatives of another country.

direct democracy A system of government in which political decisions are made by the people themselves rather than by elected representatives. This form of government was widely practiced in ancient Greece.

direct primary An election held within each of the two major parties—Democratic and Republican—to choose the party's candidates for the general election.

direct technique Any method used by an interest group to interact with government officials directly to further the group's goals.

dissenting opinion A statement written by a judge or justice who disagrees with the majority opinion.

diversity of citizenship A basis for federal court jurisdiction over a lawsuit that arises when (1) the parties in the lawsuit live in different states or when one of the parties is a foreign government or a foreign citizen, and (2) the amount in controversy is more than $75,000.

divine right theory A theory that the right to rule by a king or queen was derived directly from God rather than from the consent of the people.

division of powers A basic principle of federalism established by the U.S. Constitution. In a federal system, powers are divided between units of government (such as the federal and state governments).

domestic policy Public policy concerning issues within a national unit, such as national policy concerning welfare or crime.

double jeopardy To prosecute a person twice for the same criminal offense; prohibited by the Fifth Amendment in all but a few circumstances.

drug court A court in which persons convicted of violating certain drug laws are ordered to undergo treatment in a rehabilitation program as an alternative to serving time in a jail or prison.

dual federalism A system of government in which both the federal and state governments maintain diverse but sovereign powers.

due process clause The constitutional guarantee, set out in the Fifth and Fourteenth Amendments, that the government will not illegally or arbitrarily deprive a person of life, liberty, or property.

due process of law The requirement that the government use fair, reasonable, and standard procedures whenever it takes any legal action against an individual; required by the Fifth and Fourteenth Amendments.

E

easy-money policy A monetary policy that involves stimulating the economy by expanding the rate of growth of the money supply. An easy-money policy supposedly will lead to lower interest rates and induce consumers to spend more and producers to invest more.

economic policy All actions taken by the national government to smooth out the ups and downs in the nation's overall business activity.

economic regulation Government regulation of natural monopolies and inherently noncompetitive industries.

elector A member of the electoral college.

electoral college The group of electors who are selected by the voters in each state to officially elect the president and vice president. The number of electors in each state is equal to the number of that state's representatives in both chambers of Congress.

electorate All of the citizens eligible to vote in a given election.

electronic media Communication channels that involve electronic transmissions, such as radio, television, and, to an extent, the Internet.

entitlement program A government program (such as Social Security) that allows, or entitles, a certain class of people (such as the elderly) to receive special benefits. Entitlement programs operate under open-ended budget authorizations that, in effect, place no limits on how much can be spent.

equal employment opportunity A goal of the 1964 Civil Rights Act to end employment discrimination based on race, color, religion, gender, or national origin and to promote equal job opportunities for all individuals.

equal protection clause Section 1 of the Fourteenth Amendment, which states that no state shall "deny to any person within its jurisdiction the equal protection of the laws."

equality A concept that holds, at a minimum, that all people are entitled to equal protection under the law.

espionage The practice of spying, on behalf of a foreign power, to obtain information about government plans and activities.

establishment clause The section of the First Amendment that prohibits Congress from passing laws "respecting an establishment of religion." Issues concerning the establishment clause often center on prayer in public schools, the teaching of fundamentalist theories of creation, and government aid to parochial schools.

***ex post facto* law** A criminal law that punishes individuals for committing an act that was legal when the act was committed but that has since become a crime.

exclusionary rule A criminal procedural rule requiring that any illegally obtained evidence will not be admissible in court. The rule is based on Supreme Court interpretations of the Fourth and Fourteenth Amendments.

executive agreement A binding international agreement, or pact, that is made between the president and another head of state and that does not require Senate approval.

Executive Office of the President (EOP) A group of staff agencies that assist the president in carrying out major duties. Franklin D. Roosevelt established the EOP in 1939 to cope with the increased responsibilities brought on by the Great Depression.

executive order A presidential order to carry out a policy or policies described in a law passed by Congress.

executive privilege An inherent executive power claimed by presidents to withhold information from, or to refuse to appear before, Congress or the courts. The president can also accord the privilege to other executive officials.

expressed powers Constitutional or statutory powers that are expressly provided for by the Constitution or by congressional laws.

extraordinary majority More than a mere majority; typically, an extraordinary majority consists of two-thirds or three-fifths of the voting body (such as a legislature).

F

faction A group or clique within a larger group.

federal mandate A requirement in federal legislation that forces states and municipalities to comply with certain rules.

Federal Open Market Committee (FOMC) The most important body within the Federal Reserve System; the FOMC decides how monetary policy should be carried out by the Federal Reserve.

federal question A question that pertains to the U.S. Constitution, acts of Congress, or treaties. A federal question provides a basis for federal court jurisdiction.

federal system A form of government in which a written constitution provides for a division of powers between a central government and several regional governments. In the United States, the division of powers between the national government and the fifty states is established by the Constitution.

federalism A way of organizing separate states into a single political system in such a way that each can maintain its fundamental political identity. Federalism emphasizes negotiated policymaking among the member states. The United States has a truly federal system because the Constitution specifically describes how power to make and implement policy should be shared by the national government and the state governments.

Federalists A political group, led by Alexander Hamilton and John Adams, that supported the adoption of the Constitution and the creation of a federal form of government.

"fighting words" Words that, when uttered by a public speaker, are so inflammatory that they could provoke the average listener to violence.

filtering software Computer programs designed to block access to certain Web sites.

filibustering The Senate tradition of unlimited debate, undertaken for the purpose of preventing action on a bill.

first budget resolution A budget resolution, which is supposed to be passed in May, that sets overall revenue goals and spending targets for the next fiscal year, which begins on October 1.

First Continental Congress The first gathering of delegates from twelve of the thirteen colonies, held in 1774.

fiscal federalism The power of the national government to influence state policies through grants.

fiscal policy The use of changes in government expenditures and taxes to alter national economic variables, such as the employment rate and price stability.

fiscal year A twelve-month period that is established for book-keeping or accounting purposes. The government's fiscal year runs from October 1 through September 30.

foreign policy A systematic and general plan that guides a country's attitudes and actions toward the rest of the world. Foreign policy includes all of the economic, military, commercial, and diplomatic positions and actions that a nation takes in its relationships with other countries.

free exercise clause The provision of the First Amendment stating that the government cannot pass laws "prohibiting the free exercise" of religion. Free exercise issues often concern religious practices that conflict with established laws.

free rider problem The difficulty faced by interest groups that lobby for a public good. Individuals can enjoy the outcome of the group's efforts without having to contribute, such as by becoming members of the group.

fundamental right A basic right of all Americans, such as all First Amendment rights. Any law or action that prevents some group of persons from exercising a fundamental right will be subject to the "strict-scrutiny" standard, under which the law or action must be necessary to promote a compelling state interest and must be narrowly tailored to meet that interest.

G

general election A regularly scheduled election to elect the U.S. president, vice president, and senators and representatives in Congress; general elections are held in even-numbered years on the first Tuesday after the first Monday in November.

gender gap A term used to describe the difference between the percentage of votes cast for a particular candidate by women and the percentage of votes cast for the same candidate by men.

gerrymandering The drawing of a legislative district's boundaries in such a way as to maximize the influence of a certain group or political party.

government The individuals and institutions that make society's rules and that also possess the power and authority to enforce those rules.

government corporation An agency of the government that is run as a business enterprise. Such agencies engage in primarily commercial activities, produce revenues, and require greater flexibility than that permitted in most government agencies.

grandfather clause A clause in a state law that restricted the franchise (voting rights) to those whose grandfathers had voted; one of the techniques used in the South to prevent African Americans from exercising their right to vote.

Great Compromise A plan for a bicameral legislature in which one chamber would be based on population and the other chamber would represent each state equally. The plan, also known as the Connecticut Compromise, resolved the small-state/large-state controversy.

I

ideologue An individual who holds very strong political opinions.

ideology A set of beliefs about human nature, social inequality, and government institutions that forms the basis of a political or economic system.

impeachment A formal proceeding against a public official for misconduct or wrongdoing in office.

implied powers The powers of the federal government that are implied by the expressed powers in the Constitution, particularly in Article I, Section 8.

income redistribution The transfer of income from one group to another; income is taken from some people through taxation and given to others.

independent executive agency A federal bureaucratic agency that is not located within a cabinet department.

independent expenditure An expenditure for activities that are independent from (not coordinated with) those of a political candidate or a political party.

independent regulatory agency A federal bureaucratic organization that is responsible for creating and implementing rules that regulate private activity and protect the public interest in a particular sector of the economy.

indirect technique Any method used by interest groups to influence government officials through third parties, such as voters.

inherent powers The powers of the national government that, although not expressly granted by the Constitution, are necessary to ensure the nation's integrity and survival as a political unit. Inherent powers include the power to make treaties and the power to wage war or make peace.

initiative A procedure by which voters can propose a change in state and local laws, including state constitutions, by means of gathering signatures on a petition and submitting it to the legislature (and/or the voters) for approval.

institution An ongoing organization that performs certain functions for society. Some of the institutions in our government are the legal system, Congress, and the social-welfare system.

instructed delegate A representative (such as a member of Congress) who is expected to mirror the views of those whom he or she represents (such as a congressional member's constituents).

interest group An organized group of individuals sharing common objectives who actively attempt to influence policymakers in all three branches of the government and at all levels.

interstate commerce Trade that involves more than one state.

interventionism Direct involvement by one country in another country's affairs.

intrastate commerce Commerce that takes place within state borders. State governments have the power to regulate intrastate commerce.

iron curtain A phrase coined by Winston Churchill to describe the political boundaries between the democratic countries in Western Europe and the Soviet-controlled Communist countries in Eastern Europe.

iron triangle A three-way alliance among legislators, bureaucrats, and interest groups to make or preserve policies that benefit their respective interests.

isolationism A political policy of noninvolvement in world affairs.

issue ad A negative political advertisement that focuses on flaws in an opposing candidate's position on a particular issue.

issue networks Groups of individuals or organizations— which consist of legislators and legislative staff members, interest group leaders, bureaucrats, the media, scholars, and other experts—that support particular policy positions on a given issue.

J

judicial review The power of the courts to decide on the constitutionality of legislative enactments and of actions taken by the executive branch.

judiciary The courts; one of the three branches of the federal government in the United States.

jurisdiction The authority of a court to hear and decide a particular case.

justiciable controversy A controversy that is not hypothetical or academic but real and substantial; a requirement that must be satisfied before a court will hear a case.

K

Keynesian economics An economic theory proposed by British economist John Maynard Keynes that is typically associated with the use of fiscal policy to alter national economic variables. Keynesian economics gained prominence during the Great Depression of the 1930s.

kitchen cabinet The name given to a president's unofficial advisers. The term was coined during Andrew Jackson's presidency.

L

legislative rule An administrative agency rule that carries the same weight as a statute enacted by a legislature.

Lemon test A three-part test enunciated by the Supreme Court in the 1971 case of *Lemon v. Kurtzman* to determine whether government aid to parochial schools is constitutional. To be constitutional, the aid must (1) be for a clearly secular purpose; (2) in its primary effect, neither advance nor inhibit religion; and (3) avoid an "excessive government entanglement with religion." The *Lemon* test has also been used in other types of cases involving the establishment clause.

libel A published report of a falsehood that tends to injure a person's reputation or character.

liberal One who subscribes to a set of political beliefs that includes the advocacy of active government, government inter-

vention to improve the welfare of individuals, support for civil rights, and political change.

liberalism A set of political beliefs that includes the advocacy of active government, government intervention to improve the welfare of individuals, and civil rights.

liberty The freedom of individuals to believe, act, and express themselves freely so long as doing so does not infringe on the rights of other individuals in the society.

limited government A form of government based on the principle that the powers of government should be clearly limited either through a written document or through wide public understanding; characterized by institutional checks to ensure that government serves public rather than private interests.

literacy test A test given to voters to ensure that they could read and write and thus evaluate political information; a technique used in many southern states to restrict African American participation in elections.

lobbying All of the attempts by organizations or by individuals to influence the passage, defeat, or contents of legislation or to influence the administrative decisions of government.

lobbyist An individual who handles a particular interest group's lobbying efforts.

loophole A legal way of evading a certain legal requirement.

M

Madisonian Model The model of government devised by James Madison in which the powers of the government are separated into three branches: executive, legislative, and judicial.

Magna Carta The great charter that King John of England was forced to sign in 1215 as protection against the absolute powers of the monarchy. It included such fundamental rights as trial by jury and due process of law.

majority leader The party leader elected by the majority party in the House or in the Senate.

majority party The political party that has more members in the legislature than does the opposing party.

malapportionment A condition that results when, based on population and representation, the voting power of citizens in one district becomes more influential than the voting power of citizens in another district.

managed news coverage News coverage that is manipulated (managed) by a campaign manager or political consultant to gain media exposure for a political candidate.

markup session A meeting held by a congressional committee or subcommittee to approve, amend, or redraft a bill.

Marshall Plan A plan providing for U.S. economic assistance to European nations following World War II to help those nations recover from the war; the plan was named after George C. Marshall, secretary of state from 1947 to 1949.

mass media Communication channels, such as newspapers and radio and television broadcasts, through which people can communicate to mass audiences.

Mayflower Compact A document drawn up by Pilgrim leaders in 1620 on the ship *Mayflower*. The document stated that laws were to be made for the general good of the people.

media Newspapers, magazines, television, radio, the Internet, and any other printed or electronic means of communication.

mediating institutions Institutions that assume a mediating role between Americans and their government. Mediating institutions include political party conventions (which decide who will be candidates for political office) and network news organizations (which determine what political events should be reported to the public).

minority leader The party leader elected by the minority party in the House or in the Senate.

minority party The political party that has fewer members in the legislature than does the opposing party.

minority-majority district A congressional district whose boundaries are drawn in such a way as to maximize the voting power of a minority group.

Miranda warnings A series of statements informing criminal suspects, on their arrest, of their constitutional rights, such as the right to remain silent and the right to counsel; required by the Supreme Court's 1966 decision in *Miranda v. Arizona*.

moderate With regard to the political spectrum, a person whose views fall in the middle of the spectrum.

monarchy A form of autocracy in which a king, queen, emperor, empress, tsar, or tsarina is the highest authority in the government; monarchs usually obtain their power through inheritance.

monetary policy Actions taken by the Federal Reserve Board to change the amount of money in circulation so as to affect interest rates, credit markets, the rate of inflation, the rate of economic growth, and the rate of unemployment.

Monroe Doctrine A U.S. policy, announced in 1823 by President James Monroe, that the United States would not tolerate foreign intervention in the Western Hemisphere, and in return, the United States would stay out of European affairs.

multiculturalism The belief that the many cultures that make up American society should remain distinct and be protected and even encouraged by our laws.

multilateral Involving more than one side or nation.

mutual-assured destruction (MAD) A phrase referring to the assumption, on which the policy of deterrence was based, that if the forces of two nations are equally capable of destroying each other, neither will take a chance on war.

N

narrowcasting Catering media programming to the specialized tastes and preferences of targeted audiences.

national convention The meeting held by each major party every four years to select presidential and vice-presidential candidates, to write a party platform, and to conduct other party business.

national party chairperson An individual who serves as a political party's administrative head at the national level and directs the work of the party's national committee.

national party committee The political party leaders who direct party business during the four years between the national party conventions, organize the next national convention, and plan how to obtain a party victory in the next presidential elections.

National Security Council (NSC) A council that advises the president on domestic and foreign matters concerning the safety and defense of the nation; established in 1947.

natural rights Rights that are not bestowed by governments but are inherent within every single man, woman, and child by virtue of the fact that he or she is a human being.

necessary and proper clause Article I, Section 8, Clause 18, of the Constitution, which gives Congress the power to make all laws "necessary and proper" for the federal government to carry out its responsibilities; also called the elastic clause.

negative externality An effect of private decision making, such as pollution, that imposes social costs on the community. Negative externalities resulting from business decisions are often cited as reasons for government regulation.

negative political advertising Political advertising undertaken for the purpose of discrediting an opposing candidate in the eyes of the voters; attack ads and issue ads are forms of negative political advertising.

negotiated rulemaking A type of administrative agency rulemaking in which the industries that will be affected by the new rule participate in the rule's formulation.

neutral competency The application of technical skills to jobs without regard to political issues.

neutrality A position of not being aligned with either side in a dispute or conflict, such as a war.

New Deal A program ushered in by the Roosevelt administration in 1933 to bring the United States out of the Great Depression. The New Deal included many government spending and public-assistance programs, in addition to thousands of regulations governing economic activity.

new federalism A plan to limit the federal government's role in regulating state governments and to give the states increased power to decide how they should spend government revenues.

nominating convention An official meeting of a political party to choose its candidates. Nominating conventions at the state and local levels also select delegates to represent the people of their geographic areas at a higher-level party convention.

normal trade relations (NTR) status A status granted through an international treaty by which each member nation must treat other members at least as well as it treats the country that receives its most favorable treatment. This status was formerly known as *most-favored-nation status*.

O

obscenity Indecency or offensiveness in speech or expression, behavior, or appearance; what specific expressions or acts constitute obscenity normally are determined by community standards.

Office of Management and Budget (OMB) An agency in the Executive Office of the President that assists the president in preparing and supervising the administration of the federal budget.

office-block ballot A ballot that lists together all of the candidates for each office.

"one person, one vote" rule A rule, or principle, requiring that congressional districts must have equal population so that one person's vote counts as much as another's vote.

open primary A primary in which voters can vote for a party's candidates regardless of whether they belong to the party.

opinion A written statement by a court expressing the reasons for its decision in a case.

oral argument An argument presented to a judge in person by an attorney on behalf of his or her client.

P

parliament The name of the national legislative body in countries governed by a parliamentary system, such as England and France.

partisan politics Political actions or decisions that are influenced by a particular political party's ideology.

party elite A loose-knit group of party activists who organize and oversee party functions and planning during and between campaigns.

party identifier A person who identifies himself or herself as being a member of a particular political party.

party platform The document drawn up by each party at its national convention that outlines the policies and positions of the party.

party ticket A list of a political party's candidates for various offices.

party-column ballot A ballot (also called the Indiana ballot) that lists all of a party's candidates under the party label; voters can vote for all of a party's candidates for local, state, and national offices by making a single "X" or pulling a single lever.

patron An individual or organization that provides financial backing to an interest group.

patronage A system of rewarding the party faithful and workers with government jobs or contracts.

peer group Associates, often those close in age to oneself; may include friends, classmates, co-workers, club members, or church group members. Peer group influence is a significant factor in the political socialization process.

picket-fence federalism A model of federalism in which specific policies and programs are administered by all levels of government—national, state, and local.

pluralist theory A theory that views politics as a contest among various interest groups—at all levels of government—to gain benefits for their members.

plurality A situation in which a candidate wins an election by receiving more votes than the others but does not necessarily win a majority (over 50 percent of the votes). Most federal, state, and local laws allow for elections to be won by a plurality vote.

pocket veto A special type of veto power used by the chief executive after the legislature has adjourned. Bills that are not signed by the president die after a specified period of time and must be reintroduced if Congress wishes to reconsider them.

police powers The powers of a government body that enable it to create laws for the protection of the health, morals, safety, and welfare of the people. In the United States, most police powers are reserved to the states.

policymaking process The procedures involved in getting an issue on the political agenda; formulating, adopting, and implementing a policy with regard to the issue; and then evaluating the results of the policy.

political action committee (PAC) A committee that is established by a corporation, labor union, or special interest group to raise funds and make contributions on the establishing organization's behalf.

political advertising Advertising undertaken by or on behalf of a political candidate to familiarize voters with the candidate and his or her views on campaign issues.

political agenda The issues that politicians will address; often determined by the media.

political consultant A person who, for a large fee, devises a political candidate's campaign strategies, monitors the campaign's progress, plans all media appearances, and coaches the candidate for debates.

political culture The set of ideas, values, and attitudes about government and the political process held by a community or nation.

political party A group of individuals outside the government who organize to win elections, operate the government, and determine policy.

political socialization A learning process through which most people acquire their political attitudes, opinions, beliefs, and knowledge.

politics The process of resolving conflicts over how society should use its scarce resources and who should receive various benefits, such as wealth, status, health care, and higher education. According to Harold Lasswell, politics is the process of determining "who gets what, when, and how" in a society. According to David Easton, politics is "the authoritative allocation of values" in a society.

poll tax A fee of several dollars that had to be paid in order to vote; a device used in some southern states to prevent African Americans from voting.

poll watcher A representative from one of the two major political parties who is allowed to monitor a polling place to make sure that the election is run fairly and to avoid fraud.

power The ability to influence the behavior of others, usually through the use of force, persuasion, or rewards.

precedent A court decision that furnishes an example or authority for deciding subsequent cases involving identical or similar facts and legal issues.

precinct A political district within a city (such as a block or a neighborhood) or a portion of a rural county; the smallest voting district at the local level.

preemption A doctrine rooted in the supremacy clause of the Constitution that provides that national laws or regulations governing a certain area take precedence over conflicting state laws or regulations governing that same area.

preemptive war A strategy of striking against an enemy before the enemy is able to launch an attack. It characterizes the foreign policy of the George W. Bush administration in the war on terrorism.

press secretary A member of the White House staff who holds press conferences for reporters and makes public statements for the president.

primary A preliminary election held for the purpose of choosing a party's final candidate.

primary source of law A source of law that establishes the law. Primary sources of law include constitutions, statutes, administrative agency rules and regulations, and decisions rendered by the courts.

print media Communication channels that consist of printed materials, such as newspapers and magazines.

privatization The replacement of government agencies that provide products or services to the public by private firms that provide the same products or services.

probable cause Cause for believing that there is a substantial likelihood that a person has committed or is about to commit a crime.

public debt The total amount of money that the national government owes as a result of borrowing; also called the *national debt*.

public opinion The individual attitudes or beliefs about politics, public issues, and public policies that are shared by a significant portion of adults; a complex collection of opinions held by many people on issues in the public arena.

public opinion poll A numerical survey of the public's opinion on a particular topic at a particular moment.

public policies Plans of action to support or achieve government goals that are designed to improve the lives of citizens.

public services Essential services that individuals cannot provide for themselves, such as building and maintaining roads, providing welfare programs, operating public schools, and preserving national parks.

public-interest group An interest group formed for the purpose of working for the "public good"; examples of public-interest groups are the American Civil Liberties Union and Common Cause.

push poll A campaign tactic used to feed false or misleading information to potential voters, under the guise of taking an opinion poll, with the intent to "push" voters away from one candidate and toward another.

push technology Software that enables Internet users to customize the type of information they receive from Web sources.

The information is "pushed" to the user automatically as it is put on the Web.

Q

quota system A policy under which a specific number of jobs, promotions, or other types of selections, such as university admissions, must be given to members of selected groups.

R

racial profiling A form of discrimination in which law enforcement assumes that people of a certain race are more likely to commit crimes. Racial profiling has been linked to more frequent traffic stops of African Americans by police, and of increased security checks in airports of Arab Americans.

radical left Persons on the extreme left side of the political spectrum who would like to significantly change the political order, usually to promote egalitarianism. The radical left includes socialists, Communists, and, often, populists.

radical right Persons on the extreme right side of the political spectrum. The radical right includes reactionaries (who would like to return to the values and social systems of some previous era), fascists (who pursue strongly nationalistic policies), and libertarians (who believe in no regulation of the economy and individual behavior, except for defense).

random sample In the context of opinion polling, a sample in which each person within the entire population being polled has an equal chance of being chosen.

rational basis test A test (also known as the "ordinary scrutiny" standard) used by the Supreme Court to decide whether a discriminatory law violates the equal protection clause of the Constitution. Few laws evaluated under this test are found invalid.

realigning election An election in which the popular support for and relative strength of the parties shift so that either (1) the minority (opposition) party emerges as the majority party or (2) the majority party is reestablished with a different coalition of supporters.

recall A procedure that allows voters to dismiss an elected official from a state or local office before the official's term has expired.

referendum A form of direct democracy in which legislative or constitutional measures are proposed by a legislature and then presented to the voters for approval.

representative democracy A form of democracy in which the will of the majority is expressed through smaller groups of individuals elected by the people to act as their representatives.

republic Essentially, a term referring to a representative democracy—in which the will of the majority is expressed through smaller groups of individuals elected by the people to act as their representatives.

reverse discrimination The assertion that affirmative action programs that require preferential treatment for minorities discriminate against those who have no minority status.

rule of law A basic principle of government that requires both those who govern and those who are governed to act in accordance with established law.

rulemaking The process undertaken by an administrative agency when formally proposing, evaluating, and adopting a new regulation.

Rules Committee A standing committee in the House of Representatives that provides special rules governing how particular bills will be considered and debated by the House. The Rules Committee normally proposes time limitations on debate for any bill, which are accepted or modified by the House.

S

sabotage A destructive act intended to hinder a nation's defense efforts.

sample In the context of opinion polling, a group of people selected to represent the population being studied.

sampling error In the context of opinion polling, the difference between what the sample results show and what the true results would have been had everybody in the relevant population been interviewed.

school voucher An educational certificate, provided by the government, that allows a student to use public funds to pay for a private or a public school chosen by the student or his or her parents.

secession The act of formally withdrawing from membership in an alliance; the withdrawal of a state from the federal Union.

second budget resolution A budget resolution, which is supposed to be passed in September, that sets "binding" limits on taxes and spending for the next fiscal year, which begins on October 1.

Second Continental Congress The congress of the colonies that met in 1775 to assume the powers of a central government and establish an army.

seditious speech Speech that urges resistance to lawful authority or that advocates the overthrowing of a government.

self-incrimination Providing damaging information or testimony against oneself in court.

senatorial courtesy A practice that allows a senator of the president's party to veto a president's appointment to a federal judgeship within the senator's state.

separate-but-equal doctrine A Supreme Court doctrine holding that the equal protection clause of the Fourteenth Amendment did not forbid racial segregation as long as the facilities for blacks were equal to those provided for whites. The doctrine was overturned in the *Brown v. Board of Education of Topeka* decision of 1954.

separation of powers The principle of dividing governmental powers among the executive, the legislative, and the judicial branches of government.

sexual harassment Unwanted physical contact, verbal conduct, or abuse of a sexual nature that interferes with a recipient's job performance, creates a hostile environment, or carries with it an implicit or explicit threat of adverse employment consequences.

Shays' Rebellion A rebellion of angry farmers in western Massachusetts in 1786, led by former Revolutionary War captain Daniel Shays. This rebellion and other similar uprisings in the New England states emphasized the need for a true national government.

single-member district system A method of election in which only one candidate can win election to each office.

sit-in A tactic of nonviolent civil disobedience. Demonstrators enter a business, college building, or other public place and remain seated until they are forcibly removed or until their demands are met. The tactic was used successfully in the civil rights movement and other protest movements in the United States.

slander The public utterance (speaking) of a statement that holds a person up for contempt, ridicule, or hatred.

social conflict Disagreements among people in a society over what the society's priorities should be with respect to the use of scarce resources.

social contract A voluntary agreement among individuals to create a government and to give that government adequate power to secure the mutual protection and welfare of all individuals.

social regulation Government regulation across all industries that is undertaken for the purpose of protecting the public welfare.

social-welfare policy All government actions that are undertaken to give assistance to specific groups, such as the aged, the ill, and the poor.

soft money Campaign contributions that are made to political parties, instead of to particular candidates.

Solid South A term used to describe the tendency of the southern states to vote Democratic after the Civl War.

solidarity Mutual agreement with others in a particular group.

sound bite In televised news reporting, a brief comment, lasting for only a few seconds, that captures a thought or a perspective and has an immediate impact on the viewers.

Speaker of the House The presiding officer in the House of Representatives. The Speaker has traditionally been a long-time member of the majority party and is often the most powerful and influential member of the House.

special election An election that is held at the state or local level when the voters must decide an issue before the next general election or when vacancies occur by reason of death or resignation.

spin A reporter's slant on, or interpretation of, a particular event or action.

spin doctor A political candidate's press adviser who tries to convince reporters to give a story or event concerning the candidate a particular "spin" (interpretation, or slant).

stagflation A condition that occurs when both inflation and unemployment are rising.

standing committee A permanent committee in Congress that deals with legislation concerning a particular area, such as agriculture or foreign relations.

standing to sue The requirement that an individual must have a sufficient stake in a controversy before he or she can bring a lawsuit. The party bringing the suit must demonstrate that he or she has either been harmed or been threatened with a harm.

stare decisis A common law doctrine under which judges normally are obligated to follow the precedents established by prior court decisions.

statutory law The body of law enacted by legislatures (as opposed to constitutional law, administrative law, or case law).

straw poll A nonscientific poll; a poll in which there is no way to ensure that the opinions expressed are representative of the larger population.

subcommittee A division of a larger committee that deals with a particular part of the committee's policy area. Each of the standing committees in Congress has several subcommittees.

suffrage The right to vote; the franchise.

supremacy clause Article VI, Clause 2, of the Constitution, which makes the Constitution and federal laws superior to all conflicting state and local laws.

suspect classification A classification based on race, for example, that provides the basis for a discriminatory law. Any law based on a suspect classification is subject to strict scrutiny by the courts—meaning that the law must be justified by a compelling state interest.

symbolic speech The expression of beliefs, opinions, or ideas through forms other than speech or print; speech involving actions and other nonverbal expressions.

T

terrorism The random use of staged violence at infrequent intervals to achieve political goals.

third party In the United States, any party other than one of the two major parties (Republican and Democratic) is considered a minor party, or third party.

three-fifths compromise A compromise reached during the Constitutional Convention by which it was agreed that three-fifths of all slaves were to be counted both for tax purposes and for representation in the House of Representatives.

totalitarian A term describing a dictatorship in which a political leader (or group of leaders) seeks to control almost all aspects of social and economic life. Totalitarian dictatorships are rooted in the assumption that the needs of the nation come before the needs of individuals.

tracking poll Polls that are taken almost every day toward the end of a political campaign to find out how well the candidates are competing for votes.

trade organization An association formed by members of a particular industry, such as the oil industry or the trucking industry, to develop common standards and goals for the industry. Trade organizations, as interest groups, lobby government for legislation or regulations that specifically benefit their groups.

treason As enunciated in Article III, Section 3, of the Constitution, the act of levying war against the United States or adhering (remaining loyal) to its enemies.

treaty A formal agreement between the governments of two or more countries.

trial court A court in which trials are held and testimony taken.

trustee In regard to a legislator, one who acts according to his or her conscience and the broad interests of the entire society.

two-party system A political system in which two strong and established parties compete for political offices.

tyranny The arbitrary or unrestrained exercise of power by an oppressive individual or government.

U

unicameral legislature A legislature with only one chamber.

unilateral In international relations, an action undertaken by one nation.

unitary system A centralized governmental system in which local or subdivisional governments exercise only those powers given to them by the central government.

V

veto A Latin word meaning "I forbid"; the refusal by an official, such as the president of the United States or a state governor, to sign a bill into law.

veto power A constitutional power that enables the chief executive (president or governor) to reject legislation and return it to the legislature with reasons for the rejection. This prevents or delays the bill from becoming law.

vital center The center of the political spectrum, or those who hold moderate political views. The center is vital because without it, it may be difficult, if not impossible, to reach the compromises that are necessary to a political system's continuity.

W

ward A local unit of a political party's organization, consisting of a division or district within a city.

Watergate scandal A scandal involving an illegal break-in of the Democratic National Committee offices in 1972 by members of President Richard M. Nixon's reelection campaign staff. Before Congress could vote to impeach Nixon for his participation in covering up the break-in, Nixon resigned from the presidency.

weapons of mass destruction (WMDs) Nuclear, chemical, and biological weapons that can inflict massive civilian casualties and pose long-term health dangers to human beings.

whip A member of Congress who assists the majority or minority leader in the House or in the Senate in managing the party's legislative preferences.

whistleblower In the context of government employment, someone who "blows the whistle" (reports to authorities) on gross governmental inefficiency, illegal action, or other wrongdoing.

White House Office The personal office of the president. White House Office personnel handle the president's political needs and manage the media.

winner-take-all system A term used to describe the electoral college system, in which the candidate who receives the largest popular vote in a state is credited with all that state's electoral votes—one vote per elector.

writ of _certiorari_ An order from a higher court asking a lower court for the record of a case.

writ of _habeas corpus_ An order that requires an official to bring a specified prisoner into court and explain to the judge why the person is being held in prison.

appointments by, to Supreme Court, 318, 328, 336
armed forces ordered by
    into Panama, 281
    into Saudi Arabia, 181
election of 1988 and, 190
election of 1992 and, 22, 165, 223
First Gulf War and, 281
foreign policy and, 269
public opinion and, 181
Bush, George W., 3, 116, 176, 244, 269, 270, 289, 290
    appointments by
        African Americans and, 257
        to cabinet, 111, 113, 257
        to federal courts, 91, 328–329, 330
        Hispanics and, 113
        to Supreme Court, 91, 318, 328, 329
        women and, 111, 257
    Bipartisan Campaign Finance Reform Act of 2002 signed by, 207
    budget and, 259, 260, 312
    cabinet of, 286, 288
    candidate Web site of, 232
    choice of Dick Cheney as running mate and, 288
    democracy in the Middle East and, 11–12, 41, 202, 204
    Department of Homeland Security and, 39, 157, 196, 260, 299
    educational reform and, 82, 138, 222, 223
    elected without majority of popular vote, 22, 43, 181, 212, 284
    election of 2000 and, 22, 43, 120, 160, 181, 190, 191, 206, 212, 223, 279, 284, 318
    election of 2004 and, 3, 43, 84, 91, 112, 158, 160, 162, 167, 173, 179, 187, 189, 190, 191, 192, 197, 201, 202, 212, 223, 231, 233, 279, 284
    executive privilege claimed by, 283, 285
    Federal Marriage Amendment (FMA) supported by, 64, 102, 103, 120, 273
    federalism and, 65–66
    fund-raising by, 231, 232
    gay rights and, 120
    legislative agenda after 2004 elections and, 162, 277
    military experience and, 187
    military tribunals created by, 281, 332
    moral and religious values and, 2, 79, 277–278
    Partial Birth Abortion Ban Act signed by, 91
    "performance-based budgeting" and, 312
    power of, source of, 284
    private contractors in Iraq and, 135
    privatizing some of federal bureaucracy and, 294, 313
    public opinion and, 181, 224, 284
    public relations contracts and, 222

school dress issue and, 79
Second Gulf War and, 11–12, 135, 266
Social Security partial privatization and, 128, 138, 192, 221, 278, 279, 313
states' rights issues and, 64, 65–66
tax proposals and, 177, 192
Terri Schiavo case and, 277–278
vital center and, 191
Vladimir Putin criticized by, 224
war on terrorism and, 39, 65, 66, 157, 158, 181, 202, 260, 279, 281, 283, 284, 285, 332–333
Bush, Jeb, 112
Bush, Jenna, 3
Bush, Laura, 3
Business interest groups, 132–134
Busing, 106
Butler, Jon, 24

C

CAB (Civil Aeronautics Board), 304
Cabinet. See also Executive department(s)
    British Parliament and, 239
    defined, 285
    kitchen, 285
    as of 2005, 286
Cambodia, American invasion of, 280, 283
Camp David, 267
Campaign(s)
    campaign strategy and, 202
        Internet and, 232
    change by Internet and, 232–233
    cost of, 202–204. See also Campaign financing
        beneficiaries of, 225
    cyberspace and, 231–233
    everyday life and, 213
    financing of. See Campaign financing
    modern, 201–208
    negative, 196, 197. See also Negative political advertising
    political consultant and, 202
    professional organization of, 202–203
        illustrated, 203
    running, 162
Campaign financing
    contributions for
        independent expenditures versus, 206
        made to political parties. See Soft money
        policy decisions and, 207
        soft money and. See Soft money
        through political action committees (PACs), 141
        votes of officeholder and, 207–208
    regulations governing
        loopholes and, 205–206
        reform and, 142, 206–207
        skirting, 205–206
Campaign strategy, 202
    Internet, 232

Canada
    courts in, look to U.S. Supreme Court for guidance, 336
    importation of prescription drugs from, 57
    same-sex couples allowed to marry in, 102
Candidate(s)
    elections and. See Election(s)
    news coverage and, 223–224
    nominating, 197–201
    perception of, voting behavior and, 187
    policy choices of, voting behavior and, 187–188
    presidential, nominating, 199–201
    selection of, 159, 197–201
    television and, 220–225
    winning, 17
Cannon, Joseph G. "Uncle Joe," 247–248
Capital punishment. See Death penalty
Carmichael, Stokely, 108
Carter, Jimmy, 153, 167
    early life of, 268
    election of 1976 and, 212
    election of 1980 and, 190–191
    Panama Canal Treaty and, 273
    Vietnam War draft resisters granted amnesty by, 274
Case law, 320–321
Castro, Fidel, 7, 113
Categorical grant, 67
Catt, Carrie Chapman, 110
Caucus, 197–198, 200
CBS, 216
CBS News, 216
    poll of, 179
CDA (Communications Decency Act)(1996), 87–88
CEA (Council of Economic Advisers), 288
Censorship, 89, 224
    self-, 227–228
Census, apportionment of House seats and, 240
Center for Democracy and Technology, 97
Center for Responsive Politics, 207–208, 232
Central Intelligence Agency (CIA), 5, 6, 52
    formation of, 303
    profile of, 303
    psychics paid by, 310
    turf battles and, 314
Certiorari, writ of, 325
Chambliss, Saxby, 196
Chao, Elaine, 286
Charles I (king of England), 8
Chase, Samuel, 256
Chavez-Thompson, Linda, 330
Checks and balances, 37–38, 282
    defined, 37
    Department of Homeland Security and, 39
    illustrated, 38
    judicial restraint and, 338